Defense of the Faith

Old Western Culture Reader
Volume 10

Defense of the Faith

Scholastics of the High Middle Ages

Old Western Culture Reader
Volume 10

Companion to *Christendom: Defense of the Faith*,
a great books curriculum by Roman Roads Press

ROMAN ROADS PRESS
MOSCOW, IDAHO

Defense of the Faith: Scholastics of the High Middle Ages
Old Western Culture Reader, Vol. 10

Copyright © 2020 Roman Roads Media

Third Edition

Published by Roman Roads Press
Moscow, Idaho, USA
romanroadspress.com

General Editor: Daniel Foucachon
Editor and Interior Layout: E. Gunn Wilson and Carissa Hale
Cover Design, Valerie Anne Bost, Daniel Foucachon, and Rachel Rosales

All rights reserved. No part of this publication may be reproduced, stored in a retrieval system, or transmitted in any form by any means, electronic, mechanical, photocopy, recording, or otherwise, without prior permission of the publisher, except as provided by the USA copyright law.

Defense of the Faith, Scholastics of the High Middle Ages
Old Western Culture Reder, Volume 10
© Roman Roads Media, LLC
ISBN: 978-1-944482-39-8

Version 3.1.0 January 2022

This is a companion reader for the *Old Western Culture* curriculum by Roman Roads Press. To find out more about this course, visit www.romanroadspress.com.

Old Western Culture
Great Books Reader Series

THE GREEKS

VOLUME 1	*The Epics*
VOLUME 2	*Drama & Lyric*
VOLUME 3	*The Histories*
VOLUME 4	*The Philosophies*

THE ROMANS

VOLUME 5	*The Aeneid*
VOLUME 6	*The Historians*
VOLUME 7	*Early Christianity*
VOLUME 8	*Nicene Christianity*

CHRISTENDOM

VOLUME 9	*Early Medievals*
VOLUME 10	*Defense of the Faith*
VOLUME 11	*The Medieval Mind*
VOLUME 12	*The Reformation*

EARLY MODERNS

VOLUME 13	*Rise of England*
VOLUME 14	*Politics and Poetry*
VOLUME 15	*The Enlightenment*
VOLUME 16	*The Novels*

Contents

Anselm of Canterbury
    Proslogium (Discourse on the Existence of God)   1
    Monologium (A Monologue on the Reason for Faith)   29
    Cur Deus Homo (Why God Became Man)   119

Geoffrey of Monmouth
    History of the Kings of Britain   215

Jacobus de Vorigaine
    The Golden Legend   423
        Life of St. Nicholas   423
        Life of St. Anthony   433
        Life of St. Agnes   438
        Life of St. Juliana   444
        Life of St. Longinus   448
        Life of St. Patrick   450
        Life of St. George   453
        Life of St. Pernelle (Petronilla)   459

Geoffrey de Villehardouin
    The Conqust of Constantinople   461

Jean de Joinville
    The Life of St. Louis   611

Proslogium

Anselm of Canterbury

Translated by Sidney Norton Deane

Preface

In this brief work the author aims at proving in a single argument the existence of God, and whatsoever we believe of God. The author writes in the person of one who contemplates God, and seeks to understand what he believes. To this work he had given this title: Faith Seeking Understanding. He finally named it Proslogium—that is, A Discourse.

AFTER I had published, at the solicitous entreaties of certain brethren, a brief work (the *Monologium*) as an example of meditation on the grounds of faith, in the person of one who investigates, in a course of silent reasoning with himself, matters of which he is ignorant; considering that this book was knit together by the linking of many arguments, I began to ask myself whether there might be found a single argument which would require no other for its proof than itself alone; and alone would suffice to demonstrate that God truly exists, and that there is a supreme good requiring nothing else, which all other things require for their existence and well-being; and whatever we believe regarding the divine Being.

Although I often and earnestly directed my thought to this end, and at some times that which I sought seemed to be just within my reach, while again it wholly evaded my mental vision, at last in despair I was about to cease, as if from the search for a thing which could not be found. But when I wished to exclude this thought altogether, lest, by busying my mind to no purpose, it should keep me from other thoughts in which I might be successful; then more and more, though I was unwilling and shunned it, it began to force itself upon me with a kind of importunity. So, one day, when I was exceedingly wearied with resisting its importunity, in the very conflict of my thoughts, the proof of which I had despaired offered itself, so that I eagerly embraced the thoughts which I was strenuously repelling.

Thinking, therefore, that what I rejoiced to have found would if put in writing, be welcome to some readers, of this very matter, and of some others, I have written the following treatise in the person of one who strives to lift his mind to the contemplation of God, and seeks to understand what he believes. In my judgment, neither this work nor the other, which I mentioned above, deserved to be called a book, or to bear the name of an author; nor yet did I think they ought not to be sent forth without some title by which they might, in some sort, invite one into whose hands they fell to their perusal. I accordingly gave each a title, that the first might be known as An Example of Meditation on the Grounds of Faith, and its sequel as Faith Seeking Understanding. But, after, both had been copied by many under these titles, many urged me, and especially Hugo, the reverend Archbishop of Lyons, who discharges the apostolic office in Gaul, who instructed me to this effect on his apostolic authority—to prefix my name to these writings. And that this might be done more fitly, I named the first, *Monologium*, that is, A Soliloquy; but the second, *Proslogium*, that is, A Discourse.

1

Exhortation of the mind to the contemplation of God. It casts aside cares, and excludes all thoughts save that of God, that it may seek Him. Man was created to see God. Man by sin lost the blessedness for which he was made, and found the misery for which he was not made. He did not keep this good when he could keep it easily. Without God it is ill with us. Our labors and attempts are in vain without God. Man cannot seek God, unless God himself teaches him; nor find him, unless he reveals himself. God created man in his image, that he might be mindful of him, think of him, and love him. The believer does not seek to understand, that he may believe, but he believes that he may understand: for unless he
believed he would not understand.

UP now, slight man! Flee, for a little while, thy occupations; hide thyself, for a time, from thy disturbing thoughts. Cast aside, now, thy burdensome cares, and put away thy toilsome business. Yield room for some little time to God; and rest for a little time in him. Enter the inner chamber of thy mind; shut out all thoughts save that of God, and such as can aid thee in seeking him; close thy door and seek him. Speak now, my whole heart! Speak now to God, saying, I seek thy face; thy face, Lord, will I seek (Psalms 27:8). And come thou now, O Lord my God, teach my heart where and how it may seek thee, where and how it may find thee.

Lord, if thou art not here, where shall I seek thee, being absent? But if thou art everywhere, why do I not see thee present? Truly thou dwellest in unapproachable light. But where is unapproachable light, or how shall I come to it? Or who shall lead me to that light and into it, that I may see thee in it? Again, by what marks, under what form, shall I seek thee? I have never seen thee, O Lord, my God; I do not know thy form. What, O most high Lord, shall this man do, an exile far from thee? What shall thy servant do, anxious in his love of thee, and cast out afar from thy face? He pants to see thee, and thy face is too far from him. He longs to come to thee, and thy dwelling-place is inaccessible. He is eager to find thee, and knows not thy place. He desires to seek thee, and does not know thy face. Lord, thou art my God, and thou art my Lord, and never have

I seen thee. It is thou that hast made me, and hast made me anew, and hast bestowed upon me all the blessing I enjoy; and not yet do I know thee. Finally, I was created to see thee, and not yet have I done that for which I was made.

O wretched lot of man, when he hath lost that for which he was made! O hard and terrible fate! Alas, what has he lost, and what has he found? What has departed, and what remains? He has lost the blessedness for which he was made, and has found the misery for which he was not made. That has departed without which nothing is happy, and that remains which, in itself, is only miserable. Man once did eat the bread of angels, for which he hungers now; he eateth now the bread of sorrows, of which he knew not then. Alas! For the mourning of all mankind, for the universal lamentation of the sons of Adam! He choked with satiety[1], we sigh with hunger. He abounded, we beg. He possessed in happiness, and miserably forsook his possession; we suffer want in unhappiness, and feel a miserable longing, and alas! we remain empty.

Why did he not keep for us, when he could so easily, that whose lack we should feel so heavily? Why did he shut us away from the light, and cover us over with darkness? With what purpose did he rob us of life, and inflict death upon us? Wretches that we are, whence have we been driven out; whither are we driven on? Whence hurled? Whither consigned to ruin? From a native country into exile, from the vision of God into our present blindness, from the joy of immortality into the bitterness and horror of death. Miserable exchange of how great a good, for how great an evil! Heavy loss, heavy grief, heavy all our fate!

But alas! wretched that I am, one of the sons of Eve, far removed from God! What have I undertaken? What have I accomplished? Whither was I striving? How far have I come? To what did I aspire? Amid what thoughts am I sighing? I sought blessings, and lo! confusion. I strove toward God, and I stumbled on myself.

---

1 The quality of being fed or gratified to or beyond capacity

I sought calm in privacy, and I found tribulation and grief in my inmost thoughts. I wished to smile in the joy of my mind, and I am compelled to frown by the sorrow of my heart. Gladness was hoped for, and lo! a source of frequent sighs!

And thou too, O Lord, how long? How long, O Lord, dost thou forget us; how long dost thou turn thy face from us? When wilt thou look upon us, and hear us? When wilt thou enlighten our eyes, and show us thy face? When wilt thou restore thyself to us? Look upon us, Lord; hear us, enlighten us, reveal thyself to us. Restore thyself to us, that it may be well with us—thyself, without whom it is so ill with us. Pity our toilings and strivings toward thee since we can do nothing without thee. Thou dost invite us; do thou help us. I beseech thee, O Lord, that I may not lose hope in sighs, but may breathe anew in hope. Lord, my heart is made bitter by its desolation; sweeten thou it, I beseech thee, with thy consolation. Lord, in hunger I began to seek thee; I beseech thee that I may not cease to hunger for thee. In hunger I have come to thee; let me not go unfed. I have come in poverty to the Rich, in misery to the Compassionate; let me not return empty and despised. And if, before I eat, I sigh, grant, even after sighs, that which I may eat. Lord, I am bowed down and can only look downward; raise me up that I may look upward. My iniquities have gone over my head; they overwhelm me; and, like a heavy load, they weigh me down. Free me from them; unburden me, that the pit of iniquities may not close over me.

Be it mine to look up to thy light, even from afar, even from the depths. Teach me to seek thee, and reveal thyself to me, when I seek thee, for I cannot seek thee, except thou teach me, nor find thee, except thou reveal thyself. Let me seek thee in longing, let me long for thee in seeking; let me find thee in love, and love thee in finding. Lord, I acknowledge and I thank thee that thou hast created me in this thine image, in order that I may be mindful of thee, may conceive of thee, and love thee; but that image has been so consumed and wasted away by vices, and obscured by the smoke of wrongdoing, that it cannot achieve that for which it was made, except thou renew it, and create it anew. I do not endeavor, O Lord, to penetrate thy sublimity, for in no wise do I compare my understanding with that; but I long to understand in some degree thy truth, which my heart believes and loves. For I do not seek to understand that I may believe, but I believe in order to understand. For this also I believe—that unless I believed, I should not understand.

2

Truly there is a God, although the fool hath said in his heart, There is no God.

AND so, Lord, do thou, who dost give understanding to faith, give me, so far as thou knowest it to be profitable, to understand that thou art as we believe; and that thou art that which we believe. And indeed, we believe that thou art a being than which nothing greater can be conceived. Or is there no such nature, since the fool hath said in his heart, there is no God? (Psalms 14:1). But, at any rate, this very fool, when he hears of this being of which I speak—a being than which nothing greater can be conceived—understands what he hears, and what he understands is in his mind; although he does not understand it to exist.

For it is one thing for an object to be in the understanding, and another to understand that the object exists. When a painter first conceives of what he will afterwards perform, he has it in his understanding, but he does not yet understand it to be because he has not yet performed it. But after he has made the painting, he both has it in his understanding, and he understands that it exists because he has made it.

Hence, even the fool is convinced that something exists in the mind, at least, than which nothing greater can be conceived. For, when he hears of this, he understands it. And whatever is understood, exists in the mind. And assuredly that, than which nothing greater can be conceived, cannot exist in the mind alone. For, suppose it exists in the mind alone: then it can be conceived to exist in reality; which is greater.

Therefore, if that, than which nothing greater can be conceived, exists in the mind alone, the very being, than which nothing greater can be conceived, is one, than which a greater can be conceived. But obviously this is impossible. Hence, there is no doubt that there exists a being, than which nothing greater can be conceived, and it exists both in the mind and in reality.

3

God cannot be conceived not to exist. God is that, than which nothing greater can be conceived. That which can be conceived not to exist is not God.

AND it assuredly exists so truly, that it cannot be conceived not to exist. For, it is possible to conceive of a being which cannot be conceived not to exist; and this is greater than one which can be conceived not to exist. Hence, if that, than which nothing greater can be conceived, can be conceived not to exist, it is not that, than which nothing greater can be conceived. But this is an irreconcilable contradiction. There is, then, so truly a being than which nothing greater can be conceived to exist, that it cannot even be conceived not to exist;. and this being thou art, O Lord, our God.

So truly, therefore, dost thou exist, O Lord, my God, that thou canst not be conceived not to exist; and rightly. For, if a mind could conceive of a being better than thee, the creature would rise above the Creator; and this is most absurd. And, indeed, whatever else there is, except thee alone, can be conceived not to exist. To thee alone, therefore, it belongs to exist more truly than all other beings, and hence in a higher degree than all others. For, whatever else exists does not exist so truly, and hence in a less degree it belongs to it to exist. Why, then, has the fool said in his heart, there is no God (Psalms 14:1), since it is so evident, to a rational mind, that thou dost exist in the highest degree of all? Why, except that he is dull and a fool?

4

How the fool has said in his heart what cannot be conceived. A thing may be conceived in two ways: (1) when the word signifying it is conceived; (2) when the thing itself is understood. As far as the word goes, God can be conceived not to exist; in reality he cannot.

BUT how has the fool said in his heart what he could not conceive; or how is it that he could not conceive what he said in his heart? Since it is the same to say in the heart, and to conceive.

But if really, nay, since really, he both conceived, because he said in his heart; and did not say in his heart, because he could not conceive; there is more than one way in which a thing is said in the heart or conceived. For in one sense, an object is conceived when the word signifying it is conceived; and in another, when the very entity, which the object is, is understood.

In the former sense, then, God can be conceived not to exist; but in the latter, not at all. For no one who understands what fire and water are can conceive fire to be water, in accordance with the nature of the facts themselves, although this is possible according to the words. So, then, no one who understands what God is can conceive that God does not exist; although he says these words in his heart, either without any or with some foreign signification. For, God is that than which a greater cannot be conceived. And he who thoroughly understands this, assuredly understands that this being so truly exists, that not even in concept can it be non-existent. Therefore, he who understands that God so exists, cannot conceive that he does not exist.

I thank thee, gracious Lord, I thank thee; because what I formerly believed by thy bounty, I now so understand by thine illumination, that if I were unwilling to believe that thou dost exist, I should not be able not to understand this to be true.

5

God is whatever it is better to be than not to be; and he, as the only self-existent being, creates all things from nothing.

WHAT art thou, then, Lord God, than whom nothing greater can be conceived? But what art thou, except that which, as the highest of all beings, alone exists through itself, and creates all other things from nothing? For, whatever is not this is less than a thing which can be conceived of. But this cannot be conceived of thee. What good, therefore, does the supreme Good lack, through which every good is? Therefore, thou art just, truthful, blessed, and whatever it is better to be than not to be. For it is better to be just than not just; better to be blessed than not blessed.

6

How God is sensible (sensibilis) *although he is not a body. God is sensible, omnipotent, compassionate, passionless; for it is better to be these than not be. He who in any way knows, is not improperly said in some sort to feel.*

BUT, although it is better for thee to be sensible, omnipotent, compassionate, passionless, than not to be these things; how art thou sensible, if thou art not a body; or omnipotent, if thou hast not all powers; or at once compassionate and passionless? For, if only corporeal things are sensible, since the senses encompass a body and are in a body, how art thou sensible, although thou art not a body, but a supreme Spirit, who is superior to body? But, if feeling is only cognition, or for the sake of cognition—for he who feels obtains knowledge in accordance with the proper functions of his senses; as through sight, of colors; through taste, of flavors—whatever in any way cognises is not inappropriately said, in some sort, to feel.

Therefore, O Lord, although thou art not a body yet thou art truly sensible in the highest degree in respect of this, that thou dost cognise all things in the highest degree; and not as an animal cognises, through a corporeal sense.

7

How he is omnipotent, although there are many things of which he is not capable. To be capable of being corrupted, or of lying, is not power, but impotence. God can do nothing by virtue of impotence, and nothing has power against him.

BUT how art thou omnipotent, if thou art not capable of all things? Or, if thou canst not be corrupted, and canst not lie, nor make what is true, false—as, for example, if thou shouldst make what has been done not to have been done, and the like—how art thou capable of all things? Or else to be capable of these things is not power, but impotence. For, he who is capable of these things is capable of what is not for his good, and of what he ought not to do; and the more capable of them he is, the more power have adversity and perversity against him; and the less has he himself against these.

He, then, who is thus capable is so not by power, but by impotence. For, he is not said to be able because he is able of himself, but because his impotence gives something else power over him. Or, by a figure of speech, just as many words are improperly applied, as when we use "to be" for "not to be," and "to do" for what is really "not to do", or "to do nothing." For, often we say to a man who denies the existence of something: "It is as you say it to be," though it might seem more proper to say, "It is not, as you say it is not." In the same way we say, "This man sits just as that man does," or, "This man rests just as that man does"; although to sit is not to do anything, and to rest is to do nothing.

So, then, when one is said to have the power of doing or experiencing what is not for his good, or what he ought not to do, impotence is understood in the word power. For, the more he possesses this power, the more powerful are adversity and perversity against him, and the more powerless is he against them.

Therefore, O Lord, our God, the more truly art thou omnipotent, since thou art capable of nothing through impotence, and nothing has power against thee.

8

How he is compassionate and passionless. God is compassionate, in terms of our experience, because we experience the effect of compassion. God is not compassionate, in terms of his own being, because he does not experience the feeling (affectus) *of compassion.*

BUT how art thou compassionate, and, at the same time, passionless? For, if thou art passionless, thou dost not feel sympathy; and if thou dost not feel sympathy, thy heart is not wretched from sympathy for the wretched; but this it is to be compassionate. But if thou art not compassionate, whence cometh so great consolation to the wretched? How, then, art thou compassionate and not compassionate, O Lord, unless because thou art compassionate in terms of our experience, and not compassionate in terms of thy being.

Truly, thou art so in terms of our experience, but thou art not so in terms of thine own. For, when thou beholdest us in our wretchedness, we experience the effect of compassion, but thou dost not experience the feeling. Therefore, thou art both compassionate, because thou dost save the wretched, and spare those who sin against thee; and not compassionate because thou art affected by no sympathy for wretchedness.

9

How the all-just and supremely just God spares the wicked, and justly pities the wicked. He is better who is good to the righteous and the wicked than he who is good to the righteous alone. Although God is supremely just, the source of his compassion is hidden. God is supremely compassionate, because he is supremely just. He saveth the just, because justice goes with them; he frees sinners by the authority of justice. God spares the wicked out of justice; for it is just that God, than whom none is better or more powerful, should be good even to the wicked, and should make the wicked good. If God ought not to pity, he pities unjustly. But this it is impious to suppose. Therefore, God justly pities.

BUT how dost thou spare the wicked, if thou art all just and supremely just? For how, being all just and supremely just, dost thou aught that is not just? Or, what justice is that to give him who merits eternal death everlasting life? How then, gracious Lord, good to the righteous and the wicked, canst thou save the wicked if this is not just, and thou dost not aught that is not just? Or, since thy goodness is incomprehensible, is this hidden in the unapproachable light wherein thou dwellest? Truly, in the deepest and most secret parts of thy goodness is hidden the fountain whence the stream of thy compassion flows.

For thou art all just and supremely just, yet thou art kind even to the wicked, even because thou art all supremely good. For thou wouldst be less good if thou wert not kind to any wicked being. For, he who is good, both to the righteous and the wicked, is better than he who is good to the wicked alone; and he who is good to the wicked, both by punishing and sparing them, is better than he who is good by punishing them alone. Therefore, thou art compassionate, because thou art all supremely good. And, although it appears why thou dost reward the good with goods and the evil with evils; yet this, at least, is most wonderful, why thou, the all and supremely just, who lackest nothing, bestowest goods on the wicked and on those who are guilty toward thee.

The depth of thy goodness, O God! The source of thy compassion appears, and yet is not clearly seen! We see whence the river flows, but the spring whence it arises is not seen. For, it is from the abundance of thy goodness that thou art good to those who sin against thee; and in the depth of thy goodness is hidden the reason for this kindness.

For, although thou dost reward the good with goods and the evil with evils, out of goodness, yet this the concept of justice seems to demand. But, when thou dost bestow goods on the evil, and it is known that the supremely Good hath willed to do this, we wonder why the supremely just has been able to will this.

O compassion, from what abundant sweetness and what sweet abundance dost thou well forth to us! O boundless goodness of God, how passionately should sinners love thee! For thou savest the just, because justice goeth with them; but sinners thou dost free by the authority of justice. Those by the help of their deserts; these, although their deserts oppose. Those by acknowledging the goods thou hast granted; these by pardoning the evils thou hatest. O boundless goodness, which dost so exceed all understanding, let that compassion come upon me, which proceeds from thy so great abundance! Let it flow upon me, for it wells forth from thee. Spare, in mercy; avenge not, in justice.

For, though it is hard to understand how thy compassion is not inconsistent with thy justice; yet we must believe that it does not oppose justice at all, because it flows from goodness, which is no goodness without justice; nay, that it is in true harmony with justice. For, if thou art compassionate only because thou art supremely good, and supremely good only because thou art supremely just, truly thou art compassionate even because thou art supremely just. Help me, just and compassionate God, whose light I seek; help me to understand what I say.

Truly, then, thou art compassionate even because thou art just. Is, then, thy compassion born of thy justice? And dost thou spare the wicked, therefore, out of justice? If this is true, my Lord, if this is true, teach me how it is. Is it because it is just, that thou shouldst be so good that thou canst not be conceived better; and that thou shouldst work so powerfully that thou canst not be conceived more powerful? For what can be more just than this? Assuredly it could not be that thou shouldst be good only by requiting (*retribuendo*) and not by sparing, and that thou shouldst make good only those who are not good, and not the wicked also. In this way, therefore, it is just that thou shouldst spare the wicked, and make good souls of evil.

Finally, what is not done justly ought not to be done; and what ought not to be done is done unjustly. If, then, thou dost not justly pity the wicked, thou oughtest not to pity them. And, if thou oughtest not to pity them, thou pityest them unjustly. And if it is impious to suppose this, it is right to believe that thou justly pityest the wicked.

10

How he justly punishes and justly spares the wicked. God, in sparing the wicked, is just, according to his own nature because he does what is consistent with his goodness; but he is not just, according to our nature, because he does not inflict the punishment deserved.

BUT it is also just that thou shouldst punish the wicked. For what is more just than that the good should receive goods, and the evil, evils? How, then, is it just that thou shouldst punish the wicked, and, at the same time, spare the wicked? Or, in one way, dost thou justly punish, and, in another, justly spare them? For, when thou punishest the wicked, it is just, because it is consistent with their deserts; and when, on the other hand, thou sparest the wicked, it is just, not because it is compatible with their deserts, but because it is compatible with thy goodness.

For, in sparing the wicked, thou art as just, according to thy nature, but not according to ours, as thou art compassionate, according to our nature, and not according to thine; seeing that, as in saving us, whom it would be just for thee to destroy, thou art compassionate, not because thou feelest an affection (*affectum*), but because we feel the effect (*effectum*); so thou art just, not because thou requitest us as we deserve, but because thou dost that which becomes thee as the supremely good Being. In this way, therefore, without contradiction thou dost justly punish and justly spare.

11

How all the ways of God are compassion and truth; and yet God is just in all his ways. We cannot comprehend why, of the wicked, he saves these rather than those, through his supreme goodness: and condemns those rather than these, through his supreme justice.

BUT, is there any reason why it is not also just, according to thy nature, O Lord, that thou shouldst punish the wicked? Surely it is just that thou shouldst be so just that thou canst not be conceived more just; and this thou wouldst in no wise be if thou didst only render goods to the good, and not evils to the evil. For, he who requiteth both good and evil according to their deserts is more just than he who so requites the good alone. It is, therefore, just, according to thy nature, O just and gracious God, both when thou dost punish and when thou sparest.

Truly, then, all the paths of the Lord are mercy and truth (Psalms 25:10); and yet the Lord is righteous in all his ways (Psalms 145:17). And assuredly without inconsistency: For, it is not just that those whom thou dost will to punish should be saved, and that those whom thou dost will to spare should be condemned. For that alone is just which thou dost will; and that alone unjust which thou dost not will. So, then, thy compassion is born of thy justice.

For it is just that thou shouldst be so good that thou art good in sparing also; and this may be the reason why the supremely Just can will goods for the evil. But if it can be comprehended in any way why thou canst will to save the wicked, yet by no consideration can we comprehend why, of those who are alike wicked, thou savest some rather than others, through supreme goodness; and why thou dost condemn the latter rather than the former, through supreme justice.

So, then, thou art truly sensible (*sensibilis*), omnipotent, compassionate, and passionless, as thou art living, wise, good, blessed, eternal: and whatever it is better to be than not to be.

12

God is the very life whereby he lives; and so of other like attributes.

BUT undoubtedly, whatever thou art, thou art through nothing else than thyself. Therefore, thou art the very life whereby thou livest; and the wisdom wherewith thou art wise; and the very goodness whereby thou art good to the righteous and the wicked; and so of other like attributes.

13

How he alone is uncircumscribed and eternal, although other spirits are uncircumscribed and eternal. No place and time contain God. But he is himself everywhere and always. He alone not only does not cease to be, but also does not begin to be.

BUT everything that is in any way bounded by place or time is less than that which no law of place or time limits. Since, then, nothing is greater than thou, no place or time contains thee; but thou art everywhere and always. And since this can be said of thee alone, thou alone art uncircumscribed and eternal. How is it, then, that other spirits also are said to be uncircumscribed and eternal?

Assuredly thou art alone eternal; for thou alone among all beings not only dost not cease to be but also dost not begin to be.

But how art thou alone uncircumscribed? Is it that a created spirit, when compared with thee, is circumscribed, but when compared with matter, uncircumscribed? For altogether circumscribed is that which, when it is wholly in one place, cannot at the same time be in another. And this is seen to be true of corporeal things alone. But uncircumscribed is that which is, as a whole, at the same time everywhere. And this is understood to be true of thee alone. But circumscribed, and, at the same time, uncircumscribed is that which, when it is anywhere as a whole, can at the same time be somewhere else as a whole, and yet not everywhere. And this is recognised as true of created spirits. For, if the soul were not as a whole in the separate members of the body, it would not feel as a whole in the separate members. Therefore, thou, Lord, art peculiarly uncircumscribed and eternal; and yet other spirits also are uncircumscribed and eternal.

14

How and why God is seen and yet not seen by those who seek him.

HAST thou found what thou didst seek, my soul? Thou didst

seek God. Thou hast found him to be a being which is the highest of all beings, a being than which nothing better can be conceived; that this being is life itself, light, wisdom, goodness, eternal blessedness, and blessed eternity; and that it is everywhere and always.

For, if thou hast not found thy God, how is he this being which thou hast found, and which thou hast conceived him to be, with so certain truth and so true certainty? But, if thou hast found him, why is it that thou dost not feel thou hast found him? Why, O Lord, our God, does not my soul feel thee, if it hath found thee? Or, has it not found him whom it found to be light and truth? For how did it understand this, except by seeing light and truth? Or, could it understand anything at all of thee, except through thy light and thy truth?

Hence, if it has seen light and truth, it has seen thee; if it has not seen thee, it has not seen light and truth. Or, is what it has seen both light and truth; and still it has not yet seen thee, because it has seen thee only in part, but has not seen thee as thou art? Lord my God, my creator and renewer, speak to the desire of my soul what thou art other than it hath seen, that it may clearly see what it desires. It strains to see thee more; and sees nothing beyond this which it hath seen, except darkness. Nay, it does not see darkness, of which-there is none in thee; but it sees that it cannot see farther, because of its own darkness.

Why is this, Lord, why is this? Is the eye of the soul darkened by its infirmity, or dazzled by thy glory? Surely it is both darkened in itself, and dazzled by thee. Doubtless it is both obscured by its own insignificance, and overwhelmed by thy infinity. Truly, it is both contracted by its own narrowness and overcome by thy greatness.

For how great is that light from which shines every truth that gives light to the rational mind! How great is that truth in which is everything that is true, and outside which is only nothingness and the false! How boundless is the truth which sees at one glance whatsoever has been made, and by whom, and through whom, and how it has been made from nothing! What purity, what certainty, what splendor where it is! Assuredly more than a creature can conceive.

15

He is greater than can be conceived.

THEREFORE, O Lord, thou art not only that than which a greater cannot be conceived, but thou art a being greater than can be conceived. For, since it can be conceived that there is such a being, if thou art not this very being, a greater than thou can be conceived. But this is impossible.

16

This is the unapproachable light wherein he dwells.

TRULY, O Lord, this is the unapproachable light in which thou dwellest; for truly there is nothing else which can penetrate this light, that it may see thee there. Truly, I see it not, because it is too bright for me. And yet, whatsoever I see, I see through it, as the weak eye sees what it sees through the light of the sun, which in the sun itself it cannot look upon. My understanding cannot reach that light, for it shines too bright. It does not comprehend it, nor does the eye of my soul endure to gaze upon it long. It is dazzled by the brightness, it is overcome by the greatness, it is overwhelmed by the infinity, it is dazed by the largeness, of the light.

O supreme and unapproachable light! O whole and blessed truth, how far art thou from me, who am so near to thee! How far removed art thou from my vision, though I am so near to thine! Everywhere thou art wholly present, and I see thee not. In thee I move, and in thee I have my being; and I cannot come to thee. Thou art within me, and about me, and I feel thee not.

17

In God is harmony, fragrance, sweetness, pleasantness to the touch, beauty, after his ineffable manner.

STILL thou art hidden, O Lord, from my soul in thy light and thy blessedness; and therefore my soul still walks in its darkness and wretchedness. For it looks, and does not see thy beauty. It hearkens, and does not hear thy harmony. It smells, and does not perceive thy fragrance. It tastes, and does not recognize thy sweetness. It touches, and does not feel thy pleasantness. For thou hast these attributes in thyself, Lord God, after thine ineffable manner, who hast given them to objects created by thee, after their sensible manner; but the sinful senses of my soul have grown rigid and dull, and have been obstructed by their long listlessness.

18

God is life, wisdom, eternity, and every true good. Whatever is composed of parts is not wholly one; it is capable, either in fact or in concept, of dissolution. In God wisdom, eternity, etc., are not parts, but one, and the very whole which God is, or unity itself, not even in concept divisible.

AND lo, again confusion; lo, again grief and mourning meet him who seeks for joy and gladness. My soul now hoped for satisfaction; and lo, again it is overwhelmed with need. I desired now to feast, and lo, I hunger more. I tried to rise to the light of God, and I have fallen back into my darkness. Nay, not only have I fallen into it, but I feel that I am enveloped in it. I fell before my mother conceived me. Truly, in darkness I was conceived, and in the cover of darkness I was born. Truly, in him we all fell, in whom we all sinned. In him we all lost, who kept easily, and wickedly lost to himself and to us, that which when we wish to seek it, we do not know; when we seek it, we do not find; when we find, it is not that which we seek.

Do thou help me for thy goodness' sake! Lord, I sought thy face; thy face, Lord, will I seek; hide not thy face far from me (Psalms

27:8-9). Free me from myself toward thee. Cleanse, heal, sharpen, enlighten the eye of my mind that it may behold thee. Let my soul recover its strength, and with all its understanding let it strive toward thee, O Lord. What art thou, Lord, what art thou? What shall my heart conceive thee to be?

Assuredly thou art life, thou art wisdom, thou art truth, thou art goodness, thou art blessedness, thou art eternity, and thou art every true good. Many are these attributes: my straitened understanding cannot see so many at one view, that it may be gladdened by all at once. How, then, O Lord, art thou all these things? Are they parts of thee, or is each one of these rather the whole, which thou art? For, whatever is composed of parts is not altogether one, but is in some sort plural, and diverse from itself; and either in fact or in concept is capable of dissolution.

But these things are alien to thee, than whom nothing better can be conceived of. Hence, there are no parts in thee, Lord, nor art thou more than one. But thou art so truly a unitary being, and so identical with thyself, that in no respect art thou unlike thyself; rather thou art unity itself, indivisible by any conception. Therefore, life and wisdom and the rest are not parts of thee, but all are one; and each of these is the whole, which thou art, and which all the rest are.

In this way, then, it appears that thou hast no parts, and that thy eternity, which thou art, is nowhere and never a part of thee or of thy eternity. But everywhere thou art as a whole, and thy eternity exists as a whole forever.

19

He does not exist in place or time, but all things exist in him.

BUT if through thine eternity thou hast been, and art, and wilt be; and to have been is not to be destined to be; and to be is not to have been, or to be destined to be; how does thine eternity exist as a whole forever? Or is it true that nothing of thy eternity passes away, so that it is not now; and that nothing of it is destined to be, as if it were not yet?

Thou wast not, then, yesterday, nor wilt thou be to-morrow; but yesterday and to-day and to-morrow thou art; or, rather, neither yesterday nor to-day nor to-morrow thou art; but simply, thou art, outside all time. For yesterday and to-day and to-morrow have no existence, except in time; but thou, although nothing exists without thee, nevertheless dost not exist in space or time, but all things exist in thee. For nothing contains thee, but thou containest all.

20

He exists before all things and transcends all things, even the eternal things. The eternity of God is present as a whole with him; while other things have not yet that part of their eternity which is still to be, and have no longer that part which is past.

HENCE, thou dost permeate and embrace all things. Thou art before all, and dost transcend all. And, of a surety, thou art before all; for before they were made, thou art. But how dost thou transcend all? In what way dost thou transcend those beings which will have no end? Is it because they cannot exist at all without thee; while thou art in no wise less, if they should return to nothingness? For so, in a certain sense, thou dost transcend them. Or, is it also because they can be conceived to have an end; but thou by no means? For so they actually have an end, in a certain sense; but thou, in no sense. And certainly, what in no sense has an end transcends what is ended in any sense. Or, in this way also dost thou transcend all things, even the eternal, because thy eternity and theirs is present as a whole with thee; while they have not yet that part of their eternity which is to come, just as they no longer have that part which is past? For so thou dost ever transcend them, since thou art ever present with thyself, and since that to which they have not yet come is ever present with thee.

21

Is this the age of the age, or ages of ages? The eternity of God contains the ages of time themselves, and can be called the age of the age or ages of ages.

IS this, then, the age of the age, or ages of ages? For, as an age of time contains all temporal things, so thy eternity contains even the ages of time themselves. And these are indeed an age, because of their indivisible unity; but ages, because of their endless immeasurability. And, although thou art so great, O Lord, that all things are full of thee, and exist in thee; yet thou art so without all space, that neither midst, nor half, nor any part, is in thee.

22

He alone is what he is and who he is. All things need God for their being and their well-being.

THEREFORE, thou alone, O Lord, art what thou art; and thou art he who thou art. For, what is one thing in the whole and another in the parts, and in which there is any mutable element, is not altogether what it is. And what begins from non-existence, and can be conceived not to exist, and unless it subsists through something else, returns to non-existence; and what has a past existence, which is no longer, or a future existence, which is not yet—this does not properly and absolutely exist.

But thou art what thou art, because whatever thou art at any time, or in any way, thou art as a whole and forever. And thou art he who thou art, properly and simply; for thou hast neither a past existence nor a future, but only a present existence; nor canst thou be conceived as at any time non-existent. But thou art life, and light, and wisdom, and blessedness, and many goods of this nature. And yet thou art only one supreme good; thou art all-sufficient to thyself, and needest none; and thou art he whom all things need for their existence and well-being.

23

This good is equally Father, and Son, and Holy Spirit. And this is a single, necessary Being, which is every good, and wholly good, and the only good.—Since the Word is true, and is truth itself, there is nothing in the Father, who utters it, which is not accomplished in the Word by which he expresses himself. Neither is the love which proceeds from Father and Son unequal to the Father or the Son, for Father and Son love themselves and one another in the same degree in which what they are is good. Of supreme simplicity nothing can be born, and from it nothing can proceed, except that which is this, of which it is born, or from which it proceeds.

THIS good thou art, thou, God the Father; this is thy Word, that is, thy Son. For nothing, other than what thou art, or greater or less than thou, can be in the Word by which thou dost express thyself; for the Word is true, as thou art truthful. And, hence, it is truth itself, just as thou art; no other truth than thou; and thou art of so simple a nature, that of thee nothing can be born other than what thou art. This very good is the one love common to thee and to thy Son, that is, the Holy Spirit proceeding from both. For this love is not unequal to thee or to thy Son; seeing that thou dost love thyself and him, and he, thee and himself, to the whole extent of thy being and his. Nor is there aught else proceeding from thee and from him, which is not unequal to thee and to him. Nor can anything proceed from the supreme simplicity, other than what this, from which it proceeds, is.

But what each is, separately, this is all the Trinity at once, Father, Son, and Holy Spirit; seeing that each separately is none other than the supremely simple unity, and the supremely unitary simplicity which can neither be multiplied nor varied. Moreover, there is a single necessary Being. Now, this is that single, necessary Being, in which is every good; nay, which is every good, and a single entire good, and the only good.

24

Conjecture as to the character and the magnitude of this good. If the created life is good, how good is the creative life!

AND now, my soul, arouse and lift up all thy understanding, and conceive, so far as thou canst, of what character and how great is that good! For, if individual goods are delectable, conceive in earnestness how delectable is that good which contains the pleasantness of all goods; and not such as we have experienced in created objects, but as different as the Creator from the creature. For, if the created life is good, how good is the creative life! If the salvation given is delightful, how delightful is the salvation which has given all salvation! If wisdom in the knowledge of the created world is lovely, how lovely is the wisdom which has created all things from nothing! Finally, if there are many great delights in delectable things, what and how great is the delight in him who has made these delectable things.

25

What goods and how great, belong to those who enjoy this good. Joy is multiplied in the blessed from the blessedness and joy of others.

WHO shall enjoy this good? And what shall belong to him, and what shall not belong to him? At any rate, whatever he shall wish shall be his, and whatever he shall not wish shall not be his. For, these goods of body and soul will be such as eye hath not seen nor ear heard, neither has the heart of man conceived (Isa. 64:4, 1 Cor. 2:9).

Why, then, dost thou wander abroad, slight man, in thy search for the goods of thy soul and thy body? Love the one good in which are all goods, and it sufficeth. Desire the simple good which is every good, and it is enough. For, what dost thou love, my flesh? What dost thou desire, my soul? There, there is whatever ye love, whatever ye desire.

If beauty delights thee, there shall the righteous shine forth as the sun (Matthew 13:43). If swiftness or endurance, or freedom of body, which naught can withstand, delight thee, they shall be as angels of God—because it is sown a natural body; it is raised a spiritual body (1 Corinthians 15:44)—in power certainly, though not in nature. If it is a long and sound life that pleases thee, there a healthful eternity is, and an eternal health. For the righteous shall live for ever (Wisdom 5:15), and the salvation of the righteous is of the Lord (Psalms 37:39). If it is satisfaction of hunger, they shall be satisfied when the glory of the Lord hath appeared (Psalms 17:15). If it is quenching of thirst, they shall be abundantly satisfied with the fatness of thy house (Psalms 36:8). If it is melody, there the choirs of angels sing forever, before God. If it is any not impure, but pure, pleasure, thou shalt make them drink of the river of thy pleasures, O God (Psalms 36:8).

If it is wisdom that delights thee, the very wisdom of God will reveal itself to them. If friendship, they shall love God more than themselves, and one another as themselves. And God shall love them more than they themselves; for they love him, and themselves, and one another, through him, and he, himself and them, through himself. If concord, they shall all have a single will.

If power, they shall have all power to fulfill their will, as God to fulfill his. For, as God will have power to do what he wills, through himself, so they will have power, through him, to do what they will. For, as they will not will aught else than he, he shall will whatever they will; and what he shall will cannot fail to be. If honor and riches, God shall make his good and faithful servants rulers over many things (Luke 12:42); nay, they shall be called sons of God, and gods; and where his Son shall be, there they shall be also, heirs indeed of God, and joint heirs with Christ (Romans 8:17).

If true security delights thee, undoubtedly they shall be as sure that those goods, or rather that good, will never and in no wise fail them; as they shall be sure that they will not lose it of their own accord; and that God, who loves them, will not take it away from those who love him against their will; and that nothing more powerful than God will separate him from them against his will and theirs.

But what, or how great, is the joy where such and so great is the good! Heart of man, needy heart, heart acquainted with sorrows, nay, overwhelmed with sorrows, how greatly wouldst thou rejoice, if thou didst abound in all these things! Ask thy inmost mind whether it could contain its joy over so great a blessedness of its own.

Yet assuredly, if any other whom thou didst love altogether as thyself possessed the same blessedness, thy joy would be doubled, because thou wouldst rejoice not less for him than for thyself. But if two, or three, or many more, had the same joy, thou wouldst rejoice as much for each one as for thyself, if thou didst love each as thyself. Hence, in that perfect love of innumerable blessed angels and sainted men, where none shall love another less than himself, every one shall rejoice for each of the others as for himself.

If, then, the heart of man will scarce contain his joy over his own so great good, how shall it contain so many and so great joys? And doubtless, seeing that every one loves another so far as he rejoices in the other's good, and as, in that perfect felicity, each one should love God beyond compare, more than himself and all the others with him; so he will rejoice beyond reckoning in the felicity of God, more than in his own and that of all the others with him.

But if they shall so love God with all their heart, and all their mind, and all their soul, that still all the heart, and all the mind, and all the soul shall not suffice for the worthiness of this love; doubtless they will so rejoice with all their heart, and all their mind, and all their soul, that all the heart, and all the mind, and all the soul shall not suffice for the fullness of their joy.

26

Is this joy which the Lord promises made full? The blessed shall rejoice according as they shall love; and they shall love according as they shall know.

MY God and my Lord, my hope and the joy of my heart, speak unto my soul and tell me whether this is the joy of which thou tellest us through thy Son: Ask and ye shall receive, that your joy may be full (John 16:24). For I have found a joy that is full, and more than full. For when heart, and mind, and soul, and all the man, are full of that joy, joy beyond measure will still remain. Hence, not all of that joy shall enter into those who rejoice; but they who rejoice shall wholly enter into that joy.

Show me, O Lord, show thy servant in his heart whether this is the joy into which thy servants shall enter, who shall enter into the joy of their Lord. But that joy, surely, with which thy chosen ones shall rejoice, eye hath not seen nor ear heard, neither has it entered into the heart of man (Isa. 64:4, 1 Cor. 2:9). Not yet, then, have I told or conceived, O Lord, how greatly those blessed ones of thine shall rejoice. Doubtless they shall rejoice according as they shall love; and they shall love according as they shall know. How far they will know thee, Lord, then! And how much they will love thee! Truly, eye hath not seen, nor ear heard, neither has it entered into the heart of man in this life, how far they shall know thee, and how much they shall love thee in that life.

I pray, O God, to know thee, to love thee, that I may rejoice in thee. And if I cannot attain to full joy in this life may I at least advance from day to day, until that joy shall come to the full. Let the knowledge of thee advance in me here, and there be made full. Let the love of thee increase, and there let it be full, that here my joy may be great in hope, and there full in truth. Lord, through thy Son thou dost command, nay, thou dost counsel us to ask; and thou dost promise that we shall receive, that our joy may be full. I ask, O Lord, as thou dost counsel through our wonderful Counselor. I will receive what thou dost promise by virtue of thy truth, that my joy may be full. Faithful God, I ask. I will receive, that my joy may be full. Meanwhile, let my mind meditate upon it; let my tongue speak of it. Let my heart love it; let my mouth talk of it. Let my soul hunger for it; let my flesh thirst for it; let my whole being desire it, until I enter into thy joy, O Lord, who art the Three and the One God, blessed forever and ever. Amen.

Monologium

Anselm of Canterbury

Translated by Sidney Norton Deane

Preface

In this book Anselm discusses, under the form of a meditation, the Being of God, basing his argument not on the authority of Scripture, but on the force of reason. It contains nothing that is inconsistent with the writings of the Holy Fathers, and especially nothing that is inconsistent with those of St. Augustine. The Greek terminology is employed in Chapter 78, where it is stated that the Trinity may be said to consist of three substances, that is, three persons.

CERTAIN brethren have often and earnestly entreated me to put in writing some thoughts that I had offered them in familiar conversation, regarding meditation on the Being of God, and on some other topics connected with this subject, under the form of a meditation on these themes. It is in accordance with their wish, rather than with my ability, that they have prescribed such a form for the writing of this meditation; in order that nothing in Scripture should be urged on the authority of Scripture itself, but that whatever the conclusion of independent investigation should declare to be true, should, in an unadorned style, with common proofs and with a simple argument, be briefly enforced by the cogency of reason, and plainly expounded in the light of truth. It was their wish also, that I should not disdain to meet such simple and almost foolish objections as occur to me.

This task I have long refused to undertake. And, reflecting on the matter, I have tried on many grounds to excuse myself; for the more they wanted this work to be adaptable to practical use, the more was what they enjoined on me difficult of execution. Overcome at last, however, both by the modest importunity of their entreaties and by the not contemptible sincerity of their zeal; and reluctant as I was because of the difficulty of my task and the weakness of my talent, I entered upon the work they asked for. But it is with pleasure inspired by their affection that, so far as I was able, I have prosecuted this work within the limits they set.

I was led to this undertaking in the hope that whatever I might accomplish would soon be overwhelmed with contempt, as by men disgusted with some worthless thing. For I know that in this book I have not so much satisfied those who entreated me, as put an end to the entreaties that followed me so urgently. Yet, somehow it fell out, contrary to my hope, that not only the brethren mentioned above, but several others, by making copies for their own use, condemned this writing to long remembrance. And, after frequent consideration, I have not been able to find that I have made in it any statement which is inconsistent with the writings of the Catholic Fathers, or especially with those of St. Augustine. Wherefore, if it shall appear to any man that I have offered in this work any thought that is either too novel or discordant with the truth, I ask him not to denounce me at once as one who boldly seizes upon new ideas, or as a maintainer of falsehood; but let him first read diligently Augustine's books on the Trinity, and then judge my treatise in the light of those.

In stating that the supreme Trinity may be said to consist of three substances, I have followed the Greeks, who acknowledge three substances in one Essence, in the same faith wherein we acknowledge three persons in one Substance. For they designate by the word *substance* that attribute of God which we designate by the word *person*.

Whatever I have said on that point, however, is put in the mouth of one debating and investigating in solitary reflection questions to which he had given no attention before. And this method I knew to be in accordance with the wish of those whose request I was striving to fulfill. But it is my prayer and earnest entreaty, that if any shall wish to copy this work, he shall be careful to place this preface at the beginning of the book, before the body of the meditation itself. For I believe that one will be much helped in understanding the matter of this book, if he has taken note of the intention, and the method according to which it is discussed. It is my opinion, too, that one who has first seen this preface will not pronounce a rash judgment, if he shall find offered here any thought that is contrary to his own belief.

1

There is a being which is best, and greatest, and highest of all existing beings.

IF any man, either from ignorance or unbelief, has no knowledge of the existence of one Nature which is highest of all existing beings, which is also sufficient to itself in its eternal blessedness, and which confers upon and effects in all other beings, through its omnipotent goodness, the very fact of their existence, and the fact that in any way their existence is good; and if he has no knowledge of many other things, which we necessarily believe regarding God and his creatures, he still believes that he can at least convince himself of these truths in great part, even if his mental powers are very ordinary, by the force of reason alone.

And, although he could do this in many ways, I shall adopt one which I consider easiest for such a man. For, since all desire to enjoy only those things which they suppose to be good, it is natural that this man should, at some time, turn his mind's eye to the examination of that cause by which these things are good, which he does not desire, except as he judges them to be good. So that, as reason leads the way and follows up these considerations, he advances rationally to those truths of which, without reason, he has no knowledge. And if, in this discussion, I use any argument which no greater authority adduces, I wish it to be received in this way: although, on the grounds that I shall see fit to adopt, the conclusion is reached as if necessarily, yet it is not, for this reason, said to be absolutely necessary, but merely that it can appear so for the time being.

It is easy, then, for one to say to himself: Since there are goods so innumerable, whose great diversity we experience by the bodily senses, and discern by our mental faculties, must we not believe that there is some one thing, through which all goods whatever are good? Or are they good one through one thing and another through another? To be sure, it is most certain and clear, for all who are willing to see, that whatsoever things are said to possess any attribute in such a way that in mutual comparison they may be said to possess it in greater, or less, or equal degree, are said to possess it by virtue of some fact, which is not understood to be one thing in one case and another in another, but to be the same in different cases, whether it is regarded as existing in these cases in equal or unequal degree. For, whatsoever things are said to be just, when compared one with another, whether equally, or more, or less, cannot be understood as just, except through the quality of justness, which is not one thing in one instance, and another in another.

Since it is certain, then, that all goods, if mutually compared, would prove either equally or unequally good, necessarily they are all good by virtue of something which is conceived of as the same in different goods, although sometimes they seem to be called good, the one by virtue of one thing, the other by virtue of another. For, apparently it is by virtue of one quality, that a horse is called good, because he is strong, and by virtue of another, that he is called good, because he is swift. For, though he seems to be called good by virtue of his strength, and good by virtue of his swiftness, yet swiftness and strength do not appear to be the same thing.

But if a horse, because he is strong and swift, is therefore good, how is it that a strong, swift robber is bad? Rather, then, just as a strong, swift robber is bad, because he is harmful, so a strong, swift horse is good, because he is useful. And, indeed, nothing is ordinarily regarded as good, except either for some utility—as, for instance, safety is called good, and those things which promote safety—or for some honorable character—as, for instance, beauty is reckoned to be good, and what promotes beauty.

But, since the reasoning which we have observed is in no wise refutable, necessarily, again, all things, whether useful or honorable, if they are truly good, are good through that same being through which all goods exist, whatever that being is. But who can doubt this very being, through which all goods exist, to be a great good? This must be, then, a good through itself, since every other good is through it.

It follows, therefore, that all other goods are good through another being than that which they themselves are, and this being alone is good through itself. Hence, this alone is supremely good, which is alone good through itself. For it is supreme, in that it so surpasses other beings, that it is neither equaled nor excelled. But that which is supremely good is also supremely great. There is, therefore, some one being which is supremely good, and supremely great, that is, the highest of all existing beings.

2

The same subject continued.

BUT, just as it has been proved that there is a being that is supremely good, since all goods are good through a single being, which is good through itself; so it is necessarily inferred that there is something supremely great, which is great through itself. But, I do not mean physically great, as a material object is great, but that which the greater it is, is the better or the more worthy—wisdom, for instance. And since there can be nothing supremely great except what is supremely good, there must be a being that is greatest and best, i.e. the highest of all existing beings.

3

There is a certain Nature through which whatever is exists, and which exists through itself, and is the highest of all existing beings.

THEREFORE, not only are all good things such through something that is one and the same, and all great things such through something that is one and the same; but whatever is, apparently exists through something that is one and the same. For, everything that is, exists either through something, or through nothing. But nothing exists through nothing. For it is altogether inconceivable that anything should not exist by virtue of something.

Whatever is, then, does not exist except through something. Since this is true, either there is one being, or there are more than one, through which all things that are exist. But if there are more than one, either these are themselves to be referred to some one being, through which they exist, or they exist separately, each through itself, or they exist mutually through one another.

But, if these beings exist through one being, then all things do not exist through more than one, but rather through that one being through which these exist.

If, however, these exist separately, each through itself, there is, at any rate, some power or property of existing through self (*existendi per se*), by which they are able to exist each through itself. But there can be no doubt that, in that case, they exist through this very power, which is one, and through which they are able to exist, each through itself. More truly, then, do all things exist through this very being, which is one, than through these, which are more than one, which, without this one, cannot exist.

But that these beings exist mutually through one another, no reason can admit; since it is an irrational conception that anything should exist through a being on which it confers existence. For not even beings of a relative nature exist thus mutually, the one through the other. For, though the terms *master* and *servant* are used with mutual reference, and the men thus designated are mentioned as having mutual relations, yet they do not at all exist mutually, the one through the other, since these relations exist through the subjects to which they are referred.

Therefore, since truth altogether excludes the supposition that there are more beings than one, through which all things exist, that being, through which all exist, must be one. Since, then, all things that are exist through this one being, doubtless this one being exists through itself. Whatever things there are else then, exist through something other than themselves, and this alone through itself. But whatever exists through another is less than that, through which all things are, and which alone exists through itself. Therefore, that which exists through itself exists in the greatest degree of all things.

There is, then, some one being which alone exists in the greatest and the highest degree of all. But that which is greatest of all, and through which exists whatever is good or great, and, in short, whatever has any existence—that must be supremely good, and supremely great, and the highest of all existing beings.

4

The same subject continued.

FURTHERMORE, if one observes the nature of things, he perceives, whether he will or no, that not all are embraced in a single degree of dignity; but that certain among them are distinguished by inequality of degree. For, he who doubts that the horse is superior in its nature to wood, and man more excellent than the horse, assuredly does not deserve the name of man. Therefore, although it cannot be denied that some natures are superior to others, nevertheless reason convinces us that some nature is so preeminent among these, that it has no superior. For, if the distinction of degrees is infinite, so that there is among them no degree, than which no higher can be found, our course of reasoning reaches this conclusion: that the multitude of natures themselves is not limited by any bounds. But only an absurdly foolish man can fail to regard such a conclusion as absurdly foolish. There is, then, necessarily some nature which is so superior to some nature or natures, that there is none in comparison with which it is ranked as inferior.

Now, this nature which is such, either is single, or there are more natures than one of this sort, and they are of equal degree.

But, if they are more than one and equal, since they cannot be equal through any diverse causes, but only through some cause which is one and the same, that one cause, through which they are equally so great, either is itself what they are, that is, the very essence of these natures; or else it is another than what they are.

But if it is nothing else than their very essence itself, just as they have not more than one essence, but a single essence, so they have not more than one nature, but a single nature. For I here understand *nature* as identical with *essence*.

If, however, that through which these natures are so great is another than that which they are, then, certainly, they are less than that through which they are so great. For, whatever is great through something else is less than that through which it is great. Therefore, they are not so great that there is nothing else greater than they.

But if, neither through what they are nor through anything other than themselves, can there be more such natures than one, than which nothing else shall be more excellent, then in no wise can there be more than one nature of this kind. We conclude, then, that there is some nature which is one and single, and which is so superior to others that it is inferior to none. But that which is such is the greatest and best of all existing beings. Hence, there is a certain nature which is the highest of all existing beings. This, however, it cannot be, unless it is what it is through itself, and all existing beings are what they are through it.

For since, as our reasoning showed us not long since, that which exists through itself, and through which all other things exist, is the highest of all existing beings; either conversely, that which is the highest exists through itself, and all others through it; or, there will be more than one supreme being. But it is manifest that there cannot be more than one supreme being. There is, therefore, a certain Nature, or Substance, or Essence, which is through itself good and great, and through itself is what it is; and through which exists whatever is truly good, or great, or has any existence at all; and which is the supreme good being, the supreme great being, being or subsisting as supreme, that is, the highest of all existing beings.

5

Just as this Nature exists through itself, and other beings through it, so it derives existence from itself, and other beings from it.

SEEING, then, that the truth already discovered has been satisfactorily demonstrated, it is profitable to examine whether this Nature, and all things that have any existence, derive existence from no other source than it, just as they do not exist except through it.

But it is clear that one may say that what derives existence from something, exists through the same thing; and what exists through something, also derives existence from it. For instance, what derives existence from matter, and exists through the artificer, may also be said to exist through matter, and to derive existence from the artificer, since it exists through both, and derives existence from both. That is, it is endowed with existence by both, although it exists through matter and from the artificer in another sense than that in which it exists through, and from, the artificer.

It follows, then, that just as all existing beings are what they are, through the supreme Nature, and as that Nature exists through itself, but other beings through another than themselves, so all existing beings derive existence from this supreme Nature. And therefore, this Nature derives existence from itself, but other beings from it.

6

This Nature was not brought into existence with the help of any external cause, yet it does not exist through nothing, or derive existence from nothing.
—How existence through self, and derived from self, is conceivable.

SINCE the same meaning is not always attached to the phrase, "existence through" something, or to the phrase, "existence derived from" something, very diligent inquiry must be made in what way all existing beings exist through the supreme Nature, or derive existence from it. For, what exists through itself, and what exists through another, do not admit the same ground of existence. Let us first consider, separately, this supreme Nature, which exists through self; then these beings which exist through another.

Since it is evident, then, that this Nature is whatever it is through itself, and all other beings are what they are through it, how does it exist through itself? For, what is said to exist through anything apparently exists through an efficient agent, or through matter, or through some other external aid, as through some instrument. But, whatever exists in any of these three ways exists through another than itself, and is of later existence, and, in some sort, less than that through which it obtains existence.

But, in no wise does the supreme Nature exist through another, nor is it later or less than itself or anything else. Therefore, the supreme Nature could be created neither by itself, nor by another; nor could itself or another be the matter whence it should be created; nor did it assist itself in any way; nor did anything assist it to be what it was not before.

What is to be inferred? For that which cannot have come into existence by any creative agent, or from any matter, or with any external aids, seems either to be nothing, or, if it has any existence, to exist through nothing, and derive existence from nothing. And although, in accordance with the observations I have already made, in the light of reason, regarding the supreme Substance, I should think such propositions could in no wise be true in the case of supreme Substance; yet, I would not neglect to give a connected demonstration of this matter.

For, seeing that this my meditation has suddenly brought me to an important and interesting point, I am unwilling to pass over carelessly even any simple or almost foolish objection that occurs to me in my argument; in order that by leaving no ambiguity in my discussion up to this point, I may have the better assured strength to advance toward what follows; and in order that if, perchance, I shall wish to convince any one of the truth of my speculations, even one of the slower minds, through the removal of every obstacle, however slight, may acquiesce in what it finds here.

That this Nature, then, without which no nature exists, is nothing, is as false as it would be absurd to say that whatever is, is nothing. And, moreover, it does not exist through nothing, because it is utterly inconceivable that what is something should exist through nothing. But, if in any way it derives existence from nothing, it does so through itself, or through another, or through nothing. But it is evident that in no wise does anything exist through nothing. If, then, in any way it derives existence from nothing, it does so either through itself or through another.

But nothing can, through itself, derive existence from nothing, because if anything derives existence from nothing, through something, then that through which it exists must exist before it. Seeing that this Being, then, does not exist before itself, by no means does it derive existence from itself.

But if it is supposed to have derived existence from some other nature, then it is not the supreme Nature, but some inferior one, nor is it what it is through itself, but through another.

Again: if this Nature derives existence from nothing, through something, that through which it exists was a great good, since it was the cause of good. But no good can be understood as existing before that good, without which nothing is good; and it is sufficiently clear that this good, without which there is no good, is the supreme Nature which is under discussion. Therefore, it is not even conceivable that this Nature was preceded by any being, through which it derived existence from nothing.

Hence, if it has any existence through nothing, or derives existence from nothing, there is no doubt that either, whatever it is, it does not exist through itself, or derive existence from itself, or else it is itself nothing. It is unnecessary to show that both these suppositions are false. The supreme Substance, then, does not exist through any efficient agent, and does not derive existence from any matter, and was not aided in being brought into existence by any external causes. Nevertheless, it by no means exists through nothing, or derives existence from nothing; since, through itself and from itself, it is whatever it is.

Finally, as to how it should be understood to exist through itself, and to derive existence from itself: it did not create itself, nor did it spring up as its own matter, nor did it in any way assist itself to become what it was not before, unless, haply, it seems best to conceive of this subject in the way in which one says that *the light lights* or is *lucent*, through and from itself. For, as are the mutual relations of *the light* and *to light* and *lucent* (*lux, lucere, lucens*), such are the relations of *essence* and *to be* and *being*, that is, *existing* or *subsisting*. So the *supreme Being*, and *to be* in the highest degree, and *being* in the highest degree, bear much the same relations, one to another, as *the light* and *to light* and *lucent*.

7

In what way all other beings exist through this Nature and derive existence from it.

THERE now remains the discussion of that whole class of beings that exist through another, as to how they exist through the supreme Substance, whether because this Substance created them all, or because it was the material of all. For, there is no need to inquire whether all exist through it for this reason, namely, that there being another creative agent, or another existing material, this supreme Substance has merely aided in bringing about the existence of all things: since it is inconsistent with what has already been shown, that whatever things are should exist secondarily, and not primarily, through it.

First, then, it seems to me, we ought to inquire whether that whole class of beings which exist through another derive existence from any material. But I do not doubt that all this solid world, with its parts, just as we see, consists of earth, water, fire, and air. These four elements, of course, can be conceived of without these forms which we see in actual objects, so that their formless, or even confused, nature appears to be the material of all bodies, distinguished by their own forms. I say that I do not doubt this. But I ask, whence this very material that I have mentioned, the material of the mundane mass, derives its existence. For, if there is some material of this material, then that is more truly the material of the physical universe.

If, then, the universe of things, whether visible or invisible, derives existence from any material, certainly it not only cannot be, but it cannot even be supposed to be, from any other material than from the supreme Nature or from itself, or from some third being—but this last, at any rate, does not exist. For, indeed, nothing is even conceivable except that highest of all beings, which exists through itself, and the universe of beings which exist, not through themselves, but through this supreme Being. Hence, that which has no existence at all is not the material of anything.

From its own nature the universe cannot derive existence, since, if this were the case, it would in some sort exist through itself and so through another than that through which all things exist. But all these suppositions are false.

Again, everything that derives existence from material derives existence from another, and exists later than that other. Therefore, since nothing is other than itself, or later than itself, it follows that nothing derives material existence from itself.

But if, from the material of the supreme Nature itself, any lesser being can derive existence, the supreme good is subject to change and corruption. But this it is impious to suppose. Hence, since everything that is other than this supreme Nature is less than it, it is impossible that anything other than it in this way derives existence from it.

Furthermore: doubtless that is in no wise good, through which the supreme good is subjected to change or corruption. But, if any lesser nature derives existence from the material of the supreme good, inasmuch as nothing exists whencesoever, except through the supreme Being, the supreme good is subjected to change and corruption through the supreme Being itself. Hence, the supreme Being, which is itself the supreme good, is by no means good; which is a contradiction. There is, therefore, no lesser nature which derives existence in a material way from the supreme Nature.

Since, then, it is evident that the essence of those things which exist through another does not derive existence as if materially, from the supreme Essence, nor from itself, nor from another, it is manifest that it derives existence from no material. Hence, seeing that whatever is, exists through the supreme Being, nor can anything else exist through this Being except by its creation, or by its existence as material, it follows, necessarily, that nothing besides it exists except by its creation. And, since nothing else is or has been, except that supreme Being and the beings created by it, it could create nothing at all through any other instrument or aid than itself. But all that it has created, it has doubtless created either from something, as from material, or from nothing.

Since, then, it is most patent that the essence of all beings, except the supreme Essence, was created by that supreme Essence, and derives existence from no material, doubtless nothing can be more clear than that this supreme Essence nevertheless produced from nothing, alone and through itself, the world of material things, so numerous a multitude, formed in such beauty, varied in such order, so fitly diversified.

8

How it is to be understood that this Nature created all things from nothing.

BUT we are confronted with a doubt regarding this term *nothing*. For, from whatever source anything is created, that source is the cause of what is created from it, and, necessarily, every cause affords some assistance to the being of what it effects. This is so firmly believed, as a result of experience, by every one, that the belief can be wrested from no one by argument, and can scarcely be purloined by sophistry.

Accordingly, if anything was created from nothing, this very nothing was the cause of what was created from it. But how could that which had no existence, assist anything in coming into existence? If, however, no aid to the existence of anything ever had its source in nothing, who can be convinced, and how, that anything is created out of nothing?

Moreover, nothing either means something, or does not mean something. But if nothing is something, whatever has been created from nothing has been created from something. If, however, nothing is not something; since it is inconceivable that anything should be created from what does not exist, nothing is created from nothing; just as all agree that nothing comes from nothing. Whence, it evidently follows, that whatever is created is created from something; for it is created either from something or from nothing. Whether, then, nothing is something, or nothing is not something, it apparently follows, that whatever has been created was created from something.

But, if this is posited as a truth, then it is so posited in opposition to the whole argument propounded in the preceding chapter. Hence, since what was nothing will thus be something, that which was something in the highest degree will be nothing. For, from the discovery of a certain Substance existing in the greatest degree of all existing beings, my reasoning had brought me to this conclusion, that all other beings were so created by this Substance, that that from which they were created was nothing. Hence, if that from which they were created, which I supposed to be nothing, is something, whatever I supposed to have been ascertained regarding the supreme Being, is nothing.

What, then, is to be our understanding of the term *nothing*?—For I have already determined not to neglect in this meditation any possible objection, even if it be almost foolish.—In three ways, then—and this suffices for the removal of the present obstacle—can the statement that any substance was created from nothing be explained.

There is one way, according to which we wish it to be understood, that what is said to have been created from nothing has not been created at all; just as, to one who asks regarding a dumb man, of what he speaks, the answer is given, "of nothing," that is, he does not speak at all. According to this interpretation, to one who inquires regarding the supreme Being, or regarding what never has existed and does not exist at all, as to whence it was created, the answer "from nothing" may properly be given; that is, it never was created. But this answer is unintelligible in the case of any of those things that actually were created.

There is another interpretation which is, indeed, capable of supposition, but cannot be true; namely, that if anything is said to have been created from nothing, it was created from nothing itself (*de nihilo ipso*), that is, from what does not exist at all, as if this very nothing were some existent being from which something could be created. But, since this is always false, as often as it is assumed an irreconcilable contradiction follows.

There is a third interpretation, according to which a thing is said to have been created from nothing, when we understand that it was indeed created, but that there is not anything whence it was created. Apparently it is said with a like meaning, when a man is afflicted without cause, that he is afflicted "over nothing."

If, then, the conclusion reached in the preceding chapter is understood in this sense, that with the exception of the supreme Being all things have been created by that Being from nothing, that is, not from anything; just as this conclusion consistently follows the preceding arguments, so, from it, nothing inconsistent is inferred; although it may be said, without inconsistency or any contradiction, that what has been created by the creative Substance was created from nothing, in the way that one frequently says a rich man has been made from a poor man, or that one has recovered health from sickness; that is, he who was poor before, is rich now, as he was not before; and he who was ill before, is well now, as he was not before.

In this way, then, we can understand, without inconsistency, the statement that the creative Being created all things from nothing, or that all were created through it from nothing; that is, those things which before were nothing, are now something. For, indeed, from the very word that we use, saying that it *created* them or that they were *created*, we understand that when this Being created them, it created something, and that when they were created, they were created only as something. For so, beholding a man of very lowly fortunes exalted with many riches and honors by some one, we say, "Lo, he has made that man out of nothing"; that is, the man who was before reputed as nothing is now, by virtue of that other's making, truly reckoned as something.

9

Those things which were created from nothing had an existence before their creation in the thought of the Creator.

BUT I seem to see a truth that compels me to distinguish carefully in what sense those things which were created may be said to have been nothing before their creation. For, in no wise can anything conceivably be created by any, unless there is, in the mind of the creative agent, some example, as it were, or (as is more fittingly supposed) some model, or likeness, or rule. It is evident, then, that before the world was created, it was in the thought of the supreme Nature, what, and of what sort, and how, it should be. Hence, although it is clear that the beings that were created were nothing before their creation, to this extent, that they were not what they now are, nor was there anything whence they should be created, yet they were not nothing, so far as the creator's thought is concerned, through which, and according to which, they were created.

10

This thought is a kind of expression of the objects created (locutio rerum), *like the expression which an artisan forms in his mind for what he intends to make.*

BUT this model of things, which preceded their creation in the thought of the creator, what else is it than a kind of expression of these things in his thought itself; just as when an artisan is about to make something after the manner of his craft, he first expresses it to himself through a concept? But by the expression of the mind or reason I mean, here, not the conception of words signifying the objects, but the general view in the mind, by the vision of conception, of the objects themselves, whether destined to be, or already existing.

For, from frequent usage, it is recognised that we can express the same object in three ways. For we express objects either by the sensible use of sensible signs, that is, signs which are perceptible to the bodily senses; or by thinking within ourselves insensibly of these signs which, when outwardly used, are sensible; or not by employing these signs, either sensibly or insensibly, but by expressing the things themselves inwardly in our mind, whether by the power of imagining material bodies or of understanding thought, according to the diversity of these objects themselves.

For I express a man in one way, when I signify him by pronouncing these words, a man; in another, when I think of the same words in silence; and in another, when the mind regards the man himself, either through the image of his body, or through the reason; through the image of his body, when the mind imagines his visible form; through the reason, however, when it thinks of his universal essence, which is a rational, mortal animal.

Now, the first two kinds of expression are in the language of one's race. But the words of that kind of expression, which I have put third and last, when they concern objects well known, are natural, and are the same among all nations. And, since all other words owe their invention to these, where these are, no other word is necessary for the recognition of an object, and where they cannot be, no other word is of any use for the description of an object.

For, without absurdity, they may also be said to be the truer, the more like they are to the objects to which they correspond, and the more expressively they signify these objects. For, with the exception of those objects, which we employ as their own names, in order to signify them, like certain sounds, the vowel *a* for instance—with the exception of these, I say, no other word appears so similar to the object to which it is applied, or expresses it as does that likeness which is expressed by the vision of the mind thinking of the object itself.

This last, then, should be called the especially proper and primary *word*, corresponding to the thing. Hence, if no expression of any object whatever so nearly approaches the object as that expression which consists of this sort of words, nor can there be in the thought of any another word so like the object, whether destined to be, or already existing, not without reason it may be thought that such an expression of objects existed with (*apud*) the supreme Substance before their creation, that they might be created; and exists, now that they have been created, that they may be known through it.

11

The analogy, however, between the expression of the Creator and the expression of the artisan is very incomplete.

BUT, though it is most certain that the supreme Substance expressed, as it were, within itself the whole created world, which it established according to, and through, this same most profound expression, just as an artisan first conceives in his mind what he afterwards actually executes in accordance with his mental concept, yet I see that this analogy is very incomplete.

For the supreme Substance took absolutely nothing from any other source, whence it might either frame a model in itself, or make its creatures what they are; while the artisan is wholly unable to conceive in his imagination any bodily thing, except what he has in some way learned from external objects, whether all at once, or part by part; nor can he perform the work mentally conceived if there is a lack of material, or of anything without which a work premeditated cannot be performed. For, though a man can, by meditation or representation, frame the idea of some sort of animal such as has no existence; yet, by no means has he the power to do this, except by uniting in this idea the parts that he has gathered in his memory from objects known externally.

Hence, in this respect, these inner expressions of the works they are to create differ in the creative substance and in the artisan: that the former expression, without being taken or aided from any external source, but as first and sole cause, could suffice the Artificer for the performance of his work, while the latter is neither first, nor sole, nor sufficient, cause for the inception of the artisan's work. Therefore, whatever has been created through the former expression is only what it is through that expression, while whatever has been created through the latter would not exist at all, unless it were something that it is not through this expression itself.

12

This expression of the supreme Being is the supreme Being.

BUT since, as our reasoning shows, it is equally certain that whatever the supreme Substance created, it created through nothing other than itself; and whatever it created, it created through its own most intimate expression, whether separately, by the utterance of separate words, or all at once, by the utterance of one word; what conclusion can be more evidently necessary, than that this expression of the supreme Being is no other than the supreme Being? Therefore, the consideration of this expression should not, in my opinion, be carelessly passed over. But before it can be discussed, I think some of the properties of this supreme Substance should be diligently and earnestly investigated.

13

As all things were created through the supreme Being, so all live through it.

IT is certain, then, that through the supreme Nature whatever is not identical with it has been created. But no rational mind can doubt that all creatures live and continue to exist, so long as they do exist, by the sustenance afforded by that very Being through whose creative act they are endowed with the existence that they have. For, by a like course of reasoning to that by which it has been gathered that all existing beings exist through some one being, hence that being alone exists through itself, and others through another than themselves—by a like course of reasoning, I say, it can be proved that whatever things live, live through some one being; hence that being alone lives through itself, and others through another than themselves.

But, since it cannot but be that those things which have been created live through another, and that by which they have been created lives through itself, necessarily, just as nothing has been created except through the creative, present Being, so nothing lives except through its preserving presence.

14

This Being is in all things, and throughout all; and all derive existence from it and exist through and in it.

BUT if this is true—rather, since this must be true, it follows that, where this Being is not, nothing is. It is, then, everywhere, and throughout all things, and in all. But seeing that it is manifestly absurd that as any created being can in no wise exceed the immeasurableness of what creates and cherishes it, so the creative and cherishing Being cannot, in anyway, exceed the sum of the things it has created; it is clear that this Being itself is what supports and surpasses, includes and permeates, all other things. If we unite this truth with the truths already discovered, we find it is this same Being which is in all and through all, and from which, and through which, and in which, all exist.

15

What can or cannot be stated concerning the substance of this Being.

NOT without reason I am now strongly impelled to inquire as earnestly as I am able, which of all the statements that may be made regarding anything is substantially applicable to this so wonderful Nature. For, though I should be surprised if, among the names or words by which we designate things created from nothing, any should be found that could worthily be applied to the Substance which is the creator of all; yet, we must try and see to what end reason will lead this investigation.

As to relative expressions, at any rate, no one can doubt that no such expression describes what is essential to that in regard to which it is relatively employed. Hence, if any relative predication is made regarding the supreme Nature, it is not significant of its substance.

Therefore, it is manifest that this very expression, that this Nature, is the highest of all beings, or greater than those which have been created by it; or any other relative term that can, in like manner, be applied to it, does not describe its natural essence.

For, if none of those things ever existed, in relation to which it is called supreme or greater, it would not be conceived as either supreme or greater, yet it would not, therefore, be less good, or suffer detriment to its essential greatness in any degree. And this truth is clearly seen from the fact that this Nature exists through no other than itself, whatever there be that is good or great. If, then, the supreme Nature can be so conceived of as not supreme, that still it shall be in no wise greater or less than when it is conceived of as the highest of all beings, it is manifest that the term *supreme*, taken by itself, does not describe that Being which is altogether greater and better than whatever is not what it is. But, what these considerations show regarding the term *supreme* or *highest* is found to be true, in like manner, of other similar, relative expressions.

Passing over these relative predications, then, since none of them taken by itself represents the essence of anything, let our attention be turned to the discussion of other kinds of predication.

Now, certainly if one diligently considers separately whatever there is that is not of a relative nature, either it is such that, to be it is in general better than not to be it, or such that, in some cases, not to be it is better than to be it. But I here understand the phrases, *to be it* and *not to be it*, in the same way in which I understand *to be true* and *not to be true*, *to be bodily* and *not to be bodily*, and the like. Indeed, to be anything is, in general, better than not to be it; as to be wise is better than not to be so; that is, it is better to be wise than not to be wise. For, though one who is just, but not wise, is apparently a better man than one who is wise, but not just, yet, taken by itself, it is not better not to be wise than to be wise. For, everything that is not wise, simply in so far as it is not wise, is less than what is wise, since everything that is not wise would be better if it were wise. In the same way, to be true is altogether better than not to be so, that is, better than not to be true; and just is better than not just; and to live than not to live.

But, in some cases, not to be a certain thing is better than to be it, as not to be gold may be better than to be gold. For it is better for man not to be gold, than to be gold; although it might be better for something to be gold, than not to be gold—lead, for instance. For though both, namely, man and lead are not gold, man is something as much better than gold, as he would be of inferior nature, were he gold; while lead is something as much more base than gold, as it would be more precious, were it gold.

But, from the fact that the supreme Nature may be so conceived of as not supreme, that *supreme* is neither in general better than *not supreme*, nor *not supreme* better, in any case, than *supreme*—from this fact it is evident that there are many relative expressions which are by no means included in this classification. Whether, however, any are so included, I refrain from inquiring; since it is sufficient, for my purpose, that undoubtedly none of these, taken by itself, describes the substance of the supreme Nature.

Since, then, it is true of whatever else there is, that, if it is taken independently, *to be it* is better than *not to be it*; as it is impious to suppose that the substance of the supreme Nature is anything, than which what is not it is in any way better, it must be true that this substance is whatever is, in general, better than what is not it. For, it alone is that, than which there is nothing better at all, and which is better than all things, which are not what it is.

It is not a material body, then, or any of those things which the bodily senses discern. For, then all these there is something better, which is not what they themselves are. For, the rational mind, as to which no bodily sense can perceive what, or of what character, or how great, it is—the less this rational mind would be if it were any of those things that are in the scope of the bodily senses, the greater it is than any of these. For by no means should this supreme Being be said to be any of those things to which something, which they themselves are not, is superior; and it should by all means, as our reasoning shows, be said to be any of those things to which everything, which is not what they themselves are, is inferior.

Hence, this Being must be living, wise, powerful, and all-powerful, true, just, blessed, eternal, and whatever, in like manner, is absolutely better than what is not it. Why, then, should we make any further inquiry as to what that supreme Nature is, if it is manifest which of all things it is, and which it is not?

16

For this Being it is the same to be just that it is to be justice; and so with regard to attributes that can be expressed in the same way: and none of these shows of what character, or how great, but what this Being is.

BUT perhaps, when this Being is called just, or great, or anything like these, it is not shown what it is, but of what character, or how great it is. For every such term seems to be used with reference to quantity or magnitude; because everything that is just is so through justness, and so with other like cases, in the same way. Hence, the supreme Nature itself is not just, except through justness.

It seems, then, that by participation in this quality, that is, justness, the supremely good Substance is called just. But, if this is so, it is just through another, and not through itself. But this is contrary to the truth already established, that it is good, or great, or whatever it is at all, through itself and not through another. So, if it is not just, except through justness, and cannot be just, except through itself, what can be more clear than that this Nature is itself justness? And, when it is said to be just through justness, it is the same as saying that it is just through itself. And, when it is said to be just through itself, nothing else is understood than that it is just through justness. Hence, if it is inquired what the supreme Nature, which is in question, is in itself, what truer answer can be given, than Justness?

We must observe, then, how we are to understand the statement, that the Nature which is itself justness is just. For, since a man cannot be justness, but can possess justness, we do not conceive of a just man as being justness, but as possessing justness. Since, on the other hand, it cannot properly be said of the supreme Nature that it possesses justness, but that it is justness, when it is called just it is properly conceived of as being justness, but not as possessing justness. Hence, if, when it is said to be justness, it is not said of what character it is, but what it is, it follows that, when it is called just, it is not said of what character it is, but what it is.

Therefore, seeing that it is the same to say of the supreme Being, that it is just and that it is justness; and, when it is said that it is justness, it is nothing else than saying that it is just; it makes no difference whether it is said to be justness or to be just. Hence, when one is asked regarding the supreme Nature, what it is, the answer, Just, is not less fitting than the answer, Justness. Moreover, what we see to have been proved in the case of justness, the intellect is compelled to acknowledge as true of all attributes which are similarly predicated of this supreme Nature. Whatever such attribute is predicated of it, then, it is shown, not of what character, or how great, but what it is.

But it is obvious that whatever good thing the supreme Nature is, it is in the highest degree. It is, therefore, supreme Being, supreme Justness, supreme Wisdom, supreme Truth, supreme Goodness, supreme Greatness, supreme Beauty, supreme Immortality, supreme Incorruptibility, supreme Immutability, supreme Blessedness, supreme Eternity, supreme Power, supreme Unity; which is nothing else than supremely being, supremely living, etc.

17

It is simple in such a way that all things that can be said of its essence are one and the same in it: and nothing can be said of its substance except in terms of what it is.

IS it to be inferred, then, that if the supreme Nature is so many goods, it will therefore be compounded of more goods than one? Or is it true, rather, that there are not more goods than one, but a single good described by many names? For, everything which is composite requires for its subsistence the things of which it is compounded, and, indeed, owes to them the fact of its existence, because, whatever it is, it is through these things; and they are not what they are through it, and therefore it is not at all supreme. If, then, that Nature is compounded of more goods than one, all these facts that are true of every composite must be applicable to it. But this impious falsehood the whole cogency of the truth that was shown above refutes and overthrows, through a clear argument.

Since, then, that Nature is by no means composite and yet is by all means those so many goods, necessarily all these are not more than one, but are one. Any one of them is, therefore, the same as all, whether taken all at once or separately. Therefore, just as whatever is attributed to the essence of the supreme Substance is one; so this substance is whatever it is essentially in one way, and by virtue of one consideration. For, when a man is said to be a material body, and rational, and human, these three things are not said in one way, or in virtue of one consideration. For, in accordance with one fact, he is a material body; and in accordance with another, rational; and no one of these, taken by itself, is the whole of what man is.

That supreme Being, however, is by no means anything in such a way that it is not this same thing, according to another way, or another consideration; because, whatever it is essentially in any way, this is all of what it is. Therefore, nothing that is truly said of the supreme Being is accepted in terms of quality or quantity, but only in terms of what it is. For, whatever it is in terms of either quality or quantity would constitute still another element, in terms of what it is; hence, it would not be simple, but composite.

18

It is without beginning and without end.

FROM what time, then, as this so simple Nature which creates and animates all things existed, or until what time is it to exist? Or rather, let us ask neither from what time, nor to what time, it exists; but is it without beginning and without end? For, if it has a beginning, it has this either from or through itself, or from or through another, or from or through nothing.

But it is certain, according to truths already made plain, that in no wise does it derive existence from another, or from nothing; or exist through another, or through nothing. In no wise, therefore, has it had inception through or from another, or through or from nothing.

Moreover, it cannot have inception from or through itself, although it exists from and through itself. For it so exists from and through itself, that by no means is there one essence which exists from and through itself, and another through which, and from which, it exists. But, whatever begins to exist from or through something, is by no means identical with that from or through which it begins to exist. Therefore, the supreme Nature does not begin through or from itself.

Seeing, then, that it has a beginning neither through nor from itself, and neither through nor from nothing, it assuredly has no beginning at all. But neither will it have an end. For, if it is to have end, it is not supremely immortal and supremely incorruptible. But we have proved that it is supremely immortal and supremely incorruptible. Therefore, it will not have an end.

Furthermore, if it is to have an end, it will perish either willingly or against its will. But certainly that is not a simple, unmixed good, at whose will the supreme good perishes. But this Being is itself the true and simple, unmixed good. Therefore, that very Being, which is certainly the supreme good, will not die of its own will. If, however, it is to perish against its will, it is not supremely powerful, or all-powerful. But cogent reasoning has asserted it to be powerful and all-powerful. Therefore, it will not die against its will. Hence, if neither with nor against its will the supreme Nature is to have an end, in no way will it have an end.

Again, if the supreme nature has an end or a beginning, it is not true eternity, which it has been irrefutably proved to be above.

Then, let him who can conceive of a time when this began to be true, or when it was not true, namely, that something was destined to be; or when this shall cease to be true, and shall not be true, namely, that something has existed. But, if neither of these suppositions is conceivable, and both these facts cannot exist without truth, it is impossible even to conceive that truth has either beginning or end. And then, if truth had a beginning, or shall have an end; before it began it was true that truth did not exist, and after it shall be ended it will be true that truth will not exist. Yet, anything that is true cannot exist without truth. Therefore, truth existed before truth existed, and truth will exist after truth shall be ended, which is a most contradictory conclusion. Whether, then, truth is said to have, or understood not to have, beginning or end, it cannot be limited by any beginning or end. Hence, the same follows as regards the supreme Nature, since it is itself the supreme Truth.

19

In what sense nothing existed before or will exist after this Being.

BUT here we are again confronted by the term *nothing*, and whatever our reasoning thus far, with the concordant attestation of truth and necessity, has concluded nothing to be. For, if the propositions duly set forth above have been confirmed by the fortification of logically necessary truth, not anything existed before the supreme Being, nor will anything exist after it. Hence, nothing existed before, and nothing will exist after, it. For, either something or nothing must have preceded it; and either something or nothing must be destined to follow it.

But, he who says that nothing existed before it, appears to make this statement, "that there was before it a time when nothing existed, and that there will be after it a time when nothing will exist." Therefore, when nothing existed, that Being did not exist, and when nothing shall exist, that Being will not exist. How is it, then, that it does not take inception from nothing or how is it that it will not come to nothing?—if that Being did not yet exist, when nothing already existed; and the same Being shall no longer exist, when nothing shall still exist. Of what avail is so weighty a mass of arguments, if this nothing so easily demolishes their structure? For, if it is established that the supreme Being succeeds nothing [*Nothing is here treated as an entity, supposed actually to precede the supreme Being in existence. The fallacy involved is shown below.*—Tr.], which precedes it, and yields its place to nothing, which follows it, whatever has been posited as true above is necessarily unsettled by empty nothing.

But, rather ought this nothing to be resisted, lest so many structures of cogent reasoning be stormed by nothing; and the supreme good, which has been sought and found by the light of truth, be lost for nothing. Let it rather be declared, then, that nothing did not exist before the supreme Being, and that nothing will not exist after it, rather than that, when a place is given before or after it to nothing, that Being which through itself brought into existence what was nothing, should be reduced through nothing to nothing.

For this one assertion, namely, that nothing existed before the supreme Being, carries two meanings. For, one sense of this statement is that, before the supreme Being, there was a time when nothing was. But another understanding of the same statement is that, before the supreme Being, not anything existed. Just as, supposing I should say, "Nothing has taught me to fly," I could explain this assertion either in this way, that nothing, as an entity in itself, which signifies not anything, has taught me actually to fly—which would be false; or in this way, that not anything has taught me to fly, which would be true.

The former interpretation, therefore, which is followed by the inconsistency discussed above, is rejected by all reasoning as false. But there remains the other interpretation, which unites in perfect consistency with the foregoing arguments, and which, from the force of their whole correlation, must be true.

Hence, the statement that nothing existed before that Being must be received in the latter sense. Nor should it be so explained, that it shall be understood that there was any time when that Being did not exist, and nothing did exist; but, so that it shall be understood that, before that Being, there was not anything. The same sort of double signification is found in the statement that nothing will exist after that Being.

If, then, this interpretation of the term *nothing*, that has been given, is carefully analysed, most truly neither something nor nothing preceded or will follow the supreme Being, and the conclusion is reached, that nothing existed before or will exist after it. Yet, the solidity of the truths already established is in no wise impaired by the emptiness of nothing.

20

It exists in every place and at every time.

BUT, although it has been concluded above that this creative Nature exists everywhere, and in all things, and through all; and from the fact that it neither began, nor will cease to be, it follows that it always has been, and is, and will be; yet, I perceive a certain secret murmur of contradiction which compels me to inquire more carefully where and when that Nature exists.

The supreme Being, then, exists either everywhere and always, or merely at some place and time, or nowhere and never: or, as I express it, either in every place and at every time, or finitely, in some place and at some time, or in no place and at no time.

But what can be more obviously contradictory, than that what exists most really and supremely exists nowhere and never? It is, therefore, false that it exists nowhere and never. Again, since there is no good, nor anything at all without it; if this Being itself exists nowhere or never, then nowhere or never is there any good, and nowhere and never is there anything at all. But there is no need to state that this is false. Hence, the former proposition is also false, that that Being exists nowhere and never.

It therefore exists finitely, at some time and place, or everywhere and always. But, if it exists finitely, at some place or time, there and then only, where and when it exists, can anything exist. Where and when it does not exist, moreover, there is no existence at all, because, without it, nothing exists. Whence it will follow, that there is some place and time where and when nothing at all exists. But seeing that this is false—for place and time themselves are existing things—the supreme Nature cannot exist finitely, at some place or time. But, if it is said that it of itself exists finitely, at some place and time, but that, through its power, it is wherever and whenever anything is, this is not true. For, since it is manifest that its power is nothing else than itself, by no means does its power exist without it.

Since, then, it does not exist finitely, at some place or time, it must exist everywhere and always, that is, in every place and at every time.

21

It exists in no place or time.

BUT, if this is true, either it exists in every place and at every time, or else only a part of it so exists, the other part transcending every place and time.

But, if in part it exists, and in part does not exist, in every place and at every time, it has parts; which is false. It does not, therefore, exist everywhere and always in part.

But how does it exist as a whole, everywhere and always? For, either it is to be understood that it exists as a whole at once, in all places or at all times, and by parts in individual places and times; or, that it exists as a whole, in individual places and times as well.

But, if it exists by parts in individual places or times, it is not exempt from composition and division of parts; which has been found to be in a high degree alien to the supreme Nature. Hence, it does not so exist, as a whole, in all places and at all times that it exists by parts in individual places and times.

We are confronted, then, by the former alternative, that is, how the supreme Nature can exist, as a whole, in every individual place and time. This is doubtless impossible, unless it either exists at once or at different times in individual places or times. But, since the law of place and the law of time, the investigation of which it has hitherto been possible to prosecute in a single discussion, because they advanced on exactly the same lines, here separate one from another and seem to avoid debate, as if by evasion in diverse directions, let each be investigated independently in discussion directed on itself alone.

First, then, let us see whether the supreme Nature can exist, as a whole, in individual places, either at once in all, or at different times, in different places. Then, let us make the same inquiry regarding the times at which it can exist.

If, then, it exists as a whole in each individual place, then, for each individual place there is an individual whole. For, just as place is so distinguished from place that there are individual places, so that which exists as a whole, in one place, is so distinct from that which exists as a whole at the same time, in another place, that there are individual wholes. For, of what exists as a whole, in any place, there is no part that does not exist in that place. And that of which there is no part that does not exist in a given place, is no part of what exists at the same time outside this place.

What exists as a whole, then, in any place, is no part of what exists at the same time outside that place. But, of that of which no part exists outside any given place, no part exists, at the same time, in another place. How, then, can what exists as a whole, in any place, exist simultaneously, as a whole, in another place, if no part of it can at that time exist in another place?

Since, then, one whole cannot exist as a whole in different places at the same time, it follows that, for individual places, there are individual wholes, if anything is to exist as a whole in different individual places at once. Hence, if the supreme Nature exists as a whole, at one time, in every individual place, there are as many supreme Natures as there can be individual places; which it would be irrational to believe. Therefore, it does not exist, as a whole, at one time in individual places.

If, however, at different times it exists, as a whole, in individual places, then, when it is in one place, there is in the meantime no good and no existence in other places, since without it absolutely nothing exists. But the absurdity of this supposition is proved by the existence of places themselves, which are not nothing, but something. Therefore, the supreme Nature does not exist, as a whole, in individual places at different times.

But, if neither at the same time nor at different times does it exist, as a whole, in individual places, it is evident that it does not at all exist, as a whole, in each individual place. We must now examine, then, whether this supreme Nature exists, as a whole, at individual times, either simultaneously or at distinct times for individual times.

But, how can anything exist, as a whole, simultaneously, at individual times, if these times are not themselves simultaneous? But, if this Being exists, as a whole, separately and at distinct times for individual times, just as a man exists as a whole yesterday, to-day, and to-morrow; it is properly said that it was and is and will be. Its age, then, which is no other than its eternity, does not exist, as a whole, simultaneously, but it is distributed in parts according to the parts of time.

But its eternity is nothing else than itself. The supreme Being, then, will be divided into parts, according to the divisions of time. For, if its age is prolonged through periods of time, it has with this time present, past, and future. But what else is its age than its duration of existence, than its eternity? Since, then, its eternity is nothing else than its essence, as considerations set forth above irrefutably prove; if its eternity has past, present, and future, its essence also has, in consequence, past, present, and future.

But what is past is not present or future; and what is present is not past or future; and what is future is not past or present. How, then, shall that proposition be valid, which was proved with clear and logical cogency above, namely, that that supreme Nature is in no wise composite, but is supremely simple, supremely immutable?—how shall this be so, if that Nature is one thing, at one time, and another, at another, and has parts distributed according to times? Or rather, if these earlier propositions are true, how can these latter be possible? By no means, then, is past or future attributable to the creative Being, either its age or its eternity. For why has it not a present, if it truly *is*? But *was* means past, and *will be* future. Therefore that Being never was, nor will be. Hence, it does not exist at distinct times, just as it does not exist, as a whole, simultaneously in different individual times.

If, then, as our discussion has proved, it neither so exists, as a whole, in all places or times that it exists, as a whole, at one time in all, or by parts in individual places and times; nor so that it exists, as a whole, in individual times and places, it is manifest that it does not in any way exist, as a whole, in every time or place.

And, since, in like manner, it has been demonstrated that it neither so exists in every time or place, that a part exists in every, and a part transcends every, place and time, it is impossible that it exists everywhere and always.

For, in no way can it be conceived to exist everywhere and always, except either as a whole or in part. But if it does not at all exist everywhere and always, it will exist either finitely in some place or time, or in none. But it has already been proved, that it cannot exist finitely, in any place or time. In no place or time, that is, nowhere and never, does it exist. For it cannot exist, except in every or in some place or time.

But, on the other hand, since it is irrefutably established, not only that it exists through itself, and without beginning and without end, but that without it nothing anywhere or ever exists, it must exist everywhere and always.

22

How it exists in every place and time, and in none.

HOW, then, shall these prepositions, that are so necessary according to our exposition, and so necessary according to our proof, be reconciled? Perhaps the supreme Nature exists in place and time in some such way, that it is not prevented from so existing simultaneously, as a whole, in different places or times, that there are not more wholes than one; and that its age, which does not exist, except as true eternity, is not distributed among past, present, and future.

For, to this law of space and time, nothing seems to be subject, except the beings which so exist in space or time that they do not transcend extent of space or duration of time. Hence, though of beings of this class it is with all truth asserted that one and the same whole cannot exist simultaneously, as a whole, in different places or times; in the case of those beings which are not of this class, no such conclusion is necessarily reached.

For it seems to be rightly said, that place is predicable only of objects whose magnitude place contains by including it, and includes by containing it; and that time is predicable only of objects whose duration time ends by measuring it, and measures by ending it. Hence, to any being, to whose spatial extent or duration no bound can be set, either by space or time, no place or time is properly attributed. For, seeing that place does not act upon it as place, nor time as time, it is not irrational to say, that no place is its place, and no time its time.

But, what evidently has no place or time is doubtless by no means compelled to submit to the law of place or time. No law of place or time, then, in any way governs any nature, which no place or time limits by some kind of restraint. But what rational consideration can by any course of reasoning fail to reach the conclusion, that the Substance which creates and is supreme among all beings, which must be alien to, and free from, the nature and law of all things which itself created from nothing, is limited by no restraint of space or time; since, more truly, its power, which is nothing else than its essence, contains and includes under itself all these things which it created? Is it not impudently foolish, too, to say either, that space circumscribes the magnitude of truth, or, that time measures its duration—truth, which regards no greatness or smallness of spatial or temporal extent at all?

Seeing, then, that this is the condition of place or time; that only whatever is limited by their bounds neither escapes the law of parts—such as place follows, according to magnitude, or such as time submits to, according to duration—nor can in any way be contained, as a whole, simultaneously by different places or times; but whatever is in no wise confined by the restraint of place or time, is not compelled by any law of places or times to multiplicity of parts, nor is it prevented from being present, as a whole and simultaneously, in more places or times than one—seeing, I say, that this is the condition governing place or time, no doubt the supreme Substance, which is encompassed by no restraint of place or time, is bound by none of their laws.

Hence, since inevitable necessity requires that the supreme Being, as a whole, be lacking to no place or time, and no law of place or time prevents it from being simultaneously in every place or time; it must be simultaneously present in every individual place or time. For, because it is present in one place, it is not therefore prevented from being present at the same time, and in like manner in this, or that other, place or time.

Nor, because it was, or is, or shall be, has any part of its eternity therefore vanished from the present, with the past, which no longer is; nor does it pass with the present, which is, for an instant; nor is it to come with the future, which is not yet.

For, by no means is that Being compelled or forbidden by a law of space or time to exist, or not to exist, at any place or time—the Being which, in no wise, includes its own existence in space or time. For, when the supreme Being is said to exist in space or time, although the form of expression regarding it, and regarding local and temporal natures, is the same, because of the usage of language, yet the sense is different, because of the unlikeness of the objects of discussion. For in the latter case the same expression has two meanings, namely: (1) that these objects are present in those places and times in which they are said to be, and (2) that they are contained by these places and times themselves.

But in the case of the supreme Being, the first sense only is intended, namely, that it is present; not that it is also contained. If the usage of language permitted, it would, therefore, seem to be more fittingly said that it exists *with* place or time, than that it exists *in* place or time. For the statement that a thing exists in another implies that it is contained, more than does the statement that it exists with another.

In no place or time, then, is this Being properly said to exist, since it is contained by no other at all. And yet it may be said, after a manner of its own, to be in every place or time, since whatever else exists is sustained by its presence, lest it lapse into nothingness. It exists in every place and time, because it is absent from none; and it exists in none, because it has no place or time, and has not taken to itself distinctions of place or time, neither here nor there, nor anywhere, nor then, nor now, nor at any time; nor does it exist in terms of this fleeting present, in which we live, nor has it existed, nor will it exist, in terms of past or future, since these are restricted to things finite and mutable, which it is not.

And yet, these properties of time and place can, in some sort, be ascribed to it, since it is just as truly present in all finite and mutable beings as if it were circumscribed by the same places, and suffered change by the same times.

We have sufficient evidence, then, to dispel the contradiction that threatened us; as to how the highest Being of all exists, everywhere and always, and nowhere and never, that is, in every place and time, and in no place or time, according to the consistent truth of different senses of the terms employed.

23

How it is better conceived to exist everywhere than in every place

BUT, since it is plain that this supreme Nature is not more truly in all places than in all existing things, not as if it were contained by them, but as containing all, by permeating all, why should it not be said to be everywhere, in this sense, that it may be understood rather to be in all existing things, than merely in all places, since this sense is supported by the truth of the fact, and is not forbidden by the proper signification of the word of place?

For we often quite properly apply terms of place to objects which are not places; as, when I say that the understanding is there in the soul, where rationality is. For, though *there* and *where* are adverbs of place, yet, by no local limitation, does the mind contain anything, nor is either rationality or understanding contained.

Hence, as regards the truth of the matter, the supreme Nature is more appropriately said to be everywhere, in this sense, that it is in all existing things, than in this sense, namely that it is merely in all places. And since, as the reasons set forth above show, it cannot exist otherwise, it must so be in all existing things, that it is one and the same, perfect whole in every individual thing simultaneously.

24

How it is better understood to exist always than at every time.

IT is also evident that this supreme Substance is without beginning and without end; that it has neither past, nor future, nor the temporal, that is, transient present in which we live; since its age, or eternity, which is nothing else than itself, is immutable and without parts. Is not, therefore, the term which seems to mean all time more properly understood, when applied to this Substance, to signify eternity, which is never unlike itself, rather than a changing succession of times, which is ever in some sort unlike itself?

Hence, if this Being is said to exist always; since, for it, it is the same to exist and to live, no better sense can be attached to this statement, than that it exists or lives eternally, that is, it possesses interminable life, as a perfect whole at once. For its eternity apparently is an interminable life, existing at once as a perfect whole.

For, since it has already been shown that this Substance is nothing else than its own life and its own eternity, is in no wise terminable, and does not exist, except as at once and perfectly whole, what else is true eternity, which is consistent with the nature of that Substance alone, than an interminable life, existing as at once and perfectly whole?

For this truth is, at any rate, clearly perceived from the single fact that true eternity belongs only to that substance which alone, as we have proved, was not created, but is the creator, since true eternity is conceived to be free from the limitations of beginning and end; and this is proved to be consistent with the nature of no created being, from the very fact that all such have been created from nothing.

25

It cannot suffer change by any accidents. Accidents, as Anselm uses the term, are facts external to the essence of a being, which may yet be conceived to produce changes in a mutable being.

BUT does not this Being, which has been shown to exist as in every way substantially identical with itself, sometimes exist as different from itself, at any rate accidentally? But how is it supremely immutable, if it can, I will not say, be, but, be conceived of, as variable by virtue of accidents? And, on the other hand, does it not partake of accident, since even this very fact that it is greater than all other natures and that it is unlike them seems to be an accident in its case (*illi accidere*)? But what is the inconsistency between susceptibility to certain facts, called accidents, and natural immutability, if from the undergoing of these accidents the substance undergoes no change?

For, of all the facts, called accidents, some are understood not to be present or absent without some variation in the subject of the accident—all colors, for instance—while others are known not to effect any change in a thing either by occurring or not occurring— certain relations, for instance. For it is certain that I am neither older nor younger than a man who is not yet born, nor equal to him, nor like him. But I shall be able to sustain and to lose all these relations toward him, as soon as he shall have been born, according as he shall grow, or undergo change through diverse qualities.

It is made clear, then, that of all those facts, called accidents, a part bring some degree of mutability in their train, while a part do not impair at all the immutability of that in whose case they occur. Hence, although the supreme Nature in its simplicity has never undergone such accidents as cause mutation, yet it does not disdain occasional expression in terms of those accidents which are in no wise inconsistent with supreme immutability; and yet there is no accident respecting its essence, whence it would be conceived of, as itself variable.

Whence this conclusion, also, may be reached, that it is susceptible of no accident; since, just as those accidents, which effect some change by their occurrence or non-occurrence, are by virtue of this very effect of theirs regarded as being true accidents, so those facts, which lack a like effect, are found to be improperly called accidents. Therefore, this Essence is always, in every way, substantially identical with itself; and it is never in any way different from itself, even accidentally. But, however it may be as to the proper signification of the term *accident*, this is undoubtedly true, that of the supremely immutable Nature no statement can be made, whence it shall be conceived of as mutable.

26

How this Being is said to be substance: it transcends all substance and is individually whatever it is.

BUT, if what we have ascertained concerning the simplicity of this Nature is established, how is it substance? For, though every substance is susceptible of admixture of difference, or, at any rate, susceptible of mutation by accidents, the immutable purity of this Being is inaccessible to admixture or mutation, in any form.

How, then, shall it be maintained that it is a substance of any kind, except as it is called *substance* for *being*, and so transcends, as it is above, every substance? For, as great as is the difference between that Being, which is through itself whatever it is, and which creates every other being from nothing, and a being, which is made whatever it is through another, from nothing; so much does the supreme Substance differ from these beings, which are not what it is. And, since it alone, of all natures, derives from itself, without the help of another nature, whatever existence it has, is it not whatever it is individually and apart from association with its creatures?

Hence, if it ever shares any name with other beings, doubtless a very different signification of that name is to be understood in its case.

27

It is not included among substances as commonly treated, yet it is a substance and an indivisible spirit.

IT is, therefore, evident that in any ordinary treatment of substance, this Substance cannot be included, from sharing in whose essence every nature is excluded. Indeed, since every substance is treated either as universal, i.e. as essentially common to more than one substance, as being a man is common to individual men; or as individual, having a universal essence in common with others, as individual men have in common with individual men the fact that they are men; does any one conceive that, in the treatment of other substances, that supreme Nature is included, which neither divides itself into more substances than one, nor unites with any other, by virtue of a common essence?

Yet, seeing that it not only most certainly exists, but exists in the highest degree of all things; and since the essence of anything is usually called its substance, doubtless if any worthy name can be given it, there is no objection to our calling it substance.

And since no worthier essence than spirit and body is known, and of these, spirit is more worthy than body, it must certainly be maintained that this Being is spirit and not body. But, seeing that one spirit has not any parts, and there cannot be more spirits than one of this kind, it must, by all means, be an indivisible spirit. For since, as is shown above, it is neither compounded of parts, nor can be conceived of as mutable, through any differences or accidents, it is impossible that it is divisible by any form of division.

28

This Spirit exists simply, and created beings are not comparable with him.

IT seems to follow, then, from the preceding considerations, that the Spirit, which exists in so wonderfully singular and so singularly wonderful a way of its own, is in some sort unique; while other beings which seem to be comparable with it are not so.

For, by diligent attention it will be seen that that Spirit alone exists simply, and perfectly, and absolutely; while all other beings are almost non-existent, and hardly exist at all. For, seeing that of this Spirit, because of its immutable eternity, it can in no wise be said, in terms of any alteration, that it was or will be, but simply that it is; it is not now, by mutation, anything which it either was not at any time, or will not be in the future. Nor does it fail to be now what it was, or will be, at any time; but, whatever it is, it is, once for all, and simultaneously, and interminably. Seeing, I say, that its existence is of this character, it is rightly said itself to exist simply, and absolutely, and perfectly.

But since, on the other hand, all other beings, in accordance with some cause, have at some time been, or will be, by mutation, what they are not now; or, are what they were not, or will not be, at some time; and, since this former existence of theirs is no longer a fact; and that future existence is not yet a fact; and their existence in a transient, and most brief, and scarcely existing, present is hardly a fact—since, then, they exist in such mutability, it is not unreasonably denied that they exist simply, and perfectly, and absolutely; and it is asserted that they are almost nonexistent, that they scarcely exist at all.

Again, since all beings, which are other than this Spirit himself, have come from non-existence to existence, not through themselves, but through another; and, since they return from existence to non-existence, so far as their own power is concerned, unless they are sustained through another being, is it consistent with their nature to exist simply, or perfectly, or absolutely, and not rather to be almost non-existent?

And since the existence of this ineffable Spirit alone can in no way be conceived to have taken inception from non-existence, or to be capable of sustaining any deficiency rising from what is in nonexistence; and since, whatever he is himself, he is not through another than himself, that is, than what he is himself, ought not his existence alone to be conceived of as simple, and perfect, and absolute?

But what is thus simply, and on every ground, solely perfect, simple, and absolute, this may very certainly be justly said to be in some sort unique. And, on the other hand, whatever is known to exist through a higher cause, and neither simply, nor perfectly, nor absolutely, but scarcely to exist, or to be almost non-existent—this assuredly may be rightly said to be in some sort non-existent.

According to this course of reasoning, then, the creative Spirit alone exists, and all creatures are nonexistent; yet, they are not wholly non-existent, because, through that Spirit which alone exists absolutely, they have been made something from nothing.

29.

His expression is identical with himself, and consubstantial with him, since there are not two spirits, but one.

BUT now, having considered these questions regarding the properties of the supreme Nature, which have occurred to me in following the guidance of reason to the present point, I think it reasonable to examine this Spirit's expression (*locutio*), through which all things were created.

For, though all that has been ascertained regarding this expression above has the inflexible strength of reason, I am especially compelled to a more careful discussion of this expression by the fact that it is proved to be identical with the supreme Spirit himself. For, if this Spirit created nothing except through himself, and whatever was created by him was created through that expression, how shall that expression be anything else than what the Spirit himself is?

Furthermore, the facts already discovered declare irrefutably that nothing at all ever could, or can, exist, except the creative Spirit and its creatures. But it is impossible that the expression of this Spirit is included among created beings; for every created being was created through that expression; but that expression could not be created through itself. For nothing can be created through itself, since every creature exists later than that through which it is created, and nothing exists later than itself.

The alternative remaining is, then, that this expression of the supreme Spirit, since it cannot be a creature, is no other than the supreme Spirit. Therefore, this expression itself can be conceived of as nothing else than the intelligence (*intelligentia*) of this Spirit, by which he conceives of (*intelligit*) all things. For, to him, what is expressing anything, according to this kind of expression, but conceiving of it? For he does not, like man, ever fail to express what he conceives.

If, then, the supremely simple Nature is nothing else than what its intelligence is, just as it is identical with its wisdom, necessarily, in the same way, it is nothing else than what its expression is. But, since it is already manifest that the supreme Spirit is one only, and altogether indivisible, this his expression must be so consubstantial with him, that they are not two spirits, but one.

30

This expression does not consist of more words than one, but is one Word.

WHY, then, should I have any further doubt regarding that question which I dismissed above as doubtful, namely, whether this expression consists of more words than one, or of one? For, if it is so consubstantial with the supreme Nature that they are not two spirits, but one; assuredly, just as the latter is supremely simple, so is the former. It therefore does not consist of more words than one, but is one Word, through which all things were created.

31

This Word itself is not the likeness of created beings, but the reality of their being, while created beings are a kind of likeness of reality.—What natures are greater and more excellent than others.

BUT here, it seems to me, there arises a question that is not easy to answer, and yet must not be left in any ambiguity. For all words of that sort by which we express any objects in our mind, that is, conceive of them, are likenesses and images of the objects to which they correspond; and every likeness or image is more or less true, according as it more or less closely imitates the object of which it is the likeness.

What, then, is to be our position regarding the Word by which all things are expressed, and through which all were created? Will it be, or will it not be, the likeness of the things that have been created through itself? For, if it is itself the true likeness of mutable things, it is not consubstantial with supreme immutability; which is false.

But, if it is not altogether true, and is merely a sort of likeness of mutable things, then the Word of supreme Truth is not altogether true; which is absurd. But if it has no likeness to mutable things, how were they created after its example?

But perhaps nothing of this ambiguity will remain if—as the reality of a man is said to be the living man, but the likeness or image of a man in his picture—so the reality of being is conceived of as in the Word, whose essence exists so supremely that in a certain sense it alone exists; while in these things which, in comparison with that Essence, are in some sort non-existent, and, yet were made something through, and according to, that Word, a kind of imitation of that supreme Essence is found.

For, in this way the Word of supreme Truth, which is also itself supreme Truth, will experience neither gain nor loss, according as it is more or less like its creatures. But the necessary inference will rather be, that every created being exists in so much the greater degree, or is so much the more excellent, the more like it is to what exists supremely, and is supremely great.

For on this account, perhaps—nay, not perhaps, but certainly—does every mind judge natures in any way alive to excel those that are not alive, the sentient to excel the non-sentient, the rational the irrational. For, since the supreme Nature, after a certain unique manner of its own, not only exists, but lives, and is sentient and rational, it is clear that, of all existing beings, that which is in some way alive is more like this supreme Nature, than that which is not alive at all; and what, in any way, even by a corporeal sense, cognises anything, is more like this Nature than what is not sentient at all; and what is rational, more than what is incapable of reasoning.

But it is clear, for a like reason, that certain natures exist in a greater or less degree than others. For, just as that is more excellent by nature which, through its natural essence, is nearer to the most excellent Being, so certainly that nature exists in a greater degree, whose essence is more like the supreme Essence. And I think that this can easily be ascertained as follows. If we should conceive any substance that is alive, and sentient, and rational, to be deprived of its reason, then of its sentience, then of its life, and finally of the bare existence that remains, who would fail to understand that the substance that is thus destroyed, little by little, is gradually brought to smaller and smaller degrees of existence, and at last to non-existence? But the attributes which, taken each by itself, reduce an essence to less and less degrees of existence, if assumed in order, lead it to greater and greater degrees.

It is evident, then, that a living substance exists in a greater degree than one that is not living, a sentient than a non-sentient, and a rational than a non-rational. So, there is no doubt that every substance exists in a greater degree, and is more excellent, according as it is more like that substance which exists supremely and is supremely excellent.

It is sufficiently clear, then, that in the Word, through which all things were created, is not their likeness, but their true and simple essence; while, in the things created, there is not a simple and absolute essence, but an imperfect imitation of that true Essence. Hence, it necessarily follows, that this Word is not more nor less true, according to its likeness to the things created, but every created nature has a higher essence and dignity, the more it is seen to approach that Word.

32

The supreme Spirit expresses himself by a coeternal Word.

BUT since this is true, how can what is simple Truth be the Word corresponding to those objects, of which it is not the likeness? Since every word by which an object is thus mentally expressed is the likeness of that object, if this is not the word corresponding to the objects that have been created through it, how shall we be sure that it is the Word? For every word is a word corresponding to some object. Therefore, if there were no creature, there would be no word.

Are we to conclude, then, that if there were no creature, that Word would not exist at all, which is the supreme self-sufficient Essence? Or, would the supreme Being itself, perhaps, which is the Word still be the eternal Being, but not the Word, if nothing were ever created through that Being? For, to what has not been, and is not, and will not be, then can be no word corresponding.

But, according to this reasoning, if there were never any being but the supreme Spirit, there would be no word at all in him. If there were no word in him, he would express nothing to himself; if he expressed nothing to himself, since, for him, expressing anything is the same with understanding or conceiving of it (*intelligere*), he would not understand or conceive of anything; if he understood or conceived of nothing, then the supreme Wisdom, which is nothing else than this Spirit, would understand or conceive of nothing; which is most absurd.

What is to be inferred? For, if it conceived of nothing, how would it be the supreme Wisdom? Or, if there were in no wise anything but it, of what would it conceive? Would it not conceive of itself? But how can it be even imagined that the supreme Wisdom, at any time does not conceive of itself; since a rational mind can remember not only itself, but that supreme Wisdom, and conceive of that Wisdom and of itself? For, if the human mind could have no memory or concept of that Wisdom or of itself, it would not distinguish itself at all from irrational creatures, and that Wisdom from the whole created world, in silent meditation by itself, as my mind does now.

Hence, that Spirit, supreme as he is eternal, is thus eternally mindful of himself, and conceives of himself after the likeness of a rational mind; nay, not after the likeness of anything; but in the first place that Spirit, and the rational mind after its likeness. But, if he conceives of himself eternally, he expresses himself eternally. If he expresses himself eternally, his Word is eternally with him. Whether, therefore, it be thought of in connection with no other existing being, or with other existing beings, the Word of that Spirit must be coeternal with him.

33

He utters himself and what he creates by a single consubstantial Word.

BUT here, in my inquiry concerning the Word, by which the Creator expresses all that he creates, is suggested the word by which he, who creates all, expresses himself. Does he express himself, then, by one word, and what he creates by another; or does he rather express whatever he creates by the same word whereby he expresses himself?

For this Word also, by which he expresses himself, must be identical with himself, as is evidently true of the Word by which he expresses his creatures. For since, even if nothing but that supreme Spirit ever existed, urgent reason would still require the existence of that word by which he expresses himself, what is more true than that his Word is nothing else than what he himself is? Therefore, if he expresses himself and what he creates by a Word consubstantial with himself, it is manifest that of the Word by which he expresses himself, and of the Word by which he expresses the created world, the substance is one.

How, then, if the substance is one, are there two words? But, perhaps, identity of substance does not compel us to admit a single Word. For the Creator himself, who speaks in these words, has the same substance with them, and yet is not the Word. But, undoubtedly the word by which the supreme Wisdom expresses itself may most fitly be called its Word on the former ground, namely, that it contains the perfect likeness of that Wisdom.

For, on no ground can it be denied that when a rational mind conceives of itself in meditation, the image of itself arises in its thought, or rather the thought of the mind is itself its image, after its likeness, as if formed from its impression. For, whatever object the mind, either through representation of the body or through reason, desires to conceive of truly, it at least attempts to express its likeness, so far as it is able, in the mental concept itself. And the more truly it succeeds in this, the more truly does it think of the object itself; and, indeed, this fact is observed more clearly when it thinks of something else which it is not, and especially when it thinks of a material body. For, when I think of a man I know, in his absence, the vision of my thought forms such an image as I have acquired in memory through my ocular vision and this image is the word corresponding to the man I express by thinking of him.

The rational mind, then, when it conceives of itself in thought, has with itself its image born of itself that is, its thought in its likeness, as if formed from its impression, although it cannot, except in thought alone, separate itself from its image, which image is its word.

Who, then, can deny that the supreme Wisdom, when it conceives of itself by expressing itself, begets a likeness of itself consubstantial with it, namely, its Word? And this Word, although of a subject so uniquely important nothing can be said with sufficient propriety, may still not inappropriately be called the image of that Wisdom, its representation, just as it is called his likeness.

But the Word by which the Creator expresses the created world is not at all, in the same way, a word corresponding to the created world, since it is not this world's likeness, but its elementary essence. It therefore follows, that he does not express the created world itself by a word corresponding to the created world. To what, then, does the word belong, whereby he expresses it, if he does not express it by a word, belonging to itself? For what he expresses, he expresses by a word, and a word must belong to something, that is, it is the likeness of something. But if he expresses nothing but himself or his created world he can express nothing, except by a word corresponding to himself or to something else.

So, if he expresses nothing by a word belonging to the created world, whatever he expresses, he expresses by the Word corresponding to himself. By one and the same Word, then, he expresses himself and whatever he has made.

34

How he can express the created world by his Word.

BUT how can objects so different as the creative and the created being be expressed by one Word, especially since that Word itself is coeternal with him who expresses them, while the created world is not coeternal with him? Perhaps, because he himself is supreme Wisdom and supreme Reason, in which are all things that have been created; just as a work which is made after one of the arts, not only when it is made, but before it is made, and after it is destroyed, is always in respect of the art itself nothing else than what that art is.

Hence, when the supreme Spirit expresses himself, he expresses all created beings. For, both before they were created, and now that they have been created, and after they are decayed or changed in any way, they are ever in him not what they are in themselves, but what this Spirit himself is. For, in themselves they are mutable beings, created according to immutable reason; while in him is the true first being, and the first reality of existence, the more like unto which those beings are in any way, the more really and excellently do they exist. Thus, it may reasonably be declared that, when the supreme Spirit expresses himself, he also expresses whatever has been created by one and the same Word.

35

Whatever has been created is in his Word and knowledge, life and truth.

BUT, since it is established that his word is consubstantial with him, and perfectly like him, it necessarily follows that all things that exist in him exist also, and in the same way, in his Word. Whatever has been created, then, whether alive or not alive, or howsoever it exists in itself, is very life and truth in him.

But, since knowing is the same to the supreme Spirit as conceiving or expressing, he must know all things that he knows in the same way in which he expresses or conceives of them. Therefore, just as all things are in his Word life and truth, so are they in his knowledge.

36

In how incomprehensible a way he expresses or knows the objects created by him.

HENCE, it may be most clearly comprehended that how this Spirit expresses, or how he knows the created world, cannot be comprehended by human knowledge. For none can doubt that created substances exist far differently in themselves than in our knowledge. For, in themselves they exist by virtue of their own being; while in our knowledge is not their being, but their likeness.

We conclude, then, that they exist more truly in themselves than in our knowledge, in the same degree in which they exist more truly anywhere by virtue of their own being, than by virtue of their likeness. Therefore, since this is also an established truth, that every created substance exists more truly in the Word, that is, in the intelligence of the Creator, than it does in itself, in the same degree in which the creative being exists more truly than the created; how can the human mind comprehend of what kind is that expression and that knowledge, which is so much higher and truer than created substances; if our knowledge is as far surpassed by those substances as their likeness is removed from their being?

37

Whatever his relation to his creatures, this relation his Word also sustains: yet both do not simultaneously sustain this relation as more than one being.

BUT since it has already been clearly demonstrated that the supreme Spirit created all things through his Word, did not the Word itself also create all things? For, since it is consubstantial with him, it must be the supreme essence of that of which it is the Word. But there is no supreme Essence, except one, which is the only creator and the only beginning of all things which have been created. For this Essence, through no other than itself, alone created all things from nothing. Hence, whatever the supreme Spirit creates, the same his Word also creates, and in the same way.

Whatever relation, then, the supreme Spirit bears to what he creates, this relation his Word also bears, and in the same way. And yet, both do not bear it simultaneously, as more than one, since there are not more supreme creative essences than one. Therefore, just as he is the creator and the beginning of the world, so is his Word also; and yet there are not two, but one creator and one beginning.

38

It cannot be explained why they are two, although they must be so.

OUR careful attention is therefore demanded by a peculiarity which, though most unusual in other beings, seems to belong to the supreme Spirit and his Word. For, it is certain that in each of these separately and in both simultaneously, whatever they are so exists that it is separately perfected in both, and yet does not admit plurality in the two. For although, taken separately, he is perfectly supreme Truth and Creator, and his Word is supreme Truth and Creator; yet both at once are not two truths or two creators.

But although this is true, yet it is most remarkably clear that neither he, whose is the Word, can be his own Word, nor can the Word be he, whose Word it is, although in so far as regards either what they are substantially, or what relation they bear to the created world, they ever preserve an indivisible unity. But in respect of the fact that he does not derive existence from that Word, but that Word from him, they admit an ineffable plurality, ineffable, certainly, for although necessity requires that they be two, it can in no wise be explained why they are two.

For although they may perhaps be called two equals, or some other mutual relation may in like manner be attributed to them, yet if it were to be asked what it is in these very relative expressions with reference to which they are used, it cannot be expressed plurally, as one speaks of two equal lines, or two like men. For, neither are there two equal spirits nor two equal creators, nor is there any dual expression which indicates either their essence or their relation to the created world; and there is no dual expression which designates the peculiar relation of the one to the other, since there are neither two words nor two images.

For the Word, by virtue of the fact that it is a word or image, bears a relation to the other, because it is Word and image only as it is the Word and image of something; and so peculiar are these attributes to the one that they are by no means predicable of the other. For he, whose is the Word and image, is neither image nor Word. It is, therefore, evident that it cannot be explained why they are two, the supreme Spirit and the Word, although by certain properties of each they are required to be two. For it is the property of the one to derive existence from the other, and the property of that other that the first derives existence from him.

39

This Word derives existence from the supreme Spirit by birth.

AND this truth, it seems, can be expressed in no more familiar terms than when it is said to be the property of the one, to be born of the other; and of the other, that the first is born of him. For it is now clearly proved, that the Word of the supreme Spirit does not derive existence from him, as do those beings which have been created by him; but as Creator from Creator, supreme Being from supreme Being. And, to dispose of this comparison with all brevity, it is one and the same being which derives existence from one and the same being, and on such terms, that it in no wise derives existence, except from that being.

Since it is evident, then, that the Word of the supreme Spirit so derives existence from him alone, that it is completely analogous to the offspring of a parent; and that it does not derive existence from him, as if it were created by him, doubtless no more fitting supposition can be entertained regarding its origin, than that it derives existence from the supreme Spirit by birth (*nascendo*).

For, innumerable objects are unhesitatingly said to be born of those things from which they derive existence, although they possess no such likeness to those things of which they are said to be born, as offspring to a parent.—We say, for instance, that the hair is born of the head, or the fruit of the tree, although the hair does not resemble the head, nor the fruit the tree.

If, then, many objects of this sort are without absurdity said to be born, so much the more fittingly may the Word of the supreme Spirit be said to derive existence from him by birth, the more perfect the resemblance it bears to him, like a child's to its parent, through deriving existence from him.

40

He is most truly a parent, and that Word his offspring.

BUT if it is most properly said to be born, and is so like him of whom it is born, why should it be esteemed *like*, as a child is like his parent? Why should it not rather be declared, that the Spirit is more truly a parent, and the Word his offspring, the more he alone is sufficient to effect this birth, and the more what is born expresses his likeness? For, among other beings which we know bear the relations of parent and child, none so begets as to be solely and without accessory, sufficient to the generation of offspring; and none is so begotten that without any admixture of unlikeness, it shows complete likeness to its parent.

If, then, the Word of the supreme Spirit so derives its complete existence from the being of that Spirit himself alone, and is so uniquely like him, that no child ever so completely derives existence from its parent, and none is so like its parent, certainly the relation of parent and offspring can be ascribed to no beings so consistently as to the supreme Spirit and his Word. Hence, it is his property to be most truly parent, and its to be most truly his offspring.

41

He most truly begets, and it is most truly begotten.

BUT it will be impossible to establish this proposition, unless, in equal degree, he most truly begets, and it is most truly begotten. As the former supposition is evidently true, so the latter is necessarily most certain. Hence, it belongs to the supreme Spirit most truly to beget, and to his Word to be most truly begotten.

42

It is the property of the one to be most truly progenitor and Father, and of the other to be the begotten and Son.

I should certainly be glad, and perhaps able, now to reach the conclusion, that he is most truly the Father, while this Word is most truly his Son. But I think that even this question should not be neglected: whether it is more fitting to call them Father and Son, than mother and daughter, since in them there is no distinction of sex.

For, if it is consistent with the nature of the one to be the Father, and of his offspring to be the Son, because both are Spirit (*Spiritus*, masculine); why is it not, with equal reason, consistent with the nature of the one to be the mother, and the other the daughter, since both are truth and wisdom (*veritas et sapientia*, feminine)?

Or, is it because in these natures that have a difference of sex, it belongs to the superior sex to be father or son, and to the inferior to be mother or daughter? And this is certainly a natural fact in most instances, but in some the contrary is true, as among certain kinds of birds, among which the female is always larger and stronger, while the male is smaller and weaker.

At any rate, it is more consistent to call the supreme Spirit father than mother, for this reason, that the first and principal cause of offspring is always in the father. For, if the maternal cause is ever in some way preceded by the paternal, it is exceedingly inconsistent that the name mother should be attached to that parent with which, for the generation of offspring, no other cause is associated, and which no other precedes. It is, therefore, most true that the supreme Spirit is Father of his offspring. But, if the son is always more like the father than is the daughter, while nothing is more like the supreme Father than his offspring; then it is most true that this offspring is not a daughter, but a Son.

Hence, just as it is the property of the one most truly to beget, and of the other to be begotten, so it is the property of the one to be most truly progenitor, and of the other to be most truly begotten. And as the one is most truly the parent, and the other his offspring, so the one is most truly Father, and the other most truly Son.

43

Consideration of the common attributes of both and the individual properties of each.

NOW that so many and so important properties of each have been discovered, whereby a strange plurality, as ineffable as it is inevitable, is proved to exist in the supreme unity, I think it most interesting to reflect, again and again, upon so unfathomable a mystery.

For observe: although it is so impossible that he who begets, and he who is begotten, are the same, and that parent and offspring are the same—so impossible that necessarily one must be the progenitor and the other the begotten, and one the Father, the other the Son; yet, here it is so necessary that he who begets and he who is begotten shall be the same, and also that parent and offspring shall be the same, that the progenitor cannot be any other than what the begotten is, nor the Father any other than the Son.

And although the one is one, and the other another, so that it is altogether evident that they are two; yet that which the one and the other are is in such a way one and the same, that it is a most obscure mystery why they are two. For, in such a way is one the Father and the other the Son, that when I speak of both I perceive that I have spoken of two; and yet so identical is that which both Father and Son are, that I do not understand why they are two of whom I have spoken.

For, although the Father separately is the perfectly supreme Spirit, and the Son separately is the perfectly supreme Spirit, yet, so are the Spirit-Father and the Spirit-Son one and the same being, that the Father and the Son are not two spirits, but one Spirit. For, just as to separate properties of separate beings, plurality is not attributed, since they are not properties of two things, so, what is common to both preserves an indivisible unity, although it belongs, as a whole, to them taken separately.

For, as there are not two fathers or two sons, but one Father and one Son, since separate properties belong to separate beings, so there are not two spirits, but one Spirit; although it belongs both to the Father, taken separately, and to the Son, taken separately, to be the perfect Spirit. For so opposite are their relations, that the one never assumes the property of the other; so harmonious are they in nature, that the one ever contains the essence of the other. For they are so diverse by virtue of the fact that the one is the Father and the other the Son, that the Father is never called the Son, nor the Son the Father; and they are so identical, by virtue of their substance, that the essence of the Son is ever in the Father, and the essence of the Father in the Son.

44

How one is the essence of the other.

HENCE, even if one is called the essence of the other, there is no departure from truth; but the supreme simplicity and unity of their common nature is thus honored. For, not as one conceives of a man's wisdom, through which man is wise, though he cannot be wise through himself, can we thus understand the statement that the Father is essence of the Son, and the Son the essence of the Father. We cannot understand that the Son is existent through the Father, and the Father through the Son, as if the one could not be existent except through the other, just as a man cannot be wise except through wisdom.

For, as the supreme Wisdom is ever wise through itself, so the supreme Essence ever exists through itself. But, the perfectly supreme Essence is the Father, and the perfectly supreme Essence is the Son. Hence, the perfect Father and the perfect Son exist, each through himself, just as each is wise through himself.

For the Son is not the less perfect essence or wisdom because he is an essence born of the essence of the Father, and a wisdom born of the wisdom of the Father; but he would be a less perfect essence or wisdom if he did not exist through himself, and were not wise through himself.

For, there is no inconsistency between the subsistence of the Son through himself, and his deriving existence from his Father. For, as the Father has essence, and wisdom, and life in himself; so that not through another's, but through his own, essence he exists; through his own wisdom he is wise; through his own life he lives; so, by generation, he grants to his Son the possession of essence, and wisdom, and life in himself, so that not through an extraneous essence, wisdom, and life, but through his own, he subsists, is wise, and lives; otherwise, the existence of Father and Son will not be the same, nor will the Son be equal to the Father. But it has already been clearly proved how false this supposition is.

Hence, there is no inconsistency between the subsistence of the Son through himself, and his deriving existence from the Father, since he must have from the Father this very power of subsisting through himself. For, if a wise man should teach me his wisdom, which I formerly lacked, he might without impropriety be said to teach me by this very wisdom of his. But, although my wisdom would derive its existence and the fact of its being from his wisdom, yet when my wisdom once existed, it would be no other essence than its own, nor would it be wise except through itself.

Much more, then, the eternal Father's eternal Son, who so derives existence from the Father that they are not two essences, subsists, is wise, and lives through himself. Hence, it is inconceivable that the Father should be the essence of the Son, or the Son the essence of the Father, on the ground that the one could not subsist through itself, but must subsist through the other. But in order to indicate how they share in an essence supremely simple and supremely one, it may consistently be said, and conceived, that the one is so identical with the other that the one possesses the essence of the other.

On these grounds, then, since there is obviously no difference between possessing an essence and being an essence, just as the one possesses the essence of the other, so the one is the essence of the other, that is, the one has the same existence with the other.

45

The Son may more appropriately be called the essence of the Father, than the Father the essence of the Son: and in like manner the Son is the virtue, wisdom, etc., of the Father.

AND although, for reasons we have noted, this is true, it is much more proper to call the Son the essence of the Father than the Father the essence of the Son. For, since the Father has his being from none other than himself, it is not wholly appropriate to say that he has the being of another than himself; while, since the Son has his being from the Father, and has the same essence with his Father, he may most appropriately be said to have the essence of his Father.

Hence, seeing that neither has an essence, except by being an essence; as the Son is more appropriately conceived to have the essence of the Father than the Father to have the essence of the Son, so the Son may more fitly be called the essence of the Father than the Father the essence of the Son. For this single explanation proves, with sufficiently emphatic brevity, that the Son not only has the same essence with the Father, but has this very essence from the Father; so that, to assert that the Son is the essence of the Father is the same as to assert that the Son is not a different essence from the essence of the Father nay, from the Father essence.

In like manner, therefore, the Son is the virtue of the Father, and his wisdom, and justice, and whatever is consistently attributed to the essence of the supreme Spirit.

46

How some of these truths which are thus expounded may also be conceived of in another way.

YET, some of these truths, which may be thus expounded and conceived of, are apparently capable of another interpretation as well, not inconsistent with this same assertion. For it is proved that the Son is the true Word, that is, the perfect intelligence, conceiving of the whole substance of the Father, or perfect cognition of that substance, and knowledge of it, and wisdom regarding it; that is, it understands, and conceives of, the very essence of the Father, and cognises it, and knows it, and is wise (*sapit*) regarding it.

If, then, in this sense, the Son is called the intelligence of the Father, and wisdom concerning him, and knowledge and cognition of him, and acquaintance with him; since the Son understands and conceives of the Father, is wise concerning him, knows and is acquainted with him, there is no departure from truth.

Most properly, too, may the Son be called the truth of the Father, not only in the sense that the truth of the Son is the same with that of the Father, as we have already seen; but in this sense, also, that in him no imperfect imitation shall be conceived of, but the complete truth of the substance of the Father since he is no other than what the Father is.

47

The Son is the Intelligence of intelligence and the Truth of truth.

BUT if the very substance of the Father is intelligence, and knowledge, and wisdom, and truth, it is consequently inferred that as the Son is the intelligence, and knowledge, and wisdom, and truth, of the paternal substance, so he is the intelligence of intelligence, the knowledge of knowledge, the wisdom of wisdom, and the truth of truth.

48

How the Son is the intelligence or wisdom of memory or the memory of the Father and of memory.

BUT what is to be our notion of memory? Is the Son to be regarded as the intelligence conceiving of memory, or as the memory of the Father, or as the memory of memory? Indeed, since it cannot be denied that the supreme Wisdom remembers itself, nothing can be more consistent than to regard the Father as memory, just as the Son is the Word; because the Word is apparently born of memory, a fact that is more clearly seen in the case of the human mind.

For, since the human mind is not always thinking of itself, though it ever remembers itself, it is clear that, when it thinks of itself, the word corresponding to it is born of memory. Hence, it appears that, if it always thought of itself, its word would be always born of memory. For, to think of an object of which we have remembrance, this is to express it mentally; while the word corresponding to the object is the thought itself, formed after the likeness of that object from memory.

Hence, it may be clearly apprehended in the supreme Wisdom, which always thinks of itself, just as it remembers itself, that, of the eternal remembrance of it, its coeternal Word is born. Therefore, as the Word is properly conceived of as the child, the memory most appropriately takes the name of parent. If, then, the child which is born of the supreme Spirit alone is the child of his memory, there can be no more logical conclusion than that his memory is himself. For not in respect of the fact that he remembers himself does he exist in his own memory, like ideas that exist in the human memory, without being the memory itself; but he so remembers himself that he is his own memory.

It therefore follows that, just as the Son is the intelligence or wisdom of the Father, so he is that of the memory of the Father. But, regarding whatever the Son has wisdom or understanding, this he likewise remembers. The Son is, therefore, the memory of the Father, and the memory of memory, that is, the memory that remembers the Father, who is memory, just as he is the wisdom of the Father, and the wisdom of wisdom, that is, the wisdom wise regarding the wisdom of the Father; and the Son is indeed memory, born of memory, as he is wisdom, born of wisdom, while the Father is memory and wisdom born of none.

49

The supreme Spirit loves himself.

BUT, while I am here considering with interest the individual properties and the common attributes of Father and Son, I find none in them more pleasurable to contemplate than the feeling of mutual love. For how absurd it would be to deny that the supreme Spirit loves himself, just as he remembers himself, and conceives of himself! Since even the rational human mind is convinced that it can love both itself and him, because it can remember itself and him, and can conceive of itself and of him; for idle and almost useless is the memory and conception of any object, unless, so far as reason requires, the object itself is loved or condemned. The supreme Spirit, then, loves himself, just as he remembers himself and conceives of himself.

50

The same love proceeds equally from Father and Son.

IT is, at any rate, clear to the rational man that he does not remember himself or conceive of himself because he loves himself, but he loves himself because he remembers himself and conceives of himself; and that he could not love himself if he did not remember and conceive of himself. For no object is loved without remembrance or conception of it; while many things are retained in memory and conceived of, that are not loved.

It is evident, then, that the love of the supreme Spirit proceeds from the fact that he remember himself and conceives of himself (*se intelligit*). But if, by the memory of the supreme Spirit, we understand the Father, and by his intelligence by which he conceives of anything, the Son, it is manifest that the love of the supreme Spirit proceeds equally from Father and Son.

51

Each loves himself and the other with equal love.

BUT if the supreme Spirit loves himself, no doubt the Father loves himself, the Son loves himself, and the one the other; since the Father separately is the supreme Spirit, and the Son separately is the supreme Spirit, and both at once one Spirit. And, since each equally remembers himself and the other, and conceives equally of himself and the other; and since what is loved, or loves in the Father, or in the Son, is altogether the same, necessarily each loves himself and the other with an equal love.

52

This love is as great as the supreme Spirit himself.

HOW great, then, is this love of the supreme Spirit, common as it is to Father and Son! But, if he loves himself as much as he remembers and conceives of himself; and, moreover, remembers and conceives of himself in as great a degree as that in which his essence exists, since otherwise it cannot exist; undoubtedly his love is as great as he himself is.

53

This love is identical with the supreme Spirit, and yet it is itself with the Father and the Son one spirit.

BUT, what can be equal to the supreme Spirit, except the supreme Spirit? That love is, then, the supreme Spirit. Hence, if no creature, that is, if nothing other than the supreme Spirit, the Father and the Son, ever existed; nevertheless, Father and Son would love themselves and one another.

It therefore follows that this love is nothing else than what the Father and the Son are, which is the supreme Being. But, since there cannot be more than one supreme Being, what inference can be more necessary than that Father and Son and the love of both are one supreme Being? Therefore, this love is supreme Wisdom, supreme Truth, the supreme Good, and whatsoever can be attributed to the substance the supreme Spirit.

54

It proceeds as a whole from the Father, and as a whole from the Son, and yet does not exist except as one love.

IT should be carefully considered whether there are two loves, one proceeding from the Father, the other from the Son; or one, not proceeding as a whole from one, but in part from the Father, in part from the Son; or neither more than one, nor one proceeding in part from each separately, but one proceeding as a whole from each separately, and likewise as a whole from the two at once.

But the solution of such a question can, without doubt, be apprehended from the fact that this love proceeds not from that in which Father and Son are more than one, but from that in which they are one. For, not from their relations, which are more than one, but from their essence itself, which does not admit of plurality, do Father and Son equally produce so great a good.

Therefore, as the Father separately is the supreme Spirit, and the Son separately is the supreme Spirit, and Father and Son at once are not two, but one Spirit; so from the Father separately the love of the supreme Spirit emanates as a whole, and from the Son as a whole, and at once from Father and Son, not as two, but as one and the same whole.

55

This love is not their Son.

SINCE this love, then, has its being equally from Father and Son, and is so like both that it is in no wise unlike them, but is altogether identical with them; is it to be regarded as their Son or offspring? But, as the Word, so soon as it is examined, declares itself to be the offspring of him from whom it derives existence, by displaying a manifold likeness to its parent; so love plainly denies that it sustains such a relation, since, so long as it is conceived to proceed from Father and Son, it does not at once show to one who contemplates it so evident a likeness to him from whom it derives existence, although deliberate reasoning teaches us that it is altogether identical with Father and Son.

Therefore, if it is their offspring, either one of them is its father and the other its mother, or each is its father, or mother—suppositions which apparently contradict all truth. For, since it proceeds in precisely the same way from the Father as from the Son, regard for truth does not allow the relations of Father and Son to it to be described by different words; therefore, the one is not its father, the other its mother. But that there are two beings which, taken separately, bear each the perfect relation of father or mother, differing in no respect, to some one being—of this no existing nature allows proof by any example.

Hence, both, that is, Father and Son, are not father and mother of the love emanating from them. It therefore is apparently most inconsistent with truth that their identical love should be their son or offspring.

56

Only the Father begets and is unbegotten; only the son is begotten; only love neither begotten nor unbegotten.

STILL, it is apparent that this love can neither be said, in accordance with the usage of common speech, to be unbegotten, nor can it so properly be said to be begotten, as the Word is said to be begotten. For we often say of a thing that it is begotten of that from which it derives existence, as when we say that light or heat is begotten of fire, or any effect of its cause.

On this ground, then, love, proceeding from supreme Spirit, cannot be declared to be wholly unbegotten, but it cannot so properly be said to be begotten as can the Word; since the Word is the most true offspring and most true Son, while it is manifest that love is by no means offspring or son.

He alone, therefore, may, or rather should, be called begetter and unbegotten, whose is the Word; since he alone is Father and parent, and in no wise derives existence from another; and the Word alone should be called begotten, which alone is Son and offspring. But only the love of both is neither begotten nor unbegotten, because it is neither son nor offspring, and yet does in some sort derive existence from another.

57

This love is uncreated and creator, as are Father and Son; and yet it is with them not three, but one uncreated and creative being. And it may be called the Spirit of Father and Son.

BUT, since this love separately is the supreme Being, as are Father and Son, and yet at once Father and Son, and the love of both are not more than one, but one supreme Being, which alone was created by none, and created all things through no other than itself; since this is true, necessarily, as the Father separately, and the Son separately, are each uncreated and creator, so, too, love separately is uncreated and creator, and yet all three at once are not more than one, but one uncreated and creative being.

None, therefore, makes or begets or creates the Father, but the Father alone begets, but does not create, the Son; while Father and Son alike do not create or beget, but somehow, if such an expression may be used, breathe their love: for, although the supremely immutable Being does not breathe after our fashion, yet the truth that this Being sends forth this, its love, which proceeds from it, not by departing from it, but by deriving existence from it, can perhaps be no better expressed than by saying that this Being breathes its love.

But, if this expression is admissible, as the Word of the supreme Being is its Son, so its love may fittingly enough be called its breath (*Spiritus*). So that, though it is itself essentially spirit, as are Father and Son, they are not regarded as the spirits of anything, since neither is the Father born of any other nor the Son of the Father, as it were, by breathing; while that love is regarded as the Breath or Spirit of both since from both, breathing in their transcendent way, it mysteriously proceeds.

And this love, too, it seems, from the fact there is community of being between Father and Son, may, not unreasonably, take, as it were its own, some name which is common to Father and Son; if there is any exigency demanding that it should have a name proper to itself. And, indeed, if this love is actually designated by the name Spirit, as by its own name, since this name equally describes the Father and the Son: it will be useful to this effect also, that through this name it shall be signified that this love is identical with Father and Son, although it has its being from them.

58

As the Son is the essence or wisdom of the Father in the sense that he has the same essence or wisdom that the Father has: so likewise the Spirit is the essence and wisdom etc. of Father and Son.

ALSO, just as the Son is the substance and wisdom and virtue of the Father, in the sense that he has the same essence and wisdom and virtue with the Father; so it may be conceived that the Spirit of both is the essence or wisdom or virtue of Father and Son, since it has altogether the same essence, wisdom, and virtue with these.

59

The Father and the Son and their Spirit exist equally the one in the other.

IT is a most interesting consideration that the Father, and the Son, and the Spirit of both, exist in one another with such equality that no one of them surpasses another. For, not only is each in such a way the perfectly supreme Being that, nevertheless, all three at once exist only as one supreme Being, but the same truth is no less capable of proof when each is taken separately.

For the Father exists as a whole in the Son, and in the Spirit common to them; and the Son in the Father, and in the Spirit; and the Spirit in the Father, and in the Son; for the memory of the supreme Being exists, as a whole, in its intelligence and in its love, and the intelligence in its memory and love, and the love in its memory and intelligence. For the supreme Spirit conceives of (*intelligit*) its memory as a whole, and loves it, and remembers its intelligence as a whole, and loves it as a whole, and remembers its love as a whole, and conceives of it as a whole.

But we mean by the memory, the Father; by the intelligence, the Son; by the love, the Spirit of both. In such equality, therefore, do Father and Son and Spirit embrace one another, and exist in one another, that none of them can be proved to surpass another or to exist without it.

60

To none of these is another necessary that he may remember, conceive, or love: since each taken by himself is memory and intelligence and love and all that is necessarily inherent in the supreme Being.

BUT, while this discussion engages our attention, I think that this truth, which occurs to me as I reflect, ought to be most carefully commended to memory. The Father must be so conceived of as memory, the Son as intelligence, and the Spirit as love, that it shall also be understood that the Father does not need the Son, or the Spirit common to them, nor the Son the Father, or the same Spirit, nor the Spirit the Father, or the Son: as if the Father were able, through his own power, only to remember, but to conceive only through the Son, and to love only through the Spirit of himself and his son; and the Son could only conceive or understand (*intelligere*) through himself, but remembered through the Father, and loved through his Spirit; and this Spirit were able through himself alone only to love, while the Father remembers for him, and the Son conceives or understands (*intelligit*) for him.

For, since among these three each one taken separately is so perfectly the supreme Being and the supreme Wisdom that through himself he remembers and conceives and loves, it must be that none of these three needs another, in order either to remember or to conceive or to love. For, each taken separately is essentially memory and intelligence and love, and all that is necessarily inherent in the supreme Being.

61

Yet there are not three, but one Father and one Son and one Spirit.

AND here I see a question arises. For, if the Father is intelligence and love as well as memory, and the Son is memory and love as well as intelligence, and the Spirit is no less memory and intelligence than love; how is it that the Father is not a Son and a Spirit of some being? And why is not the Son the Father and the Spirit of some being? And why is not this Spirit the Father of some being, and the Son of some being? For it was understood, that the Father was memory, the Son intelligence, and the Spirit love.

But this question is easily answered, if we consider the truths already disclosed in our discussion. For the Father, even though he is intelligence and love, is not for that reason the Son or the Spirit of any being; since he is not intelligence, begotten of any, or love, proceeding from any, but whatever he is, he is only the begetter, and is he from whom the other proceeds.

The Son also, even though by his own power he remembers and loves, is not, for that reason, the Father or the Spirit of any; since he is not memory as begetter, or love as proceeding from another after the likeness of his Spirit, but whatever being he has he is only begotten and is he from whom the Spirit proceeds.

The Spirit, too, is not necessarily Father or Son, because his own memory and intelligence are sufficient to him; since he is not memory as begetter, or intelligence as begotten, but he alone, whatever he is, proceeds or emanates.

What, then, forbids the conclusion that in the supreme Being there is only one Father, one Son, one Spirit, and not three Fathers or Sons or Spirits?

62

How it seems that of these three more sons than one are born.

BUT perhaps the following observation will prove inconsistent with this assertion. It should not be doubted that the Father and the Son and their Spirit each expresses himself and the other two, just as each conceives of, and understands, himself and the other two. But, if this is true, are there not in the supreme Being as many words as there are expressive beings, and as many words as there are beings who are expressed?

For, if more men than one give expression to some one object in thought, apparently there are as many words corresponding to that object as there are thinkers; since the word corresponding to it exists in the thoughts of each separately. Again, if one man thinks of more objects than one, there are as many words in the mind of the thinker as there are objects thought of.

But in the thought of a man, when he thinks of anything outside his own mind, the word corresponding to the object thought of is not born of the object itself, since that is absent from the view of thought, but of some likeness or image of the object which exists in the memory of the thinker, or which is perhaps called to mind through a corporeal sense from the present object itself.

But in the supreme Being, Father and Son and their Spirit are always so present to one another—for each one, as we have already seen, exists in the others no less than in himself—that, when they express one another, the one that is expressed seems to beget his own word, just as when he is expressed by himself. How is it, then, that the Son and the Spirit of the Son and of the Father beget nothing, if each begets his own word, when he is expressed by himself or by another? Apparently as many words as can be proved to be born of the supreme Substance, so many Sons, according to our former reasoning, must there be begotten of this substance, and so many spirits proceeding from it.

63

How among them there is only one Son of one Father, that is, one Word, and that from the Father alone.

ON these grounds, therefore, there apparently are in that Being, not only many fathers and sons and beings proceeding from it, but other necessary attributes as well; or else Father and Son and their Spirit, of whom it is already certain that they truly exist, are not three expressive beings, although each taken separately is expressive, nor are there more beings than one expressed, when each one expresses himself and the other two.

For, just as it is an inherent property of the supreme Wisdom to know and conceive, so it is assuredly natural to eternal and immutable knowledge and intelligence ever to regard as present what it knows and conceives of. For, to such a supreme Spirit expressing and beholding through conception, as it were, are the same, just as the expression of our human mind is nothing but the intuition of the thinker.

But reasons already considered have shown most convincingly that whatever is essentially inherent in the supreme Nature is perfectly consistent with the nature of the Father and the Son and their Spirit taken separately; and that, nevertheless, this, if attributed to the three at once, does not admit of plurality. Now, it is established that as knowledge and intelligence are attributes of his being, so his knowing and conceiving is nothing else than his expression, that is, his ever beholding as present what he knows and conceives of. Necessarily, therefore, just as the Father separately, and the Son separately, and their Spirit separately, is a knowing and conceiving being, and yet the three at once are not more knowing and conceiving beings than one, but one knowing and one conceiving being: so, each taken separately is expressive, and yet there are not three expressive beings at once, but one expressive being.

Hence, this fact may also be clearly recognised, that when these three are expressed, either by themselves or by another, there are not more beings than one expressed. For what is therein expressed except their being? If, then, that Being is one and only one, then what is expressed is one and only one; therefore, if it is in them one and only one which expresses, and one which is expressed—for it is one wisdom which expresses and one substance which is expressed—it follows that there are not more words than one, but one alone. Hence, although each one expresses himself and all express one another, nevertheless there cannot be in the supreme Being another Word than that already shown to be born of him whose is the Word, so that it may be called his true image and his Son.

And in this truth I find a strange and inexplicable factor. For observe: although it is manifest that each one, that is, Father and Son, and the Spirit of Father and Son equally expresses himself and both the others, and that there is one Word alone among them; yet it appears that this Word itself can in no wise be called the Word of all three, but only of one.

For it has been proved that it is the image and Son of him whose Word it is. And it is plain that it cannot properly be called either the image or son of itself, or of the Spirit proceeding from it. For, neither of itself nor of a being proceeding from it, is it born, nor does it in its existence imitate itself or a being proceeding from itself. For it does not imitate itself, or take on a like existence to itself, because imitation and likeness are impossible where only one being is concerned, but require plurality of beings; while it does not imitate the spirit, nor does it exist in his likeness, because it has not its existence from that Spirit, but the Spirit from it. It is to be concluded that this sole Word corresponds to him alone, from whom it has existence by generation, and after whose complete likeness it exists.

One Father, then, and not more than one Father; one Son, and not more than one Son; one Spirit proceeding from them, and not more than one such Spirit, exist in the supreme Being. And, although there are three, so that the Father is never the Son or the Spirit proceeding from them, nor the Son at any time the Father or the Spirit, nor the Spirit of Father and Son ever the Father or the Son; and each separately is so perfect that he is self-sufficient, needing neither of the others; yet what they are is in such a way one that just as it cannot be attributed to them taken separately as plural, so, neither can it be attributed to them as plural, when the three are taken at once. And though each one expresses himself and all express one another, yet there are not among them more words than one, but one; and this Word corresponds not to each separately, nor to all together, but to one alone.

64

Though this truth is inexplicable, it demands belief.

IT seems to me that the mystery of so sublime a subject transcends all the vision of the human intellect. And for that reason I think it best to refrain from the attempt to explain how this thing is. For it is my opinion that one who is investigating an incomprehensible object ought to be satisfied if this reasoning shall have brought him far enough to recognise that this object most certainly exists; nor ought assured belief to be the less readily given to these truths which are declared to be such by cogent proofs, and without the contradiction of any other reason, if, because of the incomprehensibility of their own natural sublimity, they do not admit of explanation.

But what is so incomprehensible, so ineffable, as that which is above all things? Hence, if these truths, which have thus far been debated in connection with the supreme Being, have been declared on cogent grounds, even though they cannot be so examined by the human intellect as to be capable of explanation in words, their assured certainty is not therefore shaken. For, if a consideration, such as that above, rationally comprehends that it is incomprehensible in what way supreme Wisdom knows its creatures, of which we necessarily know so many; who shall explain how it knows and expresses itself, of which nothing or scarcely anything can be known by man? Hence, if it is not by virtue of the self-expression of this Wisdom that the Father begets and the Son is begotten, who shall tell his generation?

65

How real truth may be reached in the discussion of an ineffable subject.

BUT again, if such is the character of its ineffability—nay, since it is such—how shall whatever conclusion our discussion has reached regarding it in terms of Father, Son, and emanating Spirit be valid? For, if it has been explained on true grounds, how is it ineffable? Or, if it is ineffable, how can it be such as our discussion has shown? Or, could it be explained to a certain extent, and therefore nothing would disprove the truth of our argument; but since it could not be comprehended at all, for that reason it would be ineffable?

But how shall we meet the truth that has already been established in this very discussion, namely, that the supreme Being is so above and beyond every other nature that, whenever any statement is made concerning it in words which are also applicable to other natures, the sense of these words in this case is by no means that in which they are applied to other natures.

For what sense have I conceived of, in all these words that I have thought of, except the common and familiar sense? If, then, the familiar sense of words is alien to that Being, whatever I have inferred to be attributable to it is not its property. How, then, has any truth concerning the supreme Being been discovered, if what has been discovered is so alien to that Being? What is to be inferred?

Or, has there in some sort been some truth discovered regarding this incomprehensible object, and in some sort has nothing been proved regarding it? For often we speak of things which we do not express with precision as they are; but by another expression we indicate what we are unwilling or unable to express with precision, as when we speak in riddles. And often we see a thing, not precisely as it is in itself, but through a likeness or image, as when we look upon a face in a mirror. And in this way, we often express and yet do not express, see and yet do not see, one and the same object; we express and see it through another; we do not express it, and do not see it by virtue of its own proper nature.

On these grounds, then, it appears that there is nothing to disprove the truth of our discussion thus far concerning the supreme Nature, and yet this Nature itself remains not the less ineffable, if we believe that it has never been expressed according to the peculiar nature of its own being, but somehow described through another.

For whatever terms seem applicable to that Nature do not reveal it to me in its proper character, but rather intimate it through some likeness. For, when I think of the meanings of these terms, I more naturally conceive in my mind of what I see in created objects, than of what I conceive to transcend all human understanding. For it is something much less, nay, something far different, that their meaning suggests to my mind, than the conception of which my mind itself attempts to achieve through this shadowy signification.

For, neither is the term wisdom sufficient to reveal to me that Being, through which all things were created from nothing and are preserved from nothingness; nor is the term essence capable of expressing to me that Being which, through its unique elevation, is far above all things, and through its peculiar natural character greatly transcends all things.

In this way, then, is that Nature ineffable, because it is incapable of description in words or by any other means; and, at the same time, an inference regarding it, which can be reached by the instruction of reason or in some other way, as it were in a riddle, is not therefore necessarily false.

66

Through the rational mind is the nearest approach to the supreme Being.

SINCE it is clear, then, that nothing can be ascertained concerning this Nature in terms of its own peculiar character, but only in terms of something else, it is certain that a nearer approach toward knowledge of it is made through that which approaches it more nearly through likeness. For the more like to it anything among created beings is proved to be, the more excellent must that created being be by nature. Hence, this being, through its greater likeness, assists the investigating mind in the approach to supreme Truth; and through its more excellent created essence, teaches the more correctly what opinion the mind itself ought to form regarding the Creator. So, undoubtedly, a greater knowledge of the creative Being is attained, the more nearly the creature through which the investigation is made approaches that Being. For that every being, in so far as it exists, is like the supreme Being, reasons already considered do not permit us to doubt.

It is evident, then, that as the rational mind alone, among all created beings, is capable of rising to the investigation of this Being, so it is not the less this same rational mind alone, through which the mind itself can most successfully achieve the discovery of this same Being. For it has already been acknowledged that this approaches it most nearly, through likeness of natural essence. What is more obvious, then, than that the more earnestly the rational mind devotes itself to learning its own nature, the more effectively does it rise to the knowledge of that Being; and the more carelessly it contemplates itself, the farther does it descend from the contemplation of that Being?

67

The mind itself is the mirror and image of that Being.

THEREFORE, the mind may most fitly be said to be its own

mirror wherein it contemplates, so to speak, the image of what it cannot see face to face. For, if the mind itself alone among all created beings is capable of remembering and conceiving of and loving itself, I do not see why it should be denied that it is the true image of that being which, through its memory and intelligence and love, is united in an ineffable Trinity. Or, at any rate, it proves itself to be the more truly the image of that Being by its power of remembering, conceiving of, and loving, that Being. For, the greater and the more like that Being it is, the more truly it is recognised to be its image.

But, it is utterly inconceivable that any rational creature can have been naturally endowed with any power so excellent and so like the supreme Wisdom as this power of remembering, and conceiving of, and loving, the best and greatest of all beings. Hence, no faculty has been bestowed on any creature that is so truly the image of the Creator.

68

The rational creature was created in order that it might love this Being.

IT seems to follow, then, that the rational creature ought to devote itself to nothing so earnestly as to the expression, through voluntary performance, of this image which is impressed on it through a natural potency. For, not only does it owe its very existence to its creator; but the fact that it is known to have no power so important as that of remembering, and conceiving of, and loving, the supreme good, proves that it ought to wish nothing else so especially.

For who can deny that whatever within the scope of one's power is better, ought to prevail with the will? For, to the rational nature rationality is the same with the ability to distinguish the just from the not-just, the true from the not-true, the good from the not-good, the greater good from the lesser; but this power is altogether useless to it, and superfluous, unless what it distinguishes it loves or condemns, in accordance with the judgment of true discernment.

From this, then, it seems clear enough that every rational being exists for this purpose, that according as, on the grounds of discernment, it judges a thing to be more or less good, or not good, so it may love that thing in greater or less degree, or reject it.

It is, therefore, most obvious that the rational creature was created for this purpose, that it might love the supreme Being above all other goods, as this Being is itself the supreme good; nay, that it might love nothing except it, unless because of it; since that Being is good through itself, and nothing else is good except through it.

But the rational being cannot love this Being, unless it has devoted itself to remembering and conceiving of it. It is clear, then, that the rational creature ought to devote its whole ability and will to remembering, and conceiving of, and loving, the supreme good, for which end it recognises that it has its very existence.

69

The soul that ever loves this Essence lives at some time in true blessedness.

BUT there is no doubt that the human soul is a rational creature. Hence, it must have been created for this end, that it might love the supreme Being. It must, therefore, have been created either for this end, that it might love that Being eternally; or for this, that at some time it might either voluntarily, or by violence, lose this love.

But it is impious to suppose that the supreme Wisdom created it for this end, that at some time, either it should despise so great a good, or, though wishing to keep it, should lose it by some violence. We infer, then, that it was created for this end, that it might love the supreme Being eternally. But this it cannot do unless it lives forever. It was so created, then, that it lives forever, if it forever wills to do that for which it was created.

Hence, it is most incompatible with the nature of the supremely good, supremely wise, and omnipotent Creator, that what he has made to exist that it might love him, he should make not to exist, so long as it truly loves him; and that what he voluntarily gave to a non-loving being that it might ever love, he should take away, or permit to be taken away, from the loving being, so that necessarily it should not love; especially since it should by no means be doubted that he himself loves every nature that loves him. Hence, it is manifest that the human soul is never deprived of its life, if it forever devotes itself to loving the supreme life.

How, then, shall it live? For is long life so important a matter, if it is not secure from the invasion of troubles? For whoever, while he lives, is either through fear or through actual suffering subject to troubles, or is deceived by a false security, does he not live in misery? But, if any one lives in freedom from these troubles, he lives in blessedness. But it is most absurd to suppose that any nature that forever loves him, who is supremely good and omnipotent, forever lives in misery. So, it is plain, that the human soul is of such a character that, if it diligently observes that end for which it exists, it at some time lives in blessedness, truly secure from death itself and from every other trouble.

70

This Being gives itself in return to the creature that loves it, that that creature may be eternally blessed.

THEREFORE it cannot be made to appear true that he who is most just and most powerful makes no return to the being that loves him perseveringly, to which although it neither existed nor loved him, he gave existence that it might be able to be a loving being. For, if he makes no return to the loving soul, the most just does not distinguish between the soul that loves, and the soul that despises what ought to be supremely loved, nor does he love the soul that loves him; or else it does not avail to be loved by him; all of which suppositions are inconsistent with his nature; hence he does make a return to every soul that perseveres in loving him.

But what is this return? For, if he gave to what was nothing, a rational being, that it might be a loving soul, what shall he give to the loving soul, if it does not cease to love? If what waits upon love is so great, how great is the recompense given to love? And if the sustainer of love is such as we declare, of what character is the profit? For, if the rational creature, which is useless to itself without this love, is with it preeminent among all creatures, assuredly nothing can be the reward of love except what is preeminent among all natures.

For this same good, which demands such love toward itself, also requires that it be desired by the loving soul. For, who can love justice, truth, blessedness, incorruptibility, in such a way as not to wish to enjoy them? What return, then, shall the supreme Goodness make to the being that loves and desires it, except itself? For, whatever else it grants, it does not give in return, since all such bestowals neither compensate the love, nor console the loving being, nor satisfy the soul that desires this supreme Being.

Or, if it wishes to be loved and desired, so as to make some other return than its love, it wishes to be loved and desired, not for its own sake, but for the sake of another; and does not wish to be loved itself, but wishes another to be loved; which it is impious to suppose.

So, it is most true that every rational soul, if, as it should, it earnestly devotes itself through love to longing for supreme blessedness, shall at some time receive that blessedness to enjoy, that what it now sees as through a glass and in a riddle, it may then see face to face. But it is most foolish to doubt whether it enjoys that blessedness eternally; since, in the enjoyment of that blessedness, it will be impossible to turn the soul aside by any fear, or to deceive it by false security; nor, having once experienced the need of that blessedness, will it be able not to love it; nor will that blessedness desert the soul that loves it; nor shall there be anything powerful enough to separate them against their will. Hence, the soul that has once begun to enjoy supreme Blessedness will be eternally blessed.

71

The soul that despises this being will be eternally miserable.

FROM this it may be inferred, as a certain consequence, that the soul which despises the love of the supreme good will incur eternal misery. It might be said that it would be justly punished for such contempt if it lost existence or life, since it does not employ itself to the end for which it was created. But reason in no wise admits such a belief, namely, that after such great guilt it is condemned to be what it was before all its guilt.

For, before it existed, it could neither be guilty nor feel a penalty. If, then, the soul despising that end for which it was created, dies so as to feel nothing, or so as to be nothing at all, its condition will be the same when in the greatest guilt and when without all guilt; and the supremely wise Justice will not distinguish between what is capable of no good and wills no evil, and what is capable of the greatest good and wills the greatest evil.

But it is plain enough that this is a contradiction. Therefore, nothing can be more logical, and nothing ought to be believed more confidently than that the soul of man is so constituted that, if it scorns loving the supreme Being, it suffers eternal misery; that just as the loving soul shall rejoice in an eternal reward, so the soul despising that Being shall suffer eternal punishment; and as the former shall feel an immutable sufficiency, so the latter shall feel an inconsolable need.

72

Every human soul is immortal. And it is either forever miserable, or at some time truly blessed.

BUT if the soul is mortal, of course the loving soul is not eternally blessed, nor the soul that scorns this Being eternally miserable. Whether, therefore, it loves or scorns that for the love of which it was created, it must be immortal. But if there are some rational souls which are to be judged as neither loving nor scorning, such as the souls of infants seem to be, what opinion shall be held regarding these? Are they mortal or immortal? But undoubtedly all human souls are of the same nature. Hence, since it is established that some are immortal, every human soul must be immortal. But since every living being is either never, or at some time, truly secure from all trouble; necessarily, also, every human soul is either ever miserable, or at some time truly blessed.

73

No soul is unjustly deprived of the supreme good, and every effort must be directed toward that good.

BUT, which souls are unhesitatingly to be judged as so loving that for the love of which they were created, that they deserve to enjoy it at some time, and which as so scorning it, that they deserve ever to stand in need of it; or how and on what ground those which it seems impossible to call either loving or scorning are assigned to either eternal blessedness or misery—of all this I think it certainly most difficult or even impossible for any mortal to reach an understanding through discussion. But that no being is unjustly deprived by the supremely great and supremely good Creator of that good for which it was created, we ought most assuredly to believe. And toward this good every man ought to strive, by loving and desiring it with all his heart, and all his soul, and all his mind.

74

The supreme Being is to be hoped for.

BUT the human soul will by no means be able to train itself in this purpose, if it despairs of being able to reach what it aims at. Hence, devotion to effort is not more profitable to it than hope of attainment is necessary.

75

We must believe in this Being, that is, by believing we must reach out for it.

BUT what does not believe cannot love or hope. It is, therefore, profitable to this human soul to believe the supreme Being and those things without which that Being cannot be loved, that, by believing, the soul may reach out for it. And this truth can be more briefly and fitly indicated, I think, if instead of saying, "strive for" the supreme Being, we say, "believe in" the supreme Being.

For, if one says that he believes in it, he apparently shows clearly enough both that, through the faith which he professes, he strives for the supreme Being, and that he believes those things which are proper to this aim. For it seems that either he who does not believe what is proper to striving for that Being, or he who does not strive for that Being, through what he believes, does not believe in it. And, perhaps, it is indifferent whether we say, "believe in it," or "direct belief to it," just as by believing to strive for it and toward it are the same, except that whoever shall have come to it by striving for (*tendendo in*) it, will not remain without, but within it. And this is indicated more distinctly and familiarly if we say, "striving for" (*in*) it, than if we say, "toward" (*ad*) it.

On this ground, therefore, I think it may more fitly be said that we should believe in it, than that we should direct belief to it.

76

We should believe in Father and Son and in their Spirit equally, and in each separately, and in the three at once.

WE should believe, then, equally in the Father and in the Son and in their Spirit, and in each separately, and in the three at once, since the Father separately, and the Son separately, and their Spirit separately is the supreme Being, and at once Father and Son with their Spirit are one and the same supreme Being, in which alone every man ought to believe; because it is the sole end which in every thought and act he ought to strive for. Hence, it is manifest that as none is able to strive for that Being, except he believe in it; so to believe it avails none, except he strive for it.

77

What is living, and what is dead faith.

HENCE, with however great confidence so important a truth is believed, the faith will be useless and, as it were, dead, unless it is strong and living through love. For, that the faith which is accompanied by sufficient love is by no means idle, if an opportunity of operation offers, but rather exercises itself in an abundance of works, as it could not do without love, may be proved from this fact alone, that, since it loves the supreme Justice, it can scorn nothing that is just, it can approve nothing that is unjust. Therefore, seeing that the fact of its operation shows that life, without which it could not operate, is inherent in it; it is not absurd to say that operative faith is alive, because it has the life of love without which it could not operate; and that idle faith is not living, because it lacks that life of love, with which it would not be idle.

Hence, if not only he who has lost his sight is called blind, but also he who ought to have sight and has it not, why cannot, in like manner, faith without love be called dead; not because it has lost its life, that is, love; but because it has not the life which it ought always to have? As that faith, then, which operates through love is recognised as living, so that which is idle, through contempt, is proved to be dead. It may, therefore, be said with sufficient fitness that living faith believes in that in which we ought to believe; while dead faith merely believes that which ought to be believed.

78

The supreme Being may in some sort be called Three.

AND so it is evidently expedient for every man to believe in a certain ineffable trinal unity, and in one Trinity; one and a unity because of its one essence, but trinal and a trinity because of its three—what? For, although I can speak of a Trinity because of Father and Son and the Spirit of both, who are three; yet I cannot, in one word, show why they are three; as if I should call this Being a Trinity because of its three persons, just as I would call it a unity because of its one substance.

For three persons are not to be supposed, because all persons which are more than one so subsist separately from one another, that there must be as many substances as there are persons, a fact that is recognised in the case of more men than one, when there are as many persons as there are individual substances. Hence, in the supreme Being, just as there are not more substances than one, so there are not more persons than one.

So, if one wishes to express to any why they are three, he will say that they are Father and Son and the Spirit of both, unless perchance, compelled by the lack of a precisely appropriate term, he shall choose some one of those terms which cannot be applied in a plural sense to the supreme Being, in order to indicate what cannot be expressed in any fitting language; as if he should say, for instance, that this wonderful Trinity is one essence or nature, and three persons or substances.

For these two terms are more appropriately chosen to describe plurality in the supreme Being, because the word *person* is applied only to an individual, rational nature; and the word *substance* is ordinarily applied to individual beings, which especially subsist in plurality. For individual beings are especially exposed to, that is, are subject to, accidents, and for this reason they more properly receive the name *sub-stance*. Now, it is already manifest that the supreme Being, which is subject to no accidents, cannot properly be called a substance, except as the word *substance* is used in the same sense with the word *Essence*. Hence, on this ground, namely, of necessity, that supreme and one Trinity or trinal unity may justly be called one Essence and three Persons or three Substances.

79

This Essence itself is God, who alone is lord and ruler of all.

IT appears, then—nay, it is unhesitatingly declared, that what is called God is not nothing; and that to this supreme Essence the name God is properly given. For every one who says that a God exists, whether one or more than one, conceives of him only as of some substance which be believes to be above every nature that is not God, and that he is to be worshiped of men because of his preeminent majesty, and to be appeased for man's own sake because of some imminent necessity.

But what should be so worshiped in accordance with its majesty, and what should be so appeased on behalf of any object, as the supremely good and supremely powerful Spirit, who is Lord of all and who rules all? For, as it is established that through the supreme Good and its supremely wise omnipotence all things were created and live, it is most inconsistent to suppose that the Spirit himself does not rule the beings created by him, or that beings are governed by another less powerful or less good, or by no reason at all, but by the confused flow of events alone. For it is he alone through whom it is well with every creature, and without whom it is well with none, and from whom, and through whom, and in whom, are all things.

Therefore, since he himself alone is not only the beneficent Creator, but the most powerful Lord, and most wise ruler of all; it is clear that it is he alone whom every other nature, according to its whole ability, ought to worship in love, and to love in worship; from whom all happiness is to be hoped for; with whom refuge from adversity is to be sought; to whom supplication for all things is to be offered. Truly, therefore, he is not only God, but the only God, ineffably Three and One.

CUR DEUS HOMO

ANSELM OF CANTERBURY

Translated by Sidney Norton Deane

Preface

THE first part of this book was copied without my knowledge, before the work had been completed and revised. I have therefore been obliged to finish it as best I could, more hurriedly, and so more briefly, than I wished. For had an undisturbed and adequate period been allowed me for publishing it, I should have introduced and subjoined many things about which I have been silent. For it was while suffering under great anguish of heart, the origin and reason of which are known to God, that, at the entreaty of others, I began the book in England, and finished it when an exile in Capra. From the theme on which it was published I have called it *Cur Deus Homo*, and have divided it into two short books. The first contains the objections of infidels, who despise the Christian faith because they deem it contrary to reason; and also the reply of believers; and, in fine, leaving Christ out of view (as if nothing had ever been known of him), it proves, by absolute reasons, the impossibility that any man should be saved without him. Again, in the second book, likewise, as if nothing were known of Christ, it is moreover shown by plain reasoning and fact that human nature was ordained for this purpose, viz. that every man should enjoy a happy immortality, both in body and in soul; and that it was necessary that this design for which man was made should be fulfilled; but that it could not be fulfilled unless God became man, and unless all things were to take place which we hold with regard to Christ. I request all who may wish to copy this book to prefix this brief preface, with the heads of the whole work, at its commencement; so that, into whosesoever hands it may fall, as he looks on the face of it, there may be nothing in the whole body of the work which shall escape his notice.

BOOK ONE

1

The question on which the whole work rests.

ANSELM. I have been often and most earnestly requested by many, both personally and by letter, that I would hand down in writing the proofs of a certain doctrine of our faith, which I am accustomed to give to inquirers; for they say that these proofs gratify them, and are considered sufficient. This they ask, not for the sake of attaining to faith by means of reason, but that they may be gladdened by understanding and meditating on those things which they believe; and that, as far as possible, they may be always ready to convince any one who demands of them a reason of that hope which is in us. And this question, both infidels are accustomed to bring up against us, ridiculing Christian simplicity as absurd; and many believers ponder it in their hearts; for what cause or necessity, in sooth, God became man, and by his own death, as we believe and affirm, restored life to the world; when he might have done this, by means of some other being, angelic or human, or merely by his will. Not only the learned, but also many unlearned persons interest themselves in this inquiry and seek for its solution. Therefore, since many desire to consider this subject, and, though it seem very difficult in the investigation, it is yet plain to all in the solution, and attractive for the value and beauty of the reasoning; although what ought to be sufficient has been said by the holy fathers and their successors, yet I will take pains to disclose to inquirers what God has seen fit to lay open to me. And since investigations, which are carried on by question and answer, are thus made more plain to many, and especially to less quick minds, and on that account are more gratifying, I will take to argue with me one of those persons who agitate this subject; one, who among the rest impels me more earnestly to it, so that in this way Boso may question and Anselm reply.

2

How those things which are to be said should be received.

BOSO. As the right order requires us to believe the deep things of Christian faith before we undertake to discuss them by reason; so to my mind it appears a neglect if, after we are established in the faith, we do not seek to understand what we believe. Therefore, since I thus consider myself to hold the faith of our redemption, by the prevenient[1] grace of God, so that, even were I unable in any way to understand what I believe, still nothing could shake my constancy; I desire that you I should discover to me, what, as you know, many besides myself ask, for what necessity and cause God, who is omnipotent, should have assumed the littleness and weakness of human nature for the sake of its renewal?

ANSELM. You ask of me a thing which is above me, and therefore I tremble to take in hand subjects too lofty for me, lest, when some one may have thought or even seen that I do not satisfy him, he will rather believe that I am in error with regard to the substance of the truth, than that my intellect is not able to grasp it.

BOSO. You ought not so much to fear this, because you should call to mind, on the other hand, that it often happens in the discussion of some question that God opens what before lay concealed; and that you should hope for the grace of God, because if you liberally impart those things which you have freely received, you will be worthy to receive higher things to which you have not yet attained.

---

[1] Preceding in time or order; antecedent

ANSELM. There is also another thing on account of which I think this subject can hardly, or not at all, be discussed between us comprehensively; since, for this purpose, there is required a knowledge of Power and Necessity and Will and certain other subjects which are so related to one another that none of them can be fully examined without the rest; and so the discussion of these topics requires a separate labor, which, though not very easy, in my opinion, is by no means useless; for ignorance of these subjects makes certain things difficult, which by acquaintance with them become easy.

BOSO. You can speak so briefly with regard to these things, each in its place, that we may both have all that is requisite for the present object, and what remains to be said we can put off to another time.

ANSELM. This also much disinclines me from your request, not only that the subject is important, but as it is of a form fair above the sons of men, so is it of a wisdom fair above the intellect of men. On this account, I fear, lest, as I am wont to be incensed against sorry artists, when I see our Lord himself painted in an unseemly figure; so also it may fall out with me if I should undertake to exhibit so rich a theme in rough and vulgar diction.

BOSO. Even this ought not to deter you, because, as you allow any one to talk better if he can, so you preclude none from writing more elegantly if your language does not please him. But, to cut you off from all excuses, you are not to fulfill this request of mine for the learned but for me, and those asking the same thing with me.

ANSELM. Since I observe your earnestness and that of those who desire this thing with you, out of love and pious zeal, I will try to the best of my ability with the assistance of God and your prayers, which, when making this request, you have often promised me, not so much to make plain what you inquire about, as to inquire with you. But I wish all that I say to be received with this understanding, that, if I shall have said anything which higher authority does not corroborate, though I appear to demonstrate it by argument, yet it is not to be received with any further confidence, than as so appearing to me for the time, until God in some way make a clearer revelation to me. But if I am in any measure able to set your inquiry at rest, it should be concluded that a wiser than I will be able to do this more fully; nay, we must understand that for all that a man can say or know still deeper grounds of so great a truth lie concealed.

BOSO. Suffer me, therefore, to make use of the words of infidels; for it is proper for us when we seek to investigate the reasonableness of our faith to propose the objections of those who are wholly unwilling to submit to the same faith, without the support of reason. For although they appeal to reason because they do not believe, but we, on the other hand, because we do believe; nevertheless, the thing sought is one and the same. And if you bring up anything in reply which sacred authority seems to oppose, let it be mine to urge this inconsistency until you disprove it.

ANSELM. Speak on according to your pleasure.

3

Objections of infidels and replies of believers.

BOSO. Infidels ridiculing our simplicity charge upon us that we do injustice and dishonor to God when we affirm that he descended into the womb of a virgin, that he was born of woman, that he grew on the nourishment of milk and the food of men; and, passing over many other things which seem incompatible with Deity, that he endured fatigue, hunger, thirst, stripes, and crucifixion among thieves.

ANSELM. We do no injustice or dishonor to God, but give him thanks with all the heart, praising and proclaiming the ineffable height of his compassion. For the more astonishing a thing it is, and beyond expectation, that he has restored us from so great and deserved ills in which we were, to so great and unmerited blessings which we had forfeited; by so much the more has he shown his more exceeding love and tenderness towards us. For did they but carefully consider how fitly in this way human redemption is secured, they would not ridicule our simplicity, but would rather join with us in praising the wise beneficence of God. For, as death came upon the human race by the disobedience of man, it was fitting that by man's obedience life should be restored. And, as sin, the cause of our condemnation, had its origin from a woman, so ought the author of our righteousness and salvation to be born of a woman. And so also was it proper that the devil, who, being man's tempter, had conquered him in eating of the tree, should be vanquished by man in the suffering of the tree which man bore. Many other things also, if we carefully examine them, give a certain indescribable beauty to our redemption as thus procured.

4

How these things appear not decisive to infidels, and merely like so many pictures.

BOSO. These things must be admitted to be beautiful, and like so many pictures; but, if they have no solid foundation, they do not appear sufficient to infidels as reasons why we ought to believe that God wished to suffer the things which we speak of. For when one wishes to make a picture, he selects something substantial to paint it upon, so that his picture may remain. For no one paints in water or in air, because no traces of the picture remain in them. Wherefore, when we hold up to infidels these harmonious proportions which you speak of as so many pictures of the real thing, since they do not think this belief of ours a reality, but only a fiction, they consider us, as it were, to be painting upon a cloud. Therefore the rational existence of the truth must first be shown, I mean, the necessity, which proves that God ought to or could have condescended to those things which we affirm. Afterwards, to make the body of the truth, so to speak, shine forth more clearly, these harmonious proportions, like pictures of the body, must be described.

ANSELM. Does not the reason why God ought to do the things we speak of seem absolute enough when we consider that the human race, that work of his so very precious, was wholly ruined, and that it was not seemly that the purpose which God had made concerning man should fall to the ground; and, moreover, that this purpose could not be carried into effect unless the human race were delivered by their Creator himself?

5

How the redemption of man could not be effected by any other being but God.

BOSO. If this deliverance were said to be effected somehow by any other being than God (whether it were an angelic or a human being), the mind of man would receive it far more patiently. For God could have made some man without sin, not of a sinful substance, and not a descendant of any man, but just as he made Adam, and by this man it should seem that the work we speak of could have been done.

ANSELM. Do you not perceive that, if any other being should rescue man from eternal death, man would rightly be adjudged as the servant of that being? Now if this be so, he would in no wise be restored to that dignity which would have been his had he never sinned. For he, who was to be through eternity only the servant of God and an equal with the holy angels, would now be the servant of a being who was not God, and whom the angels did not serve.

6

How infidels find fault with us for saying that God has redeemed us by his death, and thus has shown his love towards us, and that he came to overcome the devil for us.

BOSO. This they greatly wonder at, because we call this redemption a release. For, say they, in what custody or imprisonment, or under whose power were you held, that God could not free you from it, without purchasing your redemption by so many sufferings, and finally by his own blood? And when we tell them that he freed us from our sins, and from his own wrath, and from hell, and from the power of the devil, whom he came to vanquish for us, because we were unable to do it, and that he purchased for us the kingdom of heaven; and that, by doing all these things, he manifested the greatness of his love towards us; they answer: If you say that God, who, as you believe, created the universe by a word, could not do all these things by a simple command, you contradict yourselves, for you make him powerless. Or, if you grant that he could have done these things in some other way, but did not wish to, how can you vindicate his wisdom, when you assert that he desired, without any reason, to suffer things so unbecoming? For these things which you bring up are all regulated by his will; for the wrath of God is nothing but his desire to punish. If, then, he does not desire to punish the sins of men, man is free from his sins, and from the wrath of God, and from hell, and from the power of the devil, all which things are the sufferings of sin; and, what he had lost by reason of these sins, he now regains. For, in whose power is hell, or the devil? Or, whose is the kingdom of heaven, if it be not his who created all things? Whatever things, therefore, you dread or hope for, all lie subject to his will, whom nothing can oppose. If, then, God were unwilling to save the human race in any other way than that you mention, when he could have done it by his simple will, observe, to say the least, how you disparage his wisdom. For, if a man without motive should do, by severe toil, a thing which he could have done in some easy way, no one would consider him a wise man. As to your statement that God has shown in this way how much he loved you, there is no argument to support this, unless it be proved that he could not otherwise have saved man. For, if he could not have done it otherwise, then it was, indeed, necessary for him to manifest his love in this way. But now, when he could have saved man differently, why is it that, for the sake of displaying his love, he does and suffers the things which you enumerate? For does he not show good angels how much he loves them, though he suffer no such things as these for them? As to what you say of his coming to vanquish the devil for you, with what meaning dare you allege this? Is not the omnipotence of God everywhere enthroned? How is it, then, that God must needs come down from heaven to vanquish the devil? These are the objections with which infidels think they can withstand us.

7

How the devil had no justice on his side against man; and why it was, that he seemed to have had it, and why God could have freed man in this way.

BOSO. Moreover, I do not see the force of that argument, which we are wont to make use of, that God, in order to save men, was bound, as it were, to try a contest with the devil in justice, before he did in strength, so that, when the devil should put to death that being in whom there was nothing worthy of death, and who was God, he should justly lose his power over sinners; and that, if it were not so, God would have used undue force against the devil, since the devil had a rightful ownership of man, for the devil had not seized man with violence, but man had freely surrendered to him. It is true that this might well enough be said, if the devil or man belonged to any other being than God, or were in the power of any but God. But since neither the devil nor man belong to any but God, and neither can exist without the exertion of Divine power, what cause ought God to try with his own creature (*de suo, in suo*), or what should he do but punish his servant, who had seduced his fellow-servant to desert their common Lord and come over to himself; who, a traitor, had taken to himself a fugitive; a thief, had taken to himself a fellow-thief, with what he had stolen from his Lord. For when one was stolen from his Lord by the persuasions of the other, both were thieves. For what could be more just than for God to do this? Or, should God, the judge of all, snatch man, thus held, out of the power of him who holds him so unrighteously, either for the purpose of punishing him in some other way than by means of the devil, or of sparing him, what injustice would there be in this? For, though man deserved to be tormented by the devil, yet the devil tormented him unjustly. For man merited punishment, and there was no more suitable way for him to be punished than by that being to whom he had given his consent to sin. But the infliction of punishment was nothing meritorious in the devil; on the other hand, he was even more unrighteous in this, because he was not led to it by a love of justice, but urged on by a malicious impulse. For he did not do this at the command of God, but God's inconceivable wisdom, which happily controls even wickedness, permitted it. And, in my opinion, those who think that the devil has any right in holding man, are brought to this belief by seeing that man is justly exposed to the tormenting of the devil, and that God in justice permits this; and therefore they suppose that the devil rightly inflicts it. For the very same thing, from opposite points of view, is sometimes both just and unjust, and hence, by those who do not carefully inspect the matter, is deemed wholly just or wholly unjust. Suppose, for example, that one strikes an innocent person unjustly, and hence justly deserves to be beaten himself; if, however, the one who was beaten, though he ought not to avenge himself, yet does strike the person who beat him, then he does it unjustly. And hence this violence on the part of the man who returns the blow is unjust, because he ought not to avenge himself; but as far as he who received the blow is concerned, it is just, for since he gave a blow unjustly, he justly deserves to receive one in return. Therefore, from opposite views, the same action is both just and unjust, for it may chance that one person shall consider it only just, and another only unjust. So also the devil is said to torment men justly, because God in justice permits this, and man in justice suffers it. But when man is said to suffer justly, it is not meant that his just suffering is inflicted by the hand of justice itself, but that he is punished by the just judgment of God. But if that written decree is brought up, which the Apostle says was made against us, and canceled by the death of Christ; and if any one thinks that it was intended by this decree that the devil, as if under the writing of a sort of compact, should justly demand sin and the punishment of sin, of man, before Christ suffered, as a debt for the first sin to which he tempted man, so that in this way he seems to prove his right over man, I do not by any means think that it is to be so understood. For that writing is not of the devil, because it is called the writing of a decree of the devil, but of God. For by the just judgment of God it was decreed, and, as it were, confirmed by writing, that, since man had sinned, he should not henceforth of himself have the power to avoid sin or the punishment of sin; for the spirit is out-going and not returning (*est enim spiritus vadens et non rediens*); and he who sins ought not to escape with impunity, unless pity spare the sinner, and deliver and restore him. Wherefore we ought not to believe that, on account of this writing, there can be found any justice on the part of the devil in his tormenting man. In fine, as there is never any injustice in a good angel, so in an evil angel there can be no justice at all. There was no reason, therefore, as respects the devil, why God should not make use of his own power against him for the liberation of man.

8

How, although the acts of Christ's condescension which we speak of do not belong to his divinity, it yet seems improper to infidels that these things should be said of him even as a man; and why it appears to them that this man did not suffer death of his own will.

ANSELM. The will of God ought to be a sufficient reason for us, when he does anything, though we cannot see why he does it. For the will of God is never irrational.

BOSO. That is very true, if it be granted that God does wish the thing in question; but many will never allow that God does wish anything if it be inconsistent with reason.

ANSELM. What do you find inconsistent with reason, in our confessing that God desired those things which make up our belief with regard to his incarnation?

BOSO. This in brief: that the Most High should stoop to things so lowly, that the Almighty should do a thing with such toil.

ANSELM. They who speak thus do not understand our belief. For we affirm that the Divine nature is beyond doubt impassible, and that God cannot at all be brought down from his exaltation, nor toil in anything which he wishes to effect. But we say that the Lord Jesus Christ is very God and very man, one person in two natures, and two natures in one person. When, therefore, we speak of God as enduring any humiliation or infirmity, we do not refer to the majesty of that nature, which cannot suffer; but to the feebleness of the human constitution which he assumed. And so there remains no ground of objection against our faith. For in this way we intend no debasement of the Divine nature, but we teach that one person is both Divine and human. In the incarnation of God there is no lowering of the Deity; but the nature of man we believe to be exalted.

BOSO. Be it so; let nothing be referred to the Divine nature, which is spoken of Christ after the manner of human weakness; but how will it ever be made out a just or reasonable thing that God should treat or suffer to be treated in such a manner, that man whom the Father called his beloved Son in whom he was well pleased, and whom the Son made himself? For what justice is there in his suffering death for the sinner, who was the most just of all men? What man, if he condemned the innocent to free the guilty, would not himself be judged worthy of condemnation? And so the matter seems to return to the same incongruity which is mentioned above. For if he could not save sinners in any other way than by condemning the just, where is his omnipotence? If, however, he could, but did not wish to, how shall we sustain his wisdom and justice?

ANSELM. God the Father did not treat that man as you seem to suppose, nor put to death the innocent for the guilty. For the Father did not compel him to suffer death, or even allow him to be slain, against his will, but of his own accord he endured death for the salvation of men.

BOSO. Though it were not against his will, since he agreed to the will of the Father; yet the Father seems to have bound him, as it were, by his injunction. For it is said that Christ "humbled himself, being made obedient to the Father even unto death, and that the death of the cross. For which cause God also has highly exalted him"; and that "he learned obedience from the things which he suffered"; and that God spared not his own Son, but gave him up for us all." And likewise the Son says: "I came not to do my own will, but the will of him that sent me." And when about to suffer, he says: "As the Father has given me commandment, so I do." Again: "The cup which the Father has given me, shall I not drink it?" And, at another time: "Father, if it be possible, let this cup pass from me; nevertheless, not as I will, but as you will." And again: "Father, if this cup may not pass from me except I drink it, your will be done." In all these passages it would rather appear that Christ endured death by the constraint of obedience, than by the inclination of his own free will.

9

How it was of his own accord that he died, and what this means: "he was made obedient even unto death"; and: "for which cause God has highly exalted him"; and: "I came not to do my own will"; and: "he spared not his own Son"; and: "not as I will, but as you will."

ANSELM. It seems to me that you do not rightly understand the difference between what he did at the demand of obedience, and what he suffered, not demanded by obedience, but inflicted on him, because he kept his obedience perfect.

BOSO. I need to have you explain it more clearly.

ANSELM. Why did the Jews persecute him even unto death?

BOSO. For nothing else, but that, in word and in life, he invariably maintained truth and justice.

ANSELM. I believe that God demands this of every rational being, and every being owes this in obedience to God.

BOSO. We ought to acknowledge this.

ANSELM. That man, therefore, owed this obedience to God the Father, humanity to Deity; and the Father claimed it from him.

BOSO. There is no doubt of this.

ANSELM. Now you see what he did, under the demand of obedience.

BOSO. Very true, and I see also what infliction he endured, because he stood firm in obedience. For death was inflicted on him for his perseverance in obedience and he endured it; but I do not understand how it is that obedience did not demand this.

ANSELM. Ought man to suffer death, if he had never sinned, or should God demand this of him?

BOSO. It is on this account that we believe that man would not have been subject to death, and that God would not have exacted this of him; but I should like to hear the reason of the thing from you.

ANSELM. You acknowledge that the intelligent creature was made holy, and for this purpose, viz. to be happy in the enjoyment of God.

BOSO. Yes.

ANSELM. You surely will not think it proper for God to make his creature miserable without fault, when he had created him holy that he might enjoy a state of blessedness. For it would be a miserable thing for man to die against his will.

BOSO. It is plain that, if man had not sinned, God ought not to compel him to die.

ANSELM. God did not, therefore, compel Christ to die; but he suffered death of his own will, not yielding up his life as an act of obedience, but on account of his obedience in maintaining holiness; for he held out so firmly in this obedience that he met death on account of it. It may, indeed be said, that the Father commanded him to die, when he enjoined that upon him on account of which he met death. It was in this sense, then, that "as the Father gave him the commandment, so he did, and the cup which He gave to him, he drank; and he was made obedient to the Father, even unto death"; and thus "he learned obedience from the things which he suffered," that is, how far obedience should be maintained. Now the word *didicit*, which is used, can be understood in two ways. For either *didicit* is written for this: he caused others to learn; or it is used, because he did learn by experience what he had an understanding of before. Again, when the Apostle had said: "he humbled himself, being made obedient even unto death, and that the death of the cross," he added: "wherefore God also has exalted him and given him a name, which is above every name." And this is similar to what David said: "he drank of the brook in the way, therefore did he lift up the head." For it is not meant that he could not have attained his exaltation in any other way but by obedience unto death; nor is it meant that his exaltation was conferred on him, only as a reward of his obedience (for he himself said before he suffered, that all things had been committed to him by the Father, and that all things belonging to the Father were his); but the expression is used because he had agreed with the Father and the Holy Spirit, that there was no other way to reveal to the world the height of his omnipotence, than by his death. For if a thing do not take place, except on condition of something else, it is not improperly said to occur by reason of that thing. For if we intend to do a thing, but mean to do something else first by means of which it may be done; when the first thing which we wish to do is done, if the result is such as we intended, it is properly said to be on account of the other; since that is now done which caused the delay; for it had been determined that the first thing should not be done without the other. If, for instance, I propose to cross a river only in a boat, though I can cross it in a boat or on horseback, and suppose that I delay crossing because the boat is gone; but if afterwards I cross, when the boat has returned, it may be properly said of me: the boat was ready, and therefore he crossed. And we not only use this form of expression when it is by means of a thing which we desire should take place first, but also when we intend to do something else, not by means of that thing, but only after it. For if one delays taking food because he has not to-day attended the celebration of mass; when that has been done which he wished to do first, it is not improper to say to him: now take food, for you have now done that for which you delayed taking food. Far less, therefore, is the language strange when Christ is said to be exalted on this account, because he endured death; for it was through this, and after this, that he determined to accomplish his exaltation. This may be understood also in the same way as that passage in which it is said that our Lord increased in wisdom, and in favor with God; not that this was really the case, but that he deported himself as if it were so. For he was exalted after his death, as if it were really on account of that. Moreover, that saying of his: "I came not to do mine own will, but the will of him that sent me," is precisely like that other saying: "My doctrine is not mine"; for what one does not have of himself, but of God, he ought not to call his own, but God's. Now no one has the truth which he teaches, or a holy will, of himself, but of God. Christ, therefore, came not to do his own will, but that of the Father; for his holy will was not derived from his humanity, but from his divinity. For that sentence: "God spared not his own Son, but gave him up for us all," means nothing more than that he did not rescue him. For there are found in the Bible many things like this. Again, when he says: "Father, if it be possible, let this cup pass from me; nevertheless not as I will, but as you will"; and "If this cup may not pass from me, except I drink it, your will be done"; he signifies by his own will the natural desire of safety, in accordance with which human nature shrank from the anguish of death. But he speaks of the will of the Father, not because the Father preferred the death of the Son to his life; but because the Father was not willing to rescue the human race, unless man were to do even as great a thing as was signified in the death of Christ. Since reason did not demand of another what he could not do, therefore, the Son says that he desires his own death. For he preferred to suffer, rather than that the human race should be lost; as if he were to say to the Father: "Since you do not desire the reconciliation of the world to take place in any other way, in this respect, I see that you desirest my death; let your will, therefore, be done, that is, let my death take place, so that the world may be reconciled to you." For we often say that one desires a thing, because he does not choose something else, the choice of which would preclude the existence of that which he is said to desire; for instance, when we say that he who does not choose to close the window through which the draft is admitted which puts out the light, wishes the light to be extinguished. So the Father desired the death of the Son, because he was not willing that the world should be saved in any other way, except by man's doing so great a thing as that which I have mentioned. And this, since none other could accomplish it, availed as much with the Son, who so earnestly desired the salvation of man, as if the Father had commanded him to die; and, therefore, "as the Father gave him commandment, so he did, and the cup which the Father gave to him he drank, being obedient even unto death."

10

Likewise on the same topics; and how otherwise they can be correctly explained.

ANSELM. It is also a fair interpretation that it was by that same holy will by which the son wished to die for the salvation of the world, that the Father gave him commandment (yet not by compulsion), and the cup of suffering, and spared him not, but gave him up for us and desired his death; and that the Son himself was obedient even unto death, and learned obedience from the things which he suffered. For as with regard to that will which led him to a holy life, he did not have it as a human being of himself, but of the Father; so also that will by which he desired to die for the accomplishment of so great a good, he could not have had but from the Father of lights, from whom is every good and perfect gift. And as the Father is said to draw by imparting an inclination, so there is nothing improper in asserting that he moves man. For as the Son says of the Father: "No man cometh to me except the Father draw him," he might as well have said, except he move him. In like manner, also, could he have declared: "No man layeth down his life for my sake, except the Father move or draw him." For since a man is drawn or moved by his will to that which he invariably chooses, it is not improper to say that God draws or moves him when he gives him this will. And in this drawing or impelling it is not to be understood that there is any constraint, but a free and grateful clinging to the holy will which has been given. If then it cannot be denied that the Father drew or moved the Son to death by giving him that will; who does not see that, in the same manner, he gave him commandment to endure death of his own accord and to take the cup, which he freely drank. And if it is right to say that the Son spared not himself, but gave himself for us of his own will, who will deny that it is right to say that the Father, of whom he had this will, did not spare him but gave him up for us, and desired his death? In this way, also, by following the will received from the Father invariably, and of his own accord, the Son became obedient to Him, even unto death; and learned obedience from the things which he suffered; that is, he learned how great was the work to be accomplished by obedience. For this is real and sincere obedience when a rational being, not of compulsion, but freely, follows the will received from God. In other ways, also, we can properly explain the Father's desire that the Son should die, though these would appear sufficient. For as we say that he desires a thing who causes another to desire it; so, also, we say that he desires a thing who approves of the desire of another, though he does not cause that desire. Thus when we see a man who desires to endure pain with fortitude for the accomplishment of some good design; though we acknowledge that we wish to have him endure that pain, yet we do not choose, nor take pleasure in, his suffering, but in his choice. We are, also, accustomed to say that he who can prevent a thing but does not, desires the thing which he does not prevent. Since, therefore, the will of the Son pleased the Father, and he did not prevent him from choosing, or from fulfilling his choice, it is proper to say that he wished the Son to endure death so piously and for so great an object, though he was not pleased with his suffering. Moreover, he said that the cup must not pass from him, except he drink it, not because he could not have escaped death had he chosen to; but because, as has been said, the world could not otherwise be saved; and it was his fixed choice to suffer death, rather than that the world should not be saved. It was for this reason, also, that he used those words, viz. to teach the human race that there was no other salvation for them but by his death; and not to show that he had no power at all to avoid death. For whatsoever things are said of him, similar to these which have been mentioned, they are all to be explained in accordance with the belief that he died, not by compulsion, but of free choice. For he was omnipotent, and it is said of him, when he was offered up, that he desired it. And he says himself: "I lay down my life that I may take it again; no man taketh it from me, but I lay it down of myself; I have power to lay it down, and I have power to take it again." A man cannot, therefore, be properly said to have been driven to a thing which he does of his own power and will.

BOSO. But this simple fact, that God allows him to be so treated, even if he were willing, does not seem becoming for such a Father in respect to such a Son.

ANSELM. Yes, it is of all things most proper that such a Father should acquiesce with such a Son in his desire, if it be praiseworthy as relates to the honor of God, and useful for man's salvation, which would not otherwise be effected.

BOSO. The question which still troubles us is, how the death of the Son can be proved reasonable and necessary. For otherwise, it does not seem that the Son ought to desire it, or the Father compel or permit it. For the question is, why God could not save man in some other way, and if so, why he wished to do it in this way? For it both seems unbecoming for God to have saved man in this way; and it is not clear how the death of the Son avails for the salvation of man. For it is a strange thing if God so delights in, or requires, the blood of the innocent, that he neither chooses, nor is able, to spare the guilty without the sacrifice of the innocent.

ANSELM. Since, in this inquiry, you take the place of those who are unwilling to believe anything not previously proved by reason, I wish to have it understood between us that we do not admit anything in the least unbecoming to be ascribed to the Deity, and that we do not reject the smallest reason if it be not opposed by a greater. For as it is impossible to attribute anything in the least unbecoming to God; so any reason, however small, if not overbalanced by a greater, has the force of necessity.

BOSO. In this matter, I accept nothing more willingly than that this agreement should be preserved between us in common.

ANSELM. The question concerns only the incarnation of God, and those things which we believe with regard to his taking human nature.

BOSO. It is so.

ANSELM. Let us suppose, then, that the incarnation of God, and the things that we affirm of him as man, had never taken place; and be it agreed between us that man was made for happiness, which cannot be attained in this life, and that no being can ever arrive at happiness, save by freedom from sin, and that no man passes this life without sin. Let us take for granted, also, the other things, the belief of which is necessary for eternal salvation.

BOSO. I grant it; for in these there is nothing which seems unbecoming or impossible for God.

ANSELM. Therefore, in order that man may attain happiness, remission of sin is necessary.

BOSO. We all hold this.

11

What it is to sin, and to make satisfaction for sin.

ANSELM. We must needs inquire, therefore, in what manner God puts away men's sins; and, in order to do this more plainly, let us first consider what it is to sin, and what it is to make satisfaction for sin.

BOSO. It is yours to explain and mine to listen.

ANSELM. If man or angel always rendered to God his due, he would never sin.

BOSO. I cannot deny that.

ANSELM. Therefore to sin is nothing else than not to render to God his due.

BOSO. What is the debt which we owe to God?

ANSELM. Every wish of a rational creature should be subject to the will of God.

BOSO. Nothing is more true.

ANSELM. This is the debt which man and angel owe to God, and no one who pays this debt commits sin; but every one who does not pay it sins. This is justice, or uprightness of will, which makes a being just or upright in heart, that is, in will; and this is the sole and complete debt of honor which we owe to God, and which God requires of us. For it is such a will only, when it can be exercised, that does works pleasing to God; and when this will cannot be exercised, it is pleasing of itself alone, since without it no work is acceptable. He who does not render this honor which is due to God, robs God of his own and dishonors him; and this is sin. Moreover, so long as he does not restore what he has taken away, he remains in fault; and it will not suffice merely to restore what has been taken away, but, considering the contempt offered, he ought to restore more than he took away. For as one who imperils another's safety does not enough by merely restoring his safety, without making some compensation for the anguish incurred; so he who violates another's honor does not enough by merely rendering honor again, but must, according to the extent of the injury done, make restoration in some way satisfactory to the person whom he has dishonored. We must also observe that when any one pays what he has unjustly taken away, he ought to give something which could not have been demanded of him, had he not stolen what belonged to another. So then, every one who sins ought to pay back the honor of which he has robbed God; and this is the satisfaction which every sinner owes to God.

BOSO. Since we have determined to follow reason in all these things, I am unable to bring any objection against them, although you somewhat startle me.

12

Whether it were proper for God to put away sins by compassion alone, without any payment of debt.

ANSELM. Let us return and consider whether it were proper for God to put away sins by compassion alone, without any payment of the honor taken from him.

BOSO. I do not see why it is not proper.

ANSELM. To remit sin in this manner is nothing else than not to punish; and since it is not right to cancel sin without compensation or punishment; if it be not punished, then is it passed by undischarged.

BOSO. What you say is reasonable.

ANSELM. It is not fitting for God to pass over anything in his kingdom undischarged.

BOSO. If I wish to oppose this, I fear to sin.

ANSELM. It is, therefore, not proper for God thus to pass over sin unpunished.

BOSO. Thus it follows.

ANSELM. There is also another thing which follows if sin be passed by unpunished, viz. that with God there will be no difference between the guilty and the not guilty; and this is unbecoming to God.

BOSO. I cannot deny it.

ANSELM. Observe this also. Every one knows that justice to man is regulated by law, so that, according to the requirements of law, the measure of award is bestowed by God.

BOSO. This is our belief.

ANSELM. But if sin is neither paid for nor punished, it is subject to no law.

BOSO. I cannot conceive it to be otherwise.

ANSELM. Injustice, therefore, if it is canceled by compassion alone, is more free than justice, which seems very inconsistent. And to these is also added a further incongruity, viz. that it makes injustice like God. For as God is subject to no law, so neither is injustice.

BOSO. I cannot withstand your reasoning. But when God commands us in every case to forgive those who trespass against us, it seems inconsistent to enjoin a thing upon us which it is not proper for him to do himself.

ANSELM. There is no inconsistency in God's commanding us not to take upon ourselves what belongs to Him alone. For to execute vengeance belongs to none but Him who is Lord of all; for when the powers of the world rightly accomplish this end, God himself does it who appointed them for the purpose.

BOSO. You have obviated[2] the difficulty which I thought to exist; but there is another to which I would like to have your answer. For since God is so free as to be subject to no law, and to the judgment of no one, and is so merciful as that nothing more merciful can be conceived; and nothing is right or fit save as he wills; it seems a strange thing for us to say that he is wholly unwilling or unable to put away an injury done to himself, when we are wont to apply to him for indulgence with regard to those offenses which we commit against others.

ANSELM. What you say of God's liberty and choice and compassion is true; but we ought so to interpret these things as that they may not seem to interfere with His dignity. For there is no

---

2 Removed

liberty except as regards what is best or fitting; nor should that be called mercy which does anything improper for the Divine character. Moreover, when it is said that what God wishes is just, and that what He does not wish is unjust, we must not understand that if God wished anything improper it would be just, simply because he wished it. For if God wishes to lie, we must not conclude that it is right to lie, but rather that he is not God. For no will can ever wish to lie, unless truth in it is impaired, nay, unless the will itself be impaired by forsaking truth. When, then, it is said: "If God wishes to lie," the meaning is simply this: "If the nature of God is such as that he wishes to lie"; and, therefore, it does not follow that falsehood is right, except it be understood in the same manner as when we speak of two impossible things: "If this be true, then that follows; because neither this nor that is true"; as if a man should say: "Supposing water to be dry, and fire to be moist"; for neither is the case. Therefore, with regard to these things, to speak the whole truth: If God desires a thing, it is right that he should desire that which involves no unfitness. For if God chooses that it should rain, it is right that it should rain; and if he desires that any man should die, then is it right that he should die. Wherefore, if it be not fitting for God to do anything unjustly, or out of course, it does not belong to his liberty or compassion or will to let the sinner go unpunished who makes no return to God of what the sinner has defrauded him.

BOSO. You remove from me every possible objection which I had thought of bringing against you.

ANSELM. Yet observe why it is not fitting for God to do this.

BOSO. I listen readily to whatever you say.

13

How nothing less was to be endured, in the order of things, than that the creature should take away the honor due the Creator and not restore what he takes away.

ANSELM. In the order of things, there is nothing less to be

endured than that the creature should take away the honor due the Creator, and not restore what he has taken away.

BOSO. Nothing is more plain than this.

ANSELM. But there is no greater injustice suffered than that by which so great an evil must be endured.

BOSO. This, also, is plain.

ANSELM. I think, therefore, that you will not say that God ought to endure a thing than which no greater injustice is suffered, viz. that the creature should not restore to God what he has taken away.

BOSO. No; I think it should be wholly denied.

ANSELM. Again, if there is nothing greater or better than God, there is nothing more just than supreme justice, which maintains God's honor in the arrangement of things, and which is nothing else but God himself.

BOSO. There is nothing clearer than this.

ANSELM. Therefore God maintains nothing with more justice than the honor of his own dignity.

BOSO. I must agree with you.

ANSELM. Does it seem to you that he wholly preserves it, if he allows himself to be so defrauded of it as that he should neither receive satisfaction nor punish the one defrauding him?

BOSO. I dare not say so.

ANSELM. Therefore the honor taken away must be repaid, or punishment must follow; otherwise, either God will not be just to himself, or he will be weak in respect to both parties; and this it is impious even to think of.

BOSO. I think that nothing more reasonable can be said.

14

How the honor of God exists in the punishment of the wicked.

BOSO. But I wish to hear from you whether the punishment of the sinner is an honor to God, or how it is an honor. For if the punishment of the sinner is not for God's honor when the sinner does not pay what he took away, but is punished, God loses his honor so that he cannot recover it. And this seems in contradiction to the things which have been said.

ANSELM. It is impossible for God to lose his honor; for either the sinner pays his debt of his own accord, or, if he refuse, God takes it from him. For either man renders due submission to God of his own will, by avoiding sin or making payment, or else God subjects him to himself by torments, even against man's will, and thus shows that he is the Lord of man, though man refuses to acknowledge it of his own accord. And here we must observe that as man in sinning takes away what belongs to God, so God in punishing gets in return what pertains to man. For not only does that belong to a man which he has in present possession, but also that which it is in his power to have. Therefore, since man was so made as to be able to attain happiness by avoiding sin; if, on account of his sin, he is deprived of happiness and every good, he repays from his own inheritance what he has stolen, though he repay it against his will. For although God does not apply what he takes away to any object of his own, as man transfers the money which he has taken from another to his own use; yet what he takes away serves the purpose of his own honor, for this very reason, that it is taken away. For by this act he shows that the sinner and all that pertains to him are under his subjection.

15

Whether God suffers his honor to be violated even in the least degree.

BOSO. What you say satisfies me. But there is still another point which I should like to have you answer. For if, as you make out, God ought to sustain his own honor, why does he allow it to be violated even in the least degree? For what is in any way made liable to injury is not entirely and perfectly preserved.

ANSELM. Nothing can be added to or taken from the honor of God. For this honor which belongs to him is in no way subject to injury or change. But as the individual creature preserves, naturally or by reason, the condition belonging, and, as it were, allotted to him, he is said to obey and honor God; and to this, rational nature, which possesses intelligence, is especially bound. And when the being chooses what he ought, he honors God; not by bestowing anything upon him, but because he brings himself freely under God's will and disposal, and maintains his own condition in the universe, and the beauty of the universe itself, as far as in him lies. But when he does not choose what he ought, he dishonors God, as far as the being himself is concerned, because he does not submit himself freely to God's disposal. And he disturbs the order and beauty of the universe, as relates to himself, although he cannot injure nor tarnish the power and majesty of God. For if those things which are held together in the circuit of the heavens desire to be elsewhere than under the heavens, or to be further removed from the heavens, there is no place where they can be but under the heavens, nor can they fly from the heavens without also approaching them. For both whence and whither and in what way they go, they are still under the heavens; and if they are at a greater distance from one part of them, they are only so much nearer to the opposite part. And so, though man or evil angel refuse to submit to the Divine will and appointment, yet he cannot escape it; for if he wishes to fly from a will that commands, he falls into the power of a will that punishes. And if you ask whither he goes, it is only under the permission of that will; and even this wayward choice or action of his becomes subservient, under infinite wisdom, to the order and beauty of the universe before spoken of. For when it is understood that God brings good out of many forms of evil, then the satisfaction for sin freely given, or if this be not given, the exaction of punishment, hold their own place and orderly beauty in the same universe. For if Divine wisdom were not to insist upon things, when wickedness tries to disturb the right appointment, there would be, in the very universe which God ought to control, an unseemliness springing from the violation of the beauty of arrangement, and God would appear to be deficient in his management. And these two things are not only unfitting, but consequently impossible; so that satisfaction or punishment must needs follow every sin.

BOSO. You have relieved my objection.

ANSELM. It is then plain that no one can honor or dishonor God, as he is in himself; but the creature, as far as he is concerned, appears to do this when he submits or opposes his will to the will of God.

BOSO. I know of nothing which can be said against this.

ANSELM. Let me add something to it.

BOSO. Go on, until I am weary of listening.

16

The reason why the number of angels who fell must be made up from men.

ANSELM. It was proper that God should design to make up for the number of angels that fell, from human nature which he created without sin.

BOSO. This is a part of our belief, but still I should like to have some reason for it.

ANSELM. You mistake me, for we intended to discuss only the incarnation of the Deity, and here you are bringing in other questions.

BOSO. Be not angry with me; "for the Lord loveth a cheerful giver"; and no one shows better how cheerfully he gives what he promises, than he who gives more than he promises; therefore, tell me freely what I ask.

ANSELM. There is no question that intelligent nature, which finds its happiness, both now and forever, in the contemplation of God, was foreseen by him in a certain reasonable and complete number, so that there would be an unfitness in its being either less or greater. For either God did not know in what number it was best to create rational beings, which is false; or, if he did know, then he appointed such a number as he perceived was most fitting. Wherefore, either the angels who fell were made so as to be within that number; or, since they were out of that number, they could not continue to exist, and so fell of necessity. But this last is an absurd idea.

BOSO. The truth which you set forth is plain.

ANSELM. Therefore, since they ought to be of that number, either their number should of necessity be made up, or else rational nature, which was foreseen as perfect in number, will remain incomplete. But this cannot be.

BOSO. Doubtless, then, the number must be restored.

ANSELM. But this restoration can only be made from human beings, since there is no other source.

17

How other angels cannot take the place of those who fell.

BOSO. Why could not they themselves be restored, or other angels substituted for them?

ANSELM. When you shall see the difficulty of our restoration, you will understand the impossibility of theirs. But other angels cannot be substituted for them on this account (to pass over its apparent inconsistency with the completeness of the first creation), because they ought to be such as the former angels would have been, had they never sinned. But the first angels in that case would have persevered without ever witnessing the punishment of sin; which, in respect to the others who were substituted for them after their fall, was impossible. For two beings who stand firm in truth are not equally deserving of praise, if one has never seen the punishment of sin, and the other forever witnesses its eternal reward. For it must not for a moment be supposed that good angels are upheld by the fall of evil angels, but by their own virtue. For, as they would have been condemned together, had the good sinned with the bad, so, had the unholy stood firm with the holy, they would have been likewise upheld. For, if, without the fall of a part, the rest could not be upheld, it would follow, either that none could ever be upheld, or else that it was necessary for some one to fall, in order by his punishment to uphold the rest; but either of these suppositions is absurd. Therefore, had all stood, all would have been upheld in the same manner as those who stood; and this manner I explained, as well as I could, when treating of the reason why God did not bestow perseverance upon the devil.

BOSO. You have proved that the evil angels must be restored from the human race; and from this reasoning it appears that the number of men chosen will not be less than that of fallen angels. But show, if you can, whether it will be greater.

18

Whether there will be more holy men than evil angels.

ANSELM. If the angels, before any of them fell, existed in that perfect number of which we have spoken, then men were only made to supply the place of the lost angels; and it is plain that their number will not be greater. But if that number were not found in all the angels together, then both the loss and the original deficiency must be made up from men, and more men will be chosen than there were fallen angels. And so we shall say that men were made not only to restore the diminished number, but also to complete the imperfect number.

BOSO. Which is the better theory, that angels were originally made perfect in number or that they were not?

ANSELM. I will state my views.

BOSO. I cannot ask more of you.

ANSELM. If man was created after the fall of evil angels, as some understand the account in Genesis, I do not think that I can prove from this either of these suppositions positively. For it is possible, I think, that the angels should have been created perfect in number, and that afterwards man was created to complete their number when it had been lessened; and it is also possible that they were not perfect in number, because God deferred completing the number, as he does even now, determining in his own time to create man. Wherefore, either God would only complete that which was not yet perfect, or, if it were also diminished, He would restore it. But if the whole creation took place at once, and those days in which Moses appears to describe a successive creation are not to be understood like such days as ours, I cannot see how angels could have been created perfect in number. Since, if it were so, it seems to me that some, either men or angels, would fall immediately, else in heaven's empire there would be more than the complete number required. If, therefore, all things were created at one and the same time, it should seem that angels, and the first two human beings, formed an incomplete number, so that, if no angel fell, the deficiency alone should be made up, but if any fell, the lost part should be restored; and that human nature, which had stood firm, though weaker than that of angels, might, as it were, justify God, and put the devil to silence, if he were to attribute his fall to weakness. And in case human nature fell, much more would it justify God against the devil, and even against itself, because, though made far weaker and of a mortal race, yet, in the elect, it would rise from its weakness to an estate exalted above that from which the devil was fallen, as far as good angels, to whom it should be equal, were advanced after the overthrow of the evil, because they persevered. From these reasons, I am rather inclined to the belief that there was not, originally, that complete number of angels necessary to perfect the celestial state; since, supposing that man and angels were not created at the same time, this is possible; and it would follow of necessity, if they were created at the same time, which is the opinion of the majority, because we read: "He, who liveth forever, created all things at once." But if the perfection of the created universe is to be understood as consisting, not so much in the number of beings, as in the number of natures; it follows that human nature was either made to consummate this perfection, or that it was superfluous, which we should not dare affirm of the nature of the smallest reptile. Wherefore, then, it was made for itself, and not merely to restore the number of beings possessing another nature. From which it is plain that, even had no angel fallen, men would yet have had their place in the celestial kingdom. And hence it follows that there was not a perfect number of angels, even before a part fell; otherwise, of necessity some men or angels must fall, because it would be impossible that any should continue beyond the perfect number.

BOSO. You have not labored in vain.

ANSELM. There is, also, as I think, another reason which supports, in no small degree, the opinion that angels were not created perfect in number.

BOSO. Let us hear it.

ANSELM. Had a perfect number of angels been created, and had man been made only to fill the place of the lost angels, it is plain that, had not some angels fallen from their happiness, man would never have been exalted to it.

BOSO. We are agreed.

ANSELM. But if any one shall ask: "Since the elect rejoice as much over the fall of angels as over their own exaltation, because the one can never take place without the other; how can they be justified in this unholy joy, or how shall we say that angels are restored by the substitution of men, if they (the angels) would have remained free from this fault, had they not fallen, viz., from rejoicing over the fall of others?" We reply: Cannot men be made free from this fault? Nay, how ought they to be happy with this fault? With what temerity, then, do we say that God neither wishes nor is able to make this substitution without this fault!

BOSO. Is not the case similar to that of the Gentiles who were called unto faith, because the Jews rejected it?

ANSELM. No; for had the Jews all believed, yet the Gentiles would have been called; for "in every nation he that feareth God and worketh righteousness is accepted of him." But since the Jews despised the apostles, this was the immediate occasion of their turning to the Gentiles.

BOSO. I see no way of opposing you.

ANSELM. Whence does that joy which one has over another's fall seem to arise?

BOSO. Whence, to be sure, but from the fact that each individual will be certain that, had not another fallen, he would never have attained the place where he now is?

ANSELM. If, then, no one had this certainty, there would be no cause for one to rejoice over the doom of another.

BOSO. So it appears.

ANSELM. Think you that any one of them can have this certainty, if their number shall far exceed that of those who fell?

BOSO. I certainly cannot think that any one would or ought to have it. For how can any one know whether he were created to restore the part diminished, or to make up that which was not yet complete in the number necessary to constitute the state? But all are sure that they were made with a view to the perfection of that kingdom.

ANSELM. If, then, there shall be a larger number than that of the fallen angels, no one can or ought to know that he would not have attained this height but for another's fall.

BOSO. That is true.

ANSELM. No one, therefore, will have cause to rejoice over the perdition of another.

BOSO. So it appears.

ANSELM. Since, then, we see that if there are more men elected than the number of fallen angels, the incongruity will not follow which must follow if there are not more men elected; and since it is impossible that there should be anything incongruous in that celestial state, it becomes a necessary fact that angels were not made perfect in number, and that there will be more happy men than doomed angels.

BOSO. I see not how this can be denied.

ANSELM. I think that another reason can be brought to support this opinion.

BOSO. You ought then to present it.

ANSELM. We believe that the material substance of the world must be renewed, and that this will not take place until the number of the elect is accomplished, and that happy kingdom made perfect, and that after its completion there will be no change. Whence it may be reasoned that God planned to perfect both at the same time, in order that the inferior nature, which knew not God, might not be perfected before the superior nature which ought to enjoy God; and that the inferior, being renewed at the same time with the superior, might, as it were, rejoice in its own way; yes, that every creature having so glorious and excellent a consummation, might delight in its Creator and in itself, in turn, rejoicing always after its own manner, so that what the will effects in the rational nature of its own accord, this also the irrational creature naturally shows by the arrangement of God. For we are wont to rejoice in the fame of our ancestors, as when on the birthdays of the saints we delight with festive triumph, rejoicing in their honor. And this opinion derives support from the fact that, had not Adam sinned, God might yet put off the completion of that state until the number of men which he designed should be made out, and men themselves be transferred, so to speak, to an immortal state of bodily existence. For they had in paradise a kind of immortality, that is, a power not to die, but since it was possible for them to die, this power was not immortal, as if, indeed, they had not been capable of death. But if God determined to bring to perfection, at one and the same time, that intelligent and happy state and this earthly and irrational nature; it follows that either that state was not complete in the number of angels before the destruction of the wicked, but God was waiting to complete it by men, when he should renovate the material nature of the world; or that, if that kingdom were perfect in number, it was not in confirmation, and its confirmation must be deferred, even had no one sinned, until that renewal of the world to which we look forward; or that, if that confirmation could not be deferred so long, the renewal of the world must be hastened that both events might take place at the same time. But that God should determine to renew the world immediately after it was made, and to destroy in the very beginning those things which after this renewal would not exist, before any reason appeared for their creation, is simply absurd. It therefore follows that, since angels were not complete in number, their confirmation will not be long deferred on this account, because the renewal of a world just created ought soon to take place, for this is not fitting. But that God should wish to put off their confirmation to the future renewing of the world seems improper, since he so quickly accomplished it in some, and since we know that in regard to our first parents, if they had not sinned as they did, he would have confirmed them, as well as the angels who persevered. For, although not yet advanced to that equality with angels to which men were to attain, when the number taken from among them was complete; yet, had they preserved their original holiness, so as not to have sinned though tempted, they would have been confirmed, with all their offspring, so as never more to sin; just as when they were conquered by sin, they were so weakened as to be unable, in themselves, to live afterwards without sinning. For who dares affirm that wickedness is more powerful to bind a man in servitude, after he has yielded to it at the first persuasion, than holiness to confirm him in liberty when he has adhered to it in the original trial? For as human nature, being included in the person of our first parents, was in them wholly won over to sin (with the single exception of that man whom God being able to create from a virgin was equally able to save from the sin of Adam), so had they not sinned, human nature would have wholly conquered. It therefore remains that the celestial state was not complete in its original number, but must be completed from among men.

BOSO. What you say seems very reasonable to me. But what shall we think of that which is said respecting God: "He has appointed the bounds of the people according to the number of the children of Israel"; which some, because for the expression "children of Israel" is found sometimes "angels of God," explain in this way, that the number of elect men taken should be understood as equal to that of good angels?

ANSELM. This is not discordant with the previous opinion, if it be not certain that the number of angels who fell is the same as that of those who stood. For if there be more elect than evil angels, and elect men must needs be substituted for the evil angels, and it is possible for them to equal the number of the good angels, in that case there will be more holy men than evil angels. But remember with what condition I undertook to answer your inquiry, viz. that if I say anything not upheld by greater authority, though I appear to demonstrate it, yet it should be received with no further certainty than as my opinion for the present, until God makes some clearer revelation to me. For I am sure that, if I say anything which plainly opposes the Holy Scriptures, it is false; and if I am aware of it, I will no longer hold it. But if, with regard to subjects in which opposite opinions may be held without hazard, as that, for instance, which we now discuss; for if we know not whether there are to be more men elected than the number of the lost angels, and incline to either of these opinions rather than the other, I think the soul is not in danger; if, I say, in questions like this, we explain the Divine words so as to make them favor different sides, and there is nowhere found anything to decide, beyond doubt, the opinion that should be held, I think there is no censure to be given. As to the passage which you spoke of: "He has determined the bounds of the people (or tribes) according to the number of the angels of God"; or as another translation has it: "according to the number of the children of Israel"; since both translations either mean the same thing, or are different, without contradicting each other, we may understand that good angels only are intended by both expressions, "angels of God," and "children of Israel," or that elect men only are meant, or that both angels and elect men are included, even the whole celestial kingdom. Or by angels of God may be understood holy angels only, and by children of Israel, holy men only; or, by children of Israel, angels only, and by angels of God, holy men. If good angels are intended in both expressions, it is the same as if only "angels of God" had been used; but if the whole heavenly kingdom were included, the meaning is that a people, that is, the throng of elect men, is to be taken, or that there will be a people in this stage of existence, until the appointed number of that kingdom, not yet completed, shall be made up from among men. But I do not now see why angels only, or even angels and holy men together, are meant by the expression "children of Israel"; for it is not improper to call holy men "children of Israel," as they are called "sons of Abraham." And they can also properly be called "angels of God," because they imitate the life of angels, and they are promised in heaven a likeness to and equality with angels, and all who live holy lives are angels of God. Therefore the confessors or martyrs are so called; for he who declares and bears witness to the truth, he is a messenger of God, that is, his angel. And if a wicked man is called a devil, as our Lord says of Judas, because they are alike in malice; why should not a good man be called an angel, because he follows holiness? Wherefore I think we may say that God has appointed the bounds of the people according to the number of elect men, because men will exist and there will be a natural increase among them, until the number of elect men is accomplished; and when that occurs, the birth of men, which takes place in this life, will cease. But if by "angels of God" we only understand holy angels, and by "children of Israel " only holy men; it may be explained in two ways: that "God has appointed the bounds of the people according to the number of the angels of God," viz. either that so great a people, that is, so many men, will be taken as there are holy angels of God, or that a people will continue to exist upon earth, until the number of angels is completed from among men. And I think there is no other possible method of explanation: "he has appointed the bounds of the people according to the number of the children of Israel," that is, that there will continue to be a people in this stage of existence, as I said above, until the number of holy men is completed. And we infer from either translation that as many men will be taken as there were angels who remained steadfast. Yet, although lost angels must have their ranks filled by men, it does not follow that the number of lost angels was equal to that of those who persevered. But if any one affirms this, he will have to find means of invalidating the reasons given above, which prove, I think, that there was not among angels, before the fall, that perfect number before mentioned, and that there are more men to be saved than the number of evil angels.

BOSO. I by no means regret that I urged you to these remarks about the angels, for it has not been for nought. Now let us return from our digression.

19

How man cannot be saved without satisfaction for sin.

ANSELM. It was fitting for God to fill the places of the fallen angels from among men.

BOSO. That is certain.

ANSELM. Therefore there ought to be in the heavenly empire as many men taken as substitutes for the angels as would correspond with the number whose place they shall take, that is, as many as there are good angels now; otherwise they who fell will not be restored, and it will follow that God either could not accomplish the good which he begun, or he will repent of having undertaken it; either of which is absurd.

BOSO. Truly it is fitting that men should be equal with good angels.

ANSELM. Have good angels ever sinned?

BOSO. No.

ANSELM. Can you think that man, who has sinned, and never made satisfaction to God for his sin, but only been suffered to go unpunished, may become the equal of an angel who has never sinned?

BOSO. These words I can both think of and utter, but can no more perceive their meaning than I can make truth out of falsehood.

ANSELM. Therefore it is not fitting that God should take sinful man without an atonement, in substitution for lost angels; for truth will not suffer man thus to be raised to an equality with holy beings.

BOSO. Reason shows this.

ANSELM. Consider, also, leaving out the question of equality with the angels, whether God ought, under such circumstances, to raise man to the same or a similar kind of happiness as that which he had before he sinned.

BOSO. Tell your opinion, and I will attend to it as well as I can.

ANSELM. Suppose a rich man possessed a choice pearl which had never been defiled, and which could not be taken from his hands without his permission; and that he determined to commit it to the treasury of his dearest and most valuable possessions.

BOSO. I accept your supposition.

ANSELM. What if he should allow it to be struck from his hand and cast in the mire, though he might have prevented it; and afterwards taking it all soiled by the mire and unwashed, should commit it again to his beautiful and loved casket; will you consider him a wise man?

BOSO. How can I? For would it not be far better to keep and preserve his pearl pure, than to have it polluted?

ANSELM. Would not God be acting like this, who held man in paradise, as it were in his own hand, without sin, and destined to the society of angels, and allowed the devil, inflamed with envy, to cast him into the mire of sin, though truly with man's consent? For, had God chosen to restrain the devil, the devil could not have tempted man. Now I say, would not God be acting like this, should he restore man, stained with the defilement of sin, unwashed, that is, without any satisfaction, and always to remain so; should he restore him at once to paradise, from which he had been thrust out?

BOSO. I dare not deny the aptness of your comparison, were God to do this, and therefore do not admit that he can do this. For it should seem either that he could not accomplish what he designed, or else that he repented of his good intent, neither of which things is possible with God.

ANSELM. Therefore, consider it settled that, without satisfaction, that is, without voluntary payment of the debt, God can neither pass by the sin unpunished, nor can the sinner attain that happiness, or happiness like that, which he had before he sinned; for man cannot in this way be restored, or become such as he was before he sinned.

BOSO. I am wholly unable to refute your reasoning. But what say you to this: that we pray God, "put away our sins from us," and every nation prays the God of its faith to put away its sins. For, if we pay our debt, why do we pray God to put it away? Is not God unjust to demand what has already been paid? But if we do not make payment, why do we supplicate in vain that he will do what he cannot do, because it is unbecoming?

ANSELM. He who does not pay says in vain: "Pardon"; but he who pays makes supplication, because prayer is properly connected with the payment; for God owes no man anything, but every creature owes God; and, therefore, it does not become man to treat with God as with an equal. But of this it is not now needful for me to answer you. For when you think why Christ died, I think you will see yourself the answer to your question.

BOSO. Your reply with regard to this matter suffices me for the present. And, moreover, you have so clearly shown that no man can attain happiness in sin, or be freed from sin without satisfaction for the trespass, that, even were I so disposed, I could not doubt it.

20

That satisfaction ought to be proportionate to guilt; and that man is of himself unable to accomplish this.

ANSELM. Neither, I think, will you doubt this, that satisfaction should be proportionate to guilt.

BOSO. Otherwise sin would remain in a manner exempt from control (*inordinatum*), which cannot be, for God leaves nothing uncontrolled in his kingdom. But this is determined, that even the smallest unfitness is impossible with God.

ANSELM. Tell me, then, what payment you make God for your sin?

BOSO. Repentance, a broken and contrite heart, self-denial, various bodily sufferings, pity in giving and forgiving, and obedience.

ANSELM. What do you give to God in all these?

BOSO. Do I not honor God, when, for his love and fear, in heartfelt contrition I give up worldly joy, and despise, amid abstinence and toils, the delights and ease of this life, and submit obediently to him, freely bestowing my possessions in giving to and releasing others?

ANSELM. When you render anything to God which you owe him, irrespective of your past sin, you should not reckon this as the debt which you owe for sin. But you owe God every one of those things which you have mentioned. For, in this mortal state, there should be such love and such desire of attaining the true end of your being, which is the meaning of prayer, and such grief that you have not yet reached this object, and such fear lest you fail of it, that you should find joy in nothing which does not help you or give encouragement of your success. For you do not deserve to have a thing which you do not love and desire for its own sake, and the want of which at present, together with the great danger of never getting it, causes you no grief. This also requires one to avoid ease and worldly pleasures such as seduce the mind from real rest and pleasure, except so far as you think suffices for the accomplishment of that object. But you ought to view the gifts which you bestow as a part of your debt, since you know that what you give comes not from yourself, but from him whose servant both you are and he also to whom you give. And nature herself teaches you to do to your fellow servant, man to man, as you would be done by; and that he who will not bestow what he has ought not to receive what he has not. Of forgiveness, indeed, I speak briefly, for, as we said above, vengeance in no sense belongs to you, since you are not your own, nor is he who injures you yours or his, but you are both the servants of one Lord, made by him out of nothing. And if you avenge yourself upon your fellow servant, you proudly assume judgment over him when it is the peculiar right of God, the judge of all. But what do you give to God by your obedience, which is not owed him already, since he demands from you all that you are and have and can become?

BOSO. Truly I dare not say that in all these things I pay any portion of my debt to God.

ANSELM. How then do you pay God for your transgression?

BOSO. If in justice I owe God myself and all my powers, even when I do not sin, I have nothing left to render to him for my sin.

ANSELM. What will become of you then? How will you be saved?

BOSO. Merely looking at your arguments, I see no way of escape. But, turning to my belief, I hope through Christian faith, "which works by love," that I may be saved, and the more, since we read that if the sinner turns from his iniquity and does what is right, all his transgressions shall be forgotten.

ANSELM. This is only said of those who either looked for Christ before his coming, or who believe in him since he has appeared. But we set aside Christ and his religion as if they did not exist, when we proposed to inquire whether his coming were necessary to man's salvation.

BOSO. We did so.

ANSELM. Let us then proceed by reason simply.

BOSO. Though you bring me into straits, yet I very much wish you to proceed as you have begun.

21

How great a burden sin is.

ANSELM. Suppose that you did not owe any of those things which you have brought up as possible payment for your sin, let us inquire whether they can satisfy for a sin so small as one look contrary to the will of God.

BOSO. Did I not hear you question the thing, I should suppose that a single repentant feeling on my part would blot out this sin.

ANSELM. You have not as yet estimated the great burden of sin.

BOSO. Show it me then.

ANSELM. If you should find yourself in the sight of God, and one said to you: "Look thither"; and God, on the other hand, should say: "It is not my will that you should look"; ask your own heart what there is in all existing things which would make it right for you to give that look contrary to the will of God.

BOSO. I can find no motive which would make it right; unless, indeed I am so situated as to make it necessary for me either to do this, or some greater sin.

ANSELM. Put away all such necessity, and ask with regard to this sin only whether you can do it even for your own salvation.

BOSO. I see plainly that I cannot.

ANSELM. Not to detain you too long; what if it were necessary either that the whole universe, except God himself, should perish and fall back into nothing, or else that you should do so small a thing against the will of God?

BOSO. When I consider the action itself, it appears very slight; but when I view it as contrary to the will of God, I know of nothing so grievous, and of no loss that will compare with it; but sometimes we oppose another's will without blame in order to preserve his property, so that afterwards he is glad that we opposed him.

ANSELM. This is in the case of man, who often does not know what is useful for him, or cannot make up his loss; but God is in want of nothing, and, should all things perish, can restore them as easily as he created them.

BOSO. I must confess that I ought not to oppose the will of God even to preserve the whole creation.

ANSELM. What if there were more worlds as full of beings as this?

BOSO. Were they increased to an infinite extent, and held before me in like manner, my reply would be the same.

ANSELM. You cannot answer more correctly, but consider, also, should it happen that you gave the look contrary to God's will, what payment you can make for this sin?

BOSO. I can only repeat what I said before.

ANSELM. So heinous is our sin whenever we knowingly oppose the will of God even in the slightest thing; since we are always in his sight, and he always enjoins it upon us not to sin.

BOSO. I cannot deny it.

ANSELM. Therefore you make no satisfaction unless you restore something greater than the amount of that obligation, which should restrain you from committing the sin.

BOSO. Reason seems to demand this, and to make the contrary wholly impossible.

ANSELM. Even God cannot raise to happiness any being bound at all by the debt of sin, because He ought not to.

BOSO. This decision is most weighty.

ANSELM. Listen to an additional reason which makes it no less difficult for man to be reconciled to God.

BOSO. This alone would drive me to despair, were it not for the consolation of faith.

ANSELM. But listen.

BOSO. Say on.

22

What contempt man brought upon God, when he allowed himself to be conquered by the devil; for which he can make no satisfaction.

ANSELM. Man being made holy was placed in paradise, as it were in the place of God, between God and the devil, to conquer the devil by not yielding to his temptation, and so to vindicate the honor of God and put the devil to shame, because that man, though weaker and dwelling upon earth, should not sin though tempted by the devil, while the devil, though stronger and in heaven, sinned without any to tempt him. And when man could have easily effected this, he, without compulsion and of his own accord, allowed himself to be brought over to the will of the devil, contrary to the will and honor of God.

BOSO. To what would you bring me?

ANSELM. Decide for yourself if it be not contrary to the honor of God for man to be reconciled to Him, with this calumnious[3] reproach still heaped upon God; unless man first shall have honored God by overcoming the devil, as he dishonored him in yielding to the devil. Now the victory ought to be of this kind, that, as in strength and immortal vigor, he freely yielded to the devil to sin, and on this account justly incurred the penalty of death; so, in his weakness and mortality, which he had brought upon himself, he should conquer the devil by the pain of death, while wholly avoiding sin. But this cannot be done, so long as from the deadly effect of the first transgression, man is conceived and born in sin.

BOSO. Again I say that the thing is impossible, and reason ap-

---

3 False and defamatory; slanderous

proves what you say.

ANSELM. Let me mention one thing more, without which man's reconciliation cannot be justly effected, and the impossibility is the same.

BOSO. You have already presented so many obligations which we ought to fulfill, that nothing which you can add will alarm me more.

ANSELM. Yet listen.

BOSO. I will.

23

What man took from God by his sin, which he has no power to repay.

ANSELM. What did man take from God, when he allowed himself to be overcome by the devil?

BOSO. Go on to mention, as you have begun, the evil things which can be added to those already shown, for I am ignorant of them.

ANSELM. Did not man take from God whatever He had purposed to do for human nature?

BOSO. There is no denying that.

ANSELM. Listen to the voice of strict justice; and judge according to that whether man makes to God a real satisfaction for his sin, unless, by overcoming the devil, man restore to God what he took from God in allowing himself to be conquered by the devil; so that, as by this conquest over man the devil took what belonged to God, and God was the loser, so in man's victory the devil may be despoiled, and God recover his right.

BOSO. Surely nothing can be more exactly or justly conceived.

ANSELM. Think you that supreme justice can violate this justice?

BOSO. I dare not think it.

ANSELM. Therefore man cannot and ought not by any means to receive from God what God designed to give him, unless he return to God everything which he took from him; so that, as by man God suffered loss, by man, also, he might recover his loss. But this cannot be effected except in this way: that, as in the fall of man all human nature was corrupted, and, as it were, tainted with sin, and God will not choose one of such a race to fill up the number in his heavenly kingdom; so, by man's victory, as many men may be justified from sin as are needed to complete the number which man was made to fill. But a sinful man can by no means do this, for a sinner cannot justify a sinner.

BOSO. There is nothing more just or necessary; but, from all these things, the compassion of God and the hope of man seems to fail, as far as regards that happiness for which man was made.

ANSELM. Yet wait a little.

BOSO. Have you anything further?

24

How, as long as man does not restore what he owes God, he cannot be happy, nor is he excused by want of power.

ANSELM. If a man is called unjust who does not pay his fellow-man a debt, much more is he unjust who does not restore what he owes God.

BOSO. If he can pay and yet does not, he is certainly unjust. But if he be not able, wherein is he unjust?

ANSELM. Indeed, if the origin of his inability were not in himself, there might be some excuse for him. But if in this very impotence lies the fault, as it does not lessen the sin, neither does it excuse him from paying what is due. Suppose one should assign his slave a certain piece of work, and should command him not to throw himself into a ditch, which he points out to him and from which he could not extricate himself; and suppose that the slave, despising his master's command and warning, throws himself into the ditch before pointed out, so as to be utterly unable to accomplish the work assigned; think you that his inability will at all excuse him for not doing his appointed work?

BOSO. By no means, but will rather increase his crime, since he brought his inability upon himself. For doubly has he sinned, in not doing what he was commanded to do and in doing what he was forewarned not to do.

ANSELM. Just so inexcusable is man, who has voluntarily brought upon himself a debt which he cannot pay, and by his own fault disabled himself, so that he can neither escape his previous obligation not to sin, nor pay the debt which he has incurred by sin. For his very inability is guilt, because he ought not to have it; nay, he ought to be free from it; for as it is a crime not to have what he ought, it is also a crime to have what he ought not. Therefore, as it is a crime in man not to have that power which he received to avoid sin, it is also a crime to have that inability by which he can neither do right and avoid sin, nor restore the debt which he owes on account of his sin. For it is by his own free action that he loses that power, and falls into this inability. For not to have the power which one ought to have, is the same thing as to have the inability which one ought not to have. Therefore man's inability to restore what he owes to God, an inability brought upon himself for that very purpose, does not excuse man from paying; for the result of sin cannot excuse the sin itself.

BOSO. This argument is exceedingly weighty, and must be true.

ANSELM. Man, then, is unjust in not paying what he owes to God.

BOSO. This is very true; for he is unjust, both in not paying, and in not being able to pay.

ANSELM. But no unjust person shall be admitted to happiness; for as that happiness is complete in which there is nothing wanting, so it can belong to no one who is not so pure as to have no injustice found in him.

BOSO. I dare not think otherwise.

ANSELM. He, then, who does not pay God what he owes can never be happy.

BOSO. I cannot deny that this is so.

ANSELM. But if you choose to say that a merciful God remits to the suppliant his debt, because he cannot pay; God must be said to dispense with one of two things, viz. either this which man ought voluntarily to render but cannot, that is, an equivalent for his sin, a thing which ought not to be given up even to save the whole universe besides God; or else this, which, as I have before said, God was about to take away from man by punishment, even against man's will, viz. happiness. But if God gives up what man ought freely to render, for the reason that man cannot repay it, what is this but saying that God gives up what he is unable to obtain? But it is mockery to ascribe such compassion to God. But if God gives up what he was about to take from unwilling man, because man is unable to restore what he ought to restore freely, He abates the punishment and makes man happy on account of his sin, because he has what he ought not to have. For he ought not to have this inability, and therefore as long as he has it without atonement it is his sin. And truly such compassion on the part of God is wholly contrary to the Divine justice, which allows nothing but punishment as the recompense of sin. Therefore, as God cannot be inconsistent with himself, his compassion cannot be of this nature.

BOSO. I think, then, we must look for another mercy than this.

ANSELM. But suppose it were true that God pardons the man who does not pay his debt because he cannot.

BOSO. I could wish it were so.

ANSELM. But while man does not make payment, he either wishes to restore, or else he does not wish to. Now, if he wishes to do what he cannot, he will be needy, and if he does not wish to, he will be unjust.

BOSO. Nothing can be plainer.

ANSELM. But whether needy or unjust, he will not be happy.

BOSO. This also is plain.

ANSELM. So long, then, as he does not restore, he will not be happy.

BOSO. If God follows the method of justice, there is no escape for the miserable wretch, and God's compassion seems to fail.

ANSELM. You have demanded an explanation; now hear it. I do not deny that God is merciful, who preserveth man and beast, according to the multitude of his mercies. But we are speaking of that exceeding pity by which he makes man happy after this life. And I think that I have amply proved, by the reasons given above, that happiness ought not to be bestowed upon any one whose sins have not been wholly put away; and that this remission ought not to take place, save by the payment of the debt incurred by sin, according to the extent of sin. And if you think that any objections can be brought against these proofs, you ought to mention them.

BOSO. I see not how your reasons can be at all invalidated.

ANSELM. Nor do I, if rightly understood. But even if one of the whole number be confirmed by impregnable truth, that should be sufficient. For truth is equally secured against all doubt, if it be demonstrably proved by one argument as by many.

BOSO. Surely this is so. But how, then, shall man be saved, if he neither pays what he owes, and ought not to be saved without paying? Or, with what face shall we declare that God, who is rich in mercy above human conception, cannot exercise this compassion?

ANSELM. This is the question which you ought to ask of those in whose behalf you are speaking, who have no faith in the need of Christ for man's salvation, and you should also request them to tell how man can be saved without Christ. But, if they are utterly unable to do it, let them cease from mocking us, and let them hasten to unite themselves with us, who do not doubt that man can be saved through Christ; else let them despair of being saved at all. And if this terrifies them, let them believe in Christ as we do, that they may be saved.

BOSO. Let me ask you, as I have begun, to show me how a man is saved by Christ.

25

How man's salvation by Christ is necessarily possible.

ANSELM. Is it not sufficiently proved that man can be saved by Christ, when even infidels do not deny that man can be happy somehow, and it has been sufficiently shown that, leaving Christ out of view, no salvation can be found for man? For, either by Christ or by some one else can man be saved, or else not at all. If, then, it is false that man cannot be saved all, or that he can be saved in any other way, his salvation must necessarily be by Christ.

BOSO. But what reply will you make to a person who perceives that man cannot be saved in any other way, and yet, not understanding how he can be saved by Christ, sees fit to declare that there cannot be any salvation either by Christ or in any other way?

ANSELM. What reply ought to be made to one who ascribes impossibility to a necessary truth, because he does not understand how it can be?

BOSO. That he is a fool.

ANSELM. Then what he says must be despised.

BOSO. Very true; but we ought to show him in what way the thing is true which he holds to be impossible.

ANSELM. Do you not perceive, from what we have said above, that it is necessary for some men to attain to felicity? For, if it is unfitting for God to elevate man with any stain upon him, to that for which he made him free from all stain, lest it should seem that God had repented of his good intent, or was unable to accomplish his designs; far more is it impossible, on account of the same unfitness, that no man should be exalted to that state for which he was made. Therefore, a satisfaction such as we have above proved necessary for sin, must be found apart from the Christian faith, which no reason can show; or else we must accept the Christian doctrine. For what is clearly made out by absolute reasoning ought by no means to be questioned, even though the method of it be not understood.

BOSO. What you say is true.

ANSELM. Why, then, do you question further?

BOSO. I come not for this purpose, to have you remove doubts from my faith, but to have you show me the reason for my confidence. Therefore, as you have brought me thus far by your reasoning, so that I perceive that man as a sinner owes God for his sin what he is unable to pay, and cannot be saved without paying; I wish you would go further with me, and enable me to understand, by force of reasoning, the fitness of all those things which the Catholic faith enjoins upon us with regard to Christ, if we hope to be saved; and how they avail for the salvation of man, and how God saves man by compassion; when he never remits his sin, unless man shall have rendered what was due on account of his sin. And, to make your reasoning the clearer, begin at the beginning, so as to rest it upon a strong foundation.

ANSELM. Now God help me, for you do not spare me in the least, nor consider the weakness of my skill, when you enjoin so great a work upon me. Yet I will attempt it, as I have begun, not trusting in myself but in God, and will do what I can with his help. But let us separate the things which remain to be said from those which have been said, by a new introduction, lest by their unbroken length, these things become tedious to one who wishes to read them.

BOOK TWO

1

How man was made holy by God, so as to be happy in the enjoyment of God.

ANSELM. It ought not to be disputed that rational nature was made holy by God, in order to be happy in enjoying Him. For to this end is it rational, in order to discern justice and injustice, good and evil, and between the greater and the lesser good. Otherwise it was made rational in vain. But God made it not rational in vain. Wherefore, doubtless, it was made rational for this end. In like manner is it proved that the intelligent creature received the power of discernment for this purpose, that he might hate and shun evil, and love and choose good, and especially the greater good. For else in vain would God have given him that power of discernment, since man's discretion would be useless unless he loved and avoided according to it. But it does not befit God to give such power in vain. It is, therefore, established that rational nature was created for this end, viz. to love and choose the highest good supremely, for its own sake and nothing else; for if the highest good were chosen for any other reason, then something else and not itself would be the thing loved. But intelligent nature cannot fulfill this purpose without being holy. Therefore that it might not in vain be made rational, it was made, in order to fulfill this purpose, both rational and holy. Now, if it was made holy in order to choose and love the highest good, then it was made such in order to follow sometimes what it loved and chose, or else it was not. But if it were not made holy for this end, that it might follow what it loves and chooses, then in vain was it made to love and choose holiness; and there can be no reason why it should be ever bound to follow holiness. Therefore, as long as it will be holy in loving and choosing the supreme good, for which it was made, it will be miserable; because it will be impotent despite of its will, inasmuch as it does not have what it desires. But this is utterly absurd. Wherefore rational nature was made holy, in order to be happy in enjoying the supreme good, which is God. Therefore man, whose nature is rational, was made holy for this end, that he might be happy in enjoying God.

2

How man would never have died, unless he had sinned.

ANSELM. Moreover, it is easily proved that man was so made as not to be necessarily subject to death; for, as we have already said, it is inconsistent with God's wisdom and justice to compel man to suffer death without fault, when he made him holy to enjoy eternal blessedness. It therefore follows that had man never sinned he never would have died.

3

How man will rise with the same body which he has in this world.

ANSELM. From this the future resurrection of the dead is clearly proved. For if man is to be perfectly restored, the restoration should make him such as he would have been had he never sinned.

BOSO. It must be so.

ANSELM. Therefore, as man, had he not sinned, was to have been transferred with the same body to an immortal state, so when he shall be restored, it must properly be with his own body as he lived in this world.

BOSO. But what shall we say to one who tells us that this is right enough with regard to those in whom humanity shall be perfectly restored, but is not necessary as respects the reprobate?

ANSELM. We know of nothing more just or proper than this, that as man, had he continued in holiness, would have been perfectly happy for eternity, both in body and in soul; so, if he persevere in wickedness, he shall be likewise completely miserable forever.

BOSO. You have promptly satisfied me in these matters.

4

How God will complete, in respect to human nature, what he has begun.

ANSELM. From these things, we can easily see that God will either complete what he has begun with regard to human nature, or else he has made to no end so lofty a nature, capable of so great good. Now if it be understood that God has made nothing more valuable than rational existence capable of enjoying him; it is altogether foreign from his character to suppose that he will suffer that rational existence utterly to perish.

BOSO. No reasonable being can think otherwise.

ANSELM. Therefore is it necessary for him to perfect in human nature what he has begun. But this, as we have already said, cannot be accomplished save by a complete expiation of sin, which no sinner can effect for himself.

BOSO. I now understand it to be necessary for God to complete what he has begun, lest there be an unseemly falling off from his design.

5

How, although the thing may be necessary, God may not do it by a compulsory necessity; and what is the nature of that necessity which removes or lessens gratitude, and what necessity increases it.

BOSO. But if it be so, then God seems as it were compelled, for the sake of avoiding what is unbecoming, to secure the salvation of man. How, then, can it be denied that he does it more on his own account than on ours? But if it be so, what thanks do we owe him for what he does for himself? How shall we attribute our salvation to his grace, if he saves us from necessity?

ANSELM. There is a necessity which takes away or lessens our gratitude to a benefactor, and there is also a necessity by which the favor deserves still greater thanks. For when one does a benefit from a necessity to which he is unwillingly subjected, less thanks are due him, or none at all. But when he freely places himself under the necessity of benefiting another, and sustains that necessity without reluctance, then he certainly deserves greater thanks for the favor. For this should not be called necessity but grace, inasmuch as he undertook or maintains it, not with any constraint, but freely. For if that which to-day you promise of your own accord you will give to-morrow, you do give to-morrow with the same willingness; though it be necessary for you, if possible, to redeem your promise, or make yourself a liar; notwithstanding, the recipient of your favor is as much indebted for your precious gift as if you had not promised it, for you were not obliged to make yourself his debtor before the time of giving it: just so is it when one undertakes, by a vow, a design of holy living. For though after his vow he ought necessarily to perform, lest he suffer the judgment of an apostate, and, although he may be compelled to keep it even unwillingly, yet, if he keep his vow cheerfully, he is not less but more pleasing to God than if he had not vowed. For he has not only given up the life of the world, but also his personal liberty, for the sake of God; and he cannot be said to live a holy life of necessity, but with the same freedom with which he took the vow. Much more, therefore, do we owe all thanks to God for completing his intended favor to man; though, indeed, it would not be proper for him to fail in his good design, because wanting nothing in himself he begun it for our sake and not his own. For what man was about to do was not hidden from God at his creation; and yet by freely creating man, God as it were bound himself to complete the good which he had begun. In fine, God does nothing by necessity, since he is not compelled or restrained in anything. And when we say that God does anything to avoid dishonor, which he certainly does not fear, we must mean that God does this from the necessity of maintaining his honor; which necessity is after all no more than this, viz. the immutability of his honor, which belongs to him in himself, and is not derived from another; and therefore it is not properly called necessity. Yet we may say, although the whole work which God does for man is of grace, that it is necessary for God, on account of his unchangeable goodness, to complete the work which he has begun.

BOSO. I grant it.

6

How no being, except the God-man, can make the atonement by which man is saved.

ANSELM. But this cannot be effected, except the price paid to God for the sin of man be something greater than all the universe besides God.

BOSO. So it appears.

ANSELM. Moreover, it is necessary that he who can give God anything of his own which is more valuable than all things in the possession of God, must be greater than all else but God himself.

BOSO. I cannot deny it.

ANSELM. Therefore none but God can make this satisfaction.

BOSO. So it appears.

ANSELM. But none but a man ought to do this, otherwise man does not make the satisfaction.

BOSO. Nothing seems more just.

ANSELM. If it be necessary, therefore, as it appears, that the heavenly kingdom be made up of men, and this cannot be effected unless the aforesaid satisfaction be made, which none but God can make and none but man ought to make, it is necessary for the God-man to make it.

BOSO. Now blessed be God! We have made a great discovery with regard to our question. Go on, therefore, as you have begun. For I hope that God will assist you.

ANSELM. Now must we inquire how God can become man.

7

How necessary it is for the same being to be perfect God and perfect man.

ANSELM. The Divine and human natures cannot alternate, so that the Divine should become human or the human Divine; nor can they be so commingled as that a third should be produced from the two which is neither wholly Divine nor wholly human. For, granting that it were possible for either to be changed into the other, it would in that case be only God and not man, or man only and not God. Or, if they were so commingled that a third nature sprung from the combination of the two (as from two animals, a male and a female of different species, a third is produced, which does not preserve entire the species of either parent, but has a mixed nature derived from both), it would neither be God nor man. Therefore the God-man, whom we require to be of a nature both human and Divine, cannot be produced by a change from one into the other, nor by an imperfect commingling of both in a third; since these things cannot be, or, if they could be, would avail nothing to our purpose. Moreover, if these two complete natures are said to be joined somehow, in such a way that one may be Divine while the other is human, and yet that which is God not be the same with that which is man, it is impossible for both to do the work necessary to be accomplished. For God will not do it, because he has no debt to pay; and man will not do it, because he cannot. Therefore, in order that the God-man may perform this, it is necessary that the same being should be perfect God and perfect man, in order to make this atonement. For he cannot and ought not to do it, unless he be very God and very man. Since, then, it is necessary that the God-man preserve the completeness of each nature, it is no less necessary that these two natures be united entire in one person, just as a body and a reasonable soul exist together in every human being; for otherwise it is impossible that the same being should be very God and very man.

BOSO. All that you say is satisfactory to me.

8

How it behooved God to take a man of the race of Adam, and born of a woman.

ANSELM. It now remains to inquire whence and how God shall assume human nature. For he will either take it from Adam, or else he will make a new man, as he made Adam originally. But, if he makes a new man, not of Adam's race, then this man will not belong to the human family, which descended from Adam, and therefore ought not to make atonement for it, because he never belonged to it. For, as it is right for man to make atonement for the sin of man, it is also necessary that he who makes the atonement should be the very being who has sinned, or else one of the same race. Otherwise, neither Adam nor his race would make satisfaction for themselves. Therefore, as through Adam and Eve sin was propagated among all men, so none but themselves, or one born of them, ought to make atonement for the sin of men. And, since they cannot, one born of them must fulfil this work. Moreover, as Adam and his whole race, had he not sinned, would have stood firm without the support of any other being, so, after the fall, the same race must rise and be exalted by means of itself. For, whoever restores the race to its place, it will certainly stand by that being who has made this restoration. Also, when God created human nature in Adam alone, and would only make woman out of man, that by the union of both sexes there might be increase, in this he showed plainly that he wished to produce all that he intended with regard to human nature from man alone. Wherefore, if the race of Adam be reinstated by any being not of the same race, it will not be restored to that dignity which it would have had, had not Adam sinned, and so will not be completely restored; and, besides, God will seem to have failed of his purpose, both which suppositions are incongruous: It is, therefore, necessary that the man by whom Adam's race shall be restored be taken from Adam.

BOSO. If we follow reason, as we proposed to do, this is the necessary result.

ANSELM. Let us now examine the question, whether the human nature taken by God must be produced from a father and mother, as other men are, or from man alone, or from woman alone. For, in whichever of these three modes it be, it will be produced from Adam and Eve, for from these two is every person of either sex descended. And of these three modes, no one is easier for God than another, that it should be selected on this account.

BOSO. So far, it is well.

ANSELM. It is no great toil to show that that man will be brought into existence in a nobler and purer manner, if produced from man alone, or woman alone, than if springing from the union of both, as do all other men.

BOSO. I agree with you.

ANSELM. Therefore must he be taken either from man alone, or woman alone.

BOSO. There is no other source.

ANSELM. In four ways can God create man, viz. either of man and woman, in the common way; or neither of man nor woman, as he created Adam; or of man without woman, as he made Eve; or of woman without man, which thus far he has never done. Wherefore, in order to show that this last mode is also under his power, and was reserved for this very purpose, what is more fitting than that he should take that man whose origin we are seeking from a woman without a man? Now whether it be more worthy that he be born of a virgin, or one not a virgin, we need not discuss, but must affirm, beyond all doubt, that the God-man should be born of a virgin.

BOSO. Your speech gratifies my heart.

ANSELM. Does what we have said appear sound, or is it unsubstantial as a cloud, as you have said infidels declare?

BOSO. Nothing can be more sound.

ANSELM. Paint not, therefore, upon baseless emptiness, but upon solid truth, and tell how clearly fitting it is that, as man's sin and the cause of our condemnation sprung from a woman, so the cure of sin and the source of our salvation should also be found in a woman. And that women may not despair of attaining the inheritance of the blessed, because that so dire an evil arose from woman, it is proper that from woman also so great a blessing should arise, that their hopes may be revived. Take also this view. If it was a virgin which brought all evil upon the race, it is much more appropriate that a virgin should be the occasion of all good. And this also. If woman, whom God made from man alone, was made of a virgin (*de virgine*), it is peculiarly fitting for that man also, who shall spring from a woman, to be born of a woman without man. Of the pictures which can be superadded to this, showing that the God-man ought to be born of a virgin, we will say nothing. These are sufficient.

BOSO. They are certainly very beautiful and reasonable.

9

How of necessity the Word only can unite in one person with man.

ANSELM. Now must we inquire further, in what person God, who exists in three persons, shall take upon himself the nature of man. For a plurality of persons cannot take one and the same man into a unity of person. Wherefore in one person only can this be done. But, as respects this personal unity of God and man, and in which of the Divine persons this ought to be effected, I have expressed myself, as far as I think needful for the present inquiry, in a letter on the Incarnation of the Word, addressed to my lord, the Pope Urban.

BOSO. Yet briefly glance at this matter, why the person of the Son should be incarnated rather than that of the Father or the Holy Spirit.

ANSELM. If one of the other persons be incarnated, there will be two sons in the Trinity, viz. the Son of God, who is the Son before the incarnation, and he also who, by the incarnation, will be the son of the virgin; and among the persons which ought always to be equal there will be an inequality as respects the dignity of birth. For the one born of God will have a nobler birth than he who is born of the virgin. Likewise, if the Father become incarnate, there will be two grandsons in the Trinity; for the Father, by assuming humanity, will be the grandson of the parents of the virgin, and the Word, though having nothing to do with man, will yet be the grandson of the virgin, since he will be the son of her son. But all these things are incongruous and do not pertain to the incarnation of the Word. And there is yet another reason which renders it more fitting for the Son to become incarnate than the other persons. It is, that for the Son to pray to the Father is more proper than for any other person of the Trinity to supplicate his fellow. Moreover, man, for whom he was to pray, and the devil, whom he was to vanquish, have both put on a false likeness to God by their own will. Wherefore they have sinned, as it were, especially against the person of the Son, who is believed to be the very image of God. Wherefore the punishment or pardon of guilt is with peculiar propriety ascribed to him upon whom chiefly the injury was inflicted. Since, therefore, infallible reason has brought us to this necessary conclusion, that the Divine and human natures must unite in one person, and that this is evidently more fitting in respect to the person of the Word than the other persons, we determine that God the Word must unite with man in one person.

BOSO. The way by which you lead me is so guarded by reason that I cannot deviate from it to the right or left.

ANSELM. It is not I who lead you, but he of whom we are speaking, without whose guidance we have no power to keep the way of truth.

10

How this man dies not of debt; and in what sense he can or cannot sin; and how neither he nor an angel deserves praise for their holiness, if it is impossible for them to sin.

ANSELM. We ought not to question whether this man was about to die as a debt, as all other men do. For, if Adam would not have died had he not committed sin, much less should this man suffer death, in whom there can be no sin, for he is God.

BOSO. Let me delay you a little on this point. For in either case it is no slight question with me whether it be said that he can sin or that he cannot. For if it be said that he cannot sin, it should seem hard to be believed. For to say a word concerning him, not as of one who never existed in the manner we have spoken hitherto, but as of one whom we know and whose deeds we know; who, I say, will deny that he could have done many things which we call sinful? For, to say nothing of other things, how shall we say that it was not possible for him to commit the sin of lying? For, when he says to the Jews, of his Father: "If I say that I know him not, I shall be a liar, like unto you," and, in this sentence, makes use of the words: "I know him not," who says that he could not have uttered these same four words, or expressing the same thing differently, have declared, "I know him not?" Now had he done so, he would have been a liar, as he himself says, and therefore a sinner. Therefore, since he could do this, he could sin.

ANSELM. It is true that he could say this, and also that he could not sin.

BOSO. How is that?

ANSELM. All power follows the will. For, when I say that I can speak or walk, it is understood, if I choose. For, if the will be not implied as acting, there is no power, but only necessity. For, when I say that I can be dragged or bound unwillingly, this is not my power, but necessity and the power of another; since I am able to be dragged or bound in no other sense than this, that another can drag or bind me. So we can say of Christ, that he could lie, so long as we understand, if he chose to do so. And, since he could not lie unwillingly and could not wish to lie, none the less can it be said that he could not lie. So in this way it is both true that he could and could not lie.

BOSO. Now let us return to our original inquiry with regard to that man, as if nothing were known of him. I say, then, if he were unable to sin, because, according to you, he could not wish to sin, he maintains holiness of necessity, and therefore he will not be holy from free will. What thanks, then, will he deserve for his holiness? For we are accustomed to say that God made man and angel capable of sinning on this account, that, when of their own free will they maintained holiness, though they might have abandoned it, they might deserve commendation and reward, which they would not have done had they been necessarily holy.

ANSELM. Are not the angels worthy of praise, though unable to commit sin?

BOSO. Doubtless they are, because they deserved this present inability to sin from the fact that when they could sin they refused to do so.

ANSELM. What say you with respect to God, who cannot sin, and yet has not deserved this, by refusing to sin when he had the power? Must not he be praised for his holiness?

BOSO. I should like to have you answer that question for me; for if I say that he deserves no praise, I know that I speak falsely. If, on the other hand, I say that he does deserve praise, I am afraid of invalidating my reasoning with respect to the angels.

ANSELM. The angels are not to be praised for their holiness because they could sin, but because it is owing to themselves, in a certain sense, that now they cannot sin. And in this respect are they in a measure like God, who has, from himself, whatever he possesses. For a person is said to give a thing, who does not take it away when he can; and to do a thing is but the same as not to prevent it, when that is in one's power. When, therefore, the angel could depart from holiness and yet did not, and could make himself unholy yet did not, we say with propriety that he conferred virtue upon himself and made himself holy. In this sense, therefore, has he holiness of himself (for the creature cannot have it of himself in any other way), and, therefore, should be praised for his holiness, because he is not holy of necessity but freely; for that is improperly called necessity which involves neither compulsion nor restraint. Wherefore, since whatever God has he has perfectly of himself, he is most of all to be praised for the good things which he possesses and maintains not by any necessity, but, as before said, by his own infinite unchangeableness. Therefore, likewise, that man who will be also God since every good thing which he possesses comes from himself, will be holy not of necessity but voluntarily, and, therefore, will deserve praise. For, though human nature will have what it has from the Divine nature, yet it will likewise have it from itself, since the two natures will be united in one person.

BOSO. You have satisfied me on this point; and I see clearly that it is both true that he could not sin, and yet that he deserves praise for his holiness. But now I think the question arises, since God could make such a man, why he did not create angels and our first parents so as to be incapable of sin, and yet praiseworthy for their holiness?

ANSELM. Do you know what you are saying?

BOSO. I think I understand, and it is therefore I ask why he did not make them so.

ANSELM. Because it was neither possible nor right for any one of them to be the same with God, as we say that man was. And if you ask why he did not bring the three persons, or at least the Word, into unity with men at that time, I answer: Because reason did not at all demand any such thing then, but wholly forbade it, for God does nothing without reason.

BOSO. I blush to have asked the question. Go on with what you have to say.

ANSELM. We must conclude, then, that he should not be subject to death, inasmuch as he will not be a sinner.

BOSO. I must agree with you.

11

How Christ dies of his own power, and how mortality does not inhere in the essential nature of man.

ANSELM. Now, also, it remains to inquire whether, as man's nature is, it is possible for that man to die?

BOSO. We need hardly dispute with regard to this, since he will be really man, and every man is by nature mortal.

ANSELM. I do not think mortality inheres in the essential nature of man, but only as corrupted. Since, had man never sinned, and had his immortality been unchangeably confirmed, he would have been as really man; and, when the dying rise again, incorruptible, they will no less be really men. For, if mortality was an essential attribute of human nature, then he who was immortal could not be man. Wherefore, neither corruption nor incorruption belong essentially to human nature, for neither makes nor destroys a man; but happiness accrues to him from the one, and misery from the other. But since all men die, mortality is included in the definition of man, as given by philosophers, for they have never even believed in the possibility of man's being immortal in all respects. And so it is not enough to prove that that man ought to be subject to death, for us to say that he will be in all respects a man.

BOSO. Seek then for some other reason, since I know of none, if you do not, by which we may prove that he can die.

ANSELM. We may not doubt that, as he will be God, he will possess omnipotence.

BOSO. Certainly.

ANSELM. He can, then, if he chooses, lay down his life and take it again.

BOSO. If not, he would scarcely seem to be omnipotent.

ANSELM. Therefore is he able to avoid death if he chooses, and also to die and rise again. Moreover, whether he lays down his life by the intervention of no other person, or another causes this, so that he lays it down by permitting it to be taken, it makes no difference as far as regards his power.

BOSO. There is no doubt about it.

ANSELM. If, then, he chooses to allow it, he could be slain; and if he were unwilling to allow it, he could not be slain.

BOSO. To this we are unavoidably brought by reason.

ANSELM. Reason has also taught us that the gift which he presents to God, not of debt but freely, ought to be something greater than anything in the possession of God.

BOSO. Yes.

ANSELM. Now this can neither be found beneath him nor above him.

BOSO. Very true.

ANSELM. In himself, therefore, must it be found.

BOSO. So it appears.

ANSELM. Therefore will he give himself, or something pertaining to himself.

BOSO. I cannot see how it should be otherwise.

ANSELM. Now must we inquire what sort of a gift this should be? For he may not give himself to God, or anything of his, as if God did not have what was his own. For every creature belongs to God.

BOSO. This is so.

ANSELM. Therefore must this gift be understood in this way, that he somehow gives up himself, or something of his, to the honor of God, which he did not owe as a debtor.

BOSO. So it seems from what has been already said.

ANSELM. If we say that he will give himself to God by obedience, so as, by steadily maintaining holiness, to render himself subject to his will, this will not be giving a thing not demanded of him by God as his due. For every reasonable being owes his obedience to God.

BOSO. This cannot be denied.

ANSELM. Therefore must it be in some other way that he gives himself, or something belonging to him, to God.

BOSO. Reason urges us to this conclusion.

ANSELM. Let us see whether, perchance, this may be to give up his life or to lay down his life, or to deliver himself up to death for God's honor. For God will not demand this of him as a debt; for, as no sin will be found, he ought not to die, as we have already said.

BOSO. Else I cannot understand it.

ANSELM. But let us further observe whether this is according to reason.

BOSO. Speak you, and I will listen with pleasure.

ANSELM. If man sinned with ease, is it not fitting for him to atone with difficulty? And if he was overcome by the devil in the easiest manner possible, so as to dishonor God by sinning against him, is it not right that man, in making satisfaction for his sin, should honor God by conquering the devil with the greatest possible difficulty? Is it not proper that, since man has departed from God as far as possible in his sin, he should make to God the greatest possible satisfaction?

BOSO. Surely, there is nothing more reasonable.

ANSELM. Now, nothing can be more severe or difficult for man to do for God's honor, than to suffer death voluntarily when not bound by obligation; and man cannot give himself to God in any way more truly than by surrendering himself to death for God's honor.

BOSO. All these things are true.

ANSELM. Therefore, he who wishes to make atonement for

man's sin should be one who can die if he chooses.

BOSO. I think it is plain that the man whom we seek for should not only be one who is not necessarily subject to death on account of his omnipotence, and one who does not deserve death on account of his sin, but also one who can die of his own free will, for this will be necessary.

ANSELM. There are also many other reasons why it is peculiarly fitting for that man to enter into the common intercourse of men, and maintain a likeness to them, only without sin. And these things are more easily and clearly manifest in his life and actions than they can possibly be shown to be by mere reason without experience. For who can say how necessary and wise a thing it was for him who was to redeem mankind, and lead them back by his teaching from the way of death and destruction into the path of life and eternal happiness, when he conversed with men, and when he taught them by personal intercourse, to set them an example himself of the way in which they ought to live? But how could he have given this example to weak and dying men, that they should not deviate from holiness because of injuries, or scorn, or tortures, or even death, had they not been able to recognise all these virtues in himself?

12

How, though he share in our weakness, he is not therefore miserable.

BOSO. All these things plainly show that he ought to be mortal and to partake of our weaknesses. But all these things are our miseries. Will he then be miserable?

ANSELM. No, indeed! For as no advantage which one has apart from his choice constitutes happiness, so there is no misery in choosing to bear a loss, when the choice is a wise one and made without compulsion.

BOSO. Certainly, this must be allowed.

13

How, along with our other weaknesses, he does not partake of our ignorance.

BOSO. But tell me whether, in this likeness to men which he ought to have, he will inherit also our ignorance, as he does our other infirmities?

ANSELM. Do you doubt the omnipotence of God?

BOSO. No! But, although this man be immortal in respect to his Divine nature, yet will he be mortal in his human nature. For why will he not be like them in their ignorance, as he is in their mortality?

ANSELM. That union of humanity with the Divine person will not be effected except in accordance with the highest wisdom; and, therefore, God will not take anything belonging to man which is only useless, but even a hindrance to the work which that man must accomplish. For ignorance is in no respect useful, but very prejudicial. How can he perform works, so many and so great, without the highest wisdom? Or, how will men believe him if they find him ignorant? And if he be ignorant, what will it avail him? If nothing is loved except as it is known, and there be no good thing which he does not love, then there can be no good thing of which be is ignorant. But no one perfectly understands good, save he who can distinguish it from evil; and no one can make this distinction who does not know what evil is. Therefore, as he of whom we are speaking perfectly comprehends what is good, so there can be no evil with which he is unacquainted. Therefore must he have all knowledge, though he do not openly show it in his intercourse with men.

BOSO. In his more mature years, this should seem to be as you say; but, in infancy, as it will not be a fit time to discover wisdom, so there will be no need, and therefore no propriety, in his having it.

ANSELM. Did not I say that the incarnation will be made in wisdom? But God will in wisdom assume that mortality, which he makes use of so widely, because for so great an object. But he could not wisely assume ignorance, for this is never useful, but always injurious, except when an evil will is deterred from acting, on account of it. But, in him an evil desire never existed. For if ignorance did no harm in any other respect, yet does it in this, that it takes away the good of knowing. And to answer your question in a word: that man, from the essential nature of his being, will be always full of God; and, therefore, will never want the power, the firmness or the wisdom of God.

BOSO. Though wholly unable to doubt the truth of this with respect to Christ, yet, on this very account, have I asked for the reason of it. For we are often certain about a thing, and yet cannot prove it by reason.

14

How his death outweighs the number and greatness of our sins.

BOSO. Now I ask you to tell me how his death can outweigh the number and magnitude of our sins, when the least sin we can think of you have shown to be so monstrous that, were there an infinite number of worlds as full of created existence as this, they could not stand, but would fall back into nothing, sooner than one look should be made contrary to the just will of God.

ANSELM. Were that man here before you, and you knew who he was, and it were told you that, if you did not kill him, the whole universe, except God, would perish, would you do it to preserve the rest of creation?

BOSO. No! Not even were an infinite number of worlds displayed before me.

ANSELM. But suppose you were told: "If you do not kill him, all the sins of the world will be heaped upon you."

BOSO. I should answer, that I would far rather bear all other sins, not only those of this world, past and future, but also all others that can be conceived of, than this alone. And I think I ought to say this, not only with regard to killing him, but even as to the slightest injury which could be inflicted on him.

ANSELM. You judge correctly; but tell me why it is that your heart recoils from one injury inflicted upon him as more heinous than all other sins that can be thought of, inasmuch as all sins whatsoever are committed against him?

BOSO. A sin committed upon his person exceeds beyond comparison all the sins which can be thought of, that do not affect his person.

ANSELM. What say you to this, that one often suffers freely certain evils in his person, in order not to suffer greater ones in his property?

BOSO. God has no need of such patience, for all things lie in subjection to his power, as you answered a certain question of mine above.

ANSELM. You say well; and hence we see that no enormity or multitude of sins, apart from the Divine person, can for a moment be compared with a bodily injury inflicted upon that man.

BOSO. This is most plain.

ANSELM. How great does this good seem to you, if the destruction of it is such an evil?

BOSO. If its existence is as great a good as its destruction is an evil, then is it far more a good than those sins are evils which its destruction so far surpasses.

ANSELM. Very true. Consider, also, that sins are as hateful as they are evil, and that life is only amiable in proportion as it is good. And, therefore, it follows that that life is more lovely than sins are odious.

BOSO. I cannot help seeing this.

ANSELM. And do you not think that so great a good in itself so lovely, can avail to pay what is due for the sins of the whole world?

BOSO. Yes! It has even infinite value.

ANSELM. Do you see, then, how this life conquers all sins, if it be given for them?

BOSO. Plainly.

ANSELM. If, then, to lay down life is the same as to suffer death, as the gift of his life surpasses all the sins of men, so will also the suffering of death.

15

How this death removes even the sins of his murderers.

BOSO. This is properly so with regard to all sins not affecting the person of the Deity. But let me ask you one thing more. If it be as great an evil to slay him as his life is a good, how can his death overcome and destroy the sins of those who slew him? Or, if it destroys the sin of any one of them, how can it not also destroy any sin committed by other men? For we believe that many men will be saved, and a vast many will not be saved.

ANSELM. The Apostle answers the question when he says: "Had they known it, they would never have crucified the Lord of glory." For a sin knowingly committed and a sin done ignorantly are so different that an evil which they could never do, were its full extent known, may be pardonable when done in ignorance. For no man could ever, knowingly at least, slay the Lord; and, therefore, those who did it in ignorance did not rush into that transcendental crime with which none others can be compared. For this crime, the magnitude of which we have been considering as equal to the worth of his life, we have not looked at as having been ignorantly done, but knowingly; a thing which no man ever did or could do.

BOSO. You have reasonably shown that the murderers of Christ can obtain pardon for their sin.

ANSELM. What more do you ask? For now you see how reason of necessity shows that the celestial state must be made up from men, and that this can only be by the forgiveness of sins, which man can never have but by man, who must be at the same time Divine, and reconcile sinners to God by his own death. Therefore have we clearly found that Christ, whom we confess to be both God and man, died for us; and, when this is known beyond all doubt, all things which he says of himself must be acknowledged as true, for God cannot lie, and all he does must be received as wisely done, though we do not understand the reason of it.

BOSO. What you say is true; and I do not for a moment doubt that his words are true, and all that he does reasonable. But I ask this in order that you may disclose to me, in their true rationality, those things in Christian faith which seem to infidels improper or impossible; and this, not to strengthen me in the faith, but to gratify one already confirmed by the knowledge of the truth itself.

16

How God took that man from a sinful substance, and yet without sin; and of the salvation of Adam and Eve.

BOSO. As, therefore, you have disclosed the reason of those things mentioned above, I beg you will also explain what I am now about to ask. First, then, how does God, from a sinful substance, that is, of human species, which was wholly tainted by sin, take a man without sin, as an unleavened lump from that which is leavened? For, though the conception of this man be pure, and free from the sin of fleshly gratification, yet the virgin herself, from whom he sprang, was conceived in iniquity, and in sin did her mother bear her, since she herself sinned in Adam, in whom all men sinned.

ANSELM. Since it is fitting for that man to be God, and also the restorer of sinners, we doubt not that he is wholly without sin; yet will this avail nothing, unless he be taken without sin and yet of a sinful substance. But if we cannot comprehend in what manner the wisdom of God effects this, we should be surprised, but with reverence should allow of a thing of so great magnitude to remain hidden from us. For the restoring of human nature by God is more wonderful than its creation; for either was equally easy for God; but before man was made he had not sinned so that he ought not to be denied existence But after man was made he deserved, by his sin, to lose his existence together with its design; though he never has wholly lost this, viz. that he should be one capable of being punished, or of receiving God's compassion. For neither of these things could take effect if he were annihilated. Therefore God's restoring man is more wonderful than his creating man, inasmuch as it is done for the sinner contrary to his deserts; while the act of creation was not for the sinner, and was not in opposition to man's deserts. How great a thing it is, also, for God and man to unite in one person, that, while the perfection of each nature is preserved, the same being may be both God and man! Who, then, will dare to think that the human mind can discover how wisely, how wonderfully, so incomprehensible a work has been accomplished?

BOSO. I allow that no man can wholly discover so great a mystery in this life, and I do not desire you to do what no man can do, but only to explain it according to your ability. For you will sooner convince me that deeper reasons lie concealed in this matter, by showing some one that you know of, than if, by saying nothing, you make it appear that you do not understand any reason.

ANSELM. I see that I cannot escape your importunity; but if I have any power to explain what you wish, let us thank God for it. But if not, let the things above said suffice. For, since it is agreed that God ought to become man, no doubt He will not lack the wisdom or the power to effect this without sin.

BOSO. This I readily allow.

ANSELM. It was certainly proper that that atonement which Christ made should benefit not only those who lived at that time but also others. For, suppose there were a king against whom all the people of his provinces had rebelled, with but a single exception of those belonging to their race, and that all the rest were irretrievably under condemnation. And suppose that he who alone is blameless had so great favor with the king, and so deep love for us, as to be both able and willing to save all those who trusted in his guidance; and this because of a certain very pleasing service which he was about to do for the king, according to his desire; and, inasmuch as those who are to be pardoned cannot all assemble upon that day, the king grants, on account of the greatness of the service performed, that whoever, either before or after the day appointed, acknowledged that he wished to obtain pardon by the work that day accomplished, and to subscribe to the condition there laid down, should be freed from all past guilt; and, if they sinned after this pardon, and yet wished to render atonement and to be set right again by the efficacy of this plan, they should again be pardoned, only provided that no one enter his mansion until this thing be accomplished by which his sins are removed. In like manner, since all who are to be saved cannot be present at the sacrifice of Christ, yet such virtue is there in his death that its power is extended even to those far remote in place or time. But that it ought to benefit not merely those present is plainly evident, because there could not be so many living at the time of his death as are necessary to complete the heavenly state, even if all who were upon the earth at that time were admitted to the benefits of redemption. For the number of evil angels which must be made up from men is greater than the number of men at that time living. Nor may we believe that, since man was created, there was ever a time when the world, with the creatures made for the use of man, was so unprofitable as to contain no human being who had gained the object for which he was made. For it seems unfitting that God should even for a moment allow the human race, made to complete the heavenly state, and those creatures which he made for their use, to exist in vain.

BOSO. You show by correct reasoning, such as nothing can oppose, that there never was a time since man was created when there has not been some one who was gaining that reconciliation without which every man was made in vain. So that we rest upon this as not only proper but also necessary. For if this is more fit and reasonable than that at any time there should be no one found fulfilling the design for which God made man, and there is no further objection that can be made to this view, then it is necessary that there always be some person partaking of this promised pardon. And, therefore, we must not doubt that Adam and Eve obtained part in that forgiveness, though Divine authority makes no mention of this.

ANSELM. It is also incredible that God created them, and unchangeably determined to make all men from them, as many as were needed for the celestial state, and yet should exclude these two from this design.

BOSO. Nay, undoubtedly we ought to believe that God made them for this purpose, viz. to belong to the number of those for whose sake they were created.

ANSELM. You understand it well. But no soul, before the death of Christ, could enter the heavenly kingdom, as I said above, with regard to the palace of the king.

BOSO. So we believe.

ANSELM. Moreover, the virgin, from whom that man was taken of whom we are speaking, was of the number of those who were cleansed from their sins before his birth, and he was born of her in her purity.

BOSO. What you say would satisfy me, were it not that he ought to be pure of himself, whereas he appears to have his purity from his mother and not from himself.

ANSELM. Not so. But as the mother's purity, which he partakes, was only derived from him, he also was pure by and of himself.

17

How he did not die of necessity, though he could not be born, except as destined to suffer death.

BOSO. Thus far it is well. But there is yet another matter that needs to be looked into. For we have said before that his death was not to be a matter of necessity; yet now we see that his mother was purified by the power of his death, when without this he could not have been born of her. How, then, was not his death necessary, when he could not have been, except in view of future death? For if he were not to die, the virgin of whom he was born could not be pure, since this could only be effected by true faith in his death, and, if she were not pure, he could not be born of her. If, therefore, his death be not a necessary consequence of his being born of the virgin, he never could have been born of her at all; but this is an absurdity.

ANSELM. If you had carefully noted the remarks made above, you would easily have discovered in them, I think, the answer to your question.

BOSO. I see not how.

ANSELM. Did we not find, when considering the question whether he would lie, that there were two senses of the word power in regard to it, the one referring to his disposition, the other to the act itself; and that, though having the power to lie, he was so constituted by nature as not to wish to lie, and, therefore, deserved praise for his holiness in maintaining the truth?

BOSO. It is so.

ANSELM. In like manner, with regard to the preservation of his life, there is the power of preserving and the power of wishing to preserve it. And when the question is asked whether the same God-man could preserve his life, so as never to die, we must not doubt that he always had the power to preserve his life, though he could not wish to do so for the purpose of escaping death. And since this disposition, which forever prevents him from wishing this, arises from himself, he lays down his life not of necessity, but of free authority.

BOSO. But those powers were not in all respects similar, the power to lie and the power to preserve his life. For, if he wished to lie, he would of course be able to; but, if he wished to avoid the other, he could no more do it than he could avoid being what he is. For he became man for this purpose, and it was on the faith of his coming death that he could receive birth from a virgin, as you said above.

ANSELM. As you think that he could not lie, or that his death was necessary, because he could not avoid being what he was, so you can assert that he could not wish to avoid death, or that he wished to die of necessity, because he could not change the constitution of his being; for he did not become man in order that he should die, any more than for this purpose, that he should wish to die. Wherefore, as you ought not to say that he could not help wishing to die, or that it was of necessity that he wished to die, it is equally improper to say that he could not avoid death, or that he died of necessity.

BOSO. Yes, since dying and wishing to die are included in the same mode of reasoning, both would seem to fall under a like necessity.

ANSELM. Who freely wished to become man, that by the same unchanging desire he should suffer death, and that the virgin from whom that man should be born might be pure, through confidence in the certainty of this?

BOSO. God, the Son of God.

ANSELM. Was it not above shown, that no desire of God is at all constrained; but that it freely maintains itself in his own unchangeableness, as often as it is said that he does anything necessarily?

BOSO. It has been clearly shown. But we see, on the other hand, that what God unchangeably wishes cannot avoid being so, but takes place of necessity. Wherefore, if God wished that man to die, he could but die.

ANSELM. Because the Son of God took the nature of man with this desire, viz. that he should suffer death, you prove it necessary that this man should not be able to avoid death.

BOSO. So I perceive.

ANSELM. Has it not in like manner appeared from the things which we have spoken that the Son of God and the man whose person he took were so united that the same being should be both God and man, the Son of God and the son of the virgin?

BOSO. It is so.

ANSELM. Therefore the same man could possibly both die and avoid death.

BOSO. I cannot deny it.

ANSELM. Since, then, the will of God does nothing by any necessity, but of his own power, and the will of that man was the same as the will of God, he died not necessarily, but only of his own power.

BOSO. To your arguments I cannot object; for neither your propositions nor your inferences can I invalidate in the least. But yet this thing which I have mentioned always recurs to my mind: that, if he wished to avoid death, he could no more do it than he could escape existence. For it must have been fixed that he was to die, for had it not been true that he was about to die, faith in his coming death would not have existed, by which the virgin who gave him birth and many others also were cleansed from their sin. Wherefore, if he could avoid death, he could make untrue what was true.

ANSELM. Why was it true, before he died, that he was certainly to die?

BOSO. Because this was his free and unchangeable desire.

ANSELM. If, then, as you say, he could not avoid death because he was certainly to die, and was on this account certainly to die because it was his free and unchangeable desire, it is clear that his inability to avoid death is nothing else but his fixed choice to die.

BOSO. This is so; but whatever be the reason, it still remains certain that he could not avoid death, but that it was a necessary thing for him to die.

ANSELM. You make a great ado about nothing, or, as the saying is, you stumble at a straw.

BOSO. Are you not forgetting my reply to the excuses you made at the beginning of our discussion, viz. that you should explain the subject, not as to learned men, but to me and my fellow inquirers? Suffer me, then, to question you as my slowness and dullness require, so that, as you have begun thus far, you may go on to settle all our childish doubts.

18 (a)

[This and the succeeding chapter are numbered differently in the different editions of Anselm's texts.]

How, with God there is neither necessity nor impossibility, and what is a coercive necessity, and what one that is not so.

ANSELM. We have already said that it is improper to affirm of God that he does anything, or that he cannot do it, of necessity. For all necessity and impossibility is under his control. But his choice is subject to no necessity nor impossibility. For nothing is necessary or impossible save as he wishes it. Nay, the very choosing or refusing anything as a necessity or an impossibility is contrary to truth. Since, then, he does what he chooses and nothing else, as no necessity or impossibility exists before his choice or refusal, so neither do they interfere with his acting or not acting, though it be true that his choice and action are immutable. And as, when God does a thing, since it has been done it cannot be undone, but must remain an actual fact; still, we are not correct in saying that it is impossible for God to prevent a past action from being what it is. For there is no necessity or impossibility in the case whatever but the simple will of God, which chooses that truth should be eternally the same, for he himself is truth. Also, if he has a fixed determination to do anything, though his design must be destined to an accomplishment before it comes to pass, yet there is no coercion as far as he is concerned, either to do it or not to do it, for his will is the sole agent in the case. For when we say that God cannot do a thing, we do not deny his power; on the contrary, we imply that he has invincible authority and strength. For we mean simply this, that nothing can compel God to do the thing which is said to be impossible for him. We often use an expression of this kind, that a thing can be when the power is not in itself, but in something else; and that it cannot be when the weakness does not pertain to the thing itself, but to something else. Thus we say "Such a man can be bound," instead of saying, "Somebody can bind him," and, "He cannot be bound," instead of, "Nobody can bind him." For to be able to be overcome is not power but weakness, and not to be able to be overcome is not weakness but power. Nor do we say that God does anything by necessity, because there is any such thing pertaining to him, but because it exists in something else, precisely as I said with regard to the affirmation that he cannot do anything. For necessity is always either compulsion or restraint; and these two kinds of necessity operate variously by turn, so that the same thing is both necessary and impossible. For whatever is obliged to exist is also prevented from non-existence; and that which is compelled not to exist is prevented from existence. So that whatever exists from necessity cannot avoid existence, and it is impossible for a thing to exist which is under a necessity of nonexistence, and vice versa. But when we say with regard to God, that anything is necessary or not necessary, we do not mean that, as far as he is concerned, there is any necessity either coercive or prohibitory, but we mean that there is a necessity in everything else, restraining or driving them in a particular way. Whereas we say the very opposite of God. For, when we affirm that it is necessary for God to utter truth, and never to lie, we only mean that such is his unwavering disposition to maintain the truth that of necessity nothing can avail to make him deviate from the truth, or utter a lie. When, then, we say that that man (who, by the union of persons, is also God, the Son of God) could not avoid death, or the choice of death, after he was born of the virgin, we do not imply that there was in him any weakness with regard to preserving or choosing to preserve his life, but we refer to the unchangeableness of his purpose, by which he freely became man for this design, viz. that by persevering in his wish he should suffer death. And this desire nothing could shake. For it would be rather weakness than power if he could wish to lie, or deceive, or change his disposition, when before he had chosen that it should remain unchanged. And, as I said before, when one has freely determined to do some good action, and afterwards goes on to complete it, though, if unwilling to pay his vow, he could be compelled to do so, yet we must not say that he does it of necessity, but with the same freedom with which he made the resolution. For we ought not to say that anything is done, or not done, by necessity or weakness, when free choice is the only agent in the case. And, if this is so with regard to man, much less can we speak of necessity or weakness in reference to God; for he does nothing except according to his choice, and his will no force can drive or restrain. For this end was accomplished by the united natures of Christ, viz. that the Divine nature should perform that part of the work needful for man's restoration which the human nature could not do; and that in the human should be manifested what was inappropriate to the Divine. Finally, the virgin herself, who was made pure by faith in him, so that he might be born of her, even she, I say, never believed that he was to die, save of his own choice. For she knew the words of the prophet, who said of him: "He was offered of his own will." Therefore, since her faith was well founded, it must necessarily turn out as she believed. And, if it perplexes you to have me say that it is necessary, remember that the reality of the virgin's faith was not the cause of his dying by his own free will; but, because this was destined to take place, therefore her faith was real. If, then, it be said that it was necessary for him to die of his single choice, because the antecedent faith and prophecy were true, this is no more than saying that it must be because it was to be. But such a necessity as this does not compel a thing to be, but only implies a necessity of its existence. There is an antecedent necessity which is the cause of a thing, and there is also a subsequent necessity arising from the thing itself. Thus, when the heavens are said to revolve, it is an antecedent and efficient necessity, for they must revolve. But when I say that you speak of necessity, because you are speaking, this is nothing but a subsequent and inoperative necessity. For I only mean that it is impossible for you to speak and not to speak at the same time, and not that some one compels you to speak. For the force of its own nature makes the heaven revolve; but no necessity obliges you to speak. But wherever there is an antecedent necessity, there is also a subsequent one; but not vice versa. For we can say that the heaven revolves of necessity, because it revolves; but it is not likewise true that, because you speak, you do it of necessity. This subsequent necessity pertains to everything, so that we say: Whatever has been, necessarily has been. Whatever is, must be. Whatever is to be, of necessity will be. This is that necessity which Aristotle treats of (*de propositionibus singularibus et futuris*), and which seems to destroy any alternative and to ascribe a necessity to all things. By this subsequent and imperative necessity, was it necessary (since the belief and prophecy concerning Christ were true, that he would die of his own free will), that it should be so. For this he became man; for this he did and suffered all things undertaken by him; for this he chose as he did. For therefore were they necessary, because they were to be, and they were to be because they were, and they were because they were; and, if you wish to know the real necessity of all things which he did and suffered, know that they were of necessity, because he wished them to be. But no necessity preceded his will. Wherefore if they were not save by his will, then, had he not willed they would not have existed. So then, no one took his life from him, but he laid it down of himself and took it again; for he had power to lay it down and to take it again, as he himself said.

BOSO. You have satisfied me that it cannot be proved that he was subjected to death by any necessity; and I cannot regret my importunity in urging you to make this explanation.

ANSELM. I think we have shown with sufficient clearness how it was that God took a man without sin from a sinful substance; but I would on no account deny that there is no other explanation than this which we have given, for God can certainly do what human reason cannot grasp. But since this appears adequate, and since in search of other arguments we should involve ourselves in such questions as that of original sin, and how it was transmitted by our first parents to all mankind, except this man of whom we are speaking; and since, also, we should be drawn into various other questions, each demanding its own separate consideration; let us be satisfied with this account of the matter, and go on to complete our intended work.

BOSO. As you choose; but with this condition that, by the help of God, you will sometime give this other explanation, which you owe me, as it were, but which now you avoid discussing.

ANSELM. Inasmuch as I entertain this desire myself, I will not refuse you; but because of the uncertainty of future events, I dare not promise you, but commend it to the will of God. But say now, what remains to be unraveled with regard to the question which you proposed in the first place, and which involves many others with it.

BOSO. The substance of the inquiry was this, why God became man, for the purpose of saving men by his death, when he could have done it in some other way. And you, by numerous and positive reasons, have shown that the restoring of mankind ought not to take place, and could not, without man paid the debt which he owed God for his sin. And this debt was so great that, while none but man must solve the debt, none but God was able to do it; so that he who does it must be both God and man. And hence arises a necessity that God should take man into unity with his own person; so that he who in his own nature was bound to pay the debt, but could not, might be able to do it in the person of God. In fine, you have shown that that man, who was also God, must be formed from the virgin, and from the person of the Son of God, and that he could be taken without sin, though from a sinful substance. Moreover, you have clearly shown the life of this man to have been so excellent and so glorious as to make ample satisfaction for the sins of the whole world, and even infinitely more. It now, therefore, remains to be shown how that payment is made to God for the sins of men.

18 (b)

How Christ's life is paid to God for the sins of men, and in what sense Christ ought, and in what sense he ought not, or was not bound, to suffer.

ANSELM. If he allowed himself to be slain for the sake of justice, did he not give his life for the honor of God?

BOSO. It should seem so, but I cannot understand, although I do not doubt it, how he could do this reasonably. If I saw how he could be perfectly holy, and yet forever preserve his life, I would acknowledge that he freely gave, for the honor of God, such a gift as surpasses all things else but God himself, and is able to atone for all the sins of men.

ANSELM. Do you not perceive that when he bore with gentle patience the insults put upon him, violence and even crucifixion among thieves that he might maintain strict holiness; by this he set men an example that they should never turn aside from the holiness due to God on account of personal sacrifice? But how could he have done this, had he, as he might have done, avoided the death brought upon him for such a reason?

BOSO. But surely there was no need of this, for many persons before his coming, and John the Baptist after his coming but before his death, had sufficiently enforced this example by nobly dying for the sake of the truth.

ANSELM. No man except this one ever gave to God what he was not obliged to lose, or paid a debt he did not owe. But he freely offered to the Father what there was no need of his ever losing, and paid for sinners what he owed not for himself. Therefore he set a much nobler example, that each one should not hesitate to give to God, for himself, what he must at any rate lose before long, since it was the voice of reason; for he, when not in want of anything for himself and not compelled by others, who deserved nothing of him but punishment, gave so precious a life, even the life of so illustrious a personage, with such willingness.

BOSO. You very nearly meet my wishes; but suffer me to make one inquiry, which you may think foolish, but which, nevertheless, I find no easy thing to answer. You say that when he died he gave what he did not owe. But no one will deny that it was better for him, or that so doing he pleased God more than if he had not done it. Nor will any one say that he was not bound to do what was best to be done, and what he knew would be more pleasing to God. How then can we affirm that he did not owe God the thing which he did, that is, the thing which he knew to be best and most pleasing to God, and especially since every creature owes God all that he is and all that he knows and all that he is capable of?

ANSELM. Though the creature has nothing of himself, yet when God grants him the liberty of doing or not doing a thing, he leaves the alternative with him, so that, though one is better than the other, yet neither is positively demanded. And, whichever he does, it may be said that he ought to do it; and if he takes the better choice, he deserves a reward; because he renders freely what is his own. For, though celibacy be better than marriage, yet neither is absolutely enjoined upon man; so that both he who chooses marriage and he who prefers celibacy, may be said to do as they ought. For no one says that either celibacy or marriage ought not to be chosen; but we say that what a man esteems best before taking action upon any of these things, this he ought to do. And if a man preserves his celibacy as a free gift offered to God, he looks for a reward. When you say that the creature owes God what he knows to be the better choice, and what he is able to do, if you mean that he owes it as a debt, without implying any command on the part of God, it is not always true. Thus, as I have already said, a man is not bound to celibacy as a debt, but ought to marry if he prefers it. And if you are unable to understand the use of this word "debere," when no debt is implied, let me inform you that we use the word *debere* precisely as we sometimes do the words *posse*, and *non posse*, and also *necessitas*, when the ability, etc., is not in the things themselves, but in something else. When, for instance, we say that the poor ought to receive alms from the rich, we mean that the rich ought to bestow alms upon the poor. For this is a debt not owed by the poor but by the rich. We also say that God ought to be exalted over all, not because there is any obligation resting upon him, but because all things ought to be subject to him. And he wishes that all creatures should be what they ought; for what God wishes to be ought to be. And, in like manner, when any creature wishes to do a thing that is left entirely at his own disposal, we say that he ought to do it, for what he wishes to be ought to be. So our Lord Jesus, when he wished, as we have said, to suffer death, ought to have done precisely what he did; because he ought to be what he wished, and was not bound to do anything as a debt. As he is both God and man, in connection with his human nature, which made him a man, he must also have received from the Divine nature that control over himself which freed him from all obligation, except to do as he chose. In like manner, as one person of the Trinity, he must have had whatever he possessed of his own right, so as to be complete in himself, and could not have been under obligations to another, nor have need of giving anything in order to be repaid himself.

BOSO. Now I see clearly that he did not give himself up to die for the honor of God, as a debt; for this my own reason proves, and yet he ought to have done what he did.

ANSELM. That honor certainly belongs to the whole Trinity; and, since he is very God, the Son of God, he offered himself for his own honor, as well as for that of the Father and the Holy Spirit; that is, he gave his humanity to his divinity, which is one person of the Triune God. But, though we express our idea more definitely by clinging to the precise truth, yet we may say, according to our custom, that the Son freely gave himself to the Father. For thus we plainly affirm that in speaking of one person we understand the whole Deity, to whom as man he offered himself. And, by the names of Father and Son, a wondrous depth of devotion is excited in the hearts of the hearers, when it is said that the Son supplicates the Father on our behalf.

BOSO. This I readily acknowledge.

19

How human salvation follows upon his death.

ANSELM. Let us now observe, if we can, how the salvation of men rests on this.

BOSO. This is the very wish of my heart. For, although I think I understand you, yet I wish to get from you the close chain of argument.

ANSELM. There is no need of explaining how precious was the gift which the Son freely gave.

BOSO. That is clear enough already.

ANSELM. But you surely will not think that he deserves no reward, who freely gave so great a gift to God.

BOSO. I see that it is necessary for the Father to reward the Son; else he is either unjust in not wishing to do it, or weak in not being able to do it; but neither of these things can be attributed to God.

ANSELM. He who rewards another either gives him something which he does not have, or else remits some rightful claim upon him. But anterior[4] to the great offering of the Son, all things belonging to the Father were his, nor did he ever owe anything which could be forgiven him. How then can a reward be bestowed on one who needs nothing, and to whom no gift or release can be made?

BOSO. I see on the one hand a necessity for a reward, and on the other it appears impossible; for God must necessarily render payment for what he owes, and yet there is no one to receive it.

ANSELM. But if a reward so large and so deserved is not given to him or any one else, then it will almost appear as if the Son had done this great work in vain.

BOSO. Such a supposition is impious.

ANSELM. The reward then must be bestowed upon some one else, for it cannot be upon him.

BOSO. This is necessarily so.

ANSELM. Had the Son wished to give some one else what was due to him, could the Father rightfully prevent it, or refuse to give it to the other person?

BOSO. No! But I think it would be both just and necessary that the gift should be given by the Father to whomsoever the Son wished; because the Son should be allowed to give away what is his own, and the Father cannot bestow it at all except upon some other person.

ANSELM. Upon whom would he more properly bestow the reward accruing from his death, than upon those for whose salvation, as right reason teaches, he became man; and for whose sake, as we have already said, he left an example of suffering death to preserve holiness? For surely in vain will men imitate him, if they be not also partakers of his reward. Or whom could he more justly make heirs

---

4   Coming before in time or development

of the inheritance, which he does not need, and of the superfluity of his possessions, than his parents and brethren? What more proper than that, when he beholds so many of them weighed down by so heavy a debt, and wasting through poverty, in the depth of their miseries, he should remit the debt incurred by their sins, and give them what their transgressions had forfeited?

BOSO. The universe can hear of nothing more reasonable, more sweet, more desirable. And I receive such confidence from this that I cannot describe the joy with which my heart exults. For it seems to me that God can reject none who come to him in his name.

ANSELM. Certainly not, if he come aright. And the Scriptures, which rest on solid truth as on a firm foundation, and which, by the help of God, we have somewhat examined—the Scriptures, I say, show us how to approach in order to share such favor, and how we ought to live under it.

BOSO. And whatever is built on this foundation is founded on an immovable rock.

ANSELM. I think I have nearly enough answered your inquiry, though I might do it still more fully, and there are doubtless many reasons which are beyond me and which mortal ken does not reach. It is also plain that God had no need of doing the thing spoken of, but eternal truth demanded it. For though God is said to have done what that man did, on account of the personal union made; yet God was in no need of descending from heaven to conquer the devil, nor of contending against him in holiness to free mankind. But God demanded that man should conquer the devil, so that he who had offended by sin should atone by holiness. As God owed nothing to the devil but punishment, so man must only make amends by conquering the devil as man had already been conquered by him. But whatever was demanded of man, he owed to God and not to the devil.

20

How great and how just is God's compassion.

ANSELM. Now we have found the compassion of God which appeared lost to you when we were considering God's holiness and man's sin; we have found it, I say, so great and so consistent with his holiness, as to be incomparably above anything that can be conceived. For what compassion can excel these words of the Father, addressed to the sinner doomed to eternal torments and having no way of escape: "Take my only begotten Son and make him an offering for yourself"; or these words of the Son: "Take me, and ransom your souls." For these are the voices they utter, when inviting and leading us to faith in the Gospel. Or can anything be more just than for him to remit all debt since he has earned a reward greater than all debt, if given with the love which he deserves?

21

How it is impossible for the devil to be reconciled.

ANSELM. If you carefully consider the scheme of human salvation, you will perceive the reconciliation of the devil, of which you made inquiry, to be impossible. For, as man could not be reconciled but by the death of the God-man, by whose holiness the loss occasioned by man's sin should be made up; so fallen angels cannot be saved but by the death of a God-angel who by his holiness may repair the evil occasioned by the sins of his companions. And as man must not be restored by a man of a different race, though of the same nature, so no angel ought to be saved by any other angel, though all were of the same nature, for they are not like men, all of the same race. For all angels were not sprung from one, as all men were. And there is another objection to their restoration, viz. that, as they fell with none to plot their fall, so they must rise with none to aid them; but this is impossible. But otherwise they cannot be restored to their original dignity. For, had they not sinned, they would have been confirmed in virtue without any foreign aid, simply by the power given to them from the first. And, therefore, if any one thinks that the redemption of our Lord ought to be extended even to the fallen angels, he is convinced by reason, for by reason he has been deceived. And I do not say this as if to deny that the virtue of his death far exceeds all the sins of men and angels, but because infallible reason rejects the reconciliation of the fallen angels.

22

How the truth of the Old and New Testament is shown in the things which have been said.

BOSO. All things which you have said seem to me reasonable and incontrovertible. And by the solution of the single question proposed do I see the truth of all that is contained in the Old and New Testament. For, in proving that God became man by necessity, leaving out what was taken from the Bible, viz. the remarks on the persons of the Trinity, and on Adam, you convince both Jews and Pagans by the mere force of reason. And the God-man himself originates the New Testament and approves the Old. And, as we must acknowledge him to be true, so no one can dissent from anything contained in these books.

ANSELM. If we have said anything that needs correction, I am willing to make the correction if it be a reasonable one. But, if the conclusions which we have arrived at by reason seem confirmed by the testimony of the truth, then ought we to attribute it, not to ourselves, but to God, who is blessed forever.—

Amen.

History of the Kings of Britain

Geoffrey of Monmouth

Translated by J. A. Giles

BOOK ONE

1

The epistle dedicatory to Robert Earl of Gloucester.

WHILST occupied on many and various studies, I happened to light upon the History of the Kings of Britain, and wondered that in the account which Gildas and Bede, in their elegant treatises, had given of them, I found nothing said of those kings who lived here before the Incarnation of Christ, nor of Arthur, and many others who succeeded after the Incarnation; though their actions both deserved immortal fame, and were also celebrated by many people in a pleasant manner and by heart, as if they had been written. Whilst I was intent upon these and such like thoughts, Walter, archdeacon of Oxford, a man of great eloquence, and learned in foreign histories, offered me a very ancient book in the British tongue, which, in a continued regular story and elegant style, related the actions of them all, from Brutus, the first King of the Britons, down to Cadwallader, the son of Cadwallo. At his request, therefore, though I had not made fine language my study, by collecting florid expressions from other authors, yet contented with my own homely style, I undertook the translation of that book into Latin. For if I had swelled the pages with rhetorical flourishes, I must have tired my readers, by employing their attention more upon my words than upon the history. To you, therefore, Robert, Earl of Gloucester, this work humbly sues for the favour of being so corrected by your advice, that it may not be thought to be the poor offspring of Geoffrey of Monmouth, but when polished by your refined wit and judgment, the production of him who had Henry, the glorious King of England, for his father, and whom we see an accomplished scholar and philosopher, as well as a brave soldier and expert commander; so that Britain with joy acknowledged that in you she possesses another Henry.

2

The first inhabitants of Britain.

BRITAIN, the best of islands, is situated in the Western Ocean, between France and Ireland, being eight hundred miles long, and two hundred broad. It produces everything that is useful to man, with a plenty that never fails. It abounds with all kinds of metal, and has plains of large extent, and hills fit for the finest tillage, the richness of whose soil affords variety of fruits in their proper seasons. It also has forests well stocked with all kinds of wild beasts; in its lawns cattle find good change of pasture, and bees variety of flowers for honey. Under its lofty mountains lie green meadows pleasantly situated, in which the gentle murmurs of crystal springs gliding along clear channels, give those that pass an agreeable invitation to lie down on their banks and slumber. It is likewise well watered with lakes and rivers abounding with fish; and besides the narrow sea which is on the Southern coast towards France, there are three noble rivers, stretching out like three arms, namely, the Thames, the Severn, and the Humber; by which foreign commodities from all countries are brought into it. It was formerly adorned with eight and twenty cities, of which some are in ruins and desolate, others are still standing, beautified with lofty church-towers, wherein religious worship is performed according to the Christian institution. It is lastly inhabited by five different nations, the Britons,

Romans, Saxons, Picts, and Scots; whereof the Britons before the rest did formerly possess the whole island from sea to sea, till divine vengeance, punishing them for their pride, made them give way to the Picts and Saxons. But in what manner, and from whence, they first arrived here, remains now to be related in what follows.

3

Brutus, being banished after the killing of his parents, goes into Greece.

AFTER the Trojan war, Æneas, flying with Ascanius from the destruction of their city, sailed to Italy. There he was honourably received by King Latinus, which raised against him the envy of Turnus, King of the Rutuli, who thereupon made war against him. Upon their engaging in battle, Æneas got the victory, and having killed Turnus, obtained the kingdom of Italy, and with it Lavinia the daughter of Latinus. After his death, Ascanius, succeeding in the kingdom, built Alba upon the Tiber, and begat a son named Sylvius, who, in pursuit of a private amour, took to wife a niece of Lavinia. The damsel soon after conceived, and the father Ascanius, coming to the knowledge of it, commanded his magicians to consult of what sex the child should be. When they satisfied themselves in the matter, they told him she would give birth to a boy, who would kill his father and mother, and after traveling over many countries in banishment, would at last arrive at the highest pitch of glory. Nor were they mistaken in their prediction; for at the proper time the woman brought forth a son, and died of his birth; but the child was delivered to a nurse and called Brutus.

At length, after fifteen years were expired, the youth accompanied his father in hunting, and killed him undesignedly by the shot of an arrow. For, as the servants were driving up the deer towards them, Brutus, in shooting at them, smote his father under the breast. Upon his death, he was expelled from Italy, his kinsmen being enraged at him for so heinous a deed. Thus banished he went into Greece, where he found the posterity of Helenus, son of Priamus, kept in slavery by Pandrasus, King of the Greeks. For, after the destruction of Troy, Pyrrhus, the son of Achilles had brought hither in chains Helenus and many others; and to revenge on them the death of his father, had given command that they should be held in captivity. Brutus, finding they were by descent his old countrymen, took up his abode among them, and began to distinguish himself by his conduct and bravery in war, so as to gain the affection of kings and commanders, and above all the young men of the country. For he was esteemed a person of great capacity both in council and war, and signalized his generosity to his soldiers, by bestowing on them all the money and spoil he got. His fame, therefore, spreading over all countries, the Trojans from all parts began to flock to him, desiring under his command to be freed from subjection to the Greeks; which they assured him might easily be done, considering how much their number was now increased in the country, being seven thousand strong, besides women and children. There was likewise then in Greece a noble youth named Assaracus, a favourer of their cause. For he was descended on his mother's side from the Trojans, and placed great confidence in them, that he might be able by their assistance to oppose the designs of the Greeks. For his brother had a quarrel with him for attempting to deprive him of three castles which his father had given him at his death, on account of his being only the son of a concubine; but as the brother was a Greek, both by his father's and mother's side, he had prevailed with the king and the rest of the Greeks to espouse his cause. Brutus, having taken a view of the number of his men, and seen how Assaracus' castles lay open to him, complied with their request.

4

Brutus's letter to Pandrasus.

BEING therefore, chosen their commander, he assembled the Trojans from all parts, and fortified the towns belonging to Assaracus. But he himself, with Assaracus and the whole body of men and women that adhered to him, retired to the woods and hills, and then sent a letter to the king in these words:

"Brutus, General of the remainder of the Trojans, to Pandrasus, King of the Greeks, sends greeting. As it was beneath the dignity of a nation descended from the illustrious race of Dardanus, to be treated in your kingdom otherwise than the nobility of their birth required, they have betaken themselves to the protection of the woods. For they have preferred living after the manner of wild beasts, upon flesh and herbs, with the enjoyment of liberty, to continuing longer in the greatest luxury under the yoke of slavery. If this gives your majesty any offence, impute it not to them, but pardon it; since it is the common sentiment of every captive, to be desirous of regaining his former dignity. Let pity therefore move you to bestow on them freely their lost liberty, and permit them to inhabit the thickest of the woods, to which they have retired to avoid slavery. But if you deny them this favour, then by your permission and assistance let them depart into some foreign country."

5

Brutus falling upon the forces of Pandrasus by surprise, routs them, and takes Antigonus, the brother of Pandrasus, with Anacletus, prisoner.

PANDRASUS, perceiving the purport of the letter, was beyond measure surprised at the boldness of such a message from those whom he had kept in slavery; and having called a council of his nobles, he determined to raise an army in order to pursue them. But while he was upon his march to the desert, where he thought they were, and to the town of Sparatinum, Brutus made a sally with three thousand men, and fell upon him unawares. For having intelligence of his coming, he had got into the town the night before, with a design to break forth upon them unexpectedly, while unarmed and marching without order. The sally being made, the Trojans briskly attacked them, and endeavoured to make great slaughter. The Greeks, astonished, immediately gave way on all sides, and with the king at their head, hastened to pass the River Akalon, which runs near the place; but in passing were in great danger from the rapidity of the stream. Brutus galled them in their flight, and killed some of them in the stream, and some on the banks; and running to and fro, rejoiced to see them in both places exposed to ruin. But Antigonus, the brother of Pandrasus, grieved at the sight, rallied his scattered troops, and made a quick return upon the furious Trojans; for he rather chose to die making a brave resistance, than to be drowned in a muddy pool in a shameful flight. Thus attended with a close body of men, he encouraged them to stand their ground, and employed his whole force against the enemy with great vigour, but to little or no purpose; for the Trojans had arms, but the others none; and from this advantage they were more eager in the pursuit, and made a miserable slaughter; nor did they give over the assault till they had made nearly a total destruction, and taken Antigonus, and Anacletus his companion prisoners.

6

The town of Sparatinum besieged by Pandrasus.

BRUTUS, after the victory, reinforced the town with six hundred men, and then retired to the woods, where the Trojan people were expecting his protection. In the meantime Pandrasus, grieving at his own flight and his brother's captivity, endeavoured that night to re-assemble his broken forces, and the next morning went with a body of people which he had got together, to besiege the town, into which he supposed Brutus had put himself with Antigonus and the rest of the prisoners that he had taken. As soon as he was arrived at the walls, and had viewed the situation of the castle, he divided his army into several bodies, and placed them round it in different stations. One party was charged not to suffer any of the besieged to go out; another to turn the courses of the rivers; and a third to beat down the walls with battering rams and other engines. In obedience to those commands, they laboured with their utmost force to distress the besieged; and night coming on, made choice of their bravest men to defend the camp and tents from the incursions of the enemy, while the rest, who were fatigued with labour, refreshed themselves with sleep.

7

The besieged ask assistance of Brutus.

BUT the besieged, standing on the top of the walls, were no less vigourous to repel the forces of the enemy's engines, and assault them with their own, and cast forth darts and firebrands with a unanimous resolution to make a valiant defense. And when a breach was made through the wall, they compelled the enemy to retire, by throwing upon them fire and scalding water. But being distressed through scarcity of provision and daily labour, they sent an urgent message to Brutus, to hasten to their assistance, for they were afraid they might be so weakened as to be obliged to quit the town. Brutus, though desirous of relieving them, was under great perplexity, as he had not men enough to stand a pitched battle, and therefore made use of a strategem, by which he proposed to enter the enemy's camp by night, and having deceived their watch to kill them in their sleep. But because he knew this was impracticable without the concurrence and assistance of some Greeks, he called to him Anacletus, the companion of Antigonus, and with a drawn sword in his hand, spake to him after this manner:

"Noble youth! Your own and Antigonus's life is now at an end, unless you will faithfully perform what I command you. This night I design to invade the camp of the Greeks, and fall upon them unawares, but am afraid of being hindered in the attempt if the watch should discover the strategem. Since it will be necessary, therefore, to have them killed first, I desire to make use of you to deceive them, that I may have the easier access to the rest. Do you therefore manage this affair cunningly. At the second hour of the night go to the watch, and with fair speeches tell them that you have brought away Antigonus from prison, and that he is come to the bottom of the woods, where he lies hid among the shrubs, and cannot get any farther, by reason of the fetters with which you shall pretend he that is bound. Then you shall conduct them, as if it were to deliver him, to the end of the wood, where I will attend with a band of men ready to kill them."

8

Anacletus, in fear of death, betrays the army of the Greeks.

ANACLETUS, seeing the sword threatening him with immediate death while these words were being pronounced, was so terrified as to promise upon oath, that on condition he and Antigonus should have longer life granted them, he would execute his command. Accordingly, the agreement being confirmed, at the second hour of the night he directed his way towards the Grecian camp, and when he was come near to it, the watch, who were then narrowly examining all the places where anyone could hide, ran out from all parts to meet him, and demanded the occasion of his coming, and whether it was not to betray the army. He, with a show of great joy, made the following answer:—"I come not to betray my country, but having made my escape from the prison of the Trojans, I fly thither to desire you would go with me to Antigonus, whom I have delivered from Brutus's chains. For being not able to come with me for the weight of his fetters, I have a little while ago caused him to lie hid among the shrubs at the end of the wood, till I could meet with some one whom I might conduct to his assistance." While they were in suspense about the truth of this story, there came one who knew him, and after he had saluted him, told them who he was; so that now, without any hesitation, they quickly called their absent companions, and followed him to the wood where he had told them Antigonus lay hid. But at length, as they were going among the shrubs, Brutus with his armed bands sprang forth, and fell upon them, while under the greatest astonishment, with a most cruel slaughter. From thence he marched directly to the siege, and divided his men into three bands, assigning to each of them a different part of the camp, and telling them to advance discreetly, and without noise, and when entered, not to kill any body till he with his company should be possessed of the king's tent, and should cause the trumpet to sound for a signal.

9

The taking of Pandrasus.

WHEN he had given them these instructions, they forthwith softly entered the camp in silence, and taking their appointed stations, awaited the promised signal, which Brutus delayed not to give as soon as he had got before the tent of Pandrasus, to assault which was the thing he most desired. At hearing the signal, they forthwith drew their swords, entered in among the men in their sleep, made quick destruction of them, and allowing no quarter, in this manner traversed the whole camp. The rest, awakened at the groans of the dying, and seeing their assailants, were like sheep seized with a sudden fear; for they despaired of life, since they had neither time to take arms, nor to escape by flight. They ran up and down without arms among the armed, whithersoever the fury of the assault hurried them, but were on all sides cut down by the enemy rushing in. Some that might have escaped, were in the eagerness of flight dashed against rocks, trees, or shrubs, and increased the misery of their death. Others, that had only a shield, or some such covering for their defense, in venturing upon the same rocks to avoid death, fell down in the hurry and darkness of the night, and broke either legs or arms. Others, that escaped both these disasters, but did not know whither to fly, were drowned in the adjacent rivers; and scarcely one got away without some unhappy accident befalling him. Besides, the garrison in the town, upon notice of the coming of their fellow soldiers, sallied forth, and redoubled the slaughter.

10

A consultation about what is to be asked of the captive king.

BUT Brutus, as I said before, having possessed himself of the king's tent, made it his business to keep him a safe prisoner; for he knew he could more easily attain his ends by preserving his life than by killing him; but the party that was with him, allowing no quarter, made an utter destruction in that part which they had gained. The night being spent in this manner, when the next morning discovered to their view so great an overthrow of the enemy, Brutus, in transports of joy, gave full liberty to his men to do what they pleased with the plunder, and then entered the town with the king, to stay there till they had shared it among them; which done, he again fortified the castle, gave orders for burying the slain, and retired with his forces to the woods in great joy for the victory. After the rejoicings of his people on this occasion, their renowned general summoned the oldest of them and asked their advice, what he had best desire of Pandrasus, who, being now in their power, would readily grant whatever they would request of him, in order to regain his liberty. They, according to their different fancies, desired different things; some urged him to request that a certain part of the kingdom might be assigned them for their habitation; others that he would demand leave to depart, and to be supplied with necessaries for their voyage. After they had been a long time in suspense what to do, one of them, named Mempricius, rose up, and having made silence, spoke to them thus:

"What can be the occasion of your suspense, fathers, in a matter which I think so much concerns your safety? The only thing you can request, with any prospect of a firm peace and security to yourselves and your posterity, is liberty to depart. For if you make no better terms with Pandrasus for his life than only to have some part of the country assigned you to live among the Greeks, you will never enjoy a lasting peace while the brothers, sons, or grandsons of those whom you killed yesterday shall continue to be your neighbours. So long as the memory of their fathers' deaths shall remain, they will be your mortal enemies, and upon the least trifling provocation will endeavour to revenge themselves. Nor will you be sufficiently numerous to withstand so great a multitude of people. And if you shall happen to fall out among yourselves, their number will daily increase, yours diminish. I propose, therefore, that you request of him his eldest daughter, Ignoge, for a wife for our general, and with her, gold, silver, corn, and whatever else shall be necessary for our voyage. If we obtain this, we may with his leave remove to some other country."

11

Pandrasus gives his daughter Ignoge in marriage to Brutus, who, after his departure from Greece, falls upon a desert island, where he is told by the oracle of Diana what place he is to inhabit.

WHEN he had ended his speech, in words to this effect, the whole assembly acquiesced in his advice, and moved that Pandrasus might be brought in among them, and condemned to a most cruel death unless he would grant this request. He was immediately brought in, and being placed in a chair above the rest, and informed of the tortures prepared for him unless he would do what was commanded him, he made them this answer:

"Since my ill fate has delivered me and my brother Antigonus into your hands, I can do no other than grant your request, lest a refusal may cost us our lives, which are now entirely in your power. In my opinion life is preferable to all other considerations; therefore, wonder not that I am willing to redeem it at so great a price. But though it is against my inclination that I obey your commands, yet it seems a matter of comfort to me that I am to give my daughter to so noble a youth, whose descent from the illustrious race of Priamus and Anchises is clear, both from that greatness of mind which appears in him, and the certain accounts we have had of it. For who less than he could have released from their chains the banished Trojans, when reduced under slavery to so many great princes? Who else could have encouraged them to make head against the Greeks? Or with so small a body of men vanquished so numerous and powerful an army, and taken their king prisoner in the engagement? And, therefore, since this noble youth has gained so much glory by the opposition which he has made to me, I give him my daughter Ignoge, and also gold, silver, corn, wine, and oil, and whatever you shall find necessary for your voyage. If you shall alter your resolution, and think fit to continue among the Greeks, I will grant you the third part of my kingdom for your habitation; if not, I will faithfully perform my promise, and for your greater security will stay as a hostage among you till I have made it good."

Accordingly he held a council, and directed messengers to all the shores of Greece, to get ships together; which done, he delivered them to the Trojans, to the number of three hundred and twenty-four, laden with all kinds of provision, and married his daughter to Brutus. He made also a present of gold and silver to each man according to his quality. When everything was performed the king was set at liberty; and the Trojans, released from his power, set sail with a fair wind. But Ignoge, standing upon the stern of the ship, swooned away several times in Brutus's arms, and with many sighs and tears lamented the leaving her parents and country, nor ever turned her eyes from the shore while it was in sight. Brutus, meanwhile, endeavoured to assuage her grief by kind words and embraces intermixed with kisses, and ceased not from these blandishments till she grew weary of crying and fell asleep. During these and other accidents, the winds continued fair for two days and a night together, when at length they arrived at a certain island called Leogecia, which had been formerly wasted by the incursions of pirates, and was then uninhabited. Brutus, not knowing this, sent three hundred armed men ashore to see who inhabited it; but they finding nobody, killed several kinds of wild beasts which they met in the groves and woods, and came to a desolate city, in which they found a temple of Diana, and in it a statue of that goddess which gave answers to those that came to consult her. At last, loading themselves with the prey which they had taken in hunting, they return to their ships, and gave their companions an account of this country and city. Then they advised their leader to go to the city, and after offering sacrifices, to inquire of the deity of the place, what country was allotted them for their place of settlement. To this proposal all assented; so that Brutus, attended with Gerion, the augur, and twelve of the oldest men, set forward to the temple, with all things necessary for the sacrifice. Being arrived at the place, and presenting themselves before the shrine with garlands about their temples, as the ancient rites required, they made three fires to the three deities, Jupiter, Mercury, and Diana, and offered sacrifices to each of them. Brutus himself, holding before the altar of the goddess a consecrated vessel filled with wine, and the blood of a white hart, with his face looking up to the image, broke silence in these words:

> "Diva potens nemorum, terror sylvestribus apris;
> Cui licet amfractus ire æthereos,
> Infernasque domos; terrestria jura resolve,
> Et dic quas terras nos habitare velis?
> Dic certam sedem qua te venerabor in ævum,
> Qua tibi virgineis templa dicabo choris!"
>
> Goddess of woods, tremendous in the chase
> To mountain boars, and all the savage race!
> Wide o'er the ethereal walks extends thy sway,
> And o'er the infernal mansions void of day!
> Look upon us on earth! Unfold our fate,
> And say what region is our destined seat?
> Where shall we next thy lasting temples raise?
> And choirs of virgins celebrate thy praise?

These words he repeated nine times, after which he took four turns round the altar, poured the wine into the fire, and then laid himself down upon the hart's skin, which he had spread before the altar, where he fell asleep. About the third hour of the night, the usual time for deep sleep, the goddess seemed to present herself before him, and foretell his future success as follows:—

> "Brute! Sub accasum solis trans Gallica regna
> Insula in oceano est undique clausa mari:
> Insula in oceano est habitata gigantibus olim,
> Nunc deserta quidem, gentibus apta tuis.
> Hanc pete, namque tibi sedes erit illa perennis:
> Sic fiet natis altera Troja tuis.
> Sic de prole tua reges nascentur: et ipsis
> Totius terræ subditus orbus erit."
>
> Brutus! There lies beyond the Gallic bounds
> An island which the western sea surrounds,
> By giants once possessed, now few remain
> To bar thy entrance, or obstruct thy reign.
> To reach that happy shore thy sails employ
> There fate decrees to raise a second Troy
> And found an empire in thy royal line,
> Which time shall ne'er destroy, nor bounds confine.

Awakened by the vision, he was for some time in doubt with himself, whether what he had seen was a dream or a real appearance of the goddess herself, foretelling to what land he should go. At last he called to his companions, and related to them in order the vision he had in his sleep, at which they very much rejoiced, and were urgent to return to their ships, and while the wind favoured them, to hasten their voyage towards the west, in pursuit of what the goddess had promised. Without delay, therefore, they returned to their company, and set sail again, and after a course of thirty days came to Africa, being ignorant as yet whither to steer. From thence they came to the Philenian altars, and to a place called Salinae, and sailed between Ruscicada and the Mountains of Azara, where they underwent great danger from pirates, whom, notwithstanding, they vanquished, and enriched themselves with their spoils.

12

Brutus enters Aquitaine with Corineus.

FROM thence, passing the River Malua, they arrived at Mauritania, where at last, for want of provisions, they were obliged to go ashore; and, dividing themselves into several bands, they laid waste the whole country. When they had well stored their ships, they steered to the Pillars of Hercules, where they saw some of those sea monsters, called Syrens, which surrounded their ships, and very nearly overturned them. However, they made a shift to escape, and came to the Tyrrhenian Sea, upon the shores of which they found several nations descended from the banished Trojans, that had accompanied Antenor in his flight. The name of their commander was Corineus, a modest man in matters of council, and of great courage and boldness, who, in an encounter with any person, even of gigantic stature, would immediately overthrow him, as if he were a child. When they understood from whom he was descended, they joined company with him and those under his government, who from the name of their leader were afterwards called the Cornish people, and indeed were more serviceable to Brutus than the rest in all his engagements. From there they came to Aquitaine, and entering the mouth of the Loire, cast anchor. There they stayed seven days and viewed the country. Goffarius Pictus, who was King of Aquitaine at that time, having an account brought him of the arrival of a foreign people with a great fleet upon his coasts, sent ambassadors to them to demand whether they brought with them peace or war. The ambassadors, on their way towards the fleet, met Corineus, who was come out with two hundred men, to hunt in the woods. They demanded of him, who gave him leave to enter the king's forests, and kill his game; (which by an ancient law nobody was allowed to do without leave from the prince.) Corineus answered, that as for that matter there was no occasion for asking leave; upon which one of them, named Imbertus, rushing forward, with a full drawn bow leveled a shot at him. Corineus avoided the arrow and immediately ran up to him, and with his bow in his hand broke his head. The rest narrowly escaped, and carried the news of this disaster to Goffarius. The Pictavian general was struck with sorrow for it, and immediately raised a vast army, to revenge the death of his ambassador. Brutus, on the other hand, upon hearing the rumour of his coming, sent away the women and children to the ships, which he took care to be well guarded, and commands them to stay there, while he, with the rest that were able to bear arms, should go to meet the army. At last an assault being made, a bloody fight ensued; in which after a great part of the day had been spent, Corineus was ashamed to see the Aquitanians so bravely stand their ground, and the Trojans maintaining the fight without victory. He therefore took fresh courage, and drawing off his men to the right wing, broke in upon the very thickest of the enemies, where he made such slaughter on every side, that at last he broke the line and put them all to flight. In this encounter he lost his sword, but by good fortune, met with a battle-axe, with which he clave down to the waist everyone that stood in his way. Brutus and everybody else, both friends and enemies, were amazed at his courage and strength, for he brandished about his battle-axe among the flying troops, and terrified them not a little with these insulting words, "Whither fly ye, cowards? Whither fly ye, base wretches? Stand your ground, that ye may encounter Corineus. What! For shame! Do so many thousands of you fly one man? However, take this comfort for your flight, that you are pursued by one, before whom the Tyrrhenian giants could not stand their ground, but fell down slain in heaps together."

13

Goffarius routed by Brutus.

AT these words one of them, named Subardus, who was a consul, returned with three hundred men to assault him; but Corineus with his shield warded off the blow, and lifting up his battle-axe gave him such a stroke upon the top of his helmet, that at once he clave him down to the waist; and then rushing upon the rest he made terrible slaughter by wheeling about his battle-axe among them, and, running to and fro, seemed more anxious to inflict blows on the enemy than careful to avoid those which they aimed at him. Some had their hands and arms, some their very shoulders, some again their heads, and others their legs cut off by him. All fought with him only, and he alone seemed to fight with all. Brutus seeing him thus beset, out of regard to him, ran with a band of men to his assistance: at which the battle was again renewed with vigour and with loud shouts, and great numbers slain on both sides. But now the Trojans presently gained the victory, and put Goffarius with his Pictavians to flight. The king, after a narrow escape, went to several parts of Gaul, to procure succours among such princes as were related or known to him. At that time Gaul was subject twelve princes, who with equal authority possessed the whole country. These received him courteously, and promised with one consent to expel the foreigners from Aquitaine.

14

Brutus, after his victory with Goffarius, ravages Aquitaine with fire and sword.

BRUTUS, in joy for the victory, enriched his men with the spoils of the slain, and then, dividing them into several bodies, marched into the country with a design to lay it waste, and load his fleet with the spoil. With this view he set the cities on fire, seized the riches that were in them, destroyed the fields, and made dreadful slaughter among the citizens and common people, being unwilling to leave so much as one alive of that wretched nation. While he was making this destruction over all Aquitaine, he came to a place where the city of Tours now stands, which he afterwards built, as Homer testifies. As soon as he had looked out a place convenient for the purpose, he pitched his camp there, for a place of safe retreat, when occasion should require. For he was afraid on account of Goffarius's approach with the kings and princes of Gaul, and a very great army, which was now come near the place, ready to give him battle. Having therefore finished his camp, he expected to engage with Goffarius in two days' time, placing the utmost confidence in the conduct and courage of the young men under his command.

15

Goffarius's fight with Brutus.

GOFFARIUS, being informed that the Trojans were in those parts, marched day and night, till he came within a close view of Brutus's camp; and then with a stern look and disdainful smile, broke out into these expressions, "Oh wretched fate! Have these base exiles made a camp also in my kingdom? Arm, arm, soldiers, and march through their thickest ranks: we shall soon take these pitiful fellows like sheep, and disperse them throughout our kingdom for slaves." At these words they prepared their arms, and advanced in twelve bodies towards the enemy. Brutus, on the other hand, with his forces drawn up in order, went forth boldly to meet them, and gave his men directions for their conduct, where they should assault and where they should be on the defensive. At the beginning of the attack, the Trojans had the advantage, and made a rapid slaughter of the enemy, of which there fell near two thousand, which so terrified the rest, that they were on the point of running away. But, as the victory generally falls to that side which has very much the superiority in numbers, so the Gauls, being three to one in number, though overpowered at first, yet at last joining in a great body together, broke in upon the Trojans, and forced them to retire to their camp with much slaughter. The victory thus gained, they besieged them in their camp, with a design not to suffer them to stir out until they should either surrender themselves prisoners, or be cruelly starved to death with a long famine.

In the meantime, Corineus the night following entered into consultation with Brutus, and proposed to go out that night by by-ways, and conceal himself in an adjacent wood till break of day; and while Brutus should sally forth upon the enemy in the morning twilight, he with his company would surprise them from behind and put them to slaughter. Brutus was pleased with this stratagem of Corineus, who according to his engagement got out cunningly with three thousand men, and put himself under the covert of the woods. As soon as it was day Brutus marshaled his men and opened the camp to go out to fight. The Gauls met him and began the engagement: many thousands fell on both sides, neither party giving quarter. There was present a Trojan, named Turonus, the nephew of Brutus, inferior to none but Corineus in courage and strength of body. He alone with his sword killed six hundred men, but at last was unfortunately slain himself by the number of Gauls that rushed upon him. From him the city of Tours derived its name, because he was buried there. While both armies were thus warmly engaged, Corineus came upon them unawares, and fell fiercely upon the rear of the enemy, which put new courage into his friends on the other side, and made them exert themselves with increased vigour. The Gauls were astonished at the very shout of Corineus's men, and thinking their number to be much greater than it really was, they hastily quitted the field; but the Trojans pursued them, and killed them in the pursuit, nor did they desist till they had gained a complete victory. Brutus, though in joy for this great success, was yet afflicted to observe the number of his forces daily lessened, while that of the enemy increased more and more. He was in suspense for some time, whether he had better continue the war or not, but at last he determined to return to his ships while the greater part of his followers was yet safe, and hitherto victorious, and to go in quest of the island which the goddess had told him of. So without further delay, with the consent of his company, he repaired to the fleet, and loading it with the riches and spoils he had taken, set sail with a fair wind towards the promised island, and arrived on the coast of Totness.

16

Albion divided between Brutus and Corineus.

THE island was then called Albion, and inhabited by none but a few giants. Notwithstanding this, the pleasant situation of the places, the plenty of rivers abounding with fish, and the engaging prospect of its woods, made Brutus and his company very desirous to fix their habitation in it. They therefore passed through all the provinces, forced the giants to fly into the caves of the mountains, and divided the country among them according to the directions of their commander. After this they began to till the ground and build houses, so that in a little time the country looked like a place that had been long inhabited. At last Brutus called the island after his own name Britain, and his companions Britons; for by these means he desired to perpetuate the memory of his name. From whence afterwards the language of the nation, which at first bore the name of Trojan, or rough Greek, was called British. But Corineus, in imitation of his leader, called that part of the island which fell to his share, Corinea, and his people Corineans, after his name; and though he had his choice of the provinces before all the rest, yet he preferred this country, which is called in Latin Cornubia, either from its being in the shape of a horn (in Latin *cornu*), or from the corruption of the said name. For it was a diversion to him to encounter the said giants, which were in greater numbers there than in all the other provinces that fell to the share of his companions. Among the rest was one detestable monster, named Goëmagot, in stature twelve cubits, and of such prodigious strength that at one shake he pulled up an oak as if it had been a hazel wand. On a certain day, when Brutus was holding a solemn festival to the gods, in the port where they at first landed, this giant with twenty more of his companions came in upon the Britons, among whom he made a dreadful slaughter. But the Britons at last assembling together in a body, put them to the rout, and killed them every one but Goëmagot. Brutus had given orders to have him preserved alive, out of a desire to see a combat between him and Corineus, who took a great pleasure in such encounters. Corineus, overjoyed at this, prepared himself, and throwing aside his arms, challenged him to wrestle with him. At the beginning of the encounter, Corineus and the giant, standing, front to front, held each other strongly in their arms, and panted aloud for breath, but Goëmagot presently grasping Corineus with all his might, broke three of his ribs, two on his right side and one on his left. At which Corineus, highly enraged, roused up his whole strength, and snatching him upon his shoulders, ran with him, as fast as the weight would allow him, to the next shore, and there getting upon the top of a high rock, hurled down the savage monster into the sea; where falling on the sides of craggy rocks, he was torn to pieces, and coloured the waves with his blood. The place where he fell, taking its name from the giant's fall, is called Lam Goëmagot, that is, Goëmagot's Leap, to this day.

17

The building of new Troy by Brutus, upon the River Thames.

BRUTUS, having thus at last set eyes upon his kingdom, formed a design of building a city, and, with this view, traveled through the land to find out a convenient situation, and coming to the River Thames, he walked along the shore, and at last pitched upon a place very fit for his purpose. Here, therefore, he built a city, which he called New Troy; under which name it continued a long time after, till at last, by the corruption of the original word, it came to be called Trinovantum. But afterwards when Lud, the brother of Cassibellaun, who made war against Julius Caesar, obtained the government of the kingdom, he surrounded it with stately walls, and towers of admirable workmanship, and ordered it to be called after his name, Kaer-Lud, that is, the City of Lud. But this very thing became afterward the occasion of a great quarrel between him and his brother Nennius, who took offence at his abolishing the name of

Troy in this country. Of this quarrel Gildas the historian has given a full account; for which reason I pass it over, for fear of debasing by my account of it, what so great a writer has so eloquently related.

18

New Troy being built, and laws made for the government of it, it is given to the citizens that were to inhabit it.

AFTER Brutus had finished the building of the city, he made choice of the citizens that were to inhabit it, and prescribed them laws for their peaceable government. At this time Eli the priest governed in Judea, and the ark of the covenant was taken by the Philistines. At the same time, also, the sons of Hector, after the expulsion of the posterity of Antenor, reigned in Troy; as in Italy did Sylvius Aeneas, the son of Aeneas, the uncle of Brutus, and the third King of the Latins.

BOOK TWO

1

After the death of Brutus, his three sons succeed him in the kingdom.

DURING these transactions, Brutus had by his wife Ignoge three famous sons, whose names were Locrin, Albanact, and Kamber. These, after their father's death, which happened in the twenty-fourth year after his arrival, buried him in the city which he had built, and then having divided the kingdom of Britain among them, retired each to his government. Locrin, the eldest, possessed the middle part of the island, called afterwards from his name, Loegria. Kamber had that part which lies beyond the River Severn, now called Wales, but which was for a long time named Kambria; and hence that people still call themselves in their British tongue Kambri. Albanact, the younger brother, possessed the country he called

Albania, now Scotland. After they had a long time reigned in peace together, Humber, King of the Huns, arrived in Albania, and having killed Albanact in battle, forced his people to fly to Locrin for protection.

2

Locrin, having routed Humber, falls in love with Estrildis.

LOCRIN, at hearing this news, joined his brother Kamber, and went with the whole strength of the kingdom to meet the king of the Huns, near the river now called Humber, where he gave him battle, and put him to the rout. Humber made towards the river in his flight. Locrin, after the victory, bestowed the plunder of the enemy upon his own men, reserving for himself the gold and silver which he found in the ships, together with three virgins of admirable beauty, whereof one was the daughter of a king in Germany, whom with the other two Humber had forcibly brought away with him after he had ruined their country. Her name was Estrildis, and her beauty such as was hardly to be matched. No ivory or new-fallen snow, no lily could exceed the whiteness of her skin. Locrin, smitten with love, would have gladly married her, at which Corineus was extremely incensed, on account of the engagement which Locrin had entered into with him to marry his daughter.

3

Corineus resents the affront put upon his daughter.

HE went, therefore, to the king, and wielding a battle-axe in his right hand, vented his rage against him in these words: "Do you thus reward me, Locrin, for the many wounds which I have suffered under your father's command in his wars with strange nations, that you must slight my daughter, and debase yourself to marry a barbarian? While there is strength in this right hand, that has been destructive to so many giants upon the Tyrrenian coasts, I will never put up with this affront..." And repeating this again and again with a loud voice, he shook his battle-axe as if he was going to strike him, till the friends of both interposed, and after they had appeased Corineus, obliged Locrin to perform his agreement.

4

Locrin at last marries Guendolœna, the daughter of Corineus.

LOCRIN therefore married Corineus's daughter, named Guendoloena, yet still retained his love for Estrildis, for whom he made apartments under ground, in which he entertained her, and caused her to be honourably attended. For he was resolved at least to carry on a private amour with her, since he could not live with her openly for fear of Corineus. In this manner he concealed her, and made frequent visits to her for seven years together, without the privity of any but his most intimate domestics; and all under a pretense of performing some secret sacrifices to his gods, by which he imposed on the credulity of every body. In the meantime Estrildis became with child, and was delivered of a most beautiful daughter, whom she named Sabre. Guendoloena was also with child, and brought forth a son, who was named Maddan, and put under the care of his grandfather Corineus to be educated.

5

Locrin is killed; Estrildis and Sabre are thrown into a river.

BUT in process of time, when Corineus was dead, Locrin divorced Guendoloena, and advanced Estrildis to be queen. Guendoloena, provoked beyond measure at this, retired into Cornwall, where she assembled together all the forces of that kingdom, and began to raise disturbances against Locrin. At last both armies joined battle near the River Sture, where Locrin was killed by the shot of an arrow. After his death, Guendoloena took upon her the government of the whole kingdom, retaining her father's furious spirit. For she commanded Estrildis and her daughter Sabre to be thrown into the river now called the Severn, and published an edict though all Britain, that the river should bear the damsel's name, hoping by this to perpetuate her memory, and by that the infamy of her husband. So that to this day the river is called in the British tongue Sabren, which by the corruption of the name is in another language Sabrina.

6

Guendolœna delivers up the kingdom to Maddan, her son, after whom succeeds Mempricius.

GUENDOLOENA reigned fifteen years after the death of Locrin, who had reigned ten, and then advanced her son Maddan (whom she saw now at maturity) to the throne, contenting herself with the country of Cornwall for the remainder of her life. At this time Samuel the prophet governed in Judea, Sylvius Aeneas was yet living, and Homer was esteemed a famous orator and poet. Maddan, now in possession of the crown, had by his wife two sons, Mempricius and Malim, and ruled the kingdom in peace and with care forty years. As soon as he was dead, the two brothers quarreled for the kingdom, each being ambitious of the sovereignty of the whole island. Mempricius, impatient to attain his ends, entered into treaty with Malim, under colour of making a composition with him, and, having formed a conspiracy, murdered him in the assembly where their ambassadors were met. By these means he obtained the dominion of the whole island, over which he exercised such tyranny, that he left scarcely a nobleman alive in it, and either by violence or treachery oppressed everyone that he apprehended might be likely to succeed him, pursuing his hatred to the whole race. He also deserted his own wife, by whom he had a noble youth named Ebraucus, and addicted himself to sodomy, preferring unnatural lust to the pleasures of the conjugal state. At last, in the twentieth year of his reign, while he was hunting, he retired from his company into a valley, where he was surrounded by a great multitude of ravenous wolves, and devoured by them in a horrible manner. Then did Saul reign in Judea, and Eurystheus in Lacedaemonia.

7

Ebraucus, the successor of Mempricius, conquers the Gauls and builds the towns, Kaerebrauc, &c.

MEMPRICIUS being dead, Ebraucus, his son, a man of great stature and wonderful strength, took upon him the government of Britain, which he held forty years. He was the first after Brutus who invaded Gaul with a fleet, and distressed its provinces by killing their men and laying waste their cities; and having by these means enriched himself with an infinite quantity of gold and silver, he returned victorious. After this he built a city on the other side of the Humber, which, from his own name, he called Kaerebrauc, that is, the city of Ebraucus, about the time that David reigned in Judaea, and Sylvius Latinus in Italy; and that Gad, Nathan, and Asaph prophesied in Israel. He also built the city of Alclud towards Albani, and the town of mount Agned, called at this time the Castle of Maidens, or the Mountain of Sorrow.

8

Ebraucus's twenty sons go to Germany, and his thirty daughters to Sylvius Alba, in Italy.

THIS prince had twenty sons and thirty daughters by twenty wives, and with great valour governed the kingdom of Britain sixty years. The names of his sons were: Brutus surnamed Greenshield, Margadud, Sisillius, Regin, Morivid, Bladud, Lagon, Bodloan, Kincar, Spaden, Gaul, Darden, Eldad, Ivor, Gangu, Hector, Kerin, Rud, Assarach, and Buel. The names of his daughters were: Gloigni, Ignogni, Oudas, Guenliam, Gaudid, Angarad, Guendoloe, Tangustel, Gorgon, Medlan, Methahel, Ourar, Malure, Kambreda, Ragan, Gael, Ecub, Nest, Cheum, Stadud, Gladud, Ebren, Blagan, Aballac, Angaes, Galaes (the most celebrated beauty at that time in Britain or Gaul), Edra, Anaor, Stadial, and Egron. All these daughters their father sent into Italy to Sylvius Alba, who reigned after Sylvius Latinus, where they were married among the Trojan nobility, the Latin and Sabine women refusing to associate with them. But the sons, under the conduct of their brother Assaracus, departed in a fleet to Germany, and having, with the assistance of Sylvius Alba, subdued the people there, obtained the kingdom.

9

After Ebraucus reigns Brutus his son, after him Leil, and after Leil, Hudibras.

BUT Brutus, surnamed Greenshield, stayed with his father, whom he succeeded in the government, and reigned twelve years. After him reigned Leil, his son, a peaceful and just prince, who, enjoying a prosperous reign, built in the north of Britain a city, called by his name, Kaerleil; at the same time that Solomon began to build the temple of Jerusalem, and the queen of Sheba came to hear his wisdom, at which time also Sylvius Epitus succeeded his father in Alba, in Italy. Leil reigned twenty-five years, but towards the latter end of his life grew more remiss in his government, so that his neglect of affairs speedily occasioned a civil dissension in the kingdom. After him reigned his son Hudibras, thirty-nine years, and composed the civil dissension among his people. He built Kaerlem or Canterbury, Kaerguen or Winchester, and the town of Mount Paladur, now Shaftesbury. At this place an eagle spoke, while the wall of the town was being built; and indeed I should have transmitted the speech to posterity, has I thought it true, as the rest of the history. At this time reigned Capys, the son of Epitus, and Haggai, Amos, Joel, and Azariah, were prophets in Israel.

10

Bladud succeeds Hudibras in the kingdom, and practises magical operations.

NEXT succeeded Bladud, his son, and reigned twenty years. He built Kaerbadus, now Bath, and made hot baths in it for the benefit of the public, which he dedicated to the goddess Minerva; in whose temple he kept fires that never went out nor consumed to ashes, but as soon as they began to decay were turned into balls of stone. About this time the prophet Elias prayed that it might not rain upon earth; and it did not rain for three years and six months. This prince was a very ingenious man, and taught necromancy in his kingdom, nor did he leave off pursuing his magical operations, till he attempted to fly to the upper region of the air with wings which he had prepared, and fell upon the temple of Apollo, in the city of Trinovantum, where he was dashed to pieces.

11

Leir the son of Bladud, having no son, divides his kingdom among his daughters.

AFTER this unhappy fate of Bladud, Leir, his son was advanced to the throne, and nobly governed his country sixty years. He built upon the River Sore a city called in the British tongue Kaerleir, in the Saxon, Leircestre. He was without male issue, but had three daughters, whose names were Gonorilla, Regau, and Cordeilla, of whom he was dotingly fond, but especially of the youngest, Cordeilla. When he began to grow old, he had thoughts of dividing his kingdom among them, and of bestowing them on such husbands as were fit to be advanced to the government with them. But to make trial who was worthy to have the best part of his kingdom, he went to each of them to ask which of them loved him most. The question being proposed, Gonorilla the eldest, made answer "That she called heaven to witness, she loved him more than her own soul." The father replied, "Since you have preferred my declining age before your own life, I will marry you, my dearest daughter, to whomsoever you shall make choice of, and give with you the third part of my kingdom." Then Regau, the second daughter, willing, after the example of her sister, to prevail upon her father's good nature, answered with an oath, "That she could not otherwise express her thoughts, but that she loved him above all creatures." The credulous father upon this made her the same promise that he did to her eldest sister, that is, the choice of a husband, with the third part of his kingdom. Bur Cordeilla, the youngest, understanding how easily he was satisfied with the flattering expressions of her sisters, was desirous to make trial of his affection after a different manner. "My, father," said she, "is there any daughter that can lover her father more than duty requires? In my opinion, whoever pretends it, must disguise her real sentiments under the veil of flattery. I have always loved you as a father, nor do I yet depart from my purposed duty; and if you insist to have something more extorted from me hear now the greatness of my affection, which I always bear you, and take this for a short answer to all your questions; look how much you have, so, much is your value, and so much do I love you." The father, supposing that she spoke this out of the abundance of her heart, was highly provoked, and immediately replied, "Since you have so far despised my old age as not to think me worthy the love that your sisters express for me, you shall have from me the like regard, and shall be excluded from any share with your sisters in my kingdom. Notwithstanding, I do not say but that since you are my daughter, I will marry you to some foreigner, if fortune offers you any such husband; but will never, I do assure you, make it my business to procure so honourable a match for you as for your sisters; because, though I have hitherto loved you more than them, you have in requital thought me less worthy of your affection than they." And, without further delay, after consultation with his nobility he bestowed his two other daughters upon the Dukes of Cornwall and Albania, with half the island at present, but after his death, the inheritance of the whole monarchy of Britain.

It happened after this, that Aganippus, King of the Franks, having heard of the fame of Cordeilla's beauty, forthwith sent his ambassadors to the king to demand her in marriage. The father, retaining yet his anger towards her, made answer, "That he was very willing to bestow his daughter, but without either money or territories; because he had already given away his kingdom with all his treasure to his eldest daughters, Gonorilla and Regau." When this was told Aganippus, he, being very much in love with the lady, sent again to King Leir, to tell him, "That he had money and territories enough, as he possessed the third part of Gaul, and desired no more than his daughter only, that he might have heirs by her." At last the match was concluded; Cordeilla was sent to Gaul, and married to Aganippus.

12

Leir, finding the ingratitude of his two eldest daughters, betakes himself to his youngest, Cordeilla, in Gaul.

A LONG time after this, when Leir came to be infirm through old age, the two dukes, on whom he had bestowed Britain with his two daughters, fostered an insurrection against him, and deprived him of his kingdom, and of all regal authority, which he had hitherto exercised with great power and glory. At length, by mutual agreement, Maglaunus, Duke of Albania, one of his sons-in-law, was to allow him a maintenance at his own house, together with sixty soldiers, who were to be kept for state. After two years' stay with his son-in-law, his daughter Gonorilla grudged the number of his men, who began to upbraid the ministers of the court with their scanty allowance; and, having spoken to her husband about it, she gave orders that the numbers of her father's followers should be reduced to thirty, and the rest discharged. The father, resenting this treatment, left Maglaunus, and went to Henuinus, Duke of Cornwall, to whom he had married his daughter Regau. Here he met with an honourable reception, but before the year was at an end, a quarrel happened between the two families, which raised Regau's indignation; so that she commanded her father to discharge all his attendants but five, and to be contented with their service. This second affliction was insupportable to him, and made him return again to his former daughter, with hopes that the misery of his condition might move in her some sentiments of filial piety, and that he, with his family, might find a subsistence with her. But she, not forgetting her resentment, swore by the gods he should not stay with her, unless he would dismiss his retinue, and be contented with the attendance of one man; and with bitter reproaches she told him how ill his desire of vain-glorious pomp suited his age and poverty. When he found that she was by no means to be prevailed upon, he was at last forced to comply, and, dismissing the rest, to take up with one man only. But by this time he began to reflect more sensibly with himself upon the grandeur from which he had fallen, the miserable state to which he was now reduced, and to enter upon thoughts of going beyond sea to his youngest daughter. Yet he doubted whether he should be able to move her commiseration, because (as was related above) he had treated her so unworthily. However, disdaining to bear any longer such base usage, he took ship for Gaul. In his passage he observed he had only the third place given him among the princes that were with him in the ship, at which, with deep sighs and tears, he burst forth into the following complaint:

"O irreversible decrees of the Fates, that never swerve from your stated course! Why did you ever advance me to an unstable felicity, since the punishment of lost happiness is greater than the sense of present misery? The remembrance of the time when vast numbers of men obsequiously attended me in the taking of cities and wasting the enemy's countries, more deeply pierces my heart than the view of my present calamity, which has exposed me to the derision of those who were formerly prostrate at my feet. Oh! The enmity of fortune! Shall I ever again see the day when I may be able to reward those according to their deserts who have forsaken me in my distress? How true was thy answer, Cordeilla, when I asked thee concerning thy love to me, 'As much as you have, so much is your value, and so much do I love you.' While I had anything to give they valued me, being friends, not to me, but to my gifts: they loved me then, but they loved my gifts much more: when my gifts ceased, my friends vanished. But with what face shall I presume to see you my dearest daughter, since in my anger I married you upon worse terms than your sisters, who, after all the mighty favours they have received from me, suffer me to be in banishment and poverty?"

As he was lamenting his condition in these and the like expressions, he arrived at Karitia, where his daughter was, and waited before the city while he sent a messenger to inform her of the misery he was fallen into, and to desire her relief for a father who suffered both hunger and nakedness. Cordeilla was startled at the news and wept bitterly, and with tears asked how many men her father had with him. The messenger answered, he had but one man, who had been his armour-bearer, and was staying with him without the town. Then she took what money she thought might be sufficient, and gave it to the messenger, with orders to carry her father to another city, and there give out that he was sick, and provide for him bathing, clothes, and all other nourishment. She likewise gave orders that he should take into his service forty men, well clothed and accoutred, and that when all things were thus prepared he should notify his arrival to King Aganippus and his daughter. The messenger quickly returning, carried Leir to another city, and there kept him concealed, till he had done everything that Cordeilla had commanded.

13

He is honourably received by Coredeilla and the King of Gaul.

AS soon as he was provided with his royal apparel, ornaments, and retinue, he sent word to Aganippus and his daughter, that he was driven out of his kingdom of Britain by his sons-in-law, and was come to them to procure their assistance for recovering his dominions. Upon which they, attended with their chief ministers of state and the nobility of the kingdom, went out to meet him, and received him honourably, and gave into his management the whole power of Gaul, till such time as he should be restored to his former dignity.

14

Leir, being restored to the kingdom by the help of his son-in-law and Cordeilla, dies.

IN the meantime Aganippus sent officers over all Gaul to raise an army, to restore his father-in-law to his kingdom of Britain. Which done, Leir returned to Britain with his son and daughter and the forces which they had raised, where he fought with his sons-in-law and routed them. Having thus reduced the whole kingdom to his power, he died the third year after. Aganippus also died; and Cordeilla, obtaining the government of the kingdom, buried her father in a certain vault, which she ordered to be made for him under the River Sore, in Leicester, and which had been built originally under the ground to the honour of the god Janus. And here all the workmen of the city, upon the anniversary solemnity of that festival, used to begin their yearly labours.

15

Cordeilla, being imprisoned, kills herself. Margan, aspiring to the whole kingdom, is killed by Cunedagius.

AFTER a peaceful possession of the government for five years, Cordeilla began to meet with disturbances from the two sons of her sisters, being both young men of great spirit, whereof one, named Margan, was born to Maglaunus, and the other, named Cunedagius, to Henuinus. These, after the death of their fathers, succeeding them in their dukedoms, were incensed to see Britain subject to a woman, and raised forces in order to raise a rebellion against the queen; nor would they desist from hostilities, till, after a general waste of her countries, and several battles fought, they at last took her and put her in prison, where for grief and loss of her kingdom she killed herself. After this they divided the island between them; of which the part that reaches from the north side of the Humber to Caithness, fell to Margan; the other part from the same river westward was Cunedagius's share. At the end of two years, some restless spirits that took pleasure in the troubles of the nation, had access to Margan, and inspired him with vain conceits, by representing to him how mean and disgraceful it was for him not to govern the whole island, which was his due by right of birth. Stirred up with these and the like suggestions he marched with an army through Cunedagius's country, and began to burn all before him. The war thus breaking out, he was met by Cunedagius with all his forces, who attacked Margan, killing no small number of his men, and, putting him to flight, pursued him from one province to another, till at last he killed him in a town of Kambria, which since his death has been by the country people called Margan to this day.

After the victory, Cunedagius gained the monarchy of the whole island, which he governed gloriously for three and thirty years. At this time flourished the prophets Isaiah and Hosea, and Rome was built upon the eleventh before the Kalends of May by the two brothers, Romulus and Remus.

16

The successors of Cunedagius in the kingdom. Ferrex is killed by his brother, Porrex, in a dispute for the government.

AT last Cunedagius dying, was succeeded by his son Rivallo, a fortunate youth, who diligently applied himself to the affairs of the government. In his time it rained blood three days together, and there fell vast swarms of flies, followed by a great mortality among the people. After him succeeded Gurgustius his son; after him Sisillius; after him Jago, the nephew of Gurgustius; after him Kinmarcus the son of Sisillius; after him Gorbodugo, who had two sons, Ferrex and Porrex.

When their father grew old they began to quarrel about the succession; but Porrex, who was the most ambitious of the two, formed a design of killing his brother by treachery, which the other discovering, escaped, and passed over into Gaul. There he procured aid from Suard, King of the Franks, with which he returned and made war upon his brother; coming to an engagement, Ferrex was killed and all his forces cut to pieces. When their mother whose name was Widen, came to be informed of her son's death, she fell into a great rage, and conceived a mortal hatred against the survivor. For she had a greater affection for the deceased than for him, so that nothing would appease her indignation for his death, than her revenging it upon her surviving son. She took therefore her opportunity when he was asleep, fell upon him, and with the assistance of her women tore him to pieces. From that time a long civil war oppressed the people, and the island became divided under the power of five kings, who mutually harassed one another.

17

Dunwallo Molmutius gains the sceptre of Britain, from whom came the Molmutine laws.

AT length arose a youth of great spirit, named Dunwallo Molmutius, who was the son of Cloten, King of Cornwall, and excelled all the kings of Britain in valour and gracefulness of person. When his father was dead, he was no sooner possessed of the government of that country, than he made war against Ymner, King of Loegria, and killed him in battle. Hereupon Rudaucus, King of Kambria, and Staterius, King of Albania, had a meeting, wherein they formed an alliance together, and marched thence with their armies into Dunwallo's country to destroy all before them. Dunwallo met them with thirty thousand men, and gave them battle; and when a great part of the day was spent in the fight, and the victory yet dubious, he drew off six hundred of his bravest men, and commanded them to put on the armour of the enemies that were slain, as he himself also did, throwing aside his own. Thus accoutred he marched up with speed to the enemy's ranks, as if he was of their party, and approaching the very place where Rudaucus and Staterius were, commanded his men to fall upon them. But Dunwallo Molmutius, fearing lest in this disguise his own men might fall upon him, returned with his companions to put off the enemy's armour, and take his own again; and then encouraged them to renew the assault, which they did with great vigour, by dispersing and putting to flight the enemy. From hence he marched into the enemy's countries, destroyed their towns and cities, and reduced the people under his obedience. When he had made an entire reduction of the whole island, he prepared for himself a crown of gold, and restored the kingdom to its ancient state. This prince established what the Britons call the Molmutine laws, which are famous among the English to this day. In these, among other things, of which St. Gildas wrote a long time after, he enacted that the temples of the gods, as also cities, should have the privilege of giving sanctuary and protection to any fugitive or criminal, that should flee to them from the enemy. He likewise enacted, that the ways leading to those temples and cities, as also husbandman's ploughs, should be allowed the same privilege. So that in his day, the murders and cruelties committed by robbers were prevented, and everybody passed safe, without violence offered him. At last, after a reign of forty years spent in these and other acts of government, he died, and was buried in the city of Trinovantum, near the temple of Concord, which he himself built, when he first established his laws.

BOOK THREE

1

Brennius quarrels with Belinus his brother, and in order to make war against him, marries the daughter of the King of the Norwegians.

AFTER this a violent quarrel happened between his two sons, Belinus and Brennius, who were both ambitious of succeeding to the kingdom. The dispute was which of them should have the honour of wearing the crown. After a great many sharp conflicts that passed between them, the friends of both interposed, and brought them to agree on the division of the kingdom on these terms: that Belinus should enjoy the crown of the island, with the dominions of Loegria, Kambria and Cornwall, because, according to the Trojan constitution, the right of inheritance would come to him as the elder: and Brennius, as being the younger, should be subject to his brother, and have for his share Northumberland, which extended from the Humber to Caithness. The covenant therefore being confirmed upon these conditions, they ruled the country for five years in peace and justice. But such a state of prosperity could not long stand against the endeavours of faction. For some lying incendiaries gained access to Brennius and addressed him in this manner:

"What sluggish spirit has possessed you, that you can bear subjection to Belinus, to whom by parentage and blood you are equal; besides your experience in military affairs, which you have gained in several engagements, when you so often repulsed Cheulphus, general of the Morini, in his invasions of our country, and drove him out of your kingdom? Be no longer bound by a treaty which is a reproach to you, but marry the daughter of Elsingius, King of the Norwegians, that with his assistance you may recover your lost dignity." The young man, inflamed with these and the like specious suggestions, hearkened to them, and went to Norway, where he married the king's daughter, as his flatterers had advised him.

2

Brennius's sea-fight with Guichthlac, King of the Dacians. Guichthlac and Brennius's wife are driven ashore and taken by Belinus.

IN the meantime his brother, informed of this, was violently incensed, that without his leave he had presumed to act thus against him. Whereupon he marched into Northumberland, and possessed himself of that country and the cities in it, which he garrisoned with his own men. Brennius, upon notice given him of what his brother had done, prepared a fleet to return to Britain with a great army of Norwegians. But while he was under sail with a fair wind, he was overtaken by Guichthlac, King of the Dacians, who had pursued him. This prince had been deeply in love with the young lady that Brennius had married, and out of mere grief and vexation for the loss of her, had prepared a fleet to pursue Brennius with all expedition. In the sea-fight that happened on this occasion, he had the fortune to take the very ship in which the lady was, and brought her in among his companions. But during the engagement, contrary winds arose on a sudden, which brought on a storm, and dispersed the ships upon different shores: so that the King of the Dacians being driven up and down, after a course of five days arrived with the lady at Northumberland, under dreadful apprehensions, as not knowing upon what country this unforeseen casualty had thrown him. When this came to be known to the country people, they took them and carried them to Belinus, who was upon the sea-coast, expecting the arrival of his brother. There were with Guichthlac's ship three others, one of which had belonged to Brennius's fleet. As soon as they had declared to the king who they were, he was overjoyed at this happy accident, while he was endeavouring to revenge himself on his brother.

3

Belinus in a battle routs Brennius, who thereupon flees to Gaul.

A FEW days after appeared Brennius, with his fleet again got together, and arrived in Albania; and having received information of the capture of his wife and others, and that his brother had seized the kingdom of Northumberland in his absence, he sent his ambassadors to him, to demand the restitution of his wife and kingdom; and if he refused them, to declare that he would destroy the whole island from sea to sea, and kill his brother whenever he could come to an engagement with him. On the other hand, Belinus absolutely refused to comply with his demands, and assembling together the whole power of the island, went into Albania to give him battle. Brennius, upon advice that he had suffered a repulse, and that his brother was upon his march against him, advanced to meet him in a wood called Calaterium, in order to attack him. When they were arrived on the field of battle, each of them divided his men into several bodies, and approaching one another, began the fight. A great part of the day was spent in it, because on both sides the bravest men were engaged; and much blood was shed by reason of the fury with which they encountered each other. So great was the slaughter, that the wounded fell in heaps, like standing corn cut down by reapers. At last, the Britons prevailing, the Norwegians fled with their shattered troops to their ships, but were pursued by Belinus, and killed without mercy. Fifteen thousand men fell in the battle, nor were there a thousand of the rest that escaped unhurt. Brennius, with much difficulty securing one ship, went as fortune drove him to the coasts of Gaul; but the rest that attended him, were forced to skulk up and down wherever their misfortunes led them.

4

The King of Dacia, with Brennius's wife, is released out of prison.

BELINUS, after this victory, called a council of his nobility, to advice with them what he should do with the King of the Dacians, who had sent a message to him out of prison, that he would submit himself and the kingdom of Dacia to him, and also pay a yearly tribute, if he might have leave to depart with his mistress. He offered likewise to confirm his covenant with an oath, and the giving of hostages. When this proposal was laid before the nobility, they unanimously gave their assent that Belinus should grant Guichthlac his petition on the terms offered. Accordingly he did grant it, and Guichthlac was released from prison, and returned with his mistress into Dacia.

5

Belinus revives and confirms the Molmutine laws, especially about the highways.

BELINUS now finding no body in the kingdom of Britain able to make head against him, and being possessed of the whole island from sea to sea, confirmed the laws his father had made, and gave command for a settled execution of justice through his kingdom. But above all things he ordered that cities, and the roads leading to them, should enjoy the same privilege of peace that Dunwallo had established. But there arose a controversy about the roads, because the limits determining them were unknown. The king, therefore, willing to clear the law of all ambiguities, summoned all the workmen of the island together, and commanded them to pave a causeway of stone and mortar, which should run the whole length of the island, from the sea of Cornwall, to the shores of Caithness, and lead directly to the cities that lay upon that extent. He commanded another to be made over the breadth of the kingdom, leading from Menevia, that was situated upon the Demetian Sea, to Hamo's Port, and to pass through the interjacent cities. Two others he made obliquely through the island, for a passage to the rest of the cities. He then confirmed to them all honours and privileges, and prescribed a law for the punishment of any injury committed upon them. But if anyone is curious to know all that he decreed concerning them, let him read the Molmutine Laws, which Gildas the historian translated from British into Latin, and King Alfred into English.

6

Brennius, being made Duke of the Allobroges, returns to Britain to fight with his brother.

WHILE Belinus was thus reigning in peace and tranquility, his brother Brennius, who (as we said before) was driven upon the coasts of Gaul, suffered great torments of mind. For it was a great affliction for him to be banished from his country, and to have no power of returning to retrieve his loss. Being ignorant what course to take, he went among the princes of Gaul, accompanied only with twelve men; and when he had related his misfortune to every one of them, but could procure assistance from none, he went at last to Seginus, Duke of the Allobroges, from whom he had an honourable reception. During his stay here, he contracted such an intimacy with the duke, that he became the greatest favourite in the court. For in all affairs, both of peace and war, he showed a great capacity, so that the prince loved him with a paternal affection. He was besides of a graceful aspect, tall and slender in stature, and expert in hunting and fowling, as became his princely birth. So great was the friendship between them, that the duke resolved to give him his only daughter in marriage; and in case he himself should have no male issue, he appointed him and his daughter to succeed him in his dukedom of the Allobroges after his death. But if he should yet have a son, then he promised his assistance to advance him to the kingdom of Britain. Neither was this the desire of the duke only, but of all the nobility of his court, with whom he had very much ingratiated himself. So then without father delay the marriage was solemnized, and the princes of the country paid their homage to him, as the successor to the throne. Scarcely was the year at an end before the duke died; and then Brennius took his opportunity of engaging those princes of the country firmly in his interest, whom before he had obliged with his friendship. And this he did by bestowing generously upon them the duke's treasure, which had been hoarded up from the times of his ancestors. But that which the Allobroges most esteemed him for was his sumptuous entertainments, and keeping an open house for all.

7

Belinus and Brennius being made friends by the mediation of their mother, propose to subdue Gaul.

WHEN he had thus gained universal affection, he began to consult with himself how he might take revenge upon his brother Belinus. And when he had signified his intentions concerning it to his subjects, they unanimously concurred with him, and expressed their readiness to attend him to whatever kingdom he pleased to conduct them. He therefore soon raised a vast army, and having entered into a treaty with the Gauls for a free passage through their country into Britain, fitted out a fleet upon the coast of Neustria, in which he set sail, and with a fair wind arrived at the island. Upon hearing the rumour of his coming, his brother, Belinus, accompanied with the whole strength of the kingdom, marched out to engage him. But when the two armies were drawn out in order of battle, and just ready to begin the attack, Conwenna, their mother, who was yet living, ran in great haste through the ranks, impatient to see her son whom she had not seen for a long time. As soon, therefore, as she had with trembling steps reached the place where he stood, she threw her arms about his neck, and in transports kissed him; then uncovering her bosom, she addressed herself to him, in words interrupted with sighs, to this effect:

"My son, remember these breasts which gave you suck, and the womb wherein the Creator of all things formed you, and from whence he brought you forth into the world, while endured the greatest anguish. By the pains then which I suffered for you, I entreat you to hear my request: pardon your brother, and moderate your anger. You ought not to revenge yourself upon him who has done you no injury. As for what you complain of, that you were banished your country by him, if you duly consider the result, in strictness can it be called injustice? He did not banish you to make your condition worse, but forced you to quit a meaner that you might attain a higher dignity. At first you enjoyed only a part of a kingdom, and that in subjection to your brother. As soon as you lost that, you became his equal, by gaining the kingdom of the Allobroges. What has he then done, but raised you from a vassal to be a king? Consider farther, that the difference between you began not through him, but through yourself, who, with the assistance of the King of Norway, raised an insurrection against him."

Moved by these representations of his mother, he obeyed her with a composed mind, and putting off his helmet of his own accord, went straight with her to his brother. Belinus, seeing him approach with a peaceable countenance, threw down his arms, and ran to embrace him; so that now, without more ado, they again became friends; and disarming their forces marched with them peaceably together to Trinovantum. And here, after consultation what enterprise to undertake, they prepared to conduct their confederate army into the province of Gaul, and reduce that entire country to their subjection.

8

Belinus and Brennius, after the conquest of Gaul, march with their army to Rome.

THEY accordingly passed over into Gaul the year after, and began to lay waste that country. The news of which spreading through those several nations, all the petty kings of the Franks entered into a confederacy, and went out to fight against them. But the victory falling to Belinus and Brennius, the Franks fled with their broken forces; and the Britons and Allobroges, elevated with their success, ceased not to pursue them till they had taken their kings, and reduced them to their power. Then fortifying the cities which they had taken, in less than a year they brought the whole kingdom into subjection. At last, after a reduction of the provinces, they marched with their whole army towards Rome, and destroyed the cities and villages as they passed through Italy.

9

The Romans make a covenant with Brennius, but afterwards break it, for which reason Rome is besieged and taken by Brennius.

IN those days the two consuls of Rome were Gabius and Porsenna, to whose care the government of the country was committed. When they saw that no nation was able to withstand the power of Belinus and Brennius, they came, with the consent of the senate to them, to desire peace and amity. They likewise offered large presents of gold and silver, and to pay a yearly tribute, on condition that they might be suffered to enjoy their own in peace. The two kings therefore, taking hostages of them, yielded to their petition, and drew back their forces into Germany. While they were employing their arms in harassing that people, the Romans repented of their agreement, and again taking courage, went to assist the Germans. This step highly enraged the kings against them, who concerted measures how to carry on a war with both nations. For the greatness of the Italian army was a terror to them. The result of their council was, that Belinus with the Britons stayed in Germany, to engage with the enemy there; while Brennius and his army marched to Rome. Belinus had intelligence of it, and speedily marched with his army the same night, and possessing himself of a valley through which the enemy was to pass, lay hid there in expectation of their coming. The next day the Italians came in full march to the place; but when they saw the valley glittering with the enemy's armour, they were struck with confusion, thinking Brennius and the Galli Senones were there. At this favourable opportunity, Belinus on a sudden rushed forth, and fell furiously upon them; the Romans on the other hand, thus taken by surprised, fled the field, since they neither were armed, nor marched in any order. But Belinus gave them no quarter, and was only prevented by night coming on from making a total destruction of them. With this victory he went straight to Brennius, who had now besieged Rome three days. Then joining their armies, they assaulted the city on every side, and endeavoured to level the walls; and to strike a greater terror into the besieged, erected gibbets before the gates of the city, and threatened to hang up the hostages, whom they had given, unless they would surrender. But the Romans, nothing moved by the suffering of their sons and relations, continued inflexible, and resolute to defend themselves. They therefore sometimes broke the force of the enemy's engines, by other engines of their own, sometimes repulsed them from the walls with showers of darts. This so incensed the two brothers, that they commanded four and twenty of their noblest hostages to be hanged in the sight of their parents. The Romans, however, were only more hardened by the spectacle, and having received a message from Gabius and Porsenna, their consuls, that they would come the next day to their assistance, they resolved to march out of the city, and give the enemy battle. Accordingly, just as they were ranging their troops in order, the consuls appeared with their re-assembled forces, marching up to the attack, and advancing in a close body, fell on the Britons and Allobroges by surprise, and being joined by the citizens that sallied forth, killed no small number. The brothers, in great grief to see such destruction made of their fellow soldiers, began to rally their men, and breaking in upon the enemy several times, forced them to retire. In the end, after the loss of many thousands of brave men on both sides, the brothers gained the day, and took the city, not however till Gabius was killed and Porsenna taken prisoner. This done, they divided among their men all the hidden treasure of the city.

10

Brennius oppresses Italy in a most tyrannical manner. Belinus returns to Britain.

AFTER this complete victory, Brennius stayed in Italy, where he exercised unheard-of tyranny over the people. But the rest of his actions and his death, seeing that they are given in the Roman histories, I shall here pass over, to avoid prolixity and meddling in what others have treated of, which is foreign to my design. But Belinus returned to Britain, which he governed during the remainder of his life in peace; he repaired the cities that were falling to ruin, and built many new ones. Among the rest he built one upon the River Uske, near the sea of the Severn, which was for a long time called Caerosc, and was the metropolis of Dimetia; but after the invasion of the Romans it lost its first name, and was called the City of Legions, from the Roman legions which used to take up their winter quarters in it. He also made a gate of wonderful structure in Trinovantum, upon the bank of the Thames, which the citizens call after his name Billingsgate to this day. Over it he built a prodigiously large tower, and under it a haven or quay for ships. He was a strict observer of justice, and re-established his father's laws everywhere throughout the kingdom. In his days there was so great an abundance of riches among the people, that no age before or after is said to have shown the like. At last, when he had finished his days, his body was burned, and the ashes put up in a golden urn, which they placed at Trinovantum, with wonderful art, on the top of the tower above-mentioned.

11

Gurgiunt Brabtruc, succeeding his father Belinus, reduces Dacia, which was trying to shake off the yoke.

HE was succeeded by Gurgiunt Brabtruc, his son, a sober prudent prince, who followed the example of his father in all his actions, and was a lover of peace and justice. When some neighbouring provinces rebelled against him, inheriting with them the bravery of his father, he repressed their insolence in several fierce battles, and reduced them to a perfect subjection. Among many other things, it happened that the King of the Dacians, who paid tribute in his father's time, refused not only tribute, but all manner of homage to him. This he seriously resented, and passed over in a fleet to Dacia, where he harassed the people with a most cruel war, slew their king, and reduced the country to its former dependence.

12

*Ireland is given to be inhabited by the Barclenses,
who had been banished out of Spain.*

AT that time, as he was returning home from his conquest through the Orkney islands, he found thirty ships full of men and women; and upon his inquiring of them the occasion of their coming hither, their leader, named Partholoim, approached him in a respectful and submissive manner, and desired pardon and peace, telling him that he had been driven out of Spain, and was sailing round those seas in quest of a habitation. He also desired some small part of Britain to dwell in, that they might put an end to their tedious wanderings; for it was now a year and a half since he had been driven from his country, all of which time he and his company had been out at sea. When Gurgiunt Brabtruc understood that they came from Spain, and were called Barclenses, he granted their petition, and sent men with them to Ireland, which was then wholly uninhabited, and assigned it to them. There they grew up and increased in number, and have possessed that island to this very day. Gurgiunt Brabtruc after this ended his days in peace and was buried in the City of Legions, which, after his father's death, he ornamented with buildings and fortified with walls.

13

*Guithelin reigns after Gurgiunt Brabtruc, and the Martian law
is instituted by Martia, a noble woman.*

AFTER him Guithelin wore the crown, which he enjoyed all his life, treating his subjects with mildness and affection. He had for his wife a noble lady named Martia, accomplished in all kinds of learning. Among many other admirable productions of her wit, she was the author of what the Britons call the Martian law. This also, among other things, King Alfred translated, and called it in the Saxon tongue, Pa Marchitle Lage. Upon the death of Guithelin the government of the kingdom remained in the hands of this queen and her son Sisillius, who was then but seven years old, and therefore unfit to take the government upon himself alone.

14

Guithelin's successors in the kingdom.

FOR this reason the mother had the sole management of affairs committed to her, out of regard to her great sense and judgment. But on her death, Sisillius took the crown and government. After him reigned Kimarus his son, to whom succeeded Danius his brother. After his death the crown came to Morvidus, whom he had by his concubine Tangustela. He would have been a prince of extraordinary worth, had he not been addicted to immoderate cruelty, so far that in his anger he spared nobody if any weapon were at hand. He was of a graceful aspect, extremely liberal, and of such vast strength as not to have his match in the whole kingdom.

15

Morvidus, a most cruel tyrant, after the conquest of the King of the Morini, is devoured by a monster.

IN his time a certain king of the Morini arrived with a great force in Northumberland, and began to destroy the country. But Morvidus, with all the strength of the kingdom, marched out against him, and fought him. In this battle he alone did more than the greatest part of his army, and after the victory, suffered none of the enemy to escape alive. For he commanded them to be brought to him one after the other, that he might satisfy his cruelty in seeing them killed; and when he grew tired of this, he gave orders that they should be flayed alive and burned. During these and other monstrous acts of cruelty, an accident happened which put a period to his wickedness. There came from the coasts of the Irish Sea, a most cruel monster, that was continually devouring the people on the sea-coasts. As soon as he heard of it, he ventured to go and encounter it alone;

when he had in vain spent all his darts upon it, the monster rushed upon him, and with open jaws swallowed him up like a small fish.

16

Gorbonian, a most just king of the Britons.

HE had five sons, whereof the eldest, Gorbonian, ascended the throne. There was not in his time a greater lover of justice and equity, or a more careful ruler of the people. The performance of due worship to the gods, and doing justice to the common people, were his continual employments. Through all the cities of Britain, he repaired the temples of the gods, and built many new ones. In all his days, the island abounded with riches, more than all the neighbouring countries. For he gave great encouragement to husbandmen in their tillage, by protecting them against any injury or oppression of their lords; and the soldiers he amply rewarded with money, so that no one had occasion to do wrong to another. Amidst these and many other acts of his innate goodness, he paid the debt of nature, and was buried at Trinovantum.

17

Arthgallo is deposed by the Britons, and is succeeded by Elidure, who restores him again his kingdom.

AFTER him Arthgallo, his brother, was dignified with the crown, and in all his actions he was the very reverse of his brother. He everywhere endeavoured to depress the nobility, and advance the baser sort of the people. He plundered the rich, and by those means amassed vast treasures. But the nobility, disdaining to bear his tyranny any longer, made an insurrection against him, and deposed him; and then advanced Elidure, his brother, who was afterwards surnamed the Pious, on account of his commiseration to Arthgallo in distress. For after five years' possession of the kingdom, as he happened to be hunting in the wood Calaterium, he met his brother that had been deposed. For he had traveled over several kingdoms to desire assistance for the recovery of his lost dominions, but had procured none. And being no longer able to bear the poverty to which he was reduced, he returned back to Britain, attended only by ten men, with a design to repair to those who had been formerly his friends. It was at this time, as he was passing through the wood, his brother Elidure, who little expected it, got sight of him, and forgetting all injuries, ran to him, and affectionately embraced him. Now as he had long lamented his brother's affliction, he carried him with him to the city Alclud, where he hid him in his bed-chamber. After this, he feigned himself sick, and sent messengers over the whole kingdom that they should come to visit him. Accordingly, when they were all met together at the city where he lay, he gave orders that they should come into his chamber one by one, softly, and without noise: his pretense for which was that their talk would be a disturbance to his head, should they all crowd in together. Thus, in obedience to his commands, and without the least suspicion of any design, they entered his house one after another. But Elidure had given charge to his servants, who were set ready for the purpose, to take each of them as they entered, and cut off their heads unless they would again submit themselves to Arthgallo his brother. Thus did he with every one of them apart, and compelled them, through fear, to be reconciled to Arthgallo. At last the agreement being ratified, Elidure conducted Arthgallo to York, where he took the crown from his own head, and put it on that of his brother. From this act of extraordinary affection to his brother, he obtained the surname of Pious. Arthgallo after this reigned ten years, and made amends for his former maladministration, by pursuing measures of an entirely opposite tendency, in depressing the baser sort, and advancing men of good birth; in suffering everyone to enjoy his own, and exercising strict justice towards all men. At last sickness seizing him, he died, and was buried in the city Kaerleir.

18

Elidure is imprisoned by Peredure, after whose death he is a third time advanced to the throne.

THEN Elidure was again advanced to the throne, and restored to his former dignity. But while in his government he followed the example of his eldest brother Gorbonian, in performing all acts of grace; his two remaining brothers, Vigenius and Peredure, raised an army, and made war against him in which they proved victorious; so that they took him prisoner, and shut him up in the tower at Trinovantum, where they placed a guard over him. Then they divided the kingdom betwixt them; that part which is from the River Humber westward falling to Vigenius's share, and the remainder with all Albania to Peredure's. After seven years Vigenius died, and so the whole kingdom came to Peredure, who from that time governed the people with generosity and mildness, so that he even excelled his older brothers who had preceded him, nor was any mention now made of Elidure. But irresistible fate at last removed him suddenly, and so made way for Elidure's release from prison, and advancement to the throne the third time; who finished the course of his life in just and virtuous actions, and after death left an example of piety to his successors.

19

The names of Elidure's thirty-three successors.

ELIDURE being dead, Gorbonian's son enjoyed the crown and imitated his uncle's wise and prudent government. For he abhorred tyranny, and practiced justice and mildness towards the people, nor did he ever swerve from the rule of equity. After him reigned Margan, the son of Arthgallo, who, being instructed by the examples of his immediate predecessors, held the government in peace. To him succeeded Enniaunus, his brother, who took a contrary course, and in the sixth year of his reign was deposed for having preferred a tyrannical to a just and legal administration. In his room was placed his kinsman Idwallo, the son of Vigenius, who, being admonished by Enniaunus's ill success, became a strict observer of justice and equity. To him succeeded Runno, the son of Peredure, whose successor was Geruntius, the son of Elidure. After him reigned Catellus, his son; after Catellus, Coillus; after Coillus, Porrex; after Porrex, Cherin. This prince had three sons, Fulgenius, Eldadus, and Andragius, who all reigned one after the other. Then succeeded Urianus, the son of Andragius; after whom reigned in order, Eliud, Cledaucus, Cletonus, Gurgintius, Merianus, Bleduno, Cap, Oenus, Sisillius, and Blegabred. This last prince, in singing and playing upon musical instruments, excelled all the musicians that had been before him, so that he seemed worthy of the title of the God of Jesters. After him reigned Arthmail, his brother; after Arthmail, Eldol; to whom succeeded in order, Redion, Rederchius, Samuil, Penissel, Pir, Capoir, and Cligueillus the son of Capoir, a man prudent and mild in all his actions, and who above all things made it his business to exercise true justice among his people.

20

Heli's three sons; the first of whom, viz. Lud, gives name to the city of London.

NEXT to him succeeded his son Heli, who reigned forty years. He had three sons, Lud, Cassibellaun, and Nennius; of whom Lud, being the eldest, succeeded to the kingdom after his father's death. He became famous for the building of cities, and for rebuilding the walls of Trinovantum, which he also surrounded with innumerable towers. He likewise commanded the citizens to build houses, and all other kinds of structures in it, so that no city in all foreign countries to a great distance round could show more beautiful palaces. He was withal a warlike man, and very magnificent in his feasts and public entertainments. And though he had many other cities, yet he loved this above them all, and resided in it the greater part of the year; for which reason it was afterwards called Kaerlud, and by the corruption of the word, Kaer-london; and again by change of languages, in process of time, London; as also by foreigners who arrived here, and reduced this country under their subjection, it was called Londres. At last, when he was dead, his body was buried by the gate which to this time is called in the British tongue after his name, Parthlud, and in the Saxon, Ludesgata. He had two sons, Androgeus and Tenuantius, who were incapable of governing on account of their age: and therefore their uncle Cassibeallaun was preferred to the kingdom in their room. As soon as he was crowned, he began to display his generosity and magnificence to such a degree, that his fame reached to distant kingdoms; which was the reason that the monarchy of the whole kingdom came to be invested in him, and not in his nephews. Nothwithstanding Cassibellaun, from an impulse of piety, would not suffer them to be without their share in the kingdom, but assigned a large part of it to them. For he bestowed the city of Trinovantum, with the dukedom of Kent, on Androgeus; and the dukedom of Cornwall on Tenuantius. But he himself, as possessing the crown, had the sovereignty over them, and all the other princes of the island.

BOOK FOUR

1

Julius Caesar invades Britain.

ABOUT this time it happened, (as can be found in the Roman Histories) that Julius Caesar, having subdued Gaul, came to the shore of the Ruteni. And when from thence he had got a prospect of the island of Britain, he inquired of those about him what country it was, and what people inhabited it. Then fixing his eyes upon the ocean, as soon as he was informed of the name of the kingdom and the people, he said: "In truth we Romans and the Britons have the same origin, since both are descended from the Trojan race. Our first father, after the destruction of Troy, was Aeneas; theirs, Brutus, whose father was Sylvius, the son of Ascanius, the son of Aeneas. But I am deceived, if they are not very much degenerated from us, and know nothing of the art of war, since they live separated by the ocean from the whole world. The may be easily forced to become our tributaries, and subjects to the Roman state. Before the Romans offer to invade or assault them, we must send them word that they pay tribute as other nations do, and submit themselves to the senate; for fear we should violate the ancient nobility of our father Priamus, by shedding the blood of our kinsmen." All of which he accordingly took care to signify in writing to Cassibellaun; who in great indignation returned him an answer in the following letter.

2

Cassibellaun's letter to Julius Caesar.

"CASSIBELLAUN, King of the Britons, to Caius Julius Caesar. We cannot but wonder, Caesar, at the avarice of the Roman people, since their insatiable thirst for money cannot let us alone, though the dangers of the ocean have placed us in a manner out of the world; but they must have the presumption to covet our substance, which we have hitherto enjoyed in quiet. Neither is this indeed sufficient: we must also choose subjection and slavery to them, before the enjoyment of our native liberty. Your demand, therefore, Caesar, is scandalous, since the same vein of nobility flows from Aeneas in both Britons and Romans, and one and the same chain of consanguinity unites us: which ought to be a band of firm union and friendship. It was that, which you should have demanded of us, and not slavery: we have learned to admit of the one, but never to bear the other. And so much have we been accustomed to liberty, that we are perfectly ignorant what it is to submit to slavery. And even if the gods themselves should attempt to deprive us of our liberty, we would, to the utmost of our power, resist them in defense of it. Know then, Caesar, that we are ready to fight for that and our kingdom, if, as you threaten, you shall attempt to invade Britain."

3

Caesar is routed by Cassibellaun.

ON receiving this answer, Caesar made ready his fleet, and waited for a fair wind to execute his threats against Cassibellaun. As soon as the wind stood fair, he hoisted his sails, and arrived with his army at the mouth of the River Thames. The ships were now just come close to land, when Cassibellaun with all his forces appeared on his march against them, and coming to the town of Dorobellum, he consulted with his nobility how to drive out the enemy. There was present with him Belinus, general of his army, by whose counsel the whole kingdom was governed. There were also his two nephews, Androgeus, Duke of Trinovantum, and Tenuantius Duke of Cornwall, together with three inferior kings, Cridious, King of Albania, Guerthaeth of Venedotia, and Britael of Dimetia, who, as they had encouraged the rest to fight the enemy, gave their advice to march directly to Caesar's camp, and drive them out of the country before they could take any city or town. For if he should possess himself of any fortified places, they said it would be more difficult to force him out, because he would then know whither to make a retreat with his men. To this proposal they all agreed, and advanced towards the shore where Julius Caesar had pitched his camp. And now both armies drew out in order of battle, and began the fight, wherein both bows and swords were employed. Immediately the wounded fell in heaps on each side, and the ground was drenched with the blood of the slain, as much as if it had been washed with the sudden return of the tide. While the armies were thus engaged, it happened that Nennius and Androgeus, with the citizens of Canterbury and Trinovantum, whom they commanded, had the fortune to meet with the troop in which Caesar himself was present. And upon an assault made, the general's cohort was very nearly routed by the Britons falling upon them in a close body. During this action, fortune gave Nennius an opportunity of encountering Caesar. Nennius therefore boldly made up to him, and was in great joy that he could but give so much as one blow to so great a man. On the other hand, Caesar being aware of his design, stretched out his shield to receive him, and with all his might struck him upon the helmet with his drawn sword, which he lifted up again with an intention to finish his first blow, and make it mortal; but Nennius carefully prevented him with his shield, upon which Caesar's sword glancing with great force from the helmet, became so firmly fastened therein, that when by the intervention of the troops they could no longer continue the encounter, the general was not able to draw it out again. Nennius, thus becoming master of Caesar's sword, threw away his own, and pulling the other out, made haste to employ it against the enemy. Whomsoever he struck with it, he either cut off his head, or left him wounded without hopes of recovery. While he was thus exerting himself, he was met by Labienus, a tribune, whom he killed in the very beginning of the encounter. At last, after the greatest part of the day was spent, the Britons poured in so fast, and made such vigorous efforts, that by the blessing of God they obtained the victory, and Caesar, with his broken forces, retired to his camp and fleet. The very same night, as soon as he had got his men together again, he went on board his fleet, rejoicing that he had the sea for his camp. And upon his companions dissuading him from continuing the war any longer, he acquiesced in their advice, and returned back to Gaul.

4

Nennius, the brother of Cassibellaun, being wounded in battle by Caesar, dies.

CASSIBELLAUN, in joy for this triumph, returned solemn thanks to God; and calling the companions of his victory together, amply rewarded every one of them, according as they had distinguished themselves. On the other hand, he was very much oppressed with grief for his brother Nennius, who lay mortally wounded, and at the very point of death. For Caesar had wounded him in the encounter, and the blow which he had given him proved incurable; so that fifteen days after the battle he died, and was buried at Trinovantum by the North Gate. His funeral obsequies were performed with regal pomp, and Caesar's sword put into the tomb with him, which he had kept possession of when struck into his shield in the combat.

The name of the sword was Crocea Mors (Yellow Death), as being mortal to every body that was wounded with it.

5

Caesar's inglorious return to Gaul.

AFTER this flight of Caesar, and his arrival on the Gallic coast, the Gauls attempted to rebel and throw off his yoke. For they thought he was so much weakened, that his forces could be no longer a terror to them. Besides, a general report was spread among them that Cassibellaun was now out at sea with a vast fleet to pursue him in his flight; on which account the Gauls, growing still more bold, began to think of driving him from their coasts. Caesar, aware of their designs, was not willing to engage in a doubtful war with a fierce people, but rather chose to go to all their first nobility with open treasures, and reconcile them with presents. To the common people he promised liberty, and the dispossessed the restitution of their estates, and to the slaves their freedom. Thus he that had insulted them before with the fierceness of a lion, and plundered them of all, now, with the mildness of a lamb, fawns on them with submissive abject speeches, and is glad to restore all again. To these acts of meanness he was forced to condescend till he had pacified them, and was able to regain his lost power. In the meantime not a day passed without reflecting upon his flight, and the victory of the Britons.

6

Cassibellaun forms a stratagem for sinking Caesar's ships.

AFTER two years were expired, he prepared to cross the sea again, and revenge himself on Cassibellaun, who having intelligence of his design, everywhere fortified his cities, repaired the ruined walls, and placed armed men at all the ports. In the River Thames, on which Caesar intended to sail up to Trinovantum, he caused iron and leaden stakes, each as thick as a man's thigh, to be fixed under the surface of the water that Caesar's ships might founder. He then assembled all the forces of the island, and took up his quarters with them near the sea-coasts in expectation of the enemy's coming.

7

Caesar a second time vanquished by the Britons.

AFTER he had furnished himself with all necessities, the Roman general embarked with a vast army, eager to revenge himself on a people that had defeated him; in which he undoubtedly would have succeeded, if he could but have brought his fleet safe to land; but this he was not able to do. For in sailing up the Thames to Trinovantum, the ships struck against the stakes, which so endangered them all on a sudden, that many thousands of men were drowned, while the ships being pierced sank into the river. Caesar, upon this, employed all his force to shift his sails, and hastened to get back again to land. And so those that remained, after a narrow escape, went on shore with him. Cassibellaun, who was present on the bank, with joy observed the disaster of the drowned, but grieved at the escape of the rest; and upon his giving a signal to his men, made an attack upon the Romans, who, nothwithstanding the danger they had suffered in the river, when landed, bravely withstood the Britons; and having no other fence to trust but their own courage, they made no small slaughter; but yet suffered a greater loss themselves than that which they were able to give the enemy. For their number was considerably diminished by their loss in the river; whereas the Britons being hourly increased with new recruits, were three times their number, and by that advantage defeated them. Caesar, seeing he could no longer maintain his ground, fled with a small body of men to his ships, and made the sea his safe retreat; and as the wind stood fair, he hoisted his sails, and steered to the shore of the Morini. From thence he repaired to a certain tower, which he had built at a place called Odnea before this second expedition into Britain. For he durst not trust the fickleness of the Gauls, who he feared would fall upon him a second time, as we have said already they did before, after the first flight he was forced to make before the Britons. And on that account he had built this tower for a refuge to himself, that he might be able to maintain his ground against a rebellious people if they should make insurrection against him.

8

Evelinus kills Hirelglas. Androgeus desires Caesar's assistance against Cassibellaun.

CASSIBELLAUN, elevated with joy for this second victory, published a decree to summon all the nobility of Britain with their wives to Trinovantum, in order to perform solemn sacrifices to their tutelary gods who had given them the victory over so great a commander. Accordingly, they all appeared, and prepared a variety of sacrifices, for which there was a great slaughter of cattle. At this solemnity they offered forty thousand cows, and a hundred thousand sheep, and also fowls of several kinds without number, besides thirty thousand wild beasts of several kinds. As soon as they had performed these solemn honours to their gods, they feasted themselves on the remainder, as was usual at such sacrifices, and spent the rest of the day and night in various plays and sports. Amidst these diversions, it happened that two noble youths, whereof one was nephew to the king, the other to Duke Androgeus, wrestled together, and afterwards had a dispute about the victory. The name of the king's nephew was Hirelglas, the other's Evelinus. As they were reproaching each other, Evelinus snatched up his sword and cut off the head of his rival. This sudden disaster put the whole court into a consternation, upon which the king ordered Evelinus to be brought before him, that he might be ready to undergo such punishment as the nobility should determine, and that the death of Hirelglas might be revenged upon him, if he were unjustly killed. Androgeus, suspecting the king's intentions, made answer that he had a court of his own, and that whatever should be alleged against his own men, ought to be determined there. If, therefore, he was resolved to demand justice of Evelinus, he might have it at Trinovantum, according to ancient custom. Cassibellaun, finding he could not attain his ends, threatened Androgeus to destroy his country with fire and sword, if he should not comply with his demands. But Androgeus, now incensed, scorned all compliance with him. On the other hand, Cassibellaun, in a great rage, hastened to make good his threats, and ravaged the country. This forced Androgeus to make use of daily solicitations to the king, by means of such as were related to him, or intimate with him, to divert his rage. But when he found these methods ineffectual, he began in earnest to consider how to oppose him. At last, when all other hopes failed, he resolved to request assistance from Caesar, and wrote a letter to him to this effect:

"Androgeus, Duke of Trinovantum, to Caius Julius Caesar, instead of wishing death as formerly, now wishes health. I repent that ever I acted against you, when you made war against the king. Had I never been guilty of such exploits, you would have vanquished Cassibellaun, who is so swollen with pride since his victory, that he is endeavouring to drive me out of his coasts, who procured him that triumph. Is this a fit reward for my services? I have settled him in an inheritance; and he endeavours to disinherit me. I have a second time restored him to the kingdom and he endeavours to destroy me. All this have I done for him in fighting against you. I call the gods to witness I have not deserved his anger, unless I can be said to deserve it for refusing to deliver up my nephew, whom he would have condemned to die unjustly. Of which, that you may be better able to judge, hear this account of the matter. It happened that for joy of the victory we performed solemn honours to our tutelary gods, in which after we had finished our sacrifices, our youth began to divert themselves with sports. Among the rest our two nephews, encouraged by the example of the others, entered the lists: and when mine had got the better, the other without any cause was incensed, and just going to strike him; but he avoided the blow, and taking him by the hand that held the sword, strove to wrest it from him. In this struggle the king's nephew happened to fall upon the sword's point, and died upon the spot. When the king was informed of it, he commanded me to deliver up the youth, that he might be punished for murder. I refused to do it; whereupon he invaded my provinces with all his forces, and has given me very great disturbance; flying, therefore, to your clemency, I desire your assistance, that by you I may be restored to my dignity, and by me you may gain possession of Britain. Let no doubts or suspicion of treachery in this matter detain you. Be influenced by the common motive of mankind; let past enmities beget a desire of friendship and after defeat make you more eager for victory."

9

Cassibellaun, being put to flight, and besieged by Caesar, desires peace.

CAESAR, having read the letter, was advised by his friends not to go into Britain upon a bare verbal invitation of the duke, unless he would send such hostages as might be for his security. Without delay, therefore, Androgeus sent his son Scaeva with thirty young noblemen nearly related to him. Upon delivery of the hostages, Caesar, relieved from his suspicion, reassembled his forces, and with a fair wind arrived at the port of Rutupi. In the meantime Cassibellaun had begun to besiege Trinovantum and ravage the country towns; but finding that Caesar was arrived, he raised the siege and hastened to meet him. As soon as he entered a valley near Dorobernia, he saw the Roman army preparing their camp: for Androgeus had conducted them to this place, for the convenience of making a sudden assault upon the city. The Romans, seeing the Britons advancing towards them, quickly flew to their arms, and placed themselves in their ranks. But Androgeus with five thousand men lay hid in a wood hard by, to be ready to assist Caesar, and spring forth on a sudden upon Cassibellaun and his party. Both armies now approached to begin the fight, some with bows and arrows, some with swords, so that much blood was shed on both sides, and the wounded fell down like leaves in autumn. While they were thus engaged, Androgeus sallied forth from the wood and fell upon the rear of Cassibellaun's army, upon which the hopes of the battle entirely depended. And now, what with the breach which the Romans had made through them just before, what with the furious interruption of their own countrymen, they were no longer able to stand their ground, but were obliged with their broken forces to quit the field.

Near the place stood a rocky mountain, on the top of which was a thick hazel wood. Hither Cassibellaun fled with his men after he found himself worsted; and having climbed up to the top of the mountain, bravely defended himself and killed the pursuing enemy. For the Roman forces with those of Androgeus pursued him to disperse his flying troops, and climbing up the mountain after them made many assaults, but all to little purpose; for the rockiness of the mountain and great height of its top was a defense to the Britons, and the advantage of higher ground gave them an opportunity of killing great numbers of the enemy. Caesar hereupon besieged the mountain the whole night, which had now overtaken them, and shut up all the avenues to it; intending to reduce the king by famine, since he could not do it by force of arms. Such was the wonderful valour of the British nation in those times, that they were able to put the conqueror of the world twice to flight and being ready to die for the defense of their country and liberty, they, even though defeated, withstood him whom the whole world could not withstand. Hence Lucan in their praise says of Caesar,

> "Territa quaesitis ostendit terga Britannis."
> With pride he fought the Britons, but when found,
> Dreaded their force, and fled the hostile ground.

Two days were now passed when Cassibellaun, having consumed all his provision, feared famine would oblige him to surrender himself prisoner to Caesar. For this reason he sent a message to Androgeus to make his peace with Julius, lest the honour of the nation might suffer by his being taken prisoner. He likewise represented that he did not deserve to be pursued to death for the annoyance he had given him. As soon as the messengers had told this to Androgeus, he made answer: "That prince deserves not to be loved, who in war is mild as a lamb, but in peace cruel as a lion. Ye gods of heaven and earth! Does my lord then condescend to entreat me now, whom before he took upon him to command? Does he desire to be reconciled and make his submission to Caesar, of whom Caesar himself had before desired peace? He ought therefore to have considered, that he who was able to drive so great a commander out of the kingdom, was able also to bring him back again. I ought not to have been so unjustly treated, who had then done him so much service, as well as now so much injury. He must be mad who either injures or reproaches his fellow soldiers by whom he defeats the enemy. The victory is not the commander's, but theirs who lose their blood in fighting for him. However, I will procure him peace if I can, for the injury which he has done me is sufficiently revenged upon him, since he sues for mercy to me."

10

Androgeus's speech to Caesar.

ANDROGEUS after this went to Caesar, and after a respectful salutation addressed him in this manner: "You have sufficiently revenged yourself upon Cassibellaun; and now let clemency take the place of vengeance. What more is there to be done than that he make his submission and pay tribute to the Roman state?" To this Caesar returned him no answer: upon which Androgeus said again; "My whole engagement with you, Caesar, was only to reduce Britain under your power, by the submission of Cassibellaun. Behold! Cassibellaun is now vanquished and Britain by my assistance become subject to you. What further service do I owe you? God forbid that I should suffer my sovereign who sues to me for peace, and makes me satisfaction for the injury which he has done me, to be in prison or in chains. It is no easy matter to put Cassibellaun to death while I have life; and if you do not comply with my demand, I shall not be ashamed to give him my assistance." Caesar, alarmed at these menaces of Androgeus, was forced to comply, on condition that he should pay a yearly tribute of three thousand pounds of silver. So then Julius and Cassibellaun from this time became friends, and made presents to each other. After this, Caesar wintered in Britain, and the following spring returned into Gaul. At length he assembled all his forces, and marched towards Rome against Pompey.

11

Tenuantius is made king of Britain after Cassibellaun.

AFTER seven years had expired, Cassibellaun died and was buried at York. He was succeeded by Tenuantius, Duke of Cornwall, and brother of Androgeus: for Androgeus was gone to Rome with Caesar. Tenuantius therefore, now wearing the crown, governed the kingdom with diligence. He was a warlike man, and a strict observer of justice. After him Kymbelinus, his son, was advanced to the throne, being a great soldier, and brought up by Augustus Caesar. He had contracted so great a friendship with the Romans, that he freely paid them tribute when he might have very well refused it. In his days was born our Lord Jesus Christ, by whose precious blood mankind was redeemed from the devil, under whom they had been before enslaved.

12

Upon Guiderius's refusing to pay tribute to the Romans, Claudius Caesar invades Britain.

KYMBELINUS, when he had governed Britain ten years, begat two sons, the elder named Guiderius, the other Arviragus. After his death the government fell to Guiderius. This prince refused to pay tribute to the Romans; for which reason Claudius, who was now emperor, marched against him. He was attended in this expedition by the commander of his army, who was called in the British tongue, Leuis Hamo, by whose advice the following war was to be carried on. This man, therefore, arriving at the city of Portcestre, began to block up the gates with a wall, and denied the citizens all liberty of passing out. For his design was either to reduce them to subjection by famine, or kill them without mercy.

13

Leuis Hamo, a Roman, by wicked treachery kills Guiderius.

GUIDERIUS, upon the news of Claudius's coming, assembled all the soldiery of the kingdom, and went to meet the Roman army. In the battle that ensued, he began the assault with great eagerness, and did more execution with his own sword than the greater part of his army. Claudius was now on the point of retreating to his ships, and the Romans very nearly routed, when the crafty Hamo, throwing aside his own armour, put on that of the Britons, and as a Briton fought against his own men. Then he exhorted the Britons to a vigourous assault, promising them a speedy victory. For he had learned their language and manners, having been educated among the British hostages at Rome. By these means he approached by little and little to the king, and seizing a favourable opportunity, stabbed him while under no apprehension of danger, and then escaped through the enemy's ranks to return to his men with the news of his detestable exploit. But Arviragus, his brother, seeing him killed, forthwith put on his brother's habiliments, and, as if he had been Guiderius himself, encouraged the Britons to stand their ground. Accordingly, as they knew nothing of the king's disaster they made a vigorous resistance, fought courageously, and killed no small number of the enemy. At last the Romans gave ground, and dividing themselves into two bodies, basely quitted the field. Caesar with one part, to secure himself, retired to his ships; but Hamo fled to the woods, because he had not time to get to his ships. Arviragus, therefore, thinking that Claudius fled along with him, pursued him with all speed, and did not leave off harassing him from place to place, till he overtook him on a part of the sea-coast, which, from the name of Hamo, is now called Southampton. There was at the same place a convenient haven for ships, and some merchant ships at anchor. And just as Hamo was attempting to get on board them Arviragus came upon him unawares, and forthwith killed him. And ever since that time the haven has been called Hamo's Port.

14

Arviragus, King of Britain, makes his submission to Claudius, who with his assistance conquers the Orkney islands.

IN the meantime, Claudius, with his remaining forces, assaulted the city above mentioned, which was then called Kaerperis, now Portcestre, and presently leveled the walls, and having reduced the citizens to subjection, went after Arviragus, who had entered Winchester. Afterwards he besieged that city, and employed a variety of engines against it. Arviragus, seeing himself in these straits, called his troops together, and opened the gates to march out and give him battle. But just as he was ready to begin the attack, Claudius, who feared the boldness of the king, and the bravery of the Britons, sent a message to him with a proposal of peace; choosing rather to reduce them by wisdom and policy, than run the hazard of a battle. To this purpose he offered a reconciliation with him, and promised to give him his daughter, if he would only acknowledge the kingdom of Britain subject to the Roman state. The nobility hereupon persuaded him to lay aside thoughts of war, and be content with Claudius's promise; representing to him at the same time, that it was no disgrace to be subject to the Romans, who enjoyed the empire of the whole world. By these and many other arguments he was prevailed upon to hearken to their advice, and make his submission to Caesar. After which Claudius sent to Rome for his daughter, and then, with the assistance of Arviragus, reduced the Orkneys and the provincial islands to his power.

15

Claudius gives his daughter Genuissa for a wife to Arviragus, and returns to Rome.

AS soon as the winter was over, those that were sent for Claudius's daughter returned with her, and presented her to her father. The damsel's name was Genuissa, and so great was her beauty, that it raised the admiration of all that saw her. After her marriage with the king, she gained so great an ascendant over his affections, that he in a manner valued nothing but her alone: insomuch that he was desirous to have the place honoured where the nuptials were solemnized, and moved Claudius to build a city upon it for a monument to posterity of so great and happy a marriage. Claudius consented to it, and commanded a city to be built, which after his name is called Kaerglou, that is Gloucester, to this day, and is situated on the confines of Dimetia and Loegria, upon the banks of the Severn. But some say that it derived its name from Duke Gloius, a son that was born to Claudius there, and to whom, after the death of Arviragus, fell the dukedom of Dimetia. The city being finished, and the island now enjoying peace, Claudius returned to Rome, leaving to Arviragus the government of the British islands. At the same time the apostle Peter founded the Church of Antioch; and afterwards coming to Rome, was bishop there, and sent Mark, the evangelist, into Egypt to preach the gospel which he had written.

16

Arviragus revolting from the Romans, Vespasian is sent into Britain.

AFTER the departure of Claudius, Arviragus began to show his wisdom and courage, to rebuild cities and towns, and to exercise so great authority over his own people that he became a terror to the kings of remote countries. But this so elevated him with pride that he despised the Roman power, disdained any longer subjection to the senate, and assumed to himself the sole authority in everything. Upon this news Vespasian was sent by Claudius to procure a reconciliation with Arviragus, or to reduce him to the subjection of the Romans. When, therefore, Vespasian arrived at the haven of Rutupi, Arviragus met him, and prevented him entering the port. For he brought so great an army along with him, that the Romans, for fear of his falling upon them, durst not come ashore. Vespasian upon this withdrew from that port, and shifting his sails arrived at the shore of Totness. As soon as he was landed, he marched directly to besiege Kaerpenhuelgoit, now Exeter; and after lying before it seven days, was overtaken by Arviragus and his army, who gave him battle. That day great destruction was made in both armies, but neither got the victory. The next morning, by the mediation of Queen Genuissa, the two leaders were made friends, and sent their men over to Ireland. As soon as winter was over, Vespasian returned to Rome, but Arviragus continued still in Britain. Afterwards, when he grew old, he began to show much respect to the senate, and to govern his kingdom in peace and tranquility. He confirmed the old laws of his ancestors, and enacted some new ones, and made very ample presents to all persons of merit. So that his fame spread over all Europe, and he was both loved and feared by the Romans, and became the subject of their discourse more than any king in his time. Hence Juvenal relates how a certain blind man, speaking of a turbot[1] that was taken, said:

> "Regem aliquem capies, aut de temone Britanno Decidet Arviragus."
> Arviragus shall from his chariot fall,
> Or thee his lord some captive king shall call.

In war none was more fierce than he, in peace none more mild, none more pleasing, or in his presents more magnificent. When he had finished his course of life, he was buried at Gloucester, in a certain temple which he had built and dedicated to the honour of Claudius.

17

Rodric, leader of the Picts, is vanquished by Marius.

HIS son Marius, a man of admirable prudence and wisdom, succeeded him in the kingdom. In his reign a certain king of the Picts, named Rodric, came from Scythia with a great fleet, and arrived in the north part of Britain, which is called Albania, and began to ravage that country. Marius therefore raising an army went in quest of him, and killed him in battle, and gained the victory; for a mon-

---

1   A large European flatfish

ument of which he set up a stone in the province, which from his name was afterwards called Westmorland after him, where there is an inscription retaining his memory to this day. He gave the conquered people that came with Rodric liberty to inhabit that part of Albania which is called Caithness that had been a long time desert and uncultivated. And as they had no wives, they desired to have the daughters and kinswomen of the Britons. But the Britons refused, disdaining to unite with such a people. Having suffered a repulse here, they sailed over into Ireland, and married the women of that country and by their offspring increased in number. But let thus much suffice concerning them, since I do not propose to write the history of this people, or of the Scots, who derived their original from them and the Irish. Marius, after he had settled the island in perfect peace, began to love the Roman people, paying the tribute that was demanded of him; and in imitation of his father's example practiced justice, law, peace, and everything that was honourable in his kingdom.

18

Marius dying, is succeeded by Coillus.

AS soon as he had ended his days, his son, Coillus took upon him the government of the kingdom. He had been brought up from his infancy at Rome, and having been taught the Roman manners, had contracted a most strict amity with them. He likewise paid them tribute, and declined making them any opposition, because he saw the whole world subject to them, and that no town or country was out of the limits of their power. By paying therefore what was required of him, he enjoyed his kingdom in peace: and no king ever showed greater respect to his nobility, not only permitting them to enjoy their own with quiet, but also binding them to him by his continual bounty and munificence.

19

Lucius is the first British king that embraces the Christian faith, together with his people.

COILLUS had but one son, named Lucius, who, obtaining the crown after his father's decease, imitated all his acts of goodness, and seemed to his people to be no other than Coillus himself revived. As he had made so good a beginning, he was willing to make a better end: for which purpose he sent letters to Pope Eleutherius, desiring to be instructed by him in the Christian religion. For the miracles which Christ's disciples performed in several nations wrought a conviction in his mind; so that being inflamed with an ardent love of the true faith, he obtained the accomplishment of his pious request. For that holy pope, upon receipt of this devout petition, sent to him two most religious doctors, Faganus and Duvanus, who, after they had preached concerning the incarnation of the Word of God, administered baptism to him, and made him a proselyte to the Christian faith. Immediately upon this, people from all countries, assembling together, followed the king's example, and being washed in the same holy laver, were made partakers of the kingdom of heaven. The holy doctors, after they had almost extinguished paganism over the whole island, dedicated the temples, that had been founded in honour of many gods, to the only God and his saints, and filled them with congregations of Christians. There were then in Britain eight and twenty flamens[2], as also three archflamens, to whose jurisdiction the other judges and enthusiasts were subject. These also, according to the apostolic command, were delivered from idolatry; and where they were flamens, they were made bishops, where archflamens, archbishops. The seats of the archflamens were at the three noblest cities, viz. London, York, and the City of Legions, which its old walls and buildings show to have been situated upon the River Uske in Glamorganshire. To these three, now purified from superstition, were made subject twenty-eight bishops with their dioceses. To the metropolitan of York were subject Deira

---

2   One of the principal kinds of priests in ancient Rome

and Albania, which the great River Humber divides from Loegria. To the metropolitan of London were subject Loegria and Cornwall. These two provinces the Severn divides from Kambria or Wales, which was subject to the City of Legions.

20

Faganus and Duvanus give an account to Rome, of what they had done in Britain.

AT last, when they had made an entire reformation here, the two prelates returned to Rome, and desired the pope to confirm what they had done. As soon as they had obtained a confirmation, they returned again to Britain, accompanied with many others, by whose doctrine the British nation was in a short time strengthened in the faith. Their names and acts are recorded in a book which Gildas wrote concerning the victory of Aurelius Ambrosius; and what is delivered in so bright a treatise, needs not to be repeated here in a meaner style.

BOOK FIVE

1

Lucius dies without issue, and is a benefactor to the churches.

IN the meantime, the glorious King Lucius highly rejoiced at the great progress which the true faith and worship had made in his kingdom, and permitted the possessions and territories which formerly belonged to the temples of the gods, to be converted to a better use, and appropriated to Christian churches. And because a greater honour was due to them than to the others, he made large additions of lands and manor-houses, and all kinds of privileges to them. Amidst these and other acts of his great piety, he departed this life in the city of Gloucester, and was honourably buried in the cathedral church in the hundred and fifty-sixth year after our Lord's incarnation. He had no issue to succeed him, so that after his decease there arose a dissension among the Britons, and the Roman power was much weakened.

2

Severus, a senator, subdues part of Britain; his war with Fulgenius.

WHEN this news was brought to Rome, the senate despatched Severus, a senator, with two legions, to reduce the country to subjection. As soon as he was arrived, he came to a battle with the Britons, part of whom he obliged to surrender to him, and the other part which he could not subdue he endeavoured to distress in several cruel engagements, and forced them to fly beyond Deira to Albania. Notwithstanding which they opposed him with all their might under the conduct of Fulgenius, and often made great slaughter both of their own countrymen and of the Romans. For Fulgenius brought to assistance all the people of the islands that he could find, and so frequently gained the victory. The emperor, not being able to resist the irruptions[3] which he made, commanded a wall to be built between Deira and Albania, to hinder his excursions upon them; they accordingly made one at the common charge from sea to sea, which for a long time hindered the approach of the enemy. But Fulgenius, when he was unable to make any longer resistance, made a voyage into Scythia to desire the assistance of the Picts towards his restoration. And when he had got together all the forces of that country, he returned with a great fleet into Britain, and besieged York. Upon this news being spread through the country, the greatest part of the Britons deserted Severus, and went over to Fulgenius. However this did not make Severus desist from his enterprise: but calling together the Romans, and the rest of the Britons that adhered to him, he marched to the siege, and fought with Fulgenius; but the engagement proving very sharp, he was killed with many of his followers: Fulgenius also was mortally wounded. Afterwards Severus

---

3   A sudden, violent, or forcible entry; a rushing or bursting in

was buried at York, which city was taken by his legions. He left two sons, Bassianus and Geta, whereof Geta had a Roman for his mother, but Bassianus a Briton. Therefore upon the death of their father the Romans made Geta king, favouring him on account of being a Roman by both his parents: but the Britons rejected him, and advanced Bassianus, as being their countryman by his mother's side. This proved the occasion of a battle between the two brothers, in which Geta was killed; and so Bassianus obtained the sovereignty.

3

Carausius advanced to be king of Britain.

AT that time there was in Britain one Carausius, a young man of mean birth, who, having given proof of his bravery in many engagements, went to Rome, and solicited the senate for leave to defend with a fleet the maritime coasts of Britain from the incursions of barbarians; which if they would grant him, he promised to do more for the honour and service of the commonwealth, than by delivering up to them the kingdom of Britain. The senate, deluded by his specious[4] promises, granted him his request, and so, with his commission sealed, he returned to Britain. Then by wicked practices getting a fleet together, he enlisted into his service a body of the bravest youths, and putting out to sea, sailed round the whole kingdom, causing very great disturbance among the people. In the meantime he invaded the adjacent islands, where he destroyed all before him, countries, cities, and towns, and plundered the inhabitants of all they had. By this conduct he encouraged all manner of dissolute fellows to flock to him in the hope of plunder, and in a very short time was attended by an army which no neighbouring prince was able to oppose. This made him begin to swell with pride, and to propose to the Britons that they should make him their king; for which consideration he promised to kill and banish the Romans, and free the whole island from the invasions of barbarous nations. Accordingly obtaining his request, he fell upon Bassianus and killed

---

4   Having a false look of truth or genuineness

him, and then took upon him the government of the kingdom. For Bassianus was betrayed by the Picts whom Flugenius, his mother's brother, had brought with him into Britain, and who being corrupted by the promises and presents of Carausius, instead of assisting Bassianus, deserted him in the very battle, and fell upon his men; so that the rest were put into a consternation, and not knowing their friends from their foes, quickly gave ground, and left the victory to Carausius. Then he, to reward the Picts for this success, gave them a habitation in Albania where they continued afterwards mixed with the Britons.

4

Allectus kills Carausius, but is afterwards himself slain in flight by Asclepiodotus.

WHEN the news of these proceedings of Carausius arrived in Rome, the senate commissioned Allectus, with three legions, to kill the tyrant, and restore the kingdom of Britain to the Roman power. No sooner was he arrived, than he fought with Carausius, killed him, and took upon himself the government. After which he miserably oppressed the Britons for having deserted the commonwealth, and adhered to Carausius. But the Britons, not enduring this, advanced Asclepiodotus, Duke of Cornwall, to be their king, and then unanimously marched against Allectus, and challenged him to battle. He was then at London, celebrating a feast to his tutelary gods; but being informed of the coming of Asclepiodotus, he quitted the sacrifice, and went out with all his forces to meet him, and engaged with him in a sharp fight. But Asclepiodotus had the advantage, and dispersed and put to flight Allectus's troops, and in the pursuit killed many thousands, as also King Allectus himself. After this victory, Livius Gallus, the colleague of Allectus, assembled the rest of the Romans, shut the gates of the city, and placed his men in the towers and other fortifications, thinking by these means either to make a stand against Asclepiodotus, or at least to avoid imminent death. But Asclepiodotus seeing this laid siege to the city, and sent word to all the dukes of Britain that he had killed Allectus with a great number of his men, and was besieging Gallus and the rest of the Romans in London; and therefore earnestly entreated them to hasten to his assistance, representing to them withal, how easy it was to extirpate the whole race of the Romans out of Britain, provided they would all join their forces against the besieged. At this summons came the Dimetians, Venedotians, Deirans, Albanians, and all others of the British race. As soon as they appeared before the duke, he commanded vast numbers of engines to be made to beat down the walls of the city. Accordingly everyone readily executed his orders with great bravery, and made a violent assault upon the city, the walls of which were in a very short time battered down, and a passage made into it. After these preparations, they began a bloody assault upon the Romans, who, seeing their fellow soldiers falling before them without intermission, persuaded Gallus to offer a surrender on the terms of having quarter granted them, and leave to depart: for they were now all killed except one legion which still held out. Gallus consented to the proposal, and accordingly surrendered himself and his men to Asclepiodotus, who was disposed to give them quarter; but he was prevented by a body of Venedotians, who rushed upon them, and the same day cut off all their heads upon a brook within the city, which from the name of the commander was afterwards called in the British tongue Nautgallim, and in the Saxon Gallembourne.

5

Asclepiodotus obtains the crown. Diocletian's massacre of the Christians in Britain.

THE Romans being thus defeated, Asclepiodotus, with the consent of the people, placed the crown upon his own head, and governed the country in justice and peace ten years, and curbed the insolence and outrages committed by plunderers and robbers. In his days began the persecutions of the emperor Diocletian; and Christianity, which from the time of King Lucius had continued fixed and undisturbed, was almost abolished over the whole island. This was principally owing to Maximianus Herculius, general of that tyrant's army, by whose command all the churches were pulled down, and all the copies of the Holy Scriptures that could be found were burned in the public markets. The priests, with the believers under their care, were put to death, and with emulation pressed in crowds together for a speedy passage to the joys of heaven, as their proper dwelling place. God therefore magnified his goodness to us, for as much as he did, in that time of persecution, of his mere grace, light up the bright lamps of the holy martyrs to prevent the spreading of gross darkness over the people of Britain; whose sepulchres and places of suffering might have been a means of inflaming our minds with the greatest fervency of divine love, had not the deplorable impiety of barbarians deprived us of them. Among others of both sexes who continued firm in the army of Christ, and suffered, were Alban of Verulam, and Julius and Aaron, both of the City of Legions. Of these, Alban, out of the fervour of his charity, when his confessor, Amphibalus, was pursued by the persecutors, and just ready to be apprehended, first hid him in his house, and then offered himself to die for him imitating in this Christ himself, who laid down his life for his sheep. The other two, after being torn limb from limb, in a manner unheard of, received the crown of martyrdom, and were elevated up to the gates of heavenly Jerusalem.

6

An insurrection against Asclepiodotus by Coel, whose daughter, Helena, Constantius marries.

IN the meantime Coel, Duke of Kaercolvin or Colchester, made an insurrection against King Asclepiodotus, and in a pitched battle, killed him, and took possession of his crown. The senate, hearing this, rejoiced at the king's death who had given such disturbance to the Roman power and, reflecting on the damage which they had sustained by the loss of this kingdom, they sent Constantius the senator, a man of prudence and courage, who had reduced Spain under their subjection, and who was above all the rest industrious to promote the good of the commonwealth. Coel, having information of his coming, was afraid to stand before him. Therefore, as soon as Constantius was arrived at the island, Coel sent ambassadors to him with offers of peace and submission, on condition that he should enjoy the kingdom of Britain, and pay no more than the usual tribute to the Roman state. Constantius consented to this proposal and so upon their giving hostages, peace was confirmed between them. The month after Coel was seized with a very great sickness, of which he died within eight days. After his decease, Constantius himself was crowned, and married the daughter of Coel, whose name was Helena. She surpassed all the ladies of the country in beauty, as she did all the others of the time in her skill in music and the liberal arts. Her father had no other issue to succeed him on the throne; for which reason he was very careful about her education, that she might be better qualified to govern the kingdom. Constantius, therefore, having made her partner of his bed, had a son by her called Constantine. After eleven years were expired, he died at York, and bestowed the kingdom upon his son, who, within a few years after he was raised to this dignity, began to give proofs of heroic virtue, undaunted courage, and strict observance of justice towards his people. He put a stop to the depredations of robbers, suppressed the insolence of tyrants, and endeavoured everywhere to restore peace.

7

The Romans desire Constantine's assistance against the cruelty of Maxentius.

AT that time there was a tyrant at Rome, named Maxentius, who made it his endeavour to confiscate the estates of all the best of the nobility, and oppressed the commonwealth with his grievous tyranny. Whilst he, therefore, was proceeding in his cruelty, those that were banished fled to Constantine in Britain and were honourably entertained by him. At last, when a great many such had resorted to him, they endeavoured to raise in him an abhorrence of the tyrant, and frequently expostulated with him after this manner: "How long, Constantine, will you suffer our distress and banishment? Why do you delay to restore us to our native country? You are the only person of our nation that can restore to us what we have lost, by driving out Maxentius. For what prince is to be compared with the King of Britain, either for brave and gallant soldiers, or for large treasures? We entreat you to restore us to our estates, wives, and children, by conducting us with an army to Rome."

8

Constantine, having reduced Rome, obtains the empire of the world. Octavius, Duke of the Wisseans, is put to flight by Trahern.

CONSTANTINE, moved with these and the like speeches, made an expedition to Rome, and reduced it under his power, and afterwards obtained the empire of the whole world. In this expedition he carried along with him three uncles of Helena, viz. Leolin, Trahern, and Marius, and advanced them to the degree of senators. In the meantime Octavius, Duke of the Wisseans, rebelled against the Roman proconsuls, to whom the government of the island had been committed, and having killed them, took possession of the throne. Constantine, upon information of this, sent Trahern, the uncle of Helena, with three legions to reduce the island. Trahern came to shore near the city, which in the British tongue is called Kaerperis, and having assailed it, took it in two days. This news spreading over the whole country, King Octavius assembled all the forces of the land, and went to meet him not far from Winchester, in a field called in the British tongue Maisuriam,, where he engaged with him in battle, and routed him. Trahern, upon this loss, betook himself with his broken forces to his ships, and in them made a voyage to Albania, in the provinces of which he made great destruction. When Octavius received intelligence of this, he followed him with his forces, and encountered him in Westmorland, but fled, having lost the victory. On the other hand, Trahern, when he found the day was his own, pursued Octavius, nor ever suffered him to be at rest till he had dispossessed him both of his cities and crown. Octavius, in great grief for the loss of his kingdom, went with his fleet to Norway to obtain assistance from King Gombert. In the meantime he had given orders to his most intimate adherents to watch carefully all opportunities of killing Trahern, which accordingly was not long after done by the magistrate of a certain privileged town, who had a more than ordinary love for him. For as Trahern was one day upon a journey from London, he lay hid with a hundred men in the vale of a wood, through which he was to pass, and there fell upon him unawares, and killed him in the midst of his men. This news being brought to Octavius, he returned back to Britain, where he dispersed the Romans, and recovered the throne. In a short time after this, he arrived to such greatness and wealth that he feared nobody and possessed the kingdom until the reign of Gratian and Valentinian.

9

Maximian is desired for a king of Britain.

AT last, in his old age, being willing to settle the government, he asked his council which of his family they desired to have for their king after his decease. For he had no son, and only one daughter, to whom he could leave the crown. Some, therefore, advised him to bestow his daughter with the kingdom upon some noble Roman, to the end that they might enjoy a firmer peace. Others were of the opinion that Conan Meriadoc, his nephew, ought to be preferred to the throne, and the daughter married to some prince of another kingdom with a dowry in money. While these things were in agitation among them, there came Caradoc, Duke of Cornwall, and gave his advice to invite over Maximian the senator, and to bestow the lady with the kingdom upon him, which would be a means of securing to them a lasting peace. For his father Leolin, the uncle of Constantine, whom we mentioned before, was a Briton, but by his mother and place of birth he was a Roman, and by both parents he was descended of royal blood. And there was a sure prospect of a firm and secure peace under him, on account of the right which he had to Britain by his descent from the emperors, and also from the British blood. But the Duke of Cornwall, by delivering this advice, brought upon himself the displeasure of Conan, the king's nephew, who was very ambitious of succeeding to the kingdom, and put the whole court into confusion about it. However, Caradoc, being unwilling to recede from his proposal, sent his son Mauricius to Rome to acquaint Maximian with what had passed. Mauricius was a person of large and well-proportioned stature, as well as great courage and boldness, and could not bear to have his judgment contradicted without recourse to arms and dueling. On presenting himself before Maximian, he met with a reception suitable to his quality, and had the greatest honours paid him of any that were about him. There happened to be at that time a great contest between Maximian and the two emperors, Gratian and Valentinian, on account of his being refused the third part of the empire, which he demanded. When, therefore, Mauricius saw Maximian ill-treated by the emperors, he took occasion from thence to address him in this manner: "Why need you, Maximian, stand in fear of Gratian, when you have so fair an opportunity of wresting the empire from him? Come with me into Britain, and you shall take possession of that crown. For King Octavius, being now grown old and infirm, desires nothing more than to find some such proper person to bestow his kingdom and daughter upon. He has no male issue, and therefore has asked the advice of the nobility to whom he should marry his daughter with the kingdom: and they to his satisfaction have passed a decree, that the kingdom and lady be given to you, and have sent me to acquaint you with it. So that if you go with me, and accomplish this affair, you may with the treasure and forces of Britain be able to return back to Rome, drive out the emperors, and gain the empire to yourself. For in this manner did your kinsman Constantius, and several others of our kings who raised themselves to the empire.

10

Maximian, coming into Britain, artfully declines fighting with Conan.

MAXIMIAN was pleased with the offer, and took his journey to Britain; but in his way subdued the cities of the Franks by which he amassed a great treasure of gold and silver, and raised men for his service in all parts. Afterwards he set sail with a fair wind, and arrived at Hamo's Port; the news of which struck the king with fear and astonishment, who took this to be a hostile invasion. Whereupon he called to him his nephew Conan, and commanded him to raise all the forces of the kingdom, and go and meet the enemy. Conan, having made the necessary preparations, marched accordingly to Hamo's Port, where Maximian had pitched his tents, who upon seeing the approach of so numerous an army, was under the greatest perplexities what course to take. For as he was attended with a smaller body of men, and had no hopes of being entertained peaceably, he dreaded both the number and courage of the enemy. Under these difficulties he called a council of the oldest men, together with Mauricius, to ask their advice what was to be done at this critical juncture. "It is not for us," said Mauricius, "to hazard a battle with such a numerous and powerful army: neither was the reduction of Britain by arms the end of our coming. Our business must be to desire peace and a hospitable treatment till we can learn the king's mind. Let us say that we are sent by the emperors upon an embassy to Octavius, and let us with artful speeches pacify the people." When all had shown themselves pleased with this advice, he took with him twelve aged men with grey hairs, eminent beyond the rest for their quality and wisdom, and, bearing olive-branches in their right hands, went to meet Conan. The Britons, seeing they were men of venerable age, and that they bore olive-branches as a token of peace, rose up before them in a respectful manner, and opened a way for their free access to their commander. Then presenting themselves before Conan Meriadoc, they saluted him in the name of the emperors and the senate, and told him that Maximian was sent to Octavius upon an embassy from Gratian and Valentinian. Conan made answer: "Why is he then attended with so great a multitude? This does not look like the appearance of ambassadors, but the invasion of enemies." To which Mauricius replied: "It did not become so great a man to appear as a mean figure, or without soldiers for his guard; especially considering, that by reason of Roman power, and the actions of his ancestors, he is become obnoxious to many kings. If he had but a small retinue, he might have been killed by the enemies of the commonwealth. He is come in peace, and it is peace which he desires. For, from the time of our arrival, our behaviour has been such as to give no offence to any body. We have brought necessaries at our own expenses, as peaceable people do, and have taken nothing from any by violence." While Conan was in suspense, whether to give them peace, or begin the battle, Caradoc, Duke of Cornwall with others of the nobility, came to him, and dissuaded him from proceeding in the war after this representation; whereupon, though much against his will, he laid down his arms, and granted them peace. Thus he conducted Maximian to London, where he gave the king an account of the whole proceeding.

11

The kingdom of Britain is bestowed on Maximian.

CARADOC, after this, taking along with him his son Mauricius, commanded everybody to withdraw from the king's presence, and then addressed him in these words: "Behold, that which your more faithful and loyal subjects have long wished for, is now by the good providence of God brought about. You commanded your nobility to give their advice how to dispose of your daughter and kingdom, as being willing to hold the government no longer on account of your great age. Some, therefore, were for having the kingdom delivered up to Conan your nephew, and a suitable match procured for your daughter elsewhere; as fearing the ruin of our people, if any prince that is a stranger to our language should be set over us. Others were for granting the kingdom to your daughter and some nobleman of our own country, who should succeed you after your death. But the greater number recommended some person descended from the family of the emperors, on whom you should bestow your daughter and crown. For they promised themselves a firm and lasting peace, as the consequence of such a marriage, since they would be under the protection of the Roman state. See then! God has vouchsafed to bring to you a young man, who is both a Roman, and also of the royal family of Britain; and to whom, if you follow my advice, you will not delay to marry your daughter. And indeed, should you refuse him, what right could you plead to the crown of Britain against him? For he is the cousin of Constantine, and the nephew of King Coel, whose daughter Helena possessed the crown by an undeniable hereditary right." When Caradoc had represented these things to him, Octavius acquiesced, and with the general consent of the people bestowed the kingdom and his daughter upon him. Conan Meriadoc, finding how things went, was beyond all expression incensed, and, retiring into Albania, used all his interest to raise an army that he might give disturbance to Maximian. And when he had got a great body of men together, he passed the Humber, and wasted the provinces on each side of it. At the news whereof, Maximian hastened to assemble his forces against him, and then gave him battle, and returned with victory. But this proved no decisive blow to Conan, who with his re-assembled troops still continued to ravage the provinces, and provoked Maximian to return again and renew the war, in which he had various success, being sometimes victorious, sometimes defeated. At last, after great damages done to both sides, they were brought by the mediation of friends to a reconciliation.

12

Maximian overthrows the Armoricans: his speech to Conan.

FIVE years after this, Maximian, proud of the vast treasures that daily flowed in upon him, fitted out a great fleet, and assembled together all the forces in Britain. For this kingdom was not now sufficient for him; he was ambitious of adding Gaul also to it. With this view he set sail, and arrived first at the kingdom of Armorica, now called Bretagne, and began hostilities upon the Gallic people that inhabited it. But the Gauls, under the command of Imbaltus, met him, and engaged him in battle, in which the greater part being in danger, they were forced to fly, and leave Imbaltus with fifteen thousand men killed, all of them Armoricans. This severe overthrow was matter of the greatest joy to Maximian, who knew the reduction of that country would be very easy after the loss of so many men. Upon this occasion he called Conan aside from the army, and smiling said: "See, we have already conquered one of the best kingdoms in Gaul; we may now have hopes of gaining all the rest. Let us make haste to take the cities and towns, before the rumours of their danger spread to the remoter parts of Gaul, and raise all the people up in arms. For if we can but get possession of this kingdom, I make no doubt of reducing all Gaul under our power. Be not therefore concerned that you have yielded up the island of Britain to me, nothwithstanding the hopes you once had of succeeding to it; because whatever you have lost in it, I will restore to you in this kingdom; and this shall be another Britain which we will people with our own countrymen, and drive out the old inhabitants. The land is fruitful in corn, the rivers abound with fish, the woods afford a beautiful prospect, and the forests are everywhere pleasant; nor is there in my opinion anywhere a more delightful country." Upon this, Conan, with a submissive bow, gave him his thanks, and promised to continue loyal to him as long as he lived.

13

Redonum taken by Maximian.

AFTER this they marched with their forces to Redonum and took it the same day. For the citizens, hearing of the bravery of the Britons, and what slaughter they had made, fled away with haste, leaving their wives and children behind them. And the rest of the cities and towns soon followed their example; so that there was an easy entrance into them for the Britons, who wherever they entered killed all they found left of the male sex, and spared only the women. At last, when they had wholly extirpated the inhabitants of all those provinces, they garrisoned the cities and towns with British soldiers and made fortifications in several places. The fame of Maximian's exploits spreading over the rest of the provinces of Gaul, all their dukes and princes were in a dreadful consternation, and had no other hopes left but in their prayers to their gods. Maximian, finding that he had struck terror into them, began to think of still bolder attempts, and by profusely distributing presents, augmented his army. For all persons that he knew to be eager for plunder, he enlisted into his service, and by plentifully bestowing his money and other valuable things among them, kept them firm to his interest.

14

Maximian, after the conquest of Gaul and Germany, makes Triers the seat of his empire.

BY these means he raised such a numerous army as he thought would be sufficient for the conquest of all Gaul. Notwithstanding which he suspended his arms for a time, till he had settled the kingdom which he had taken, and peopled it with Britons. To this end he published a decree for the assembling together of a hundred thousand of the common people of Britain, who were to come over to settle in the country; besides thirty thousand soldiers, to defend them from hostile attack. As soon as the people were arrived according to his orders, he distributed them through all the countries of Armorica, and made another Britain of it, and then bestowed it on Conan Meriadoc. But he himself, with the rest of his follow soldiers marched into the further part of Gaul, which, after many bloody battles, he subdued, as he did also all Germany, being everywhere victorious. But the seat of his empire he made at Triers, and fell so furiously upon the two emperors, Gratian and Valentinian, that he killed the one, and forced the other to flee from Rome.

15

A fight between the Aquitanians and Conan.

IN the meantime, the Gauls and Aquitanians gave disturbance to Conan and the Armorican Britons, and harassed them with their frequent incursions; but he as often defeated them, and bravely defended the country committed to him. After he had entirely vanquished them, he had a mind to bestow wives on his fellow soldiers, by whom they might have issue to keep perpetual possession of the country; and to avoid all mixture with the Gauls, he sent over to the island of Britain for wives for them. In order to accomplish this, messengers were sent to recommend the management of this affair to Dianotus, King of Cornwall, who had succeeded his brother Caradoc in that kingdom. He was a very noble and powerful prince, and to him Maximian had committed the government while he was employed in affairs abroad. He had also a daughter of wonderful beauty, named Ursula, with whom Conan was most passionately in love.

16

Guanius and Melga murder eleven thousand virgins. Maximian is killed at Rome.

DIANOTUS, upon this message sent him by Conan, was very ready to execute his orders, and summoned together the daughters of the nobility from all provinces, to the number of eleven thousand; but of the meaner sort, sixty thousand; and commanded them all to appear together in the city of London. He likewise ordered ships to be brought from all shores for their transportation to their future husbands. And though in so great a multitude many were pleased with this order, yet it was displeasing to the greater part, who had a greater affection for their relations and native country. Nor, perhaps, were there wanting some who, preferring virginity to the married state, would rather have lost their lives in any country, than enjoyed the greatest plenty in wedlock. In short, most of them had views and wishes different from one another, had they been left on their own liberty. But now the ships being ready, they went on board, and sailing down the Thames, made towards the sea. At last, as they were steering towards the Armorican coast, contrary winds arose and dispersed the whole fleet. In this storm the greater part of the ships foundered; but the women that escaped the danger of the sea, were driven upon strange islands, and by a barbarous people either murdered or made slaves. For they happened to fall into the hands of the cruel army of Guanius and Melga, who, by the command of Gratian, were making terrible destruction in Germania, and the nations on the sea-coast. Guanius was King of the Huns, and Melga of the Picts, whom Gratian had engaged in his part and had sent into Germany to harass those of Maximian's party along the sea-coasts. While they were thus exercising their barbarous rage, they happened to light upon those virgins who had been driven on those parts, and were so inflamed with their beauty, that they courted them to their brutish embraces; which, when the women would not submit, the Ambrons fell upon them, and without remorse murdered the greatest part of them. This done, the two wicked leaders of the Picts and the Huns, Guanius and Melga, being the partisans of Gratian and Valentinian, when they had learned that the island of Britain was drained of all its soldiers, made a speedy voyage towards it; and, taking into their assistance the people of the adjacent islands, arrived in Albania. Then joining in a body, they invaded the kingdom, which was left without either a government or defense, and made miserable destruction among the common people. For Maximian, as we have already related, had carried away with him all the warlike youth that could be found, and had left behind him only the husbandmen, who had neither sense nor arms for the defense of their country. Guanius and Melga, finding that they were not able to make the least opposition, began to domineer most insolently, and to lay waste their cities and countries, as if they had only been pens of sheep. The news of this grievous calamity coming to Maximian, he sent away Gratian Municeps, with two legions to their assistance; who, as soon as they arrived, fought with the enemy, and after a most bloody victory over them forced them to fly over into Ireland. In the meantime, Maximian was killed at Rome by Gratian's friends, and the Britons whom he had carried with him were also slain or dispersed. Those of them that could escape, went to their countrymen in Armorica, which was now called the other Britain.

BOOK SIX

1

Gratian, being advanced to the throne, is killed by the common people. The Britons desire the Romans to defend them against Guanius and Melga.

BUT Gratian Municeps, hearing of the death of Maximian, seized the crown, and made himself king. After this he exercised such tyranny that the common people fell upon him in tumultuous manner and murdered him. When this news reached other countries, their former enemies returned back from Ireland, and bringing with them the Scots, Norwegians, and Dacians, made dreadful devastations with fire and sword over the whole kingdom, from sea to sea. Upon this most grievous calamity and oppression, ambassadors were despatched with letters to Rome, to beseech, with tears and vows of perpetual subjection, that a body of men might be sent to revenge their injuries, and drive out the enemy from them. The ambassadors in a short time prevailed so far, that, unmindful of past injuries, the Romans granted them one legion, which was transported in a fleet to their country, and there, speedily encountered the enemy. At last, after the slaughter of a vast multitude of them, they drove them entirely out of the country, and rescued the miserable people from their outrageous cruelty. Then they gave orders for a wall to be built between Albania and Deira, from one sea to the other, for a terror to the enemy, and safeguard to the country. At that time Albania was wholly laid waste by the frequent invasions of barbarous nations; and whatever enemies made an attempt upon the country met with a convenient landing-place there. So that the inhabitants were diligent in working upon the wall, which they finished partly at the public, partly upon private charge.

2

Guithelin's speech to the Britons when the Romans left them.

THE Romans, after this, declared to the Britons that they should not be able for the future to undergo the fatigue of such laborious expeditions; and that it was beneath the dignity of the Roman state to harass so great and brave an army, both by land and sea, against base and vagabond robbers; but that they ought to apply themselves to the use of arms, and to fight bravely in defending to the utmost of their power their country, riches, wives, children, and, what is dearer to them than all these, their liberty and lives. As soon as they had given this exhortation, they commanded all the men of the island that were fit for war to appear together at London, because the

Romans were about to return home. When, therefore, they were all assembled, Guithelin, the Metropolitan of London, had orders to make a speech to them, which he did in these words:

"Though I am appointed by the princes here present to speak to you, I find myself rather ready to burst into tears, than to make an eloquent oration. It is a most sensible affliction to me to observe the weak and destitute state into which you are fallen since Maximian drew away with him all the forces and youth of this kingdom. You that were left were people wholly inexperienced in war, and occupied with other employments, as tilling the ground, and several kinds of mechanical trades. So that when your enemies from foreign countries came upon you, as sheep wandering without a shepherd, they forced you to quit your folds, till the Roman power restored you to them again. Must your hopes, therefore, always depend on foreign assistance? And will you never use yourselves to handle arms against a band of robbers, that are by no means stronger than yourselves, if you are not dispirited by sloth and cowardice? The Romans are now tired with the continual voyages wherewith they are harassed to defend you against your enemies: they rather choose to remit to you the tribute you pay to them than undergo any longer this fatigue by land and sea. Because you were only the common people at this time when we had soldiers of our own, do you therefore think that manhood has quite forsaken you? Are not men in the course of human generation often the reverse of one another? Is not a ploughman often the father of a soldier, and a soldier of a ploughman? Does not the same diversity happen in a mechanic and a soldier? Since then, in this manner, one produces another, I cannot think it possible for manhood to be lost among them. As then you are men, behave yourselves like men: call upon the name of Christ, that he may inspire you with courage to defend your liberties."

No sooner had he concluded his speech, than the people raised such a shout that one would have thought them on a sudden inspired with courage from heaven.

3

The Britons are again cruelly harassed by Guanius and Melga.

AFTER this the Romans encouraged the timorous people as much as they could, and left them patterns of their arms. They likewise commanded towers, having a prospect towards the sea, to be placed at proper distances along all the south coast, where their ships were, and from whence they feared the invasions of the barbarians. But, according to the proverb, "It is easier to make a hawk of a kite, than a scholar of a ploughman"; all learning to him is but as a pearl thrown before swine. Thus, no sooner had the Romans taken their farewell of them, than the two leaders, Guanius and Melga, issued forth from their ships in which they had fled over into Ireland, and with their band of Scots, Picts, Norwegians, Dacians, and others, whom they had brought along with them, seized upon all Albania as far as the very wall. Understanding likewise that the Romans were gone, never to return any more, they, now, in a more insolent manner than before, began their devastations in the island. Hereupon the country fellows upon the battlements of the walls sat night and day with quaking hearts, not daring to stir from their seats, and readier for flight than making the least resistance. In the meantime the enemies ceased not with their hooks to pull them down headlong, and dash the wretched herd to pieces upon the ground; who gained at least this advantage by their speedy death, that they avoided the sight of that most deplorable calamity which forthwith threatened their relations and dearest children. Such was the terrible venegeance of God for that most wicked madness of Maximian in draining the kingdom of all its forces, who, had they been present, would have repulsed any nation that invaded them; an evident proof of which they gave by the vast conquests they made abroad, even in remote countries; and also by maintaining their own country in peace, while they continued here. But thus it happens when a country is left to the defense of country clowns. In short, quitting their high wall and their cities, the country people were forced again to fly, and to suffer a more fatal dispersion, a more furious pursuit of the enemy, a more cruel and more general slaughter than before;

and like lambs before wolves, so was that miserable people torn to pieces by the merciless barbarians. Again, therefore, the wretched remainder sent letters to Agitius, a man of great power among the Romans, to this effect. "To Agitius, thrice consul, the groans of the Britons." And after some few other complaints they add: "The sea drives us to the barbarians, and the barbarians drive us back to the sea: thus we are tossed to and fro between two kinds of death, being either drowned or put to the sword." Notwithstanding this most moving address they procured no relief, and the ambassadors returning back in great heaviness, declared to their countrymen the repulse which they had suffered.

4

Guithelin desires succour of Aldroen.

HEREUPON, after a consultation together, Guithelin, Archbishop of London, passed over into Lesser Britain, called then Armorica, or Letavia, to desire assistance of their brethren. At that time Aldroen reigned there, being the fourth king from Conan, to whom, as has been already related, Maximian had given that kingdom. This prince, seeing a prelate of so great dignity arrive, received him with homour, and inquired after the occasion of his coming. To whom Guithelin answered:

"Your majesty can be no stranger to the misery which we, your Britons, have suffered (which may even demand your tears) since the time that Maximian drained our island of its soldiers to people the kingdom which you enjoy, and which God grant you may long enjoy in peace. For against us, the poor remains of the British race, all the people of the adjacent islands have risen up, and made an utter devastation in our country, which then abounded with all kinds of riches; so that the people are now wholly destitute of all manner of sustenance, but what they can get in hunting. Nor had we any power or knowledge of military affairs left among us to encounter the enemy. For the Romans are tired of us, and have absolutely refused their assistance. So that now, deprived of all other hope we come to implore your clemency, that you would furnish us with forces, and protect a kingdom which is of right your own, from the incursions of barbarians. For who but yourself ought, without your consent, to wear the crown of Constantine and Maximian, since the right your ancestors had to it is now devolved upon you? Prepare your fleet, and go with me. Behold! I deliver the kingdom of Britain into your hands."

To this Aldroen made answer: "There was a time formerly when I would not have refused to accept the island of Britain, if it had been offered me; for I do not think there was anywhere a more fruitful country while it enjoyed peace and tranquility. But now, since the calamities that have befallen it, it is become of less value, and odious both to me and all other princes. But above all things the power of the Romans was so destructive to it, that nobody could enjoy any settled state or authority in it without loss of liberty, and bearing the yoke of slavery under them. And who would not prefer the possession of a lesser country with liberty, to all the riches of that island in servitude? The kingdom that is now under my subjection I enjoy with honour, and without paying homage to any superior; so that I prefer it to all other countries, since I can govern it without being controlled. Nevertheless, out of respect to the right that my ancestors for many generations have had to your islands I deliver to you my brother Constantine with two thousand men, that with the good providence of God, he may free your country from the inroads of barbarians, and obtain the crown for himself. For I have a brother called by that name, who is an expert soldier, and in all other respects an accomplished man. If you please to accept of him, I will not refuse to send him with you, together with the said number of men; for indeed a larger number I do not mention to you, because I am daily threatened with disturbance from the Gauls." He had scarcely done speaking before the archbishop returned him thanks, and when Constantine was called in, broke out into these expressions of joy: "Christ conquers; Christ commands; Christ reigns: behold the King of desolate Britain! Be Christ only present, and behold our defense, our hope and joy." In short, the ships being got ready, the men who were chosen out from all parts of the kingdom, were delivered to Guithelin.

5

Constantine, being made king of Britain, leaves three sons.

WHEN they had made all necessary preparations, they embarked, and arrived at the port of Totness; and then without delay assembled together the youth that was left in the island, and encountered the enemy; over whom, by the merit of the holy prelate, they obtained the victory. After this the Britons, before dispersed, flocked together from all parts, and in a council held at Silchester, promoted Constantine to the throne, and there performed the ceremony of his coronation. They also married him to a lady, descended from a noble Roman family, whom Archbishop Guithelin had educated and by whom the king had afterwards three sons, Constans, Aurelius Ambrosius, and Uther Pendragon. Constans, who was the eldest, he delivered to the church of Amphibalus in Winchester, that he might there take upon him the monastic order. But the other two, viz. Aurelius and Uther, he committed to the care of Guithelin for their education. At last, after ten years were expired, there came a certain Pict, who had entered in his service, and under pretense of holding some private discourse with him, in a nursery of young trees where nobody was present, stabbed him with a dagger.

6

Constans is by Vortigern crowned king of Britain.

UPON the death of Constantine, a dissension arose among the nobility about a successor to the throne. Some were for setting up Aurelius Ambrosius; others Uther Pendragon; others again some other persons of the royal family. At last, when they could come to no conclusion, Vortigern, King of the Gewisseans, who was himself very ambitious of the crown, went to Constans the monk, and thus addressed himself to him: "You see your father is dead, and your brothers on account of their age are incapable of government; neither do I see any of your family besides yourself whom the people ought to promote to the kingdom. If you will therefore follow my advice, I will, on condition of your increasing my private estate, dispose the people to favour your advancement, and free you from that habit, nothwithstanding that it against the rule of your order." Constans, overjoyed at the proposal, promised, with an oath, that upon these terms he would grant him whatever he would desire. Then Vortigern took him, and investing him in his regal habiliments, conducted him to London, and made him king, though not with the free consent of the people. Archbishop Guithelin was then dead, nor was there any other that durst perform the ceremony of his unction on account of his having quitted the monastic order. However, this proved no hindrance to his coronation, for Vortigern himself performed the ceremony instead of a bishop.

7

Vortigern treacherously contrives to get King Constans assassinated.

CONSTANS, being thus advanced, committed the whole government of the kingdom to Vortigern, and surrendered himself up so entirely to his counsels that he did nothing without his order. His own incapacity for government obliged him to do this, for he had learned anything else rather than state affairs within his cloister. Vortigern became sensible of this, and therefore began to deliberate with himself what course to take to obtain the crown of which he had been before extremely ambitious. He saw that now was his proper time to gain his end easily, when the kingdom was wholly entrusted to his management; and Constans, who bore the title of King, was no more than the shadow of one, for he was of soft temper, a bad judge in matters of right, and not in the least feared, either by his own people, or by the neighbouring states. And as for his two bothers, Uther Pendragon and Aurelius Ambrosius, they were only children in their cradles, and therefore incapable of the government. There was likewise this farther misfortune, that all the older persons of the nobility were dead, so that Vortigern seemed to be the only man surviving that had craft, policy, and experience in matters of state; and all the rest in a manner children, or raw youths, who only inherited the honours of their parents and relations that had been killed in the former wars. Vortigern, finding a concurrence of so many favourable circumstances, contrived how he might easily and cunningly depose Constans the monk, and immediately establish himself in his place. But in order to do this, he waited until he had first well established his power and interest in several countries. He therefore petitioned to have the king's treasures, and his fortified cities, in his own custody; pretending there was a rumour that the neighbouring islanders designed an invasion of the kingdom. This being granted him, he placed his own creatures in those cities to secure them for himself. Then having formed a scheme how to execute his treasonable designs, he went to the king and represented to him the necessity of augmenting the number of his domestics, that he might more safely oppose the invasion of the enemy. "Have I not left all things to your disposal?" said Constans. "Do what you will as to that, so that they be but faithful to me." Vortigern replied, "I am informed that the Picts are going to bring the Dacians and Norwegians in upon us with a design to give us very great annoyance. I would therefore advise you, and in my opinion it is the best course you can take, that you maintain some Picts in your court who may do you good service among those of that nation. For if it is true that they are preparing to begin a rebellion, you may employ them as spies upon their countrymen in their plots and stratagems, so as easily to escape them." This was the dark treason of a secret enemy; for he did not recommend this out of regard for the safety of Constans, but because he knew the Picts to be a giddy people, and ready for all manner of wickedness; so that, in a fit of drunkenness or passion, they might easily be incensed against the king, and make no scruple to assassinate him. And such an accident, when it should happen, would make an open way for his accession to the throne, which he so often had in view. Hereupon he despatched messengers into Scotland, with an invitation to a hundred Pictish soldiers, whom accordingly he received into the king's household; and when admitted, he showed them more respect than all the rest of the domestics, by making them several presents, and allowing them a luxurious table, insomuch as they looked upon him as the king. So great was the regard they had for him, that they made songs of him about the streets, the subject of which was that Vortigern deserved the government, deserved the sceptre of Britain; but that Constans was unworthy of it. This encouraged Vortigern to show them still more favour, in order the more firmly to engage them in his interests; and when by these practices he had made them entirely his creatures, he took an opportunity, when they were drunk, to tell them that he was going to retire out of Britain to see if he could get a better estate; for the small revenue he had then, he said, would not so much as enable him to maintain a retinue of fifty men. Then putting on a look of sadness, he withdrew to his own apartment, and left them drinking in the hall. The Picts at this sight were in inexpressible sorrow, as thinking what he had said was true, and murmuring said to one another, "Why do we suffer this monk to live? Why do we not kill him, that Vortigern may enjoy his crown? Who is so fit to succeed as he? A man so generous to us is worthy to rule, and deserves all the honour and dignity that we can bestow upon him."

8

Aurelius Ambrosius and Uther Pendragon flee from Vortigern, and go to Lesser Britain.

AFTER this, breaking into Constans's bed-chamber, they fell upon him and killed him, and carried his head to Vortigern. At the sight of it, he put on a mournful countenance, and burst forth into tears, though at the same time he was almost transported with joy. However, he summoned together the citizens of London (for there the act was committed), and commanded all the assassins to be bound, and their heads to be cut off for this abominable parricide. In the meantime, there were some who had a suspicion that this piece of villainy was wholly the contrivance of Vortigern, and the Picts were only his instruments to execute it. Others again as positively asserted his innocence. At last the matter being left in doubt, those who had the care of the two brothers, Aurelius Ambrosius and Uther Pendragon, fled over with them into Lesser Britain, for fear of being killed by Vortigern. There they were kindly received by King Budes who took care to give them an education suitable to their royal birth.

9

Vortigern makes himself king of Britain.

NOW Vortigern, seeing nobody to rival him in the kingdom, placed the crown on his own head, and thus gained the pre-eminence over all the rest of the princes. At last his treason being discovered, the people of the adjacent islands, whom the Picts had brought into Albania, made insurrection against him. For the Picts were enraged on account of the death of their fellow soldiers who had been slain for the murder of Constans, and endeavoured to revenge that injury upon him. Vortigern therefore was daily in great distress, and lost a considerable part of his army in a war with them. He had likewise no less trouble from another quarter, for fear of Aurelius Ambrosius, and his brother Uther Pendragon, who, as we said before, had fled, on his account, into Lesser Britain. For he heard it rumoured, day after day, that they had now arrived at man's estate, and had built a vast fleet with a design to return back to the kingdom, which was their undoubted right.

10

Vortigern takes the Saxons that were new-comers to his assistance.

IN the meantime there arrived in Kent three bringandines, or long galleys, full of armed men, under the command of two brothers, Horsa and Hengist. Vortigern was then at Dorobernia, now Canterbury, which city he used often to visit; and being informed of the arrival of some tall strangers in large ships, he ordered that they should be received peaceably, and conducted into his presence. As soon as they were brought before him, he cast his eyes upon the two brothers, who excelled all the rest both in nobility and gracefulness of person; and having taken a view of the whole company, asked them of what country they were, and what was the occasion of their coming into his kingdom. To whom Hengist (whose years and wisdom entitled him to precedence), in the name of the rest, made the following answer:

"Most noble King, Saxony, which is one of the countries of Germany, was the place of our birth; and the occasion of our coming was to offer our service to you or some other prince. For we were driven out of our native country for no other reason, but that the laws of the kingdom required it. It is customary among us, that when we come to be overstocked with people, our princes from all the provinces meet together, and command all the youths of the kingdom to assemble before them; then casting lots they make choice of the strongest and ablest of them to go into foreign nations, to procure themselves a subsistence, and free their native country from a superfluous multitude of people. Our country, therefore, being of late overstocked, our princes met, and after having cast lots, made choice of the youth which you see in your presence, and have obliged us to obey the custom which has been established of old. And us two brothers, Hengist and Horsa, they made generals over them, out of respect to our ancestors, who enjoyed the same honour. In obedience, therefore, to the laws so long established, we put out to sea, and under the good guidance of Mercury have arrived in your kingdom."

The king, at the name of Mercury, looking earnestly upon them, asked them what religion they professed. "We worship," replied Hengist, "our country's gods, Saturn and Jupiter, and the other deities that govern the world, but especially Mercury, whom in our language we call Woden, and to whom our ancestors consecrated the fourth day of the week, still called after his name Wodensday. Next to him we worship the powerful goddess, Frea, to whom they also dedicated the sixth day, which after her name we call Friday." Vortigern replied, "For your credulity, or rather incredulity, I am much grieved, but I rejoice at your arrival, which, whether by God's providence or some other agency, happens very seasonably for me in my present difficulties. For I am oppressed by my enemies on every side, and if you will engage with me in my wars, I will entertain you honourably in my kingdom, and bestow upon you lands and possessions." The barbarians readily accepted his offer, and the agreement between them being ratified, they resided at his court. Soon after this, the Picts, issuing forth from Albania, with a very great army, began to lay waste the northern parts of the island. When Vortigern had information of it, he assembled his forces, and went to meet them beyond the Humber. Upon their engaging, the battle proved very fierce on both sides, though there was but little occasion for the Britons to exert themselves, for the Saxons fought so bravely that the enemy, formerly so victorious, were speedily put to flight.

11

Hengist brings over great numbers of Saxons into Britain: his crafty petition to Vortigern.

VORTIGERN, therefore, as he owed the victory to them, increased his bounty to them, and gave their general, Hengist, large possessions of land in Lindesia, for the subsistence of himself and his fellow soldiers. Hereupon Hengist, who was a man of experience and subtlety, finding how much interest he had with the king, addressed him in this manner:

"Sir, your enemies give you disturbance from all quarters, and few of your subjects love you. They all threaten you, and say they are going to bring over Aurelius Ambrosius from Armorica to depose you, and make him king. If you please, let us send to our country to invite over some more soldiers, that with our forces increased we may be better able to oppose them. But there is one thing which I would desire of your clemency if I did not fear a refusal." Vortigern made answer, "Send your messengers to Germany, and invite over whom you please, and you shall have no refusal from me in whatever you shall desire." Hengist, with a low bow, returned him thanks, and said, "The possessions which you have given me in land and houses are very large, but you have not yet done me that honour which becomes my station and birth, because, among other things, I should have had some town or city granted me, that I might be entitled to greater esteem among the nobility of your kingdom. I ought to have been made a consul or prince, since my ancestors enjoyed both those dignities." "It is not in my power," replied Vortigern, "to do you so much honour, because you are strangers and pagans; neither am I yet so far acquainted with your manners and customs, as to set you on a level with my natural born subjects. And, indeed, if I did esteem you as my subjects, I should not be forward to do so, because the nobility of my kingdom would strongly dissuade me from it." "Give your servant," said Hengist, "only so much ground in the place you have assigned me, as I can encompass with a leathern thong, for me to build a fortress upon, as a place of retreat if occasion should require. For I will always be faithful to you, as I have been hitherto, and pursue no other design in the request which I have made." With these words the king was prevailed upon to grant him his petition; and ordered him to dispatch messengers to Germany, to invite more men over speedily to his assistance. Hengist immediately executed his orders, and taking a bull's hide, made one thong out of the whole, with which he encompassed a rocky place that had been carefully made choice of, and within that circuit began to build a castle, which, when finished, took its name from the thong wherewith it had been measured; for it was afterwards called, in the British tongue, Kaercorrei; in Saxon, Thancastre, that is, Thong Castle.

12

Vortigern marries Rowen, the daughter of Hengist.

IN the meantime, the messengers returned from Germany with eighteen ships full of the best soldiers they could get. They also brought along with them Rowen, the daughter of Hengist, one of the most accomplished beauties of that age. After their arrival, Hengist invited the king to his house, to view his new buildings, and the new soldiers that were come over. The king readily accepted of his invitation, but privately, and having highly commended the magnificence of the structure, enlisted the men into his service. Here he was entertained at a royal banquet; and when that was over, the young lady came out of her chamber bearing a golden cup full of wine, with which she approached the king, and making a low courtesy, said to him, "Lauerd King wacht heil!" The king, at the sight of the lady's face, was on a sudden both surprised and inflamed with her beauty; and calling to his interpreter, asked him what she said, and what answer he should make her. "She called you 'Lord King,'" said the interpreter, "and offered to drink your health. Your answer must be, 'Drinc heil'!" Vortigern accordingly answered, "Drinc heil" and bade her drink; after which he took the cup from her hand, kissed her, and drank himself. From that time to this, it has been the custom in Britain, that he who drinks to any one says, "Wacht heil!" And he that pledges him answers "Drinc heil!" Vortigern being now drunk with the variety of liquors, the devil took this opportunity to enter into his heart, and make him in love with the damsel, so that he became suitor to her father for her. It was, I say, by the devil's entering into his heart, that he, who was a Christian, should fall in love with a pagan. By this example, Hengist, being a prudent man, discovered the king's levity, and consulted with his brother Horsa, and the other ancient men present, what to do in relation to the king's request. They unanimously advised him to give him his daughter, and in consideration of her to demand the province of Kent. Accordingly the daughter was without delay delivered to Vortigern, and the province of Kent to Hengist, without the knowledge of Gorangon, who had the government of it. The king the same night married the pagan lady, and became extremely delighted with her; by which he quickly brought upon himself the hatred of the nobility, and of his own sons. For he had already three sons, whose names were Vortimer, Catigern, and Pascentius.

13

The bishops, Germanus and Lupus, restore the Christian faith that had been corrupted in Britain. Octa and Ebissa are four times routed by Vortimer.

AT that time came St. Germanus, Bishop of Auxerre, and Lupus, Bishop of Troyes, to preach the gospel to the Britons. For the Christian faith had been corrupted among them, partly by the pagans whom the king had brought into society with them, partly by the Pelagian heresy, with the poison whereof they had been a long time infected. But by the preaching of these holy men, the true faith and worship was again restored, the many miracles they wrought giving success to their labours. Gildas has in his elegant treatise given an account of the many miracles God wrought by them. The king being now, as we have said, possessed of the lady, Hengist said to him: "As I am your father, I claim the right of being your counselor: do not therefore slight my advice, since it is to my countrymen you must owe the conquest of all your enemies. Let us invite over my son Octa and his brother Ebissa, who are brave soldiers, and give them the countries that are in the northern parts of Britain, by the wall, between Deira and Albania. For they will hinder the inroads of the barbarians, and so you shall enjoy peace on the other side of the Humber." Vortigern complied with this request, and ordered them to invite over whomsoever they knew able to assist him. Immediately upon the receipt of this message came Octa, Ebissa, and Cherdich, with three hundred ships filled with soldiers, who were all kindly received by Vortigern, and had ample presents made them. For by their assistance he vanquished his enemies, and in every engagement proved victorious. Hengist in the meantime continued to invite over more and more ships, and to augment his numbers daily. Which when the Britons observed, they were afraid of being betrayed by them, and moved the king to banish them out of his coasts. For it was contrary to the rule of the gospel that Christians should hold fellowship, or have any intercourse, with pagans. Besides which, the number of these that were come over was now so great, that they were a terror to his subjects; and nobody could now know who was a pagan, and who a Christian, since pagans married the daughters and kinswomen of Christians. These things they represented to the king, and endeavoured to dissuade him from entertaining them, lest they might, by some treacherous conspiracy, prove an overmatch for the native inhabitants. But Vortigern, who loved them above all other nations on account of his wife, was deaf to their advice. For this reason the Britons quickly deserted him, and unanimously set up Vortimer his son for their king; who at their instigation began to drive out the barbarians, and to make dreadful incursions upon them. Four battles he fought with them, and was victorious in all: the first upon the River Dereuent; the second upon the Ford of Epsford, where Horsa and Catigern, another son of Vortigern, met and, after a sharp encounter, killed each other; the third upon the sea-shore, where the enemies fled shamefully to their ships, and betook themselves for refuge to the isle of Thanet. But Vortimer besieged them there, and daily distressed them with his fleet. And when they were no longer able to bear the assaults of the Britons, they sent King Vortigern, who was present with them in all those wars, to his son Vortimer, to desire leave to depart, and return back safe to Germany. And while a conference upon this subject was being held, they in the meantime went on board their long galleys, and, leaving their wives and children behind them, returned back to Germany.

14

Vortimer's kindness to his soldiers at his death.

VORTIMER, after this great success, began to restore his subjects to their possessions which had been taken from them, and to show them all marks of his affection and esteem, and at the instance of St. Germanus to rebuild their churches. But his goodness quickly stirred up the enmity of the devil against him, who entering into the heart of his stepmother Rowen, excited her to contrive his death. For this purpose she consulted with the poisoners, and procured one who was intimate with him, whom she corrupted with large and numerous presents, to give him a poisonous draught; so that this brave soldier, as soon as he had taken it, was seized with a sudden illness, that deprived him of all hopes of life. Hereupon he forthwith ordered all his men to come to him, and having shown them how near he was to his end, distributed among them all the treasure his predecessors had heaped up, and endeavoured to comfort them in their sorrow and lamentation for him, telling them, he was only going the way of all flesh. But he exhorted those brave and warlike young men, who had attended him in all his victories, to persist courageously in the defense of their country against all hostile invasion; and with wonderful greatness of mind, commanded a brazen pyramid to be placed in the port where the Saxons used to land, and his body when dead to be placed on the top of it, that the sight of his tomb might frighten back the barbarians to Germany.

For he said none of them would dare approach the country, that should but get a sight of his tomb. Such was the admirable bravery of this great man, who, as he had been a terror to them while living, endeavoured to be no less so when dead. Notwithstanding which, he was no sooner dead than the Britons had no regard to his orders, and buried him at London.

15

Hengist, having wickedly murdered the princes of Britain, keeps Vortigern prisoner.

VORTIGERN, after the death of his son, was again restored to the kingdom, and at the request of his wife sent messengers into Germany to Hengist with an invitation to return into Britain, but privately and with a small retinue to prevent a quarrel between the barbarians and his subjects. But Hengist, hearing that Vortimer was dead, raised an army of not less than three hundred thousand men, and fitting out a fleet returned with them to Britain. When Vortigern and the nobility heard of the arrival of so vast a multitude they were immoderately incensed, and, after consultation together, resolved to fight them, and drive them from their coasts. Hengist, being informed of their design by messengers sent by his daughter, immediately entered into deliberation what course to pursue against them. After several stratagems had been considered, he judged it most feasible to impose upon the nation by making show of peace. With this view he sent ambassadors to the king to declare to him that he had not brought so great a number of men for the purpose either of staying with him, or offering any violence to the country. But the reason why he brought them, was because he thought Vortimer was yet living, and that he should have occasion for them against him, in case of an assault. But now since he no longer doubted of his being dead, he submitted himself and his people to the disposal of Vortigern; so that he might retain as many of them as he should think fit, and whomsoever he rejected Hengist would allow to return back without delay to Germany. And if these terms pleased Vortigern, he desired him to appoint a time and place for their meeting and adjusting matters according to his pleasure. When these things were represented to the king, he was mightily pleased, as being very unwilling to part with Hengist; and at last ordered his subjects and the Saxons to meet upon the Kalends of May, which were now very near, at the monastery of Ambrius for the settling of the matters above mentioned. The appointment being agreed to on both sides, Hengist, with a new design of villainy in his head, ordered his soldiers to carry every one of them a long dagger under their garments, and while the conference should be held with the Britons, who would have no suspicion of them, he would give this word of command, "Nemet oure Saxas"; at which moment they were all to be ready to seize boldly every one his next man, and with his drawn dagger stab him. Accordingly they all met at the time and place appointed, and began to treat of peace; and when a fit opportunity offered for executing his villain, Hengist cried out, "Nemet oure Saxas," and the same instant seized Vortigern, and held him by his cloak. The Saxons, upon the signal given, drew their daggers, and falling upon the princes, who little suspected any such design, assassinated them to the number of four hundred and sixty barons and consuls; to whose bodies St. Eldad afterwards gave Christian burial, not far from Kaercaradauc, now Salisbury, in a burying-place near the monastery of Ambrius, the abbot who was the founder of it. For they all came without arms, having no thoughts of anything but treating of peace; which gave the others a fairer opportunity of exercising their villainous design against them. But the pagans did not escape unpunished while they acted this wickedness; a great number of them being killed during this massacre of their enemies. For the Britons, taking up clubs and stones from the ground, resolutely defended themselves, and did good execution upon the traitors.

16

Eldol's valiant exploit. Hengist forces Vortigern to yield up the strongest fortifications in Britain, in consideration of his release.

THERE was present one Eldol, Consul of Gloucester, who, at the sight of this treachery, took up a stake which he happened to find, and with that made his defense. Every blow he gave carried death along with it; and by breaking either the head, arms, shoulders or legs of a great many, he struck no small terror into the traitors, nor did he move from the spot before he had killed with that weapon seventy men. But being no longer able to stand his ground against such numbers, he made his escape from them, and retired to his own city. Many fell on both sides but the Saxons got the victory; because the Britons, having no suspicion of treachery, came unarmed, and therefore made a weaker defense. After the commission of this detestable villainy, the Saxons would not kill Vortigern; but having threatened him with death and bound him, demanded his cities and fortified places in consideration of their granting him his life. He, to secure himself, denied them nothing; and when they had made him confirm his grants with an oath, they released him from his chains, and then marched first to London, which they took, as they did afterwards York, Lincoln, and Winchester; wasting the countries through which they passed, and destroying the people, as wolves do sheep when left by their shepherds. When Vortigern saw the desolation which they made, he retired into the parts of Cambria, not knowing what to do against so barbarous a people.

17

Vortigern, after consultation with magicians, orders a youth to be brought that never had a father.

AT last he had recourse to magicians for their advice, and commanded them to tell him what course to take. They advised him to build a very strong tower for his own safety, since he had lost all his other fortified places. Accordingly he made a progress about the country to find out a convenient situation, and came at last to Mount Erir, or Mount Erith, where he assembled workmen from several countries, and ordered them to build the tower. The builders, therefore, began to lay the foundation; but whatever they did one day the earth swallowed up the next, so as to leave no appearance of their work. Vortigern being informed of this again consulted with his magicians concerning the cause of it, who told him that he must find a youth that never had a father, and kill him, and then sprinkle the stones and cement with his blood; for by those means, they said, he would have a firm foundation. Hereupon messengers were despatched away over all the provinces to inquire out such a man. In their travels they came to a city, called afterwards Kaermerdin, where they saw some young men playing before the gate, and went up to them; but being weary with their journey, they sat down in the ring to see if they could meet with what they were in quest of. Towards evening, there happened on a sudden a quarrel between two of the young men, whose names were Merlin and Dabutius. In the dispute Dabutius said to Merlin, "You fool, do you presume to quarrel with me? Is there any equality in our birth? I am descended from a royal race, both by my father and mother's side. As for you, nobody knows what you are, for you never had a father." At that word the messengers looked earnestly upon Merlin, and asked the bystanders who he was. They told him it was not known who was his father; but that his mother was daughter to the King of Dimetia, and that she lived in St. Peter's church among the nuns of that city.

18

Vortigern inquires of Merlin's mother concerning her conception of him.

UPON this the messengers hastened to the governor of the city, and ordered him, in the king's name, to send Merlin and his mother to the king. As soon as the governor understood the occasion of their message, he readily obeyed the order, and sent them to Vortigern to complete his design. When they were introduced into the king's presence, he received the mother in a very respectful manner on account of her noble birth; and began to inquire of her by what man she had conceived. "My sovereign lord," said she, "by the life of your soul and mine, I know nobody that begot him of me. Only this I know, that as I was once with my companions in our chambers, there appeared to me a person in the shape of a beautiful young man, who often embraced me eagerly in his arms, and kissed me; and when he had stayed a little time, he suddenly vanished out of my sight. But many times after this he would talk with me when

I sat alone, without making any visible appearance. When he had a long time haunted me in this manner, he at last laid with me several times in the shape of a man, and left me with child. And I do affirm to you, my sovereign lord, that excepting that young man, I know nobody that begot him of me." The king, full of admiration at this account, ordered Maugantius to be called that he might satisfy him as to the possibility of what the woman had related. Maugantius, being introduced, and having the whole matter repeated to him, said to Vortigern: "In the books of our philosophers, and in a great many histories, I have found that several men have had the like original. For, as Apuleius informs us in his book concerning the Demon of Socrates, between the moon and the earth inhabit those spirits, which we will call incubuses. These are of the nature partly of men, and partly of angels, and whenever they please assume human shapes, and lie with women. Perhaps one of them appeared to this woman, and begot that young man of her."

19

Merlin's speech to the king's magicians, and advice about the building of the tower.

MERLIN in the meantime was attentive to all that had passed, and then approached the king, and said to him, "For what reason am I and my mother introduced into your presence?" "My magicians," answered Vortigern, "advised me to seek out a man that had no father, with whose blood my building is to be sprinkled, in order to make it stand." "Order your magicians," said Merlin, "to come before me, and I will convict them of a lie." The king was surprised at his words, and presently ordered the magicians to come, and sit down before Merlin, who spoke to them after this manner: "Because you are ignorant of what it is that hinders the foundation of the tower, you have recommended the shedding of my blood to cement it, as if that would presently make it stand. But tell me now, what is there under the foundation? For something there is that will not suffer it to stand." The magicians at this began to be afraid, and made no answer. Then said Merlin, who was also called Ambrose, "I entreat your majesty would command your workmen to dig into the ground, and you will find a pond which causes the foundation to sink." This accordingly was done, and then presently they found a pond deep underground, which had made it give way. Merlin after this went again to the magicians, and said, "Tell me ye false sycophants, what is there under the pond?" But they were silent. Then again he said to the king, "Command the pond to be drained, and at the bottom you will see two hollow stones, and in them two dragons asleep." The king made no scruple of believing him, since he had found true what he said of the pond, and therefore ordered it to be drained: which done, he found as Merlin had said; and now was possessed with the greatest admiration of him. Nor were the rest that were present less amazed at his wisdom, thinking it to be no less than divine inspiration.

BOOK SEVEN

1

Geoffrey of Monmouth's preface to Merlin's prophesy.

I HAD not got thus far in my history, when the subject of public discourse happening to be concerning Merlin, I was obliged to publish his prophecies at the request of my acquaintances, but especially of Alexander, bishop of Lincoln, a prelate of the greatest piety and wisdom. There was not any person, either among the clergy or the laity, that was attended with such a train of knights and noblemen, who his settled piety and great munificence engaged in his service. Out of a desire, therefore, to gratify him, I translated these prophesies, and sent them to him with the following letter.

2

Geoffrey's letter to Alexander, Bishop of Lincoln.

THE regard which I owe to your great worth, most noble prelate, has obliged me to undertake the translation of Merlin's prophecies out of British into Latin, before I had made an end to the history which I had begun concerning the acts of the British kings. For my design was to have finished that first, and afterwards to have taken this work in hand; lest being engaged on both at once, I should be less capable of attending with any exactness to either. Notwithstanding, since the deference which is paid to your penetrating judgment will screen me from censure, I have employed my rude pen, and in a coarse style present you with a translation out of a language with which you are unacquainted. At the same time, I cannot but wonder at your recommending this matter to one of my low genius, when you might have caused so many men of greater learning, and a richer vein of intellect, to undertake it; who, with their sublime strains, would much more agreeably have entertained you. Besides, without any disparagement to all the philosophers in Britain, I must take liberty to say that you yourself, if the business of your high station would give you leisure, are capable of furnishing us with loftier productions of this kind than any man living. However, since it was your pleasure that Geoffrey of Monmouth should be employed in this prophecy, he hopes that you will favourably accept of his performance, and vouchsafe to give a finer turn to whatever you shall find unpolished, or otherwise faulty in it.

3

The prophecy of Merlin.

AS Vortigern, King of the Britons, was sitting upon the bank of the drained pond, the two dragons, one of which was white, the other red, came forth, and, approaching one another, began a terrible fight, and cast forth fire with their breath. But the white dragon had the advantage, and made the other fly to the end of the lake. And he, for grief at his flight, renewed the assault upon his pursuer, and forced him to retire. After this battle of the dragons, the king commanded Ambrose Merlin to tell him what it portended. Upon which he, bursting into tears, delivered what his prophetical spirit suggested to him, as follows:

"Woe to the red dragon, for his banishment hasteneth on. His lurking holes shall be seized by the white dragon, which signifies the Saxons whom you invited over; but the red denotes the British nation, which shall be oppressed by the white. Therefore shall its mountains be leveled as the valleys, and the rivers of the valleys shall run with blood. The exercise of religion shall be destroyed, and churches laid open to ruin. At last the oppressed shall prevail, and oppose the cruelty of foreigners. For a boar of Cornwall shall give his assistance, and trample their necks under his feet. The islands of the ocean shall be subject to his power, and he shall possess the forests of Gaul. The house of Romulus shall dread his courage, and his end shall be doubtful. He shall be celebrated in the mouths of the people; and his exploits shall be food to those that relate them. Six of his posterity shall sway the sceptre, but after them shall arise a German worm. He shall be advanced by a sea-wolf, whom the woods of Africa shall accompany. Religion shall again be abolished, and there shall be a translation of the metropolitan sees. The dignity of London shall adorn Dorobernia, and the seventh pastor of York shall be resorted to in the kingdom of Armorica. St David's shall put on the pall of the City of Legions, and a preacher of Ireland shall be dumb on account of an infant growing in the womb. It shall rain a shower of blood, and a raging famine shall afflict mankind. When these things happen, the red one shall be grieved; but when his fatigue is over, shall grow strong. Then shall misfortunes hasten upon the white one, and the buildings of his gardens shall be pulled down. Seven that sway the sceptre shall be killed, one of whom shall become a saint. The wombs of mothers shall be ripped up, and infants be abortive. There shall be a most grievous punishment of men, that the natives may be restored. He that shall do these things shall put on the brazen man, and upon a brazen horse shall for a long time guard the gates of London. After this, shall the red dragon return to his proper manners, and turn his rage upon himself. Therefore shall the revenge of the Thunderer show itself, for every field shall disappoint the husbandmen. Mortality shall snatch away the people, and make a desolation over all countries. The remainder shall quit their native soil, and make foreign plantations. A blessed king shall prepare a fleet, and shall be reckoned the twelfth in the court among the saints. There shall be a miserable desolation of the kingdom, and the floors of the harvests shall return to the fruitful forests. The white dragon shall rise again, and invite over a daughter of Germany. Our gardens shall be again replenished with foreign seed, and the red one shall pine away at the end of the pond. After that shall the German worm be crowned, and the brazen prince buried. He has his bounds assigned him, which he shall not be able to pass. For a hundred and fifty years he shall continue in trouble and subjection, but shall bear sway three hundred. Then shall the north wind rise against him, and shall snatch away the flowers which the west wind produced. There shall be gilding in the temples, nor shall the edge of the sword cease. The German dragon shall hardly get to his holes, because the revenge of his treason shall overtake him. At last he shall flourish for a little time, but the decimation of Neustria shall hurt him. For a people in wood and in iron coats shall come, and revenge on him his wickedness. They shall restore the ancient inhabitants to their dwellings, and there shall be an open destruction of foreigners. The seed of the white dragon shall be swept out of our gardens, and the remainder of his generation shall be decimated. They shall bear the yoke of slavery, and wound their mother with spades and ploughs. After this shall succeed two dragons, whereof one shall be killed with the sting of envy, but the other shall return under the shadow of a name. Then shall succeed a lion of justice, at whose roar the Gallican towers and the island dragons shall tremble. In those days gold shall be squeezed from the lily and the nettle, and silver shall flow from the hoofs of bellowing cattle. The frizzled shall put on various fleeces, and the outward habit denote the inward parts. The feet of barkers shall be cut off; wild beasts shall enjoy peace; mankind shall be grieved at their punishment; the form of commerce shall be divided; the half shall be round. The ravenousness of kites shall be destroyed, and the teeth of wolves blunted. The lion's whelps shall be transformed into sea-fishes; and an eagle shall build her nest upon Mount Aravius. Venedotia shall grow red with the blood of mothers, and the house of Corineus kill six brethren. The island shall be wet with night tears; so that all shall be provoked to all things. Woe to thee, Neustria, because the lion's brain shall be poured upon thee: and he shall be banished with shattered limbs from his native soil. Posterity shall endeavour to fly above the highest places; but the favour of newcomers shall be exalted. Piety shall hurt the possessor of things got by impiety, till he shall have put on his Father; therefore, being armed with the teeth of a boar, he shall ascend above the tops of the mountains, and the shadow of him that wears a helmet. Albania shall be enraged, and, assembling her neighbours, shall be employed in shedding blood. There shall be put into her jaws a bridle that shall be made on the coast of Armorica. The eagle of the broken covenant shall gild it over, and rejoice in her third nest. The roaring whelps shall watch, and, leaving the woods, shall hunt within the walls of cities. They shall make no small slaughter of those that oppose them, and shall cut off the tongues of bulls. They shall load the necks of roaring lions with chains, and restore the times of their ancestors. Then from the first to the fourth, from the fourth to the third, from the third to the second, the thumb shall roll in oil. The sixth shall overturn the walls of Ireland, and change the woods into a plain. He shall reduce several parts to one, and be crowned with the head of a lion. His beginning shall lay open to wandering affection, but his end shall carry him up to the blessed, who are above. For he shall restore the seats of saints in their countries, and settle pastors in convenient places. Two cities he shall invest with two palls, and shall bestow virgin-presents upon virgins. He shall merit by this the favour of the Thunderer, and shall be placed among the saints. From him shall proceed a lynx penetrating all things, who shall be bent upon the ruin of his own nation; for, through him, Neustria shall lose both islands, and be deprived of its ancient dignity. Then shall the natives return back to the island; for there shall arise a dissension among foreigners. Also a hoary old man, sitting upon a snow-white horse, shall turn the course of the River Periron, and shall measure out a mill upon it with a white rod. Then shall break forth the fountains of Armorica, and they shall be crowned with the diadem of Brutus. Cambria shall be filled with joy; and the oaks of Cornwall shall flourish. The island shall be called by the name of Brutus: and the name given it by foreigners shall be abolished. From Conan shall proceed a warlike boar, that shall exercise the sharpness of his tusks within the Gallic woods. For he shall cut down all the larger oaks, and shall be a defense to the smaller. The Arabians and Africans shall dread him; for he shall pursue a furious course to the farther part of Spain. There shall succeed the goat of the Venereal castle, having golden horns and a silver beard, who shall breathe such a cloud out of his nostrils as shall darken the whole surface of the island. There shall be peace in his time; and corn shall abound by reason of the fruitfulness of the soil. Women shall become serpents in their gait, and all their motions shall be full of pride. The camp of Venus shall be restored; nor shall the arrows of Cupid cease to wound. The fountain of a river shall be turned into blood; and two kings shall fight a duel at Stafford for a lioness. Luxury shall overspread the whole ground; and fornication not cease to debauch mankind. All these things shall three ages see; till the buried kings shall be exposed to public view in the city of London. Famine shall again return; and the inhabitants shall grieve for the destruction of their cities. Then shall come the board of commerce, who shall recall the scattered flocks to the pasture they had lost. His breast shall be food to the hungry, and his tongue drink to the thirsty. Out of his mouth shall flow rivers that shall water the parched jaws of men. After this shall be produced a tree upon the Tower of London, which, having no more than three branches, shall overshadow the surface of the whole island with the breadth of its leaves. Its adversary, the north wind, shall come upon it, and with its noxious blast shall snatch away the third branch, but the two remaining ones shall possess its place till they shall destroy one another by the multitude of their leaves; and then shall it obtain the place of those two, and shall give sustenance to birds of foreign nations. It shall be esteemed hurtful to native fowls; for they shall not be able to fly freely for fear of its shadow. There shall succeed the ass of wickedness, swift against the goldsmiths, but slow against the ravenousness of wolves. In those days the oaks of the forests shall burn, and acorns grow upon the branches of other trees. The Severn sea shall discharge itself through seven mouths, and the River Uske burn seven months. Fishes shall die with the heat thereof; and of them shall be engendered serpents. The baths of Badon shall grow cold, and their salubrious waters engender death. London shall mourn for the death of twenty thousand; and the River Thames shall be turned to blood. The monks in their cowls shall be forced to marry, and their cry shall be heard upon the mountains of the Alps."

4

The continuation of the prophecy.

"THREE springs shall break forth in the city of Winchester, whose rivulets shall divide the island into three parts, Whoever shall drink of the first, shall enjoy long life, and shall never be afflicted with sickness. He that shall drink of the second, shall die of hunger, and paleness and horror shall sit in his countenance. He that shall drink of the third, shall be surprised with sudden death, neither shall his body be capable of burial. Those that are willing to escape so great a surfeit, will endeavour to hide it with several coverings: but whatever bulk shall be laid upon it, shall receive the form of another body. For earth shall be turned into stones; stones into water; wood into ashes; ashes into water, if cast over it. Also a damsel shall be sent from the city of the forest of Cantune to administer a cure, who, after she shall have practised all her arts, shall dry up the noxious fountains only with her breath. Afterwords, as soon as she shall have refreshed herself with the wholesome liquor, she shall bear in her right hand the wood of Caledon, and in her left the forts of the walls of London. Wherever she shall go, she shall make sulphurous steps which will smoke with a double flame. That smoke shall rouse up the city of the Ruteni, and shall make food for the inhabitants of the deep. She shall overflow with rueful tears, and shall fill the island with her dreadful cry. She shall be killed by a hart with ten branches, four of which shall bear golden diadems; but the other six shall be turned into buffalo's horns whose hideous sounds shall astonish the three islands of Britain. The Daneian wood shall be stirred up, and breaking forth into a human voice, shall cry: Come, O Cambria, and join Cornwall to thy side, and say to Winchester, the earth shall swallow thee up. Translate the seat of thy pastor to the place where ships come to harbour, and the rest of the members will follow the head. For the day hasteneth, in which thy citizens shall perish on account of the guilt of perjury. The whiteness of wool has been hurtful to thee, and the variety of its tinctures. Woe to the perjured nation, for whose sake the renowned city shall come to ruin. The ships shall rejoice at so great an augmentation, and one shall be made out of two. It shall be rebuilt by Eric, loaded with apples, to the smell whereof the birds of several woods shall flock together. He shall add to it a vast palace, and wall it round with six hundred towers. Therefore shall London envy it, and triply increase her walls. The River Thames shall encompass it round, and the fame of the work shall pass beyond the Alps. Eric shall hide his apples within it, and shall make subterraneous passages. At that time shall the stones speak, and the sea towards the Gallic coast be contracted into a narrow space. On each bank shall one man hear another, and the soil of the island shall be enlarged. The secrets of the deep shall be revealed, and Gaul shall tremble for fear. After these things shall come forth a heron from the forest of Calaterium, which shall fly round the island for two years together. With her nocturnal cry she shall call together the winged kind, and assemble to her all sorts of fowls. They shall invade the tillage of a husbandman, and devour all the grain of the harvests. Then shall follow a famine upon the people, and a grievous mortality upon the famine. But when this calamity shall be over, a detestable bird shall go to the Valley of Galabes, and shall raise it to be a high mountain. Upon the top thereof it shall also plant an oak, and build its nest in its branches. Three eggs shall be produced in the nest, from whence shall come forth a fox, a wolf, and a bear. The fox shall devour her mother, and bear the head of an ass. In this monstrous form shall she frighten her brothers, and make them fly into Neustria. But they shall stir up the tusky boar, and returning in a fleet shall encounter with the fox; who at the beginning of the fight shall feign herself dead, and move the boar to compassion. Then shall the boar approach her carcass, and standing over her, shall breathe upon her face and eyes. But she, not forgetting her cunning, shall bite his left foot, and pluck it off from his body. Then shall she leap upon him, and snatch away his right ear and tail, and hide herself in the caverns of the mountains. Therefore shall the deluded boar require the wolf and bear to restore him his members; who, as soon as they shall enter into the cause, shall promise two feet of the fox, together with the ear and tail, and of these they shall make up the members of a hog. With this he shall be satisfied, and expect the promised restitution. In the meantime shall the fox descend from the mountains, and change herself into a wolf, and under pretense of holding a conference with the boar, she shall go to him, and craftily devour him. After that she shall transform herself into a boar, and feigning a loss of some members, shall wait for her brothers; but as soon as they are come, she shall suddenly kill them with her tusks, and shall be crowned with the head of a lion. In her days shall a serpent be brought forth, which shall be a devourer of mankind. With its length it shall encompass London, and devour all that pass by it. The mountain ox shall take the head of a wolf, and whiten his teeth in the Severn. He shall gather to him the flocks of Albania and Cambria, which shall drink the River Thames dry. The ass shall call the goat with the long beard, and shall borrow his shape. Therefore shall the mountain ox be incensed, and having called the wolf, shall become a horned bull against them. In the exercise of his cruelty he shall devour their flesh and bones, but shall be burned upon the top of Urian. The ashes of his funeral-pile shall be turned into swans, that shall swim on dry ground as on a river. They shall devour fishes in fishes, and swallow up men in men. But when old age shall come upon them, they shall become sea-wolves, and practice their frauds in the deep. They shall drown ships, and collect no small quantity of silver. The Thames shall again flow, and assembling together the rivers shall pass beyond the bounds of its channel. It shall cover the adjacent cities, and overturn the mountains that oppose its course. Being full of deceit and wickedness, it shall make use of the fountain Galabes. Hence shall arise factions provoking the Venedotians to war. The oaks of the forest shall meet together, and encounter the rocks of the Gewisseans. A raven shall attend with the kites, and devour the carcasses of the slain. An owl shall build her nest upon the walls of Gloucester, and in her nest shall be brought forth an ass. The Serpent of Malvernia shall bring him up, and put him upon many fraudulent practices. Having taken the crown, he shall ascend on high, and frighten the people of the country with his hideous braying. In his days shall the Pachaian Mountains tremble, and the provinces be deprived of their woods. For there shall come a worm with a fiery breath, and with the vapor it sends forth shall burn up the trees. Out of it shall proceed seven lions deformed with the heads of goats. With the stench of their nostrils they shall corrupt women, and make wives turn common prostitutes. The father shall not know his own son, because they shall grow wanton like brute beasts. Then shall come the giant of wickedness, and terrify all with the sharpness of his eyes. Against him shall arise the Dragon of Worcester, and shall endeavour to banish him. But in the engagement the dragon shall be worsted, and oppressed by the wickedness of the conqueror. For he shall mount upon the dragon, and putting off his garment shall sit upon him naked. The dragon shall bear him up on high, and beat his naked rider with his tail erected. Upon this the giant rousing up his whole strength, shall break his jaws with his sword. At last the dragon shall fold itself up under its tail, and die of poison. After him shall succeed the boar of Totness, and oppress the people with grievous tyranny. Gloucester shall send forth a lion, and shall disturb him in his cruelty in several battles. He shall trample him under his feet, and terrify him with open jaws. At last the lion shall quarrel with the kingdom, and get upon the backs of the nobility. A bull shall come into the quarrel, and strike the lion with his right foot. He shall drive him through all the inns in the kingdom, but shall break his horns against the walls of Oxford. The Fox of Kaerdubalem shall take revenge on the lion, and destroy him entirely with her teeth. She shall be encompassed by the Adder of Lincoln who with a horrible hiss shall give notice of his presence to a multitude of dragons. Then shall the dragons encounter, and tear one another to pieces. The winged shall oppress that which wants wings, and fasten its claws into the poisonous cheeks. Others shall come into the quarrel, and kill one another. A fifth shall succeed those that are slain, and by various stratagems shall destroy the rest. He shall get upon the back of one with his sword, and sever his head from his body. Then throwing off his garment, he shall get upon another, and put his rights and left hand upon his tail. Thus being naked shall he overcome him, whom when clothed he was not able to deal with. The rest he shall gall in their flight, and drive them round the kingdom. Upon this shall come a roaring lion dreadful for his monstrous cruelty. Fifteen parts shall he reduce to one, and shall alone possess the people. The giants of the snow-white colour shall shine, and cause the white people to flourish. Pleasures shall effeminate the princes, and they shall suddenly be changed into beasts. Among them shall arise a lion swelled with human gore. Under him shall a reaper be placed in the standing corn, who, while he is reaping, shall be oppressed by him. A charioteer of York shall appease them, and having banished his lord, shall mount upon the chariot which he shall drive. With his sword unsheathed shall he threaten the East, and fill the tracks of his wheels with blood. Afterwards he shall become a sea-fish, who, being roused up with the hissing of a serpent, shall engender with him. From hence shall be produced three thundering bulls, who having eaten up their pastures shall be turned into trees. The first shall carry a whip of vipers, and turn his back upon the next. He shall endeavour to snatch away the whip, but shall be taken by the last. They shall turn away their faces from one another, till they have thrown away the poisoned cup. To him shall succeed a husbandman of Albania, at whose back shall be a serpent. He shall be employed in ploughing the ground, that the country may become white with corn. The serpent shall endeavour to diffuse his poison in order to blast the harvest. A grievous mortality shall sweep away the people, and the walls of cities shall be made desolate. There shall be given for a remedy the city of Claudius, which shall interpose the nurse of the scourger. For he shall bear a dose of medicine, and in a short time the island shall be restored. Then shall two successively sway the sceptre, whom a horned dragon shall serve. One shall come in armour, and shall ride upon a flying serpent. He shall sit upon his back with his naked body, and cast his right hand upon his tail. With his cry shall the seas be moved, and he shall strike terror into the second. The second therefore shall enter into confederacy with the lion; but a quarrel happening, they shall encounter one another. They shall distress one another, but the courage of the beast shall gain the advantage. Then shall come one with a drum, and appease the rage of the lion. Therefore shall the people of the kingdom be at peace, and provoke the lion to a dose of physic. In his established seat he shall adjust the weights, but shall stretch out his hands into Albania. For which reason the northern provinces shall be grieved, and open the gates of the temples. The sign-bearing wolf shall lead his troops, and surround Cornwall with his tail. He shall be opposed by a soldier in a chariot, who shall transform that people into a boar. The boar therefore shall ravage the provinces, but shall hide his head in the depth of the Severn. A man shall embrace a lion in wine, and the dazzling brightness of gold shall blind the eyes of beholders. Silver shall whiten in the circumference, and torment several wine presses. Men shall be drunk with wine, and, regardless of heaven, shall be intent upon the earth. From them shall the stars turn away their faces, and confound their usual course. Corn will wither at their malign aspects; and there shall fall no dew from heaven. The roots and branches will change their places, and the novelty of the thing shall pass for a miracle. The brightness of the sun shall fade at the amber of Mercury, and horror shall seize the beholders. Silbon of Arcadia shall change his shield; the helmet of Mars shall call Venus. The helmet of Mars shall make a shadow; and the rage of Mercury pass his bounds. Iron Orion shall unsheath his sword: the marine Phoebus shall torment the clouds; Jupiter shall go out of his lawful paths; and Venus forsake her stated lines. The malignity of the star Saturn shall fall down in rain, and slay mankind with a crooked sickle. The twelve houses of the star shall lament the irregular excursions of their guests; and Gemini omit their usual embraces, and call the urn to the fountains. The scales of Libra shall hang obliquely, till Aries puts his crooked horns under them. The tail of Scorpio shall produce lightning, and Cancer quarrel with the Sun. Virgo shall mount upon the back of Sagittarius, and darken her virgin flowers. The chariot of the moon shall disorder the zodiac, and the Pleiades break forth into weeping. No offices of Janus shall hereafter return, but his gate being shut shall lie hid in the chinks of Ariadne. The seas shall rise up in the twinkling of an eye, and the dust of the ancients shall be restored. The winds shall fight together with a dreadful blast, and their sound shall reach the stars.

BOOK EIGHT

1

Vortigern asks Merlin concerning his own death.

MERLIN, by delivering these and many other prophecies, caused in all that were present an admiration at the ambiguity of his expressions. But Vortigern above all the rest both admired and applauded the wisdom and prophetical spirit of the young man: for that age had produced none that ever talked in such a manner before him. Being therefore curious to learn his own fate, he desired the young man to tell him what he knew concerning that particular. Merlin answered: "Fly the fire of the sons of Constantine, if you are able to do it: already they are fitting out their ships; already are they leaving the Armorican shore; already are they spreading out their sails to the wind. They will steer towards Britain; they will invade the Saxon nation; they will subdue that wicked people; but they will first burn you being shut up in a tower. To your own ruin did you prove a traitor to their father, and invite the Saxons into the island. You invited them for your safeguard; but they came for a punishment to you. Two deaths instantly threaten you; nor is it easy to determine which you can best avoid. For on the one hand the Saxons shall lay waste your country, and endeavour to kill you; on the other shall arrive the two brothers, Aurelius Ambrosius and Uther Pendragon, whose business will be to revenge their father's murder on you. Seek out some refuge if you can: to-morrow they will be on the shore of Totness. The faces of the Saxons shall look red with blood, Hengist shall be killed, and Aurelius Ambrosius shall be crowned. He shall bring peace to the nation; he shall restore the churches; but shall die of poison. His brother Uther Pendragon shall succeed him, whose days also shall be cut short by poison. There shall be present at the commission of this treason your own issue, whom the boar of Cornwall shall devour." Accordingly the next day early, arrived Aurelius Ambrosius and his brother, with ten thousand men.

2

Aurelius Ambrosius, being anointed king of Britain, burns Vortigern besieged in a tower.

AS soon as news of his coming was divulged, the Britons, who had been dispersed by their great calamities, met together from all parts, and gaining this new accession of strength from their countrymen, displayed unusual vigour. Having assembled together the clergy, they anointed Aurelius king, and paid him the customary homage. And when the people were urgent to fall upon the Saxons, he dissuaded them from it, because his desire was to pursue Vortigern first. For the treason committed against his father so very much affected him, that he thought nothing done till that was first avenged. In pursuance therefore of his design, he marched with his army into Cambria, to the town of Genroreu, whither Vortigern had fled for refuge. That town was in the country of Hergin, upon the River Gania, in the mountains called Cloarius. As soon as Ambrosius was arrived there, bearing in mind the murder of his father and brother, he spake thus to Eldol, Duke of Gloucester:

"See, most noble Duke, whether the walls of this city are able to protect Vortigern against my sheathing this sword in his bowels. He deserves to die, and you cannot, I suppose, be ignorant of his desert. Oh most villainous of men, whose crimes deserve inexpressible tortures! First he betrayed my father Constantine, who had delivered him and his country from the inroads of the Picts; afterwards my brother, Constans, whom he made king on purpose to destroy him. Again, when by his craft he had usurped the crown, he introduced pagans among the natives, in order to abuse those who continued steadfast in their loyalty to me: but by the good providence of God, he unwarily fell into the snare which he had laid for my faithful subjects. For the Saxons, when they found him out in his wickedness, drove him from the kingdom; for which nobody ought to be concerned. But this I think matter of just grief, that this odious people, whom that detestable traitor invited over, has expelled the nobility, laid waste a fruitful country, destroyed the holy churches, and almost extinguished Christianity over the whole kingdom. Now, therefore, my countrymen, show yourselves men: first revenge yourselves upon him that was the occasion of all these disasters; then let us turn our arms against our enemies, and free our country from their brutish tyranny."

Immediately, therefore, they set their engines to work, and laboured to beat down the walls. But at last, when all other attempts failed, they had recourse to fire, which meeting with proper fuel, ceased not to rage till it had burned down the tower and Vortigern in it.

3

The praise of Aurelius's valour. The levity of the Scots exposed. Forces raised against Hengist.

HENGIST, with his Saxons, was struck with terror at this news, for he dreaded the valour of Aurelius. Such was the bravery and courage this prince was master of, that while he was in Gaul, there was none that durst encounter with him. For in all encounters he either dismounted his adversary, or broke his spear. Besides, he was magnificent in his presents, constant at his devotions, temperate in all respects, and above all things hated a lie. A brave soldier on foot, a better on horseback, and expert in the discipline of an army. Reports of these his noble accomplishments, while he yet continued in Armorican Britain, were daily brought over into the island. Therefore the Saxons, in fear of him, retired beyond the Humber, and in those parts fortified the cities and towns; for that country always was a place of refuge to them; their safety lying in the neighbourhood of Scotland, which used to watch all opportunities of distressing the nation; for that country being in itself a frightful place to live in, and wholly uninhabited, had been a safe retreat for strangers. By its situation it lay open to the Picts, Scots, Dacians, Norwegians, and others, that came to plunder the island. Being, therefore, secure of a safe reception in this country, they fled towards it, that, if there should be occasion, they might retreat into it as into their own camp. This was good news to Aurelius, and made him conceive greater hopes of victory. So assembling his people quickly together, he augmented his army, and made an expeditious march towards the north. In his passage through the countries, he was grieved to see the desolation made in them, but especially that the churches were leveled with the ground; and he promised to rebuild them if he gained the victory.

4

Hengist marches with his army against Aurelius, into the field of Maisbeli.

BUT Hengist, upon his approach, took courage again, and chose out the bravest of his men, whom he exhorted to make a gallant defense, and not be daunted at Aurelius, who, he told them, had but few Armorican Britons with him, since their number did not exceed ten thousand. And as for the native Britons, he made no account of them, since they had been so often defeated by him. He therefore promised them the victory, and that they should come off safely, considering the superiority of their number which amounted to two hundred thousand men in arms. After he had in this manner animated his men, he advanced with them towards Aurelius into a field called Maisbeli, through which Aurelius was to pass. For his intention was to make a sudden assault by a surprise, and fall upon the Britons before they were prepared. But Aurelius perceived the design, and yet did not, on that account, delay going to the field, but rather pursued his march with more expedition. When he was come within sight of the enemy, he put his troops in order, commanding three thousand Armoricans to attend the cavalry, and drew out the rest together with the islanders into line of battle. The Dimetians he placed upon the hills, and the Venedotians in the adjacent woods.

His reason for which was, that they might be there ready to fall upon the Saxons in case they should flee in that direction.

5

A battle between Aurelius and Hengist.

IN the meantime, Eldol, Duke of Gloucester, went to the king, and said, "This one day should suffice for all the days of my life, if by good providence I could but get an opportunity to engage with Hengist; for one of us should die before we parted. I still retain deeply fixed in my memory the day appointed for our peaceably treating together, but which he villainously made use of to assassinate all that were present at the treaty, except myself only, who stood upon my defense with a stake which I accidentally found, until I made my escape. That very day proved fatal, through his treachery, to no less than four hundred and sixty barons and consuls who all went unarmed. From that conspiracy God was pleased to deliver me by throwing a stake in my way, wherewith I defended myself and escaped." Thus spoke Eldol. Then Aurelius exhorted his companions to place all their hope on the Son of God, and to make a brave assault with one consent upon the enemy in defense of their country. Nor was Hengist less busy on the other hand in forming his troops, and giving them directions how to behave themselves in the battle; and he walked himself through their several ranks, the more to spirit themselves up. At last, both armies, being drawn out in order of battle, began the attack, which they maintained with great bravery, and no small loss of blood, both to the Britons and Saxons. Aurelius animated the Christians, Hengist the pagans; and all the time of the engagement, Eldol's chief endeavour was to encounter Hengist, but he had no opportunity for it. For Hengist, when he found that his own men were routed, and that the Christians, by the especial favour of God, had the advantage, fled to the town called Kaerconan, now Cunungeburg. Aurelius pursued him, and either killed or made slaves of all he found in the way. When Hengist saw that he was pursued by Aurelius, he would not enter the town, but assembled his troops, and prepared them to stand another engagement. For he knew the town would not hold out against Aurelius, and that his whole security now lay in his sword. At last Aurelius overtook him, and after marshaling his forces, began another most furious fight. And here the Saxons steadily maintained their ground, notwithstanding the numbers that fell. On both side there was a great slaughter, the groans of the dying causing a greater rage in those that survived. In short, the Saxons would have gained the day, had not a detachment of horse from the Armorican Britons come in upon them. For Aurelius had appointed them the same station which they had in the former battle; so that, upon their advancing, the Saxons gave ground, and when once a little dispersed, were not able to rally again. The Britons, encouraged by this advantage, exerted themselves, and laboured with all their might to distress the enemy. All the time Aurelius was fully employed, not only in giving commands, but encouraging his men by his own example; for with his own hand he killed all that stood in his way, and pursued those that fled. Nor was Eldol less active in all parts of the field, running to and fro to assault his adversaries; but still his main endeavour was to find opportunity of encountering Hengist.

6

Hengist, in a duel with Eldol, is taken by him. The Saxons are slain by the Britons without mercy.

AS there were therefore several movements made by the parties engaged on each side, an opportunity occurred for their meeting and briskly engaging each other. In this encounter of the two greatest champions in the field, the fire sparked with the clashing of their arms, and every stroke in a manner produced both thunder and lightning. For a long time was the victory in suspense, as it seemed sometimes to favour one, sometimes the other. While they were thus hotly engaged, Gorlois, Duke of Cornwall, came up to them with the party he commanded, and did great execution upon the enemy's troops. At the sight of him, Eldol, assured of victory, seized on the helmet of Hengist, and by main force dragged him in among the Britons, and then in transports of joy cried out with a loud voice, "God has fulfilled my desire! My brave soldiers, down, down, with your enemies the Ambrons. The victory is now in your hands: Hengist is defeated, and the day is your own." In the meantime the Britons failed not to perform every one his part against the pagans, upon whom they made many vigorous assaults; and though they were obliged sometimes to give ground, yet their courage did not fail them in making a good resistance; so that they gave the enemy no respite till they had vanquished them. The Saxons therefore fled whithersoever their consternation hurried them, some to the cities, some to the woods upon the hills, and others to their ships. But Octa, the son of Hengist, made his retreat with a great body of men to York: and Eosa, his kinsman, to the city of Alclud, where he had a very large army for his guard.

7

Hengist is beheaded by Eldol.

AURELIUS, after this victory, took the city of Conan above-mentioned, and stayed there three days. During this time he gave orders for the burial of the slain, for curing the wounded, and for the ease and refreshment of his forces that were fatigued. Then he called a council of his principal officers to deliberate what was to be done with Hengist. There was present at the assembly Eldad, Bishop of Gloucester, and brother of Eldol, a prelate of very great wisdom and piety. As soon as he beheld Hengist standing in the king's presence, he demanded silence, and said, "Though all should be unanimous for setting him at liberty, yet would I cut him to pieces. The prophet Samuel is my warrant, who when he had Agag, King of Amalek, in his power, hewed him in pieces, saying, As thy sword hath made women childless, so shall thy mother be childless among women. Do the same to Hengist, who is a second Agag." Accordingly Eldol took his sword, and drew him out of the city, and then cut off his head. But Aurelius, who showed moderation in all his conduct, commanded him to be buried and a heap of earth to be raised over his body, according to the custom of the pagans.

8

Octa, being besieged in York, surrenders himself to the mercy of Aurelius.

FROM hence Aurelius conducted his army to York to besiege Octa, Hengist's son. When the city was invested, Octa was doubtful whether he should give any opposition, and stand a siege against such a powerful army. After consultation upon it, he went out with his principal nobility that were present, carrying a chain in his hand, and sand upon his head, and presented himself to the king with this address: "My gods are vanquished, and I doubt not that the sovereign power is in your God, who has compelled so many noble persons to come before you in this suppliant manner. Be pleased therefore to accept of us, and of this chain. If you do not think us fit objects of your clemency, we here present ourselves ready to be fettered, and to undergo whatever punishment you shall adjudge to us." Aurelius was moved with pity at the spectacle, and demanded the advice of his council what should be done with them. After various proposals upon this subject, Eldad the bishop rose up, and delivered his opinion in these words: "The Gibeonites came voluntarily to the children of Israel to desire mercy, and they obtained it. And shall we Christians be worse than the Jews, in refusing them mercy? It is mercy which they beg, and let them have it. The island of Britain is large, and in many places uninhabited. Let us make a covenant with them, and suffer them at least to inhabit the desert places, that they may be our vassals for ever." The king acquiesced in Eldad's advice, and suffered them to partake of his clemency. After this Eosa and the rest that fled, being encouraged by Octa's success, came also, and were admitted to the same favour. The king therefore granted them the country bordering upon Scotland, and made a firm covenant with them.

9

Aurelius, having entirely routed the enemies, restores all things in Britain, especially ecclesiastical affairs, to their ancient state.

THE enemies being now entirely reduced, the king summoned

the consuls and princes of the kingdom together at York, where he gave orders for the restoration of the churches, which the Saxons had destroyed. He himself undertook the rebuilding of the metropolitan church of that city, as also the other cathedral churches in that province. After fifteen days, when he had settled workmen in various places, he went to London, which city had not escaped the fury of the enemy. He beheld with great sorrow the destruction made in it, and recalled the remainder of the citizens from all parts, and began the restoration of it. Here he settled the affairs of the whole kingdom, revived the laws, restored the right heirs to the possessions of their ancestors; and those estates whereof the heirs had been lost in the late grievous calamity, he distributed among his fellow soldiers. In these important concerns, of restoring the nation to its ancient state, repairing the churches, re-establishing peace and law, and settling the administration of justice, was his time wholly employed. From hence he went to Winchester to repair the ruins of it, as he did of other cities; and when the work was finished there, he went, at the instance of Bishop Eldad, to the monastery near Kaercaradoc, now Salisbury, where the consuls and princes, whom the wicked Hengist had treacherously murdered, lay buried. At this place was a convent that maintained three hundred friars, situated on the Mountain of Ambrius, who, as is reported, had been the founder of it. The sight of the place where the dead lay made the king, who was of a compassionate temper, shed tears, and at last enter upon thoughts, what kind of monument to erect upon it. For he thought something ought to be done to perpetuate the memory of that piece of ground, which was honoured with the bodies of so many noble patriots, that died for their country.

10

Aurelius is advised by Merlin to remove the Giant's Dance from the Mountain Killaraus.

FOR this purpose he summoned together several carpenters and masons, and commanded them to employ the utmost of their art in contriving some new structure for a lasting monument to those great men. But they, in diffidence of their own skill, refused to undertake it; and Tremounus, Archbishop of the City of Legions, went to the king, and said, "If anyone living is able to execute your commands, Merlin, the prophet of Vortigern, is the man. In my opinion there is not in all your kingdom a person of brighter genius, either in predicting future events, or in mechanical contrivances. Order him to come to you, and exercise his skill in the work which you design." Whereupon Aurelius, after he had asked a great many questions concerning him, despatched several messengers into the country to find him out, and bring him to him. After passing through several provinces, they found him in the country of the Gewisseans, at the fountain of Galabes, which he frequently resorted to. As soon as they had delivered their message to him, they conducted him to the king, who received him with joy, and, being curious to hear some of his wonderful speeches, commanded him to prophesy. Merlin made answer: "Mysteries of this kind are not to be revealed but when there is the greatest necessity for it. If I should pretend to utter them for ostentation or diversion, the spirit that instructs me would be silent, and would leave me when I should have occasion for it." When he had made the same refusal to all the rest present, the king would not urge him any longer about his predictions, but spoke to him concerning the monument which he designed. "If you are desirous," said Merlin, "to honour the burying-place of these men with an everlasting monument, send for the Giant's Dance, which is in Killaraus, a mountain in Ireland. For there is a structure of stones there, which none of this age could raise, without a profound knowledge of the mechanical arts. They are stones of a vast magnitude and wonderful quality; and if they can be placed here, as they are there, round this spot of ground, they will stand forever."

11

Uther Pendragon is appointed with Merlin to bring over the Giant's Dance.

AT these words of Merlin, Aurelius burst into laughter, and said, "How is it possible to remove such vast stones from so distant a country, as if Britain was not furnished with stones fit for the work?" Merlin replied, "I entreat your majesty to forbear vain laughter, for what I say is without vanity. They are mystical stones, and of a medicinal virtue. The giants of old brought them from the farthest coast of Africa, and placed them in Ireland, while they inhabited that country. Their design in this was to make baths in them, when they should be taken with any illness. For their method was to wash the stones, and put their sick into the water, which infallibly cured them. With the like success they cured wounds also, adding only the application of some herbs. There is not a stone there which has not some healing virtue." When the Britons heard this, they resolved to send for the stones, and to make war upon the people of Ireland if they should offer to detain them. And to accomplish this business, they made choice of Uther Pendragon, who was to be attended with fifteen thousand men. They chose also Merlin himself, by whose direction the whole affair was to be managed. A fleet being therefore got ready, they set sail, and with a fair wind arrived in Ireland.

12

Gillomanius being routed by Uther, the Britons bring over the Giant's Dance into Britain.

AT that time Gillomanius, a youth of wonderful valour, reigned in Ireland; who, upon the news of the arrival of the Britons in his kingdom, levied a vast army, and marched out against them. And when he had learned the occasion of their coming, he smiled, and said to those about him, "No wonder a cowardly race of people were able to make such devastation in the island of Britain, when the Britons are such brutes and fools. Was ever the like folly heard of? What are the stones of Ireland better than those of Britain, that our kingdom must be put to this disturbance for them? To arms, soldiers, and defend your country; while I have life they shall not take from us the least stone of the Giant's Dance." Uther, seeing them prepared for a battle, attacked them; nor was it long ere the Britons had the advantage, who, having dispersed and killed the Irish, forced Gillomanius to flee. After the victory they went to the Mountain Killaraus, and arrived at the structure of stones, the sight of which filled them both with joy and admiration. And while they were all standing round them, Merlin came up to them and said, "Now try your forces, young men, and see whether strength or art can do the most towards taking down these stones." At this word they all set to their engines with one accord, and attempted the removing of the Giant's Dance. Some prepared cables, others small ropes, others ladders for the work, but all to no purpose. Merlin laughed at their vain efforts, and then began his own contrivances. When he had placed in order the engines that were necessary, he took down the stones with an incredible facility, and gave directions for carrying them to the ships, and placing them therein. This done, they with joy set sail again to return to Britain, where they arrived with a fair gale, and repaired to the burying place with the stones. When Aurelius had notice of it, he sent messengers to all parts of Britain to summon the clergy and people together to the mount of Ambrius, in order to celebrate with joy and honour the erection of the monument. Upon this summons appeared the bishops, abbots, and people of all other orders and qualities; and upon the day and place appointed for their general meeting, Aurelius placed the crown upon his head, and with royal pomp celebrated the feast of Pentecost, the solemnity whereof he continued the three following days. In the meantime, all places of honour that were vacant, he bestowed upon his domestics as rewards for their good services. At that time the two metropolitan sees of York and Legions were vacant; and with the general consent of the people, whom he was willing to please in this choice, he granted York to Sanxo, a man of great quality, and much celebrated for his piety; and the City of Legions to Dubricius, whom divine providence had pointed out as a most useful pastor in that place. As soon as he had settled these and other affairs in the kingdom, he ordered Merlin to set up the stones brought over from Ireland about the sepulchre; which he accordingly did, and placed them in the same manner as they had been in the Mountain Killaraus, and thereby gave a manifest proof of the prevalence of art above strength.

13

Pascentius brings in the Saxons against the Britons.

AT the same time Pascentius, the son of Vortigern, who had fled over into Germany, was levying all the forces of that kingdom against Aurelius Ambrosius with a design to revenge his father's death; and promised his men an immense treasure of gold and silver if with their assistance he could succeed in reducing Britain under his power. When he had at last corrupted all the youth of the country with his large promises, he prepared a vast fleet, and arrived in the northern parts of the island, upon which he began to make great devastations. The king, on the other hand, hearing this news, assembled his army, and marching against them challenged the enraged enemy to a battle; the challenge was accepted, and by the blessing of God the enemy was defeated and put to flight.

14

Pascentius, assisted by the King of Ireland, again invades Britain. Aurelius dies by the treachery of Eopa, a Saxon.

PASCENTIUS, after this flight, durst not return to Germany, but shifting his sails, went over to Gillomanius, in Ireland, by whom he was well received. And when he had given him an account of his misfortune, Gillomanius, in pity to him, promised him his assistance, and at the same time vented his complaint of the injuries done him by Uther, the brother of Aurelius, when he came for the Giant's Dance. At last, entering into confederacy together, they made ready their fleet, in which they embarked, and arrived at the city of Menevia. The news caused Uther Pendragon to levy his forces, and march into Cambria to fight them. For his brother Aurelius then lay sick at Winchester, and was not able to go himself. When Pascentius, Gillomanius, and the Saxons heard of it, they highly rejoiced, flattering themselves that his sickness would facilitate to them the conquest of Britain. While this occurrence was the subject of the people's discourse, one of the Saxons, named Eopa, came to Pascentius, and said, "What reward will you give the man that shall kill Aurelius Ambrosius for you?" To whom Pascentius answered, "O that I could find a man of such resolution! I would give him a thousand pounds of silver, and my friendship for life; and if by good fortune I can but gain the crown, I promise upon oath to make him a centurion." To this Eopa replied, "I have learned the British language, and know the manners of the people, and have skill in physic. If, therefore, you will perform this promise, I will pretend to be a Christian and a Briton, and when, as a physician, I shall be admitted into the king's presence, I will make him a potion that shall dispatch him. And to gain the readier access to him, I will put on the appearance of a devout and learned monk." Upon this offer, Pascentius entered into covenant with him, and confirmed what he had promised with an oath. Eopa, therefore, shaved his beard and head, and in the habit of a monk hastened to Winchester, loaded with vessels full of medical preparations. As soon as he arrived there, he offered his service to those that attended about the king, and was graciously received by them; for to them nobody was now more acceptable than a physician. Being introduced into the king's presence, he promised to restore him to health, if he would but take his potions. Upon which he had his orders forthwith to prepare one of them, into which when he had secretly conveyed a poisonous mixture, he gave it to the king. As soon as Aurelius had drunk it up, the wicked Ambron ordered him presently to cover himself close up, and fall asleep, that the detestable poison might the better operate. The king readily obeyed his prescriptions, and in hopes of his speedy recovery fell asleep. But the poison quickly diffused itself through all the pores and veins of his body, so that the sleep ended in death. In the meantime the wicked traitor, having cunningly withdrawn himself first from one and then from another, was no longer to be found in the court. During these transactions at Winchester, there appeared a star of wonderful magnitude and brightness, darting forth a ray, at the end of which was a globe of fire in form of a dragon, out of whose mouth issued forth two rays; one of which seemed to stretch out itself beyond the extent of Gaul, the other towards the Irish Sea, and ended in seven lesser rays.

15

A comet pre-signifies the reign of Uther.

AT the appearance of this star, a general fear and amazement seized his people; and even Uther, the king's brother, who was then upon his march with his army into Cambria, being not a little terrified at it, was very curious to know of the learned men what it portended. Among others, he ordered Merlin to be called, who also attended in this expedition to give his advice in the management of the war; and who, being now presented before him, was commanded to discover to him the significance of the star. At this he burst out into tears, and with a loud voice cried out, "O irreparable loss! O distressed people of Britain! Alas! The illustrious prince is departed! The renowned King of the Britons, Aurelius Ambrosius, is dead! Whose death will prove fatal to us all, unless God be our helper. Make haste, therefore, most noble Uther, make haste to engage the enemy: the victory will be yours, and you shall be King of all Britain. For the star, and the fiery dragon under it, signifies yourself, and the ray extending towards the Gallic coast portends that you shall have a most potent son, to whose power all those kingdoms shall be subject over which the ray reaches. But the other ray signifies a daughter, whose sons and grandsons shall successively enjoy the kingdom of Britain."

16

Pascentius and Gillomanius are killed in battle.

UTHER, though he doubted the truth of what Merlin had declared, pursued his march against the enemy, for he was not come within half a day's march of Menevia. When Gillomanius, Pascentius, and the Saxons were informed of his approach, they went out to give him battle. As soon as they were come within sight of each other, both armies began to form themselves into several bodies, and then advanced in a close attack, in which both sides suffered a loss of men, as usually happens in such engagements. At last, towards the close of the day, the advantage was on Uther's side, and the death of Gillomanius and Pascentius made a way for complete victory. So that the barbarians, being put to flight, hastened to their ships, but were slain by their pursuers. Thus, by the favour of Christ, the general had triumphant success, and then with all possible expedition, after so great a fatigue, returned back to Winchester: for he had now been informed by messengers that arrived of the king's sad fate, and of his burial by the bishops of the country, near the convent of Ambrius, within the Giant's Dance, which in his lifetime he had commanded to be made. For upon hearing the sad news of his death, the bishops, abbots, and all the clergy of that province, had met together at Winchester, to solemnize his funeral. And because in his lifetime he had given orders for his being buried in the sepulchre which he had prepared, and therefore carried his corpse thither, and performed his exsequies[5] with royal magnificence.

17

Uther Pendragon is made king of Britain.

BUT Uther his brother, having assembled the clergy of the kingdom, took the crown, and by universal consent was advanced to the kingdom. And remembering the explanation which Merlin had made of the star above-mentioned, he commanded two dragons to be made of gold in likeness of the dragon which he had seen at the ray of the star. As soon as they were finished, which was done with a wonderful nicety of workmanship, he made a present of one to the cathedral church of Winchester, but reserved the other for himself to be carried along with him to his wars. From this time, therefore, he was called Uther Pendragon, which in the British tongue signifies the dragon's head; the occasion of this appellation being Merlin's predicting, from the appearance of a dragon, that he should be king.

---

5 Funeral procession, ceremonies of burial

18

Octa and Eosa are taken in battle.

IN the meantime Octa the son of Hengist, and his kinsman Eosa, seeing they were no longer bound by the treaty which they had made with Aurelius Ambrosius, began to raise disturbances against the king, and infest his countries. For they were now joining with the Saxons whom Pascentius had brought over, and sending messengers into Germany for the rest. Being therefore attended with a vast army, he invaded the northern provinces, and in an outrageous manner destroyed all the cities and fortified places, from Albania to York. At last, as he was beginning the siege of that city, Uther Pendragon came upon him with the whole power of the kingdom, and gave him battle. The Saxons behaved with great gallantry, and having sustained the assaults of the Britons, forced them to fly; and upon this advantage pursued them with slaughter to the Mountain Damen, which was as long as they could do it with day-light. The mountain was high, and had a hazel-wood upon the top of it, and about the middle broken and cavernous rocks, which were a harbour to wild beasts. The Britons made up to it, and stayed there all night among the rocks and hazel-bushes. But as it began to draw towards day, Uther commanded the consuls and princes to be called together that he might consult with them in what manner to assault the enemy. Whereupon they forthwith appeared before the king, who commanded them to give their advice; and Gorlois, Duke of Cornwall, had orders to deliver his opinion first, out of regard to his years and great experience. "There is no occasion," said he, "for ceremonies or speeches, while we see that it is still night: but there is for boldness and courage, if you desire any longer enjoyment of your life and liberty. The pagans are very numerous, and eager to fight, and we much inferior to them in number; so that if we stay till daybreak, we cannot, in my opinion, attack them to advantage. Come on, therefore, while we have the favour of the night, let us go down in a close body, and surprise them in their camp with a sudden assault. There can be no doubt of success, if with one consent we fall upon them boldly, while they think themselves secure, and have no expectation of our coming in such a manner." The king and all that were present were pleased with his advice, and pursued it. For as soon as they were armed and placed in their ranks, they made towards the enemy's camp, designing a general assault. But upon approaching to it, they were discovered by the watch, who with sound of trumpet awaked their companions. The enemies being hereupon put into confusion and astonishment, part of them hastened towards the sea, and part of them ran up and down whithersoever their fear or precipitation drove them. The Britons, finding their coming discovered, hastened their march, and keeping still close together in their ranks, assailed the camp; into which when they had found an entrance, they ran with their drawn swords upon the enemy; who in this sudden surprise made but a faint defence against their vigorous and regular attack; and pursuing this blow with great eagerness they destroyed some thousands of the pagans, took Octa and Eosa prisoners, and entirely dispersed the Saxons.

19

Uther, falling in love with Igerna, enjoys her by the assistance of Merlin's magical operations.

AFTER this victory Uther repaired to the city of Alclud, where he settled the affairs of that province, and restored peace everywhere. He also made a progress round all the countries of the Scots, and tamed the fierceness of that rebellious people, by such a strict administration of his justice, as none of his predecessors had exercised before: so that in his time offenders were everywhere under great terror, since they were sure of being punished without mercy. At last, when he had established peace in the northern provinces, he went to London, and commanded Octa and Eosa to be kept in prison there. The Easter following he ordered all the nobility in the kingdom to meet at that city, in order to celebrate that great festival, in honour of which he designed to wear his crown. The summons was everywhere obeyed, and there was a great concourse from all cities to celebrate the day. So the king observed the festival with great solemnity, as he had designed, and very joyfully entertained his nobility, of whom there was a very great muster, with their wives and daughters, suitably to the magnificence of the banquet prepared for them. And having been received with joy by the king, they also expressed the same in their deportment before him. Among the rest was present Gorlois, Duke of Cornwall, with his wife Igerna, the greatest beauty in all Britain. No sooner had the king cast his eyes upon her among the rest of the ladies, than he fell passionately in love with her, and little regarding the rest, made her the subject of all his thoughts. She was the only lady that he continually served with fresh dishes, and to whom he sent golden cups by his confidants; on her he bestowed all his smiles, and to her addressed all his discourse. The husband, discovering this, fell into a great rage, and retired from the court without taking leave: nor was there anybody that could stop him while he was under fear of losing the chief object of his delight. Uther, therefore, in great wrath commanded him to return back to court, and make him satisfaction for this affront. But Gorlois refused to obey; upon which the king was highly incensed, and swore he would destroy his country, if he did not speedily compound for his offense. Accordingly, without delay, while their anger was hot against each other, the king got together a great army, and marched into Cornwall, the cities and towns thereof he set on fire. But Gorlois durst not engage with him, on account of the inferiority of his numbers; and thought it a wiser course to fortify his towns till he could get succour from Ireland. And as he was under more concern for his wife than himself, he put her into the town of Tintagel, upon the sea-shore, which he looked upon as a place of great safety. But he himself entered the castle of Dimilioc, to prevent their being both at once involved in the same danger, if any should happen. The king, informed of this, went to the town where Gorlois was, which he besieged, and shut up all the avenues to it. A whole week was now past, when, retaining in mind his love to Igerna, he said to one of his confidants, named Ulfin de Ricaradoch: "My passion for Igerna is such that I can neither have ease of mind, nor health of body, till I obtain her: and if you cannot assist me with your advice how to accomplish my desire, the inward torments I endure will kill me." "Who can advise you in this matter," said Ulfin, "when no force will enable us to have access to her in the town of Tintagel? For it is situated upon the sea, and on every side surrounded by it; and there is but one entrance into it, and that through a straight rock, which three men shall be able to defend against the whole power of the kingdom. Notwithstanding, if the prophet Merlin would in earnest set about this attempt, I am of the opinion you might, with his advice, obtain your wishes." The king readily believed what he was so well inclined to, and ordered Merlin, who was also come to the siege, to be called. Merlin, therefore, being introduced into the king's presence, was commanded to give his advice, how the king might accomplish his desire with respect to Igerna. And he, finding the great anguish of the king, was moved by such excessive love, and said, "To accomplish your desire, you must make use of such arts as have not been heard of in your time. I know how, by the force of my medicines, to give you the exact likeness of Gorlois, so that in all respects you shall seem to be no other than himself. If you will therefore obey my prescriptions, I will metamorphose you into the true semblance of Gorlois, and Ulfin into Jordan of Tintagel, his familiar friend; and I myself, being transformed into another shape, will make the third in the adventure; and in this disguise you may go safely to the town where Igerna is, and have admittance to her." The king complied with the proposal, and acted with great caution in this affair; and when he had committed the care of the siege to his intimate friends, underwent the medical applications of Merlin by whom he was transformed into the likeness of Gorlois; as was Ulfin also into Jordan, and Merlin himself into Bricel; so that nobody could see any remains now of their former likeness. They then set forward on their way to Tintagel, at which they arrived in the evening twilight, and forthwith signified to the porter that the consul was come; upon which the gates were opened, and the men let in. For what room could there be for suspicion, when Gorlois himself seemed to be there present? The king therefore stayed that night with Igerna, and had the full enjoyment of her, for she was deceived with the false disguise which he had put on, and the artful and amourous discourses wherewith he entertained her. He told her he had left his own place besieged, purely to provide for the safety of her dear self, and the town she was in; so that believing all that he said, she refused him nothing which he desired. The same night therefore she conceived the most renowned Arthur, whose heroic and wonderful actions have justly rendered his name famous to posterity.

20

Gorlois being killed, Uther marries Igerna.

IN the meantime, as soon as the king's absence was discovered at the siege, his army unadvisedly made an assault upon the walls, and provoked the besieged count to a battle, who himself also, acting as inconsiderately as they, sallied forth with his men, thinking with such a small handful to oppose a powerful army; but happened to be killed in the very first brunt of the fight, and had all his men routed. The town also was taken; but all the riches of it were not shared equally among the besiegers, but every one greedily took what he could get, according as fortune or his own strength favoured him. After this bold attempt, came messengers to Igerna, with the news both of the duke's death, and of the event of the siege. But when they saw the king in the likeness of the consul, sitting close by her, they were struck with shame and astonishment at his safe arrival there, whom they had left dead at the siege; for they were wholly ignorant of the miracles which Merlin had wrought with his medicines. The king therefore smiled at the news, and embracing the countess, said to her: "Your own eyes may convince you that I am not dead, but alive. But notwithstanding, the destruction of the town and the slaughter of my men is what very much grieves me, so that there is reason to fear the king's coming upon us, and taking us in this place. To prevent which, I will go out to meet him, and make my peace with him for fear of a worse disaster." Accordingly, as soon as he was out of the town, he went to his army, and having put off the disguise of Gorlois, was Uther Pendragon again. Then he returned to the town of Tintagel, which he took, and in it, what he impatiently wished for, Igerna herself. After this they continued to live together with much affection for each other, and had a son and daughter, whose names were Arthur and Anne.

21

Octa and Eosa renew the war. Lot, a consul, marries the king's daughter.

IN the process of time the king was taken ill of a lingering distemper, and meanwhile the keepers of the prison wherein Octa and Eosa (as we related before) led a weary life, had fled over with them into Germany, and occasioned great fear over the kingdom. For there was a report of their great levies in Germany, and the vast fleet which they had prepared for their return to destroy the island: which the event verified. For they returned in a great fleet and with a prodigious number of men, and invaded the parts of Albania where they destroyed both cities and inhabitants with fire and sword. Wherefore, in order to repulse the enemies, the command of the British army was committed to Lot of Londonesia, who was a consul, and a most valiant knight, and grown up to maturity both of years and wisdom. Out of respect to his eminent merits, the king had given him his daughter Anne, and entrusted him with the care of the kingdom during his illness. In his expedition against the enemies he had various success, being often repulsed by them, and forced to retreat to the cities; but he oftener routed and dispersed them, and compelled them to flee sometimes into the woods, sometimes to their ships. So that in a war attended with so many turns of fortune, it was hard to know which side had the better. The greatest injury to the Britons was their own pride in disdaining to obey the consul's commands; for which reason all their efforts against the enemy were less vigourous and successful.

22

Uther, being ill, is carried in a horse-litter against the enemy.

THE island being by this conduct now almost laid waste, the king, having information of the matter, fell into a greater rage than his weakness could bear, and commanded all his nobility to come before him that he might reprove them severely for their pride and cowardice. And as soon as they were all entered into his presence, he sharply rebuked them in menacing language, and swore he himself would lead them against the enemy. For this purpose he ordered a horse-litter to be made in which he designed to be carried, for his infirmity would not suffer him to use any other sort of vehicle; and he charged them to be all ready to march against the enemy at the first opportunity. So, without delay, the horse-litter and all his attendants were got ready and the day arrived which had been appointed for their march.

23

Octa and Eosa, with a great number of their men, are killed.

THE king, therefore, being put into his vehicle, they marched directly to Verulam, where the Saxons were grievously oppressing the people. When Octa and Eosa had intelligence that the Britons were come, and that the king was brought in a horse-litter, they disdained to fight with him saying, it would be a shame for such brave men to fight with one that was half dead. For which reason they retired into the city, and, as it were in contempt of any danger from the enemy, left their gates wide open. But Uther, upon information of this, instantly commanded his men to lay siege to the city, and assault the walls on all sides; which orders they strictly executed; and were just entering the breaches which they had made in the walls, and ready to begin a general assault, when the Saxons, seeing the advantages which the Britons had gained, and being forced to abate somewhat of their haughty pride, condescended so far as to put themselves into a posture of defense. They therefore mounted the walls, from whence they poured down showers of arrows, and repulsed the Britons. On both sides the contest continued till night released them from the fatigue of their arms, which was what many of the Britons desired, though the greater part of them were for having the matter quickly decided with the enemy. The Saxons, on the other hand, finding how prejudicial their own pride had been to them, and that the advantage was on the side of the Britons, resolved to make a sally at break of day, and try their fortune with the enemy in the open field; which accordingly was done. For no sooner was it daylight, than they marched out with this design, all in their proper ranks. The Britons, seeing them, divided their men into several bodies, and advancing towards them, began the attack first, their part being to assault, while the others were only upon the defensive. However, much blood was shed on both sides, and the greatest part of the day spent in the fight, when at last, Octa and Eosa being killed, the Saxons turned their backs, and left the Britons a complete victory. The king at this was in such an ecstasy of joy, that whereas before he could hardly raise up himself without the help of others, he now without any difficulty sat upright in his horse-litter of himself, as if he was on a sudden restored to health; and said with a laughing and merry countenance, "These Ambrons called me the half-dead king, because my sickness obliged me to lie on a horse-litter; and indeed so I was. Yet victory to me half-dead, is better than to be safe and sound and vanquished. For to die with honour is preferable to living with disgrace."

24

Uther, upon drinking spring water that was treacherously poisoned by the Saxons, dies.

THE Saxons, notwithstanding this defeat, persisted in their malice, and entering the northern provinces, without respite infested the people there. Uther's purpose was to have pursued them, but his princes dissuaded him from it because his illness had increased since the victory. This gave new courage to the enemy, who left nothing unattempted to make conquest of the kingdom. And now they had recourse to their former treacherous practices, and contrive how to compass the king's death by secret villainy. And because they could have no access to him otherwise, they resolved to take him off by poison; in which they succeeded. For while he was lying ill at Verulam, they sent away some spies in a poor habit, to learn the state of the court; and when they had thoroughly informed themselves of the posture of affairs, they found out an expedient by which they might accomplish their villainy. For there was near the court a spring of very clear water, which the king used to drink of when his distemper had made all other liquors nauseous to him. This the detestable conspirators made use of to destroy him by so poisoning the whole mass of water which sprang up, that the next time the king drank of it, he was seized with sudden death, as were also a hundred other persons after him, till the villainy was discovered, and a heap of earth thrown over the well. As soon as the king's death was divulged, the bishops and clergy of the kingdom assembled, and carried his body to the convent of Ambrius where they buried it with regal solemnity, close by Aurelius Ambrosius, within the Giant's Dance.

BOOK NINE

1

Arthur succeeds his father Uther in the kingdom of Britain, and besieges Colgrin.

UTHER Pendragon being dead, the nobility from several provinces assembled together at Silchester, and proposed to Dubricius, Archbishop of Legions, that he should consecrate Arthur, Uther's son, to be their king. For they were now in great straits, because, upon hearing of the king's death, the Saxons had invited over their countrymen from Germany, and, under the command of Colgrin, were attempting to exterminate the whole British race. They had also entirely subdued all that part of the island which extends from the Humber to the sea of Caithness. Dubricius, therefore, grieving for the calamities of his country, in conjunction with the other bishops, set the crown upon Arthur's head. Arthur was then fifteen years old, but a youth of such unparalleled courage and generosity, joined with that sweetness of temper and innate goodness, as gained him universal love. When his coronation was over, he, according to usual custom, showed his bounty and munificence to the people. And such a number of soldiers flocked to him upon it, that his treasury was not able to answer that vast expense. But such a spirit of generosity, joined with valour, can never long want means to support itself. Arthur, therefore, the better to keep up his munificence, resolved to make use of his courage, and to fall upon the Saxons, that he might enrich his followers with their wealth. To this he was also moved by the justice of the cause, since the entire monarchy of Britain belonged to him by hereditary right. Hereupon assembling the youth under his command, he marched to York, of which, when Colgrin had intelligence, he met him with a very great army, composed of Saxons, Scots, and Picts, by the River Duglas; where a battle happened, with the loss of the greater part of both armies. Nothwithstanding, the victory fell to Arthur, who pursued Colgrin to York, and there besieged him. Badulph, upon the news of his brother's flight, went towards the siege with a body of six thousand men to his relief, for at the time of the battle he was upon the sea-coast, waiting for the arrival of Duke Cheldric with succours from Germany. And being now no more than ten miles distant from the city, his purpose was to make a speedy march in the night-time, and fall upon the enemy by way of surprise. But Arthur, having intelligence of his design, sent a detachment of six hundred horse and three thousand foot under the command of Cador, Duke of Cornwall, to meet him the same night. Cador, therefore, falling into the same road along which the enemy was passing, made a sudden assault upon them, and entirely defeated the Saxons, and put them to flight. Badulph was excessively grieved at this disappointment in the relief which he intended for his brother, and began to think of some other stratagem to gain access to him, in which if he could but succeed, he thought they might concert measures together for their safety. And since he had no other way for it, he shaved his head and beard, and put on the habit of a jester with a harp, and in this disguise walked up and down in the camp, playing upon his instrument as if he had been a harper. He thus passed unsuspected, and by a little and little went up to the walls of the city, where he was at last discovered by the besieged, who thereupon drew him up with cords, and conducted him to his brother. At this unexpected, though much desired meeting, they spent some time in joyfully embracing each other, and then began to consider various stratagems for their delivery. At last, just as they were considering their case desperate, the ambassadors returned from Germany, and brought with them to Albania a fleet of six hundred sail, laden with brave soldiers, under the command of Cheldric. Upon this news, Arthur was dissuaded by his council from continuing the siege any longer, for fear of hazarding a battle with so powerful and numerous an army.

2

Hoel sends fifteen thousand men to Arthur's assistance.

ARTHUR complied with their advice, and made his retreat to London, where he called an assembly of all the clergy and nobility of the kingdom, to ask their advice, what course to take against the formidable power of the pagans. After some deliberation, it was agreed that ambassadors should be despatched to Armorica, to King Hoel, to represent to him the calamitous state of Britain. Hoel was the son of Arthur's sister by Dubricius, King of the Armorican Britons; so that, upon the advice of the disturbances his uncle was threatened with, he ordered his fleet to be got ready, and, having assembled fifteen thousand men, he arrived with the first fair wind at Hamo's Port, and was received with all suitable honour by Arthur, and most affectionately embraced by him.

3

Arthur makes the Saxons his tributaries.

AFTER a few days they went to relieve the city Kaerliudcoit that was besieged by the pagans; which being situated upon a mountain, between two rivers in the province of Lindisia, is called by another name Lindocolinum. As soon as they arrived there with all their forces, they fought with the Saxons, and made a grievous slaughter of them, to the number of six thousand; part of whom were drowned in the rivers, part fell by the hands of the Britons. The rest in a great consternation quitted the siege and fled, but were closely pursued by Arthur, till they came to the wood of Celidon, where they endeavoured to form themselves into a body again, and make a stand. And here they again joined battle with the Britons, and made a brave defense, whilst the trees that were in the place secured them against the enemy's arrows. Arthur, seeing this, commanded the trees that were in that part of the wood to be cut down, and the trunks to be placed quite round them, so as to hinder their getting out; resolving to keep them pent up here till he could reduce them by famine. He then commanded his troops to besiege the wood, and continued three days in that place. The Saxons, having now no provisions to sustain them, and being just ready to starve with hunger, begged for leave to go out; in consideration whereof they offered to leave all their gold and silver behind them, and return back to Germany with nothing but their empty ships. They promised also that they would pay him tribute from Germany, and leave hostages with him. Arthur, after consultation about it, granted their petition, allowing them only leave to depart, and retaining all their treasures, and also hostages for payment of the tribute. But as they were under sail on their return home, they repented of their bargain, and tacked about again towards Britain, and went on shore at Totness. No sooner were they landed, than they made an utter devastation of the country as far as the Severn sea, and put all the peasants to the sword. From thence they pursued their furious march to the town of Bath, and laid siege to it. When the king had intelligence of it, he was beyond measure surprised at their proceedings, and immediately gave orders for the execution of the hostages. And desisting from an attempt which he had entered upon to reduce the Scots and Picts, he marched with the utmost expedition to raise the siege; but laboured under very great difficulties, because he had left his nephew Hoel sick at Alclud. At length, having entered the province of Somerset, and beheld how the siege was carried on, he addressed himself to his followers in these words: "Since these impious and detestable Saxons have disdained to keep faith with me, I, to keep faith in God, will endeavour to revenge the blood of my countrymen this day upon them. To arms, soldiers, and courageously fall upon the perfidious wretches, over whom we shall, with Christ assisting us, undoubtedly obtain the victory."

4

Dubricius's speech against the treacherous Saxons. Arthur with his own hand kills four hundred and seventy Saxons in one battle. Colgrin and Badulph are killed in the same.

WHEN he had done speaking, St. Dubricius, Archbishop of Legions, going to the top of a hill, cried out with a loud voice, "You that have the honour to profess the Christian faith, keep fixed in your minds the love which you owe to your country and fellow subjects, whose sufferings by the treachery of the pagans will be an everlasting reproach to you, if you do not courageously defend them. It is your country which you fight for, and for which you should, when required, voluntarily suffer death; for that itself is victory and the cure of the soul. For he that shall die for his brethren, offers himself as a living sacrifice to God, and has Christ for his example, who condescended to lay down his life for his brethren. If therefore any of you shall be killed in this war, that death itself, which is suffered in so glorious a cause, shall be to him for penance and absolution of all his sins." At these words, all of them, encouraged with the benediction of the holy prelate, instantly armed themselves, and prepared to obey his orders. Also Arthur himself, having put on a coat of mail suitable to the grandeur of so powerful a king, placed a golden helmet on his head on which was engraved the figure of a dragon; and on his shoulders his shield called Priwen; upon which the picture of the blessed Mary, mother of God, was painted in order to put him frequently in mind of her. Then girding on his Caliburn, which was an excellent sword made in the isle of Avallon, he graced his right hand with his lance, named Ron, which was hard, broad, and fit for slaughter. After this, having placed his men in order, he boldly attacked the Saxons who were drawn out in the shape of a wedge, as their manner was. And they, notwithstanding that the Britons fought with great eagerness, made a noble defense all that day; but at length, towards sunsetting, climbed up the next mountain, which served them for a camp: for they desired no larger extent of ground, since they confided very much in their numbers. The next morning Arthur, with his army, went up the mountain, but lost many of his men in the ascent by the advantage which the Saxons had in their station on the top, from whence they could pour down upon him with much greater speed than he was able to advance against them. Notwithstanding, after a very hard struggle, the Britons gained the summit of the hill, and quickly came to a close engagement with the enemy, who again gave them a warm reception, and made a vigorous defense. In this manner was a great part of that day also spent, whereupon Arthur, provoked to see the little advantage he had yet gained, and that victory still continued in suspense, drew out his Caliburn, and, calling upon the name of the blessed Virgin, rushed forward with great fury into the thickest of the enemy's ranks; of whom (such was the merit of his prayers) not one escaped alive that felt the fury of his sword; neither did he give over the fury of his assault until he had, with his Caliburn alone, killed four hundred and seventy men. The Britons, seeing this, followed their leader in great multitudes, and made slaughter on all sides; so that Colgrin, and Badulph his brother, and many thousands more, fell before them. But Cheldric, in this imminent danger to his men, betook himself to flight.

5

The Saxons, after their leader Cheldric was killed, are all compelled by Cador to surrender.

THE victory being thus gained, the king commanded Cador, Duke of Cornwall, to pursue them, while he himself should hasten his march into Albania: from whence he had advice that the Scots and Picts were besieging Alclud, in which, as we said before, Hoel lay sick. Therefore he hastened to his assistance, for fear he might fall into the hands of the barbarians. In the meantime the Duke of Cornwall, who had the command of ten thousand men, would not as yet pursue the Saxons in their flight, but speedily made himself master of their ships to hinder their getting on board, and manned them with his best soldiers who were to beat back the pagans in case they should flee thither: after this he hastily pursued the enemy, according to Arthur's command, and allowed no quarter to those he could overtake. So that they whose behaviour before was so cruel and insolent, now with timorous hearts fled for shelter, sometimes to the coverts of the woods, sometimes to mountains and caves, to prolong a wretched life. At last, when none of these places could afford them a safe retreat, they entered the Isle of Thanet with their broken forces; but neither did they there get free from the Duke of Cornwall's pursuit, for he still continued slaughtering them, and gave them no respite till he had killed Cheldric, and taken hostages for the surrender of the rest.

6

Arthur grants a pardon to the Scots and Picts, besieged at the Lake Lumond.

HAVING therefore settled peace here, he directed his march to Alclud, which Arthur had relieved from the oppression of the barbarians, and from thence conducted his army to Mureif, where the Scots and Picts were besieged; after three several battles with the king and his nephew, they had fled as far as this province, and entering upon the lake Lumond, sought for refuge in the islands that are upon it. This lake contains sixty islands, and receives sixty rivers into it, which empty themselves into the sea by no more than one mouth. There is also an equal number of rocks in these islands, as also of eagles' nests in those rocks, which flocked together there every year, and, by the loud and general noise which they now made, foreboded some remarkable event that should happen to the kingdom. To these islands, therefore, had the enemy fled, thinking the lake would serve them instead of a fortification, but it proved of little advantage to them. For Arthur, having got together a fleet, sailed round the rivers, and besieged the enemy fifteen days together, by which they were so straitened with hunger, that they died by thousands. While he was harassing them in this manner Guillamurius, King of Ireland, came up in a fleet with a very great army of barbarians, in order to relieve the besieged. This obliged Arthur to raise the siege, and turn his arms against the Irish, whom he slew without mercy, and compelled the rest to return back to their country. After this victory, he proceeded in his first attempt, which was to extirpate the whole race of the Scots and Picts, and treated them with an unparalleled severity. And as he allowed quarter to none, the bishops of that miserable country, with all the inferior clergy, met together, and bearing the relics of the saints and other consecrated things of the church before them, barefooted, came to implore the king's mercy for their people. As soon as they were admitted into his presence, they fell down upon their knees, and humbly besought him to have pity on their distressed country, since the sufferings which he had already made it undergo were sufficient; nor was there any necessity to cut off the small remainder to a man; and that he would allow them the enjoyment of a small part of the country, since they were willing to bear the yoke which he should impose upon them. The king was moved at the manner of their delivering this petition, and could not forbear expressing his clemency to them with tears; and at the request of those holy men, granted them pardon.

7

Arthur relates the wonderful nature of some ponds.

THIS affair being concluded, Hoel had the curiosity to view the situation of the lake, and wondered to find the number of rivers, islands, rocks, and eagles' nests so exactly correspond: and while he was reflecting upon it as something that appeared miraculous, Arthur came to him, and told him of another pond in the same province which was yet more wonderful. For not far from thence was one whose length and breadth were each twenty feet, and depth five feet. But whether its square figure was natural or artificial, the wonder of it was, there were four different sorts of fishes in the four several corners of it, none of which were ever found in any other part of the pond but their own. He told him likewise of another pond in Wales, near the Severn, called by the people Linligwan, into which when the sea flows, it receives it in the manner of a gulf, but so as to swallow up the tide, and never be filled, or have its banks covered by it. But at the ebbing of the sea, it throws out the waters which it had swallowed, as high as a mountain, and at last dashes and covers the banks with them. In the meantime, if all the people of that country should stand near with their faces towards it, and happened to have their clothes sprinkled with the dashing of the waves, they would hardly, if at all, escape being swallowed up by the pond. But with their backs towards it, they need not fear being dashed, though they stood upon the very banks.

8

Arthur restores York to its ancient beauty, especially as to its churches.

THE king, after his general pardon granted to the Scots, went to York to celebrate the feast of Christ's nativity which was now at hand. On entering the city, he beheld with grief the desolation of the churches; for upon the expulsion of the holy Archbishop Sanxo, and all of the clergy there, the temples which were half burned down, had no longer divine service performed in them: so much had the impious rage of the pagans prevailed. After this, in an assembly of the clergy and the people, he appointed Pyramus his chaplain metropolitan of that see. The churches that lay level with the ground, he rebuilt, and (which was their chief ornament) saw them filled with assemblies of devout persons of both sexes. Also the nobility that were driven out by the disturbances of the Saxons, he restored to their country.

9

Arthur honours Augusel with the sceptre of the Scots; Urian with that of Mureif; and Lot with the consulship of Londonesia.

THERE were three brothers of royal blood, viz. Lot, Urian, and Augusel, who, before the Saxons had prevailed, held the government of those parts. Being willing therefore to bestow on these, as he did on others, the rights of their ancestors, he restored to Augusel the sovereignty over the Scots; his brother Urian he honoured with the sceptre of Mureif; and Lot, who in the time of Aurelius Ambrosius had married his sister, by whom he had two sons, Walgan and Modred, he reestablished in the consulship of Londonesia and the other provinces belonging to him. At length, when the whole country was reduced by him to its ancient state, he took to wife Guanhumara, descended from a noble family of Romans, who was educated under Duke Cador, and in beauty surpassed all the women of the island.

10

Arthur adds to his government Ireland, Iceland, Gothland, and the Orkneys.

THE next summer he fitted out a fleet, and made an expedition into Ireland, which he was desirous to reduce. Upon landing there, he was met by King Guillamurius before mentioned, with a vast number of men, who came with a design to fight him; but at the very beginning of the battle, those naked and unarmed people were miserably routed, and fled to such places as lay open to them for shelter. Guillamurius also in a short time was taken prisoner, and forced to submit; as were also all the other princes of the country after the king's example, being under great consternation at what had happened. After an entire conquest of Ireland, he made a voyage with his fleet to Iceland, which he also subdued. And now a rumour spreading over the rest of the islands, that no country was able to withstand him, Doldavius, King of Gothland, and Gunfasius, King of the Orkneys, came voluntarily, and made their submission, on a promise of paying tribute. Then, as soon as winter was over, he returned back to Britain, where having established the kingdom, he resided in it for twelve years together in peace.

11

Arthur subdues Norway, Dacia, Aquitaine, and Gaul.

AFTER this, having invited over to him all persons whatsoever that were famous for valour in foreign nations, he began to augment the number of his domestics, and introduced such politeness into his court, as people of the remotest countries thought worthy of their imitation. So that there was not a nobleman who thought himself worthy of any consideration, unless his clothes and arms were made in the same fashion as those of Arthur's knights. At length the fame of his munificence and valour spreading over the whole world, he became a terror to the kings of other countries, who grievously feared the loss of their dominions if he should make any attempt upon them. Being much perplexed with these anxious cares, they repaired their cities and towers, and built towns in convenient places, the better to fortify themselves against any enterprise of Arthur, when occasion should require. Arthur, being informed of what they were doing, was delighted to find how much they stood in awe of him, and formed a design for the conquest of all Europe. Then having prepared his fleet, he first attempted Norway that he might procure the crown of it for Lot, his sister's husband. This Lot was the nephew of Sichelin, King of the Norwegians, who being then dead, had appointed him his successor in the kingdom. But the Norwegians, disdaining to receive him, had advanced one Riculf to the sovereignty, and having fortified their cities, thought they were able to oppose Arthur. Walgan, the son of Lot, was then a youth twelve years old, and was recommended by his uncle to the service of pope Supplicius, from whom he received arms. But to return to the history: as soon as Arthur arrived on the coast of Norway, King Riculf, attended with the whole power of that kingdom, met him, and gave him battle, in which, after a great loss of blood on both sides, the Britons at length had the advantage, and making a vigorous charge, killed Riculf and many others with him. Having thus defeated them, they set the cities on fire, dispersed the country people, and pursued the victory till they had reduced all Norway, as also Dacia, under the dominion of Arthur. After the conquest of these countries, and establishment of Lot upon the throne of Norway, Arthur made a voyage to Gaul, and dividing his army into several bodies, began to lay waste that country on all sides. The province of Gaul was then committed to Flollo, a Roman tribune, who held the government of it under the emperor Leo. Upon intelligence of Arthur's coming, he raised all the forces that were under his command, and made war against him, but without success. For Arthur was attended with the youth of all the islands that he had subdued; for which reason he was reported to have such an army as was thought invincible. And even the greater part of the Gallic army, encouraged by his bounty, came over to his service. Therefore Flollo, seeing the disadvantages he lay under, left his camp, and fled with a small number to Paris. There having recruited his army, he fortified the city, and resolved to stand another engagement with Arthur. But while he was thinking of strengthening himself with auxiliary forces in the neighbouring countries, Arthur came upon him unawares, and besieged him in the city. When a month had passed, Flollo, with grief observing his people perish with hunger, sent a message to Arthur, that they two alone should decide the conquest for the kingdom in a duel: for being a person of great stature, boldness, and courage, he gave this challenge in confidence of success. Arthur was extremely pleased at Flollo's proposal, and sent him word back again, that he would give him the meeting which he desired. A treaty, therefore, being on both sides agreed to, they met together in the island without the city, where the people waited to see the event. They were both gracefully armed, and mounted on admirably swift horses; and it was hard to tell which gave the greater hopes of victory. When they had presented themselves against each other with their lances aloft, they put spurs to their horses, and began a fierce encounter. But Arthur, who handled his lance more warily, struck it into the upper part of Flollo's breast, and avoiding his enemy's weapon, laid him prostrate upon the ground, and was just going to dispatch him with his drawn sword, when Flollo, starting up on a sudden, met him with his lance couched, wherewith he mortally stabbed the breast of Arthur's horse, and caused both him and his rider to fall. The Britons, when they saw their king lying on the ground, fearing he was killed, could hardly be restrained from breach of covenant, and falling with one consent upon the Gauls. But just as they were upon rushing into the lists, Arthur hastily got up, and guarding himself with his shield, advanced with speed against Flollo. And now they renewed the assault with great rage, eagerly bent upon one another's destruction. At length Flollo, watching his advantage, gave Arthur a blow on the forehead, which might have proved mortal, had he not blunted the edge of his weapon against the helmet. When Arthur saw his coat of mail and shield red with blood, he was inflamed with still greater rage, and lifting up his Caliburn with his utmost strength struck it through the helmet into Flollo's head, and made a terrible gash. With this wound Flollo fell down, tearing the ground with his spurs, and expired. As soon as this news was spread through the army, the citizens ran together, and opening the gates, surrendered the city to Arthur. After this victory, he divided his army into two parts; one of which he committed to the conduct of Hoel, whom he ordered to march against Guitard, commander of the Pictavians; while he with the other part should endeavour to reduce the other provinces. Hoel upon this entered Aquitaine, possessed himself of the cities of that country, and after distressing Guitard in several battles, forced him to surrender. He also destroyed Gascony with fire and sword, and subdued the princes of it. At the end of nine years, in which time all the parts of Gaul were entirely reduced, Arthur returned back to Paris, where he kept his court, and calling an assembly of the clergy and people, established peace and the just administration of the laws in that kingdom. Then he bestowed Neustria, now called Normandy, upon Bedver, his butler; the province of Andegavia upon Caius, his sewer; and several other provinces upon his great men that attended him. Thus having settled the peace of the cities and countries there, he returned back in the beginning of spring to Britain.

12

Arthur summons a great many kings, princes, bishops, archbishops, &c., to a solemn assembly at the City of Legions.

UPON the approach of the feast of Pentecost, Arthur, the better to demonstrate his joy after such triumphal success, and for the more solemn observation of that festival, and reconciling the minds of the princes that were now subject to him, resolved, during that season, to hold a magnificent court, to place the crown upon his head, and to invite all the kings and dukes under his subjection to the solemnity. And when he had communicated his design to his familiar friends, he pitched upon the City of Legions as a proper place for his purpose. For besides its great wealth above the other cities, its situation, which was in Glamorganshire upon the River Usk, near the Severn Sea, was most pleasant and fit for so great a solemnity. For on one side it was washed by that noble river, so that the kings and princes from the countries beyond the seas might have the convenience of sailing up to it. On the other side, the beauty of the meadows and groves, and magnificence of the royal palaces with lofty gilded roofs that adorned it, made it even rival the grandeur of Rome. It was also famous for two churches; whereof one was built in honour of the martyr, Julius, and adorned with a choir of virgins, who had devoted themselves wholly to the service of God; but the other, which was founded in memory of St. Aaron, his companion, and maintained a convent of canons, was the third metropolitan church of Britain. Besides, there was a college of two hundred philosophers, who, being learned in astronomy and the other arts, were diligent in observing the courses of the stars, and gave Arthur true predictions of the events that would happen at that time. In this place, therefore, which afforded such delights, were preparations made for the ensuing festival. Ambassadors were then sent into several kingdoms, to invite to court the princes both of Gaul and all the adjacent islands. Accordingly came Augusel, King of Albania, now Scotland; Urian, King of Mureif; Cadwallo Lewirh, King of the Venedotians, now called the North Wales men; Sater, King of the Demetians, or South Wales men; Cador, King of Cornwall, also the archbishops of the three metropolitan sees, London, York, and Dubricius of the City of Legions. This prelate, who was primate of Britain, and legate of the apostolical see, was so eminent for his piety that he could cure any sick person by his prayers. There came also the consuls of the principal cities, viz. Morvid, Consul of Gloucester; Mauron, of Worcester; Anaraut, of Salisbury; Arthgal, of Cargueit or Wargueit; Jugein, of Legecester; Cursalen, of Kaicester; Kinmare, Duke of Dorobernia; Galluc, of Salisbury; Urgennius, of Bath; Jonathal, of Dorchester; and Boso, of Ridoc, that is, Oxford. Besides the consuls, came the following worthies of no less dignity: Danaut map papo; Cheneus map coil; Peredur map Peridur; Guiful map Nogoit; Regin map claut; Eddelein map Oledauc; Kincar map Bagan; Kimmare; Gorboroniam map Goit; Clofaut; Run map Neton; Kimbelim; Edelnauth pap Trunat; Cathleus map Catel; Kinlich map Teton; and many others too tedious to enumerate. From the adjacent islands came Guillamurius, King of Ireland; Malvasius, King of Iceland; Doldavius, King of Gothland; Gunfasius, King of the Orkneys; Lot, King of Norway; Aschillius, King of the Dacians. From the parts beyond the seas, came Holdin King of Ruteni; Leodegarius, Consul of Bolonia; Bedver, the butler, Duke of Normandy; Borellus of Cenomania; Caius, the sewer, Duke of Andegavia; Guitard, of Pictavia; also the twelve peers of Gaul, whom Guerinus Carnotensis brought along with him; Hoel, Duke of the Armorican Britons, and his nobility, who came with such a train of mules, horses, and rich furniture, as it is difficult to describe. Besides these, there remained no prince of any consideration on this side of Spain, who came not upon this invitation. And no wonder, when Arthur's munificence, which was celebrated over the whole world, made him beloved by all people.

13

A description of the royal pomp at the coronation of Arthur.

WHEN all were assembled together in the city, upon the day of the solemnity, the archbishops were conducted to the palace, in order to place the crown upon the king's head. Therefore Dubricius, inasmuch as the court was kept in his diocese, made himself ready to celebrate the office, and undertook the ordering of whatever related to it. As soon as the king was invested with his royal habiliments, he was conducted in great pomp to the metropolitan church, supported on each side by two archbishops, and having four kings, viz. of Albania, Cornwall, Demetia, and Venedotia, whose right it was, bearing four golden swords before him. He was also attended with a concert of all sorts of music, which made most excellent harmony. On another part was the queen, dressed out in her richest ornaments, conducted by the archbishops and bishops to the Temple of Virgins; the four queens also of the kings last mentioned, bearing before her four white doves according to ancient custom; and after her there followed a retinue of women, making all imaginable demonstrations of joy. When the whole procession was ended, so transporting was the harmony of the musical instruments and voices, whereof there was a vast variety in both churches, that the knights who attended were in doubt which to prefer, and therefore crowded from the one to the other by turns, and were far from being tired with the solemnity, though the whole day had been spent in it. At last, when the divine service was over at both churches, the king and queen put off their crowns, and putting on their lighter ornaments, went to the banquet; he to one palace with the men, and she to another with the women. For the Britons still observed the ancient custom of Troy, by which the men and women used to celebrate the festivals apart. When they had all taken their seats according to precedence, Caius the sewer, in rich robes of ermine, with a thousand young noblemen, served up the dishes. From another part, Bedver the butler was followed with the same number of attendants, in various habits, who waited with all kinds of cups and drinking vessels. In the queen's palace were innumerable waiters, dressed with variety of ornaments, all performing their respective offices; which if I should describe particularly, I should draw out the history to a tedious length. For at that time Britain had arrived at such a pitch of grandeur, that in abundance of riches, luxury of ornaments, and politeness of inhabitants, it far surpassed all other kingdoms. The knights in it that were famous for feats of chivalry, wore their clothes and arms all of the same colour and fashion: and the women also no less celebrated for their wit, wore all the same kind of apparel; and esteemed none worthy of their love, but such as had given a proof of their valour in three several battles. Thus was the valour of the men an encouragement for the women's chastity, and the love of the women a spur to the soldier's bravery.

14

After a variety of sports at the coronation, Arthur amply rewards his servants.

AS soon as the banquets were over, they went into the fields without the city, to divert themselves with various sports. The military men composed a kind of diversion in imitation of a fight on horseback; and the ladies, placed on the top of the walls as spectators, in a sportive manner darted their amorous glances at the courtiers, the more to encourage them. Others spent the remainder of the day in other diversions, such as shooting with bows and arrows, tossing the pike, casting of heavy stones and rocks, playing at dice and the like, and all these inoffensively and without quarreling. Whoever gained the victory in any of these sports, was rewarded with a rich prize by Arthur. In this manner were the first three days spent; and on the fourth, all who, upon account of their titles, bore any kind of office at this solemnity, were called together to receive honours and preferments in reward of their services, and to fill up the vacancies in the governments of cities and castles, archbishoprics, bishoprics, abbeys, and other posts of honour.

15

A letter from Lucius Tiberius, general of the Romans, to Arthur being read, they consult about an answer to it.

BUT St. Dubricius, from a pious desire of leading a hermit's life, made a voluntary resignation of his archiepiscopal[6] dignity; and in his room was consecrated David, the king's uncle, whose life was a perfect example of that goodness which by his doctrine he taught. In place of St. Samson, archbishop of Dole, was appointed, with the consent of Hoel, King of the Armorican Britons, Chelianus [Kilian], a priest of Llandaff, a person highly recommended for his good life and character. The bishopric of Silchester was conferred on Mauganius, that of Winchester upon Diwanius, and that of Alclud to Eldanius. While he was disposing of these preferments upon them, it happened that twelve men of an advanced age, and venerable aspect, and bearing olive branches in their right hands, for a token that they were come upon an embassy, appeared before the king, moving towards him with a slow pace, and speaking with a soft voice; and after their compliments paid, presented him with a letter from Lucius Tiberius, in these words:

---

6 Of or relating to an archbishop

"Lucius, procurator of the commonwealth, to Arthur, King of Britain, according to his desert. The insolence of your tyranny is what fills me with the highest admiration, and the injuries you have done to Rome still increase my wonder. But it is provoking to reflect that you are grown so much above yourself, as willfully to avoid seeing this: nor do you consider what it is to have offended by unjust deeds a Senate, to whom you cannot be ignorant the whole world owes vasselage. For the tribute of Britain, which the senate had enjoined you to pay, and which used to be paid to the Roman emperors successively from the time of Julius Caesar, you have had the presumption to withhold, in contempt of their imperial authority. You have seized the province of the Allobroges, and all the islands of the ocean, whose kings, while the Roman power prevailed in those parts, paid tribute to our ancestors. And because the senate have decreed to demand justice of you for such repeated injuries, I command you to appear at Rome before the middle of August the next year, there to make satisfaction to your masters, and undergo such sentence as they shall in justice pass upon you. Which if you refuse to do, I shall come to you, and endeavour to recover with my sword, what you in your madness have robbed us of."

As soon as the letter was read in the presence of the king and consuls, Arthur withdrew with them into the Giant's Tower, which was at the entrance to the palace, to think what answer was fit to be returned to such an insolent message. As they were going up the stairs, Cador, Duke of Cornwall, who was a man of a merry disposition, said to the king in a jocose manner: "I have been till now under fear, lest the easy life which the Britons lead, by enjoying a long peace, might make them cowards, and extinguish the fame of their gallantry, by which they have raised their name above all other nations. For where the exercise of arms is wanting, and the pleasures of women, dice, and other diversions take place, no doubt what remains of virtue, honour, courage, and thirst of praise will be tainted with the rust of idleness. For now almost five years have passed, since we have been abandoned to these delights, and have had no exercise of war. Therefore, to deliver us from sloth, God has stirred up this spirit of the Romans, to restore our military virtues to their ancient state." In this manner did he entertain them with discourse, till they were come to their seats, on which when they were all placed, Arthur spoke to them after this manner.

16

Arthur, holding council with the kings, desires every one of them to deliver their opinions.

"MY companions in both good and bad fortune, whose abilities both in counsel and war I have hitherto experienced; the present exigence of affairs, after the message which we have received, requires your careful deliberation and prudent resolutions; for whatever is wisely concerted, is easily executed. Therefore we shall be the better able to bear the annoyance which Lucius threatens to give us, if we unanimously apply ourselves to consider how to overcome it. In my opinion we have no great reason to fear him, when we reflect on the unjust pretence on which he demands tribute of us. He says he has a right to it, because it was paid to Julius Caesar, and his successors, who invaded Britain with an army at the invitation of the ancient Britons, when they were quarreling among themselves, and by force reduced the country under their power, when weakened by civil dissension. And because they gained it in this manner, they had the injustice to take tribute of it. For that can never be possessed justly, which is gained by force and violence. So that he has no reasonable grounds to pretend we are of right his tributaries. But since he has the presumption to make an unjust demand of us, we have certainly as good reason to demand of him tribute from Rome; let the longer sword therefore determine the right between us. For if Rome has decreed that tribute ought to paid to it from Britain, on account of it having been formerly under the yoke of Julius Caesar, and other Roman emperors; I for the same reason now decree, that Rome ought to pay tribute to me, because my predecessors formerly held the government of it. For Belinus, that glorious King of the Britons, with the assistance of his brother Brennus, Duke of the Allobroges, after they had hanged up twenty noble Romans in the middle of the market-place, took their city, and kept possession of it a long time. Likewise Constantine, the son of Helena, and Maximian, who were both my kinsmen, gained the imperial throne of Rome. Do not you, therefore, think that we ought to demand tribute of the Romans? As for Gaul and the adjacent islands of the ocean, we have no occasion to return them any answer, since they did not defend them, when we attempted to free them from their power." As soon as he had done speaking to this effect, Hoel, King of the Armorican Britons, who had the precedence of the rest, made answer in these words.

17

The opinion of Hoel, King of Armorica, concerning a war with the Romans.

"AFTER the most profound deliberation that any of us shall be able to make, I think better advice cannot be given, than what your majesty in your great wisdom and policy now offers. Your speech, which is no less wise than eloquent, has superseded all consultation on our part; and nothing remains for us to do, but to admire and gratefully acknowledge your majesty's firmness of mind, and depth of policy, to which we owe such excellent advice. For if upon this notice you are pleased to make an expedition to Rome, I doubt not but it will be crowned with glorious success, since it will be undertaken for the defense of our liberties, and to demand justly of our enemies, what they have unjustly demanded of us. For that person who would rob another, deserves to lose his own by him against whom the attempt is made. And, therefore, since the Romans threatened us with this injury, it will undoubtedly turn to their own loss, if we can have but an opportunity of engaging with them. This is what the Britons universally desire; this is what we have promised us in the Sibylline prophecies, which expressly declare that the Roman empire shall be obtained by three persons, natives of Britain. The oracle is fulfilled in two of them, since it is manifest (as your majesty observed) that those two celebrated princes, Belinus and Constantine, governed the Roman empire: and now you are the third to whom this supreme dignity is promised. Make haste, therefore, to receive what God makes no delay to give you; to subdue those who are ready to receive your yoke; and to advance us all, who for your advancement will spare neither limbs nor life. And that if you accomplish this, I myself will attend you in person with ten thousand men."

18

The opinion of Augusel.

WHEN Hoel concluded his speech, Augusel, King of Albania, declared his good affection to the cause after this manner. "I am not able to express the joy that has transported me, since my lord has declared to us his designs. For we seem to have done nothing by all our past wars with so many and potent princes, if the Romans and Germans can be suffered to enjoy peace, and we do not severely revenge on them the grievous oppressions which they formerly brought upon this country. But now, since we are at liberty to encounter them, I am overwhelmed with joy and eagerness of desire to see a battle with them, when the blood of those cruel oppressors will be no less acceptable to me than a spring of water is to one who is parched with thirst. If I shall but live to see that day, how sweet will be the wounds which I shall then either receive or give? Nay, how sweet will be even death itself, when suffered in revenging the injuries done to our ancestors, in defending our liberties, and in promoting the glory of our king! Let us then begin with these poltroons[7], and spoil them of all their trophies, by making an entire conquest of them. And I for my share will add to the army two thousand horse, besides foot."

19

They unanimously agree upon a war with the Romans.

TO the same effect spoke all the rest, and promised each of them

---

7   A spiritless coward

their full quota of forces; so that besides those promised by the Duke of Armorica, the number of men from the island of Britain alone was sixty thousand, all completely armed. But the kings of the other islands, as they had not been accustomed to any cavalry, promised their quota of infantry; and, from the six provincial islands, viz. Ireland, Iceland, Gothland, the Orkneys, Norway, and Dacia, were reckoned a hundred and twenty thousand. From the duchies of Gaul, that is, of the Ruteni, the Portunians, the Etrusians, the Cenomanni, the Andegavians, and Pictavians, were eighty thousand. From the twelve consulships of those who came along with Guerinus Carnotensis, twelve hundred. All together they made up a hundred and eighty-three thousand two hundred, besides foot which did not easily fall under number.

20

Arthur prepares for a war, and refuses to pay tribute to the Romans.

KING Arthur, seeing all unanimously ready for his service, ordered them to return back to their countries with speed, and get ready the forces which they had promised, and to hasten to the general rendezvous upon the Kalends of August, at the mouth of the River Barba, that from thence they might advance with them to the borders of the Allobroges to meet the Romans. Then he sent word to the emperors by their ambassadors; that as to paying them tribute, he would in no wise obey their commands; and that the journey he was about to make to Rome was not to stand the award of their sentence, but to demand of them what they had judicially decreed to demand of him. With this answer the ambassadors departed; and at the same time also departed all the kings and noblemen to perform with all expedition the orders that had been given them.

BOOK TEN

1

Lucius Tiberius calls together the eastern kings against the Britons.

LUCIUS Tiberius, on receiving this answer, by order of the senate published a decree for the eastern kings to come with their forces, and assist in the conquest of Britain. In obedience to which there came in a very short time, Epistrophius, King of the Grecians; Mustensar, King of the Africans; Alifantinam, King of Spain; Hirtacius, King of the Parthians; Boccus of the Medes; Sertorius of Libya; Teucer, King of Phrygia; Serses, King of the Itureans; Pandrasus, King of Egypt; Micipsa, King of Babylon; Polytetes, Duke of Bithynia; Teucer, Duke of Phrygia; Evander of Syria; Aethion of Boeotia; Hippolytus of Crete, with the generals and nobility under them. Of the senatorian order also came Lucius Catellus, Marius Lepidus, Caius Metellus Cotta, Quintus Milvius Catulus, Quintus Carutius, and as many others as made up the number of forty thousand one hundred and sixty.

2

Arthur commits to his nephew Modred the government of Britain. His dream at Hamo's Port.

AFTER the necessary dispositions were made, upon the Kalends of August, they began their march towards Britain, which when Arthur had intelligence of, he committed the government of the kingdom to his nephew Modred and Queen Guanhumara, and marched with his army to Hamo's Port, where the wind stood fair for him. But while he, surrounded with all his numerous fleet, was sailing joyfully with a brisk gale, it happened that about midnight he fell into a very sound sleep, and in a dream saw a bear flying in the air, at the noise of which all the shores trembled; also a terrible dragon flying from the west, which enlightened the country with the brightness of its eyes. When these two met, they began a dreadful fight; but the dragon with its fiery breath burned the bear which often assaulted him, and threw him down scorched to the ground. Arthur upon this awaking, related his dream to those that stood about him, who took upon them to interpret it, and told him that the dragon signified himself, but the bear, some giant that should encounter with him; and that the fight portended the duel that would be between them, and the dragon's victory the same that would happen to himself. But Arthur conjectured it portended something else, and that the vision was applicable to himself and the emperor. As soon as the morning after this night's sail appeared, they found themselves arrived at the mouth of the River Barba. And there they pitched their tents, to wait the arrival of the kings of the islands and the generals of the other provinces.

3

Arthur kills a Spanish giant who had stolen away Helena, the niece of Hoel.

IN the meantime, Arthur had news brought to him that a giant of monstrous size was come from the shores of Spain, and had forcibly taken away Helena, the niece of Duke Hoel, from her guard, and fled with her to the top of that which is now called Michael's Mount; and that the soldiers of the country who pursued him were able to do nothing against him. For whether they attacked him by sea or land, he either overturned the ships with vast rocks, or killed them with several sorts of darts, besides many of them that he took and devoured half alive. The next night, therefore, at the second hour, Arthur, taking along with him Caius the sewer, and Bedver the butler, went out privately from the camp, and hastened towards the mountain. For being a man of undaunted courage, he did not care to lead his army against such monsters; both because he could in this manner animate his men by his own example, and also because he was alone sufficient to deal with them. As soon as they came near the mountain, they saw a fire burning upon the top of it, and another on a lesser mountain, that was not far from it. And being in doubt upon which of them the giant dwelt, they sent away

Bedver to know the certainty of the matter. So he, finding a boat, sailed over in it first to the lesser mountain, to which he could in no other way have access, because it was situated in the sea. When he had begun to climb up to the top of it, he was at first frightened by a dismal howling cry of a woman from above, and imagined the monster to be there: but quickly rousing his courage, he drew his sword, and having reached the top, found nothing but the fire which he had before seen at a distance. He discovered also a grave newly made, and an old woman weeping and howling by it, who at the sight of him instantly cried out in words interrupted with sighs, "O unhappy man, what misfortune brings you to this place? O the inexpressible tortures of death that you must suffer! I pity you, I pity you, because the detestable monster will this night destroy the flower of your youth. For that most wicked and odious giant, who brought the duke's niece, whom I have just now buried here, and me, her nurse, along with her into this mountain, will come and immediately murder you in a most cruel manner. O deplorable fate! This most illustrious princess, sinking under the fear her tender heart conceived, while the foul monster would have embraced her, fainted away and expired. And when he could not satiate his brutish lust upon her, who was the very soul, joy, and happiness of my life, being enraged at the disappointment of his bestial desire, he forcibly committed a rape upon me, who (let God and my old age witness) abhorred his embraces. Fly, dear sir, fly, for fear he may come, as he usually does, to lie with me, and finding you here most barbarously butcher you." Bedver, moved at what she said, as much as it is possible for human nature to be, endeavoured with kind words to assuage her grief, and to comfort her with the promise of speedy help: and then returned back to Arthur, and gave him an account of what he had met with. Arthur very much lamented the damsel's sad fate, and ordered his companions to leave him to deal with him alone; unless there was an absolute necessity, and then they were to come in boldly to his assistance. From hence they went directly to the next mountain, leaving their horses with their armour-bearers, and ascended to the top, Arthur leading the way. The deformed savage was then by the fire, with his face besmeared with the clotted blood of swine, part of which he already devoured, and was roasting the remainder upon spits by the fire. But at the sight of them, whose appearance was a surprise to him, he hastened to his club, which two strong men could hardly lift from the ground. Upon this the king drew his sword, and guarding himself with his shield, ran with all his speed to prevent his getting it. But the other, who was not ignorant of his design, had by this time snatched it up, and gave the king such a terrible blow upon his shield, that he made the shores ring with the noise, and perfectly stunned the king's ears with it. Arthur, fired with rage at this, lifted up his sword, and gave him a wound in the forehead, which was not indeed mortal, but yet such as made the blood gush out over his face and eyes, and so blinded him; for he had partly warded off the stroke from his forehead with his club, and prevented its being fatal. However, his loss of sight, by reason of the blood flowing over his eyes, made him exert himself with greater fury, and like an enraged boar against a hunting-spear, so did he rush in against Arthur's sword, and grasping him about the waist, force him down upon his knees. But Arthur, nothing daunted, slipped out of his hands, and so exerted himself with his sword, that he gave the giant no respite till he had struck it up to the very back through his skull. At this the hideous monster raised a dreadful roar, and like an oak torn up from the roots by the winds, so did he make the ground resound with his fall. Arthur, bursting out into a fit of laughter at the sight, commanded Bedver to cut of his head, and give it to one of the armour-bearers, who was to carry it to the camp, and there expose it to public view, but with orders for the spectators of this combat to keep silence. He told them he had found none of so great strength, since he killed the Giant Ritho, who had challenged him to fight upon the Mountain Aravius. This giant had made himself furs of the beards of kings he had killed, and had sent word to Arthur to carefully cut his beard and send it to him; and then, out of respect to his pre-eminence over other kings, his beard should have the honour of the principal place. But if he refused to do it, he challenged him to a duel, with this offer, that the conqueror should have the furs, and also the beard of the vanquished for a trophy of his victory. In this conflict, therefore, Arthur proved victorious, and took the beard and spoils of the giant: and, as he said before, he had met with none that could be compared to him for strength till his last engagement. After this victory, they returned at the second watch of the night to the camp with the head; to see which there was a great concourse of people, all extolling this wonderful exploit of Arthur by which he had freed the country from a most destructive and voracious monster. But Hoel, in great grief for the loss of his niece, commanded a mausoleum to be built over her body in the mountain where she was buried, which, taking the damsel's name, is called Helena's Tomb to this day.

4

Arthur's ambassadors to Lucius Tiberius deliver Petreius Cotta, whom they took prisoner, to Arthur.

AS soon as all the forces were arrived where Arthur expected, he marched from thence to Augustodunum, where he supposed the general was. But when he came to the River Alba, he had intelligence brought him of his having encamped not far off, and that he was come with so vast an army, that he would not be able to withstand it. However, this did not deter him from pursuing his enterprise; but he pitched his camp upon the bank of the river to facilitate the bringing up of his forces, and to secure his retreat if there should be occasion, and sent Boso, the Consul of Oxford, and Guerinus Carnotensis, with his nephew Walgan, to Lucius Tiberius, requiring him either to retire from the coasts of Gaul, or come the next day that they might try their right to that country with their swords. The retinue of young courtiers that attended Walgan, highly rejoicing at this opportunity, were urgent with him to find some occasion for a quarrel in the commander's camp, that so they might engage the Romans. Accordingly they went to Lucius, and commanded him to retire out of Gaul, or hazard a battle the next day. But while he was answering them, that he was not come to retire, but to govern the country, there was present Caius Quintilianus, his nephew, who said that the Britons were better at boasting and threatening, than they were at fighting. Walgan immediately took fire at this, and ran upon him with his drawn sword, wherewith he cut off his head, and then retreated speedily with his companions to their horses. The

Romans, both horse and foot, pursued to revenge the loss of their countryman upon the ambassadors, who fled with great precipitation. But Guerinus Carnotensis, just as one of them was come up to him, rallied on a sudden, and with his lance struck at once through his armour and the very middle of his body, and laid him prostrate on the ground. The sight of this noble exploit raised the emulation of Boso of Oxford, who, wheeling about his horse, struck his lance into the throat of the first man he met with, and dismounted him mortally wounded. In the meantime, Marcellus Mutius, with great eagerness to revenge Quintilian's death, was just upon the back of Walgan, and laid hold of him; which the other quickly obliged him to quit, by cleaving both his helmet and head to the breast with his sword. He also bade him, when he arrived at the infernal regions, tell the man he had killed in the camp, that in this manner the Britons showed their boasting and threatening. Then having reassembled his men, he encouraged them to dispatch every one his pursuer in the same manner as he had done; which accordingly they did not fail to accomplish. Notwithstanding, the Romans continued their pursuit with lances and swords, wherewith they annoyed the others, though without slaughter or taking any prisoners. But as they came near a certain wood, a party of six thousand Britons, who seeing the flight of the consuls, had hid themselves to be in readiness for their assistance, sallied forth, and putting spurs to their horses, rent the air with loud shouts, and being well fenced with their shields, assaulted the Romans suddenly, and forced them to fly. And now it was the Britons' turn to pursue, which they did with better success, for they dismounted, killed, or took several of the enemy. Petreius, the senator, upon this news, hastened to the assistance of his countrymen with ten thousand men, and compelled the Britons to retreat to the wood from whence they had sallied forth; though not without loss of his own men. For the Britons, being well acquainted with the ground, in their flight killed a great number of their pursuers. The Britons thus giving ground, Hider, with another reinforcement of five thousand men, advanced with speed to sustain them; so that they again faced those upon whom they had turned their backs, and renewed the assault with great vigour. The Romans also stood their ground, and continued the fight with various success. The great fault of the Britons was, that though they had been very eager to begin the fight, yet when begun they were less careful of the hazard they ran. Whereas the Romans were under better discipline, and had the advantage of a prudent commander, Petreius Cotta, to tell them where to advance, and where to give ground, and by these means did great injury to the enemy. When Boso observed this, he drew off from the rest a large party of those whom he knew to be the stoutest men, and spoke to them after this manner: "Since we have begun this fight without Arthur's knowledge, we must take care that we be not defeated in the enterprise. For, if we should, we shall both very much endanger our men, and incur the king's high displeasure. Rouse up your courage, and follow me through the Roman squadrons, that with the favour of good fortune we may either kill or take Petreius prisoner." With this they put spurs to their horses, and piercing through the enemy's thickest ranks, reached the place where Petrius was giving his commands. Boso hastily ran in upon him, and grasping him about the neck, fell with him to the ground, as he had intended. The Romans hereupon ran to his delivery, as did the Britons to Boso's assistance; which occasioned on both sides great slaughter, noise, and confusion, while one party strove to rescue their leader, and the other to keep him prisoner. So that this proved the sharpest part of the whole fight, and wherein their spears, swords, and arrows had the fullest employment. At length, the Britons, joining in a close body, and sustaining patiently the assaults of the Romans, retired to the main body of their army with Petreius: which they had no sooner done than they again attacked them, who being now deprived of their leader, were very much weakened, dispirited, and just beginning to flee. They, therefore, eagerly pursued, beat down, and killed several of them, and as soon as they had plundered them, pursued the rest: but they took the greatest number of them prisoners, being desirous to present them to the king. When they had at last sufficiently harassed them, they returned with their plunder and prisoners to the camp; where they gave an account of what had happened, and presented Petreius Cotta with the other prisoners before Arthur, with great joy for the victory. Arthur congratulated them upon it, and promised them advancement to greater honours for behaving themselves so gallantly when he was absent from them. Then he gave his command to some of his men to conduct the prisoners the next day to Paris, and deliver them to be kept in custody there till further orders. The party that were to undertake this charge, he ordered to be conducted by Cador, Bedver, and the two consuls, Borellus and Richerius, with their servants, till they should be out of all fear of disturbance from the Romans.

5

The Romans attack the Britons with a very great force, but are put to flight by them.

BUT the Romans, happening to get intelligence of their design, at the command of their general chose out fifteen thousand men who that night were to get before the others in their march, and rescue their fellow soldiers out of their hands. They were to be commanded by Vulteius Catellus and Quintus Carutius, senators, and also Evander, King of Syria, and Sertorius, King of Libya. Accordingly they began their march that very night, and possessed themselves of a place convenient for lying in ambush, through which they supposed the others would pass. In the morning the Britons set forward along the same road with their prisoners, and were now approaching the place in perfect ignorance of the cunning stratagem of the enemy. No sooner had they entered it, than the Romans, to their great surprise, sprang forth and fell furiously upon them. Notwithstanding, the Britons, at length recovering from their consternation, assembled together, and prepared for a bold opposition by appointing a party to guard the prisoners, and drawing out the rest in order of battle against the enemy. Richerius and Bedver had the command of the party that were set over the prisoners, but Cador, Duke of Cornwall, and Borellus headed the others. But all the Romans had made their sally without being placed in any order, and cared not to form themselves that they might lose no time in the slaughter of the Britons, whom they saw busied in marshaling their troops, and preparing only for their defense. By this conduct the Britons were extremely weakened, and would have shamefully lost their prisoners had not good fortune rendered them assistance. For Guitard, commander of the Pictavians, happened to get information of the designed strategem, and was come up with three thousand men, by the help of which they at last got the advantage, and paid back the slaughter upon their insolent assailants. Nevertheless, the loss which they sustained at the beginning of this action was very considerable. For they lost Borellus, the famous Consul of the Cenomanni, in an encounter with Evander, King of Syria, who stuck his lance into his throat; besides four noblemen, viz. Hirelgas Deperirus, Mauricius Cadorcanensis, Aliduc of Tintagel, and Hider his son, than whom braver men were hardly to be found. But yet neither did this loss dispirit the Britons, but rather made them more resolute to keep the prisoners and kill the enemy. The Romans, now finding themselves unable to maintain the fight any longer, suddenly quitted the field, and made towards their camp; but were pursued with slaughter by the Britons, who also took many of them, and allowed them no respite till they had killed Vulteius Catellus and Evander, King of Syria, and wholly dispersed the rest. After which they sent away their former prisoners to Paris, whither they were to conduct them, and returned back with those newly taken to the king; to whom they gave great hopes of a complete conquest of their enemies, since very few of the great number that came against them had met with any success.

6

Lucius Tiberius goes to Lengriae. Arthur, designing to vanquish him, by a stratagem possesses himself of the valley of Suesia.

THESE repeated disasters wrought no small disturbance in the mind of Lucius Tiberius, and made him hesitate whether to bring it to a general battle with Arthur, or to retire into Augustodunum, and stay till the emperor Leo with his forces could come to his assistance. At length, giving way to his fears, he entered Lengria with his army, intending to reach the other city the night following. Arthur, finding this, and being desirous to get before him in his march, left the city on the left hand, and the same night entered a certain valley called Suesia, through which Lucius was to pass. There he divided his men into several bodies, commanding one legion, over which Morvid, Consul of Gloucester, was appointed general, to wait close by that he might retreat to them if there should be occasion, and from thence rally his broken forces for a second battle. The rest he divided into seven parts, in each of which he placed five thousand five hundred and fifty-five men, all completely armed. He also appointed different stations to his horse and foot, and gave command that just as the foot should advance to the attack, the horse, keeping close together in their ranks, should at the same moment march up obliquely, and endeavour to put the enemy into disorder. The companies of foot were, after the British manner, drawn out into a square, with a right and left wing, under the command of Augusel, King of Albania, and Cador, Duke of Cornwall; the one presiding over the right wing, the other over the left. Over another party were placed the two famous consuls, Guerinus of Chartres and Boso of Richiden, called in the Saxon tongue Oxineford; over a third were Aschillius, King of the Dacians, and Lot, King of the Norwegians; the fourth being commanded by Hoel, Duke of the Armoricans, and Walgan, the king's nephew. After these were four other parties placed in the rear; the first commanded by Caius the sewer, and Bedver the butler; the second by Holdin, Duke of the Ruteni, and Guitard of the Pictavians; the third by Vigenis of Legecester, Jonathal of Dorchester, and Cursalem of Caicester; the fourth by Urtgennius of Bath. Behind all these, Arthur, for himself and the legion that was to attend near him, made choice of a place where he set up a golden dragon for a standard, whither the wounded or fatigued might in case of necessity retreat, as into their camp. The legion that was with him consisted of six thousand six hundred and sixty-six men.

7

Arthur's exhortation to his soldiers.

AFTER he had thus placed them all in their stations, he made the following speech to his soldiers:

"My brave countrymen, who have made Britain the mistress of thirty kingdoms, I congratulate you on your noble exploit which to me is proof that your valour is so far from being impaired, that it is rather increased. Though you have been five years without exercise, wherein the softening pleasures of an easy life had a greater share of your time than the use of arms; yet all this has not made you degenerate from your natural bravery, which you have shown in forcing the Romans to flee. The pride of their leaders has animated them to attempt the invasion of your liberties. They have tried you in battle with numbers superior to yours, and have not been able to stand before you; but have basely withdrawn themselves into that city, from which they are now ready to march out, and to pass through this valley in their way to Augustodunum; so that you may have an opportunity of falling upon them unawares like a flock of sheep. Certainly they expected to find in you the cowardice of the Eastern nations, when they thought to make your country tributary, and you their slaves. What, have they never heard of your wars, with the Dacians, Norwegians, and princes of the Gauls, whom you reduced under my power, and freed from their shameful yoke? We, then, that have had success in a greater war, need not doubt of it in a less, if we do but endeavour with the same spirit to vanquish these poltroons. You shall want no rewards of honour, if as faithful soldiers you do but strictly obey my commands. For as soon as we have routed them, we will march straight to Rome, and take it: and then all the gold, silver, palaces, towers, towns, cities, and other riches of the vanquished shall be yours." He had hardly done speaking before they all with one voice declared that they were ready to suffer death, rather than quit the field while he had life.

8

Lucius Tiberius, discovering Arthur's design, in a speech animates his followers to fight.

BUT Lucius Tiberius, discovering the designs that were formed against him, would not flee, as he had at first intended, but taking new courage, resolved to march to the same valley against them; and calling together his principal commanders, spoke to them in these words:

"Venerable fathers, to whose empire both the Eastern and Western kingdoms owe obedience, remember the virtues of your ancestors, who were not afraid to shed their blood when the vanquishing of the enemies of the commonwealth required it; but to leave an example of their courage and military virtues to their posterity, behaved themselves in all battles with the contempt of death, as if God had given them some security against it. By this conduct they often triumphed, and by triumphing escaped death. Such was the reward of their virtue from Divine Providence, which overrules all events. This increase of the commonwealth, and of their own valour was owing to this; and all those virtues that usually adorn the great, as integrity, honour, and munificence, flourishing a long time in them, raised them and their posterity to the empire of the whole world. Let their noble examples animate you: rouse up the spirit of the ancient Romans, and be not afraid to march out against our enemies that are lying in ambush before us in the valley, but boldly with your swords demand of them your just rights. Do not think that I retired into this city for fear of engaging with them; but I thought that, as their pursuit of us was rash and foolish, so we might hence on a sudden intercept them in it, and by dividing their main body make a great slaughter of them. But now, since they have altered the measures which we supposed they had taken, let us also alter ours. Let us go in quest of them and bravely fall upon them; or if they shall happen to have the advantage in the beginning of the battle, let us only stand our ground during the fury of their first assault, and the victory will undoubtedly be ours; for in many battles this manner of conduct has been attended with victory." As soon as he had made an end of speaking these and other things, they all declared their assent, promised with an oath to stand by him, and hastened to arm themselves. Which when they had done, they marched out of Lengriae to the valley where Arthur had drawn out his forces in order of battle. Then they also began to marshal their army, which they divided into twelve companies, and according to the Roman manner of battle, drew out each company in the form of a wedge, consisting of six thousand six hundred and sixty six men. Each company also had its respective leaders, who were to give direction when to advance, or when to be on the defensive. One of them was headed by Lucius Catellus the senator, and Alifantinam, King of Spain; another by Hirtacius, King of the Parthians, and Marius Lepidus, a senator; the third by Boccus, of the Medes, and Gaius Metellus, a senator; and the fourth by Sertorius, of Libya, and Quintus Milvius, a senator. These four companies were placed in front of the army. In the rear of these were four others, whereof one was commanded by Serses, King of the Itureans; another by Pandrasus, King of Egypt; a third by Polytetes, Duke of Bithynia; a fourth by Teucer, Duke of Phrygia. And again behind all these four others, whereof the commanders were Quintus Carucius, a senator, Laelius Ostiensis, Sulpitius Subuculus, and Mauricius Sylvanus. As for the general himself, he was sometimes in one place, sometimes in another, to encourage and direct as there should be occasion. For a standard he ordered a golden eagle to be firmly set up in the center, for his men to repair to when they should happen to be separated from their company.

9

A battle between Arthur and Lucius Tiberius.

AND now the Britons and Romans stood presenting their arms at one another; when forthwith at the sound of trumpets, the company that was headed by the King of Spain and Lucius Catellus, boldly rushed forward against that which the King of Scotland and Duke of Cornwall led, but were not able to make the least breach in their firm ranks. So that while these stood their ground, up came Guerinus and Boso with a body of horse upon their full speed, broke through the party that began the assault, and met with another which the King of the Parthians was leading up against Aschillius, King of Dacia. After this first onset, there followed a general engagement of both armies with great violence, and several breaches were made on each side. The shouts, the slaughter, the quantity of blood spilled, and the agonies of the dying made a dreadful scene of horror. At first, the Britons sustained a great loss, by having Bedver the butler killed, and Caius the sewer mortally wounded. For, as Bedver met Boccus, King of the Medes, he fell dead by a stab of his lance amidst the enemy's troops. And Caius, in endeavouring to revenge his death, was surrounded by the Median troops, and there received a mortal wound; yet as a brave soldier he opened himself a way with the wing which he led, killed and dispersed the Medes, and would have made a safe retreat with all his men, had he not met the King of Libya with the forces under him, who put his whole company into disorder; yet not so great, but that he was still able to get off with a few, and flee with Bedver's corpse to the golden dragon. The Neustrians grievously lamented the sight of their leader's mangled body; and so did the Andegavians, when they beheld their consul wounded. But there was now no room for complaints, for the furious and bloody shocks of both armies made it necessary to provide for their own defense. Therefore Hirelgas, the nephew of Bedver, being extremely enraged at his death, called up to him three hundred men, and like a wild boar amongst a pack of dogs, broke through the enemy's ranks with his horse, making towards the place where he had seen the standard of the King of the Medes; little regarding what might befall him, if he could but revenge the loss of his uncle. At length he reached the place, killed the king, brought off his body to his companions, and laid it by that of his uncle, where he mangled it in the same manner. Then calling with a loud voice to his countrymen, he animated their troops, and vehemently pressed them to exert themselves to the utmost, now that their spirits were raised, and the enemy disheartened; and especially as they had the advantage of them in being placed in better order, and so might the more grievously annoy them. Encouraged with this exhortation, they began a general assault upon the enemy, which was attended with a terrible slaughter on both sides. For on the part of the Romans, besides many others, fell Alifantinam, King of Spain, Micipsa of Babylon, as also Quintus Milvius and Marius Lepidus, senators. On the part of the Britons, Holdin, King of the Ruteni, Loedegarius of Bolonia, and three consuls of Britain, Cursalem of Caicester, Galluc of Salisbury, and Urtgennius of Bath. So that the troops which they commanded, being extremely weakened, retreated till they came to the army of the Armorican Britons, commanded by Hoel and Walgan. But these, being inflamed at the retreat of their friends, encouraged them to stand their ground, and caused them with the help of their own forces to put their pursuers to flight. When they continued this pursuit, they beat down and killed several of them, and gave them no respite till they came to the general's troop; who, seeing the distress of his companions, hastened to their assistance.

10

Hoel and Walgan signalize their valour in the fight.

AND now in this latter encounter the Britons were worsted, with the loss of Kimarcoc, Consul of Trigeria, and two thousand men with him; besides three famous noblemen, Richomarcus, Bloccovius, and Jagivius of Bodloan, who, had they but enjoyed the dignity of princes, would have been celebrated for their valour through all succeeding ages. For, during this assault which they made in conjunction with Hoel and Walgan, there was not an enemy within their reach that could escape the fury of their sword or lance. But upon their falling in among Lucius's party, they were surrounded by them, and suffered the same fate with the consul and the other men. The loss of these men made those matchless heroes, Hoel and Walgan, much more eager to assault the general's ranks. And to try on all sides where to make the greatest impression. But Walgan, whose valour was never to be foiled, endeavoured to gain access to Lucius himself that he might encounter him, and with this view beat down and killed all that stood in his way. And Hoel, not inferior to him, did no less service in another part by spiriting up his men, and giving and receiving blows among the enemy with the same undaunted courage. It was hard to determine which of them was the stoutest soldier.

11

Lucius Tiberius being killed, the Britons obtain the victory.

BUT Walgan, by forcing his way through the enemy's troops, as we said before, found at last (what he had wished for) access to the general, and immediately encountered him. Lucius, being then in the flower of his youth, and a person of great courage and vigour, desired nothing more than to engage with such a one as might put his strength to its full trial. Putting himself, therefore, into a posture of defense, he received Walgan with joy, and was not a little proud to try his courage with one of whom he had heard such great things. The fight continued between them a long time with great force of blows, and no less dexterity in warding them off, each being resolved upon the other's destruction. During this sharp conflict between them, the Romans, on a sudden, recovering their courage, made an assault upon the Armoricans, and having relieved their general, repulsed Hoel and Walgan, with their troops, till they found themselves unawares met by Arthur and the forces under him. For he, hearing of the slaughter that was a little before made of his men, had speedily advanced with his legion, and drawing out his Caliburn, spoke to them with a loud voice, after this manner: "What are you doing, soldiers? Will you suffer these effeminate wretches to escape? Let not one of them get off alive. Remember the force of your arms that have reduced thirty kingdoms under my subjection. Remember your ancestors whom the Romans, when at the height of their power, made tributary. Remember your liberties which these pitiful fellows, that are much your inferiors, attempt to deprive you of. Let none of them escape alive. What are you doing?" With these expostulations, he rushed upon the enemy, made terrible havoc among them, and not a man did he meet but at one blow he laid either him or his horse dead upon the ground. They, therefore, in astonishment fled from him, as a flock of sheep from a fierce lion, whom raging hunger provokes to devour whatever happens to come near him. Their arms were no manner of protection to them against the force with which this valiant prince wielded his Caliburn. Two kings, Sertorius of Libya and Polyetes of Bithynia, unfortunately felt its fury, and had their heads cut off by it. The Britons, when they saw the king performing such wonders, took courage again. With one consent they assaulted the Romans, kept close together in their ranks, and while they assailed the foot in one part, endeavoured to beat down and pierce through the horse in another. Notwithstanding, the Romans made a brave defense, and at the instigation of Lucius laboured to pay back their slaughter upon the Britons. The eagerness and force that were now shown on both sides were as great as if it was the beginning of the battle. Arthur continued to do great execution with his own hand, and encouraged the Britons to maintain the fight, as Lucius Tiberius did the Romans, and made them perform many memorable exploits. He himself, in the meantime, was very active in going from place to place, and suffered none to escape with life that happened to come within the reach of his sword or lance. The slaughter that was now made on both sides was very dreadful, and the turns of fortune various, sometimes the Britons prevailing, sometimes the Romans. At last, while this sharp dispute continued, Morvid, Consul of Gloucester, with his legion which, as we said before, was placed between the hills, came up with speed upon the rear of the enemy, and to their great surprise assaulted, broke through, and dispersed them with great slaughter. This last and decisive blow proved fatal to many thousands of Romans, and even to the general Lucius himself, who was killed among the crowds with a lance by an unknown hand. But the Britons, by long maintaining the fight, at last with great difficulty gained the victory.

12

Part of the Romans flee; the rest, of their own accord, surrender themselves for slaves.

THE Romans, being now, therefore, dispersed, betook themselves through fear, some to the by-ways and woods, some to the cities and towns, and all other places where they could be most safe; but were either killed or taken and plundered by the Britons who pursued: so that a great part of them voluntarily and shamefully held forth their hands to receive their chains, in order to prolong for a while a wretched life. In all which the justice of Divine Providence was very visible, considering how unjustly the ancestors of the Britons were formerly invaded and harassed by those of the Romans; and that these stood only in defense of that liberty, which the others would have deprived them of; and refused the tribute, which the others had no right to demand.

13

The bodies of the slain are decently buried, each in their respective countries.

ARTHUR, after he had completed his victory, gave orders for separating the bodies of his nobility from those of the enemy, and preparing a pompous funeral for them; and that, when ready, they should be carried to the abbeys of their respective countries, there to be honourably buried. But Bedver the butler was, with great lamentation of the Neustrians, carried to his own city Bajocae, which Bedver the first, his great grandfather, had built. There he was, with great solemnity, laid close by the wall, in a burying-place on the south side of the city. But Caius was carried, grievously wounded to Camus, a town which he had himself built, where in a short time he died of his wounds, and was buried, as became a duke of Andegavia, in a convent of hermits which was in a wood not far from the town. Also Holdin, Duke of Ruteni, was carried to Flanders, and buried in his own city Terivana. The other consuls and noblemen were conveyed to the neighbouring abbeys, according to Arthur's orders. Out of great clemency, also, he ordered the country people to take care of the burial of the enemy, and to carry the body of Lucius to the senate, and tell them that was the only tribute which Britain ought to pay them. After this he stayed in those parts till the next winter was over, and employed his time in reducing the cities of the Allobroges. But at the beginning of the following summer, as he was on his march towards Rome, and was beginning to pass the Alps, he had news brought to him that his nephew Modred, to whose care he had entrusted Britain, had by tyrannical and treasonable practices set the crown upon his own head; and that Queen Guanhumara, in violation of her first marriage, had wickedly married him.

BOOK ELEVEN

1

Modred makes a great slaughter of Arthur's men, but is beaten, and flees to Winchester

OF the matter now to be treated of, most noble consul, Geoffrey of Monmouth shall be silent; but will, nevertheless, though in a mean style, briefly relate what he found in the British book above mentioned, and heard from that most learned historian, Walter, archdeacon of Oxford, concerning the wars which this renowned king, upon this return to Britain after this victory, waged against his nephew. As soon, therefore, as the report of this flagrant wickedness reached him, he immediately desisted from his enterprise against Leo, King of the Romans; and having sent away Hoel, Duke of the Armoricans, with the army of Gaul, to restore peace in those parts, returned back with speed to Britain, attended only by the kings of the islands, and their armies. But the wicked traitor, Modred, had sent Cheldric, the Saxon leader, into Germany, there to raise all the forces he could find, and return with all speed: and in consideration of this service, had promised him all that part of the island which reaches from the Humber to Scotland, and whatever Hengist and Horsa had possessed of Kent in the time of Vortigern. So that he, in obedience to his commands, had arrived with eight hundred ships filled with pagan soldiers, and had entered into a covenant to obey the traitor as his sovereign; who had also drawn to his assistance the Scots, Picts, Irish, and all others whom he knew to be enemies of his uncle. His whole army, taking pagans and Christians together, amounted to eighty thousand men; and with the help of whom he met Arthur just after his landing at the port of Rutupi, and joining battle with him, made a very great slaughter of his men. For the same day fell Augusel, King of Albania, and Walgan, the king's nephew, with innumerable others. Augusel was succeeded in his kingdom by Eventus, his brother Urian's son, who afterwards performed many famous exploits in those wars. After they had at last, with much difficulty, got ashore, they paid back the slaughter, and put Modred and his army to flight. For, by long practice in war, they had learned an excellent way of ordering their forces; which was so managed, that while their foot were employed either in an assault or upon the defensive, the horse would come in at full speed obliquely, break through the enemy's ranks, and so force them to flee. Nevertheless, the perjured usurper got his forces together again, and the night following entered Winchester. As soon as Queen Guanhumara heard this, she immediately, despairing of success, fled from York to the City of Legions, where she resolved to live a chaste life among the nuns in the church of Julius the Martyr, and entered herself one of their order.

2

Modred, after being twice besieged and routed, is killed. Arthur, being wounded, gives up the kingdom to Constantine.

BUT Arthur, whose anger was now much more inflamed upon the loss of so many hundreds of fellow soldiers, after he had buried his slain, went on the third day to the city, and there besieged the traitor, who, notwithstanding, was unwilling to desist from his enterprise, but used all methods to encourage his adherents, and marching out with his troops prepared to fight his uncle. In the battle that followed hereupon, great numbers lost their lives on both sides; but at last Modred's army suffered most, so that he was forced to quit the field shamefully. From hence he made a precipitate flight, and, without taking any care for the burial of his slain, marched in haste towards Cornwall. Arthur, being inwardly grieved that he should so often escape, forthwith pursued him into that country as far as the River Cambula, where the other was expecting his coming. And Modred, as he was the boldest of men, and always the quickest at making an attack, immediately placed his troops in order, resolving either to conquer or to die, rather than continue his flight any longer. He had yet remaining with him sixty thousand men, out of whom he composed three bodies, which contained each of them six thousand six hundred and sixty six men: but all the rest he joined in one body; and having assigned to each of the other parties their leaders, he took the command of this upon himself.

After he had made this disposition of forces, he endeavoured to animate them, and promised them the estates of their enemies if they came off with victory. Arthur, on the other side, also marshaled his army which he divided into nine square companies, with a right and left wing; and having appointed to each of them their commanders, exhorted them to make a total rout of those robbers and perjured villains, who, being brought over into the island from foreign countries at the instance of the arch-traitor, were attempting to rob them of all their honours. He likewise told them that a mixed army composed of barbarous people of so many different countries, and who were all raw soldiers and inexperienced in war, would never be able to stand against such brave veteran troops as they were, provided they did their duty. After this encouragement given by each general to his fellow soldiers, the battle on a sudden began with great fury; wherein it would be both grievous and tedious to relate the slaughter, the cruel havoc, and the excess of fury that was to be seen on both sides. In this manner they spent a good part of the day, till Arthur at last made a push with his company, consisting of six thousand six hundred and sixty-six men, against that in which he knew Modred was; and having opened a way with their swords, they pierced quite through it, and made a grievous slaughter. For in this assault fell the wicked traitor himself, and many thousands with him. But notwithstanding the loss of him, the rest did not flee, but running together from all parts of the field maintained their ground with undaunted courage. The fight now grew more furious than ever, and proved fatal to almost all their commanders and their forces. For on Modred's side fell Cheldric, Elasius, Egbrict, and Bunignus, all of them Saxons; the Irishmen Gillapatric, Gillamor, Gistafel, and Gallarius; also the Scots and Picts, with almost all their leaders. On Arthur's side, Olbrict, King of Norway; Aschillius, King of Dacia; Cador Limenic; and Cassibellaun, with many thousands of others, Britons as well as foreigners that he had brought with him. And even the renowned King Arthur himself was mortally wounded; and being carried thence to the isle of Avallon to be cured of his wounds, he gave up the crown of Britain to his kinsman Constantine, the son of Cador, Duke of Cornwall, in the five hundred and forty-second year of our Lord's incarnation.

3

Constantine meets with disturbances from the Saxons and Modred's sons.

UPON Constantine's advancement to the throne, the Saxons, with the two sons of Modred, made insurrection against him, though without success; for after many battles they fled, one to London, the other to Winchester, and possessed themselves of those places. Then died Saint Daniel, the pious prelate of the church of Bangor; and Theon, Bishop of Gloucester, was elected Archbishop of London. At the same time also died David, the pious Archbishop of Legions, at the city of Menevia in his own abbey; which he loved above all the other monasteries of his diocese, because Saint Patrick, who had prophetically foretold his birth, was the founder of it. For during his residence there among the friars, he was taken with a sudden illness of which he died, and, at the command of Malgo, King of the Venedotians, was buried in that church. He was succeeded in the metropolitan see by Cynoc, Bishop of the church of Llan-Patern, who was thus promoted to a higher dignity.

4

Constantine, having murdered the two sons of Modred, is himself killed by Conan.

BUT Constantine pursued the Saxons, and reduced them under his yoke. He also took the two sons of Modred; and one of them, who had fled for sanctuary to the church of St. Amphibalus in Winchester, he murdered before the altar. The other had hidden himself in a convent of friars at London, but at last was found out by him, brought before the altar, and there put to death. Three years after this, he himself, by the vengeance of God pursuing him, was killed by Conan, and buried close by Uther Pendragon within the structure of stones which was set up not far from Salisbury, and called in the English tongue, Stonehenge.

5

Aurelius Conan reigns after Constantine.

AFTER him reigned Aurelius Conan, his nephew, a youth of wonderful valour; who, as he gained the monarch of the whole island, would have been worthy the crown of it, had he not delighted in civil war. He raised disturbances against his uncle, who ought to have reigned after Constantine, and cast him in prison; and then killing his two sons, obtained the kingdom, but died in the second year of his reign.

6

Wortiporius, being declared king, conquers the Saxons.

AFTER Conan succeeded Wortiporius, against whom the Saxons made insurrection, and brought over their countrymen from Germany in a very great fleet. But he gave them battle and came off with victory, so that he obtained the monarch of the whole kingdom, and governed the people carefully and peacefully four years.

7

Malgo, King of Britain, and a most graceful person, addicts himself to sodomy.

AFTER him succeeded Malgo, one of the handsomest of men in Britain, a great scourge of tyrants, and a man of great strength, extraordinary munificence, and matchless valour, but addicted very much to the detestable vice of sodomy, by which he made himself abominable to God. He also possessed the whole island, to which, after a cruel war, he added the six provincial islands, viz. Ireland, Iceland, Gothland, the Orkneys, Norway, and Dacia.

8

Britain, in the flame of a civil war under King Careticus, is miserably wasted by the Saxons and Africans.

AFTER Malgo succeeded Careticus, a lover of civil war, and hateful to God and to the Britons. The Saxons, discovering his fickle disposition, went to Ireland for Gormund, King of the Africans, who had arrived there with a very great fleet, and had subdued that country. From thence, at their traitorous instigation, he sailed over into Britain, which the perfidious Saxons in one part, in another the Britons by their continual wars among themselves were wholly laying waste. Entering therefore into alliance with the Saxons, he made war upon King Careticus, and after several battles fought, drove him from city to city, till at length he forced him to Cirencester, and there besieged him. Here Isembard, the nephew of Lewis, King of the Franks, came and made a league of amity with him, and out of respect to him renounced the Christian faith, on condition that he would assist him to gain the kingdom of Gaul from his uncle, by whom, he said, he was forcibly and unjustly expelled out of it. At last, after taking and burning the city, he had another fight with Careticus, and made him flee beyond the Severn into Wales. He then made an utter devastation of the country, set fire to the adjacent cities, and continued these outrages until he had almost burned up the whole surface of the island from the one sea to the other; so that the tillage was everywhere destroyed, and a general destruction made of the husbandmen and clergy, with fire and sword. This terrible calamity caused the rest to flee whithersoever they had any hopes of safety.

9

The author upbraids the Britons.

WHY foolish nation! oppressed with the weight of your abominable wickedness, why did you, in your insatiable thirst after civil wars, so weaken yourself by domestic confusions, that whereas formerly you brought distant kingdoms under your yoke, now, like a good vineyard degenerated and turned to bitterness, you cannot defend your country, your wives, and children, against your enemies? Go on, go on in your civil dissensions, little understanding the saying in the Gospel: "Every kingdom divided against itself shall fall." Since then your kingdom was divided against itself; since the rage of civil discord, and the fumes of envy, have darkened your minds, since your pride would not suffer you to pay obedience to one king; you see, therefore, your country made desolate by impious pagans, and your houses falling one upon another; which shall be the cause of lasting sorrow to your posterity. For the barbarous lionesses shall see their whelps enjoying the towns, cities, and other possessions of your children; from which they shall be miserably expelled, and hardly if ever recover their former flourishing state.

10

Loegria is again inhabited by the Saxons. The Britons, with their bishops, retire into Cornwall and Wales.

BUT to return to the history; when the inhuman tyrant, with many thousands of his Africans, had made a devastation almost over the whole island, he yielded up the greater part of it, called Loegria, to the Saxons, whose villainy had been the occasion of his arrival. Therefore the remainder of the Britons retired into the western parts of the kingdom, that is Cornwall and Wales; from whence they continually made frequent and fierce irruptions upon the enemy. The three archbishops, viz. the Archbishop of Legions, Theon of London, and Thadiocus of York, when they beheld all the churches in their jurisdiction lying level with the ground, fled with all the clergy that remained after so great a destruction to the coverts of the woods in Wales, carrying with them the relics of the saints for fear the sacred bones of so many holy men of old might be destroyed by the barbarians if they should leave them in that imminent danger, and themselves instantly suffer martyrdom. Many more went over in a great fleet into Armorican Britain; so that the whole church of the two provinces, Loegria and Northumberland, had its convents destroyed. But these things I shall relate elsewhere, when I translate the book concerning their banishment.

11

The Britons lose their kingdom.

FOR a long time after this the Britons were dispossessed of the crown of the kingdom, and the monarchy of the island, and made no endeavours to recover their ancient dignity; but even that part of the country which yet remained to them, being subject not to one king, but three tyrants, was often wasted by civil wars. But neither did the Saxons yet obtain the crown, but were also subject to three kings who harassed sometimes one another, sometimes the Britons.

12

Augustine, being sent by pope Gregory into Britain, preaches the gospel to the Angles.

IN the meantime, Augustine was sent by Pope Saint Gregory into Britain to preach the word of God to the Angles who, being blinded with pagan superstition, had entirely extinguished Christianity in that part of the island which they possessed. But among the Britons the Christian faith still flourished, and never failed among them from the time of Pope Eleutherius when it was first planted here. But when Augustine came, he found in their province seven bishoprics and an archbishopric all filled with most devout prelates, and a great number of abbeys; by which the flock of Christ was still kept in good order. Among the rest, there was in the city of Bangor a most noble church in which it is reported there was so great a number of monks, that when the monastery was divided into seven parts, having each their priors over them, not one of them had less than three hundred monks who all lived by the labour of their own hands. The name of their abbot was Dinooth, a man admirably skilled in the liberal arts; who, when Augustine required the subjection of the British bishops, and would have persuaded them to undertake the work of the gospel with him among the Angles, answered him with several arguments that they owed no subjection to him, neither would they preach to their enemies; since they had their own archbishop, and because the Saxon nation persisted in depriving them of their country. For this reason they esteemed them their mortal enemies, reckoned their faith and religion as nothing, and would no more communicate with the Angles than with dogs.

13

Ethelfrid kills a great number of the British monks, but is at last routed by the Britons.

THEREFORE Ethelbert, King of Kent, when he saw that the Britons disdained subjection to Augustine, and despised his preaching, was highly provoked, and stirred up Ethelfrid, King of the Northumbrians, and the other petty kings of the Saxons to raise a great army, and march to the city of Bangor to destroy the Abbot Dinooth, and the rest of the clergy who held them in contempt. At his instigation, therefore, they assembled a prodigious army, and in their march to the province of the Britons came to Legecester where Brocmail, consul of the city, was awaiting their coming. To the same city were come innumerable monks and hermits from several provinces of the Britons, but especially from the city of Bangor, to pray for the safety of their people. Whereupon Ethelfrid, King of the Northumbrians, collecting all his forces, joined battle with Brocmail who, having a less army to withstand him, at last quitted the city and fled, though not without having made a great slaughter of the enemy. But Ethelfrid, when he had taken the city, and understood upon what occasion the monks were come thither, commanded his men to turn their arms first against them; and so two hundred of them were honoured with the crown of martyrdom, and admitted into the kingdom of heaven that same day. From thence this Saxon tyrant proceeded on his march to Bangor; but upon the news of his outrageous madness, the leaders of the Britons, viz. Blederic, Duke of Cornwall, Margaduc, King of the Demetians, and Cadwan of the Venedotians, came from all parts to meet him and joining battle with him, wounded him, and forced him to flee; and killed of his army to the number of ten thousand and sixty-six men. On the Britons' side fell Blederic, Duke of Cornwall, who was their commander in those wars.

BOOK TWELVE

1

Cadwan acquires by treaty all Britain on this side of the Humber, and Ethelfrid the rest.

AFTER this all the princes of the Britons met together at the city of Legecester, and consented to make Cadwan their king that under his command they might pursue Ethelfrid beyond the Humber. Accordingly, as soon as he was crowned, they flocked together from all parts, and passed the Humber; of which when Ethelfrid received intelligence, he entered into a confederacy with all the Saxon kings, and went to meet Cadwan. At last, as they were forming their troops for a battle, their friends came, and made peace between them on these terms: that Cadwan should enjoy that part of Britain which lies on this side of the Humber, and Ethelfrid that which is beyond it. As soon as they had confirmed this agreement with an oath made to their hostages, there commenced such a friendship between them, that they had all things common. In the meantime it happened that Ethelfrid banished his own wife and married another, and bore so great a hatred to her that was banished that he would not suffer her to live in the kingdom of Northumberland. Whereupon she, being with child, went to King Cadwan that by his mediation she might be restored to her husband. But when Ethelfrid could by no means be brought to consent to it, she continued to live with Cadwan till she was delivered of the son which she had conceived. A short time after her delivery, Cadwan also had a son born to him by the queen, his wife. Then were the two boys brought up together in a manner suitable to their royal birth, one of which was Cadwalla, the other

Edwin. When they were nearly arrived at men's estate, their parents sent them to Salomon, King of the Armorican Britons, that in his court they might learn the discipline of war, and other princely qualifications. This prince, therefore, received them graciously, and admitted them to an intimacy with him; so that there was none of their age in the whole court that had a free access, or more familiarly discoursed with the king, than they. At last he himself was an eye-witness of their exploits against the enemy, in which they very much signalized their valour.

2

Cadwalla breaks the covenant he had made with Edwin.

IN process of time, when their parents were dead, they returned to Britain, where they took upon them the government of the kingdom, and began to form the same friendship as their fathers. Two years after this, Edwin asked leave of Cadwalla to wear a crown, and to celebrate the same solemnities as had been used of old in Northumberland. And, when they had begun a treaty upon this subject by the River Duglas that the matter might be adjusted according to the advice of their wise counselors, it happened that Cadwalla was lying on the other side of the river in the lap of a certain nephew of his, whose name was Brian. While ambassadors were negotiating between them, Brian wept, and shed tears so plentifully that the king's beard and face were wet with them. The king, imagining that it rained, lifted up his face, and seeing the young man in tears, asked him the occasion of his sudden grief. "Good reason," said he, "have I to weep continually, as well as the whole British nation which has groaned under the oppression of barbarians ever since the time of Malgo, and has not yet got a prince to restore it to its ancient flourishing state. And even the little honour that it had left, is lessened by your indulgence; since the Saxons, who are only strangers, and always traitors to our country, must now be permitted to wear the same crown as you do. For once they shall attain to regal dignity, it will be a great addition to their glory in the country from whence they came; and they will the sooner invite over their countrymen for the utter extirpation of our race. For they have been always accustomed to treachery, and never to keep faith with any; which I think should be a reason for our keeping them under, and not for exalting them. When King Vortigern first retained them in his service, they made a show of living peaceably, and fighting for our country till they had an opportunity of practicing their wickedness; and then they returned evil for good, betraying him, and made a cruel massacre of the people of the kingdom. Afterwards they betrayed Aurelius Ambrosius to whom, even after the most tremendous oaths of fidelity, at a banquet with him they gave a draught of poison. They also betrayed Arthur when, setting aside the covenant by which they were bound, they joined with his nephew Modred, and fought against him. Lastly, they broke faith with King Careticus, and brought upon him Gormund, King of the Africans, by whose disturbances our people were robbed of their country, and the king disgracefully driven out."

3

A quarrel between Cadwalla and Edwin.

AT the mention of these things, Cadwalla repented of entering into this treaty, and sent word to Edwin that he could by no means induce his counselors to consent to his petition. For they alleged that it was contrary to law and the ancient establishment that an island, which has always had no more than one crown, should now be under subjection to two crowned heads. This message incensed Edwin, and made him break off the conference, and retire into Northumberland, saying, he would be crowned without Cadwalla's leave. When Cadwalla was told this, he declared to him by his ambassadors that he would cut off his crowned head if he presumed to wear a crown within the kingdom of Britain.

4

Cadwalla is vanquished by Edwin, and driven out of the kingdom.

THIS proved the occasion of a war between them, in which, after several engagements between their men, they had at last met together themselves beyond the Humber, and had a battle, wherein Cadwalla lost many thousands of his followers, and was put to flight. From hence he marched with precipitation through Albania, and went over to Ireland. But Edwin, after this victory, led his army through the provinces of the Britons, and burning the cities before him, grievously afflicted the citizens and country people. During this exercise of his cruelty, Cadwalla never ceased endeavouring to return back to his country in a fleet, but without success; because to whatever port he steered, Edwin met him with his forces, and hindered his landing. For there was come to him from Spain a very skillful soothsayer, named Pellitus, who, by the flight of the birds and the courses of the stars, foretold all the disasters that would happen. By these means Edwin, getting knowledge of Cadwalla's return, prepared to meet him, and shattered his ships so that he drowned his men, and beat him off from all his ports. Cadwalla, not knowing what course to take, was almost in despair of ever returning. At last it came into his head to go to Salomon, King of the Armorican Britons, and desire his assistance and advice to enable him to return to his kingdom. And so, as he was steering towards Armorica, a strong tempest rose on a sudden, which dispersed the ships of his companions, and in a short time left no two of them together. The pilot of the king's ship was seized immediately with so great a fear, that quitting the stern, he left the vessel to the disposal of fortune; so that all night it was tossed up and down in great danger by the raging waves. The next morning the arrived at a certain island called Garnareia, where with great difficulty they got ashore. Cadwalla was forthwith seized with such grief for the loss of his companions, that for three days and nights together he refused to eat, but lay sick upon his bed. The fourth day he was taken with a very great longing for some venison, and causing Brian to be called, made him acquainted with it. Whereupon Brian took his bow and quiver, and went through the island, that if he could light on any wild beast, he might make booty of it. And when he had walked over the whole island without finding what he was in quest of, he was extremely concerned that he could not gratify his master's desire; and was afraid his sickness would prove mortal if his longing were not satisfied. He, therefore, fell upon a new device, and cut a piece of flesh out of his own thigh, which he roasted on a spit, and carried to the king for venison. The king, thinking it to be real venison, began to eat of it to his great refreshment, admiring the sweetness of it, which he fancied exceeded any flesh he had ever tasted before. At last, when he had fully satisfied his appetite, he became more cheerful, and in three days was perfectly well again. Then the wind standing fair, he got ready his ship, and hoisting sails they pursued their voyage, and arrived at the city, Kidaleta. From thence they went to King Salomon, by whom they were received kindly and with all suitable respect; and as soon as he had learned the occasion of their coming, he made them a promise of assistance, and spoke to them as follows:

5

The speech of Salomon, King of Armorica, to Cadwalla.

"IT is a grief to us, noble youths, that the country of your ancestors is oppressed by a barbarous nation, and that you are ignominiously driven out of it. But since other men are able to defend their kingdoms, it is a wonder your people should lose so fruitful an island, and not be able to withstand the nation of the Angles, whom our countrymen hold in contempt. While the people of this country lived together with yours in Britain, they bore sway over all the provincial kingdoms, and could never be subdued by any nation but the Romans. Neither did the Romans do this by their own power, as I have been lately informed, but by a dissension among the nobility of the island. And even the Romans, though they held it under their subjection for a time, yet upon the loss and slaughter of their rulers, were driven out with disgrace. But after the Britons came into this province under the conduct of Maximian and Conan, those that remained never had the happiness afterwards of holding an uninterrupted possession of the crown. For though many of the princes maintained the ancient dignity of their ancestors, yet their weak heirs that succeeded, though more in number, entirely lost it upon the invasion of their enemies. Therefore I am grieved for the weakness of your people, since we are of the same race with you, and the name of Britons is common to you, and to the nation that bravely defends their country, which you see at war with all its neighbours."

6

Cadwalla's answer to Salomon.

WHEN he had concluded his speech, Cadwalla, who was a little put to the blush, answered him after this manner: "Royal sir, whose descent is from a race of kings, I give you many thanks for your promise of assisting me to recover my kingdom. But what you say is a wonder, that my people have not maintained the dignity of their ancestors, since the time that the Britons came to these provinces, I am far from thinking to be such. For the noblest men of the whole kingdom followed those leaders, and there remained only the baser sort to enjoy their honours; who being raised to a high quality, on a sudden were puffed up above their station; and growing wanton with riches gave themselves up to commit such fornication as is not so much named among the Gentiles; and (as Gildas the historian testifies) were not only guilty of this vice, but of all the enormities that are incident to human nature. And what chiefly prevailed, to the entire overthrow of all goodness, was the hatred of truth, the love of a lie with the inventors of it, the embracing of evil for good, the veneration of wickedness for grace, the receiving of Satan for an angel of light. Kings were anointed, not for the sake of God, but such as were more cruel than the rest; and were soon after murdered by their anointers, without examination, having chosen others yet more cruel in their room. But if any of them showed any mildness, or seemed a favourer of truth, against him, as the subverter of Britain, were all their malice and their weapons bent. In short, things pleasing to God or displeasing, with them had the same weight, even if the worse were not the weightier. Therefore were all affairs managed contrary to public safety, as if the true physician of all had left them destitute of cure. And thus was everything done without discretion, and that not only by secular men, but by the Lord's flock and its pastors. Therefore it is not to be wondered that such a degenerate race, so odious to God for their vices, lost a country which they had so heinously corrupted. For God was willing to execute his vengeance upon them, by suffering a foreign people to come upon them, and drive them out of their possessions. Notwithstanding it would be a worthy act, if God would permit it, to restore our subjects to their ancient dignity, to prevent the reproach that may be thrown upon our race, that we were weak rulers who did not exert ourselves in our own defense. And I do the more freely ask your assistance, as you are of the same blood with us. For the great Malgo, who was the fourth King of Britain after Arthur, had two sons named Ennianus and Runo. Ennianus begot Belin; Belin, Jago; Jago, Cadwan, who was my father. Runo, who, after his brother's death, was driven out by the Saxons, came to this province and bestowed his daughter on Duke Hoel, the son of that great Hoel who shared with Arthur on his conquests. Of her was born Alan; of Alan, Hoel your father, who while he lived was a terror to all Gaul."

7

Brian kills Edwin's magician.

IN the meantime, while he was spending the winter with Salomon, they entered into a resolution that Brian should pass over into Britain, and take some method to kill Edwin's magician, lest he might by his usual art inform him of Cadwalla's coming. And when with this design he had arrived at Hamo's Port, he took upon him the habit of a poor man, and made himself a staff of iron sharp at one end with which he might kill the magician if he should happen to meet with him. From thence he went to York where Edwin then resided; and having entered that city joined himself to the poor people that waited for alms before the king's gate. But as he was going to and fro, it happened that his sister came out of the hall, with a basin in her hand, to fetch water for the queen. She had been taken by Edwin at the city of Worcester, when after Cadwalla's flight he was acting his hostilities upon the provinces of the Britons. As she was therefore passing by Brian, he immediately knew her, and, breaking forth into tears, called to her with a low voice; at which the damsel turning her face, was in doubt at first who it could be, but upon a nearer approach discovered it to be her brother, and was near falling into a swoon for fear that he might by some unlucky accident be known and taken by the enemy. She therefore refrained from saluting him, or entering into familiar discourse with him, but told him, as if she was talking upon some other subject, the state of the court, and showed him the magician that he was inquiring for, who was at that very time walking among the poor people, while the alms were being distributed among them. Brian, as soon as he had taken knowledge of the man, ordered his sister to steal out privately from her apartment the night following, and come to him near an old church without the city where he would conceal himself in expectation of her. Then dismissing her, he thrust himself in among the crowd of poor people in that part where Pellitus was placing them. And the same moment he got access to him, he lifted up his staff, and at once gave him a stab under the breast which killed him. This done, he threw away his staff, and passed among the rest undistinguished and unsuspected by any of the by-standers, and by good providence got to the place of concealment which he had appointed. His sister, when night came on, endeavoured all she could to get out, but was not able; because Edwin, being terrified at the killing of Pellitus, had set a strict watch about the court, who, making a narrow search, refused to let her go out. When Brian found this, he retired from that place, and went to Exeter, where he called together the Britons, and told them what he had done. Afterwards having despatched away messengers to Cadwalla, he fortified the city, and sent word to all the British nobility that they should bravely defend their cities and towns, and joyfully expect Cadwalla's coming to their relief in a short time with auxiliary forces from Salomon. Upon the spreading of this news over the whole island, Penda, King of the Mercians, with a very great army of Saxons, came to Exeter, and besieged Brian.

8

Cadwalla takes Penda, and routs his army.

IN the meantime, Cadwalla arrived with ten thousand men whom King Salomon had delivered to him; and with them he marched straight to the siege against King Penda. But, as he was going, he divided his forces into four parts, and then made no delay to advance and join battle with the enemy. Wherein Penda was forthwith taken, and his army routed. For, finding no other way for his own safety, he surrendered himself to Cadwalla, and gave hostages with a promise that he would assist him against the Saxons. Cadwalla, after this success against him, summoned together his nobility that had been a long time in a decaying state, and marched to Northumberland against Edwin, and made continual devastations in that country. When Edwin was informed of it, he assembled all the petty kings of the Angles, and meeting the Britons in a field called Heathfield, presently gave them battle, but was killed, and almost all the people with him, together with Osfrid, his son, and Godbold, King of the Orkneys, who had come to their assistance.

9

Cadwalla kills Osric and Aidan in fight.

HAVING thus obtained the victory, Cadwalla marched through the provinces of the Angles, and committed such outrages upon the Saxons that he spared neither age nor sex; for his resolution being to extirpate the whole race out of Britain, all that he found he put to extreme tortures. After this he had a battle with Osric, Edwin's successor, and killed him together with his two nephews, who ought to have reigned after him. He also killed Aidan, King of the Scots, who came to their assistance.

10

Oswald routs Penda in fight, but is killed by Cadwalla coming in upon him.

THEIR deaths made room for Oswald to succeed to the kingship of Northumberland; but Cadwalla drove him, with the rest that had given him disturbance, to the very wall which the emperor Severus had formerly built between Britain and Scotland. Afterwards he sent Penda, King of the Mercians, and the greatest part of his army, to the same place, to give him battle. But Oswald, as he was besieged one night by Penda in the place called Heavenfield, that is the Heavenly Field, set up there our Lord's cross, and commanded his men to speak with a very loud voice these words: "Let us all kneel down, and pray the Almighty, living and true God, to defend us from the proud army of the King of Britain, and his wicked leader Penda. For he knows how justly we wage this war for the safety of our people." They all therefore did as he commanded them, and advanced at break of day against the enemy, and by their faith gained the victory. Cadwalla, upon hearing this news, being inflamed with rage, assembled his army, and went in pursuit of the holy King Oswald; and in a battle which he had with him at a place called Burne, Penda broke in upon him and killed him.

11

Oswy submits to Cadwalla. Penda desires leave of Cadwalla to make war against him.

OSWALD, with many thousands of his men, being killed, his brother Oswy succeeded him in the kingdom of Northumberland, and by making large presents of gold and silver to Cadwalla, who was now possessed of the government of all Britain, made his peace and submission to him. Upon this Alfrid, his brother, and Ethelwald, his brother's son, began an insurrection; but, not being able to hold out against him, they fled to Penda, King of the Mercians, desiring him to assemble his army and pass the Humber with them, that he might deprive Oswy of his kingdom. But Penda, fearing to break the peace which Cadwalla had settled through the kingdom of Britain, deferred beginning any disturbance without his leave till he could some way work him up, either to make war himself upon Oswy, or allow him the liberty of doing it. At a certain Pentecost therefore, when Cadwalla was celebrating that festival at London, and for the greater solemnity wore the crown of Britain, all the kings of the Angles, excepting only Oswy, being present, as also all the dukes of the Britons; Penda went to the king, and inquired of him the reason why Oswy alone was wanting, when all the princes of the Saxons were present. Cadwalla answered, that his sickness was the cause of it; to which the other replied, that he had sent over to Germany for more Saxons, to revenge the death of his brother Oswald upon them both. He told him further that he had broken the peace of the kingdom, as being the sole author of the war and dissension among them; since Ethelfrid, King of Northumberland, and Ethelwald, his brother's son, had been by him harassed with a war, and driven out of their own country. He also desired leave, either to kill him, or banish him the kingdom.

12

Cadwalla is advised to suffer Penda to make an insurrection against Oswy.

THIS matter caused the king to enter upon much deliberation, and hold a private consultation with his intimate friends, what course to take. Among the rest that offered their proposals, Margadud, King of the Dimetians, spoke as follows: "Royal sir, since you have proposed to expel the race of the Angles from the coasts of Britain, why do you alter your resolution, and suffer them to continue in peace among us? At least you should permit them to fall out among themselves, and let our country owe its deliverance to their own civil broils. No faith is to be kept with one that is treacherous, and is continually laying snares for him to whom he owes fidelity. Such have the Saxons always been to our nation, from the very first time of their coming among us. What faith ought we to keep with them? Let Penda immediately have leave to go against Oswy, that by this civil dissension and destruction of one another, our island may get rid of them."

13

Penda is killed by Oswy. Cadwalla dies.

BY these and other words to the same effect, Cadwalla was prevailed upon to grant the permission desired. And Penda, having assembled a vast army, and laying waste that country, began a fierce war upon the king. Oswy was at last reduced to such extremity that he was forced to promise him innumerable royal ornaments, and other presents more than one would believe, if he would desist from ruining his country, and return home without committing any more hostilities. But when the other could by no entreaties be prevailed upon to do it, the king, in hopes of divine assistance, though he had a less army, however, gave him battle near the River Winwid, and having killed Penda and thirty other commanders, gained the victory. Penda's son, Wulfred, by a grant from Cadwalla, succeeded to the kingdom, and joining with Eafa and Eadbert, two leaders of the Mercians, rebelled against Oswy; but at last, by Cadwalla's command, made peace with him. At length, after forty-eight years were expired, that most noble and potent King of the Britons, Cadwalla, being grown infirm with age and sickness, departed this life upon the fifteenth before the Kalends of December. The Britons embalmed his body, and placed it with wonderful art in a brazen statue, which was cast according to the measure of his stature. This statue they set up with complete armour, on an admirable and beautiful brazen horse, over the western gate of London, for a monument of the above-mentioned victory, and for a terror to the Saxons. They also built under it a church in honour of St. Martin, in which divine ceremonies are celebrated for him and others who departed in the faith.

14

Cadwallader succeeds Cadwalla.

HE was succeeded in the kingdom by Cadwallader, his son, whom Bede calls the youth Elidwalda. At first he maintained the government with peace and honour; but after twelve years' enjoyment of the crown, he fell into a fit of sickness, and a civil war broke out among the Britons. His mother was Penda's sister, by the same father but a different mother, descended from the noble race of the Gewisseans. For Cadwalla, after his reconciliation with her brother, made her the partner of his bed, and had Cadwallader by her.

15

The Britons are compelled, by pestilence and famine, to leave Britain. Cadwallader's lamentation.

DURING his sickness, the Britons (as we said before), quarreling among themselves, made a wicked destruction of a rich country; and this again was attended with another misfortune. For this besotted people was punished with a grievous and memorable famine; so that every province was destitute of all sustenance, except what could be taken in hunting. After the famine followed a terrible pestilence, which in a short time destroyed such multitudes of people, that the living were not sufficient to bury the dead. Those of them that remained, flying their country in whole troops together, went to the countries beyond the sea, and while they were under sail, they with a mournful howling voice sang, "Thou hast given us, O God, like sheep appointed for meat, and hast scattered us among the heathen." Also Cadwallader himself, in his voyage, with his miserable fleet to Armorica, made this addition to the lamentation, "Woe to us sinners, for our grievous impieties, wherewith we have not ceased to provoke God, while we had space for repentance. Therefore the revenge of his power lies heavy upon us, and drives us out of our native soil, which neither the Romans of old, nor the Scots or Picts afterwards, nor yet the treacherous Saxons with all their craft, were able to do. But in vain have we recovered our country so often from them; since it was not the will of God that we should perpetually hold the government of it. He who is the true Judge, when he saw we were by no means to be reclaimed from our wickedness, and that no human power could expel our race, was willing to chastise our folly himself; and has turned his anger against us, by which we are driven out in crowds from our native country. Return, therefore, ye Romans; return, Scots and Picts; return, Ambrons and Saxons: behold, Britain lies open to you, being by the wrath of God made desolate, which you were never able to do. It is not your valour that expels us; but the power of the supreme King, whom we have never ceased to provoke."

16

Cadwallader with his people goes to Alan. The Saxons seize all Britain.

WITH these dolorous complaints he arrived at the Armorican coast, and went with his whole company to King Alan, the nephew of Salomon, by whom he was honourably received. So that Britain, being now destitute of its ancient inhabitants, excepting a few in Wales that escaped the general mortality, became a frightful place even to the Britons themselves for eleven years after. Neither was it at the same time more favourable to the Saxons, who died in it without intermission. Notwithstanding the remainder of them, after this raging plague was ceased, according to their old custom sent word over to their countrymen, that the island of Britain was now freed of its native inhabitants, and lay open to them if they would come over and inhabit it. As soon as they had received this information, that odious people, gathering together an innumerable multitude of men and women, arrived in Northumberland, and inhabited the provinces that lay desolate from Albania to Cornwall. For there was now nobody to hinder them, excepting the poor remains of the Britons, who continued together in the thickets of the woods of Wales. From that time the power of the Britons ceased in the island, and the Angles began their reign.

17

Cadwallader is by the voice of an angel deterred from returning to Britain.

AFTER some time, when the people had recovered strength, Cadwallader, being mindful of his kingdom, which was now free from the contagion of the pestilence, desired assistance of Alan towards the recovery of his dominions. The king granted his request; but as he was getting ready a fleet, he was commanded by the loud voice of an angel to desist from his enterprise. For God was not willing that the Britons should reign any longer in the island, before the time came of which Merlin prophetically foretold Arthur. It also commanded him to go to Rome to Pope Sergius, where, after doing penance, he should be enrolled among the saints. It told him withal, that the Britons, by the merit of their faith, should again recover the island when the time decreed for it was come. But this would not be accomplished before they should be possessed of his relics, and transport them from Rome into Britain. At the same time also the relics of the other saints should be found, which had been hidden on account of the invasion of pagans; and then at last would they recover their lost kingdom. When the holy prince had received the heavenly message, he went straight to King Alan, and gave him an account of what had been told him.

18

Cadwallader goes to Rome and dies.

THEN Alan had recourse to several books, as the prophecies of the eagle that prophesied at Shaftesbury, and the verses of Sibyl and Merlin; and made diligent search in them to see whether the revelation made to Cadwallader agreed with those written oracles. And when he could find nothing contradictory to it, he admonished Cadwallader to submit to the divine dispensation, and laying aside the thoughts of Britain, perform what the angelical voice had commanded him. But he urged him to send his son, Ivor, and his nephew, Ini, over into the island to govern the remainder of the Britons; lest a nation, descended of so ancient a race, should lose their liberty by the incursions of barbarians. Then Cadwallader, renouncing worldly cares for the sake of God and his everlasting kingdom, went to Rome, and was confirmed by Pope Sergius: and being seized with a sudden illness, was, upon the twelfth before the Kalends of May, in the six hundred and eighty-ninth year of our Lord's incarnation, freed from the corruption of the flesh, and admitted into the glories of the heavenly kingdom.

19

The two Britons, Ivor and Ini, in vain attack the nation of the Angles. Athelstan, the first King of the Angles.

AS soon as Ivor and Ini had got together their ships, they with all the forces they could raise, arrived in the island, and for forty-nine years together fiercely attacked the nation of the Angles, but to little purpose. For the above-mentioned mortality and famine, together with the inveterate spirit of faction that was among them, had made this proud people so much degenerate, that they were not able to gain any advantage of the enemy. And being now also overrun with barbarism, they were no longer called Britons, but Gualenses, Welshmen; a name derived either from Gualo their leader, or Guales their queen, or from their barbarism. But the Saxons managed affairs with more prudence, maintained peace and concord among themselves, tilled their grounds, rebuilt their cities and towns, and so throwing off the dominance of the Britons, bore sway over all Loegria under their leader Athelstan, who first wore a crown amongst them. But the Welshmen, being very much degenerated from the nobility of the Britons, never after recovered the monarchy of the island; on the contrary, by quarrels among themselves, and wars with the Saxons, their country was a perpetual scene of misery and slaughter.

20

Geoffrey of Monmouth's conclusion.

BUT as for the kings that have succeeded among them in Wales since that time, I leave the history of them to Caradoc of Lancarvan, my contemporary; as I do also the kings of the Saxons to William of Malmesbury, and Henry of Huntingdon. But I advise them to be silent concerning the Kings of the Britons, since they have not that book written in the British tongue which Walter, Archdeacon of Oxford, brought out of Brittany, and which being a true history, published in honour of those princes, I have thus taken care to translate.

The Golden Legend

Jacobus de Voragine

Translated by William Caxton

Life of St. Nicholas

Here followeth of St. Nicholas the Bishop, and first the interpretation of his name

Nicholas is said of *nichos*, which is to say victory, and of *laos*, people, so Nicholas is as much as to say as victory of people, that is, victory of sins, which be foul people. Or else he is said, victory of people, because he taught many people by his doctrine to overcome vices and sins. Or Nicholas is said of *nichor*, that is the resplendour or shining of the people, for he had in him things that make shining and clearness. After this St. Ambrose saith: The word of God, very confession, and holy thought, make a man clean. And the doctors of Greece write his legend, and some others say that Methodius the patriarch wrote it in Greek, and John the deacon translated it into Latin and adjousted thereto many things.

Of the Life of St. Nicholas

Nicholas, citizen of the city of Patras, was born of rich and holy kin, and his father was Epiphanes and his mother Johane. He was begotten in the first flower of their age, and from that time forth on they lived in continence and led a heavenly life. From the first day that he was washed and bathed, he addressed him right up in the basin, and he would not take the breast nor the pap but once on the Wednesday and once on the Friday, and in his young age he eschewed the plays and jokes of other young children. He used and haunted gladly holy church; and all that he might understand of holy scripture he executed it in deed and work after his power.

And when his father and mother were departed out of this life, he began to think how he might distribute his riches, and not to the praising of the world but to the honour and glory of God. And it was so that one, his neighbour, had then three daughters, virgins, and he was a nobleman: but for the poverty of them together, they were constrained, and in very purpose to abandon them to the sin of lechery, so that by the gain and winning of their infamy they might be sustained. And when the holy man Nicholas knew hereof he had great horror of this villainy, and threw by night secretly into the house of the man a mass of gold wrapped in a cloth. And when the man arose in the morning, he found this mass of gold, and rendered to God therefore great thankings, and therewith he married his oldest daughter. And a little while after this holy servant of God threw in another mass of gold which the man found, and thanked God, and purposed to stay awake for to know him that so had aided him in his poverty. And after a few days Nicholas doubled the mass of gold, and cast it into the house of this man. He awoke by the sound of the gold, and followed Nicholas, who fled from him, and he said to him: "Sir, flee not away so but that I may see and know thee." Then he ran after him more hastily, and knew that it was Nicholas; and immediately he kneeled down, and would have kissed his feet, but the holy man would not, but required him not to tell nor discover this thing as long as he lived.

After this the bishop of Mirea died and other bishops assembled for to purvey to this church a bishop. And there was, among the others, a bishop of great authority, and all the election was in him. And when he had warned all for to be in fastings and in prayers, this bishop heard that night a voice which said to him that, at the hour of matins, he should take heed to the doors of the church, and him that should come first to the church, and have the name of Nicholas they should consecrate him bishop. And he showed this to the other bishops and admonished them for to be all in prayers; and he kept the doors. And this was a marvelous thing, for at the hour of matins, like as he had been sent from God, Nicholas arose before all others. And the bishop took him when he was come and demanded of him his name. And he, who was simple as a dove, inclined his head, and said: "I have to name Nicholas." Then the bishop said to him: "Nicholas, servant and friend of God, for your holiness ye shall be bishop of this place." So they brought him to the church, and though he refused it strongly, yet they set him in the chair. And he followed, as he did before in all things, in humility and honesty of manners. He woke in prayer and made his body lean, he eschewed company of women, he was humble in receiving all things, profitable in speaking, joyous in admonishing, and cruel in correcting.

It is read in a chronicle that the blessed Nicholas was at the Council of Nice; and on a day, as a ship with mariners were perishing on the sea, they prayed and required devoutly of Nicholas, servant of God, saying: "If those things that we have heard of thee said be true, prove them now." And immediately a man appeared in his likeness, and said: "Lo! See ye me not? Ye called me," and then he began to help them in their exploit of the sea, and immediately the tempest ceased. And when they were come to his church, they knew him without any man to show him to them, and yet they had never seen him. And then they thanked God and him of their deliverance. And he bade them to attribute it to the mercy of God, and to their belief, and nothing to his merits.

It was so on a time that all the province of St. Nicolas suffered great famine, in such wise that victual failed. And then this holy man heard it said that certain ships laden with wheat were arrived in the haven. And immediately he went thither and prayed the mariners that they would succour the perished at least with an hundred muyes[1] of wheat of every ship. And they said: "Father we dare not,

---

1 About 400 bushels

for it is meted and measured, and we must give reckoning thereof in the garners of the Emperor in Alexandria." And the holy man said to them: "Do this that I have said to you, and I promise, in the truth of God, that it shall not be lessened or diminished when ye shall come to the garners." And when they had delivered so much out of every ship, they came into Alexandria and delivered the measure that they had received. And then they recounted the miracle to the ministers of the Emperor, and worshiped and praised strongly God and his servant Nicholas. Then this holy man distributed the wheat to every man as much as he had need, in such wise that it sufficed for two years, not only for to sell, but also to sow.

And in this country the people served idols and worshiped the false image of the cursed Diana. And to the time of this holy man, many of them had some customs of the pagans, for to sacrifice to Diana under a sacred tree; but this good man made them of all the country to cease then these customs, and commanded to cut off the tree. Then the devil was angry and wroth against him, and made an oil that burned, against nature, in water, and burned stones also. And then he transformed himself into the guise of a religious woman, and put himself in a little boat, and encountered pilgrims that sailed in the sea towards this holy saint, and reasoned with them thus, and said: "I would fain go to this holy man, but I may not, wherefore I pray you to bear this oil into his church, and for the remembrance of me, that ye anoint the walls of the hall." And immediately he vanished away. Then they saw immediately after another ship with honest persons, among whom there was one like to Nicholas, who spake to them softly: "What hath this woman said to you, and what hath she brought?" And they told to him all in order. And he said to them: "This is the evil and foul Diana; and to the end that ye know that I say truth, cast that oil into the sea." And when they had cast it, a great fire caught in the sea, and they saw it long burn against nature. Then they came to this holy man and said to him: "Verily thou art he who appeared to us in the sea and delivered us from the sea and snares of the devil."

And in this time certain men rebelled against the emperor; and the emperor sent against them three princes—Nepotian, Ursyn, and Apollyn. And they came into the port Adriatic for the wind was contrary to them; and the blessed Nicholas commanded them to dine with him. And whilst they were at dinner, the consul, corrupt by money, had commanded three innocent knights to be beheaded. And when the blessed Nicholas knew this, he prayed these three princes that they would hastily go with him. And when they were come where they should be beheaded, he found them on their knees, and blindfolded, and the executioner brandished his sword over their heads. Then St. Nicholas, embraced with the love of God, set him hardily against the executioner, and took the sword out of his hand, and threw it from him, and unbound the innocents, and led them with him all safe. And immediately he went to the judgment to the consul, and found the gates closed, which immediately he opened by force. And the consul came immediately and saluted him. And this holy man holding this salutation in contempt, said to him: "Thou enemy of God, corrupter of the law, wherefore hast thou consented to so great evil and felony, how darest thou look on us?" And when he had sorely chidden and reproved him, he repented, and at the prayer of the three princes he received him to penance. After, when the messengers of the emperor had received his benediction, they made their gear ready and departed, and subdued their enemies to the empire without shedding of blood and so returned to the emperor, and were worshipfully received. And after this it happed that some other in the emperor's house had envy of the wealth of these three princes, and accused them to the emperor of high treason, and did so much by prayer and by gifts that they caused the emperor to be so full of ire that he commanded them to prison, and without other demand, he commanded that they should be slain that same night. And when they knew it by their keeper, they rent their clothes and wept bitterly; and then Nepotian remembered him how St. Nicholas had delivered the three innocents, and counseled the others that they should require his aid and help. And thus as they prayed, St. Nicholas appeared to them, and after appeared to Constantine the emperor, and said to him: "Wherefore hast thou taken these three princes with so great wrong, and hast judged them to death without trespass? Arise up hastily, and command that they be not executed, or I shall pray to God that he move battle against thee in which thou shalt be overthrown, and shalt be made meat to beasts." And the emperor demanded: "What art thou that art entered by night into my palace and durst say to me such words?" And he said to him: "I am Nicholas bishop of Mirea." And likewise he appeared to the provost, and frightened him, saying with a fearful voice: "Thou that hast lost mind and wit, wherefore hast thou consented to the death of innocents? Go forth immediately and do thy part to deliver them, or else thy body shall rot, and be eaten with worms, and thy household shall be destroyed." And he asked him: "Who art thou that so menaces me?" And he answered: "Know thou that I am Nicholas, the bishop of the city of Mirea." Then that one woke the other, and each told to the other their dream, and immediately sent for them that were in prison, to whom the emperor said: "What kind of magic or sorcery know ye, that ye have this night by illusion caused us to have such dreams?" And they said that they were not enchanters and knew no witchcraft, and also that they had not deserved the sentence of death. Then the emperor said to them: "Know ye well a man named Nicholas?" And when they heard speak of the name of the holy saint, they held up their hands towards heaven, and prayed our Lord that by the merits of St. Nicholas they might be delivered of this present peril. And when the emperor had heard of them the life and miracles of St. Nicholas, he said to them: "Go ye forth, and yield ye thankings to God, who hath delivered you by the prayer of this holy man, and worship ye him; and bear ye to him of your jewels, and pray ye him that he threaten me no more, but that he pray for me and for my realm unto our Lord." And a while after, the said princes went unto the holy man, and fell down on their knees humbly at his feet, saying: "Verily thou art the sergeant of God, and the very worshiper and lover of Jesus Christ." And when they had all told these things in order, he lifted up his hands to heaven and gave thankings and praisings to God, and sent again the princes, well informed, into their countries.

And when it pleased our Lord to have him depart out this world, he prayed our Lord that he would send him his angels; and inclining his head he saw the angels come to him, whereby he knew well that he should depart, and began this holy psalm: "*In te domine speravi, unto, in manus tuas*", and so saying: "Lord, into thine hands I commend my spirit," he rendered up his soul and died, in the year of our Lord three hundred and forty-three, with great melody sung of the celestial company. And when he was buried in a tomb of marble, a fountain of oil sprang out from the head unto his feet; and unto this day holy oil issueth out of his body, which is much available to the health of sicknesses of many men. And after him in his see succeeded a man of good and holy life, who by envy was put out of his bishopric. And when he was out of his see the oil ceased to run, and when he was restored again thereto, the oil ran again.

Long after this the Turks destroyed the city of Mirea, and then came thither forty-seven knights of Bari, and four monks showed to them the sepulchre of St. Nicholas. And they opened it and found the bones swimming in the oil, and they bare them away honourably into the city of Bari, in the year of our Lord ten hundred and eighty-seven.

There was a man that had borrowed of a Jew a sum of money, and sware upon the altar of St. Nicholas that he would render and pay it again as soon as he might, and gave no other pledge. And this man held this money so long, that the Jew demanded and asked his money, and he said that he had paid him. Then the Jew made him to come before the law in judgment, and the oath was given to the debtor. And he brought with him an hollow staff, in which he had put the money in gold, and he leant upon the staff. And when he should make his oath and swear, he delivered his staff to the Jew to keep and hold whilst he should swear, and then swore that he had delivered to him more than he ought to him. And when he had made the oath, he demanded his staff again of the Jew, and he nothing knowing of his malice delivered it to him. Then this deceiver went his way, and immediately after, he had a sore desire to sleep, and laid him in the way, and a cart with four wheels came with great force and slew him, and broke the staff with gold that it spread abroad. And when the Jew heard this, he came thither sore moved, and saw the fraud, and many said to him that he should take to him the gold;

and he refused it, saying, that if he that was dead were not raised again to life by the merits of St. Nicholas, he would not receive it, and if he came again to life, he would receive baptism and become Christian. Then he that was dead arose, and the Jew was christened.

Another Jew saw the virtuous miracles of St. Nicholas, and made an image of the saint, and set it in his house, and commanded him that he should keep well his house when he went out, and that he should keep well all his goods, saying to him: "Nicholas, lo! here be all my goods, I charge thee to keep them, and if thou keep them not well, I shall avenge me on thee in beating and tormenting thee." And on a time, when the Jew was out, thieves came and robbed all his goods, and left, unborne away, only the image. And when the Jew came home he found him robbed of all his goods. And he reasoned with the image saying these words: "Sir Nicholas, I had set you in my house for to keep my goods from thieves, wherefore have ye not kept them? Ye shall receive sorrow and torments, and shall have pain for the thieves. I shall avenge my loss, and subdue my anger in beating thee." And then the Jew took the image, and beat it, and tormented it cruelly. Then happed a great marvel, for when the thieves divided the goods, the holy saint, like as he had been in his array, appeared to the thieves, and said to them: "Wherefore have I been beaten so cruelly for you and have so many torments? See how my body is hewed and broken; see how the red blood runneth down by my body; go ye fast and restore it again, or else the ire of God Almighty shall make you as to be one out of his wit, and that all men shall know your felony, and that each of you shall be hanged." And they said: "Who art thou that sayest to us such things?" And he said to them: "I am Nicholas the servant of Jesus Christ, whom the Jew hath so cruelly beaten for his goods that ye bore away." Then they were afraid, and came to the Jew, and heard what he had done to the image, and they told him the miracle, and delivered to him again all his goods. And thus came the thieves to the way of truth, and the Jew to the way of Jesus Christ.

A man, for the love of his son, that went to school for to learn, hallowed, every year, the feast of St. Nicholas much solemnly. On a time it happed that the father had made ready the dinner, and called many clerks to this dinner. And the devil came to the gate in the habit of a pilgrim for to demand alms: and the father immediately commanded his son that he should give alms to the pilgrim. He followed him as he went for to give to him alms, and when he came to the gate the devil caught the child and strangled him. And when the father heard this he sorrowed greatly and wept, and bore the body into his chamber, and began to cry for sorrow, and say: "Bright sweet son, how is it with thee? St. Nicholas, is this the reward that ye have done to me because I have so long served you?" And as he said these words, and others similar, the child opened his eyes, and awoke like he had been asleep, and arose up as before, and was raised from death to life.

Another nobleman prayed to St. Nicholas that he would, by his merits, get of our Lord that he might have a son, and promised that he would bring his son to the church, and would offer up to him a cup of gold. Then the son was born and came to age, and the father commanded to make a cup, and the cup pleased him much that he retained it for himself, and made another of the same value. And they went sailing in a ship toward the church of St. Nicholas, and when the child would have filled the cup, he fell into the water with the cup, and immediately was lost, and came no more up. Yet nevertheless the father performed his avow, in weeping much tenderly for his son; and when he came to the altar of St. Nicholas he offered the second cup, and when he had offered it, it fell down, like as one had cast it under the altar. And he took it up and set it again upon the altar, and then yet was it cast further than before and yet he took it up and placed it the third time upon the altar; and it was thrown again further than before. Of which thing all they that were there marveled, and men came for to see this thing. And immediately, the child that had fallen in the sea, came again before them all, and brought in his hands the first cup, and recounted to the people that immediately as he was fallen in the sea, the blessed St. Nicholas came and kept him that he had none harm. And thus his father was glad and offered to St. Nicholas both the two cups.

There was another rich man that by the merits of St. Nicholas had a son, and called him: *Deus dedit*, God gave. And this rich man made a chapel of St. Nicholas in his dwelling place; and hallowed every year the feast of St. Nicholas. And this manor was set by the land of the Agarians. This child was taken prisoner, and appointed to serve the king. The year following, and the day that his father held devoutly the feast of St. Nicholas, the child held a precious cup before the king, and remembered his capture, the sorrow of his friends, and the joy that was made that day in the house of his father, and began for to sigh sore high. And the king demanded him what ailed him and the cause of his sighing; and he told him every word wholly. And when the king knew it he said to him: "Whatsomever thy Nicholas do or do not, thou shalt abide here with us." And suddenly there blew a much strong wind, that made all the house to tremble, and the child was taken away with the cup, and was set before the gate where his father held the solemnity of St. Nicholas, in such wise that they all possessed great joy. And some say that this child was of Normandy, and went overseas, and was taken by the Sultan, who made him oft to be beaten before him. And as he was beaten on a St. Nicholas day, and was after set in prison, he prayed to St. Nicholas as well for his beating that he suffered, as for the great joy that he was wont to have on that day of St. Nicholas. And when he had long prayed and sighed he fell asleep, and when he awoke he found himself in the chapel of his father, whereat was much joy made for him. Let us then pray to this blessed saint that he will pray for us to our Lord Jesus Christ which is blessed in *secula seculorum*. Amen.

Life of St. Anthony

Here followeth of St. Anthony, and first the interpretation of his name.

Anthony is said of *ana*, which is as much to say as high, and *tenens* that is holding, which is as much as to say as holding high things and despising the world. He despised the world and said: "It is deceiving, transitory, and bitter," and Athanasius wrote his life.

Of the Life of St. Anthony.

St. Anthony was born in Egypt of good and religious father and mother, and when he was but twenty years old, he heard on a time in the church read in the gospel, that said: "If thou wilt be perfect go sell all that thou hast and give it to poor men"; and then according thereto he sold all that he had, and gave it to the poor people and became a hermit.

He had overmany temptations of the devil. Then on a time when he had overcome the spirit of fornication which tempted him therein by the virtue of his faith, the devil came to him in the form of a little child all black, and fell down at his feet and confessed that he was the devil of fornication, who St. Anthony had desired and prayed to see, for to know him that so tempted young people. Then said St. Anthony: "Since I have perceived that thou art so foul a thing I shall never doubt thee.

After, he went into a hole or cave to hide him, and immediately he found there a great multitude of devils, that so much beat him that his servant bore him upon his shoulders into his house as if he had been dead. When the other hermits were assembled and wept his death, and would have done his service, suddenly St. Anthony revived and made his servant to bear him into the pit again where the devils had so cruelly beaten him, and he began to summon the devils again, which had beaten him, to battles. And immediately they came in form of diverse beasts wild and savage, of whom that one howled, another hissed, and another cried, and another brayed and assailed St. Anthony, that one with the horns, the others with their teeth, and the others with their paws and fingernails, and ruined, and tore up his body that he supposed well to die. Then came a clear brightness, and all the beasts fled away, and St. Anthony understood that in this great light our Lord came, and he said twice: "Who art thou?" The good Jesu answered: "I am here, Anthony." Then said St. Anthony: "O good Jesu! Where hast thou been so long? Why wert thou not here with me at the beginning to help me and to heal my wounds?" Then our Lord said: "I was here but I would see and abide to see thy battle, and because thou hast manly fought and well maintained thy battle, I shall make thy name to be spread through all the world."

St. Anthony was of so great fervour and burning love to God, that when Maximus, the emperor, slew and martyred Christian men, he followed the martyrs that he might be a martyr with them and deserve it, and was sorry that martyrdom was not given to him.

After this, as St. Anthony went in desert he found a platter of silver in his way; then he thought whence this platter should come, seeing it was in no way for any man to pass, and also if it had fallen from any man he should have heard it sound in the falling. Then said he well that the devil had laid it there for to tempt him, and said: "Ha! Devil, thou seekest to tempt me and deceive me, but it shall not be in thy power." Then the platter vanished away as a little smoke. And in likewise he chanced upon a mass of gold that he found in this way, which the devil had cast for to deceive him, which he took and cast into the fire and immediately it vanished away. After, it happed that St. Anthony on a time was in prayer, and saw in a vision all the world full of snares and gins. Then cried St. Anthony and said: "O good Lord, who may escape from these snares?" And a voice said to him: "Very humility shall escape them without more."

When St. Anthony on a time was lifted up in the air, the devils came against him and laid to him all the evils that he had done from his childhood, before the angels. Then said the angels: "Thou oughtest not to tell the evils that have been defeated, but say if thou know any evil since he was made a monk." Then the devils contrived many evils, and when they might not prove them, the angels bore him higher than before, and after set him again in his place. St. Anthony recordeth of himself that he had seen a man so great and so high that he vaunted himself to be the virtue and the providence of God, and said to me: "Demand of me what thou wilt and I shall give it to thee." And I spit in the midst of his visage, and immediately I armed me with the sign of the cross, and ran upon him, and immediately he vanished away. And after this the devil appeared to him in so great a stature that he touched the heaven, and when St. Anthony had demanded him what he was, he answered: "I am the devil and demand thee why these monks and these cursed Christian men do me thus much shame?" St. Anthony said: "They do it by good right, for thou dost to them the worst thou canst," and the devil answered: "I do to them no harm; unless they trouble each other, I am destroyed and come to naught because that Jesus Christ reigneth over all."

A young man passed by St. Anthony and his bow in his hand, and beheld how St. Anthony played with his fellows, and was displeased. Then St. Anthony said to him that he should bend his bow, and so he did, and shot two or three shots before him, and immediately he unbent his bow. Then St. Anthony demanded why he held not his bow bent. And he answered that it should then be over weak and feeble; then St. Anthony said to him: "In likewise play the monks, for to be after more strong to serve God."

A man demanded of St. Anthony what he might do to please God, and he answered: "Over all where thou shalt be or shalt go, have God before thine eyes, and the holy scripture, and hold thee in one place all still, and walk not nor wander about in the country; do these three things and thou shalt be safe."

An abbot came to St. Anthony for to be counseled of him what he might do for to be saved. St. Anthony answered to him: "Have no confidence in the good that thou hast done, nor that thou hast kept thy belly and thy tongue well soberly, and repent thee not of penance that thou hast done I say, for like as fishes that have been long in the water, when they come in to dry land they must die, in likewise the monks that go out of their cloister or cells, if they converse long with seculars, they must needs lose their holiness and leave their good life. It behooveth the monks that they be solitary, and that they have three battles, that is of hearing, of speaking, and of seeing, and if they have but one of these battles, that is of the heart, yet they have overmuch."

Some hermits came to St. Anthony for to visit him, and their abbot was with them; then said St. Anthony to the hermits: "Ye have a good wise man with you," and after he said to the abbot: "Thou hast founden good brethren." Then answered the abbot: "Truly I have good brethren, but there is no door on their house, each body may enter that will, and go into the stable and unbind the ass within." And this said he because the brethren had overmuch their mouths open to speak, for immediately as they have thought on a thing is it come to the mouth. Then St. Anthony said: "Ye ought to know that there be three bodily movings, that one is of nature, another of overmuch plenty of meats, and the third of the devil."

There was a hermit that had renounced the world, but not perfectly, for he had somewhat private to himself, whom St. Anthony sent to the market to buy flesh, and as he was coming and brought the flesh, the dogs assailed him, and all tore at him, and took the flesh from him; and when he came to St. Anthony he told him what had happened to him; and then said St. Anthony to him: "Thus as the hounds have done to thee, so do the devils to monks that keep money and have some private to themselves."

On a time as St. Anthony was in the wilderness in his prayer and was weary, he said to our Lord: "Lord, I have great desire to be saved, but my thoughts hinder me." Then appeared an angel to him and said: "Do as I do, and thou shalt be safe," and he went out and saw him one while labour and another while pray, do thus and thou shalt be saved.

On a time when the brethren hermits were assembled before St. Anthony, they demanded of him of the state of souls when they be departed from the body, and the next night after a voice called St. Anthony and said: "Arise, and go out and see up on high." When St. Anthony beheld upward on high he saw one long and terrible, whose head touched the clouds, which kept people from having wings that would have fled to heaven, and this great man retained and caught some, and others he did not retain nor hinder for they flew forth up. Then he heard a noise full of joy, and another full of sorrow, and he understood that this was the devil that retained some souls that went not to heaven, and the other he might not hold nor retain, wherefore he made sorrow, and for the other he made joy, and so he heard the sorrow and the joy meddled together.

It happed on a time that St. Anthony laboured with his brethren the hermits, and he saw a vision much sorrowful, and therefore he kneeled down on his knees and prayed our Lord that he would prevent the great sorrow that was to come. Then the other hermits demanded what thing it was, and he said: "It is a great sorrow. I have seen a great plenty of beasts which environed me, which frightened all the country, and I know well that this is to say that there shall come a great trouble of men like unto beasts, that shall defoul the sacraments of holy church." Then came a voice from heaven to St. Anthony saying: "Great abomination shall come to mine altar." And immediately after, the heresy of Arius began, and much troubled the holy church, and did many evils. They beat monks and others all naked before the people, and slew Christian men like sheep upon the altars, and especially one Balachyn did great persecution to whom St. Anthony wrote a letter which said: "I see the ire and displeasure of our Lord coming upon thee if thou suffer not the Christians to live in peace. Then I command thee that thou do to them no more villainy or thou shalt have a mischance hastily." The unhappy man received this letter and began to mock St. Anthony, and spit on it, and beat well him that brought the letter, and sent again to St. Anthony these words: "If thou hast so great charge of thy monks come to me and I shall give to thee my discipline." But it happed that the fifteenth day after, he mounted upon a horse quite gently, and nevertheless when the horse felt him upon him he bit him on the legs and thighs that he died on the third day.

It happed another time that the hermits were come to St. Anthony and demanded of him a collation[2]. Then said St. Anthony: "Do ye this that is written in the gospel, if one give to the other a stroke on that one cheek show him that other?" And they made answer: "We may not do so"; then said he: "Suffer ye it once gently"; they answered: "We may not." Then said St. Anthony to his servant: "Give them to drink good wine, for these monks be over delicious. Fair brethren, put yourselves to prayer, for ye have much great need." At the last St. Anthony assembled the hermits and gave to them the peace, and died and departed out of this world holily when he was of the age of an hundred and five years. Pray we to him that he pray for us.

Life of St. Agnes

And next followeth of St. Agnes, and first the interpretation of her name.

Agnes is said of *agna* a lamb, for she was humble and gentle as a lamb, or of *agnos* in Greek, which is to say gentle and piteous, for she was gentle and merciful. Or Agnes of *agnoscendo*, for she knew the way of truth, and after this St. Austin saith: "Truth is opposed against vanity, falseness, and doubleness, for these three things were taken from her for the truth that she had."

The Life of St. Agnes.

The blessed virgin St. Agnes was much wise, and well taught, as St. Ambrose witnesseth, and wrote her passion. She was fair of visage, but much fairer in the Christian faith; she was young of age, and aged in wit, for in the thirteenth year of her age she lost the death that the world giveth, and found life in Jesus Christ.

---
2 A light meal allowed on fast days in place of lunch or supper

When she came from school the son of the prefect of Rome, for the emperor, loved her, and when his father and mother knew it, they offered to give much riches with him if he might have her in marriage; and offered to St. Agnes precious gems and jewels, which she refused to take, whereof it happed that the young man was ardently inflamed for the love of St. Agnes, and came again and took with him more precious and richer adornments, made with all manner of precious stones, and as well by his parents as by himself offered to St. Agnes rich gifts and possessions, and all the delights and pleasures of the world, and all to the end to have her in marriage. But St. Agnes answered to him in this matter: "Go from me thou bundle of sin, nourishing of evils and morsel of death, and depart, and know thou that I am spoken for and am loved of another, who hath given to me many better jewels, who hath fianced me by his faith, and is much more noble of lineage than thou art, and of estate. He hath clad me with precious stones and with jewels of gold, he hath set in my visage a sign that I receive no other spouse but him, and hath showed me over-great treasures which he must give me if I abide with him. I will have no other spouse but him, I will seek none other, in no manner may I leave him, with him am I firm and fastened in love, which is more noble, more puissant, and fairer than any other, whose love is much sweet and gracious, of whom the chamber is now for to receive me where the virgins sing merrily. I am now embraced of him of whom the mother is a virgin, and his father knew never woman, to whom the angels serve. The sun and the moon marvel them of his beauty, whose works never fail, whose riches never diminish, by whose odour dead men rise again to life, by whose touching the sick men be comforted, whose love is chastity. To him I have given my faith, to him I have commanded my heart; when I love him then am I chaste, and when I touch him then am I pure and clean, and when I take him then am I a virgin, this is the love of my God."

When the young man had heard all this he was despaired, as he that was taken in blind love, and was over sore tormented, in so much that he lay down sick in his bed for the great sorrow that he had. Then came the physicians and immediately knew his malady, and said to his father that he languished of carnal love that he had to some woman. Then the father inquired and knew that it was this woman, and spoke to St. Agnes for his son, and said to her how his son languished for her love. St. Agnes answered that in no wise she would break the faith of her first husband. Upon that the provost demanded who was her first husband, of whom she so much boasted, and in his power so much trusted. Then one of her servants said she was Christian, and that she was so enchanted that she said Jesus Christ was her spouse. And when the provost heard that she was Christian, he was very glad because to have power over her, for then the Christian people were in the will of the Lord, and if they would not deny their God and their belief, all their goods should be forfeited. Wherefore then the provost made St. Agnes to come in justice and he examined her sweetly, and after cruelly by menaces. St. Agnes, well comforted, said to him: "Do what thou wilt, for my purpose shalt thou never change." And when she saw him now flattering and now terribly angry, she scorned him. And the provost said to her, being all angry: "One of two things thou shalt choose, either do sacrifice to our gods with the virgins of the goddess Vesta, or go to the brothel to be abandoned to all that thither come, to the great shame and blame of all thy lineage." St. Agnes answered: "If thou knewest who is my God thou wouldst not say to me such words, but for as much as I know the virtue of my God, I set nothing by thy menaces, for I have his angel which is keeper of my body." Then the judge all enraged made her take off her clothes, and all naked to be led to the brothel. And thus St. Agnes, who refused to do sacrifice to the idols, was delivered naked to go to the brothel, but immediately as she was unclothed God gave to her such grace that the hairs of her head became so long that they covered all her body to her feet, so that her body was not seen. And when St. Agnes entered into the brothel, immediately she found the angel of God ready for to defend her, and environed St. Agnes with a bright clearness in such wise that no man might see her nor come to her. Then made she of the brothel her oratory, and in making her prayers to God she saw before her a white vesture, and immediately therewith she clad her and said: "I thank thee Jesus Christ which accountest me with thy virgins and hast sent me this vesture." All they that entered made honour and reverence to the great clearness that they saw about St. Agnes, and came out more devout and more clean than they entered. At last came the son of the provost with a great company for to accomplish his foul desires and lusts. And when he saw his fellows come out and issue all abashed, he mocked them and called them cowards. And then he, all araged, entered for to accomplish his evil will. And when he came to the clearness, he advanced him for to take the virgin, and immediately the devil took him by the throat and strangled him that he fell down dead.

And when the prefect heard these tidings of his son he ran weeping to the brothel, and crying, began to say to St. Agnes: "O thou cruel woman, why hast thou showed thy enchantment on my son?" And demanded of her how his son was dead, and by what cause. To whom St. Agnes answered: "He took him into his power to whom he had abandoned his will." "Why be not all they dead," said he, "that entered here before him?" "His fellows saw the miracle of the great clearness and were afraid and went their way unhurt, for they did honour to my God who hath clad me with this vestment and hath kept my body, but your villainous son, as soon as he entered into this house began to bray and cry, and when he would have laid hand upon me, immediately the devil slew him as thou seest." "If thou mayst raise him," said he, "it may well appear that thou hast not put him to death." And St. Agnes answered: "Even though thy religious faith is not worthy to make a request, nevertheless because it is time that the virtue of God be showed, go ye all out that I may make my prayer to God." And when she was on her prayers the angel came and raised him to life, and immediately he went out and began to cry, with a loud voice, that the God of Christian men was very God in heaven, and in earth, and in the sea, and that the idols were vain that they worshiped, which might not help them nor one other.

Then the bishops of the idols made a great discord among the people, so that all they cried: "Take away this sorceress and witch that turned men's minds and alieneth their wits." When the prefect saw these marvels he would gladly have delivered St. Agnes because she had raised his son, but he feared to be banished, and set in his place a lieutenant named Aspasius for to satisfy the people, and because he could not deliver her he departed sorrowfully. This Aspasius made a great fire among all the people and cast St. Agnes therein. Immediately this was done, the flame divided in two parts, and burnt them that made the discords, and she abode all whole without feeling the fire. The people thought that she had done all by enchantment. Then made St. Agnes her orison[3] to God, thanking him that she was escaped from the peril to lose her virginity, and also from the burning of the flame. And when she had made her orison the fire lost all his heat, and quenched it. Aspasius, for fear of the people, commanded to put a sword in her body, and so she was martyred. Immediately came the Christian men and the parents of St. Agnes and buried the body, but the heathen defended it, and so cast stones at them, that hardly they escaped. She suffered martyrdom in the time of Constantine the great, who began to reign the year of our Lord three hundred and nine.

Among them that buried her body was one Emerentiana who had been fellow to St. Agnes, how be it she was not yet christened, but a holy virgin. She came also to the sepulchre of St. Agnes, which constantly reproved the gentiles, and of them she was stoned to death and slain. Immediately there came an earthquake, lightning, and thunder, that many of the pagans perished, so that from then on the Christian people might surely come to the sepulchre unhurt, and the body of Emerentiana was buried by the body of St. Agnes.

It happed that when the friends of St. Agnes watched at her sepulchre on a night, they saw a great multitude of virgins clad in vestments of gold and silver, and a great light shone before them, and on the right side was a lamb more white than snow, and they saw also St. Agnes among the virgins who said to her parents: "Take heed and see that ye bewail me no more as dead, but be ye joyful with me, for with all these virgins Jesus Christ hath given me most brightest habitation and dwelling, and I am with him joined in heaven whom on earth I loved with I my thought." And this was the

---

3 Prayer

eighth day after her passion. And because of this vision holy church maketh memory of her the eight days of the feast after, which is called *Agnetis secundo*.

Of her we read an example that in the church of St. Agnes was a priest who was named Paulus and always served in that church, and had right great temptation of his flesh, but because he feared to anger our Lord he kept him from sin, and prayed to the pope that he would give him leave for to marry. The pope considered his simpleness, and for his bounty he gave him a ring in which was an emerald, and commanded that he should go to the image of St. Agnes which was in his church, and pray her that she would be his wife. This simple man did so, and the image put forth her finger and he set the ring thereon, and then she drew her finger again and kept the ring fast. And then immediately all his carnal temptation was quenched and taken away from him, and yet it is said the ring is on the finger of the image.

Constance the daughter of Constantine was smitten with a sore and foul leprosy. When she had heard of the vision of St. Agnes at her tomb shown to her friends, she came to the sepulchre of St. Agnes, and when she was in her prayers she fell asleep, and she saw in her sleep St. Agnes saying to her: "Constance, work constantly, and if thou wilt believe in Christ, thou shalt immediately be delivered of thy sickness," wherewith she awoke and found herself perfectly whole, and immediately she received baptism, and founded a church upon the body of the virgin and there abode in her virginity, and assembled there many virgins, because of her good example.

In another place it is read that when the church of St. Agnes was void, the pope said to a priest that he would give to him a wife for to nourish and keep, and he meant to commit the church of St. Agnes to his cure. And he delivered to him a ring and bade him to wed the image, and the image put forth her finger and he set on it a ring and immediately she closed the finger to her hand and kept the ring, and so he espoused her.

Of this virgin saith St. Ambrose in the book of virgins: "This virgin, young men, old men, and children praise, there is none more to be praised than that may be praised of all." St. Ambrose saith in his preface that this blessed St. Agnes despised the delights of noblesse, and deserved heavenly dignity; she left the desires of man's fellowship, and she found the fellowship of the everlasting King. And she, receiving a precious death for the confession of Jesus Christ, is made conformable to him everlastingly to reign in joy in heaven, to which he brings us, for whose glorious name and faith this glorious virgin St. Agnes suffered martyrdom of death.

Life of St. Juliana

Here followeth the Life of St. Juliana, and first the interpretation of her name.

Juliana is as much to say as burning plainly, for she burnt herself against the temptation of the devil who would have deceived her, and she helped many others to believe in the faith of our Lord Jesus Christ.

Of St. Juliana.

St. Juliana was given in marriage to the provost of Nicomedia, who was named Eulogius, and he was a pagan, and therefore she would not assent to the marriage nor assemble with him, unless he would first take the faith of Christ and be baptized. When her father saw this, immediately he stripped her bare, and made her to be beaten sore, and after delivered her to the provost. And after when the provost beheld her, and saw the great beauty in her, he said to her: "My most sweet Juliana, why hast thou brought me in such confusion that I am mocked because thou refusest to take me?" She said: "If thou wilt adore my God, I shall assent and agree to take thee, and otherwise shalt thou never be my lord." To whom the provost said: "Fair lady, that may I not do, for the emperor should then smite off my head." And she said: "If thou doubtest so much the emperor, who is mortal, why should not I doubt mine emperor Jesus Christ, who is immortal; do what thou wilt, for thou mayst not deceive me." Then the provost caused her to be beaten most cruelly with rods, and half a day to hang by the hairs of her head, and molten lead to be cast on her head. And when he saw that all this grieved her not, he bound her in chains, and set her in prison. To whom the devil came then in the likeness of an angel, who said to her in this manner: "Juliana, I am the angel of God, who hath sent me to thee to warn thee and say that thou make sacrifice to the idols for to escape the torments of evil death." Then she began to weep, and made to God this prayer: "Lord God, suffer not me to be lost, but of thy grace show to me who he is that maketh to me this warning." The same time came to her a voice that said that she should set hand on him, and constrain him to confess who he was, and immediately she took him and demanded of him, and he said that he was the devil, and that his father had sent him thither for to deceive her. She demanded of him: "Who is thy father?" And he answered: "Beelzebub, who sendeth us for to do all evil, and maketh us grievously to be beaten when we come vanquished of the Christian people. And therefore I am certain I shall have much harm because I may not overcome thee." She said to him: "Of what craft is thy father Beelzebub?" The devil said: "He contriveth all evil, and when we come into hell he sendeth us for to tempt the souls of the people." She demanded: "What torments suffereth he that cometh vanquished of a Christian creature?" The devil said: "We suffer then much grievous torment, and because when we be vanquished of a good man we dare not return, and when we be sought and cannot be found, then commandeth our master to other devils that they torment us wheresomever they find us, and therefore we must obey to him as to our father." "And of what craft art thou?" "I take solace in the shrewdness of the people; I love homicide, luxury, battle, and make debate and war." And she demanded of him: "Goest thou never to do good works and profitable?" The devil answered: "Madam, to the end that I answer the truth, to my right great harm and evil am I come hither, for I had well supposed to have deceived thee, and made thee to make sacrifice to the idols and to renounce thy God. When we come to a good Christian man and we find him ready to do service to God, we send into him many thoughts vain and evil, and also many evil desires, and turn his thought by this that we set before him, and we send errors into his thoughts, and we let him not persevere in his orisons nor in good works; yet if we see any that will go to the church or in other place for any good, immediately we be in their ways, and cast into their hearts diverse thoughts and occasions by which they be turned away from doing well. But whosomever may understand our temptations and comprehend them, to the end that he put away from him evil cogitations and thoughts, and will make his prayers, and do his good works, and hear the words of God and the divine service, of him we be cast out, and when they receive the body of Jesus Christ we depart forthwith from them. We set our intent on nothing but to deceive good persons that lead a holy life, and when we see them do good works, we send into them bitter and grievous thoughts for to leave all and do our will." St. Juliana said: "O thou spirit! How art thou so hardy to tempt any Christian person?" And the devil answered: "How darest thou thus hold me, if thou were not pledged to Jesus Christ? So trust I in my father, who is a malefactor, and I do that which pleaseth him; I have pained me to do oft many evils, and sometime I come to mine intent, and accomplish my desire, but at this time I have failed: I would I had not come hither! Alas! How understood my father of this that should not hap. Madam, let me go, and give me leave to go to some other place, for it is no need that I accuse thee to my father." At the last she let him go.

On the morn the provost commanded that St. Juliana should be brought before him in judgment; and when he saw her so well healed, and her visage so fair and so shining, then said the provost to her: "Juliana, who hath taught thee, and how mayest thou vanquish the torments?" And she said: "Hearken to me and I shall say to thee: My Lord Jesus Christ hath taught me to adore the Father, the Son, and the Holy Ghost, for I have overcome and vanquished Satan thy father, and all his other devils; for God hath sent his angel for to comfort and to help me. Merchant man, knowest thou not that the torments made ready for thee are everlasting, where thou shalt be tormented perpetually in a perpetual darkness and obscurity?" Immediately the provost made to be brought a wheel of iron between two pillars, and four horses to draw it forth, and four knights at one side, and four knights on that other to draw, and four to draw forth the wheel, so that all her body was broken in such wise that the marrow came out of the bones, and the wheel was all bloody. Then came an angel of God and broke the wheel, and healed the wounds of St. Juliana perfectly. And for this miracle were converted all they that were present. And immediately after, for the faith of Jesus Christ were beheaded men and women to the number of one hundred and thirty persons. After, the provost commanded that she should be put in a great pot full of boiling lead, and when she entered into the said pot, all the lead became cold, so that she felt no harm. And the provost cursed his gods because they might not punish a maid that so vanquished them. And then he commanded to smite off her head. And when she was led to be beheaded, the devil appeared to the provost in figure of a young man, and said: "Spare not good people, and of her have no mercy, for she hath blamed your gods and done much harm, and me she hath beaten this night past, therefore render to her that she hath deserved." With these words St. Juliana looked behind her for to wit who said such words of her. Immediately the devil said: "Alas! alas! caitiff[4] that I am, I doubt not that yet she will take and bind me," and so he vanished away. After this, she admonished the people to love and serve Jesus Christ, and she prayed them all to pray for her, and then her head was smitten off.

The provost entered into a ship with thirty-four men for to pass an arm of the sea; immediately came a great rage and tempest, which drowned the provost and all his company in the sea, and the sea threw their bodies to the shore, and wild beasts came thither and ate them. Thus this holy virgin St. Juliana suffered martyrdom for our Lord the fourteenth Kalends of the month of March. Let us pray to her that she pray for us, etc.

---

4 A base, cowardly, or despicable person

Life of St. Longinus

Here followeth the Life of St. Longinus.

Longinus, who was a puissant knight, was with other knights, by the commandment of Pilate, on the side of the cross of our Lord, and pierced the side of our Lord with a spear; and when he saw the miracles, how the sun lost his light, and great quaking of the earth when our Lord suffered death and passion in the tree of the cross, then believed he in Jesus Christ. Some say that when he smote our Lord with the spear in the side, the precious blood ran down the shaft of the spear upon his hands, and it happened that with his hands he touched his eyes, and immediately he that had been before blind saw immediately clearly, wherefore he refused all chivalry and abode with the apostles, of whom he was taught and christened, and after, he abandoned him to lead an holy life in doing alms and in keeping the life of a monk about thirty-eight years in Cæsarea and in Cappadocia, and by his words and his example he converted many men to the faith of Christ.

And when this came to the knowledge of Octavian the provost, he took him and would have constrained him to do sacrifice to the idols, and St. Longinus said: "There may no man serve two lords who be contrary to each other; thine idols be lords of thy malices, corrupters of all good works, and enemies to chastity, humility, and to bounty, and friends to all filthiness of luxury, of gluttony, of idleness, of pride, and of avarice, and my Lord is Lord of soberness that bringeth the people to the everlasting life." Then said the provost: "It is nought that thou sayest; make sacrifice to the idols and thy God shall forgive thee because of the commandment that is made to thee." Longinus said: "If thou wilt become Christian, God shall pardon thee thy trespasses." Then the provost was angry, and made the teeth of St. Longinus to be drawn out of his mouth, and cut his mouth open. And yet for all that Longinus lost not his speech, but took an axe that he there found, and hewed and broke therewith the idols and said: "Now may we see if they be very gods or not." And immediately the devils issued out and entered into the body of the provost and his fellows, and they brayed like beasts and fell down to the feet of St. Longinus and said: "We know well that thou art servant unto the sovereign God." And St. Longinus demanded of the devils why they dwelt in these idols, and they answered: "We have found place in these idols for us, for over all where Jesus Christ is not named nor is his sign showed, there dwell we gladly; and because when these pagans come to these idols for to adore and make sacrifice in the name of us, then we come and dwell in these idols; wherefore we pray thee, man of God, that thou send us not into the abyss of hell." And St. Longinus said to the people that there were: "What say ye: will ye have these devils for your gods and worship them or are ye more willing that I hunt them out of this world in the name of Jesus Christ?" And the people said with a high voice: "Much greater is the God of Christian people, holy man, we pray thee that thou suffer not the devils to dwell in this city." Then St. Longinus commanded the devils that they should issue out of these people, in such wise that the people had great joy and believed in our Lord.

A little time after the evil provost made St. Longinus to come before him, and said to him that all the people were departed, and by his enchantment had refused the idols; if the king knew it he should destroy us and the city also. Aphrodisius answered: "How wilt thou yet torment this good man, who hath saved us and hath done so much good to the city?" And the provost said: "He hath deceived us by enchantments." Aphrodisius said: "His God is great and hath no evil in him." Then did the provost cut out the tongue of Aphrodisius, wherefore St. Longinus signed unto God, and immediately the provost became blind and lost all his members. When Aphrodisius saw that, he said: "Lord God, thou art just and thy judgment is veritable." And the provost said to Aphrodisius: "Fair brother, pray to St. Longinus that he pray for me, for I have done ill to him," and Aphrodisius said: "Have not I well told it to thee, do no more so to Longinus? Seest not thou me speak without tongue?" And the provost said: "I have not only lost mine eyes, but also my heart and my body is in great pain." And St. Longinus said: "If thou wilt be whole and healed, put me to death, and I shall pray for thee to our Lord, after that I shall be dead, that he heal thee." And immediately then the provost did smite off his head, and after, he came and fell on the body of St. Longinus and said all in weeping: "Sire, I have sinned; I acknowledge and confess my filth," and immediately came again his sight, and he received health of his body and buried honorably the body of St. Longinus. And the provost believed in Jesus Christ and abode in the company of Christian men, and thanked God, and died in good estate. All this happed in Cæsarea of Cappadocia to the honour of our Lord God, to whom be given laud and glory *in secula seculorum.*

Life of St. Patrick

Here followeth the Life of St. Patrick, and first the interpretation of his name.

Patrick is as much to say as knowledge, for by the will of God he knew many of the secrets of heaven and of the joys there, and also he saw a part of the pains of hell.

Of the Life of St. Patrick.

St. Patrick was born in Britain, which is called England, and was learned at Rome and there flourished in virtues; and after departed out of the parts of Italy, where he had long dwelled, and came home into his country in Wales named Pendyac, and entered into a fair and joyous country called the valley Rosine. To whom the angel of God appeared and said: "O Patrick, this see nor bishopric God hath not provided to thee, but unto one not yet born, but shall thirty years hereafter be born," and so he left that country and sailed over into Ireland. And as Higden saith in Polycronicon, the fourth book, the twenty-fourth chapter, that St. Patrick's father was named Caprum, who was a priest and a deacon's son who was called Fodum. And St. Patrick's mother was named Conchessa, Martin's sister of France. In his baptism he was named Sucate, and St. Germain called him

Magonius, and Celestinus the pope named him Patrick. That is as much to say as father of the citizens.

St. Patrick on a day as he preached a sermon of the patience and sufferance of the passion of our Lord Jesus Christ to the king of the country, he leaned upon his crook or cross, and it happened by adventure that he set the end of the crook, or his staff, upon the king's foot, and pierced his foot with the pike, which was sharp beneath. The king had supposed that St. Patrick had done it wittingly, for to move him the sooner to patience and to the faith of God, but when St. Patrick perceived it he was much abashed, and by his prayers he healed the king. And furthermore he entreated and received grace of our Lord that no venomous beast might live in all the country, and yet unto this day is no venomous beast in all Ireland.

After it happened on a time that a man of that country stole a sheep, which belonged to his neighbour, whereupon St. Patrick admonished the people that whomsoever had taken it should deliver it again within seven days. When all the people were assembled within the church, and the man who had stolen it made no semblance to deliver again this sheep, then St. Patrick commanded, by the virtue of God, that the sheep should bleat and cry in the belly of him that had eaten it, and so it happened that, in the presence of all the people, the sheep cried and bleated in the belly of him that had stolen it. And the man that was culpable repented him of his trespass, and the others from then on kept them from stealing sheep from any other man.

Also St. Patrick was wont for to worship and do reverence unto all the crosses devoutly that he might see, but on a time before the sepulchre of a pagan stood a fair cross, which he passed and went forth by as he had not seen it, and he was demanded of his fellows why he saw not that cross. And then he prayed to God for to know whose it was, and he said he heard a voice under the earth saying: "Thou sawest it not because I am a pagan that am buried here, and am unworthy that the sign of the cross should stand there,: wherefore he made the sign of the cross to be taken thence.

On a time as St. Patrick preached in Ireland the faith of Jesus Christ, and did but little profit by his predication, for he could not convert the evil, rude, and wild people, he prayed to our Lord Jesus Christ that he would show them some sign openly, fearful and ghastful[5], by which they might be converted and be repentant of their sins. Then, by the commandment of God, St. Patrick made in the earth a great circle with his staff, and immediately the earth after the quantity of the circle opened and there appeared a great pit and a deep, and St. Patrick, by the revelation of God, understood that there was a place of purgatory, into which whomsoever entered therein he should never have other penance nor feel no other pain, and there was showed to him that many should enter which should never return nor come again. And they that should return should abide but from one morn to another, and no more, and many entered that came not again. As touching this pit or hole which is named St. Patrick's purgatory, some hold opinion that the second Patrick, who was an abbot and no bishop, that God showed to him this place of purgatory; but certainly such a place there is in Ireland wherein many men have been, and yet daily go in and come again, and some have had there marvelous visions and seen grisly and horrible pains, of whom there be books made as of Tundale and others. Then this holy man St. Patrick, the Bishop, lived till he was one hundred and twenty-two years old, and was the first that was bishop in Ireland, and died in Aurelius Ambrose's time that was King of Britain. In his time was the Abbot Columba, otherwise named Colinkillus, and St. Bride whom St. Patrick professed and veiled, and she over-lived him forty years. All these three holy saints were buried in Ulster, in the city of Dunence, as it were in a cave with three chambers. Their bodies were found at the first coming of King John, King Harry the second's son, into Ireland. Upon whose tombs these verses following were written: "*Hic jacent in Duno qui tumulo tumulantur in uno, Brigida, Patricius atque Columba plus,*" which is for to say in English: "In Duno these three be buried all in one sepulchre: Bride, Patrick, and Columba the mild."

---

5   Such as to cause fright; dreadful, terrible, or alarming

Men say that this holy bishop, St. Patrick, did three great things. One is that he drove with his staff all the venomous beasts out of Ireland. The second, that he had grant of our Lord God that no Irish man shall abide the coming of Antichrist. The third wonder is read of his purgatory, which is more referred to the less St. Patrick, the Abbot. And this holy abbot, because he found the people of that land rebel, he went out of Ireland and came in to England in the Abbey of Glastonbury, where he died on a St. Bartholomew's day. He flourished about the year of our Lord eight hundred and fifty, and the holy bishop died the year of our Lord four hundred and ninety in the one hundred and twenty-second year of his age, to whom pray we that he pray for us.

Life of St. George

Here followeth of St. George, Martyr, and first the interpretation of his name.

George is said of *geos*, which is as much to say as earth, and *orge* that is tilling. So George is to say as tilling the earth, that is his flesh. And St. Austin saith, *in libro de Trinitate* that is, good earth is in the height of the mountains, in the temperance of the valleys, and in the plain of the fields. The first is good for herbs being green, the second to vines, and the third to wheat and corn. Thus the blessed George was high in despising low things, and therefore he had verdure in himself, he was tempered by discretion, and therefore he had wine of gladness, and within he was plane of humility, and thereby put he forth wheat of good works. Or George may be said of *gerar*, that is holy, and of *gyon*, that is a wrestler, that is an holy wrestler, for he wrestled with the dragon. Or George is said of *gero*, that is a pilgrim, and *gir*, that is cut out, and *ys*, that is a councilor. He was a pilgrim in the sight of the world, and he was cut by the crown of martyrdom, and he was a good councilor in preaching. And his legend is numbered among other scriptures apocryphal in the council of Nicene, because his martyrdom hath no certain relation. For in the calendar of Bede it is said that he suffered martyrdom in Persia in the city of Diaspolin, and in other places it is read that he resteth in the city of Diaspolin which before was called Lidda, which is by the city of Joppa or Japh. And in another place it is said that he suffered death under Diocletian and Maximian, who were emperors at that time. And in another place under Diocletian emperor of Persia, being present seventy kings of his empire. And it is said here that he suffered death under Dacian the provost, then Diocletian and Maximian being emperors.

Of the Life of St. George, Martyr.

St. George was a knight and born in Cappadocia. On a time he came in to the province of Libya, to a city which is said Silene. And by this city was a stagne or a pond like a sea, wherein was a dragon which envenomed all the country. And on a time the people were assembled for to slay him, and when they saw him they fled. And when he came nigh the city he venomed the people with his breath, and therefore the people of the city gave to him every day two sheep for to feed him, because he should do no harm to the people, and when the sheep failed there was taken a man and a sheep. Then was an ordinance made in the town that there should be taken the children and young people of the town by lot, and every each one as it fell, were he gentle or poor, should be delivered when the lot fell on him or her. So it happed that many of them of the town were then delivered, insomuch that the lot fell upon the king's daughter, whereof the king was sorry, and said unto the people: "For the love of the gods take gold and silver and all that I have, and let me have my daughter." They said: "How sir! Ye have made and ordained the law, and our children be now dead, and ye would do the contrary. Your daughter shall be given, or else we shall burn you and your house."

When the king saw he might no more do, he began to weep, and said to his daughter: "Now shall I never see thine espousals." Then returned he to the people and demanded eight days' respite, and they granted it to him. And when the eight days were passed they came to him and said: "Thou seest that the city perisheth." Then did the king array his daughter like as she should be wedded, and embraced her, kissed her, and gave her his benediction, and after led her to the place where the dragon was.

When she was there St. George passed by, and when he saw the lady he demanded of her what she made there, and she said: "Go ye your way, fair young man, that ye perish not also." Then said he: "Tell to me what have ye and why weep ye, and doubt ye of nothing." When she saw that he would know, she said to him how she was delivered to the dragon. Then said St. George: "Fair daughter, doubt ye nothing hereof for I shall help thee in the name of Jesus Christ." She said: "For God's sake, good knight, go your way, and abide not with me, for ye may not deliver me." Thus as they spake together the dragon appeared and came running to them, and St. George was upon his horse, and drew out his sword and garnished him with the sign of the cross, and rode hardily against the dragon which came towards him, and smote him with his spear and hurt him sore and threw him to the ground. And after said to the maid: "Deliver to me your girdle, and bind it about the neck of the dragon and be not afraid." When she had done so, the dragon followed her as if it had been a meek beast and gentle. Then she led him into the city, and the people fled by mountains and valleys, and said: "Alas! alas! We shall be all dead." Then St. George said to them: "Doubt ye nothing, and without delay, believe ye in God, Jesus Christ, and do ye be baptized and I shall slay the dragon." Then the king was baptized and all his people, and St. George slew the dragon and smote off his head, and commanded that he should be thrown in the fields, and they took four carts with oxen that drew him out of the city.

Then were there well fifteen thousand men baptized, without women and children, and the king made a church there of our Lady and of St. George, in which yet riseth a fountain of living water, which healeth sick people that drink thereof. After this the king offered to St. George as much money as there might be numbered, but he refused all and commanded that it should be given to poor people for God's sake; and enjoined the king four things, that is, that he should have charge of the churches, and that he should honour the priests and hear their service diligently, and that he should have pity on the poor people, and after he kissed the king and departed.

Now it happed that in the time of Diocletian and Maximian, who were emperors, was so great persecution of Christian men that within a month were martyred well twenty-two thousand, and therefore they had so great dread that some denied and forsook God and did sacrifice to the idols. When St. George saw this, he left the habit of a knight and sold all that he had, and gave it to the poor, and took the habit of a Christian man, and went into the middle of the pagans and began to cry: "All the gods of the pagans and gentiles be devils, my God made the heavens and is very God." Then said the provost to him: "Of what presumption cometh this to thee, that thou sayest that our gods be devils? And say to us who thou art and what is thy name." He answered immediately and said: "I am named George, I am a gentleman, a knight of Cappadocia, and have left all for to serve the God of heaven." Then the provost enforced himself to draw him unto his faith by fair words, and when he might not bring him thereto he raised him on a gibbet; and so much beat him with great staves and implements of iron, that his body was all broken in pieces. And after he took brands of iron and joined them to his sides, and his bowels which then appeared he did rub with salt, and so sent him into prison, but our Lord appeared to him the same night with great light and comforted him much sweetly. And by this great consolation he took to him so good heart that he doubted no torment that they might make him suffer.

Then, when Dacian the provost saw that he might not surmount him, he called his enchanter and said to him: "I see that these Christian people doubt not our torments." The enchanter bound himself, upon his head to be smitten off, if he overcame not his crafts. Then he did take strong venom and meddled it with wine, and made invocation of the names of his false gods, and gave it to St. George to drink. St. George took it and made the sign of the cross on it, and immediately drank it without grieving him anything. Then the enchanter made it more strong than it was before of venom, and gave it him to drink, and it grieved him nothing. When the enchanter saw that, he kneeled down at the feet of St. George and prayed him that he would make him Christian. And when Dacian knew that he was become Christian he smote off his head. And after, on the morn, he made St. George to be set between two wheels, which were full of swords, sharp and cutting on both sides, but immediately the wheels were broken and St. George escaped without hurt. And then commanded Dacian that they should put him in a cauldron full of molten lead, and when St. George entered therein, by the virtue of our Lord it seemed that he was in a bath well at ease. Then Dacian seeing this began to assuage his ire, and to flatter him by fair words, and said to him: "George, the patience of our gods is over great unto thee who hast blasphemed them, and done to them great despite; then fair, and right sweet son, I pray thee that thou return to our law and make sacrifice to the idols, and leave thy folly, and I shall enhance thee to great honour and worship." Then began St. George to smile, and said to him: "Wherefore saidst thou not to me thus at the beginning? I am ready to do as thou sayest." Then was Dacian glad and made to cry over all the town that all the people should assemble for to see George make sacrifice who so much had striven there against. Then was the city arrayed and feast kept throughout all the town, and all came to the temple for to see him.

When St. George was on his knees, and they supposed that he would have worshiped the idols, he prayed our Lord God of heaven that he would destroy the temple and the idol in the honour of his name, for to make the people to be converted. And immediately the fire descended from heaven and burnt the temple, and the idols, and their priests, and the earth opened and swallowed all the cinders and ashes that were left. Then Dacian made him to be brought before him, and said to him: "What be the evil deeds that thou hast done and also great untruth?" Then said to him St. George: "Ah, sir, believe it not, but come with me and see how I shall sacrifice." Then said Dacian to him: "I see well thy fraud and thy deception, thou wilt make the earth to swallow me, like as thou hast the temple and my gods." Then said St. George: "O caitiff, tell me how may thy gods help thee when they may not help themselves!" Then was

Dacian so angry that he said to his wife: "I shall die for anger if I may not surmount and overcome this man." Then said she to him: "Evil and cruel tyrant! Seest thou not the great virtue of the Christian people? I said to thee well that thou shouldst not do to them any harm, for their God fighteth for them, and know thou well that I will become Christian." Then was Dacian much abashed and said to her: "Wilt thou be Christian?" Then he took her by the hair, and beat her cruelly. Then demanded she of St. George: "What may I become because I am not christened?" Then answered the blessed George: "Doubt thee nothing, fair daughter, for thou shalt be baptized in thy blood." Then began she to worship our Lord Jesus Christ, and so she died and went to heaven.

On the morn Dacian gave his sentence that St. George should be drawn through all the city, and after, his head should be smitten off. Then made he his prayer to our Lord that all they that desired any boon might get it of our Lord God in his name, and a voice came from heaven which said that it which he had desired was granted; and after he had made his orison his head was smitten off, about the year of our Lord two hundred and eighty-seven. When Dacian went homeward from the place where he was beheaded towards his palace, fire fell down from heaven upon him and burnt him and all his servants.

Gregory of Tours telleth that there were some that bore certain relics of St. George, and came into a certain oratory in a hospital, and on the morning when they should depart they could not move the door till they had left there part of their relics. It is also found in the history of Antioch, that when the Christian men went over sea to conquer Jerusalem, that one, a right fair young man, appeared to a priest of the host and counseled him that he should bear with him a little of the relics of St. George. For he was conductor of the battle, and so he did so much that he had some. And when it was so that they had assieged Jerusalem and durst not mount nor go up on the walls for the quarrels and defense of the Saracens, they saw clearly St. George who had white arms with a red cross, that went up before them on the walls, and they followed him, and so was Jerusalem taken by his help. And between Jerusalem and port Jaffa, by a town called Ramys, is a chapel of St. George which is now desolate and uncovered, and therein dwell Christian Greeks. And in the said chapel lieth the body of St. George, but not the head. And there lie his father and mother and his uncle, not in the chapel but under the wall of the chapel; and the keepers will not suffer pilgrims to come therein, but if they pay two ducats, and therefore come but few therein, but offer without the chapel at an altar. And there is seven years and seven lents of pardon; and the body of St. George lieth in the middle of the quire or choir of the said chapel, and in his tomb is a hole that a man may put in his hand. And when a Saracen, being mad, is brought thither, if he put his head in the hole he shall immediately be made perfectly whole, and have his wit again.

This blessed and holy martyr St. George is patron of this realm of England and the cry of men of war. In the worship of whom is founded the noble order of the garter, and also a noble college in the castle of Windsor by Kings of England, in which college is the heart of St. George, which Sigismund, the Emperor of Almayne[6], brought and gave for a great and a precious relic to King Harry the fifth. And also the said Sigismund was a brother of the said garter, and also there is a piece of his head, which college is nobly endowed to the honour and worship of Almighty God and his blessed martyr St. George. Then let us pray unto him that he be special protector and defender of this realm.

Life of St Pernelle (Petronilla)

Here followeth of St. Pernelle, and first the interpretation of her name.

Petronilla is said of *petens*, that is demanding, and of *tronus*, that is a throne or a seat, as who saith she was demanding the throne or seat of virgins.

---

6 Germany

Of the Life of St. Pernelle.

St. Pernelle, whose life St. Marcel writeth, was daughter of St. Peter the apostle, who was right fair and beauteous, and by the will of her father she was vexed with the fevers and axes. It happed on a time that the disciples dined with St. Peter, and one, Titus, said to him: "Peter, how is it that all sick people be healed of thee and thou sufferest Pernelle, thy daughter, to lie sick?" To whom St. Peter said: "For it is expedient to her to be sick; nevertheless because it shall not be imputed impossibility of her health for to be excused by my words," he said to her: "Arise, Pernelle, hastily, and serve us." And immediately she arose all whole, and ministered and served them. And when the service was all done and accomplished, Peter said to her: "Pernelle, go again to thy bed." And she immediately went again to her bed, and the fevers vexed her as they did before, and whereas she began to be perfect in the love of God, so he healed her perfectly.

Then was there an earl called Flaccus who came to her, and for her beauty would have her unto his wife. To whom she answered: "If thou desirest me to have unto thy wife, command thou certain virgins to come to me for to accompany me unto thine house." And while he was busy to make ready the said maidens, St. Pernelle set herself in fastings and prayers, and received the holy body of our Lord and reclined in to her bed, and after the third day she died, and she passed out of this world rendering her soul unto our Lord. Then Flaccus, seeing himself disappointed and mocked, turned himself unto Felicula, fellow of St. Pernelle, and said that she should wed him or offer unto the idols, which both two she refused.

Then the prefect set her in prison and there kept her seven days and seven nights without meat and drink, and after he hung her body on a gibbet, and there slew her and threw her body into a foul privy, which holy Nicodemus took up and buried. Wherefore Nicodemus was called of Flaccus, and because he would not sacrifice to the idols he was beaten with plummets and his body cast into the Tiber, but it was taken up by Justin his clerk and honorably buried.

The Conquest of Constantinople

Geoffry de Villehardouin

Translated by Frank T. Marzials

1

The first preaching of the crusade

BE it known to you that eleven hundred and ninety-seven years after the Incarnation of our Lord Jesus Christ, in the time of Innocent, Pope of Rome, and Philip, King of France, and Richard, King of England, there was in France a holy man named Fulk of Neuilly—which Neuilly is between Lagni-sur-Marne and Paris—and he was a priest and held the cure of the village. And this said Fulk began to speak of God throughout the Isle-de-France, and the other countries round about; and you must know that by him the Lord wrought many miracles.

Be it known to you further, that the fame of this holy man so spread, that it reached the Pope of Rome, Innocent; and the Pope sent to France, and ordered the right worthy man to preach the cross (the Crusade) by his authority. And afterwards the Pope sent a cardinal of his, Master Peter of Capua, who himself had taken the cross, to proclaim the Indulgence of which I now tell you, viz., that all who should take the cross and serve in the host for one year, would be delivered from all the sins they had committed, and acknowledged in confession. And because this indulgence was so great, the hearts of men were much moved, and many took the cross for the greatness of the pardon.

2

Of those who took the cross

THE other year after that right worthy man Fulk had so spoken of God, there was held a tourney in Champagne, at a castle called Ecri, and by God's grace it so happened that Thibaut, Count of Champagne and Brie, took the cross, and the Count Louis of Blois and Chartres likewise; and this was at the beginning of Advent (28th November 1199). Now you must know that this Count Thibaut was but a young man, and not more than twenty-two years of age, and the Count Louis not more than twenty-seven. These two counts were nephews and cousins-german to the King of France, and, on the other part, nephews to the King of England.

With these two counts there took the cross two very high and puissant barons of France, Simon of Montfort, and Renaud of Montmirail. Great was the fame thereof throughout the land when these two high and puissant men took the cross.

In the land of Count Thibaut of Champagne took the cross Garnier, Bishop of Troyes, Count Walter of Brienne, Geoffry of Joinville, who was seneschal of the land, Robert his brother, Walter of Vignory, Walter of Montbéliard, Eustace of Conflans, Guy of Plessis his brother, Henry of Arzilliéres, Oger of Saint-Chéron, Villain of Neuilly, Geoffry of Villehardouin, Marshal of Champagne, Geoffry his nephew, William of Nully, Walter of Fuligny, Everard of Montigny, Manasses of L'isle, Macaire of Sainte-Menehould, Miles the Brabant, Guy of Chappes, Clerembaud his nephew, Renaud of Dampierre, John Foisnous, and many other right worthy men whom this book does not here mention by name.

With Count Louis took the cross Gervais of Châtel Hervée, his son John of Virsin, Oliver of Rochefort, Henry of Montreuil, Payen of Orléans, Peter of Bracietix, Hugh his brother, William of Sains, John of Frialze, Walter of Gaudonville, Hugh of Cormeray, Geoffry his brother, Hervée of Beauvoir, Robert of Frouville, Peter his brother, Orri of L'isle, Robert of Quartier, and many more whom this book does not here mention by name.

In the Isle-de-France took the cross Nevelon, Bishop of Soissons, Matthew of Montmorency, Guy the Castellan of Coucy, his nephew, Robert of Ronsoi, Ferri of Yerres, John his brother, Walter of Saint-Denis, Henry his brother, William of Aunoi, Robert Mauvoisin, Dreux of Cressonsacq, Bernard of Moreuil, Enguerrand of Boves, Robert his brother, and many more right worthy men with regard to whose names this book is here silent.

At the beginning of the following Lent, on the day when folk are marked with ashes (23rd February 1200), the cross was taken at Bruges by Count Baldwin of Flanders and Hainault, and by the Countess Mary his wife, who was sister to the Count Thibaut of Champagne. Afterwards took the cross, Henry his brother, Thierri his nephew, who was the son of Count Philip of Flanders, William the advocate of Béthune, Conon his brother, John of Nêle Castellan of Bruges, Renier of Trit, Reginald his son, Matthew of Wallincourt, James of Avesnes, Baldwin of Beauvoir, Hugh of Beaumetz, Gérard of Mancicourt, Odo of Ham, William of Gommegnies, Dreux of Beaurain, Roger of Marck, Eustace of Saubruic, Francis of Colemi, Walter of Bousies, Reginald of Mons, Walter of Tombes, Bernard of Somergen, and many more right worthy men in great number, with regard to whom this book does not speak further.

Afterwards took the cross, Count Hugh of St. Paul. With him took the cross, Peter of Amiens his nephew, Eustace of Canteleu, Nicholas of Mailly, Anscau of Cayeaux, Guy of Houdain, Walter of Nêle, Peter his brother, and many other men who are unknown to us.

Directly afterwards took the cross Geoffry of Perche, Stephen his brother, Rotrou of Montfort, Ives of La Jaille, Aimery of Villeroi, Geoffry of Beaumont, and many others whose names I do not know.

3

The crusaders send six envoys to Venice

AFTERWARDS the barons held a parliament at Soissons to settle when they should start, and whither they should wend. But they could come to no agreement, because it did not seem to them that enough people had taken the cross. So during all that year (1200) no two months passed without assemblings in parliament at Compiègne. There met all the counts and barons who had taken the cross. Many were the opinions given and considered; but in the end it was agreed that envoys should be sent, the best that could be found, with full powers, as if they were the lords in person, to settle such matters as needed settlement.

Of these envoys, Thibaut, Count of Champagne and Brie, sent two; Baldwin, Count of Flanders and Hainault, two; and Louis, Count of Blois and Chartres, two. The envoys of the Count Thibaut were Geoffry of Villehardouin, Marshal of Champagne, and Miles the Brabant; the envoys of Count Baldwin were Conon of Béthune and Alard Maquereau, and the envoys of Count Louis were John of Friaise, and Walter of Gaudonville.

To these six envoys the business in hand was fully committed, all the barons delivering to them valid charters with seals attached to the effect that they would undertake to maintain and carry out whatever conventions and agreements the envoys might enter into, in all sea ports, and whithersoever else the envoys might fare.

Thus were the six envoys despatched, as you have been told; and they took counsel among themselves, and this was their conclusion: that in Venice they might expect to find a greater number of vessels than in any other port. So they journeyed day by day, till they came thither in the first week of Lent (February 1201).

4

The envoys arrive in Venice, and proffer their request

THE Doge of Venice, whose name was Henry Dandolo and who was very wise and very valiant, did them great honour, both he and the other folk, and entertained them right willingly, marveling, however, when the envoys had delivered their letters, what might be the matter of import that had brought them to that country. For the letters were letters of credence only, and declared no more than that the bearers were to be accredited as if they were the counts in person, and that the said counts would make good whatever the six envoys should undertake.

So the Doge replied: "Signors, I have seen your letters; well do we know that of men uncrowned your lords are the greatest, and they advise us to put faith in what you tell us, and that they will maintain whatsoever you undertake. Now, therefore, speak, and let us know what is your pleasure."

And the envoys answered: "Sire, we would that you should assemble your council; and before your council we will declare the wishes of our lords; and let this be tomorrow, if it so pleases you." And the Doge replied asking for respite till the fourth day, when he would assemble his council, so that the envoys might state their requirements.

The envoys waited then till the fourth day, as had been appointed them, and entered the palace, which was passing rich and beautiful; and found the Doge and his council in a chamber. There they delivered their message after this manner: "Sire, we come to thee on the part of the high barons of France, who have taken the sign of the cross to avenge the shame done to Jesus Christ, and to reconquer Jerusalem, if so be that God will suffer it. And because they know that no people have such great power to help them as you and your people, therefore we pray you by God that you take pity on the land overseas and the shame of Christ, and use diligence that our lords 'have ships for transport and battle.'"

"And after what manner should we use diligence?" said the Doge. "After all manners that you may advise and propose," rejoined the envoys, "in so far as what you propose may be within our means." "Certes[1]," said the Doge, "it is a great thing that your lords require of us, and well it seems that they have in view a high enterprise. We will give you our answer eight days from to-day. And marvel not if the term be long, for it is meet that so great a matter be fully pondered."

5

Conditions proposed by the Doge

WHEN the term appointed by the Doge was ended, the envoys returned to the palace. Many were the words then spoken which I cannot now rehearse. But this was the conclusion of that parliament: "Signors," said the Doge, "we will tell you the conclusions at which we have arrived, if so be that we can induce our great council and the commons of the land to allow of them; and you, on your part, must consult and see if you can accept them and carry them through.

"We will build transports to carry four thousand five hundred horses, and nine thousand squires, and ships for four thousand five hundred knights, and twenty thousand sergeants of foot. And we will agree also to purvey food for these horses and people during nine months. This is what we undertake to do at the least, on condition that you pay us for each horse four marks, and for each man two marks.

"And the covenants we are now explaining to you, we undertake to keep, wheresoever we may be, for a year, reckoning from the day on which we sail from the port of Venice in the service of God and of Christendom. Now the sum total of the expenses above named amounts to 85,000 marks.

---

1 Assuredly

"And this will we do moreover. For the love of God, we will add to the fleet fifty armed galleys on condition that, so long as we act in company, of all conquests in land or money, whether at sea or on dry ground, we shall have the half, and you the other half. Now consult together to see if you, on your parts, can accept and fulfill these covenants."

The envoys then departed, and said that they would consult together and give their answer on the morrow. They consulted, and talked together that night, and agreed to accept the terms offered. So the next day they appeared before the Doge, and said: "Sire, we are ready to ratify this covenant." The Doge thereon said he would speak of the matter to his people, and, as he found them affected, so would he let the envoys know the issue.

On the morning of the third day, the Doge, who was very wise and valiant, assembled his great council, and the council was of forty men of the wisest that were in the land. And the Doge, by his wisdom and wit, that were very clear and very good, brought them to agreement and approval. Thus he wrought with them; and then with a hundred others, then two hundred, then a thousand, so that at last all consented and approved. Then he assembled well ten thousand of the people in the church of St. Mark, the most beautiful church that there is, and bade them hear a mass of the Holy Ghost, and pray to God for counsel on the request and messages that had been addressed to them. And the people did so right willingly.

6

Conclusion of the treaty, and return of the envoys

WHEN mass had been said, the Doge desired the envoys to humbly ask the people to assent to the proposed covenant. The envoys came into the church. Curiously were they looked upon by many who had not before had sight of them.

Geoffry of Villehardouin, the Marshal of Champagne, by will

and consent of the other envoys, acted as spokesman and said unto them: "Lords, the barons of France, most high and puissant, have sent us to you; and they cry to you for mercy, that you take pity on Jerusalem, which is in bondage to the Turks, and that, for God's sake, you help to avenge the shame of Christ Jesus. And for this end they have elected to come to you, because they know full well that there is none other people having so great power on the seas, as you and your people. And they commanded us to fall at your feet, and not to rise till you consent to take pity on the Holy Land which is beyond the seas."

Then the six envoys knelt at the feet of the people, weeping many tears. And the Doge and all the others burst into tears of pity and compassion, and cried with one voice, and lifted up their hands, saying: "We consent, we consent!" Then was there so great a noise and tumult that it seemed as if the earth itself were falling to pieces.

And when this great tumult and passion of pity—greater did never any man see—were appeased, the good Doge of Venice, who was very wise and valiant, went up into the reading-desk, and spoke to the people, and said to them: "Signors, behold the honour that God has done you; for the best people in the world have set aside all other people, and chosen you to join them in so high an enterprise as the deliverance of our Lord!"

All the good and beautiful words that the Doge then spoke, I cannot repeat to you. But the end of the matter was, that the covenants were to be made on the following day; and made they were, and devised accordingly. When they were concluded, it was notified to the council that we should go to Babylon (Cairo), because the Turks could better be destroyed in Babylon than in any other land; but to the folk at large it was only told that we were bound to go overseas. We were then in Lent (March 1201), and by St. John's Day, in the following year—which would be twelve hundred and two years after the Incarnation of Jesus Christ—the barons and pilgrims were to be in Venice, and the ships ready against their coming.

When the treaties were duly indited and sealed, they were brought to the Doge in the grand palace, where had been assembled the great and the little council. And when the Doge delivered the treaties to the envoys, he knelt greatly weeping, and swore on holy relics faithfully to observe the conditions thereof, and so did all his council, which numbered fifty-six persons. And the envoys, on their side, swore to observe the treaties, and in all good faith to maintain their oaths and the oaths of their lords; and be it known to you that for great pity many a tear was there shed. And forthwith were messengers sent to Rome, to the Pope Innocent, that he might confirm this covenant—the which he did right willingly.

Then did the envoys borrow five thousand marks of silver, and gave them to the Doge so that the building of the ships might be begun. And taking leave to return to their own land, they journeyed day by day till they came to Placentia in Lombardy. There they parted. Geoffry, the Marshal of Champagne and Alard Maquereau went straight to France, and the others went to Genoa and Pisa to learn what help might there be had for the land overseas.

When Geoffry, the Marshal of Champagne, passed over Mont Cenis, he came in with Walter of Brienne going into Apulia to conquer the land of his wife, whom he had married since he took the cross, and who was the daughter of King Tancred. With him went Walter of Montbéliard, and Eustace of Conflans, Robert of Joinville, and a great part of the people of worth in Champagne who had taken the cross.

And when he told them the news how the envoys had fared, great was their joy, and much did they prize the arrangements made. And they said, "We are already on our way; and when you come, you will find us ready." But events fall out as God wills, and never had they power to join the host. This was much to our loss; for they were of great prowess and valiant. And thus they parted, and each went on his way.

So rode Geoffry the Marshal, day by day, that he came to Troyes in Champagne, and found his lord the Count Thibaut sick and languishing, and right glad was the count of his coming. And when he had told the count how he had fared, the count was so rejoiced that he said he would mount horse, a thing he had not done of a long time. So he rose from his bed and rode forth. But alas, how great the pity! For never again did he bestride horse but that once.

His sickness waxed and grew worse, so that at the last he made his will and testament, and divided the money which he would have taken with him on pilgrimage among his followers and companions, of whom he had many that were very good men and true—no one at that time had more. And he ordered that each one, on receiving his money, should swear on holy relics to join the host at Venice, according as he had promised. Many there were who kept that oath badly, and so incurred great blame. The count ordered that another portion of his treasure should be retained, and taken to the host, and there expended as might seem best.

Thus died the count; and no man in this world made a better end. And there were present at that time a very great assemblage of men of his lineage and of his vassals. But of the mourning and funeral pomp it is unmeet that I should here speak. Never was more honour paid to any man. And right well that it was so, for never was man of his age more beloved by his own men, nor by other folk. Buried he was beside his father in the church of our lord St. Stephen at Troyes. He left behind him the Countess, his wife, whose name was Blanche, very fair, very good, the daughter of the King of Navarre. She had borne him a little daughter, and was then about to bear a son.

7

The crusaders look for another chief

WHEN the Count was buried, Matthew of Montmorency, Simon of Montfort, Geoffry of Joinville who was seneschal, and Geoffry the Marshal went to Odo, Duke of Burgundy, and said to him, "Sire, your cousin is dead. You see what evil has befallen the land overseas. We pray you by God that you take the cross, and succour the land overseas in his stead. And we will cause you to have all his treasure, and will swear on holy relics, and make the others swear also, to serve you in all good faith, even as we should have served him."

Such was his pleasure that he refused. And be it known to you that he might have done much better. The envoys charged Geoffry of Joinville to make the self-same offer to the Count of Bar-le-Duc, Thibaut, who was cousin to the dead count, and he refused also.

Very great was the discomfort of the pilgrims, and of all who were about to go on God's service, at the death of Count Thibaut of Champagne; and they held a parliament at the beginning of the month, at Soissons, to determine what they should do. There were present Count Baldwin of Flanders and Hainault, the Count Louis of Blois and Chartres, the Count Geoffry of Perche, the Count Hugh of Saint-Paul, and many other men of worth.

Geoffry the Marshal spake to them and told them of the offer made to the Duke of Burgundy, and to the Count of Bar-le-Duc, and how they had refused it. "My lords," said he, "listen, I will advise you of somewhat if you will consent thereto. The Marquis of Montferrat is very worthy and valiant, and one of the most highly prized of living men. If you asked him to come here, and take the sign of the cross and put himself in place of the Count of Champagne, and you gave him the lordship of the host, full soon would he accept thereof."

Many were the words spoken for and against; but in the end all agreed, both small and great. So were letters written, and envoys chosen, and the marquis was sent for. And he came, on the day appointed, through Champagne and the Isle-de-France, where he received much honour, and specially from the King of France, who was his cousin.

8

Boniface, Marquis of Montferrat, becomes chief of the crusade; new crusaders; death of Geoffry, Count of Perche

SO he came to a parliament assembled at Soissons; and the main part of the counts and barons and of the other Crusaders were there assembled. When they heard that the marquis was coming, they went out to meet him, and did him much honour. In the morning the parliament was held in an orchard belonging to the abbey of our Lady of Soissons. There they besought the marquis to do as they had desired of him, and prayed him, for the love of God, to take the cross, and accept the leadership of the host, and stand in the place of Thibaut Count of Champagne, and accept of his money and of his men. And they fell at his feet with many tears; and he, on his part, fell at their feet, and said he would do it right willingly.

Thus did the marquis consent to their prayers, and receive the lordship of the host. Whereupon the Bishop of Soissons, and Master Fulk, the holy man, and two white monks whom the marquis had brought with him from his own land, led him into the Church of Notre Dame, and attached the cross to his shoulder. Thus ended this parliament, and the next day he took leave to return to his own land and settle his own affairs—telling them all to settle their own affairs likewise, for that he would meet them at Venice.

Thence did the marquis go to attend the Chapter at Citeaux, which is held on Holy Cross Day in September (14th September 1241). There he found a great number of abbots, barons, and other people of Burgundy; and Master Fulk went thither to preach the Crusade. And at that place took the cross Odo the Champenois of Champlitte, and William his brother, Richard of Dampierre, Odo his brother, Guy of Pesmes, Edmund his brother, Guy of Conflans, and many other good men of Burgundy whose names are not recorded. Afterwards took the cross the Bishop of Autun, Guignes Count of Forez, Hugh of Bergi (father and son), Hugh of Colemi. Further on in Provence took the cross Peter Bromont, and many others whose names are unknown to us.

Thus did the pilgrims make ready in all lands. Alas! a great mischance befell them in the following Lent (March 1202) before they had started, for the Count Geoffry of Perche fell sick, and made his will in such fashion that he directed that Stephen, his brother, should have his goods, and lead his men in the host. Of this exchange the pilgrims would willingly have been quit, had God so ordered. Thus did the count make an end and die; and much evil ensued, for he was a baron high and honoured, and a good knight. Greatly was he mourned throughout all his lands.

9

First starting of the pilgrims for Venice, and of some who went not thither

AFTER Easter and towards Whitsuntide (June 1202) began the pilgrims to leave their own country. And you must know that at their departure many were the tears shed for pity and sorrow, by their own people and by their friends. So they journeyed through Burgundy, and by the Mountains of Mont Jura by Mont Cenis, and through Lombardy, and began to assemble at Venice, where they were lodged on an island which is called St. Nicholas in the port.

At that time started from Flanders a fleet that carried a great number of good men-at-arms. Of this fleet were captains John of Nêle, Castellan of Bruges, Thierri, who was the son of Count Philip of Flanders, and Nicholas of Mailly. And these promised Count Baldwin, and swore on holy relics, that they would go through the straits of Morocco, and join themselves to him, and to the host of Venice, at whatsoever place they might hear that the count was faring. And for this reason the Count of Flanders and Henry his brother had confided to them certain ships loaded with cloth and food and other wares.

Very fair was this fleet, and rich, and great was the reliance that the Count of Flanders and the pilgrims placed upon it, because very many of their good sergeants were journeying therein. But ill did these keep the faith they had sworn to the count, they and others like them, because they and such others of the same sort became fearful of the great perils that the host of Venice had undertaken.

Thus did the Bishop of Autun fail us, and Guignes the Count of Forez, and Peter Bromont, and many people besides, who were greatly blamed therein; and of little worth were the exploits they performed there where they did go. And of the French failed us Bernard of Moreuil, Hugh of Chaumont, Henry of Araines, John of Villers, Walter of Saint-Denis, Hugh his brother, and many others who avoided the passage to Venice because of the danger, and went instead to Marseilles—whereof they received shame, and much were they blamed—and great were the mishaps that afterwards befell them.

10

Of the pilgrims who came to Venice, and of those who went to Apulia

NOW let us for this present speak of them no further, but speak of the pilgrims, of whom a great part had already come to Venice. Count Baldwin of Flanders had already arrived there, and many others, and thither were tidings brought to them that many of the pilgrims were traveling by other ways, and from other ports. This troubled them greatly, because they would thus be unable to fulfill the promise made to the Venetians, and find the moneys that were due.

So they took counsel together, and agreed to send good envoys to meet the pilgrims, and to meet Count Louis of Blois and Chartres, who had not yet arrived, and to put them in good heart, and beseech them to have pity of the Holy Land beyond the sea, and show them that no other passage, save that from Venice, could be of profit.

For this embassy they made choice of Count Hugh of Saint-Paul and Geoffry the Marshal of Champagne, and these rode till they came to Pavia in Lombardy. There they found Count Louis with a great many knights and men of note and worth; and by encouragements and prayers prevailed on many to proceed to Venice who would otherwise have fared from other ports, and by other ways.

Nevertheless from Placentia many men of note proceeded by other ways to Apulia. Among them were Villain of Neuilly who was one of the best knights in the world, Henry of Arzilliéres, Renaud of Dampierre, Henry of Longchamp, and Giles of Trasegnies, liegeman to Count Baldwin of Flanders and Hainault, who had given him, out of his own purse, five hundred livres to accompany him on this journey. With these went a great company of knights and sergeants, whose names are not recorded.

Thus was the host of those who went by Venice greatly weakened; and much evil befell them therefrom, as you shall shortly hear.

11

The pilgrims lack money wherewith to pay the Venetians

THUS did Count Louis and the other barons wend their way to Venice; and they were there received with feasting and joyfully, and took lodging in the Island of St. Nicholas with those who had come before. Goodly was the host, and right worthy were the men. Never did man see goodlier or worthier. And the Venetians held a market, rich and abundant, of all things needful for horses and men. And the fleet they had got ready was so goodly and fine that never did Christian man see one goodlier or finer; as well galleys as transports, and sufficient for at least three times as many men as were in the host.

Ah! the grievous harm and loss when those who should have come thither sailed instead from other ports! Right well, if they had kept their tryst, would Christendom have been exalted, and the land of the Turks abased! The Venetians had fulfilled all their undertakings, and above measure, and they now summoned the barons and counts to fulfill theirs and make payment, since they were ready to start.

The cost of each man's passage was now levied throughout the host; and there were people enough who said they could not pay for their passage, and the barons took from them such moneys as they had. So each man paid what he could. When the barons had thus claimed the cost of the passages, and when the payments had been collected, the moneys came to less than the sum due—yea, by more than one half.

Then the barons met together and said: "Lords, the Venetians have well fulfilled all their undertakings, and above measure. But we cannot fulfill ours in paying for our passages, seeing we are too few in number; and this is the fault of those who have journeyed by other ports. For God's sake therefore let each contribute all that he has, so that we may fulfill our covenant; for better is it that we should give all that we have, than lose what we have already paid, and prove false to our covenants; for if this host remains here, the rescue of the land overseas comes to naught."

Great was then the dissension among the main part of the barons and the other folk, and they said: "We have paid for our passages, and if they will take us, we shall go willingly; but if not, we shall inquire and look for other means of passage." And they spoke thus because they wished that the host should fall to pieces and each return to his own land. But the other party said, "Much rather would we give all that we have and go penniless with the host, than that the host should fall to pieces and fail; for God will doubtless repay us when it so pleases Him."

Then the Count of Flanders began to give all that he had and all that he could borrow, and so did Count Louis, and the Marquis, and the Count of Saint-Paul, and those who were of their party. Then might you have seen many a fine vessel of gold and silver borne in payment to the palace of the Doge. And when all had been brought together, there was still wanting, of the sum required, 34,000 marks of silver. Then those who had kept back their possessions and not brought them into the common stock, were right glad, for they thought now surely the host must fail and go to pieces. But God, who advises those who have been ill-advised, would not so suffer it.

12

The crusaders obtain a respite by promising to help the Venetians against Zara

THEN the Doge spoke to his people, and said unto them: "Signors, these people cannot pay more; and in so far as they have paid at all, we have benefited by an agreement which they cannot now fulfill. But our right to keep this money would not everywhere be acknowledged; and if we so kept it we should be greatly blamed, both us and our land. Let us therefore offer them terms.

"The King of Hungary has taken from us Zara in Sclavonia, which is one of the strongest places in the world; and never shall we recover it with all the power that we possess, save with the help of these people. Let us therefore ask them to help us to reconquer it, and we will remit the payment of the debt of 34,000 marks of silver, until such time as it shall please God to allow us to gain the money by conquest, we and they together." Thus was agreement made. Much was it contested by those who wished that the host should be broken up. Nevertheless the agreement was accepted and ratified.

13

The Doge and a number of Venetians take the cross

THEN, on a Sunday, was assemblage held in the church of St. Mark. It was a very high festival, and the people of the land were there, and the most part of the barons and pilgrims.

Before the beginning of High Mass, the Doge of Venice, who bore the name of Henry Dandolo, went up into the reading-desk, and spoke to the people, and said to them: "Signors, you are associated with the most worthy people in the world, and for the highest enterprise ever undertaken; and I am a man old and feeble, who should have need of rest, and I am sick in body; but I see that no one could command and lead you like myself, who am your lord. If you will consent that I take the sign of the cross to guard and direct you, and that my son remain in my place to guard the land, then shall I go to live or die with you and with the pilgrims."

And when they had heard him, they cried with one voice: "We pray you by God that you consent, and do it, and that you come with us!"

Very great was then the pity and compassion on the part of the people of the land and of the pilgrims; and many were the tears shed, because that worthy and good man would have had so much reason to remain behind, for he was an old man, and albeit his eyes were unclouded, yet he saw naught, having lost his sight through a wound in the head. He was of a great heart. Ah! How little like him were those who had gone to other ports to escape the danger.

Thus he came down from the reading-desk, and went before the altar, and knelt upon his knees greatly weeping. And they sewed the cross on to a great cotton hat, which he wore, in front, because he wished that all men should see it. And the Venetians began to take the cross in great numbers, a great multitude, for up to that day very few had taken the cross. Our pilgrims had much joy in the cross that the Doge took, and were greatly moved because of the wisdom and the valour that were in him.

Thus did the Doge take the cross, as you have heard. Then the Venetians began to deliver the ships, the galleys, and the transports to the barons for departure; but so much time had already been spent since the appointed term, that September drew near (1202).

14

Message of Alexius, the son of Isaac, the dethroned emperor of Constantinople; death of Fulk of Neuilly; arrival of the Germans

NOW give ear to one of the greatest marvels, and most wonderful adventures that you have ever heard tell of. At that time there was an emperor in Constantinople whose name was Isaac, and he had a brother, Alexius by name, whom he had ransomed from captivity among the Turks. This Alexius took his brother the emperor, tore the eyes out of his head, and made himself emperor by the aforesaid treachery. He kept Isaac a long time in prison, together with a son whose name was Alexius. This son escaped from prison, and fled in a ship to a city on the sea which is called Ancona. Thence he departed to go to King Philip of Germany, who had his sister for wife; and he came to Verona in Lombardy, and lodged in the town, and found there a number of pilgrims and other people who were on their way to join the host.

And those who had helped him to escape, and were with him, said: "Sire, here is an army in Venice, quite near to us, the best and most valiant people and knights that are in the world, and they are going overseas. Cry to them therefore for mercy, that they have pity on thee and on thy father who have been so wrongfully dispossessed. And if they be willing to help thee, thou shalt be guided by them. Perchance they will take pity on thy estate." And Alexius said he would do this right willingly, and that the advice was good.

Thus he appointed envoys, and sent them to the Marquis Boniface of Montferrat, who was chief of the host, and to the other barons. And when the barons saw them, they marveled greatly, and said to the envoys: "We understand right well what you tell us. We will send an envoy with the prince to King Philip, whither he is going. If the prince will help to recover the land overseas, we will help him to recover his own land, for we know that it has been wrested from him and from his father wrongfully." So were envoys sent into Germany, both to the heir of Constantinople and to King Philip of Germany.

Before this happened, of which I have just told you, there came news to the host which greatly saddened the barons and the other folk, viz. that Fulk, the good man, the holy man, who first preached the Crusade, had made an end and was dead.

And after this adventure, there came to the host a company of very good and worthy people from the empire of Germany, of whose arrival they of the host were full fain[2]. There came the Bishop of Halberstadt, Count Berthold of Katzenelenbogen, Gamier of Borland, Thierri of Loos, Henry of Orme, Thierri of Diest, Roger of Suitre, Alexander of Villers, Ulric of Tone, and many other good folk whose names are not recorded in this book.

15

The crusaders leave Venice to besiege Zara

THEN were the ships and transports apportioned by the barons. Ah, God, what fine war-horses were put therein. And when the ships were filled with arms and provisions, and knights and sergeants, the shields were ranged round the bulwarks and castles of the ships, and the banners displayed, many and fair.

And be it known to you that the vessels carried more than three hundred petraries and mangonels[3], and all such engines as are needed for the taking of cities, in great plenty. Never did finer fleet sail from any port. And this was in the octave of the Feast of St. Remigius (October) in the year of the Incarnation of Jesus Christ twelve hundred and two. Thus did they sail from the port of Venice, as you have been told.

On the Eve of St. Martin (10th November) they came before Zara in Sclavonia, and beheld the city enclosed by high walls and high towers; and vainly would you have sought for a fairer city, or one of greater strength, or richer. And when the pilgrims saw it, they marveled greatly, and said one to another, "How could such a city be taken by force, save by the help of God himself?"

The first ships that came before the city cast anchor, and waited for the others; and in the morning the day was very fine and very

---

2   Pleased

3   Medieval stone-throwing siege engines

clear, and all the galleys came up with the transports, and the other ships which were behind; and they took the port by force, and broke the chain that defended it though it was very strong and well-wrought; and they landed in such order that the port was between them and the town. Then might you have seen many a knight and many a sergeant swarming out of the ships, and taking from the transports many a good war-horse, and many a rich tent, and many a pavilion. Thus did the host encamp. And Zara was besieged on St. Martin's Day (11th November 1202).

At this time all the barons had not yet arrived. Thus the Marquis of Montferrat had remained behind for some business that detained him. And Stephen of Perche had remained at Venice sick, and Matthew of Montmorency. When they were healed of their sickness Matthew of Montmorency came to rejoin the host at Zara; but Stephen of Perche dealt less worthily, for he abandoned the host, and went to sojourn in Apulia. With him went Rotrou of Montfort and Ives of La Jaille, and many others, who were much blamed therein; and they journeyed to Syria in the following spring.

16

The inhabitants of Zara offer to capitulate, and then draw back; Zara is taken

ON the day following the feast of St. Martin, certain of the people of Zara came forth, and spoke to the Doge of Venice, who was in his pavilion, and said to him that they would yield up the city and all their goods—their lives being spared—to his mercy. And the Doge replied that he would not accept these conditions, nor any conditions, save by consent of the counts and barons, with whom he would go and confer.

While he went to confer with the counts and barons, that party, of whom you have already heard, who wished to disperse the host, spoke to the envoys and said, "Why should you surrender your city? The pilgrims will not attack you—have no care of them. If you can defend yourselves against the Venetians, you will be safe enough." And they chose one of themselves, whose name was Robert of Boves, who went to the walls of the city, and spoke the same words. Therefore the envoys returned to the city, and the negotiations were broken off.

The Doge of Venice, when he came to the counts and barons, said to them: "Signors, the people who are therein desire to yield the city to my mercy, on condition only that their lives are spared. But I will enter into no agreement with them—neither this nor any other—save with your consent." And the barons answered: "Sire, we advise you to accept these conditions, and we even beg of you so to do." He said he would do so; and they all returned together to the pavilion of the Doge to make the agreement, and found that the envoys had gone away by the advice of those who wished to disperse the host.

Then rose the abbot of Vaux, of the order of the Cistercians, and said to them: "Lords, I forbid you, on the part of the Pope of Rome, to attack this city; for those within it are Christians, and you are pilgrims." When the Doge heard this, he was very wroth, and much disturbed, and he said to the counts and barons: "Signors, I had this city, by their own agreement, at my mercy, and your people have broken that agreement; you have covenanted to help me to conquer it, and I summon you to do so."

Whereon the counts and barons all spoke at once, together with those who were of their party, and said: "Great is the outrage of those who have caused this agreement to be broken, and never a day has passed that they have not tried to break up the host. Now are we shamed if we do not help to take the city." And they came to the Doge, and said: "Sire, we will help you to take the city in despite of those who would hinder us."

Thus was the decision taken. The next morning the host encamped before the gates of the city, and set up their petraries and manoonels, and other engines of war, which they had in plenty, and on the side of the sea they raised ladders from the ships. Then they began to throw stones at the walls of the city and at the towers. So did the assault last for about five days. Then were the sappers[4] set to mine one of the towers, and began to sap the wall. When those within the city saw this, they proposed an agreement, such as they had before refused by the advice of those who wished to break up the host.

17

The crusaders establish themselves in the city; a fray between the Venetians and the Franks

THUS did the city surrender to the mercy of the Doge, on condition only that all lives should be spared. Then came the Doge to the counts and barons, and said to them: "Signors, we have taken this city by the grace of God, and your own. It is now winter, and we cannot stir hence till Eastertide; for we should find no market in any other place; and this city is very rich, and well furnished with all supplies. Let us therefore divide it in the midst, and we will take one half, and you the other."

As he had spoken, so was it done. The Venetians took the part of the city towards the port, where were the ships, and the Franks took the other part. There were quarters assigned to each, according as was right and convenient. And the host raised the camp, and went to lodge in the city.

On the third day after they were all lodged, there befell a great misadventure in the host, at about the hour of Vespers[5]; for there began a fray, exceeding fell and fierce, between the Venetians and the Franks, and they ran to arms from all sides. And the fray was so fierce that there were but few streets in which battle did not rage with swords and lances and cross-bows and darts; and many people were killed and wounded.

---

4   Military engineers involved in breaching fortifications

5   Sunset or evening prayer

But the Venetians could not abide the combat, and they began to suffer great losses. Then the men of mark, who did not want this evil to befall, came fully armed into the strife, and began to separate the combatants; and when they had separated them in one place, they began again in another. This lasted the better part of the night. Nevertheless with great labour and endurance at last they were separated. And be it known to you that this was the greatest misfortune that ever befell a host, and little did it lack that the host was not lost utterly. But God would not suffer it.

Great was the loss on either side. There was slain a high lord of Flanders, whose name was Giles of Landas: he was struck in the eye, and with that stroke he died in the fray; and many another of whom less was spoken. The Doge of Venice and the barons laboured much, during the whole of that week, to appease the fray, and they laboured so effectually that peace was made. God be thanked therefore.

18

On what conditions Alexius proposes to obtain the help of the crusaders for the conquest of Constantinople

A FORTNIGHT after came to Zara the Marquis Boniface of Montferrat, who had not yet joined, and Matthew of Montmorency, and Peter of Bracieux, and many another man of note. And after another fortnight came also the envoys from Germany, sent by King Philip and the heir of Constantinople. Then the barons, and the Doge of Venice assembled in a palace where the Doge was lodged. And the envoys addressed them and said: "Lords, King Philip sends us to you, as does also the brother of the king's wife, the son of the emperor of Constantinople.

"'Lords,' says the king, 'I will send you the brother of my wife; and I commit him into the hands of God—may He keep him from death!—and into your hands. And because you have fared forth for God, and for right, and for justice, therefore you are bound, in so far as you are able, to restore to their own inheritance those who have been unrighteously despoiled. And my wife's brother will make with you the best terms ever offered to any people, and give you the most puissant help for the recovery of the land overseas.

"'And first, if God grant that you restore him to his inheritance, he will place the whole empire of Romania in obedience to Rome, from which it has long been separated. Further, he knows that you have spent of your substance, and that you are poor, and he will give you 200,000 marks of silver, and food for all those of the host, both small and great. And he, of his own person, will go with you into the land of Babylon, or, if you hold that will be better, send thither 10,000 men, at his own charges. And this service he will perform for one year. And all the days of his life he will maintain, at his own charges, five hundred knights in the land overseas to guard that land.'"

"Lords, we have full power," said the envoys, "to conclude this agreement, if you are willing to conclude it on your parts. And be it known to you, that so favourable an agreement has never before been offered to anyone; and that he that would refuse it can have but small desire of glory and conquest."

The barons and the Doge said they would talk this over; and a parliament was called for the morrow. When all were assembled, the matter was laid before them.

19

Discord among the crusaders; of those who accept the proposals of the young Alexius

THEN arose much debate. The abbot of Vaux, of the order of the Cistercians, spoke, and that party that wished for the dispersal of the host; and they said they would never consent: that it was not to fall on Christians that they had left their homes, and that they would go to Syria.

And the other party replied: "Fair lords, in Syria you will be able to do nothing; and that you may right well perceive by considering how those have fared who abandoned us, and sailed from other ports. And be it known to you that it is only by way of Babylon, or of Greece, that the land overseas can be recovered, if so be that it ever is recovered. And if we reject this covenant we shall be shamed to all time."

There was discord in the host, as you hear. Nor need you be surprised if there was discord among the laymen, for the white monks of the order of Citeaux were also at issue among themselves in the host. The abbot of Loos, who was a holy man and a man of note, and other abbots who held with him, prayed and besought the people, for pity's sake and the sake of God, to keep the host together, and agree to the proposed convention, in that "it afforded the best means by which the land overseas might be recovered"; while the abbot of Vaux, on the other hand, and those who held with him, preached full oft, and declared that all this was naught, and that the host ought to go to the land of Syria, and there do what they could.

Then came the Marquis of Montferrat, and Baldwin Count of Flanders and Hainault, and Count Louis, and Count Hugh of St. Paul, and those who held with them, and they declared that they would enter into the proposed covenant, for that they should be shamed if they refused. So they went to the Doge's hostel, and the envoys were summoned, and the covenant, in such terms as you have already heard, was confirmed by oath, and by charters with seals appended.

And the book tells you that only twelve persons took the oaths on the side of the Franks, for more (of sufficient note) could not be found. Among the twelve were first the Marquis of Montferrat, the Count Baldwin of Flanders, the Count Louis of Blois and of Chartres, and the Count of St. Paul, and eight others who held with them. Thus was the agreement made, and the charters prepared, and a term fixed for the arrival of the heir of Constantinople; and the term so fixed was the fifteenth day after the following Easter.

20

Of those who separated themselves from the host to go to Syria, and of the fleet of the count of Flanders

THUS did the host sojourn at Zara all that winter (1202-1203) in the face of the King of Hungary. And be it known to you that the hearts of the people were not at peace, for the one party used all efforts to break up the host, and the other to make it hold together.

Many of the lesser folk escaped in the vessels of the merchants. In one ship escaped well nigh five hundred, and they were all drowned, and so lost. Another company escaped by land, and thought to pass through Sclavonia; and the peasants of that land fell upon them, and killed many, so that the remainder came back flying to the host. Thus did the host greatly dwindle day by day. At that time a great lord of the host, who was from Germany, Garnier of Borland by name, so wrought that he escaped in a merchant vessel, and abandoned the host, whereby he incurred great blame.

Not long afterwards, a great baron of France, Renaud of Monmirail by name, besought so earnestly, with the countenance of Count Louis, that he was sent to Syria on an embassy in one of the vessels of the fleet; and he swore with his right hand on holy relics, he and all the knights who went with him, that within fifteen days after they had arrived in Syria, and delivered their message, they would return to the host. On this condition he left the host, and with him Hervée of Chitel, his nephew, William the *vidame* of Chartres, Geoffry of Beaumont, John of Frouville, Peter his brother, and many others. And the oaths that they swore were not kept; for they did not rejoin the host.

Then came to the host news that was heard right willingly, viz. that the fleet from Flanders, of which mention has been made above, had arrived at Marseilles. And John of Nêle, Castellan of Bruges, who was captain of that host, and Thierri, who was the son of Count Philip of Flanders, and Nicholas of Mailly, advised the Count of Flanders, their lord, that they would winter at Marseilles, and asked him to let them know what was his will, and said that whatever was his will, that they would do. And he told them, by the advice of the Doge of Venice and the other barons, that they should sail at the end of the following March, and come to meet him at the port of Modon in Romania. Alas! They acted very evilly, for never did they keep their word, but went to Syria, where, as they well knew, they would achieve nothing.

Now be it known to you, lords, that if God had not loved the host, it could never have held together, seeing how many people wished evil to it!

21

The crusaders obtain the Pope's absolution for the capture of Zara

THEN the barons spoke together and said that they would send to Rome, to the Pope, because he had taken the capture of Zara in evil part. And they chose as envoys such as they knew were fitted for this office, two knights, and two clerks. Of the two clerks one was Nevelon, Bishop of Soissons, and the other Master John of Noyon, who was chancellor to Count Baldwin of Flanders; and of the knights one was John of Friaize, the other Robert of Boves. These swore on holy relics that they would perform their embassy loyally and in good faith, and that they would come back to the host.

Three kept their oath right well, and the fourth evilly, and this one was Robert of Boves. For he executed his office as badly as he could, and perjured himself, and went away to Syria as others had done. But the remaining three executed their office right well, and delivered their message as the barons had directed, and said to the Pope: "The barons cry mercy to you for the capture of Zara, for they acted as people who could do no better, owing to the default of those who had gone to other ports, and because, had they not acted as they did, they could not have held the host together. And as to this they refer themselves to you, as to their good Father, that you should tell them what are your commands, which they are ready to perform."

And the Pope said to the envoys that he knew full well that it was through the default of others that the host had been impelled to do this great mischief, and that he had them in great pity. And then he notified to the barons and pilgrims that he sent them his blessing, and absolved them as his sons, and commanded and besought them to hold the host together, inasmuch as he well knew that without that host God's service could not be done. And he gave full powers to Nevelon, Bishop of Soissons, and Master John of Noyon, to bind and to unloose the pilgrims until the cardinal joined the host.

22

Departure of the crusaders for Corfu; arrival of the young Alexius; capture of Duras

SO much time had passed that it was now Lent, and the host prepared their fleet to sail at Easter. When the ships were laden on the day after Easter (7th April 1203), the pilgrims encamped by the port, and the Venetians destroyed the city, and the walls and the towers.

Then there befell an adventure which weighed heavily upon the host; for one of the great barons of the host, by name Simon of Montfort, had made private covenant with the King of Hungary, who was at enmity with those of the host, and went to him, abandoning the host. With him went Guy of Montfort his brother, Simon of Nauphle, and Robert Mauvoisin, and Dreux of Cressonsacq, and the abbot of Vaux, who was a monk of the order of the Cistercians, and many others. And not long after another great lord of the host, called Enguerrand of Boves, joined the King of Hungary, together with Hugh, Enguerrand's brother, and such of the other people of their country as they could lead away.

These left the host, as you have just heard; and this was a great misfortune to the host, and to such as left it a great disgrace.

Then the ships and transports began to depart; and it was settled that they should take port at Corfu, an island of Romania, and that the first to arrive should wait for the last; and so it was done.

Before the Doge, the Marquis, and the galleys left Zara, Alexius, the son of the Emperor Isaac of Constantinople, had arrived. He was sent by the King Philip of Germany, and received with great joy and great honour; and the Doge gave him as many galleys and ships as he required. So they left the port of Zara, and had a fair wind, and sailed onwards till they took port at Duras. And those of the land, when they saw their lord, yielded up the city right willingly and sware fealty to him.

They departed thence and came to Corfu, and found there the host encamped before the city; and those of the host had spread their tents and pavilions, and taken the horses out of the transports for ease and refreshment. When they heard that the son of the Emperor of Constantinople had arrived in the port, then might you have seen many a good knight and many a good sergeant leading many a good war-horse and going to meet him. Thus they received him with very great joy, and much high honour. And he had his tent pitched in the midst of the host; and quite near was pitched the tent of the Marquis of Montferrat, to whose ward he had been commended by King Philip who had his sister to wife.

23

How the chiefs of the crusaders held back those who wanted to abandon the host

THE host sojourned thus for three weeks in that island, which was very rich and plenteous. And while they sojourned, there happened a misadventure fell and grievous. For a great part of those who wished to break up the host, and had previously been hostile to it, spoke together and said that the adventure to be undertaken seemed very long and very perilous, and that they, for their part, would remain in the island, suffering the host to depart, and that—when the host had so departed—they would, through the people of Corfu, send to Count Walter of Brienne, who then held Brandis, so that he might send ships to take them thither.

I cannot tell you the names of all those who wrought in this matter, but I will name some among the most notable of the chiefs, viz. Odo the Champenois of Champlitte, James of Avesnes, Peter of Amiens, Guy the Castellan of Coucy, Oger of Saint-Chéron, Guy of Chappes and Clerembaud his nephew, William of Aunoi, Peter Coiseau, Guy of Pesmes and Edmund his brother, Guy of Conflans, Richard of Dampierre, Odo his brother, and many more who had promised privily to be of their party, but who dared not for shame openly so to avow themselves; in such sort that the book testifies that more than half the host were in this mind.

And when the Marquis of Montferrat heard thereof, and Count Baldwin of Flanders, and Count Louis, and the Count of St. Paul, and the barons who held with them, they were greatly troubled, and said: "Lords, we are in evil case. If these people depart from us, after so many who have departed from us aforetime, our host is doomed, and we shall make no conquests. Let us then go to them, and fall at their feet, and cry to them for mercy, and for God's sake to have compassion upon themselves and upon us, and not to dishonour themselves, and ravish from us the deliverance of the land overseas."

Thus did the council decide; and they went, all together, to a valley where those of the other part were holding their parliament; and they took with them the son of the Emperor of Constantinople, and all the bishops and all the abbots of the host. And when they had come to the place they dismounted and went forward, and the barons fell at the feet of those of the other part, greatly weeping, and said they would not stir till those of the other part had promised not to depart from them.

And when those of the other part saw this, they were filled with very great compassion; and they wept very bitterly at seeing their lords, and their kinsmen, and their friends, thus lying at their feet. So they said they would consult together, and drew somewhat apart, and there communed. And the sum of their communing was this:

that they would remain with the host till Michaelmas, on condition that the other part would swear, loyally, on holy relics, that from that day and thenceforward, at whatever hour they might be summoned to do so, they would in all good faith, and without guile, within fifteen days, furnish ships wherein they might betake themselves to Syria.

Thus was covenant made and sworn to; and then was there great joy throughout all the host. And all got themselves to the ships, and the horses were put into the transports.

24

Departure from Corfu; capture of Andros and Abydos

THEN did they sail from the port of Corfu on the eve of Pentecost (24th May), which was twelve hundred and three years after the Incarnation of our Lord Jesus Christ. And there were all the ships assembled, and all the transports, and all the galleys of the host, and many other ships of merchants that fared with them. And the day was fine and clear, and the wind soft and favourable, and they unfurled all their sails to the breeze.

And Geoffry, the Marshal of Champagne, who dictates this work and has never lied therein by one word to his knowledge, and who was moreover present at all the councils held—he bears witness that never was yet seen so fair a sight. And well might it appear that such a fleet would conquer and gain lands, for, far as the eye could reach, there was no space without sails, and ships, and vessels, so that the hearts of men rejoiced greatly.

Thus they sailed over the sea till they came to Malea, to straits that are by the sea. And there they met two ships with pilgrims, and knights and sergeants returning from Syria, and they were of the parties that had gone to Syria by Marseilles. And when these saw our fleet so rich and well appointed, they conceived such shame that they dared not show themselves. And Count Baldwin of Flanders sent a boat from his ship to ask what people they were; and they said who they were.

And a sergeant let himself down from his ship into the boat, and said to those in the ship, "I cry quits to you for any goods of mine that may remain in the ship, for I am going with these people, for well I deem that they will conquer lands." Much did we make of the sergeant, and gladly was he received in the host. For well may it be said, that even after following a thousand crooked ways a man may find his way right in the end.

The host fared forward till it came to Nigra. Nigra is a very fair island, and there is on it a very good city called Negropont. Here the barons took council. Then went forward the Marquis Boniface of Montferrat, and Count Baldwin of Flanders and Hainault, with a great part of the transports and galleys, taking with them the son of the Emperor Isaac of Constantinople; and they came to an island called Andros, and there landed. The knights took their arms, and over-rode the country; and the people of the land came to crave mercy of the son of the Emperor of Constantinople, and gave so much of their goods that they made peace with him.

Then they returned to the ships, and sailed over the sea; when a great mishap befell, for a great lord of the host, whose name was Guy, Castellan of Coucy, died, and was cast into the sea.

The other ships, which had not sailed thitherward, had entered the passage of Abydos, and it is there that the straits of St. George (the Dardanelles) open into the great sea. And they sailed up the straits to a city called Abydos, which lies on the straits of St. George, towards Turkey, and is very fair, and well situated. There they took port and landed, and those of the city came to meet them, and surrendered the city, as men without stomach to defend themselves. And such guard was established that those of the city lost not one stiver current[6].

---

6   A small coin

They sojourned there eight days to wait for the ships transports and galleys that had not yet come up. And while they thus sojourned, they took corn from the land, for it was the season of harvest, and great was their need thereof, for before they had but little. And within those eight days all the ships and barons had come up. God gave them fair weather.

25

Arrival at St. Stephen; deliberation as to plan of attack

ALL started from the port of Abydos together. Then might you have seen the Straits of St. George, as it were, in flower with ships and galleys sailing upwards, and the beauty thereof was a great marvel to behold. Thus they sailed up the Straits of St. George till they came, on St. John the Baptist's Eve, in June (23rd June 1203) to St. Stephen, an abbey that lay three leagues from Constantinople. There had those on board the ships and galleys and transports full sight of Constantinople; and they took port and anchored their vessels.

Now you may know that those who had never before seen Constantinople looked upon it very earnestly, for they never thought there could be in all the world so rich a city; and they marked the high walls and strong towers that enclosed it round about, and the rich palaces, and mighty churches of which there were so many that no one would have believed it who had not seen it with his eyes—and the height and the length of that city which above all others was sovereign. And be it known to you, that no man there was of such hardihood but his flesh trembled: and it was no wonder, for never was so great an enterprise undertaken by any people since the creation of the world.

Then landed the counts and barons and the Doge of Venice, and a parliament was held in the church of St. Stephen. There were many opinions set forth, this way and that. All the words then spoken shall not be recorded in this book; but in the end the Doge rose on his feet and said: "Signors, I know the state of this land better than you do, for I have been here formerly. We have undertaken the greatest enterprise, and the most perilous, that ever people have undertaken. Therefore it behooves us to go to work warily. Be it known to you that if we go on dry ground, the land is great and large, and our people are poor and ill-provided. Thus they will disperse to look for food; and the people of the land are in great multitude, and we cannot keep such good watch but that some of ours will be lost. Nor are we in case to lose any, for our people are but few indeed for the work in hand.

"Now there are islands close by which you can see from here, and these are inhabited, and produce corn, and food, and other things. Let us take port there, and gather the corn and provisions of the land. And when we have collected our supplies, let us go before the city, and do as our Lord shall provide. For he that has supplies, wages war with more certainty than he that has none." To this counsel the lords and barons agreed, and all went back to their ships and vessels.

26

The crusaders land at Chalcedon and Scutari

THEY rested thus that night. And in the morning, on the day of the feast of my lord St. John the Baptist in June (24th June 1203), the banners and pennants were flown on the castles of the ships, and the coverings taken from the shields, and the bulwarks of the ships garnished. Everyone looked to his arms, such as he should use, for well each man knew that full soon he would have need of them.

The sailors weighed the anchors, and spread the sails to the wind, and God gave them a good wind, such as was convenient to them. Thus they passed before Constantinople, and so near to the walls and towers that we shot at many of their vessels. There were so many people on the walls and towers that it seemed as if there could be no more people in the world.

Then did God our Lord set to naught the counsel of the day before, and keep us from sailing to the islands: that counsel fell to naught as if none had ever heard thereof. For lo, our ships made for the mainland as straight as ever they could, and took port before a palace of the Emperor Alexius, at a place called Chalcedon. This was opposite to Constantinople, on the other side of the straits, towards Turkey. The palace was one of the most beautiful and delectable that ever eyes could see, with every delight therein that the heart of man could desire, and convenient for the house of a prince.

The counts and barons landed and lodged themselves in the palace; and in the city round about, the main part pitched their tents. Then were the horses taken out of the transports, and the knights and sergeants got to land with all their arms, so that none remained in the ships save the mariners only. The country was fair, and rich, and well supplied with all good things, and the sheaves of corn which had been reaped were in the fields, so that all—and they stood in no small need—might take thereof.

They sojourned thus in that palace the following day; and on the third day God gave them a good wind, and the mariners raised their anchors, and spread their sails to the wind. They went thus up the straits, a good league above Constantinople, to a palace that belonged to the Emperor Alexius, and was called Scutari. There the ships anchored, and the transports, and all the galleys. The horsemen who had lodged in the palace of Chalcedon went along the shore by land.

The host of the French encamped thus on the straits of St. George, at Scutari, and above it. And when the Emperor Alexius saw this, he caused his host to issue from Constantinople, and encamp over against us on the other side of the straits, and there pitched his tents, so that we might not take land against him by force. The host of the French sojourned thus for nine days, and those obtained supplies who needed them, and that was everyone in the host.

27

The foragers defeat the Greeks

DURING this time, a company of good and trustworthy men issued from the camp to guard the host, for fear it should be attacked, and the foragers searched the country. In the said company were Odo the Champenois of Champlitte, and William his brother, and Oger of Saint-Chéron, and Manasses of L'isle, and Count Girard, a count of Lombardy, a retainer of the Marquis of Montferrat; and they had with them at least eighty knights who were good men and true.

And they espied, at the foot of a mountain, some three leagues distant from the host, certain tents belonging to the Grand Duke of the Emperor of Constantinople, who had with him at least five hundred Greek knights. When our people saw them, they formed their men into four battalions, and decided to attack. And when the Greeks saw this, they formed their battalions, and arrayed themselves in rank before their tents, and waited. And our people went forward and fell upon them right vigorously.

By the help of God our Lord, this fight lasted but a little while, and the Greeks turned their backs. They were discomfited at the first onset, and our people pursued them for a full great league. There they won plenty of horses, and stallions, and palfreys, and mules, and tents, and pavilions, and such spoil as is usual in such case. So they returned to the host, where they were right well received, and their spoils were divided, as was fit.

28

Message of the emperor Alexius; reply of the crusaders

THE next day after, the Emperor Alexius sent an envoy with letters to the counts and to the barons. This envoy was called Nicholas Roux, and he was a native of Lombardy. He found the barons in the rich palace of Scutari where they were holding council and he saluted them on the part of the Emperor Alexius of Constantinople, and tendered his letters to the Marquis of Montferrat who received them. And the letters were read before all the barons; and there were in them words, written after various manners, which the book does not here relate, and at the end of the other words so written, came words of credit, accrediting the bearer of the letters, whose name was Nicholas Roux.

"Fair sir," said the barons, "we have seen your letters, and they tell us that we are to give credit to what you say, and we credit you right well. Now speak as it pleases you."

And the envoy was standing before the barons, and spoke thus: "Lords," said he, "the Emperor Alexius would have you know that he is well aware that you are the best people uncrowned, and come from the best land on earth. And he marvels much why, and for what purpose, you have come into his land and kingdom. For you are Christians, and he is a Christian, and well he knows that you are on your way to deliver the Holy Land overseas, and the Holy Cross, and the Sepulchre. If you are poor and in want, he will right willingly give you of his food and substance, provided you depart out of his land. Neither would he otherwise wish to do you any hurt, though he has full power therein, seeing that if you were twenty times as numerous as you are, you would not be able to get away without utter discomfiture if so be that he wished to harm you."

By agreement and desire of the other barons, and of the Doge of Venice, then rose to his feet Conon of Béthune, who was a good knight, and wise, and very eloquent, and he replied to the envoy: "Fair sir, you have told us that your lord marvels much why our signors and barons should have entered into his kingdom and land. Into his land they have not entered, for he holds this land wrongfully and wickedly, and against God and against reason. It belongs to his nephew, who sits upon a throne among us, and is the son of his brother, the Emperor Isaac. But if he is willing to throw himself on the mercy of his nephew, and to give him back his crown and empire, then we will pray his nephew to forgive him, and bestow upon him as much as will enable him to live wealthily. And if you come not as the bearer of such a message, then be not so bold as to come here again." So the envoy departed and went back to Constantinople to the Emperor Alexius.

29

The crusaders show the young Alexius to the people of Constantinople, and prepare for the battle

THE barons consulted together on the morrow, and said that they would show the young Alexius, the son of the Emperor of Constantinople, to the people of the city. So they assembled all the galleys. The Doge of Venice and the Marquis of Montferrat entered into one, and took with them Alexius, the son of the Emperor Isaac; and into the other galleys entered the knights and barons, as many as would.

They went thus quite close to the walls of Constantinople and showed the youth to the people of the Greeks, and said, "Behold your natural lord; and be it known to you that we have not come to do you harm, but have come to guard and defend you, if so be that you return to your duty. For he whom you now obey as your lord holds rule by wrong and wickedness, against God and reason. And you know full well that he has dealt treasonably with him who is your lord and his brother, that he has blinded his eyes and robbed from him his empire by wrong and wickedness. Now behold the rightful heir. If you hold with him, you will be doing as you ought; and if not we will do to you the very worst that we can." But for fear and terror of the Emperor Alexius, not one person on the land or in the city made show as if he held for the prince. So all went back to the host, and each sought his quarters.

On the morrow, when they had heard mass, they assembled in parliament, and the parliament was held on horseback in the midst of the fields. There might you have seen many a fine war-horse, and many a good knight thereon. And the council was held to discuss the order of the battalions, how many they should have, and of what strength. Many were the words said on one side and the other. But in the end it was settled that the advanced guard should be given to Baldwin of Flanders, because he had a very great number of good men, and archers and crossbowmen, more than any other chief that was in the host.

And after, it was settled that Henry his brother, and Matthew of Wallincourt, and Baldwin of Beauvoir, and many other good knights of their land and country, should form the second division.

The third division was formed by Count Hugh of St. Paul, Peter of Amiens his nephew, Eustace of Canteleu, Anseau of Cayeux, and many good knights of their land and country.

The fourth division was formed by Count Louis of Blois and Chartres, and was very numerous and rich and formidable; for he had placed therein a great number of good knights and men of worth.

The fifth division was formed by Matthew of Montmorency and the men of Champagne. Geoffry the Marshal of Champagne formed part of it, and Oger of Saint-Chéron, Manasses of L'isle, Miles the Brabant, Macaire of Sainte-Menehould, John Foisnous, Guy of Chappes, Clerembaud his nephew, Robert of Ronsoi; all these people formed part of the fifth division. Be it known to you that there was many a good knight therein.

The sixth division was formed by the people of Burgundy. In this division were Odo the Champenois of Champlitte, William his brother, Guy of Pesmes, Edmund his brother, Otho of la Roche, Richard of Dampierre, Odo his brother, Guy of Conflans, and the people of their land and country.

The seventh division, which was very large, was under the command of the Marquis of Montferrat. In it were the Lombards and Tuscans and the Germans, and all the people who were from beyond Mont Cenis to Lyons on the Rhone. All these formed part of the division under the marquis, and it was settled that they should form the rearguard.

30

The crusaders seize the port

THE day was fixed on which the host should embark on the ships and transports to take the land by force, and either live or die. And be it known to you that the enterprise to be achieved was one of the most redoubtable ever attempted. Then did the bishops and clergy speak to the people, and tell them how they must confess, and make each one his testament, seeing that no one knew what might be the will of God concerning him. And this was done right willingly throughout the host, and very piously.

The term fixed was now come; and the knights went on board the transports with their war-horses; and they were fully armed, with their helmets laced, and the horses covered with their housings, and saddled. All the other folk, who were of less consequence in battle, were on the great ships; and the galleys were fully armed and made ready.

The morning was fair a little after the rising of the sun; and the Emperor Alexius stood waiting for them on the other side, with great forces, and everything in order. The trumpets sounded, and every galley took a transport in tow, so as to reach the other side more readily. None asked who shall go first, but each made the land as soon as he could. The knights issued from the transports, and leapt into the sea up to their waists, fully armed, with helmets laced, and lances in hand; and the good archers, and the good sergeants, and the good crossbowmen, each in his company, landed as soon as they touched ground.

The Greeks made a goodly show of resistance; but when it came to the lowering of the lances, they turned their backs, and went away flying, and abandoned the shore. And be it known to you that never was port more proudly taken. Then began the mariners to open the ports of the transports, and let down the bridges, and take out the horses; and the knights began to mount, and they began to marshal the divisions of the host in due order.

31

Capture of the tower of Galata

COUNT Baldwin of Flanders and Hainault, with the advanced guard, rode forward, and the other divisions of the host after him, each in due order of march; and they came to where the Emperor Alexius had been encamped. But he had turned back towards Constantinople, and left his tents and pavilions standing. And there our people had much spoil.

Our barons were minded to encamp by the port before the tower of Galata, where the chain was fixed that closed the port of Constantinople. And be it known to you, that anyone must perforce pass that chain before he could enter into the port. Well did our barons then perceive that if they did not take the tower, and break the chain, they were but as dead men, and in very evil case. So they lodged that night before the tower, and in the Jewry[7] that is called Stenon, where there was a good city, and very rich.

Well did they keep guard during the night; and on the morrow, at the hour of Terce[8], those who were in the tower of Galata made a sortie, and those who were in Constantinople came to their help in barges; and our people ran to arms. There came first to the onset James of Avesnes and his men on foot; and be it known to you that he was fiercely charged, and wounded by a lance in the face, and in peril of death. And one of his knights, whose name was Nicholas of Jenlain, got to horse, and came to his lord's rescue, and succoured him right well, and so won great honour.

---

7 The quarter of the Jews

8 The third hour

Then a cry was raised in the host, and our people ran together from all sides, and drove back the foe with great fury, so that many were slain and taken. And some of them did not go back to the tower, but ran to the barges by which they had come, and there many were drowned, and some escaped.

As to those who went back to the tower, the men of our host pressed them so hard that they could not shut the gate. Then a terrible fight began again at the gate, and our people took it by force, and made prisoners of all those in the tower. Many were there killed and taken.

32

Attack on the city by land and sea

SO was the tower of Galata taken, and the port of Constantinople won by force. Much were those of the host comforted thereby, and much did they praise the Lord God; and greatly were those of the city discomforted. And on the next day, the ships, the vessels, the galleys, and the transports were drawn into the port.

Then did those of the host take council together to settle what thing they should do, and whether they should attack the city by sea or by land. The Venetians were firmly minded that the scaling ladders ought to be planted on the ships, and all the attack made from the side by the sea. The French, on the other hand, said that they did not know so well how to help themselves on sea as on land, but that when they had their horses and their arms they could help themselves on land right well. So in the end it was devised that the Venetians should attack by sea, and the barons and those of the host by land.

They sojourned thus for four days. On the fifth day, the whole host were armed, and the divisions advanced on horseback, each in the order appointed, along the harbour, till they came to the palace of Blachernae; and the ships drew inside the harbour till they came over against the self-same place, and this was near to the end of the harbour. And there is at that place a river that flows into the sea, and can only be passed by a bridge of stone. The Greeks had broken down the bridge, and the barons caused the host to labour all that day and all that night in repairing the bridge. Thus was the bridge repaired, and in the morning the divisions were armed, and rode one after the other in the order appointed, and came before the city. And no one came out from the city against them; and this was a great marvel, seeing that for every man that was in the host there were over two hundred men in the city.

Then did the barons decide that they should quarter themselves between the palace of Blachernae and the castle of Boemond, which was an abbey enclosed with walls. So the tents and pavilions were pitched—which was a right proud thing to look upon; for of Constantinople, which had three leagues of front towards the land, the whole host could attack no more than one of the gates. And the Venetians lay on the sea, in ships and vessels, and raised their ladders, and mangonels, and petraries, and made order for their assault right well. And the barons for their part made ready their petraries and mangonels on land.

And be it known to you that they did not have their time in peace and quiet; for there passed no hour of the night or day but one of the divisions had to stand armed before the gate, to guard the engines, and provide against attack. And, notwithstanding all this, the Greeks ceased not to attack them, by this gate and by others, and held them so short that six or seven times a day the whole host was forced to run to arms. Nor could they forage for provisions more than four bow-shots' distance from the camp. And their stores were but scanty, save of flour and bacon, and of those they had a little; and of fresh meat none at all, save what they got from the horses that were killed. And be it known to you that there was only food generally in the host for three weeks. Thus were they in very perilous case, for never did so few people besiege so many people in any city.

33

First incidents of the assault

THEN did they bethink themselves of a very good device; for they enclosed the whole camp with good lists, and good palisades, and good barriers, and were thus far stronger and much more secure. The Greeks meanwhile came on to the attack so frequently that they gave them no rest, and those of the host drove them back with great force; and every time that the Greeks issued forth they lost heavily.

One day the Burgundians were on guard, and the Greeks made an attack upon them, with part of the best forces that they had. And the Burgundians ran upon the Greeks and drove them in very fiercely, and followed so close to the gate that stones of great weight were hurled upon them. There was taken one of the best Greeks of the city, whose name was Constantine Lascaris; William of Neuilly took him all mounted upon his horse. And there did William of Champlitte have his arm broken with a stone, and great pity it was, for he was very brave and very valiant.

I cannot tell you of all the good strokes that were there stricken, nor of all the wounded, nor all the dead. But before the fight was over, there came into it a knight of the following of Henry, the brother of Count Baldwin of Flanders and Hainault, and his name was Eustace of Marchais; and he was armed only in padded vest and steel cap, with his shield at his neck; and he did so well in the fray that he won to himself great honour. Few were the days on which no sorties were made; but I cannot tell you of them all. So hardly did they hold us, that we could not sleep, nor rest, nor eat, save in arms.

Yet another sortie was made from a gate further up; and there again did the Greeks lose heavily. And there a knight was slain whose name was William of Gi; and there Matthew of Wallincourt did right well, and lost his horse, which was killed at the drawbridge of the gate; and many others who were in that fight did right well.

From this gate, which was beyond the palace of Blachernae, the Greeks issued most frequently, and there Peter of Bracieux got himself more honour than any, because he was quartered the nearest, and so came most often into the fray.

34

Assault of the city

THUS their peril and toil lasted for nearly ten days, until, on a Thursday morning (17th July 1203) all things were ready for the assault, and the ladders in trim; the Venetians also had made them ready by sea. The order of the assault was so devised, that of the seven divisions, three were to guard the camp outside the city, and other four to give the assault. The Marquis Boniface of Montferrat guarded the camp towards the fields with the division of the Burgundians, the division of the men of Champagne, and Matthew of Montmorency. Count Baldwin of Flanders and Hainault went to the assault with his people, and Henry his brother; and Count Louis of Blois and Chartres, and Count Hugh of St. Paul, and those who held with them went also to the assault.

They planted two ladders at a barbican near the sea; and the wall was well defended by Englishmen and Danes; and the attack was stiff and good and fierce. By main strength certain knights and two sergeants got up the ladders and made themselves masters of the wall; and at least fifteen got upon the wall, and fought there, hand to hand, with axes and swords, and those within redoubled their efforts and cast them out in very ugly sort, keeping two as prisoners. And those of our people who had been taken were led before the Emperor Alexius; much was he pleased thereat. Thus did the assault leave matters on the side of the French. Many were wounded and many had their bones broken, so that the barons were very wroth.

Meanwhile the Doge of Venice had not forgotten to do his part, but had ranged his ships and transports and vessels in line, and that line was well three crossbow-shots in length; and the Venetians began to draw near to the part of the shore that lay under the walls and the towers. Then might you have seen the mangonels shooting from the ships and transports, and the crossbow bolts flying, and the bows letting fly their arrows deftly and well; and those within defending the walls and towers very fiercely; and the ladders on the ships coming so near that in many places swords and lances crossed; and the tumult and noise were so great that it seemed as if the very earth and sea were melting together. And be it known to you that the galleys did not dare to come to the shore.

35

Capture of twenty-five towers

NOW may you hear of a strange deed of prowess; for the Doge of Venice, who was an old man, and saw naught, stood, fully armed, on the prow of his galley, and had the standard of St. Mark before him; and he cried to his people to put him on land, or else that he would do justice upon their bodies with his hands. And so they did, for the galley was run aground, and they leapt therefrom, and bore the standard of St. Mark before him on to the land.

And when the Venetians saw the standard of St. Mark on land, and the galley of their lord touching ground before them, each held himself for shamed, and they all got to the land; and those in the transports leapt forth, and landed; and those in the big ships got into barges, and made for the shore, each and all as best they could. Then might you have seen an assault, great and marvelous; and to this bears witness Geoffry of Villehardouin, who makes this book, that more than forty people told him forsooth that they saw the standard of St. Mark of Venice at the top of one of the towers, and that no man knew who bore it thither. At which miraculous sight, those who were within the city fled and abandoned the walls, and the Venetians entered in, each as fast and as best he could, and seized twenty-five of the towers, and manned them with their people. And the Doge took a boat, and sent messengers to the barons of the host to tell them that he had taken twenty-five towers, and that they would know forsooth that such towers could not be retaken. The barons were so overjoyed that they could not believe their ears; and the Venetians began to send to the host in boats the horses and palfreys they had taken.

When the Emperor Alexius saw that his foes had thus entered into the city, he sent his people against them in such numbers that our people saw they would be unable to endure the onset. So they set fire to the buildings between them and the Greeks; and the wind blew from our side, and the fire began to wax so great that the Greeks could not see our people who retired to the towers they had seized and conquered.

36

The emperor Alexius comes out for battle, but retires without attacking

THEN the Emperor Alexius issued from the city, with all his forces, by other gates which were at least a league from the camp; and so many began to issue forth that it seemed as if the whole world were there assembled. The emperor marshaled his troops in the plain, and they rode towards the camp; and when our Frenchmen saw them coming, they ran to arms from all sides. On that day Henry, the brother of Count Baldwin of Flanders, was mounting guard over the engines of war before the gate of Blachernae, together with Matthew of Wallincourt, and Baldwin of Beauvoir, and their followers. Against their encampment the Emperor Alexius had made ready a great number of his people, who were to issue by three gates, while he himself should fall upon the host from another side.

Then the six divisions issued from our camp as had been devised, and were marshaled in ranks before the palisades: the sergeants and squires on foot behind the horses, and the archers and crossbowmen in front. And there was a division of the knights on foot, for we had at least two hundred who were without horses. Thus they stood still before the palisades. And this showed great good sense, for if they had moved to the attack, the numbers of the enemy were such that they must have been overwhelmed and (as it were) drowned among them.

It seemed as if the whole plain was covered with troops, and they advanced slowly and in order. Well might we appear in perilous case, for we had but six divisions, while the Greeks had full forty, and there was not one of their divisions but was larger than any of ours. But ours were ordered in such sort that none could attack them save in front. And the Emperor Alexius rode so far forward that either side could shoot at the other. And when the Doge of Venice heard this, he made his people come forth, and leave the towers they had taken, and said he would live or die with the pilgrims. So he came to the camp, and was himself the first to land, and brought with him such of his people as he could.

Thus, for a long space, the armies of the pilgrims and of the Greeks stood one against the other; for the Greeks did not dare to throw themselves upon our ranks, and our people would not move from their palisades. And when the Emperor Alexius saw this, he began to withdraw his people, and when he had rallied them, he turned back. And seeing this, the host of the pilgrims began to march towards him with slow steps, and the Greek troops began to move backwards, and retreated to a palace called Philopas.

And be it known to you, that never did God save any people from such peril as He saved the host that day; and be it known to you further that there was none in the host so hardy but he had great joy thereof. Thus did the battle remain for that day. As it pleased God nothing further was done. The Emperor Alexius returned to the city, and those of the host to their quarters-the latter taking off their armour, for they were weary and overwrought; and they ate and drank little, seeing that their store of food was but scanty.

37

Alexius abandons Constantinople; his brother Isaac is replaced on the throne; the crusaders send him a message

NOW listen to the miracles of our Lord—how gracious are they whithersoever it pleases Him to perform them! That very night the Emperor Alexius of Constantinople took of his treasure as much as he could carry, and took with him as many of his people as would go, and so fled and abandoned the city. And those of the city who remained were dismayed, and they repaired to the prison in which lay the Emperor Isaac, whose eyes had been put out. Him they clothed imperially, and bore to the great palace of Blachernae, and seated on a high throne; and there they did to him obeisance as their lord. Then they took messengers, by the advice of the Emperor Isaac, and sent them to the host, to apprise the son of the Emperor Isaac, and the barons, that the Emperor Alexius had fled, and that they had again raised up the Emperor Isaac as emperor.

When the young man knew of this he summoned the Marquis Boniface of Montferrat, and the marquis summoned the barons throughout the host. And when they were met in the pavilion of the Emperor Isaac's son, he told them the news. And when they heard it, their joy was such as cannot be uttered, for never was greater joy in all this world. And greatly and most devoutly was our Lord praised by all, in that He had succoured them within so short a term, and exalted them so high from such a low estate. And therefore well may one say: "Him whom God will help can no man injure."

Then the day began to dawn, and the host to put on their armour; and all got them to their arms throughout the host, because they did not greatly trust the Greeks. And messengers began to come out from the city, two or three together, and told the same tale. The barons, and counts, and the Doge of Venice had agreed to send envoys into the city, to know how matters really stood; and, if that was true which had been reported, to demand of the father that he should ratify the covenants made by the son; and, if he would not, to declare that they on their part should not suffer the son to enter into the city. So envoys were chosen: one was Matthew of Montmorency, and Geoffry the Marshal of Champagne was the other, and two Venetians on the part of the Doge of Venice.

The envoys were conducted to the gate, and the gate was opened to them, and they dismounted from their horses. The Greeks had set Englishmen and Danes, with their axes, at the gate and right up to the palace of Blachernae. Thus were the envoys conducted to the great palace. There they found the Emperor Isaac, so richly clad that you would seek in vain throughout the world for a man more richly appareled than he, and by his side the empress, his wife, a most fair lady, the sister of the King of Hungary; and of great men and great ladies there were so many, that you could not stir foot for the press, and the ladies were so richly adorned that richer adornment might not be found. And all those who, the day before, had been against the emperor were, on that day, subject in everything to his good pleasure.

38

The emperor Isaac ratifies the covenants entered into by his son

THE envoys came before the Emperor Isaac, and the emperor and all those about him did them great honour. And the envoys said that they desired to speak to him privily, on the part of his son, and of the barons of the host. And he rose and entered into a chamber, and took with him only the empress, and his chancellor, and his dragoman[9] and the four envoys. By consent of the other envoys, Geoffry of Villehardouin, the Marshal of Champagne, acted as spokesman, and he said to the Emperor Isaac: "Sire, thou seest the service we have rendered to thy son, and how we have kept our covenants with him. But he cannot come hither till he has given us surety for the covenants he has made with us. And he asks of thee, as thy son, to confirm those covenants in the same form, and the

---

9 Interpreter

same manner, that he has done." "What covenants are they?" said the emperor. "They are such as we shall tell you," replied the envoys. "In the first place to put the whole empire of Romania in obedience to Rome, from which it has been separated this long while; further to give 200,000 marks of silver to those of the host, with food for one year for small and great; to send 10,000 men, horse and foot—many on foot as we shall devise and as many mounted—in his own ships, and at his own charges, to the land of Babylon, and keep them there for a year; and during his lifetime to keep, at his own charges, five hundred knights in the land overseas so that they may guard that land. Such is the covenant that your son made with us, and it was confirmed by oath, and charters with seals appended, and by King Philip of Germany who has your daughter to wife. This covenant we desire you to confirm."

"Certes" said the emperor, "this covenant is very onerous, and I do not see how effect can be given to it; nevertheless, you have done us such service, both to my son and to myself, that if we bestowed upon you the whole empire, you would have deserved it well." Many words were then spoken in this sense and that, but in the end the father confirmed the covenants, as his son had confirmed them, by oath and by charters with gold seals appended. These charters were delivered to the envoys. Then they took their leave of the Emperor Isaac, and went back to the host, and told the barons that they had fulfilled their mission.

39

Entry of the crusaders into Constantinople; coronation of the young Alexius

THEN did the barons mount their horses, and lead the young man, with great rejoicings, into the city to his father; and the Greeks opened the gate to him, and received him with very much rejoicing and great feasting. The joy of the father and of the son was very great, because of a long time they had not seen one another, and because, by God's help and that of the pilgrims, they had passed from so great poverty and ruin to such high estate. Therefore the joy was great inside Constantinople; and also without, among the host of the pilgrims, because of the honour and victory that God had given them.

And on the morrow the emperor and his son also besought the counts and the barons, for God's sake, to go and quarter themselves on the other side of the straits, toward Estanor and Galata; for if they quartered themselves in the city, it was to be feared that quarrels would ensue between them and the Greeks, and it might well chance that the city would be destroyed. And the counts and barons said that they had already served him in so many ways that they would not now refuse any request of his. So they went and quartered themselves on the other side, and sojourned there in peace and quiet, and with great store of good provisions.

Now you must know that many of those in the host went to see Constantinople, and the rich palaces and great churches of which there were many, and all the great wealth of the city—for never was there city that possessed so much. Of relics it does not behoove me to speak, for at that day there were as many there as in all the rest of the world. Thus did the Greeks and French live in good fellowship in all things, both as regards trafficking and other matters.

By common consent of Franks and Greeks it was settled that the new emperor should be crowned on the feast of my lord St. Peter (1st August 1203). So was it settled, and so it was done. He was crowned full worthily and with honour according to the use for Greek emperors at that time. Afterwards he began to pay the moneys due to the host; and such moneys were divided among the host, and each repaid what had been advanced in Venice for his passage.

40

Alexius begs the crusaders to prolong their stay

THE new emperor went oft to see the barons in the camp, and did them great honour, as much as he could; and this was but fitting, seeing that they had served him right well. And one day he came to the camp, to see the barons privily in the quarters of Count Baldwin of Hainault and Flanders. Thither were summoned the Doge of Venice, and the great barons, and he spoke to them and said: "Lords, I am emperor by God's grace and yours, and you have done me the highest service that ever yet was done by any people to Christian man. Now be it known to you that there are folk enough who show me a fair seeming, and yet love me not; and the Greeks are full of despite because it is by your help that I have entered into my inheritance.

Now the term of your departure is nigh, and your fellowship with the Venetians is timed only to last till the feast of St. Michael. And within so short a term I cannot fulfill our covenant. Be it known to you therefore, that, if you abandon me, the Greeks hate me because of you: I shall lose my land, and they will kill me. But now do this thing that I ask of you: remain here till March, and I will entertain your ships for one year from the feast of St. Michael, and bear the cost of the Venetians, and will give you such things as you may stand in need of till Easter. And within that term I shall have placed my land in such case that I cannot lose it again; and your covenant will be fulfilled, for I shall have paid such moneys as are due to you, obtaining them from all my lands; and I shall be ready also with ships either to go with you myself, or to send others, as I have covenanted; and you will have the summer from end to end in which to carry on the war against the Saracens."

The barons thereupon said they would consult together apart; knowing full well that what the young man said was sooth, and that it would be better, both for the emperor and for themselves, to consent unto him. But they replied that they could not so consent save with the common agreement of the host, and that they would therefore lay the matter before the host, and then give such answer as might be devised. So the Emperor Alexius departed from them, and went back to Constantinople. And they remained in the camp and assembled a parliament the next day. To this parliament were summoned all the barons and the chieftains of the host, and of the knights the greater part; and in their hearing were repeated all the words that the emperor had spoken.

41

Debate among the crusaders; death of Matthew of Montmorency

THEN was there much discord in the host, as had been oft times before on the part of those who wished that the host should break up; for to them it seemed to be holding together too long. And the party that had raised the discord at Corfu reminded the others of their oaths, and said: "Give us ships as you swore to us, for we purpose to go to Syria."

And the others cried to them for pity and said: "Lords, for God's sake, let us not bring to naught the great honour that God has given us. If we go to Syria at this present, we shall come thither at the beginning of winter and so not be able to make war, and the Lord's work will thus remain undone. But if we wait till March, we shall leave this emperor in good estate, and go hence rich in goods and in food. Thus shall we go to Syria, and over-run the land of Babylon. And the fleet will remain with us till Michaelmas, yes, and onwards from Michaelmas to Easter, seeing it will be unable to leave us because of the winter. So shall the land overseas fall into our hands."

Those who wished the host to be broken up, cared not for reasons good or bad so long as the host fell to pieces. But those who wished to keep the host together, wrought so effectually, with the help of God, that in the end the Venetians made a new covenant to maintain the fleet for a year, reckoning from Michaelmas, the Emperor Alexius paying them for so doing; and the pilgrims, on their side, made a new covenant to remain in the same fellowship as theretofore, and for the same term. Thus were peace and concord established in the host.

Then there befell a very great mischance in the host; for Matthew of Montmorency, who was one of the best knights in the kingdom of France, and of the most prized and most honoured, took to his bed for sickness, and his sickness so increased upon him that he died. And much dole was made for him, for great was the loss-one of the greatest that had befallen the host by any man's death. He was buried in a church of my lord St. John, of the Hospital of Jerusalem.

42

Progress of the young Alexius through the empire

AFTERWARDS, by the advice of the Greeks and the French, the Emperor Alexius issued from Constantinople with a very great company, purposing to quiet the empire and subject it to his will. With him went a great part of the barons; and the others remained to guard the camp. The Marquis Boniface of Montferrat went with him, and Count Hugh of St. Paul, and Henry, brother to Count Baldwin of Flanders and Hainault, and James of Avesnes, and William of Champlitte, and Hugh of Colerni, and many others whom the book does not here mention by name. In the camp remained Count Baldwin of Flanders and Hainault, and Count Louis of Blois and Chartres, and the greater part of the pilgrims of lesser note.

And you must know that during this progress all the Greeks on either side of the straits came to the Emperor Alexius to do his will and commandment, and did him fealty and homage as to their lord—all except John, who was King of Wallachia and Bulgaria. This John was a Wallachian, who had rebelled against his father and uncle, and had warred against them for twenty years, and had won from them so much land that he had become a very wealthy king. And be it known to you, that of the land lying on the west side of the Straits of St. George, he had conquered very nearly the half. This John did not come to do the will of the emperor, nor to submit himself to him.

43

Conflict between the Greeks and Latins in Constantinople; burning of the city

WHILE the Emperor Alexius was away on this progress, there befell a very grievous misadventure; for a conflict arose between the Greeks and the Latins who inhabited Constantinople, and of these last there were many. And certain people—who they were I know not—out of malice, set fire to the city; and the fire waxed so great and horrible that no man could put it out or abate it. And when the barons of the host, who were quartered on the other side of the port, saw this, they were sore grieved and filled with pity—seeing the great churches and the rich palaces melting and falling in, and the great streets filled with merchandise burning in the flames; but they could do nothing.

Thus did the fire prevail, and win across the port even to the densest part of the city, and to the sea on the other side quite near to the church of St. Sophia. It lasted two days and two nights, nor could it be put out by the hand of man. And the front of the fire, as it went flaming, was well over half a league broad. What was the damage then done, what the possessions and riches swallowed up, could no man tell, nor what the number of men and women and children who perished for many were burned.

All the Latins, to whatever land they might belong, who were lodged in Constantinople, dared no longer to remain therein; but they took their wives and their children, and such of their possessions as they could save from the fire, and entered into boats and vessels, and passed over the port and came to the camp of the pilgrims. Nor were they few in number, for there were of them some fifteen thousand, small and great; and afterwards it proved to be of advantage to the pilgrims that these should have crossed over to them. Thus was there division between the Greeks and the Franks; nor were they ever again as much at one as they had been before, for neither side knew on whom to cast the blame for the fire; and this rankled in men's hearts upon either side.

At that time did a thing befall whereby the barons and those of the host were greatly saddened; for the Abbot of Loos died, who was a holy man and a worthy, and had wished well to the host. He was a monk of the order of the Cistercians.

44

The young Alexius returns to Constantinople; he fails in his promises to the crusaders

THE Emperor Alexius remained for a long time on progress till St. Martin's Day, and then he returned to Constantinople. Great was the joy at his home-coming, and the Greeks and ladies of Constantinople went out to meet their friends in great cavalcades, and the pilgrims went out to meet their friends, and had great joy of them. So did the emperor re-enter Constantinople and the palace of Blachernae; and the Marquis of Montferrat and the other barons returned to the camp.

The emperor, who had managed his affairs right well and thought he had now the upper hand, was filled with arrogance towards the barons and those who had done so much for him, and never came to see them in the camp, as he had done aforetime. And they sent to him and begged him to pay them the moneys due, as he had covenanted. But he led them on from delay to delay, making them, at one time and another, payments small and poor; and in the end the payments ceased and came to naught.

The Marquis Boniface of Montferrat, who had done more for him than any other, and stood better in his regard, went to him oftentimes and showed him what great services the Crusaders had rendered him, and that greater services had never been rendered to any one. And the emperor still entertained them with delays, and never carried out such things as he had promised, so that at last they saw and knew clearly that his intent was wholly evil.

Then the barons of the host held a parliament with the Doge of

Venice, and they said that they now knew that the emperor would fulfill no covenant, nor ever speak sooth to them; and they decided to send good envoys to demand the fulfillment of their covenant, and to show what services they had done him; and if he would now do what was required, they were to be satisfied; but, if not, they were to defy him, and right well might he rest assured that the barons would by all means recover their due.

45

The crusaders defy the emperors

FOR this embassy were chosen Conon of Béthune and Geoffry of Villehardouin, the Marshal of Champagne, and Miles the Brabant of Provins; and the Doge also sent three chief men of his council. So these envoys mounted their horses, and, with swords girt, rode together till they came to the palace of Blachernae. And be it known to you that by reason of the treachery of the Greeks, they went in great peril, and on a hard adventure.

They dismounted at the gate and entered the palace, and found the Emperor Alexius and the Emperor Isaac seated on two thrones, side by side. And near them was seated the empress, who was the wife of the father, and stepmother of the son, and sister to the King of Hungary—a lady both fair and good. And there were with them a great company of people of note and rank, so that well did the court seem the court of a rich and mighty prince.

By desire of the other envoys Conon of Béthune, who was very wise and eloquent of speech, acted as spokesman: "Sire, we have come to thee on the part of the barons of the host and of the Doge of Venice. They would put thee in mind of the great service they have done to thee—a service known to the people and manifest to all men. Thou hast sworn, thou and thy father, to fulfill the promised covenants, and they have your charters in hand. But you have not fulfilled those covenants well, as you should have done. Many times have they called upon you to do so, and now again we call upon you, in the presence of all your barons, to fulfill the covenants that are between you and them. Should you do so, it shall be well. If not, be it known to you that from this day forth they will not hold you as lord or friend, but will endeavour to obtain their due by all the means in their power. And of this they now give you warning, seeing that they would not injure you, nor any one, without first defiance given; for never have they acted treacherously, nor in their land is it customary to do so. You have heard what we have said. It is for you to take counsel thereon according to your pleasure."

Much were the Greeks amazed and greatly outraged by this open defiance; and they said that never had any one been so hardy as to dare defy the Emperor of Constantinople in his own hall. Very evil were the looks now cast on the envoys by the Emperor Alexius and by all the Greeks, who aforetime were wont to regard them very favourably.

Great was the tumult there within, and the envoys turned about and came to the gate and mounted their horses. When they got outside the gate, there was not one of them but felt glad at heart; nor is that to be marveled at, for they had escaped from very great peril, and it was a mercy that they were not all killed or taken. So they returned to the camp, and told the barons how they had fared.

46

The war begins; the Greeks endeavour to set fire to the fleet of the crusaders

THUS did the war begin; and each side did to the other as much harm as they could, by sea and by land. The Franks and the Greeks fought often; but never did they fight, let God be praised therefore, that the Greeks did not lose more than the Franks. So the war lasted a long space, till the heart of the winter.

Then the Greeks bethought themselves of a very great device, for they took seven large ships, and filled them full of big logs, and shavings, and tow, and resin, and barrels, and then waited until such time as the wind should blow strongly from their side of the straits. And one night, at midnight, they set fire to the ships, and unfurled their sails to the wind. And the flames blazed up high, so that it seemed as if the whole world were a-fire. Thus did the burning ships come towards the fleet of the pilgrims; and a great cry arose in the host, and all sprang to arms on every side. The Venetians ran to their ships, and so did all those who had ships in possession, and they began to draw them away out of the flames very vigorously.

And to this bears witness Geoffry the Marshal of Champagne, who dictates this work, that never did people help themselves better at sea than the Venetians did that night; for they sprang into the galleys and boats belonging to the ships, and seized upon the fire ships, all burning as they were, with hooks, and dragged them by main force before their enemies, outside the port, and set them into the current of the straits, and left them to go burning down the straits. So many of the Greeks had come down to the shore that they were without end and innumerable, and their cries were so great that it seemed as if the earth and sea would melt together. They got into barges and boats, and shot at those on our side who were battling with the flames, so that some were wounded.

All the knights of the host, as soon as they heard the clamour, armed themselves; and the battalions marched out into the plain, each according to the order in which they had been quartered, for they feared lest the Greeks should also attack them on land.

They endured thus in labour and anguish till daylight; but by God's help those on our side lost nothing, save a Pisan ship which was full of merchandise, and was burned with fire. Deadly was the peril in which we stood that night, for if the fleet had been consumed, all would have been lost, and we should never have been able to get away by land or sea. Such was the guerdon[10] which the Emperor Alexius would have bestowed upon us in return for our services.

---

10 Reward or recompense

47

Mourzuphles usurps the empire; Isaac dies, and the young Alexius is strangled

THEN the Greeks, being thus embroiled with the Franks, saw that there was no hope of peace; so they privily took counsel together to betray their lord. Now there was a Greek who stood higher in his favour than all others, and had done more to make him embroil himself with the Franks than any other. This Greek was named Mourzuphles.

With the advice and consent of the others, one night towards midnight, when the Emperor Alexius was asleep in his chamber, those who ought to have been guarding him, and specially Mourzuphles, took him in his bed and threw him into a dungeon in prison. Then Mourzuphles assumed the scarlet buskins with the help and by the counsel of the other Greeks (January 1204). So he made himself emperor. Afterwards they crowned him at St. Sophia. Now see if ever people were guilty of such horrible treachery!

When the Emperor Isaac heard that his son was taken and Mourzuphles crowned, great fear came upon him, and he fell into a sickness that lasted no long time. So he died. And the Emperor Mourzuphles caused the son, whom he had in prison, to be poisoned two or three times; but it did not please God that he should thus die. Afterwards the emperor went and strangled him, and when he had strangled him, he caused it to be reported everywhere that he had died a natural death, and had him mourned for, and buried honourably and as an emperor, and made great show of grief.

But murder cannot be hid. Soon was it clearly known, both to the Greeks and to the French, that this murder had been committed, as has just been told to you. Then did the barons of the host and the Doge of Venice assemble in parliament, and with them met the bishops and the clergy. And all the clergy, including those who had powers from the Pope, showed to the barons and to the pilgrims that any one guilty of such a murder had no right to hold lands, and that those who consented thereto were abettors of the murder; and beyond all this, that the Greeks had withdrawn themselves from obedience to Rome. "Wherefore we tell you," said the clergy, "that this war is lawful and just, and that if you have a right intention in conquering this land, to bring it into the Roman obedience, all those who die after confession shall have part in the indulgence granted by the Pope." And you must know that by this the barons and pilgrims were greatly comforted.

48

The crusaders continue the war; defeat of Mourzuphles

DIRE was the war between the Franks and the Greeks, for it abated not, but rather increased and waxed fiercer, so that few were the days on which there was not fighting by sea or land. Then Henry, the brother of Count Baldwin of Flanders, rode forth, and took with him a great part of the good men in the host. With him went James of Avesnes, and Baldwin of Beauvoir, Odo the Champenois of Champlitte, William his brother, and the people of their country. They started at vesper time and rode all night, and on the morrow, when it was full day, they came to a good city called Phile, and took it; and they had great gain of beasts, and prisoners, and clothing, and food which they sent in boats down the straits to the camp, for the city lies on the sea of Russia.

So they sojourned two days in that city with food in great plenty, enough and to spare. The third day they departed with the beasts and the booty, and rode back towards the camp. Now the Emperor Mourzuphles heard tell how they had issued from the camp, and he left Constantinople by night with a great part of his people, and set himself in ambush at a place by which they must needs pass. And he watched them pass with their beasts and their booty, each division, the one after the other, till it came to the rear-guard. The rear-guard was under the command of Henry, the brother of Count Baldwin of Flanders, and formed of his people, and the Emperor Mourzuphles fell upon them at the entrance to a wood; whereupon they turned against him. Very fiercely did the battle rage there.

By God's help the Emperor Mourzuphles was discomfited, and came near to being taken captive; and he lost his imperial banner and holy standard that was borne before him, in which he and the other Greeks had great confidence—it was a standard that figured our Lady—and he lost at least twenty knights of the best people that he had. Thus was discomfited the Emperor Mourzuphles, as you have just heard, and fiercely did the war rage between him and the Franks; and by this time a great part of the winter had already passed, and it was near Candlemas (2nd February 1204), and Lent was approaching.

49

Of the pilgrims who had gone to Syria

NOW we will leave off speaking of the host before Constantinople, and speak of those who sailed from other ports than Venice, and of the ships of Flanders that had sojourned during the winter at Marseilles, and had all gone over in the summer to the land of Syria; and these were far more in number than the host before Constantinople. Listen now, and you shall hear what a great mischance it was that they had not joined themselves to the host, for in that case would Christendom have been forever exalted. But because of their sins, God would not so have it, for some died of the sickness of the land, and some turned back to their own homes. Nor did they perform any great deeds, or achieve aught of good, in the land overseas.

And there started also a company of very good men to go to Antioch, to join Boemond, prince of Antioch and Count of Tripoli, who was at war with King Leon, the Lord of the Armenians. This company was going to the prince to be in his pay; and the Turks of the land knew of it, and made an ambush there where the men of the company needs must pass. And they came thither, and fought, and the Franks were discomfited, so that not one escaped that was not killed or taken.

There were slain Villain of Neuilly, who was one of the best knights in the world, and Giles of Trasegnies, and many others; and were taken Bernard of Moreuil, and Renaud of Dampierre, and John of Villers, and William of Neuilly. And you must know that eighty knights were in this company, and every one was either killed or taken. And well does this book bear witness, that of those who avoided the host of Venice, there was not one but suffered harm or shame. He therefore must be accounted wise who holds to the better course.

50

Agreement between the Franks and Venetians before attacking Constantinople

NOW let us leave speaking of those who avoided the host, and speak of those before Constantinople. Well had these prepared all their engines, and mounted their petraries and mangonels on the ships and on the transports, and got ready all such engines of war as are needful for the taking of a city, and raised ladders from the yards and masts of the vessels, so high that they were a marvel to behold. And when the Greeks saw this, they began, on their side, to strengthen the defences of the city which was enclosed with high walls and high towers. Nor was any tower so high that they did not raise thereon two or three stages of wood to heighten it still more. Never was city so well fortified.

Thus did the Greeks and the Franks bestir themselves on the one side and the other during the greater part of Lent.

Then those of the host spoke together, and took counsel what they should do. Much was advanced this way and that, but in the end, they devised that if God granted them entry into the city by force, all the booty taken was to be brought together, and fittingly distributed; and further, if the city fell into their power, six men should be taken from among the Franks, and six from among the Venetians, and these twelve should swear on holy relics to elect as emperor the man who, as they deemed, would rule with most profit to the land. And whosoever was thus elected emperor would have one quarter of whatever was captured, whether within the city or without, and moreover would possess the palace of Bucoleon and that of Blachernae; and the remaining three parts would be divided into two, and one of the halves awarded to the Venetians and the other to those of the host.

And there should be taken twelve of the wisest and most experienced men among the host of the pilgrims, and twelve among the Venetians, and those twenty-four would divide fiefs and honours, and appoint the service to be done therefore to the emperor.

This covenant was made sure and sworn to on the one side and the other by the Franks and the Venetians; with provision that at the end of March, a year thence, any who so desired might depart hence and go their way, but that those who remained in the land would be held to the service of the emperor in such manner as might be ordained. Thus was the covenant devised and made sure; and such as should not observe it were excommunicated by the clergy.

51

Attack of the crusaders repulsed; they make ready for another assault

THE fleet was very well prepared and armed, and provisions were got together for the pilgrims. On the Thursday after mid-Lent (8th April 1204), all entered into the vessels, and put their horses into the transports. Each division had its own ships, and all were ranged side by side; and the ships were separated from the galleys and transports. A marvelous sight it was to see; and well does this book bear witness that the attack, as it had been devised, extended over full half a French league.

On the Friday morning the ships and the galleys and the other vessels drew near to the city in due order, and then began an assault most fell and fierce. In many places the pilgrims landed and went up to the walls, and in many places the scaling ladders on the ships approached so close, that those on the towers and on the walls and those on the ladders crossed lances, hand to hand. Thus lasted the assault, in more than a hundred places, very fierce, and very dour, and very proud, till near upon the hour of Nones.[11]

But, for our sins, the pilgrims were repulsed in that assault, and those who had landed from the galleys and transports were driven back into them by main force. And you must know that on that day those of the host lost more than the Greeks, and much were the Greeks rejoiced thereat. And some there were who drew back from the assault, with the ships in which they were. And some remained with their ships at anchor so near to the city that from either side they shot at one another with petraries and mangonels.

Then, at vespers, those of the host and the Doge of Venice called together a parliament, and assembled in a church on the other side of the straits—on the side where they had been quartered. There were many opinions given and discussed; and much were those of the host moved for the mischief that had that day befallen them. And many advised that they should attack the city on another side—the side where it was not so well fortified. But the Venetians, who had fuller knowledge of the sea, said that if they went to that other side, the current would carry them down the straits, and that they would be unable to stop their ships. And you must know that there were those who would have been well pleased if the current had borne them down the straits, or the wind, they cared not whither, so long as they left that land behind, and went on their way. Nor is this to be wondered at, for they were in sore peril.

Enough was there spoken, this way and in that; but the conclusion of their deliberation was this: that they would repair and refit on the following day, which was Saturday, and during the whole of Sunday, and that on the Monday they would return to the assault; and they devised further that the ships that carried the scaling ladders should be bound together, two and two, so that two ships

---

11 The ninth hour or mid-afternoon prayer

should be ready to attack one tower; for they had perceived that day how only one ship had attacked each tower, and that this had been too heavy a task for the ship, seeing that those in the tower were more in number than those on the ladder. For this reason was it well seen that two ships would attack each tower with greater effect than one. As had been settled, so was it done, and they waited thus during the Saturday and Sunday.

52

The crusaders take a part of the city

BEFORE the assault, the Emperor Mourzuphles had come to encamp with all his power in an open space, and had there pitched his scarlet tents. Thus matters remained till the Monday morning, when those on the ships, transports, and galleys were all armed. And those of the city stood in much less fear of them than they did at the beginning, and were in such good spirits that on the walls and towers you could see nothing but people. Then began an assault proud and marvelous, and every ship went straight before it to the attack. The noise of the battle was so great that it seemed to rend the earth.

Thus did the assault last for a long while, till our Lord raised a wind called Boreas which drove the ships and vessels further up on to the shore. And two ships that were bound together, of which the one was called the Pilgrim and the other the Paradise, approached so near to a tower, the one on the one side and the other on the other—so as God and the wind drove them—that the ladder of the Pilgrim joined on to the tower. Immediately a Venetian and a knight of France, whose name was Andrew of Urboise, entered into the tower, and other people began to enter after them, and those in the tower were discomfited and fled.*

[NOTE: I should like to quote here another feat of arms related by Robert of Clari, one of those feats that serve to explain how the Crusaders obtained mastery—the mastery of perfect fearlessness—

over the Greeks. Robert of Clari, then, relates how a small body of the besiegers, ten knights and nine sergeants, had come before a postern which had been newly bricked up.

"Now there was there a clerk, Aleaume of Clari by name, who had shown his courage whenever there was need, and was always first in any assault at which he might be present; and when the tower of Galata was taken, this same clerk had performed more deeds of prowess with his body, man for man, than any one in the host, save only the Lord Peter of Bracuel; for the Lord Peter it was who surpassed all others, whether of high or low degree, so that there was none other that performed such feats of arms, or acts of prowess with his body, as the Lord Peter of Bracuel. So when they came to the postern they began to hew and pick at it very hardily; but the bolts flew at them so thick, and so many stones were hurled at them from the wall, that it seemed as if they would be buried beneath the stones such was the mass of quarries and stones thrown from above. And those who were below held up targes[12] and shields to cover those who were picking and hewing underneath; and those above threw down pots of boiling pitch, and Greek fire, and large rocks, so that it was one of God's miracles that the assailants were not utterly confounded; for my Lord Peter and his men suffered more than enough of blows and grievous danger. However, so did they hack at the postern, both above and below, with their axes and good swords, that they made a great hole therein; and when the postern was broken through, they all swarmed to the aperture, but saw so many people above and below, that it seemed as if half the world were there, and they dared not be so bold as to enter.

"Now when Aleaume, the clerk, saw that no one dared to go in, he sprang forward, and said that go in he would. And there was there present a knight, a brother to the clerk (the knight's name was Robert of Clari) who forbade him, and said he should not go in. And the clerk said he would, and scrambled in on his hands and feet. And when the knight saw this, he took hold upon him, by the

---

12 A general word for "shield" in Old English

foot, and began to drag him back. But in his brother's despite, and whether his brother would or not, the clerk went in. And when he was within, many were the Greeks who ran upon him, and those on the walls cast big stones upon him. And the clerk drew his knife, and ran at them; and he drove them before him as if they had been cattle, and cried to those who were without, to the Lord Peter of Amiens and his folk, 'Sire, come in boldly, I see that they are falling back discomfited and flying.' When my Lord Peter heard this, he and his people who were without entered in; and there were no more than ten knights with him, but there were some sixty sergeants, and they were all on foot. And when those who were on the wall at that place saw them, they had such fear that they did not dare to remain there, but avoided a great space on the wall, and fled helter-skelter.

"Now the Emperor Mourzuphles, the traitor, was near by at less than a stone's throw of distance, and he caused the silver horns to be sounded, and the cymbals, and a great noise to be made. And when he saw my Lord Peter, and his people who had entered in on foot, he made a great show of falling upon them, and spurring forward, came about half-way to where they stood. But my Lord Peter, when he saw him coming, began to encourage his people, and to say: 'Now, Lord God, grant that we may do well, and the battle is ours. Here comes the emperor! Let no one dare to think of retreat, but each bethink himself to do well.' Then Mourzuphles, seeing that they would in no wise give way, stayed where he was, and then turned back to his tents."

After this, according to Robert of Clari, Lord Peter's men broke open a gate, and the Crusaders entered into the city. See *Li Estoires de chiaus qus conquisent Constantinoble. De Robert de Clari en aminois, chevalier*, pp. 60-62. The volume in the British Museum is undated, and there is this note in the catalogue, "No more printed." The volume itself is noteless, though there are printed marks here and there which would suggest that notes were intended. The Chronicle of Robert of Clari will also be found in Hopf's *Chroniques Gréco-romanes inédites ou peu connues*, etc., pp. 1-85, Berlin, 1873.]

When the knights, who were in the transports, saw this, they landed, and raised their ladders against the wall, and scaled the top of the wall by main force, and so took four of the towers. And all begin to leap out of the ships and transports and galleys, helter-skelter, each as best he could; and they broke in some three of the gates and entered in; and they drew the horses out of the transports; and the knights mounted and rode straight to the quarters of the Emperor Mourzuphles. He had his battalions arrayed before his tents, and when his men saw the mounted knights coming, they lost heart and fled; and so went the emperor flying through the streets to the castle of Bucoleon.

Then might you have seen the Greeks beaten down; and horses and palfreys captured, and mules, and other booty. Of killed and wounded there was neither end nor measure. A great part of the Greek lords had fled towards the gate of Blachernae. And vesper-time was already past, and those of the host were weary of the battle and of the slaying. And they began to assemble in a great open space that was in Constantinople, and decided that they would take up their quarters near the walls and towers they had captured. Never had they thought that in a whole month they should be able to take the city, with its great churches, and great palaces, and the people that were in it.

53

Flight of Mourzuphles; second fire in Constantinople

AS they had settled, so was it done, and they encamped before the walls and before the towers by their ships. Count Baldwin of Flanders and Hainault quartered himself in the scarlet tents that the Emperor Mourzuphles had left standing, and Henry his brother before the palace of Blachernae; and Boniface, Marquis of Montferrat, he and his men, towards the thickest part of the city. So were the host encamped as you have heard, and Constantinople taken on the Monday after Palm Sunday (12th April 1204).

Now Count Louis of Blois and Chartres had languished all the winter with a quartan fever[13], and could not bear his armour. And you must know that this was a great misfortune to the host, seeing he was a good knight of his body; and he lay in one of the transports.

Thus did those of the host, who were very weary, rest that night. But the Emperor Mourzuphles rested not, for he assembled all his people, and said he would go and attack the Franks. Nevertheless he did not do as he had said, for he rode along other streets, as far as he could from those held by the host, and came to a gate which is called the Golden Gate, whereby he escaped, and avoided the city; and afterwards all who could fled also. And of all this those of the host knew nothing.

During that night, towards the quarters of Boniface Marquis of Montferrat, certain people, whose names are unknown to me, being in fear lest the Greeks should attack them, set fire to the buildings between themselves and the Greeks. And the city began to take fire, and to burn very direfully; and it burned all that night and all the next day, till vesper-time. And this was the third fire there had been in Constantinople since the Franks arrived in the land; and more houses had been burned in the city than there are houses in any three of the greatest cities in the kingdom of France.

That night passed and the next day came, which was a Tuesday morning (13th April 1204); and all armed themselves throughout the host, both knights and sergeants, and each repaired to his post. Then they issued from their quarters, and thought to find a sorer battle than the day before, for no word had come to them that the emperor had fled during the night. But they found none to oppose them.

54

The crusaders occupy the city

THE Marquis Boniface of Montferrat rode all along the shore to

---

[13] A form of malaria

the palace of Bucoleon, and when he arrived there it surrendered on condition that the lives of all therein should be spared. At Bucoleon were found the larger number of the great ladies who had fled to the castle, for there were found the sister [Agnes, sister of Philip Augustus, married successively to Alexius II, to Andronicus, and to Theodore Branas] of the King of France, who had been empress, and the sister [Margaret, sister of Emeric, King of Hungary, married to the Emperor Isaac, and afterwards to the Marquis of Montferrat] of the King of Hungary, who had also been empress, and very many other ladies. Of the treasure that was found in that palace I cannot well speak, for there was so much that it was beyond end or counting.

At the same time that this palace was surrendered to the Marquis Boniface of Montferrat, did the palace of Blachernae surrender to Henry, the brother of Count Baldwin of Flanders, on condition that no hurt should be done to the bodies of those who were therein. There too was found much treasure, not less than in the palace of Bucoleon. Each garrisoned with his own people the castle that had been surrendered to him, and set a guard over the treasure. And the other people, spread abroad throughout the city, also gained much booty. The booty gained was so great that none could tell you the end of it: gold, and silver, and vessels, and precious stones, and samite, and cloth of silk, and robes of vair[14] and grey and ermine, and every choicest thing found upon the earth. And well does Geoffry of Villehardouin the Marshal of Champagne bear witness that never, since the world was created, had so much booty been won in any city.

Every man took quarters where he pleased, and of lodgings there was no stint. So the host of the pilgrims and of the Venetians found quarters, and greatly did they rejoice and give thanks because of the victory God had vouchsafed to them—for those who before had been poor were now in wealth and luxury. Thus they celebrated Palm Sunday and the Easter Day following (25th April 1204) in the

---

14 Squirrel fur used in medieval robes

joy and honour that God had bestowed upon them. And well might they praise our Lord, since in all the host there were no more than twenty thousand armed men, one with another, and with the help of God they had conquered four hundred thousand men, or more, and in the strongest city in all the world—yea, a great city—and very well fortified.

55

Division of the spoil

THEN was it proclaimed throughout the host by the Marquis Boniface of Montferrat, who was lord of the host, and by the barons, and by the Doge of Venice, that all the booty should be collected and brought together, as had been covenanted under oath and pain of excommunication. Three churches were appointed for the receiving of the spoils, and guards were set to have them in charge, both Franks and Venetians, the most upright that could be found.

Then each began to bring in such booty as he had taken, and to collect it together. And some brought in loyally, and some in evil sort, because covetousness, which is the root of all evil, hindered them. So from that time forth the covetous began to keep things back, and our Lord began to love them less. Ah God! how loyally they had borne themselves up to now! And well had the Lord God shown them that in all things He was ready to honour and exalt them above all people. But full oft do the good suffer for the sins of the wicked.

The spoils and booty were collected together, and you must know that all was not brought into the common stock, for not a few kept things back, despite the excommunication of the Pope. That which was brought to the churches was collected together and divided, in equal parts, between the Franks and the Venetians, according to the sworn covenant. And you must know further that the pilgrims, after the division had been made, paid out of their share fifty thousand marks of silver to the Venetians, and then divided at least one hundred thousand marks between themselves, among their own people. And shall I tell you in what wise? Two sergeants on foot counted as one mounted, and two sergeants mounted as one knight. And you must know that no man received more, either on account of his rank or because of his deeds, than that which had been so settled and ordered, save in so far as he may have stolen it.

And as to theft, and those who were convicted thereof, you must know that stern justice was meted out to such as were found guilty, and not a few were hung. The Count of St. Paul hung one of his knights, who had kept back certain spoils, with his shield to his neck; but many there were, both great and small, who kept back part of the spoils, and it was never known. Well may you be assured that the spoil was very great, for if it had not been for what was stolen and for the part given to the Venetians, there would have been at least four hundred thousand marks of silver and at least ten thousand horses—one with another. Thus were divided the spoils of Constantinople, as you have heard.

56

Baldwin, Count of Flanders, elected emperor

THEN a parliament assembled, and the commons of the host declared that an emperor must be elected, as had been settled aforetime. And they parliamented so long that the matter was adjourned to another day, and on that day would they choose the twelve electors who were to make the election. Nor was it possible that there should be lack of candidates, or of men covetous, seeing that so great an honour was in question as the imperial throne of Constantinople. But the greatest discord that arose was the discord concerning Count Baldwin of Flanders and Hainault and the Marquis Boniface of Montferrat; for all the people said that either of those two should be elected.

And when the chief men of the host saw that all held either for Count Baldwin or for the Marquis of Montferrat, they conferred together and said: "Lords, if we elect one of these two great men, the other will be so filled with envy that he will take away with him all his people. And then the land that we have won may be lost, just as the land of Jerusalem came nigh to be lost when, after it had been conquered, Godfrey of Bouillon was elected king, and the Count of St. Giles became so filled with envy that he enticed the other barons, and whomsoever he could, to abandon the host. Then did many people depart, and there remained so few that, if God had not sustained them, the land of Jerusalem would have been lost. Let us therefore beware lest the same mischance befall us also, and rather bethink ourselves how we may keep both these lords in the host. Let the one on whom God shall bestow the empire so devise that the other is well content; let him grant to that other all the land on the further side of the straits, towards Turkey, and the Isle of Greece, and that other shall be his liegeman. Thus shall we keep both lords in the host."

As had been proposed, so was it settled, and both consented right willingly. Then came the day for the parliament, and the parliament assembled. And the twelve electors were chosen, six on one side and six on the other; and they swore on holy relics to elect, duly, and in good faith, whomsoever would best meet the needs of the host, and bear rule over the empire most worthily.

Thus were the twelve chosen, and a day appointed for the election of the emperor; and on the appointed day the twelve electors met at a rich palace, one of the fairest in the world, where the Doge of Venice had his quarters. Great and marvelous was the concourse, for everyone wished to see who should be elected. Then were the twelve electors called, and set in a very rich chapel within the palace, and the door was shut, so that no one remained with them. The barons and knights stayed without in a great palace.

The council lasted till they were agreed; and by consent of all they appointed Nevelon, Bishop of Soissons, who was one of the twelve, to act as spokesman. Then they came out to the place where all the barons were assembled, and the Doge of Venice. Now you must know that many set eyes upon them to know how the election had turned. And the bishop, lifting up his voice while all listened intently, spoke as he had been charged, and said: "Lords, we are agreed—let God be thanked!—upon the choice of an emperor; and you have all sworn that he whom we shall elect as emperor shall be held by you to be emperor indeed, and that if any one gainsay him, you will be his helpers. And we name him now at the self-same hour when God was born, the Count Baldwin of Flanders and Hainault!"

A cry of joy was raised in the palace, and they bore the count out of the palace, and the Marquis Boniface of Montferrat bore him on one side to the church, and showed him all the honour he could. So was the Count Baldwin of Flanders and Hainault elected emperor, and a day appointed for his coronation, three weeks after Easter (16th May 1204). And you must know that many a rich robe was made for the coronation; nor did they want for the wherewithal.

57

Boniface weds Isaac's widow, and after Baldwin's coronation obtains the kingdom of Salonika

BEFORE the time appointed for the coronation, the Marquis Boniface of Montferrat espoused the empress who had been the wife of the Emperor Isaac, and was sister to the King of Hungary. And within that time also did one of the most noble barons of the host, who bore the name of Odo the Champenois of Champlitte, make an end and die. Much was he mourned and bewept by William his brother, and by his other friends; and he was buried in the church of the Apostles with great honour.

The time for the coronation drew near, and the Emperor Baldwin was crowned with great joy and great honour in the church of St. Sophia, in the year of the Incarnation of Jesus Christ one thousand twelve hundred and four. Of the rejoicings and feasting there is no need to speak further, for the barons and knights did all they could; and the Marquis Boniface of Montferrat and Count Louis of Blois and Chartres did homage to the emperor as their lord. After the great rejoicings and ceremonies of the coronation, he was taken in great pomp, and with a great procession, to the rich palace of Bucoleon. And when the feastings were over he began to discuss his affairs.

Boniface the Marquis of Montferrat called upon him to carry out the covenant made, and give him, as he was bound to do, the land on the other side of the straits towards Turkey and the Isle of Greece. And the emperor acknowledged that he was bound so to do, and said he would do it right willingly. And when the Marquis of Montferrat saw that the emperor was willing to carry out this covenant so debonairly, he besought him, in exchange for this land, to bestow upon him the kingdom of Salonika, because it lay near the land of the King of Hungary, whose sister he had taken to wife.

Much was this matter debated in various ways; but in the end the emperor granted the land of Salonika to the marquis, and the marquis did homage therefore. And at this there was much joy throughout the host because the marquis was one of the knights most highly prized in all the world, and one whom the knights most loved, inasmuch as no one dealt with them more liberally than he. Thus the marquis remained in the land, as you have heard.

58

Baldwin marches against Mourzuphles

THE Emperor Mourzuphles had not yet removed more than four days' journey from Constantinople; and he had taken with him the empress who had been the wife of the Emperor Alexius, who aforetime had fled, and his daughter. This Emperor Alexius was in a city called Messinopolis, with all his people, and still held a great part of the land. And at that time the men of note in Greece departed, and a large number passed over the straits towards Turkey; and each one, for his own advantage, made himself master of such lands as he could lay hands upon; and the same thing happened also throughout the other parts of the empire.

The Emperor Mourzuphles made no long tarrying before he took a city which had surrendered to my lord the Emperor Baldwin, a city called Tchorlu. So he took it and sacked it, and seized whatever he found there. When the news thereof came to the Emperor Baldwin, he took counsel with the barons, and with the Doge of Venice, and they agreed to this, that he should issue forth with all his host to make conquest of the land, and leave a garrison in Constantinople to keep it sure, seeing that the city had been newly taken and was peopled with the Greeks.

So did they decide, and the host was called together, and decision made as to who should remain in Constantinople, and who should go in the host with the Emperor Baldwin. In Constantinople remained Count Louis of Blois and Chartres, who had been sick and was not yet recovered, and the Doge of Venice. And Conon of Béthune remained in the palaces of Blachemoe and Bucoleon to keep the city; and with him Geoffry the Marshal of Champagne, and Miles the Brabant of Provins, and Manasses of Isle, and all their people. All the rest made ready to go in the host with the emperor.

Before the Emperor Baldwin left Constantinople, his brother Henry departed thence, by his command, with a hundred very good knights; and he rode from city to city, and in every city to which he came the people swore fealty to the emperor. So he fared forward till he came to Adrianople, which was a good city, and wealthy; and those of the city received him right willingly and swore fealty to the emperor. Then he lodged in the city, he and his people, and sojourned there till the Emperor Baldwin came thither.

59

Mourzuphles takes refuge with Alexius, the brother of Isaac, who puts out his eyes

THE Emperor Mourzuphles, when he heard that they thus advanced against him, did not dare to abide their coming, but remained always two or three days' march in advance.

So he fared forward till he came near Messinopolis, where the Emperor Alexius was sojourning, and he sent on messengers telling Alexius that he would give him help, and do all he behests. And the Emperor Alexius answered that he should be as welcome as if he were his own son, and that he would give him his daughter to wife, and make of him his son. So the Emperor Mourzuphles encamped before Messinopolis, and pitched his tents and pavilions, and Alexius was quartered within the city. So they conferred together, and Alexius gave him his daughter to wife, and they entered into alliance, and said they should be as one.

They sojourned thus for I know not how many days, the one in the camp and the other in the city, and then did the Emperor Alexius invite the Emperor Mourzuphles to come and eat with him, and to go with him to the baths. So were matters settled. The Emperor Mourzuphles came privately, and with few people, and when he was within the house, the Emperor Alexius called him into a privy chamber, and had him thrown on to the ground, and the eyes drawn out of his head. And this was done in such treacherous wise as you have heard. Now say whether this people, who wrought such cruelty one to another, were fit to have lands in possession! And when the host of the Emperor Mourzuphles heard what had been done, they scattered, and fled this way and that; and some joined themselves to the Emperor Alexius, and obeyed him as their lord, and remained with him.

60

Baldwin marches against Alexius; he is joined by Boniface

THEN the Emperor Baldwin moved from Constantinople, with all his host, and rode forward till he came to Adrianople. There he found Henry his brother, and the men with him. All the people whithersoever the emperor passed, came to him, and put themselves at his mercy and under his rule. And while they were at Adrianople, they heard the news that the Emperor Alexius had pulled out the eyes of the Emperor Mourzuphles. Of this there was much talk among them; and well did all say that those who betrayed one another so disloyally and treacherously had no right to hold land in possession.

Then was the Emperor Baldwin minded to ride straight to Messinopolis, where the Emperor Alexius was. And the Greeks of Adrianople besought him, as their lord, to leave a garrison in their city because of Johannizza, King of Wallachia and Bulgaria, who oftentimes made war upon them. And the Emperor Baldwin left there Eustace of Saubruic, who was a knight of Flanders, very worthy and very valiant, together with forty right good knights, and a hundred mounted sergeants.

So departed the Emperor Baldwin from Adrianople, and rode towards Messinopolis, where he thought to find the Emperor Alexius. All the people of the lands through which he passed put themselves under his rule and at his mercy, and when the Emperor Alexius saw this, he avoided Messinopolis and fled. And the Emperor Baldwin rode on till he came before Messinopolis; and those of the city went out to meet him and surrendered the city to his commandment.

Then the Emperor Baldwin said he would sojourn there, waiting for the arrival of Boniface, Marquis of Montferrat, who had not yet joined the host, seeing he could not move as fast as the emperor, because he was bringing with him the empress, his wife. However, he also rode forward till he came to Messinopolis by the river, and there encamped, and pitched his tents and pavilions. And on the morrow he went to speak to the Emperor Baldwin, and to see him, and reminded him of his promise.

"Sire," said he, "tidings have come to me from Salonika that the people of the land would have me know that they are ready to receive me willingly as their lord. And I am your liegeman, and hold the land from you. Therefore, I pray you, let me go thither; and when I am in possession of my land and of my city, I will bring you out such supplies as you may need, and come ready prepared to do your behests. But do not go and ruin my land. Let us rather, if it so pleases you, march against Johannizza, the King of Wallachia and

Bulgaria, who holds a great part of the land wrongfully."

61

Rupture between Baldwin and Boniface; the one marches on Salonika, the other on Demotica

I KNOW not by whose counsel it was that the emperor replied that he was determined to march towards Salonika, and would afterwards attend to his other affairs. "Sire," said Boniface, Marquis of Montferrat, "I pray thee, since I am able without thee to get possession of my land, that thou wilt not enter therein; but if thou dost enter therein, I shall deem that thou art not acting for my good. And be it known to thee that I shall not go with thee, but depart from among you." And the Emperor Baldwin replied that, notwithstanding all this, he should most certainly go.

Alas! how ill-advised were they, both the one and the other, and how great was the sin of those who caused this quarrel! For if God had not taken pity upon them, now would they have lost all the conquests they had made, and Christendom been in danger of ruin. So by ill fortune was there division between the Emperor Baldwin of Constantinople and Boniface, Marquis of Montferrat, and by ill advice. The Emperor Baldwin rode towards Salonika, as he devised, with all his people, and with all his power. And Boniface, the Marquis of Montferrat, went back, and he took with him a great number of right worthy people. With him went James of Avesnes, William of Champlitte, Hugh of Colemi, Count Berthold of Katzenellenbogen, and the greater part of those who came from the Empire of Germany and held with the marquis. Thus did the marquis ride back till he came to a castle, very goodly, very strong, and very rich, which is called Demotica; and it was surrendered by a Greek of the city, and when the marquis had entered therein he garrisoned it. Then because of their knowledge of the empress his wife, the Greeks began to turn towards him, and to surrender to his rule from all the country round about, within a day or two's journey.

The Emperor Baldwin rode straight on to Salonika, and came to a castle called Christopolis, one of the strongest in the world. And it surrendered, and those of the city did homage to him. Afterwards he came to another place called Blache, which was very strong and very rich, and this too surrendered, and the people did homage. Next he came to Cetros, a city strong and rich, and it also came to his rule and order, and did homage. Then he rode to Salonika, and encamped before the city, and was there for three days. And those within surrendered the city, which was one of the best and wealthiest in Christendom at that day, on condition that he would maintain the uses and customs theretofore observed by the Greek emperor.

62

Message of the crusaders to Boniface; he suspends the siege of Adrianople

WHILE the Emperor Baldwin was thus at Salonika, and the land surrendering to his good pleasure and commandment, the Marquis Boniface of Montferrat, with all his people and a great quantity of Greeks who held to his side, marched to Adrianople and besieged it, and pitched his tents and pavilions round about. Now Eustace of Saubruic was therein, with the people whom the emperor had left there, and they mounted the walls and towers and made ready to defend themselves.

Then took Eustace of Saubruic two messengers and sent them, riding night and day, to Constantinople. And they came to the Doge of Venice, and to Count Louis, and to those who had been left in the city by the Emperor Baldwin, and told them that Eustace of Saubruic would have them know that the emperor and the marquis were embroiled together, and that the marquis had seized Demotica, which was one of the strongest castles in Romania, and one of the richest, and that he was besieging them in Adrianople. And when those in Constantinople heard this they were moved with anger, for they thought most surely that all their conquests would be lost.

Then assembled in the palace of Blachernae the Doge of Venice, and Count Louis of Blois and Chartres, and the other barons that were in Constantinople; and much were they distraught, and greatly were they angered, and fiercely did they complain of those who had put enmity between the emperor and the marquis. At the prayer of the Doge of Venice and of Count Louis, Geoffry of Villehardouin, the Marshal of Champagne, was enjoined to go to the siege of Adrianople, and appease the war, if he could, because he was well in favour with the marquis, and therefore they thought he would have more influence than any other. And he, because of their prayers, and of their great need, said he would go willingly; and he took with him Manasses of L'isle, who was one of the good knights of the host, and one of the most honoured.

So they departed from Constantinople, and rode day by day till they came to Adrianople where the siege was going on. And when the marquis heard thereof, he came out of the camp and went to meet them. With him came James of Avesnes, and William of Champlitte, and Hugh of Colemi, and Otho of la Roche, who were the chief counselors of the marquis. And when he saw the envoys, he did them much honour and showed them much fair seeming.

Geoffry the Marshal, with whom he was on very good terms, spoke to him very sharply, reproaching him with the fashion in which he had taken the land of the emperor and besieged the emperor's people in Adrianople, and that without apprising those in Constantinople, who surely would have obtained such redress as was due if the emperor had done him any wrong. And the marquis disculpated[15] himself much, and said it was because of the wrong the emperor had done him that he had acted in such sort.

So wrought Geoffry, the Marshal of Champagne, with the help of God, and of the barons who were in the confidence of the marquis, and who loved the said Geoffry well, that the marquis assured him he would leave the matter in the hands of the Doge of Venice, and of Count Louis of Blois and Chartres, and of Conon of Béthune, and of Geoffry of Villehardouin, the Marshal—all of

---

15 Absolved from blame; exonerated

whom well knew what was the covenant made between himself and the emperor. So was a truce established between those in the camp and those in the city.

And you must know that Geoffry the Marshal, and Manasses of Isle, were right joyously looked upon, both by those in the camp and those in the city, for very strongly did either side wish for peace. And in such measure as the Franks rejoiced, so were the Greeks dolen, because right willingly would they have seen the Franks quarreling and at war. Thus was the siege of Adrianople raised, and the marquis returned with all his people to Demotica, where was the empress his wife.

63

Message of the crusaders to Baldwin; death of several knights

THE envoys returned to Constantinople, and told what they had done. Greatly did the Doge of Venice, and Count Louis of Blois, and all besides, then rejoice that to these envoys had been committed the negotiations for a peace; and they chose good messengers, and wrote a letter, and sent it to the Emperor Baldwin, telling him that the marquis had referred himself to them, with assurances that he would accept their arbitration, and that he (the emperor) was even more strongly bound to do the same, and that they besought him to do so—for they would in no wise countenance war—and promise to accept their arbitration, as the marquis had done.

While this was in progress the Emperor Baldwin had settled matters at Salonika and departed thence, garrisoning it with his people, and had left there as chief Renier of Mons, who was a good knight and a valiant. And tidings had come to him that the marquis had taken Demotica, and established himself therein, and conquered a great part of the land lying round about, and besieged the emperor's people in Adrianople. Greatly enraged was the Emperor Baldwin when these tidings came to him, and much did he hasten so as to raise the siege of Adrianople, and do to the marquis all the harm that he could. Ah God! what mischief their discord might have caused! If God had not seen to it, Christendom would have been undone.

So did the Emperor Baldwin journey day by day. And a very great mischance had befallen those who were before Salonika, for many people of the host were stricken down with sickness. Many who could not be moved had to remain in the castles by which the emperor passed, and many were brought along in litters, journeying in sore pain; and many there were who died at Cetros (La Serre). Among those who so died at Cetros was Master John of Noyon, chancellor to the Emperor Baldwin. He was a good clerk, and very wise, and much had he comforted the host by the word of God, which he well knew how to preach. And you must know that by his death the good men of the host were much discomforted.

Nor was it long ere another great misfortune befell the host, for Peter of Amiens died, who was a man rich and noble, and a good and brave knight, and great dole was made for him by Hugh of St. Paul, who was his cousin; and heavily did his death weigh upon the host. Shortly after died Gerard of Mancicourt, who was a knight much prized, and Giles of Annoy, and many other good people. Forty knights died during this expedition, and by their death was the host greatly enfeebled.

64

Baldwin's reply to the message of the crusaders

THE Emperor Baldwin journeyed so day by day that he met the messengers sent by those of Constantinople. One of the messengers was a knight belonging to the land of Count Louis of Blois, and the count's liegeman; his name was Bègue of Fransures, and he was wise and eloquent. He spoke the message of his lord and the other barons right manfully, and said: "Sire, the Doge of Venice, and Count Louis, my lord, and the other barons who are in Constantinople send you health and greeting as to their lord, and they complain to God and to you of those who have raised discord between you and the Marquis of Montferrat, whereby it failed but little that Christendom was not undone; and they tell you that you did very ill when you listened to such counselors. Now they apprise you that the marquis has referred to them the quarrel that there is between him and you, and they pray you, as their lord, to refer that quarrel to them likewise, and to promise to abide by their ruling. And be it known to you that they will in no wise, nor on any ground, suffer that you should go to war."

The Emperor Baldwin went to confer with his council, and said he would reply immediately. Many there were in the emperor's council who had helped to cause the quarrel, and they were greatly outraged by the declaration sent by those at Constantinople, and they said: "Sire, you hear what they declare to you, that they will not suffer you to take vengeance on your enemy. Truly it seems that if you will not do as they order, they will set themselves against you."

Very many big words were then spoken; but, in the end, the council agreed that the emperor had no wish to lose the friendship of the Doge of Venice, and Count Louis, and the others who were in Constantinople; and the emperor replied to the envoys: "I will not promise to refer the quarrel to those who sent you, but I will go to Constantinople without doing aught to injure the marquis." So the Emperor Baldwin journeyed day by day till he came to Constantinople, and the barons, and the other people, went to meet him, and received him as their lord with great honour.

65

Reconciliation of Baldwin and Boniface

ON the fourth day the emperor knew clearly that he had been ill-advised to quarrel with the marquis, and then the Doge of Venice and Count Louis came to speak to him and said: "Sire, we would pray you to refer this matter to us, as the marquis has done." And the emperor said he would do so right willingly. Then were envoys chosen to fetch the marquis, and bring him thither. Of the envoys one was Gervais of Chatel, and the second Renier of Trit, and Geoffry, Marshal of Champagne the third, and the Doge of Venice sent two of his people.

The envoys rode day by day till they came to Demotica, and they found the marquis with the empress his wife, and a great number of right worthy people, and they told him how they had come to fetch him. Then did Geoffry the Marshal desire him to come to Constantinople as he had promised, and make peace in such wise as might be settled by those in whose hands he had remitted his cause; and they promised him safe conduct, as also to those who might go with him.

The marquis took counsel with his men. Some there were who agreed that he should go, and some who advised that he should not go. But the end of the debate was such that he went with the envoys to Constantinople, and took full a hundred knights with him; and they rode day by day till they came to Constantinople. Very gladly were they received in the city; and Count Louis of Blois and Chartres, and the Doge of Venice went out to meet the marquis, together with many other right worthy people, for he was much loved in the host.

Then was a parliament assembled, and the covenants were rehearsed between the Emperor Baldwin and the Marquis Boniface; and Salonika was restored to Boniface, with the land, he placing Demotica, which he had seized, in the hands of Geoffry the Marshal of Champagne, who undertook to keep it till he heard, by accredited messenger, or letters duly sealed, that the marquis was in possession of Salonika, when he would give back Demotica to the emperor, or to whomsoever the emperor might appoint. Thus was peace made between the emperor and the marquis, as you have heard. And great was the joy thereof throughout the host, for out of this quarrel might very great evil have arisen.

66

The kingdom of Salonika is restored to Boniface; division of the land between the crusaders

THE marquis then took leave, and went towards Salonika with his people, and with his wife; and with him rode the envoys of the emperor; and as they went from castle to castle, each, with all its lordship, was restored to the marquis on the part of the emperor. So they came to Salonika, and those who held the place for the emperor surrendered it. Now the governor, whom the emperor had left there, and whose name was Renier of Mons, had died; he was a man most worthy, and his death a great mischance.

Then the land and country began to surrender to the marquis, and a great part thereof to come under his rule. But a Greek, a man of great rank, whose name was Leon Sgure, would in no wise come under the rule of the marquis, for he had seized Corinth and Napoli, two cities that lie upon the sea, and are among the strongest cities under heaven. He then refused to surrender, but began to make war against the marquis, and a very great many of the Greeks held with him. And another Greek whose name was Michael, and who had come with the marquis from Constantinople, and was thought by the marquis to be his friend, departed without any word said, and went to a city called Durazzo and took to wife the daughter of a rich Greek, who held the land from the emperor, and seized the land, and began to make war on the marquis.

Now the land from Constantinople to Salonika was quiet and at peace, for the ways were so safe that all could come and go at their pleasure, and from the one city to the other there were full twelve long days' journey. And so much time had now passed that we were at the beginning of September (1204). And the Emperor Baldwin was in Constantinople, and the land at peace, and under his rule. Then died two right good knights in Constantinople, Eustace of Canteleu, and Aimery of Villeroi, whereof their friends had great sorrow.

Then did they begin to divide the land. The Venetians had their part, and the pilgrims the other. And when each one was able to go to his own land, the covetousness of this world, which has worked so great evil, suffered them not to be at peace, for each began to deal wickedly in his land, some more, and some less, and the Greeks began to hate them and to nourish a bitter heart.

Then did the Emperor Baldwin bestow on Count Louis the duchy of Nice, which was one of the greatest lordships in the land of Romania, and situate on the other side of the straits, towards Turkey. Now all the land on the other side of the straits had not surrendered to the emperor, but was against him. Then afterwards he gave the duchy of Philippopolis to Renier of Trit.

So Count Louis sent his men to conquer his land—some hundred and twenty knights. And over them were set Peter of Bracieux and Payen of Orleans. They left Constantinople on All Saints Day (1st November 1204), and passed over the Straits of St. George on ship-board, and came to Piga, a city that lies on the sea, and is inhabited by Latins. And they began to war against the Greeks.

67

Execution of Mourzuphles and imprisonment of Alexius

IN those days it happened that the Emperor Mourzuphles, whose eyes had been put out—the same who had murdered his lord, the Emperor Isaac's son, the Emperor Alexius, whom the pilgrims had brought with them to that land—it happened, I say, that the Emperor Mourzuphles fled privily, and with but few people, and took refuge beyond the straits. But Thierri of Loos heard of it, for Mourzuphles' flight was revealed to him, and he took Mourzuphles and brought him to the Emperor Baldwin at Constantinople. And the Emperor Baldwin rejoiced thereat, and took counsel with his men what he should do with a man who had been guilty of such a murder upon his lord.

And the council agreed to this: There was in Constantinople, towards the middle of the city, a column, one of the highest and the most finely wrought in marble that eye had ever seen; and Mourzuphles should be taken to the top of that column and made to leap down, in the sight of all the people, because it was fit that an act of justice so notable should be seen of the whole world. So they led the Emperor Mourzuphles to the column, and took him to the top, and all the people in the city ran together to behold the event. Then they cast him down, and he fell from such a height that when he came to the earth he was all shattered and broken.

Now hear of a great marvel! On that column from which he fell were images of divers kinds, wrought in the marble. And among these images was one, worked in the shape of an emperor, falling headlong; for of a long time it had been prophesied that from that column an emperor of Constantinople should be cast down. So did the semblance and the prophecy come true.

It came to pass at this time also, that the Marquis Boniface of Montferrat, who was near Salonika, took prisoner the Emperor Alexius—the same who had put out the eyes of the Emperor Isaac—and the empress his wife with him. And he sent the scarlet buskins, and the imperial vestments, to the Emperor Baldwin, his lord, at Constantinople, and the emperor took the act in very good part. Shortly after the marquis sent the Emperor Alexius and the empress his wife, to Montferrat, there to be imprisoned.

68

Capture of Abydos, of Philippopolis, and of Nicomedia; Theodore Lascaris pretends to the empire

AT the feast of St. Martin after this (11th November 1204), Henry, the brother of the Emperor Baldwin, went forth from Constantinople, and marched down by the straits to the mouth of Abydos; and he took with him some hundred and twenty good knights. He crossed the straits near a city which is called Abydos, and found it well furnished with good things, with corn and meats, and with all things of which man has need. So he seized the city, and lodged therein, and then began to war with the Greeks who were before him. And the Armenians of the land, of whom there were many, began to turn towards him, for they greatly hated the Greeks.

At that time Renier of Trit left Constantinople, and went towards Philippopolis, which the emperor had given him; and he took with him some hundred and twenty very good knights, and rode day by day till he passed beyond Adrianople, and came to Philippopolis. And the people of the land received him, and obeyed him as their lord, for they beheld his coming very willingly. And they stood in great need of succour, for Johannizza, the King of Wallachia, had mightily oppressed them with war. So Renier helped them right well, and held a great part of the land, and most of those who had sided with Johannizza, now turned to him. In those parts the war with Johannizza raged fiercely.

The emperor had sent some hundred knights over the straits of Saint George opposite Constantinople. Macaire of Sainte-Menehould was in command, and with him went Matthew of Wallincourt, and Robert of Ronsoi. They rode to a city called Nicomedia, which lies on a gulf of the sea, and is well two days journey from Constantinople. When the Greeks saw them coming, they avoided the city, and went away; so the pilgrims lodged therein, and garrisoned it, and enclosed it with walls, and began to wage war before them on that side also.

The land on the other side of the straits had for lord a Greek named Theodore Lascaris. He had for wife the daughter of the Emperor Alexius, through whom he laid claim to the land—this was the Alexius whom the Franks had driven from Constantinople, and who had put out his brother's eyes. The same Lascaris maintained the war against the Franks on the other side of the straits, in whatsoever part they might be.

In Constantinople remained the Emperor Baldwin and Count Louis with but few people, and the Count of St. Paul, who was grievously sick with gout that held him by the knees and feet; and the Doge of Venice, who saw naught.

69

Reinforcements from Syria; death of Mary, the wife of Baldwin

AFTER this time came from the land of Syria a great company of those who had abandoned the host, and gone thither from other ports than Venice. With this company came Stephen of Perche, and Renaud of Montmirail, who was cousin to Count Louis, and they were by him much honoured, for he was very glad of their coming. And the Emperor Baldwin, and the rest of the people also received them very gladly, for they were of high rank, and very rich, and brought very many good people with them.

From the land of Syria came Hugh of Tabarie, and Raoul his brother, and Thierri of Tenremonde, and very many people of the land, knights and light horsemen, and sergeants.

And the Emperor Baldwin gave to Stephen of Perche the duchy of Philadelphia.

Among other tidings came news at this time to the Emperor Baldwin whereby he was made very sorrowful; for the Countess Mary [she was the daughter of Henry Count of Champagne and of Mary, daughter of Philip Augustus, King of France] his wife, whom he had left in Flanders, seeing she could not go with him because she was with child—he was then but count—had brought forth a daughter; and afterwards, on her recovery, she started to go to her lord overseas and passed to the port of Marseilles, and coming to Acre, she had but just landed, when the tidings came to her from Constantinople—told by the messengers whom her lord had sent—that Constantinople was taken, and her lord made emperor to the great joy of all Christendom. On hearing this the lady was minded to come to him forthwith. Then a sickness took her, and she made an end and died, whereof there was great dole throughout all Christendom, for she was a gracious and virtuous lady and greatly honoured. And those who came in this company brought the tidings of her death, whereof the Emperor Baldwin had sore affliction, as also the barons of the land, for much did they desire to have her for their lady.

70

Defeat of Theodore and Constantine Lascaris

AT that time those who had gone to the city of Piga—Peter of Bracieux and Payen of Orléans being the chiefs—fortified a castle called Palormo; and they left therein a garrison of their people, and rode forward to conquer the land. Theodore Lascaris had collected all the people he could, and on the day of the feast of my lord St. Nicholas (6th December 1204), which is before the Nativity, he joined battle in the plain before a castle called Poemaninon. The battle was engaged with great disadvantage to our people, for those of the other part were in such numbers as was marvelous; and on our side there were but one hundred and forty knights, without counting the mounted sergeants.

But our Lord orders battles as it pleases Him. By His grace and by His will, the Franks vanquished the Greeks and discomfited them, so that they suffered very great loss. And within the week, they surrendered a very large part of the land. They surrendered Poemaninon, which was a very strong castle, and Lopadium, which was one of the best cities of the land, and Polychna, which is seated on a lake of fresh water, and is one of the strongest and best castles that can be found. And you must know that our people fared very excellently, and by God's help had their will of that land.

Shortly after, by the advice of the Armenians, Henry, the brother of the Emperor Baldwin of Constantinople, started from the city of Abydos, leaving therein a garrison of his people, and rode to a city called Adramittium, which lies on the sea, a two days' journey from Abydos. This city yielded to him, and he lodged therein, and a great part of the land surrendered; for the city was well supplied with corn, and meats, and other goods. Then he maintained the war in those parts against the Greeks.

Theodore Lascaris, who had been discomfited at Poemaninon, collected as many people as he could, and assembled a very great army, and gave the command thereof to Constantine, his brother, who was one of the best Greeks in Romania, and then rode straight towards Adramittium. And Henry, the brother of the Emperor Baldwin, had knowledge, through the Armenians, that a great host was marching against him, so he made ready to meet them, and set his battalions in order; and he had with him some very good men, as Baldwin of Beauvoir, and Nicholas of Mailly, and Anseau of Cayeux, and Thierri of Loos, and Thierri of Tenremonde.

So it happened that on the Saturday which is before mid Lent (19th March 1205), came Constantine Lascaris with his great host before Adramittium. And Henry, when he knew of his coming, took counsel, and said he would not suffer himself to be shut up in the city, but would issue forth. And those of the other part came on with all their host in great companies of horse and foot, and those on our part went out to meet them, and began the onslaught. Then was there a dour battle and fighting hand to hand; but by God's help the Franks prevailed, and discomfited their foes, so that many were killed and taken captive, and there was much booty. Then were the Franks at ease, and very rich, so that the people of the land turned to them, and began to bring in their tributes.

71

Boniface attacks Leon Sgure; he is joined by Geoffry of Villehardouin, the nephew

NOW let us leave speaking further for the time being of those at Constantinople, and return to the Marquis Boniface of Montferrat. The marquis had gone, as you have heard, towards Salonika, and then ridden forth against Leon Sgure who held Napoli and Corinth, two of the strongest cities in the world. Boniface besieged both cities at once. James of Avesnes, with many other good men, remained before Corinth, and the rest encamped before Napoli, and laid siege to it.

Then befell a certain adventure in the land. For Geoffry of Villehardouin, who was nephew to Geoffry of Villehardouin, Marshal of Champagne, being his brother's son, was moved to leave Syria with the company that came to Constantinople. But wind and chance carried him to the port of Modon, and there his ship was injured, so that, of necessity, it behooved him to winter in that country. And a Greek, who was a great lord of the land, knew of it, and came to him, and did him much honour, and said: "Fair Sir, the Franks have conquered Constantinople, and elected an emperor. If thou wilt make alliance with me, I will deal with thee in all good faith, and we together will conquer much land." So they made alliance on oath, the Greek and Geoffry of Villehardouin, and conquered together a great part of the country, and Geoffry of Villehardouin found much good faith in the Greek.

But adventures happen as God wills, and sickness laid hold of the Greek, and he made an end and died. And the Greek's son rebelled against Geoffry of Villehardouin, and betrayed him, and the castles in which Geoffry had set a garrison turned against him. Now he heard tell that the marquis was besieging Napoli, so he went towards him with as many men as he could collect, and rode through the land for some six days in very great peril, and thus came to the camp, where he was received right willingly, and much honoured by the marquis and all who were there. And this was but right, seeing he was very honourable and valiant, and a good knight.

72

Exploits of William of Champlitte and Geoffry of Villehardouin, the nephew, in Morea

THE marquis would have given him land and possessions so that he might remain with him, but he would not, and spoke to William of Champlitte, who was his friend, and said: "Sir, I come from a land that is very rich, and is called Morea. Take as many men as you can collect, and leave this host, and let us go and conquer that land by the help of God. And that which you will give me out of our conquests, I will hold from you, and I will be your liegeman." And William of Champlitte, who greatly trusted and loved him, went to the marquis, and told him of the matter, and the marquis allowed of their going.

So William of Champlitte and Geoffry of Villehardouin (the nephew) departed from the host, and took with them about a hundred knights, and a great number of mounted sergeants, and entered into the land of Morea, and rode onwards till they came to the city of Modon. Michael heard that they were in the land with so few people, and he collected together a great number of people, a number that was marvelous, and he rode after them as one thinking they were all no better than prisoners, and in his hand.

And when they heard tell that he was coming, they refortified Modon, where the defences had long since been pulled down, and there left their baggage, and the lesser folk. Then they rode out a day's march, and ordered their array with as many people as they had. But the odds seemed too great, for they had no more than five hundred men mounted, whereas on the other part there were well over five thousand. But events happen as God pleases; for our people fought with the Greeks and discomfited and conquered them. And the Greeks lost very heavily, while those on our side gained horses and arms enough, and other goods in very great plenty, and so returned very happy, and very joyously, to the city of Modon.

Afterwards they rode to a city called Coron, on the sea, and besieged it. And they had not besieged it long before it surrendered, and William gave it to Geoffry of Villehardouin (the nephew) and he became his liegeman, and set therein a garrison of his men. Next they went to a castle called Chalemate which was very strong and fair, and besieged it. This castle troubled them for a very long space, but they remained before it till it was taken. Then did more of the Greeks of that land surrender than had done aforetime.

73

Siege of Napoli and Corinth; alliance between the Greeks and Johannizza

THE Marquis of Montferrat besieged Napoli, but he could there do nothing for the place was too strong, and his men suffered greatly. James of Avesnes, meanwhile, continued to besiege Corinth, where he had been left by the marquis. Leon Sgure, who was in Corinth, and very wise and wily, saw that James had not many people with him, and did not keep good watch. So one morning, at the break of day, he issued from the city in force, and got as far as the tents, and killed many before they could get to their armour. There was killed Dreux of Estruen, who was very honourable and valiant, and greatly was he lamented. And James of Avesnes, who was in command, waxed very wroth at the death of his knight, and did not leave the fray till he was wounded in the leg right grievously. And well did those who were present bear witness that it was to his doughtiness that they owed their safety; for you must know that they came very near to being all lost. But by God's help they drove the Greeks back into the castle by force.

Now the Greeks, who were very disloyal, still nourished treachery in their hearts. They perceived at that time that the Franks were so scattered over the land that each had his own matters to attend to. So they thought they could the more easily betray them. They took envoys therefore privily, from all the cities in the land, and sent them to Johannizza, the King of Wallachia and Bulgaria, who was still at war with them as he had been aforetime. And they told Johannizza they would make him emperor, and give themselves wholly to him, and slay all the Franks. So they swore that they would obey him as their lord, and he swore that he would defend them as though they were his own people. Such was the oath sworn.

74

Uprising of the Greeks at Demotica and Adrianople; their defeat at Arcadiopolis

AT that time there happened a great misfortune at Constantinople, for Count Hugh of St. Paul, who had long been in bed, sick of the gout, made an end and died; and this caused great sorrow, and was a great mishap, and much was he bewept by his men and by his friends. He was buried with great honour in the church of my lord St. George of Mangana.

Now Count Hugh in his lifetime had held a castle called Demotica, which was very strong and rich, and he had therein some of his knights and sergeants. The Greeks, who had made oath to the King of Wallachia that they would kill and betray the Franks, betrayed them in that castle, and slaughtered many and took many captive. Few escaped, and those who escaped went flying to a city called Adrianople, which the Venetians held at that time.

Not long after the Greeks in Adrianople rose in arms; and such of our men as were therein, and had been set to guard it, came out in great peril, and left the city. Tidings thereof came to the Emperor Baldwin of Constantinople, who had but few men with him, he and Count Louis of Blois. Much were they then troubled and dismayed. And thenceforth, from day to day, did evil tidings begin to come to them, that everywhere the Greeks were rising, and that wherever the Greeks found Franks occupying the land, they killed them.

And those who had left Adrianople, the Venetians and the others who were there, came to a city called Tzurulum, that belonged to the Emperor Baldwin. There they found William of Blanvel, who kept the place for the emperor. By the help and comfort that he gave them, and because he accompanied them with as many men as he could, they turned back to a city, some twelve leagues distant, called Arcadiopolis, which belonged to the Venetians, and they found it empty. So they entered in, and put a garrison there.

On the third day the Greeks of the land gathered together, and came at the break of dawn before Arcadiopolis; and then began, from all sides, an assault, great and marvelous. The Franks defended themselves right well, and opened their gates, and issued forth, attacking vigorously. As was God's will, the Greeks were discomfited, and those on our side began to cut them down and to slay them, and then chased them for a league, and killed many, and captured many horses and much other spoil.

So the Franks returned with great joy to Arcadiopolis, and sent tidings of their victory to the Emperor Baldwin, in Constantinople, who was much rejoiced thereat. Nevertheless they dared not hold the city of Arcadiopolis, but left it on the morrow, and abandoned it, and returned to the city of Tzurulum. Here they remained in very great doubt, for they misdoubted the Greeks who were in the city as much as those who were without, because the Greeks in the city had also taken part in the oath sworn to the King of Wallachia, and were bound to betray the Franks. And many there were who did not dare to abide in Tzurulum, but made their way back to Constantinople.

75

The crusaders on the other side of the straits are recalled to march on Adrianople; expedition of Geoffry of Villehardouin

THEN the Emperor Baldwin, and the Doge of Venice, and Count Louis took counsel together, for they saw they were losing the whole land. And they settled that the emperor should tell his brother Henry, who was at Adramittium, to abandon whatsoever conquests he had made, and come to their succour.

Count Louis, on his side, sent to Payen of Orléans and Peter of Bracieux, who were at Lopadium, and to all the people that were with them, telling them to leave whatsoever conquests they had made, save Pioa only, that lay on the sea, where they were to set a garrison—the smallest they could—and that the remainder were to come to their succour.

The emperor directed Macaire of Sainte-Menehould, and Matthew of Wallincourt, and Robert of Ronsoi, who had some hundred knights with them in Nicomedia, to leave Nicomedia and come to their succour.

By command of the Emperor Baldwin, Geoffry of Villehardouin, Marshal of Champagne, issued from Constantinople, with Manasses of L'isle, and with as many men as they could collect, and these were few enough, seeing that all the land was being lost. And they rode to the city of Tzurulum, which is distant a three days' journey. There they found William of Blanvel, and those that were with him, in very great fear, and much were these reassured at their coming. At that place they remained four days. The Emperor Baldwin sent after Geoffry the Marshal as many as he could of such people as were coming into Constantinople, so that on the fourth day there were at Tzurulum eighty knights.

Then did Geoffry the Marshal move forward, and Manasses of L'isle, and their people, and they rode on, and came to the city of Arcadiopolis, and quartered themselves therein. There they remained a day, and then moved to a city called Bulgaropolis. The Greeks had avoided this city and the Franks quartered themselves therein. The following day they rode to a city called Neguise, which was very fair and strong, and well furnished with all good things. And they found that the Greeks had abandoned it, and were all gone to Adrianople. Now Adrianople was distant nine French leagues, and therein were gathered all the great multitude of the Greeks. And the Franks decided that they should wait where they were till the coming of the Emperor Baldwin.

76

Renier of Trit abandoned at Philippopolis by his son and the greater part of his people

NOW does this book relate a great marvel: for Renier of Trit, who was at Philippopolis, a good nine days' journey from Constantinople, with at least one hundred and twenty knights, was deserted by Reginald his son, and Giles his brother, and James of Bondies, who was his nephew, and Achard of Verdun, who had his daughter to wife. And they had taken some thirty of his knights, and thought to come to Constantinople; and they had left him, you must know, in great peril. But they found the country raised against them, and were discomfited; and the Greeks took them, and afterwards handed them over to the King of Wallachia, who had their heads cut off. And you must know that they were but little pitied by the people, because they had behaved in such evil sort to one whom they were bound to treat quite otherwise.

And when the other knights of Renier of Trit saw that he was thus abandoned by those who were much more bound to him than themselves, they felt the less shame, and some eighty together left him, and departed by another way. So Renier of Trit remained among the Greeks with very few men, for he had not more than fifteen knights at Philippopolis and Stanimac—which is a very strong castle which he held, and where he was for a long time besieged.

77

Baldwin undertakes the siege of Adrianople

WE will speak no further now of Renier of Trit but return to the Emperor Baldwin, who was in Constantinople with but very few people, and greatly angered and much distracted. He was waiting for Henry his brother, and all the people on the other side of the straits, and the first who came to him from the other side of the straits came from Nicomedia, viz. Macaire of Sainte-Menehould, and Matthew of Wallincourt, and Robert of Ronsoi, and with them full a hundred knights.

When the emperor saw them, he was right glad, and he consulted with Count Louis, who was Count of Blois and Chartres. And they settled to go forth, with as many men as they had, to follow Geoffry the Marshal of Champagne, who had gone before. Alas, what a pity it was they did not wait till all had joined them who were on the other side of the straits, seeing how few people they had, and how perilous the adventure on which they were bound.

So they started from Constantinople, some one hundred and forty knights, and rode from day to day till they came to the castle of Neguise, where Geoffry the Marshal was quartered. That night they took counsel together, and the decision to which they came was, that on the morrow they should go before Adrianople, and lay siege to it. So they ordered their battalions, and did for the best with such people as they had.

When the morning came, and full daylight, they rode as had been arranged, and came before Adrianople. And they found it very well defended, and saw the flags of Johannizza, King of Wallachia and Bulgaria, on the walls and towers; and the city was very strong and very rich, and very full of people. Then they made an assault, with very few people, before two of the gates, and this was on the Tuesday of Palmtide (29th March 1205). So did they remain before the city for three days, in great discomfort, and but few in number.

78

The siege of Adrianople continued without result

THEN came Henry Dandolo, the Doge of Venice, who was an old man and saw naught. And he brought with him as many people as he had, and these were quite as many as the Emperor Baldwin and Count Louis had brought, and he encamped before one of the gates. On the morrow they were joined by a troop of mounted sergeants, but these might well have been better men than they proved themselves to be. And the host had small store of provisions, because the merchants could not come with them; nor could they go foraging, because of the many Greeks that were spread throughout the land.

Johannizza, King of Wallachia, was coming to succour Adrianople with a very great host; for he brought with him Wallachians and Bulgarians, and full fourteen thousand Comans who had never been baptised.

Now because of the dearth of provisions, Count Louis of Blois and Chartres went foraging on Palm Sunday. With him went Stephen of Perche, brother of Count Geoffry of Perche, and Renaud of Montmirail, who was brother of Count Hervée of Nevers, and Gervais of Châtel, and more than half of the host. They went to a castle called Peutace, and found it well garrisoned with Greeks, and assailed it with great force and fury; but they were able to achieve nothing, and so retreated without taking any spoils. Thus they remained during the week of the two Easters (Palm Sunday to Easter Day), and fashioned engines of diverse sorts, and set such miners as they had to work underground and so undermine the wall. And thus did they celebrate Easter (10th April) before Adrianople, being but few in number and scant of provisions.

79

Johannizza, King of Wallachia, comes to relieve Adrianople

THEN came tidings that Johannizza, King of Wallachia, was coming upon them to relieve the city. So they set their affairs in order, and it was arranged that Geoffry the Marshal, and Manasses of L'isle should guard the camp, and that the Emperor Baldwin and all the remainder of the host should issue from the camp if so be that Johanizza came and offered battle.

Thus they remained till the Wednesday of Easter week, and Johannizza had by that time approached so near that he encamped at about five leagues from us. And he sent his Comans running before our camp, and a cry was raised throughout the camp, and our men issued therefrom helter-skelter, and pursued the Comans for a full league very foolishly; for when they wished to return, the Comans began to shoot at them in grievous wise, and wounded a good many of their horses.

So our men returned to the camp, and the barons were summoned to the quarters of the Emperor Baldwin. And they took counsel, and all said that they had dealt foolishly in thus pursuing people who were so lightly armed. And in the end they settled that if Johannizza came on again, they would issue forth, and set themselves in array of battle before the camp, and there wait for him, and not move from thence. And they had it proclaimed throughout the host that none should be so rash as to disregard this order, and move from his post for any cry or tumult that might come to his ears. And it was settled that Geoffry the Marshal should keep guard on the side of the city, with Manasses of L'isle.

So they passed that night till the Thursday morning in Easter week, when they heard mass and ate their dinner. And the Comans ran up to their tents, and a cry arose, and they ran to arms, and issued from the camp with all their battalions in array, as had afore been devised.

80

Defeat of the crusaders; Baldwin taken prisoner

COUNT Louis went out first with his battalion, and began to follow after the Comans, and sent to urge the emperor to come after him. Alas! how ill did they keep to what had been settled the night before! For they ran in pursuit of the Comans for at least two leagues, and joined issue with them, and chased them a long space. And then the Comans turned back upon them, and began to cry out and to shoot.

On our side there were battalions made up of other people than knights, people having too little knowledge of arms, and they began to wax afraid and be discomfited. And Count Louis, who had been the first to attack, was wounded in two places full sorely; and the Comans and Wallachians began to invade our ranks; and the count had fallen, and one of his knights, whose name was John of Friaise, dismounted, and set him on his horse. Many were Count Louis' people who said: "Sir, get you hence, for you are too sorely wounded, and in two places." And he said: "The Lord God forbid that ever I should be reproached with flying from the field, and abandoning the emperor."

The emperor, who was in great straits on his side, recalled his people, and he told them that he would not fly, and that they were to remain with him: and well do those who were there present bear witness that never did knight defend himself better with his hands than did the emperor. This combat lasted a long time. Some were there who did well, and some were there who fled. In the end, for so God suffers misadventures to occur, they were discomfited. There on the field remained the Emperor Baldwin, who never would fly, and Count Louis; the Emperor Baldwin was taken alive and Count Louis was slain.

Alas! how woeful was our loss! There was lost the Bishop Peter of Bethlehem, and Stephen of Perche, brother to Count Geoffry, and Renaud of Montmirail, brother of the Count of Nevers, and Matthew of Wallincourt, and Robert of Ronsoi, John of Friaise, Walter of Neuilli, Ferri of Yerres, John his brother, Eustace of Heumont, John his brother, Baldwin of Neuville, and many more of whom the book does not here make mention. Those who were able to escape came back flying to the camp.

81

The crusaders raise the siege of Adrianople

WHEN Geoffry, the Marshal of Champagne, who was keeping guard at one of the gates of the city, saw this he issued from the camp as soon as he could, with all the men that were with him, and gave command to Manasses of L'isle, who was on guard at another gate, that he should follow after him. And he rode forth with all his force at full speed, and in full array, to meet the fugitives, and the fugitives all rallied round him. And Manasses of L'isle followed as soon as he was able, with his men, and joined himself to him, so that together they formed a very strong body; and all those who came out of the rout, and whom they could stop, were taken into their ranks.

The rout was thus stayed between nones and vespers. But the most part of the fugitives were so afeared that they fled right before them till they came to the tents and quarters. Thus was the rout stayed, as you have heard; and the Comans, with the Wallachians and Greeks, who were in full chase, ceased their pursuit. But these still galled our force with their bows and arrows, and the men of our force kept still with their faces turned towards them. Thus did both sides remain till nightfall, when the Comans and Wallachians began to retire.

Then did Geoffry of Villehardouin, the Marshal of Champagne, summon to the camp the Doge of Venice, who was an old man and saw naught, but very wise and brave and vigorous; and he asked the Doge to come to him there where he stood with his men, holding the field; and the Doge did so. And when the Marshal saw him, he called him into council, aside, all alone, and said to him: "Lord, you see the misadventure that has befallen us. We have lost the Emperor Baldwin and Count Louis, and the larger part of our people, and of the best. Now let us bethink ourselves how to save what is left. For if God does not take pity on them, we are but lost."

And in the end they settled it thus: that the Doge would return to the camp, and put heart into the people, and order that every one should arm and remain quiet in his tent or pavilion; and that Geoffry the Marshal would remain in full order of battle before the camp till it was night, so that their enemies might not see the host move; and that when it was night all would move from before the city; the Doge of Venice would go before, and Geoffry the Marshal would form the rear-guard, with those who were with him.

82

Retreat of the crusaders

THUS they waited till it was night; and when it was night the Doge of Venice left the camp, as had been arranged, and Geoffry the Marshal formed the rear-guard. And they departed at foot pace, and took with them all their people mounted and dismounted, the wounded as well those who were whole—they left not one behind. And they journeyed towards a city that lies upon the sea, called Rodosto, and that was full three days' journey distant. So they departed from Adrianople, as you have heard; and this adventure befell in the year of the Incarnation of Jesus Christ twelve hundred and five.

And in the night that the host left Adrianople, it happened that a company started to get to Constantinople earlier, and by a more direct way; and they were greatly blamed therefore. In this company was a certain count from Lombardy named Gerard, who came from the land of the marquis, and Odo of Ham, who was lord of a castle called Ham in Vermandois, and John of Maseroles, and many others to the number of twenty-five knights, whom the book does not name. And they went away so fast after the discomfiture which had taken place on the Thursday evening, that they came to Constantinople on the Saturday night, though it was ordinarily a good five days' journey. And they told the news to the Cardinal Peter of Capua, who was there by the authority of Innocent Pope of Rome, and to Conon of Béthune, who guarded the city, and to Miles the Brabant, and to the other good men in the city. And you must know that these were greatly affeared, and thought of a certainty that all the rest, who had been left before Adrianople, were lost, for they had no news of them

83

Peter of Bracieux and Payen of Orleans meet the retreating host

NOW will we say no more about those at Constantinople, who

were in sore trouble, but go back to the Doge of Venice and Geoffry the Marshal, who marched all the night that they left Adrianople, till the dawn of the following day; and then they came to a city called Pamphyle. Now listen and you shall hear how adventures befall as God wills: for in that city had lain during the night, Peter of Bracieux and Payen of Orléans, and all the men belonging to the land of Count Louis, at least a hundred very good knights and one hundred and forty mounted sergeants, and they were coming from the other side of the straits to join the host at Adrianople.

When they saw the host coming, they ran to their arms right nimbly, for they thought we were the Greeks. So they armed themselves, and sent to know what people we were, when their messengers discovered that we were the host retreating after our discomfiture. So the messengers went back, and told them that the Emperor Baldwin was lost, and their lord, Count Louis, of whose land and country they were, and of whose following.

Sadder news could they not have heard. There might you have seen many tears wept, and many hands wrung for sorrow and pity. And they went on, all armed as they were, till they came to where Geoffry, the Marshal of Champagne, was keeping guard in the rear, in very great anxiety and misease. For Johannizza, the King of Wallachia and Bulgaria, had come at the point of day before Adrianople with all his host, and found that we had departed, and so ridden after us till it was full day; and when he found us not, he was full of grief; and well was it that he found us not, for if he had found us we must all have been lost beyond recovery.

"Sir," said Peter of Bracieux and Payen of Orléans to Geoffry the Marshal, "what would you have us do? We will do whatever you wish." And he answered them: "You see how matters stand with us. You are fresh and unwearied, and your horses also; therefore do you keep guard in the rear, and I will go forward and hold in hand our people, who are greatly dismayed and in sore need of comfort." To this they consented right willingly. So they established the rearguard duly and efficiently, and as men who well knew how, for they were good knights and honourable.

84

The host reaches Rodosto

GEOFFRY the Marshal rode before and led the host, and rode till he came to a city called Cariopolis. Then he saw that the horses were weary with marching all night, and entered into the city, and put them up till noon. And they gave food to their horses, and ate themselves of what they could find, and that was but little.

So they remained all the day in that city until night. And Johannizza, the King of Wallachia, had followed them all the day with all his powers, and encamped about two leagues from them. And when it was night, those in the city all armed themselves and departed. Geoffry the Marshal led the van, and those formed the rear-guard who had formed it during the day. So they rode through that night, and the following day (16th April) in great fear and much hardship, till they came to the city of Rodosto, a city very rich and very strong, and inhabited by Greeks. These Greeks did not dare to defend themselves, so our people entered in and took quarters; so at last were they in safety.

Thus did the host escape from Adrianople, as you have heard. Then was a council held in the city of Rodosto; and it seemed to the council that Constantinople was in greater jeopardy than they were. So they took messengers, and sent them by sea, telling them to travel night and day, and to advise those in the city not to be anxious about them—for they had escaped—and that they would repair back to Constantinople as soon as they could.

85

Seven thousand pilgrims leave the crusaders

AT the time when the messengers arrived, there were in Constantinople five ships of Venice, very large and very good, laden with pilgrims, and knights, and sergeants who were leaving the land and returning to their own countries. There were at least seven thousand men at arms in the ships, and one was William the advocate of Béthune, and there were besides Baldwin of Aubigny, and John of Virsin who belonged to the land of Count Louis, and was his liegeman, and at least one hundred other knights, whom the book does not here name. Master Peter of Capua, who was cardinal from the Pope of Rome, Innocent, and Conon of Béthune, who commanded in Constantinople, and Miles the Brabant, and a great number of other men of mark, went to the five ships, and prayed those who were in them, with sighs and tears, to have mercy and pity upon Christendom, and upon their liege lords who had been lost in battle, and to remain for the love of God. But they would not listen to a single word, and left the port. They spread their sails, and went their way, as God ordained, in such sort that the wind took them to the port of Rodosto; and this was on the day following that on which those who had escaped from the discomfiture came thither.

The same prayers, with tears and weeping, that had been addressed to them at Constantinople—those same prayers were now addressed to them at Rodosto; and Geoffry the Marshal, and those who were with him, besought them to have mercy and pity on the land, and remain, for never would they be able to succour any land in such dire need. They replied that they would consult together, and give an answer on the morrow.

And now listen to the adventure which befell that night in the city. There was a knight from the land of Count Louis, called Peter of Frouville, who was held in honour, and of great name. The same fled by night, and left all his baggage and his people, and got himself to the ship of John of Virsin, who was from the land of Count Louis of Blois and Chartres. And those on board the five ships, who in the morning were to give their answer to Geoffry the Marshal and to the Doge of Venice, so soon as they saw the day, they spread their sails, and went their way without word said to anyone. Much and great blame did they receive, both in the land whither they went, and in the land they had left; and he who received most blame of all was Peter of Frouville. For well has it been said that he is but ill-advised who, through fear of death, does what will be a reproach to him for ever.

86

Meeting of many of the crusaders; Henry, the brother of Baldwin, is made regent

NOW let us speak of these last no farther, but speak of Henry, brother to the Emperor Baldwin of Constantinople, who had left Adramittium, which he had conquered, and passed the straits at the city of Abydos, and was coming towards Adrianople to succour the Emperor Baldwin, his brother. And with him had come the Armenians of the land, who had helped him against the Greeks—some twenty thousand with all their wives and children—for they dared not remain behind.

Then came to him the news, by certain Greeks, who had escaped from the discomfiture, that his brother the Emperor Baldwin was lost, and Count Louis, and the other barons. Afterwards came the news of those who had escaped and were at Rodosto; and these asked him to make all the haste he could, and come to them. And because he wanted to hasten as much as he could, and reach them earlier, he left behind the Armenians, who traveled on foot, and had with them chariots, and their wives and children; and inasmuch as these could not come on so fast, and he thought they would travel safely and without hurt, he went forward and encamped in a village called Cartopolis.

On that very day came thither the nephew of Geoffry the Marshal, Anseau of Courcelles, whom Geoffry had summoned from the parts of Macre, Trajanopolis, and the Baie, lands that had been bestowed upon him; and with Anseau came the people from Philippopolis, who had left Renier of Trit. This company held full a hundred good knights, and full five hundred mounted sergeants, who all were on their way to Adrianople to succour the Emperor Baldwin. But tidings had come to them, as to the others, that the emperor had been defeated, so they turned to go to Rodosto, and came to encamp at Cartopolis, the village where Henry, the brother of the Emperor Baldwin, was then encamped. And when Baldwin's men saw them coming, they ran to arms, for they thought they were Greeks, and the others thought the same of Baldwin's men. And so they advanced till they became known to one another, and each was right glad of the other's coming, and felt all the safer; and they quartered themselves in the village that night until the morrow.

On the morrow they left, and rode straight towards Rodosto, and came that night to the city; and there they found the Doge of Venice and Geoffry the Marshal, and all who had escaped from the late discomfiture; and right glad were these to see them. Then were many tears shed for sorrow by those who had lost their friends. Ah, God! What pity it was that those men now assembled had not been at Adrianople with the Emperor Baldwin, for in that case would nothing have been lost. But such was not God's pleasure.

So they sojourned there on the following day, and the day after, and arranged matters; and Henry, the brother of the Emperor Baldwin, was received into lordship, as regent of the empire, in lieu of his brother.

And then misfortune came upon the Armenians, who were coming after Henry, the brother of the Emperor Baldwin, for the people of the land gathered together and discomfited the Armenians, so that they were all taken, killed or lost.

87

Return to Constantinople; appeals for help sent to the Pope, and to France, and to other lands; death of the Doge

JOHANNIZZA, King of Wallachia and Bulgaria, had with him all his power, and he occupied the whole land; and the country, and the cities, and the castles held for him; and his Comans over-ran the land as far as Constantinople. Henry the regent of the empire, and the Doge of Venice, and Geoffry the Marshal, were still at Rodosto, which is a three days' journey from Constantinople. And they took council, and the Doge of Venice set a garrison of Venetians in Rodosto—for it was theirs. And on the morrow they put their forces in array, and rode, day by day, towards Constantinople.

When they reached Selymbria, a city which is two days' journey from Constantinople, and belonged to the Emperor Baldwin, Henry his brother set there a garrison of his people, and they rode with the rest to Constantinople, where they were received right willingly, for the people were in great terror. Nor is that to be wondered at, for they had lost so much of the country, that outside Constantinople they only held Rodosto and Selymbria; the whole of the rest of the country being held by Johannizza, King of Wallachia and Bulgaria. And on the other side of the straits of St. George, they held no more than the castle of Piga, while the rest of the land was in the hands of Theodore Lascaris.

Then the barons decided to send to the Apostle of Rome, Innocent, and to France and Flanders, and to other lands, to ask for succour. And for this purpose were chosen as envoys Nevelon, Bishop of Soissons, and Nicholas of Mailly, and John Bliaud. The rest remained in Constantinople, in great distress, as men who stood in fear of losing the land. So they remained till Pentecost (29th May 1205). And within this time a very great misfortune happened to the host, for Henry Dandolo was taken sick; so he made an end and died, and was buried with great honour in the church of St. Sophia.

When Pentecost had come, Johannizza, the King of Wallachia and Bulgaria, had pretty well had his will of the land; and he could no longer hold his Comans together, because they were unable to keep the field during the summer; so the Comans departed to their own country. And he, with all his host of Bulgarians and Greeks, marched against the marquis towards Salonika. And the marquis, who had heard the news of the discomfiture of the Emperor Baldwin, raised the siege of Napoli, and went to Salonika with as many men as he could collect, and garrisoned it.

88

The regent obtains certain advantages over the Greeks

HENRY, the brother of the Emperor Baldwin of Constantinople, with as many people as he could gather, marched against the Greeks to a city called Tzurulum, which is a three days' journey from Constantinople. This city surrendered, and the Greeks swore fealty to him—an oath which at that time men observed badly. From thence he marched to Arcadiopolis, and found it void, for the Greeks did not dare to await his coming. And from thence again he rode to the city of Bizye, which was very strong, and well garrisoned with Greeks; and this city too surrendered. Afterwards he rode to the city of Napoli which also remained well garrisoned with Greeks.

As our people were preparing for an assault, the Greeks within the city asked to negotiate for capitulation. But while they thus negotiated, the men of the host effected an entrance into the city on another side, and Henry the Regent of the empire and those who were negotiating knew nothing of it. And this proved very disastrous to the Greeks. For the Franks, who had effected an entrance, began to slaughter them, and to seize their goods, and to take all that they had. So were many killed and taken captive. In this wise was Napoli captured; and the host remained there three days. And the Greeks were so terrified by this slaughter, that they abandoned all the cities and castles of the land, and fled for refuge to Adrianople and Demotica, which were very strong and good cities.

89

Seres surrenders to Johannizza; he forfeits his word

AT that time it happened that Johannizza, the King of Wallachia and Bulgaria, with all his host, marched against the marquis, towards a city called Seres. And the marquis had set a strong garrison of his people in the city, for he had set there Hugh of Colemi, who was a very good knight, and high in rank, and William of Arles, who was his marshal, and great part of his best men. And Johannizza, the King of Wallachia besieged them; nor had he been there long before he took the burgh by force. And at the taking of the burgh a great misfortune befell, for Hugh of Colemi was killed; he was struck through the eye.

When he was killed, who was the best of them all, the rest of the garrison were greatly afeared. They drew back into the castle, which was very strong; and Johannizza besieged them, and erected his petraries and mangonels. Nor had he besieged them long before they began to talk about surrendering, for which they were afterwards blamed, and incurred great reproach. And they agreed to yield up the castle to Johannizza, and Johannizza on his side caused twenty-five of his highest ranking men to swear to them that they should be taken, safe and sound, with all their horses, and all their arms, and all their baggage, to Salonika, or Constantinople, or Hungary—whichever of the three they liked best.

In this manner was Seres surrendered, and Johannizza caused the besieged to come forth from the castle and encamp near him in the fields; and he treated them with much fair seeming, and sent them presents. So he kept them for three days, and then he lied and foreswore his promises; for he had them taken, and spoiled of their goods, and led away to Wallachia, naked, and unshod, and on foot. The poor and the mean people, who were of little worth, he sent into Hungary; and as for the others, he caused their heads to be cut off. Of such mortal treachery was the King of Wallachia guilty, as you have heard. Here did the host suffer grievous loss, one of the most dolorous that ever it suffered. And Johannizza had the castle and city razed, and went on after the marquis.

90

The regent besieges Adrianople in vain

HENRY, the regent of the empire, with all his power, rode towards Adrianople, and laid siege to it; and he was in great peril, for there were many, both within and without the city who so hemmed him in, he and his people, that they could scantly buy provisions, or go foraging. Therefore they enclosed their camp with palisades and barriers, and told off part of their men to keep guard within the palisades and barriers, while the others attacked the city.

And they devised machines of diverse kinds, and scaling ladders, and many other engines, and wrought diligently to take the city. But they could not take it, for the city was very strong and well furnished for defence. So matters went ill with them, and many of their people were wounded; and one of their good knights, Peter of Bracieux, was struck on the forehead from a mangonel, and brought near to death; but he recovered, by the will of God, and was taken away in a litter.

When they saw that they could in no wise prevail against the city, Henry the Regent of the empire, and the French host departed. And greatly were they harassed by the people of the land and by the Greeks; and they rode from day to day till they came to a city called Pamphyle, and lodged there, and sojourned in it for two months. And they made thence many forays towards Demotica and the country round about, where they captured much cattle, and other booty. So the host remained in those parts till the beginning of winter; and supplies came to them from Rodosto, and from the sea.

91

Destruction of Philippopolis by Johannizza

NOW let us leave speaking of Henry, the Regent of the empire, and speak of Johannizza, the King of Wallachia and Bulgaria, who had taken Seres, as you have already heard, and killed by treachery those who had surrendered to him. Afterwards he had ridden towards Salonika, and sojourned thereby a long while, and wasted a great part of the land. The Marquis Boniface of Montferrat was at Salonika, very wroth, and sorrowing greatly for the loss of his lord, the Emperor Baldwin, and for the other barons, and for his castle of Seres that he had lost, and for his men.

And when Johannizza saw that he could do nothing more, he retired towards his own land, with all his force. And the people in Philippopolis—which belonged to Renier of Trit, for the Emperor Baldwin had bestowed it upon him—heard tell how the Emperor Baldwin was lost, and many of his barons, and that the marquis had lost Seres; and they saw that the relatives of Renier of Trit, and his own son and his nephew, had abandoned him, and that he had with him but very few people; and they deemed that the Franks would never be in power again. So a great part of the people, who were Paulicians, betook themselves to Johannizza, and surrendered themselves to him, and said: "Sire, ride to Philippopolis, or send thither thy host, and we will deliver the whole city into thy hands."

When Renier of Trit, who was in the city, knew of this, he doubted not that they would yield up the city to Johannizza. So he issued forth with as many people as he could collect, and left at the point of day, and came to one of the outlying quarters of the city where dwelt the Paulicians who had repaired to Johannizza, and he set fire to that quarter of the city, and burned a great part of it. Then he went to the castle of Stanimac, which was at three leagues' distance, and garrisoned by his people, and entered therein. And in this castle he lay besieged for a long while, some thirteen months, in great distress and great poverty, so that for famine they ate their horses. He was distant a nine days' journey from Constantinople, and could neither obtain tidings therefrom, nor send tidings thither.

Then did Johannizza send his host before Philippopolis; nor had he been there long before those who were in the city surrendered it to him, and he promised to spare their lives. And after he had promised to spare their lives, he first caused the archbishop of the city to be slain, and the men of rank to be flayed alive, and certain others to be burned, and certain others to have their heads cut off, and the rest he caused to be driven away in chains. And the city he caused to be pulled down, with its towers and walls; and the high palaces and rich houses to be burned and utterly destroyed. Thus was destroyed the noble city of Philippopolis, one of the three finest cities in the empire of Constantinople.

92

The regent sets garrisons in such places as he still held

NOW let us leave off speaking of those who were at Philippopolis, and of Renier of Trit, who is shut up in Stanimac, and return to Henry, the brother of the Emperor Baldwin, who had sojourned at Pamphyle till the beginning of winter. Then he took council with his men and with his barons; and they decided to set a garrison in a city called Rusium, which was situated at a place rich and fertile in the middle of the land; and the chiefs placed over this garrison were Thierri of Loos, who was seneschal, and Thierri of Tenremonde, who was constable. And Henry, the regent of the empire, gave to them at least seven score knights, and a great many mounted sergeants, and ordered them to maintain the war against the Greeks, and to guard the marches.

And he himself went with the rest of his people to the city of Bizye, and placed a garrison there; and left in command Anseau of Cayeux, and confided to him at least six score knights, and a great many mounted sergeants. Another city, called Arcadiopolis was garrisoned by the Venetians. And the city of Napoli was restored by the brother of the Emperor Baldwin to Vemas, who had to wife the sister of the King of France, and was a Greek who sided with us; and except he, no other Greek was on our part. And those who were in these cities maintained the war against the Greeks, and made many forays. Henry himself returned to Constantinople with the rest of his men.

Now Johannizza, the King of Wallachia and Bulgaria, though rich and of great possessions, never forgot his own interests, but raised a great force of Comans and Wallachians. And when it came to three weeks after Christmas, he sent these men into the land of Romania to help those at Adrianople and Demotica; and the latter, being now in force, grew bolder and rode abroad with the greater assurance.

93

Defeat of the Franks near Rusium

THIERRI of Tenremonde, who was chief and constable, made a foray on the fourth day before the feast of St. Mary Candlemas (30th January 1206); and he rode all night, having six score knights with him, and left Rusium with but a small garrison. When it was dawn, he came to a village where the Comans and Wallachians were encamped, and surprised them in such sort that those who were in the village were unaware of their coming. They killed a good many of the Comans and Wallachians, and captured some forty of their horses; and when they had done this execution, they turned back towards Rusium.

And on that very night the Comans and Wallachians had ridden forth to do us hurt; and there were some seven thousand of them. They came in the morning before Rusium, and the garrison, which was but small, closed the gates, and mounted the walls; and the Comans and Wallachians turned back. They had not gone more than a league and a half from the city, when they met the company of the French under the command of Thierri of Tenremonde. So soon as the French saw them advancing, they formed into their four battalions, with intent to draw into Rusium in slow time; for they knew that if, by God's grace, they could come thither, they would then be in safety.

The Comans, and the Wallachians, and the Greeks of the land rode towards them, for they were in very great force. And they came upon the rear-guard, and began to harass it full sorely. Now the rear-guard was formed of the men of Thierri of Loos, who was seneschal, and had returned to Constantinople, and his brother Villain was now in command.

And the Comans and Wallachians and Greeks pressed them very hard, and wounded many of their horses. Loud were the cries and fierce the onslaught, so that by main force and pure distress they drove the rear-guard back on the battalion of Andrew of Urboise and John of Choisy; and in this manner the Franks retreated, suffering greatly.

The enemy renewed their onslaught so fiercely that they drove the Franks who were nearest to them back on the battalion of Thierri of Tenremonde, the constable. Nor was it long before they drove them back still further on to the battalions led by Charles of the Frêne. And now the Franks had retreated, sore harassed, till they were within half a mile of Rusium. And the others ever pressed upon them more hardily; and the battle went sore against them, and many were wounded, and of their horses. So, as God will suffer misadventures, they could endure no further, but were discomfited; for they were heavily armed, and their enemies lightly; and the latter began to slaughter them.

Alas! well might Christendom rue that day! For of all those six score knights did not more than ten escape who were not killed or taken; and those who escaped came flying into Rusium, and rejoined their own people. There was slain Thierri of Tenremonde, the constable, Orri of L'isle, who was a good knight and highly esteemed, and John of Pompone, Andrew of Urboise, John of Choisy, Guy of Conflans, Charles of the Frêne, Villain the brother of Thierri the Seneschal. Nor can this book tell the names of all who were then killed or taken. On that day happened one of the greatest mishaps, and the most grievous that ever befell to the Christendom of the land of Romania, and one of the most pitiful.

The Comans, and Greeks, and Wallachians retired, having done according to their will in the land, and won many good horses and good hauberks. And this misadventure happened on the day before the eve of our Lady St. Mary Candlemas (31st January 1206). And the remnant who had escaped from the discomfiture, together with those who had been in Rusium, escaped from the city, so soon as it was night, and went all night flying, and came on the morrow to the city of Rodosto.

94

New invasion of Johannizza; ruin of Napoli

THIS dolorous news came to Henry the Regent of the empire, while he was going in procession to the shrine of our Lady of Blachemae, on the day of the feast of our Lady St. Mary Candlemas. And you must know that many were then dismayed in Constantinople, and they thought of a truth that the land was but lost. And Henry, the regent of the empire, decided that he would place a garrison in Selymbria, which was a two days' journey from Constantinople, and he sent thither Macaire of Sainte-Menehould, with fifty knights to garrison the city.

Now when tidings came to Johannizza, King of Wallachia, as to how his people had fared, he very greatly rejoiced; for they had killed or taken a very great part of the best men in the French host. So he sent throughout all his lands to collect as many people as he could, and raised a great host of Comans, and Greeks and Wallachians, and entered into Romania. And the greater part of the cities held for him, and all the castles; and he had so large a host that it was a marvel.

When the Venetians heard tell that he was coming with so great a force, they abandoned Arcadiopolis. And Johannizza rode with all his hosts till he came to Napoli, which was garrisoned by Greeks and Latins, and belonged to Vemas, who had to wife the empress, the sister of the King of France; and of the Latins was chief Bègue of Fransures, a knight of the land of the Beauvaisais. And Johannizza, the King of Wallachia, caused the city to be assaulted, and took it by force.

There was so great a slaughter of people killed, that it was a marvel. And Bègue of Fransures was taken before Johannizza, who had him killed incontinently, together with all, whether Greek or Latin, who were of any account; and all the meaner folk, and women and children, he caused to be led away captive to Wallachia. Then did he cause all the city—which was very good and very rich, and in a good land—to be cast down and utterly destroyed. Thus was the city of Napoli razed to the ground as you have heard.

95

Destruction of Rodosto

TWELVE leagues thence lay the city of Rodosto on the sea. It was very strong, and rich, and large, and very well garrisoned by Venetians, And besides all this, there had come thither a body of sergeants, some two thousand strong, and they had also come to guard the city. When they heard that Napoli had been taken by force, and that Johannizza had caused all the people that were therein to be put to death, they fell in to such terror that they were utterly confounded and foredone[16]. As God suffers misadventures to fall upon men, so the Venetians rushed to their ships, helter-skelter, pell-mell, and in such sort that they almost drowned one another; and the mounted sergeants, who came from France and Flanders, and other countries, went flying through the land.

Now listen and hear how little this served them, and what a misadventure was their flight; for the city was so strong, and so well enclosed by good walls and good towers, that no one would ever have ventured to assault it, and that Johannizza had no thought of going thither. But when Johannizza, who was full half a day's journey distant, heard tell that they had fled, he rode thither. The Greeks who had remained in the city, surrendered, and he incontinently caused them to be taken, small and great—save those who escaped—and led captive into Wallachia; and the city he ordered to be destroyed and razed to the ground. Ah! the loss and damage! For the city was one of the best in Romania, and of the best situated.

---

16   Exhausted with fatigue

96

Johannizza continues his conquests and ravages

NEAR there was another city called Panedor, which surrendered to him; and he caused it to be utterly destroyed, and the people to be led captive to Wallachia like the people of Rodosto. Afterwards he rode to the city of Heraclea, that lay by a good seaport, and belonged to the Venetians, who had left in it but a weak garrison; so he assaulted it, and took it by force. There again was a mighty slaughter, and the remnant that escaped the slaughter he caused to be led captive to Wallachia, while the city itself he destroyed, as he had destroyed the others.

Thence he marched to the city of Daonium, which was very strong and fine; and the people did not dare to defend it. So he caused it to be destroyed and razed to the ground. Then he marched to the city of Tzurulum, which had already surrendered to him, and caused it to be destroyed and razed to the ground, and the people to be led away captive. And thus he dealt with every castle and city that surrendered; even though he had promised them safety, he caused the buildings to be destroyed, and the men and women to be led away captive; and no covenant that he made did he ever keep.

Then the Comans and Wallachians scoured the land up to the gates of Constantinople, where Henry the regent then was with as many men as he could command; and very dolorous was he and very wroth, because he could not get men enough to defend his land. So the Comans seized the cattle off the land, and took captive men, women, and children, and destroyed the cities and castles, and caused such ruin and desolation that never has man heard tell of greater.

So they came to a city called Athyra, which was twelve leagues from Constantinople, and had been given to Payen of Orléans by Henry, the emperor's brother. This city held a very great number of people, for the dwellers in the country round about had fled thither; and the Comans assaulted it, and took it by force. There the slaughter was so great, that there had been none such in any city where they had been. And you must know that all the castles and all the cities that surrendered to Johannizza under promise of safety were destroyed and razed to the ground, and the people led away captive to Wallachia in such manner as you have heard.

And you must know that within five days' journey from Constantinople there remained nothing to destroy save only the city of Bizye, and the city of Selymbria, which were garrisoned by the French. And in Bizye abode Anseau of Cayeux, with six score knights, and in Salymbria abode Macaire of Sainte-Menehould with fifty knights; and Henry the brother of the Emperor Baldwin remained in Constantinople with the remainder of the host. And you may know that their fortunes were at the lowest, seeing that outside of Constantinople they had kept possession of no more than these two cities.

97

The Greeks are reconciled to the crusaders; Johannizza besieges Demotica

WHEN the Greeks who were in the host with Johannizza—the same who had yielded themselves up to him, and rebelled against the Franks—when they saw how he destroyed their castles and cities, and kept no covenant with them, they held themselves to be but dead men, and betrayed. They spoke one to another, and said that as Johannizza had dealt with other cities, so would he deal with Adrianople and Demotica when he returned thither, and that if these two cities were destroyed, then was Romania forever lost.

So they took messengers privily, and sent them to Vemas in Constantinople. And they besought Vemas to cry for pity to Henry, the brother of the Emperor Baldwin, and to the Venetians, so that they might make peace with them; and they themselves, in turn, would restore Adrianople and Demotica to the Franks; and the Greeks would all turn to Henry; and the Greeks and Franks dwell together in good accord.

So a council was held, and many words were spoken this way and that, but in the end it was settled that Adrianople and Demotica, with all their appurtenances, should be bestowed on Vemas and the empress his wife, who was sister to the King Philip of France, and that they should do service therefore to the emperor and to the empire. Such was the convention made and concluded, and so was peace established between the Greeks and the Franks.

Johanizza, the King of Wallachia and Bulgaria, who had sojourned long in Romania, and wasted the country during the whole of Lent, and for a good while after Easter (2nd April 1206), now retired towards Adrianople and Demotica, and had it in mind to deal with those cities as he had dealt with the other cities of the land. And when the Greeks who were with him saw that he turned towards Adrianople, they began to steal away, both by day and by night, some twenty, thirty, forty, a hundred, at a time.

When he came to Adrianople, he required of those that were within that they should let him enter, as he had entered elsewhere. But they said they would not, and spoke thus: "Sire, when we surrendered to thee, and rebelled against the Franks, thou didst swear to protect us in all good faith, and to keep us in safety. Thou hast not done so, but hast utterly ruined Romania; and we know full well that thou wilt do unto us as thou hast done unto others." And when Johannizza heard this, he laid siege to Demotica, and erected round it sixteen large petraries, and began to construct engines of every kind for the siege, and to waste all the country round.

Then did those in Adrianople and Demotica take messengers, and send them to Constantinople, to Henry, the Regent of the empire, and to Vemas, and prayed them, for God's sake, to rescue Demotica, which was being besieged. And when those at Constantinople heard these tidings, they decided to succour Demotica. But some there were who did not dare to advise that our people should issue from Constantinople, and so place in jeopardy the few Christian folk that remained. Nevertheless, in the end, as you have heard, it was decided to issue forth, and move on Selymbria.

The cardinal, who was there as legate on the part of the Pope of Rome, preached thereon to the people, and promised a full indulgence to all such as should go forth and lose their lives on the way. So Henry issued from Constantinople with as many men as he could collect, and marched to the city of Selymbria; and he encamped before the city for full eight days. And from day to day came messengers from Adrianople praying him to have mercy upon them, and come to their relief, for if he did not come to their relief, they were but lost.

98

The crusaders march to the relief of Demotica

THEN did Henry take council with his barons, and their decision was that they would go to the city of Bizye, which was a fair city, and strong. So they did as they had devised, and came to Bizye, and encamped before the city on the eve of the feast of my lord St. John the Baptist, in June (23rd June 1206). And on the day that they so encamped came messengers from Adrianople, and said to Henry, the brother of the Emperor Baldwin: "Sire, be it known to thee that if thou dost not relieve the city of Demotica, it cannot hold out more than eight days, for Johannizza's petraries have breached the walls in four places, and his men have twice got on to the walls."

Then he asked for counsel as to what he should do. Many were the words spoken, to and fro; but in the end they said: "Lord, we have come so far that we shall be forever shamed if we do not succour Demotica. Let every man now confess and receive the communion; and then let us set our forces in array." And it was reckoned that they had with them about four hundred knights, and of a certainty no more. So they summoned the messengers who had come from Adrianople, and asked them how matters stood, and what number of men Johannizza had with him. And the messengers answered that he had with him at least forty thousand men-at-arms, not reckoning those on foot, of whom they had no count.

Ah God! what a perilous battle—so few against so many! In the morning, on the day of the feast of my lord St. John the Baptist, all confessed and received the communion, and on the following day they marched forward. The van was commanded by Geoffry, the Marshal of Champagne, and with him was Macaire of Sainte-Menehould. The second division was under Conon of Béthune and Miles the Brabant; the third under Payen of Orléans and Peter of Bracieux; the fourth was under Anseau of Cayeux; the fifth under Baldwin of Beauvoir; the sixth under Hugh of Beaumetz; the seventh under Henry, brother of the Emperor Baldwin; the eighth, with the Flemings, under Walter of Escornai; Thierri of Loos, who was seneschal, commanded the rear-guard.

So they rode for three days, all in order; nor did any host ever advance seeking battle so perilously. For they were in peril on two accounts; first because they were so few, and those they were about to attack so many; and secondly, because they did not believe the Greeks, with whom they had just made peace, would help them heartily. For they stood in fear lest, when need arose, the Greeks would go over to Johannizza, who, as you have already heard, had been so near to taking Demotica.

99

Johannizza retreats, followed by the crusaders

WHEN Johannizza heard that the Franks were coming, he did not dare to abide, but burned his engines of war, and broke up his camp. So he departed from Demotica; and you must know that this was accounted by all the world as a great miracle. And Henry, the regent of the empire, came on the fourth day (28th June) before Adrianople, and pitched his camp near the river of Adrianople, in the fairest meadows in the world. When those who were within the city saw his host coming, they issued forth, bearing all their crosses, and in procession, and showed such joy as had never been seen. And well might they rejoice for they had been in evil case.

Then came tidings to the host that Johannizza was lodged at a castle called Rodosto. So in the morning they set forth and marched to those parts to seek battle; and Johannizza broke up his camp, and marched back towards his own land. The host followed after him for five days, and he as constantly retired before them. On the fifth day they encamped at a very fair and pleasant place by a castle called Fraim; and there they sojourned three days.

And at this place there was a division in the host, and a company of valiant men separated themselves therefrom because of a quarrel that they had with Henry, the brother of the Emperor Baldwin. Of this company Baldwin of Beauvoir was chief; and Hugh of Beaumetz went with him, and William of Gommegnies, and Dreux of Beaurain. There were some fifty knights who departed together in that company; and they never thought the rest would dare to remain in the land in the midst of their enemies.

100

Renier of Trit relieved and delivered

THEN did Henry, the regent of the empire, take council with the barons that were with him; and they decided to ride forward. So they rode forward for two days, and encamped in a very fair valley, near a castle called Moniac. The castle yielded itself to them, and they remained there five days; and then said they would go and relieve Renier of Renier of Trit, who was besieged in Stanimac, and had been shut up therein for thirteen months. So Henry the Regent of the empire, remained in the camp, with a great part of the host, and the remainder went forward to relieve Renier of Trit at Stanimac.

And you must know that those who went forward went in very great peril, and that any rescue so full of danger has but seldom been undertaken, seeing that they rode for three days through the land of their enemies. In this rescue took part Conon of Béthune, and Geoffry of Villehardouin, Marshal of Champagne, and Macaire of Sainte-Menehould, and Miles the Brabant, and Peter of Bracieux, and Payen of Orléans, and Anseau of Cayeux, and Thierri of Loos, and William of Perchoi, and a body of Venetians under command of Andrew Valère. So they rode forward till they came to the castle of Stanimac, and approached so near that they could now see it.

Renier of Trit was on the walls, and he perceived the advanced guard, which was under Geoffry the Marshal, and the other battalions, approaching in very good order; and he knew not what people they might be. And no wonder that he was in doubt, for of a long time he had heard no tidings of us; and he thought we were Greeks coming to besiege him.

Geoffry, the Marshal of Champagne, took certain Turcoples[17] and mounted cross-bowmen and sent them forward to see if they could learn the condition of the castle; for they knew not if those within it were alive or dead, seeing that of a long time they had heard no tidings of them. And when these came before the castle, Renier of Trit and his men knew them; and you may well think what joy they had! They issued forth and came to meet their friends, and all made great joy of each other.

The barons quartered themselves in a very good city that lay at the foot of the castle, and had aforetime besieged the castle. Then said the barons that they had often heard tell that the Emperor Baldwin had died in Johannizza's prison, but that they did not believe it. Renier of Trit, however, told them of a truth that the emperor was dead, and then they believed it. Greatly did many then grieve; alas! if only their grief had not been beyond remedy!

So they lay that night in the city; and on the morrow they departed, and abandoned Stanimac. They rode for two days, and on the third they came to the camp, below the castle of Moniac, that lies on the River Arta, where Henry, the emperor's brother, was waiting for them. Greatly did those of the host rejoice over Renier of Trit, who had thus been rescued from durance, and great was the credit given to those who had brought him back, for they had gone for him in great peril.

---

17   Soldiers born of a Turkish father and a Greek mother

101

Henry crowned emperor; Johannizza ravages the country again; the emperor marches against him

THE barons now resolved that they would go to Constantinople, and crown Henry, the brother of the Emperor Baldwin, as emperor, and leave in the country Vemas, and all the Greeks of the land, together with forty knights, whom Henry, the regent of the empire, would leave with him. So Henry, the regent of the empire, and the other barons, went towards Constantinople, and they rode from day to day till they came thither, and right well were they received. They crowned Henry as emperor with great joy and great honour in the church of St. Sophia on the Sunday (20th August) after the festival of our lady St. Mary, in August. And this was in the year of the Incarnation of our Lord Jesus Christ twelve hundred and six.

Now when Johannizza, the King of Wallachia and Bulgaria, heard that the emperor had been crowned in Constantinople, and that Vemas had remained in the land of Adrianople and Demotica, he collected together as large a force as he could. And Vemas had not rebuilt the walls of Demotica where they had been breached by Johannizza with his petraries and mangonels, and he had set but a weak garrison therein. So Johannizza marched on Demotica, and took it, and destroyed it, and razed the walls to the ground, and overran the whole country, and took men, women, and children for a prey, and wrought devastation. Then did those in Adrianople beseech the Emperor Henry to succour them, seeing that Demotica had been lost in such cruel sort.

Then did the Emperor Henry summon as many people as he could, and issued from Constantinople, and rode day by day towards Adrianople, with all his forces in order. And Johannizza, the King of Wallachia, who was in the land, when he heard that the emperor was coming, drew back into his own land. And the Emperor Henry rode forward till he came to Adrianople, and he encamped outside the city in a meadow.

Then came the Greeks of the land, and told him that Johannizza, the King of Wallachia, was carrying off men and women and cattle, and that he had destroyed Demotica, and wasted the country round; and that he was still within a day's march. The emperor settled that he would follow after, and do battle—if so be that Johannizza would abide his coming—and deliver the men and women who were being led away captive. So he rode after Johannizza, and Johannizza retired as the emperor advanced, and the emperor followed him for four days. Then they came to a city called Veroi.

When those who were in the city saw the host of the Emperor Henry approaching, they fled into the mountains and abandoned the city. And the emperor came with all his host, and encamped before the city, and found it well furnished with corn and meat, and such other things as were needful. So they sojourned there for two days, and the emperor caused his men to overrun the surrounding country, and they obtained a large booty in cows and buffaloes, and other beasts in very great plenty. Then he departed from Veroi with all his booty, and rode to another city, a day's journey distant, called Blisnon. And as the other Greeks had abandoned Veroi, so did the dwellers in Blisnon abandon their city; and he found it furnished with all things necessary, and quartered himself there.

102

The emperor meets Johannizza and recaptures his prisoners

THEN came tidings that in a certain valley, three leagues distant from the host, were the men and women whom Johannizza was leading away captive, together with his plunder, and all his chariots. Then did Henry appoint the Greeks from Adrianople and Demotica to go and recover the captives and the plunder, two battalions of knights going with them; and as had been arranged, so was this done on the morrow. The command of the one battalion was given to Eustace, the brother of the Emperor Henry of Constantinople, and the command of the other to Macaire of Sainte-Menehould.

So they rode, they and the Greeks, till they came to the valley of which they had been told; and there they found the captives. And Johannizza's men engaged the Emperor Henry's men, and men and horses were killed and wounded on either side; but by the goodness of God, the Franks had the advantage, and rescued the captives, and caused them to turn again, and brought them away.

And you must know that this was a mighty deliverance; for the captives numbered full twenty thousand men, women, and children; and there were full three thousand chariots laden with their clothes and baggage, to say nothing of other booty in good quantity. The line of the captives, as they came to the camp, was two great leagues in length, and they reached the camp that night. Then was the Emperor Henry greatly rejoiced, and all the other barons; and they had the captives lodged apart, and well guarded, with their goods, so that they lost not one pennyworth of what they possessed. On the morrow the Emperor Henry rested for the sake of the people he had delivered. And on the day after he left that country, and rode day by day till he came to Adrianople.

There he set free the men and women he had rescued; and each one went whithersoever he listed, to the land where he was born, or to any other place. The booty, of which he had great plenty, was divided in due shares among the host. So the Emperor Henry sojourned there five days, and then rode to the city of Demotica, to see how far it had been destroyed, and whether it could again be fortified. He encamped before the city, and saw, both he and his barons, that in the state in which it then was, it were not well to refortify it.

103

Projected marriage between the emperor and the daughter of Boniface; the crusaders ravage the land of Johannizza

THEN came to the camp, as envoy, a baron, Otho of La Roche by name, belonging to the Marquis Boniface of Montferrat. He came to speak of a marriage that had been spoken of aforetime between the daughter of Boniface, the Marquis of Montferrat, and the Emperor Henry; and brought tidings that the lady had come from Lombardy, whence her father had sent to summon her, and that she was now at Salonika. Then did the emperor take council, and it was decided that the marriage should be ratified on either side. So the envoy, Otho of La Roche, returned to Salonika.

The emperor had reassembled his men, who had gone to place in safe holding the booty taken at Veroi. And he marched day by day from Adrianople till he came to the land of Johannizza, the King of Wallachia and Bulgaria. They came to a city called Ferme, and took it, and entered in, and won much booty. They remained there for three days, and overran all the land, got very much spoil, and destroyed a city called Aquilo.

On the fourth day they departed from Ferme, which was a city fair and well situated, with hot water springs for bathing, the finest in the world; and the emperor caused the city to be burned and destroyed, and they carried away much spoil in cattle and goods. Then they rode day by day till they came back to the city of Adrianople; and they sojourned in the land till the feast of All Saints (1st November 1206), when they could no longer carry on the war because of the winter. So Henry and all his barons, who were much aweary of campaigning, turned their faces towards Constantinople; and he left at Adrianople, among the Greeks, a man of his named Peter of Radinghem, with ten knights.

104

The emperor resumes the war against Theodore Lascaris

AT that time Theodore Lascaris, who held the land on the other side of the straits towards Turkey, was at truce with the Emperor Henry; but that truce he had not kept well, having broken and violated it. So the emperor held council, and sent to the other side of the straits, to the city of Piga, to Peter of Bracieux, to whom land had been assigned in those parts, and with him Payen of Orléans, and Anseau of Cayeux, and Eustace, the emperor's brother, and a great part of his best men to the number of seven score knights. These began to make war in very grim and earnest fashion against Theodore Lascaris, and greatly wasted his land.

They marched to a land called Skiza, which was surrounded by the sea except on one side. And in old days the way of entry had been defended with walls, and towers, and moats, but these were now decayed. So the host of the French entered in, and Peter of Bracieux, to whom the land had been devised, began to restore the defenses, and built two castles, and made two fortified ways of entry. From thence they overran the land of Lascaris, and gained much booty and cattle, and brought such booty and cattle into their island: Theodore Lascaris, on the other hand, harked back upon Skiza, so that there were frequent battles and skirmishes, and losses on the one side and on the other; and the war in those parts was fierce and perilous.

Now let us leave speaking of those who were at Skiza, and speak of Thierri of Loos, who was seneschal, and to whom Nicomedia should have belonged; and Nicomedia lay a day's journey from Nice the Great, the capital of the land of Theodore Lascaris. Thierri then went thither, with a great body of the emperor's men, and found that the castle had been destroyed. So he enclosed and fortified the church of St. Sophia, which was very large and fair, and maintained the war in that place.

105

Advantages obtained by Boniface; marriage of his daughter with the emperor

AT that time the Marquis Boniface of Montferrat departed from Salonika, and went to Seres, which Johannizza had destroyed; and he rebuilt it; and afterwards rebuilt a castle called Drama in the valley of Philippi. All the country round about surrendered to him, and came under his rule; and he wintered in the land.

Meanwhile, so much time had gone by that Christmas was now past. Then came messengers from the marquis to the emperor at Constantinople to say that the marquis had sent his daughter in a galley to the city of Abydos. So the Emperor Henry sent Geoffry, the Marshal of Champagne, and Miles the Brabant, to bring the lady; and these rode day by day till they came to Abydos.

They found the lady, who was very good and fair, and saluted her on behalf of their lord, Henry the Emperor, and brought her to Constantinople in great honour. So the Emperor Henry was wedded to her in the Church of St. Sophia, on the Sunday after the feast of our lady St. Mary Candlemas (4th February 1207), with great joy and in great pomp; and they both wore a crown; and high were the marriage-feastings in the palace of Bucoleon. Thus, as you have just heard, was the marriage celebrated between the emperor and the daughter of the Marquis Boniface, Agnes the empress by name.

106

Theodore Lascaris forms an alliance with Johannizza

THEODORE Lascaris, who was warring against the Emperor Henry, took messengers and sent them to Johannizza, the King of Wallachia and Bulgaria. And he advised Johannizza that all the forces of the Emperor Henry were fighting against him (Lascaris) on the other side of the straits towards Turkey; that the emperor was in Constantinople with but very few people; and that now was the time for vengeance, inasmuch as he himself would be attacking the emperor on the one side, and Johannizza on the other, and the emperor had so few men that he would not be able to defend himself against both. Now Johannizza had already engaged a great host of Comans who were on their way to join his host; and had collected together as large a force of Wallachians and Bulgarians as ever he could. And so much time had now gone by, that it was the beginning of Lent (7th March 1207).

Macaire of Sainte-Menehould had begun to build a castle at

Charax, which lies on a gulf of the sea, six leagues from Nicomedia, towards Constantinople. And William of Sains began to build another castle at Cibotos, that lies on the gulf of Nicomedia, on the other side, towards Nice. And you must know that the Emperor Henry had as much as he could do near Constantinople; as also the barons who were in the land. And well does Geoffry of Villehardouin, the Marshal of Champagne, who is dictating this work, bear witness that never at any time were people so distracted and oppressed by war; this was by reason that the host were scattered in so many places.

107

Siege of Adrianople by Johannizza; siege of Skiza and Cibotos by Lascaris

THEN Johannizza left Wallachia with all his hosts, and with a great host of Comans who joined themselves to him, and entered Roumania. And the Comans overran the country up to the gates of Constantinople; and he himself besieged Adrianople, and erected there thirty-three great petraries which hurled stones against the walls and the towers. And inside Adrianople were only the Greeks and Peter of Radinghem, who had been set there by the emperor, with ten knights. Then the Greeks and the Latins together sent to tell the Emperor Henry how Johannizza had besieged them, and prayed for succour.

Much was the emperor distraught when he heard this; for his forces on the other side of the straits were so scattered, and were everywhere so hard pressed, that they could do no more than they were doing, while he himself had but few men in Constantinople. Nonetheless he undertook to take the field with as many men as he could collect in the Easter fortnight; and he sent word to Skiza, where most of his people were, that they should come to him. So these began to come to him by sea; Eustace, the brother of the Emperor Henry, and Anseau of Cayeux, and the main part of their men, and thus only Peter of Bracieux, and Payen of Orléans, with but few men, remained in Skiza.

When Theodore Lascaris heard tidings that Adrianople was besieged, and that the Emperor Henry, through utter need, was recalling his people, and did not know which way to turn—whether to this side or to that—so heavily was he oppressed by the war, then did Lascaris with the greater zeal gather together all the people he could, and pitched his tents and pavilions before the gates of Skiza; and many were the battles fought before Skiza, some lost and some won. And when Theodore Lascaris saw that there were few people remaining in the city, he took a great part of his host, and such ships as he could collect on the sea, and sent them to the castle of Cibotos, which William of Sains was fortifying; and they set siege to the castle by sea and land, on the Saturday in mid-Lent (31st March 1207).

Within were forty knights, very good men, and Macaire of Sainte-Menehould was their chief; and their castle was as yet but little fortified, so that their foes could come at them with swords and lances. The enemy attacked them by land and by sea very fiercely; and the assault lasted during the whole of Saturday, and our people defended themselves very well. And this book bears witness that never did fifty knights defend themselves at greater disadvantage against such odds. And well may this appear, for of the knights that were there, all were wounded save five only; and one was killed, who was nephew to Miles the Brabant, and his name was Giles.

108

The emperor attacks the fleet of Theodore Lascaris, and rescues Cibotos

BEFORE this assault began, on the Saturday morning, there came a messenger flying to Constantinople. He found the Emperor Henry in the palace of Blachernae, sitting at meat, and spoke to him thus: "Sire, be it known to you that those at Cibotos are being attacked by land and sea; and if you do not speedily deliver them, they will be taken, and be but dead men."

With the emperor were Conon of Béthune, and Geoffry, the

Marshal of Champagne, and Miles the Brabant, and but very few people. And they held a council, and the council was but short, and the emperor went down to the shore, and entered into a galleon; and each one was to take ship such as he could find. And it was proclaimed throughout the city that all were to follow the emperor in the utter need wherein he stood, to go and rescue his men, seeing that without help they were but lost. Then might you have seen the whole city of Constantinople all a-swarm with Venetians and Pisans and other seafaring folk, running to their ships, helter-skelter and pell-mell; and with them entered into the ships the knights, fully armed; and whosoever was first ready, he first left port to go after the emperor.

So they went rowing hard all the evening, as long as the light lasted, and all through the night till the dawn of the following day. And the emperor had used such diligence, that a little after sun-rising he came in sight of Cibotos, and of the host surrounding it by sea and land. And those who were within the castle had not slept that night, but had kept guard through the whole night, however sick or wounded they might be, as men who expected nothing but death.

The emperor saw that the Greeks were close to the walls and about to assault the city. Now he himself had but few of his people with him—among them were Geoffry the Marshal in another ship, and Miles the Brabant, and certain Pisans, and other knights—so that he had some sixteen ships great and small, while on the other side there were full sixty. Nevertheless they saw that if they waited for their people, and suffered the Greeks to assault Cibotos, then those within must be all killed or taken; and when they saw this they decided to sail against the enemy's ships.

They sailed thitherward therefore in line; and all those on board the ships were fully armed, and with their helms laced. And when the Greeks, who were about to attack the castle, saw us coming, they perceived that help was at hand for the besieged, and they avoided the castle, and came to meet us; and all this great host, both horse and foot, drew up on the shore. And the Greeks on ship-board [*The meaning here is a little obscure in the original*] when they saw that the emperor and his people meant to attack them in any case, drew back towards those on shore, so that the latter might give them help with bows and darts.

So the emperor held them close with his seventeen ships till the shouts of those coming from Constantinople began to reach him; and when the night fell so many had come up, that the Franks were everywhere in force upon the sea; and they lay all armed during the night, and cast anchor. And they settled that as soon as they saw the day, they would go and do battle with the enemy on the shore, and also seize their ships. But when it came to about midnight, the Greeks dragged all their ships to land, and set fire to them, and burned them all, and broke up their camp, and went away flying.

The Emperor Henry and his host were right glad of the victory that God had given them, and that they had thus been able to succour their people. And when it came to be morning, the emperor and his barons went to the castle of Cibotos, and found those who were therein very sick, and for the most part sore wounded. And the emperor and his people looked at the castle, and saw that it was so weak as not to be worth the holding. So they gathered all their people into the ships, and left the castle and abandoned it. Thus did the Emperor Henry return to Constantinople.

109

Johannizza raises the siege of Adrianople

JOHANNIZZA, the King of Wallachia, who had besieged Adrianople, gave himself no rest for his petraries, of which he had many, cast stones night and day against the walls and towers, and damaged the walls and towers very greatly. And he set his sappers to mine the walls, and made many assaults. And well did those who were within, both Greeks and Latins, maintain themselves, and often did they beg the Emperor Henry to succour them, and warn him that, if he did not succour them, they were utterly undone. The emperor was much distraught; for when he wished to go and succour his people at Adrianople on the one side, then Theodore Lascaris pressed upon him so straitly on the other side, that of necessity he was forced to draw back.

So Johannizza remained during the whole month of April (1207) before Adrianople; and he came so near to taking it that in two places he beat down the walls and towers to the ground, and his men fought hand to hand, with swords and lances, against those who were within. Also he made assaults in force, and the besieged defended themselves well; and there were many killed and wounded on one side and on the other.

As it pleases God that adventures should be ordered, so it befell that the Comans who had overrun the land, and gained much booty, and returned to the camp before Adrianople with all their spoils, now said they would remain with Johannizza no longer, but go back to their own land. Thus the Comans abandoned Johannizza. And without them he dared not remain before Adrianople. So he departed from before the city, and left it.

And you must know that this was held to be a great miracle: that the siege of a city so near to the taking should be abandoned, and by a man possessed of such power. But as God wills, so do events befall. Those in Adrianople made no delay in begging the emperor, for the love of God, to come to them as soon as he could; forsooth it was that if Johannizza, the King of Wallachia returned, they would all be killed or taken.

110

Skiza again besieged by Theodore Lascaris; the emperor delivers the city

THE emperor, with as many men as he possessed, had prepared to go to Adrianople, when tidings came, very grievous, that Escurion, who was admiral of the galleys of Theodore Lascaris, had entered with seventeen galleys into the straits of Abydos, in the channel of St. George, and come before Skiza, where Peter of Bracieux then was, and Payen of Orléans; and that the said Escurion was besieging the city by sea, while Theodore Lascaris was besieging it by land. Moreover, the people of the land of Skiza had rebelled against Peter of Bracieux, as also those of Marmora, and had wrought him great harm, and killed many of his people.

When these tidings came to Constantinople, they were greatly dismayed. Then did the Emperor Henry take council with his men, and his barons, and the Venetians also; and they said that if they did not succour Peter of Bracieux, and Payen of Orléans, they were but dead men, and the land would be lost. So they armed fourteen galleys in all diligence, and set in them the Venetians of most note, and all the barons of the emperor.

In one galley entered Conon of Béthune and his people; in another Geoffry of Villehardouin and his people; in the third Macaire of Sainte-Menehould and his people; in the fourth Miles the Brabant; in the fifth Anscau of Cayeux; in the sixth Thierri of Loos, who was seneschal of Roumania; in the seventh William of Perchoi; and in the eighth Eustace the Emperor's brother. Thus did the Emperor Henry put into all these galleys the best people that he had; and when they left the port of Constantinople, well did all say that never had galleys been better armed, nor manned with better men. And thus, for this time, the march on Adrianople was again put off.

Those who were in the galleys sailed down the straits, right towards Skiza. How Escurion, the admiral of Theodore Lascaris' galleys, heard of it, I know not; but he abandoned Skiza, and went away, and fled down the straits. And the others chased him two days and two nights, beyond the straits of Abydos, forty miles. And when they saw they could not come up with him, they turned back, and came to Skiza, and found there Peter of Bracieux and Payen of Orléans; and Theodore Lascaris had dislodged from before the city and repaired to his own land. Thus was Skiza relieved, as you have just heard; and those in the galleys turned back to Constantinople, and prepared once more to march on Adrianople.

111

The emperor twice delivers Nicomedia besieged by Theodore Lascaris

THEODORE Lascaris sent the most part of his force into the land of Nicomedia. And the people of Thierri of Loos, who had fortified the church of St. Sophia, and were therein, besought their lord and the emperor to come to their relief; for if they received no help they could not hold out, especially as they had no provisions. Through sheer distress and sore need, the Emperor Henry and his people agreed that they must once more abandon thought of going to Adrianople, and cross the straits of St. George to the Turkish side with as many people as they could collect, and succour Nicomedia.

And when the people of Theodore Lascaris heard that the emperor was coming, they avoided the land, and retreated towards Nice the Great. And when the emperor knew of it, he took council, and it was decided that Thierri of Loos, the Seneschal of Roumania, should abide in Nicomedia with all his knights, and all his sergeants to guard the land; and Macaire of Sainte-Menehould should abide at Charax, and William of Perchoi in Skiza; and each defend the land where he abode.

Then did the Emperor Henry, and the remainder of his people return to Constantinople, and prepare once again to go towards Adrianople. And while he was so preparing, Thierri of Loos, the seneschal, who was in Nicomedia, and William of Perchoi, and all their people, went out foraging on a certain day. And the people of Theodore Lascaris knew of it, and surprised them, and fell upon them. Now the people of Theodore Lascaris were very many, and our people very few. So the battle began, and they fought hand to hand, and before very long the few were not able to stand against the many.

Thierri of Loos did right well, as also his people; he was twice struck down, and by main strength his men remounted him. And William of Perchoi was also struck down, and remounted and rescued. But numbers hemmed them in too sore, and the Franks were discomfited. There was taken Thierri of Loos, wounded in the face, and in peril of death. There, too, were most of his people taken for few escaped. William of Perchoi fled on a hackney, wounded in the hand.

Those that escaped from the discomfiture rallied in the church of St. Sophia.

He who dictates this history heard blame attached in this affair—whether rightly or wrongly he knows not—to a certain knight named Anseau of Remi, who was liegeman of Thierri of Loos, the seneschal, and chief of his men; and who abandoned him in the fray.

Then did those who had returned to the church of St. Sophia in Nicomedia, viz. William of Perchoi and Anseau of Remi, take a messenger, and send him flying to Constantinople, to the Emperor Henry; and they told the emperor what had befallen, how the seneschal had been taken with his men; how they themselves were besieged in the church of St. Sophia, in Nicomedia; and how they had food for no more than five days; and they told him he must know of a certainty that if he did not succour them they must be killed or taken. The emperor, as one hearing a cry of distress, passed over the straits of St. George, he and his people, each as best he could, to go to the relief of those in Nicomedia. And so the march to Adrianople was put off once more.

When the emperor had passed over the straits of St. George, he set his troops in array, and rode day by day till he came to Nicomedia. When the people of Theodore Lascaris, and his brothers, who formed the host, heard thereof, they drew back, and passed over the mountain on the other side, towards Nice. And the emperor encamped by Nicomedia in a very fair field that lay beside the river on this side of the mountain. He had his tents and pavilions pitched; and caused his men to overrun and harry the land, because the people had rebelled when they heard that Thierri of Loos, the seneschal, was taken; and the emperor's men captured much cattle and many prisoners.

112

Truce with Theodore Lascaris; the emperor invades the lands of Johannizza

THE Emperor Henry sojourned after this manner for five days in the meadow by Nicomedia. And while he was thus sojourning, Theodore Lascaris took messengers, and sent them to him, asking him to make a truce for two years, on condition that the emperor would suffer him to demolish Skiza and the fortress of the church of St. Sophia of Nicomedia, while he, on his side, would yield up all the prisoners taken in the last victory, and at other times, of whom he had a great many in his land.

Now the emperor took council with his people; and they said that they could not maintain two wars at the same time, and that it was better to suffer loss as proposed than suffer the loss of Adrianople, and the land on the other side of the straits; and moreover that they would (by agreeing to this truce) cause division between their enemies, viz. Johannizza, the King of Wallachia and Bulgaria, and Theodore Lascaris who were now friends, and helped one another in the war.

The matter was thus settled and agreed to. Then the Emperor Henry summoned Peter of Bracieux from Skiza; and he came to him; and the Emperor Henry so wrought with him that he gave up Skiza into his hands, and the emperor delivered it to Theodore Lascaris to be demolished, as also the church of St. Sophia of Nicomedia. So was the truce established, and so were the fortresses demolished. Thierri of Loos was given up, and all the other prisoners.

Then the Emperor Henry repaired to Constantinople, and undertook once more to go to Adrianople with as many men as he could collect. He assembled his host at Selymbria; and so much time had already passed that this did not take place till after the feast of St. John, in June (1207). And he rode day by day till he came to Adrianople, and encamped in the fields before the city. And those within the city, who had greatly desired his coming, went out to meet him in procession, and received him very gladly. And all the Greeks of the land came with them.

The emperor remained only one day before the city to see all the damage that Johannizza had done to the walls and towers, with mines and petraries; and these had worked great havoc to the city. And on the morrow he departed, and marched towards the country of Johannizza, and so marched for four days. On the fifth day he came to the foot of the Mountain of Wallachia, to a city called Euloi which Johannizza had newly re-peopled with his folk. And when the people of the land saw the host coming, they abandoned the city, and fled into the mountains.

113

The emperor's foragers suffer loss

THE Emperor Henry and the host of the French encamped before the city; and the foraging parties overran the land and captured oxen, and cows in great plenty, and other beasts. And those from Adrianople who had brought their chariots with them, and were poor and ill-furnished with food, loaded their chariots with corn and other grain; and they found also provisions in plenty and loaded with them, in great quantities, the other chariots that they had captured. So the host sojourned there for three days; and every day the foraging parties went foraging throughout the land; but the land was full of mountains, and strong defiles, and the host lost many foragers who adventured themselves madly.

In the end, the Emperor Henry sent Anscau of Cayeux to guard the foragers, and Eustace his brother, and Thierri of Flanders, his nephew, and Walter of Escomai, and John Bliaud. Their four battalions went to guard the foragers, and entered into a land rough and mountainous. And when their people had overrun the land, and wished to return, they found the defiles very well guarded. For the Wallachians of the country had assembled, and fought against them, and did them great hurt, both to men and horses. Hardly were our men put to it to escape discomfiture; and the knights had, of necessity, to dismount and go on foot. But by God's help they returned to the camp, though not without great loss and damage.

On the morrow the Emperor Henry, and the host of the French departed thence, and marched day by day till they came to Adrianople; and they stored therein the corn and other provisions that they brought with them. The emperor sojourned in the field before the city some fifteen days.

114

Homage rendered by Boniface to the emperor, and by Geoffry of Villehardouin to Boniface

AT that time Boniface, the Marquis of Montferrat, who was at Seres, which he had fortified, rode forth as far as Messinopolis, and all the land surrendered to his will. Then he took messengers, and sent them to the Emperor Henry, and told him that he would right willingly speak with him by the river that runs below Cypsela. Now they two had never been able to speak together face to face since the conquest of the land, for so many enemies lay between them that the one had never been able to come to the other. And when the emperor and those of his council heard that the marquis Boniface was at Messinopolis, they rejoiced greatly; and the emperor sent back word by the messengers that he would speak with the marquis on the day appointed.

So the emperor went thitherward, and he left Conon of Béthune to guard the land near Adrianople, with one hundred knights. And they came on the set day to the place of meeting in a very fair field, near the city of Cypsela. The emperor came from one side, and the marquis from the other, and they met with very great joy; nor is that to be wondered at, seeing they had not, of a long time, beheld one another. And the marquis asked the emperor for tidings of his daughter Agnes; and the emperor told him she was with child, and the marquis was glad thereof and rejoiced. Then did the marquis become liegeman to the emperor, and held from him his land, as he had done from the Emperor Baldwin, his brother. And the marquis gave to Geoffry of Villehardouin, Marshal of Champagne, the city of Messinopolis, and all its appurtenances, or else that of Seres, whichever he liked best; and the Marshal became his liegeman, save in so far as he owed fealty to the emperor of Constantinople.

They sojourned thus in that field for two days in great joy, and said that, as God had granted that they should come together, so might they yet again defeat their enemies. And they made agreement to meet at the end of the summer, in the month of October, with all their forces, in the meadow before the city of Adrianople, and make war against the King of Wallachia. So they separated joyous and well content. The marquis went to Messinopolis, and the Emperor Henry towards Constantinople.

115

Boniface is killed in a battle against the Bulgarians

WHEN the marquis had come to Messinopolis, he did not remain there more than five days before he rode forth, by the advice of the Greeks of the land, on an expedition to the Mountain of Messinopolis, which was distant a long day's journey. And when he had been through the land, and was about to depart, the Bulgarians of the land collected and saw that the marquis had but a small force with him. So they came from all parts and attacked the rear-guard. And when the marquis heard the shouting, he leapt on a horse, all unarmed as he was, with a lance in his hand. And when he came together, where the Bulgarians were fighting with the rear-guard, hand to hand, he ran in upon them, and drove them a great way back.

Then was the Marquis Boniface of Montferrat wounded with an arrow in the thick of the arm, beneath the shoulder, mortally, and he began to lose blood. And when his men saw it, they began to be dismayed, and to lose heart, and to bear themselves badly. Those who were round the marquis held him up, and he was losing much blood that he began to faint. And when his men perceived that he could give them no further help, they were the more dismayed, and began to desert him. So were they discomfited by misadventure; and those who remained by him—and they were but few—were killed.

The head of the Marquis Boniface of Montferrat was cut off, and the people of the land sent it to Johannizza; and that was one of the greatest joys that ever Johannizza had. Alas! what a dolorous mishap for the Emperor Henry, and for all the Latins of the land of Roumania, to lose such a man by such a misadventure—one of the best barons and most liberal, and one of the best knights in the world! And this misadventure befell in the year of the Incarnation of Jesus Christ, twelve hundred and seven.

End.

THE LIFE OF ST. LOUIS

JEAN DE JOINVILLE

Ethel Wedgewood

INTRODUCTION

The Lord of Joinville dedicates his book to Louis, son of Philippe le Bel and Jeanne of Navarre (afterwards Louis X, "le Hutin"), and divides it into two parts.

To his good lord, Louis, son of the King of France, by the grace of God, King of Navarre, Count Palatine of Champagne and Brie, greeting, love, honour, and ready service from John, Lord of Joinville, his Seneschal of Champagne.

Dear Lord, I give you to know that your Lady Mother the Queen, who loved me well—may God have mercy on her!—desired of me right earnestly that I would make her a book of the holy words and good deeds of our King, Saint Louis; and I did promise her the same; and by God's aid the book is completed in two parts.

The first part tells how he ordered his time according to God and the Church and to the profit of his realm.

The second part of the book treats of his knightly prowess and great feats of arms.

Sir, in that it is written: "Do first that which pertains to God, and He will direct all the rest for thee," have I caused to be written such matters as pertain to the three things aforesaid: to wit, to soul, body, and the government of the people.

These other things, moreover, have I caused to be written to the honour of his true and holy relics, that by them it may be plainly seen that never a layman of our times lived so holily as he did all his days, from the beginning of his reign unto the end of his life. Not that I was present at his life's end, but his son, Count Peter of Alençon, was there, who loved me well and related to me the fair ending that he made, as you will find it written at the end of this book. Whereby methinks they fell short of his due in not ranking him among the martyrs, seeing the great hardships that he underwent in the pilgrimage of the Cross for the space of six years that I was in his company; and specially in that he followed our Lord in the matter of the Cross. For if God died by the Cross, even so did he; for he was crossed when he was at Tunis.

The second book will tell us of his deeds of knightly prowess and great daring; which were such, that four times I beheld him put his person in jeopardy of death, as you shall hear, to save his followers from harm.

The first occasion was when we touched land before Damietta; when all his council urged him, so I heard, to tarry until he should see how his knights should fare at their landing; and for this reason: that if he went ashore with them, and were slain along with his followers, the cause would be lost; whereas, if he tarried in his ship, he in himself might make good the loss and win back the land of Egypt. And he would hearken to none of them but leaped all armed into the sea, his shield about his neck and his spear in his hand, and was one of the first ashore.

The second occasion was when we left Mansourah to go to Damietta and his council urged him, as I was given to understand, to travel to Damietta in the galleys; and he would hearken to never a one, saying rather that he would never desert his followers, but that their fate should be his.

The third occasion was when we had dwelt a year in the Holy Land, after his brothers had left it. In great peril of death were we at that time; since, whilst the King was sojourning in Acre, for one man-of-arms that he had in his company the inhabitants had full thirty, when the town was seized. Indeed, I know no other reason wherefore the Turks did not come and take us in the town, save for the love God bore the King, who put fear into the hearts of our enemies, so that they did not dare attack us.

The fourth occasion when he jeopardized his person was when we returned from overseas and came before the Isle of Cyprus, where our ship ran so heavily aground, that three spans-length of the keel whereon she was built was torn away. Whereupon the King sent for fourteen master mariners to advise him what he should do; and they all advised him, as you will hear, to go into another ship. But to all their arguments the King replied: "Sirs, I see, that if I go out of this ship, she will be abandoned, and no one will remain in her, but they will choose to remain in Cyprus; wherefore please God, I will never cause the ruin of so great a number of men as are here, rather will I stay here to safeguard them." Thus the King warded off the mischief of eight hundred persons that were in his ship.

In the last part of this book we will speak of his end and in what a holy fashion he passed away.

Now to you, my Lord King of Navarre, I say, that I promised your lady mother the Queen—God rest her soul!—that I would make this book; and to acquit me of my promise I have made it. And since I see none that has so good a right to it as you who are her heir, to you I send it to the end that you and your brothers and all others who shall hear it may take good example thereby, and show forth the example in their works, that God may be well pleased with them.

PART I

Sayings and customs of the King

IN the name of Almighty God, I, John, Lord of Joinville, Seneschal of Champagne, do cause to be written the life of our Saint Louis, that which I saw and heard during the space of six years that I was in his company on the pilgrimage overseas and after we returned. And before I tell you of his great deeds and knightliness, I will tell you what I saw and heard of his holy words and good teachings, so that they may be found in sequence, to the edification of those that shall hear them.

The love he bore his people appeared in what he said to his son during a sore sickness he had at Fountainebleau: "Fair son," quoth he, "I pray thee, win the love of the people of thy kingdom. For truly, I would rather that a Scot should come out of Scotland and rule the people of the kingdom well and justly, than that thou shouldst govern them ill-advisedly."

The holy man so loved truth that he would not play even the Saracens false, as hereafter you shall hear.

Touching his mouth he was sober, for never in my life did I hear him discourse of dishes, as many rich men do; but contentedly he ate whatever his cooks set before him. In words he was temperate, for never did I hear him speak ill of others, nor ever hear him name the Devil; the which is not common throughout the kingdom, and thereat, I trow, God is ill pleased. His wine he tempered moderately, according as he saw that the wine could bear it. He asked me in Cyprus: Why I put no water to my wine. And I told him: "It was the physicians' doing, who told me that I had a thick head and a cold belly, and that it was not in me to get drunk." And he said: They deceived me; for unless I used myself whilst young to drink it watered, if, when old, I desired to do so, I should then be seized with gouts and stomach complaints and never have my health: whereas, if in old age I were to take my wine neat, I should be drunk every evening, and that it was a passing foul thing for a gallant gentleman to get drunk.

He asked me: Whether I wished to be honoured in this world and win Heaven at my death. "Yea!" said I. "Then," said he, "see that you be not wittingly guilty of any word or deed whereof if all the world knew it you could not acknowledge." So I said; so I did.

He bade me avoid contradicting or disagreeing with anything that anyone said before me, provided there would be no blame nor harm to myself in letting it pass; for that hard words provoke quarrels that are the death of thousands.

He used to say that we ought so to clothe and care for our bodies that sober men of the world might not deem us over-nice, nor young men deem us slovens. And this reminds me of the father of the present king and the embroidered coats-of-arms that they make nowadays. For I told him that never in my travels overseas did I see embroidered coats, neither belonging to the king nor to anyone else. And he told me that he had garments embroidered with his arms such as had cost him eight hundred pounds. And I told him that he would have employed them better, had he given them to God, and had made his clothes of good taffety as his father was wont to do.

He called me once, and said to me: "You are of such subtle perception in all matters touching religion, that I am afraid to talk to you, and for that reason I have called in these friars here, for I wish to ask you a question." The question was: "Seneschal, what sort of thing is God?" I answered: "Such a good thing, sir, that there is none better." "Well answered indeed," said he "for the very same answer is written in this book that I hold. Next I ask you," said he, "which would you rather: be a leper, or have committed a deadly sin?" And I, who never lied to him, replied that I would rather have committed thirty deadly sins than be a leper. And when the friars were gone, he called me all alone, and made me sit at his feet, and said to me: "What was that you said to me yesterday?" And I replied that I still said the same. "You talk like a hasty rattlepate," said he, "for there is no leprosy so foul as deadly sin, seeing that a soul in deadly sin is in the image of the Devil. And truly when a man dies, he is healed of the leprosy of the body, but when a man dies that has committed deadly sin, great fear must he needs have lest such leprosy should endure so long as God shall be in Heaven."

He asked me whether I washed the feet of the poor on Maundy Thursday. "Sorrow take it, sir!" said I. "The feet of those wretches will I never wash!" "Truly," quoth he "that was ill said; for you should not despise that which God did for our instruction. Wherefore I pray you, for the love of God and of me, that henceforth you will accustom yourself to wash them."

He so loved all manner of God-fearing men, that he bestowed the Constableship of France on my lord Giles le Brun, who was not of the realm of France, because he had a great reputation as a God-fearing man. And truly so I think he was.

There was Master Robert of Sorbonne, whom, because of his high reputation for honour and virtue, the King would have to dine at his table.

It chanced one day, that he and I were next one another at table, and the King reproved us, and said: "Speak aloud, for your fellows here fancy that you are backbiting them. If your discourse at table be of pleasant matters, then speak aloud, or if not, then keep silence."

When the King was merry, he would say to me: "Come, Seneschal, tell me the reasons why a gallant man is better than a Begouin?" Then would begin the argument between Master Robert and me; and when we had disputed a good while, he would give judgment thus: "Master Robert, I would wish to have the name of a gallant man, provided that I were one, and give you all the rest. For a gallant man is such a great thing and such a fine thing, that the very sound of it fills one's mouth."

He used to say, on the contrary, that it was a bad business to borrow from anyone, for that the restoring was so disagreeable that the very "R's" in it flayed one's throat, and betokened the Devil's rakes, always dragging back the man who set about restoring his neighbour's property. And the Devil is so cunning about it, that in the case of great usurers and robbers, he wiles them into giving to God that which they ought to restore to its owners. He bade me tell King Tibald from him, that he should beware of the house of Preachers of Provence which he was building, lest all the money he was putting into it should be a clog to his soul; for that wise men during their lifetime should deal with their possessions as executors: to wit, that good executors first of all redress any wrongs done by the dead man, and restore whatever was not his, and the remainder of his wealth they spend in alms.

The holy King was at Corbeuil one Pentecost, where there were four-score knights. After dinner, he came down into a meadow by the chapel, and stood in the gateway, talking to the Count of Brittany, the father of the present duke, whom God preserve! Thither came Master Robert of Sorbonne, seeking me, and took me by the flap of my cloak, and led me to the King, all the other knights following us. "Master Robert, what do you want with me?" asked I. "I ask you," said he, "if the King were sitting in this meadow, and you went and sat above him on the bench, would you not be to blame?" I answered: Yes. "Then," said he, "you are just as much to blame in being more richly clad than the King; for you clothe yourself in green and miniver, which the King does not." Said I to him: "Master Robert, I am in no wise to blame, though I do dress in green and miniver; for this dress was handed down to me from my father and mother. But you are to blame, for you are the son of villein[1] parents, and have laid aside their dress, and attired yourself in finer cloth than the King." Then I took hold of the lappet of his surcoat and that of the King's, and said: "Look and see if what I say is true." Thereupon the King set to work to defend Master Robert by words with all his might.

---

1 A feudal tenant subject to a lord or manor to whom he pays dues and services in return for land

Afterwards, my lord the King called my lord Philip his son (father to the present king) and King Tibald, and sat down by the door of his oratory, and put his hand on the ground, and said: "Sit down here close beside me, that we may not be overheard." "Oh, Sir!" said they, "we should not venture to sit so close to you!" "Seneschal," said he, "sit you here." Which I did, so close to him, that my gown touched his. He made them sit down beyond me, and said to them: "It was great ill breeding in you, that are my sons, not to do at once what I bade you, and take care that it never happens again." And they said it should not. Then he told me that he had called us in order to confess to me that he had been wrong in defending Master Robert against me. "But," said he, "when I saw him in such confusion, I was obliged to come to his assistance. But all the same do not hold by anything I said in Master Robert's defense; for, as the seneschal says, you should dress well and neatly, so that your wives may love you the better, and your followers esteem you the more."

The holy King strove with all his might, by his conversation, to make me believe firmly in the Christian law. He told me once, that some Albigenses had come to the Count of Montfort (who at that time was holding the Albigenses' country for the King) and told him they had come to see the body of our Lord which had turned to flesh and blood in the priest's hands. "Go and see it, you that disbelieve it," said he, "for as for me, I firmly believe it, according to the teaching of Holy Church. And know, that it is I that shall be the winner," said the Count, "because in this mortal life I believe it; wherefore I shall have a crown in Heaven above the angels, for they see it face to face, and so cannot choose but believe it."

He told me that there was a great conference of clergy and Jews in the monastery of Clugny, and there was a knight to whom the abbot had given bread out of charity, and he desired the abbot to let him have the first word, and with some difficulty he got permission. Then the knight rose, and leaned upon his crutch, and bade them bring forth the greatest scholar and master among the Jews, and they did so. And he put a question to him as follows: "Master," said he, "I ask you, whether you believe that the Virgin Mary, who carried God in her womb and in her arms, brought forth as a maid, and that she is the Mother of God?" And the Jew replied that he did not believe a word of it. The knight replied that he was a great fool to trust himself inside her monastery and house, when he neither believed in nor loved her; "And truly you shall pay for it," quoth he. And thereupon he lifted up his staff, and smote the Jew behind the ear, and stretched him on the ground. And the Jews took to their heels, carrying their master off with them, all wounded. And that was the end of the conference. Then the abbot came to the knight, and said that he had acted very foolishly; and the knight replied that he himself had acted still more foolishly in calling such a conference; for that there were numbers of Christians there, who by the close of the conference would have gone away infidels, through not seeing through the fallacies of the Jews. "And so I tell you," said the King, "that no one ought to argue with them unless he be a very good scholar; but a layman, if he hear the Christian law defamed, should undertake its defense with the sword alone, and that he should use to run them straight through the body as far in as it will go!"

He governed his dominions in this wise: Every day he heard his Hours by note, and a Requiem mass without note and afterwards the mass for the day, or for the saint (if it fell on a saint's day) by note. Every day he used to rest in his bed after dinner; and when he had slept and rested, then the office for the Dead used to be said in his chamber by himself and one of his chaplains before he heard vespers. In the evening he heard complines[2].

He had arranged his business in such a fashion, that my lord of Nesle, and the good Count of Soissons, and we others who were about his person after hearing mass used to go and listen to the Pleas of the Gate (which they call now "Petitions"). And when he came back from the minster, he used to send for us, and would sit down at the foot of his bed and make us sit all round him, and would ask us whether there were any cases to be despatched that could not be despatched without him, and we named them, and he

---

[2] The final church service of the day, also known as Night Prayers

would send for the parties, and ask them: "Why do you not accept what our officers offer you?" And they would say: "It is very little, sir." And he would talk to them as follows: "You ought really to take what people are ready to concede." And in this way the holy man laboured with all his might to bring them into the right and reasonable course.

Many a time it chanced in summer, that he would go and sit in the forest of Vincennes, after mass, and all who had business would come and talk with him, without hindrance from ushers or anyone. Then he would ask them with his own lips: "Is there anyone here, that has a suit?" And those that had suits stood up. Then he would say: "Keep silence, all of you; and you shall be dealt with in order." Then he would call up my lord Peter of Fontaines and my lord Geoffrey of Villette, and say to one of them: "Dispatch me this suit!" And if, in the speech of those who were speaking on behalf of others, he saw that a point might be better put, he himself would put it for them with his own lips. I have seen him sometimes in summer, when to hear his people's suits, he would come into the gardens of Paris clad in a camel's-hair coat, with a sleeveless surcoat of tiretaine, a cloak of black taffety round his neck, his hair well combed and without a quoif, and a white swansdown hat upon his head. He would cause a carpet to be spread, that we might sit round him; and all the people who had business before him stood round about, and then he caused their suits to be despatched— just as I told you before about the forest of Vincennes.

The King's loyalty may be seen in the affair of my lord of Trie, who sent the saint some letters which stated that the King had granted the county of Danmartin in Govelle to the heirs of the Countess of Boulogne, who had died recently. The seal of the letter was broken, so that there was nothing left of the King's seal but half the legs of the figure and the stool on which the King had his feet, and he showed it to all us who were of his council, and asked us to assist him with our counsel. We all declared with one accord that he was in no wise bound to carry out the terms of the letter. Then he bade John Saracen, his chamberlain, bring him the letter which he had given into his keeping. When he had the letter in his hand, he said to us: "Sirs, look at this seal which I used before I went overseas: it is plain to see, that the impress of the broken seal is exactly like the perfect seal, so that I could not venture in all conscience to withhold the county in question." And thereupon he called my lord Reynold of Trie, and said to him: "I deliver the county to you."

PART II

In France and Egypt

1

Of the King's birth and coronation, and how the Count of Brittany and the barons of France rebelled against him.

IN the name of Almighty God, having heretofore written part of the good words and teachings of Saint Louis, our King, we will next begin upon his deeds, in the name of God and of himself.

He was born, as I have heard him say, on the day of Saint Mark the Evangelist, after Easter. On that day, in many places they carry the Cross in procession, and in France it is called "Black Cross Day," and this was, as it were, a foreshadowing of the great host of people who died on those two crusades: to wit, on the Egyptian crusade, and on that other where he died at Carthage; for very great sorrowing there was in this world, and very great rejoicing there is in Heaven over those who on those two pilgrimages died true crusaders. He was crowned on the first Sunday in Advent. The mass for that Sunday begins: "To Thee have I lifted up my soul" and what follows after. In God he trusted firmly till his death; for at the point of death, with his last words he called on God and His Saints, especially upon my lord Saint James and my lady Saint Genevieve.

Great need had he in childhood that God should guard him; as by the good teachings of his mother, who taught him to love and believe in God, and set men of religion about him. Child as he was, she used to make him repeat his Hours and hear the lessons on Feast-days, and often told him as he recorded later, that she were rather he were dead than that he should commit a deadly sin.

Great need had he in his youth of God's aid; for his mother was from Spain, and had neither kindred nor friends in all the realm of France; and the barons of France, seeing the King but a child, and his mother a foreign woman, made the Count of Boulogne, the King's uncle, their leader, and looked upon him as actually their liege lord.

After the King was crowned, there were some of the barons who requested the Queen to grant them certain large territories; and because she would do none of it, they gathered themselves together, all the barons, at Corbeuil. And the holy King told me that he and his mother, who were at Montl'hery, durst not return to Paris until the men of Paris came under arms to fetch them. And he told me, how, all the way from Montl'hery to Paris, the road was thronged with people, armed and unarmed, all loudly praying Christ to give him health and long life, and to defend and keep him from his enemies.

At this parliament of the barons at Corbeuil, so it is said, those of them that were present decided that the good knight Count Peter of Brittany should rebel against the King, and further, that when the King should summon them to march against the Count, they should attend in person and each bring only two knights with him; and this to see whether the Count of Brittany would be able to crush the Queen, she being but a foreign woman, as you have heard. And many people say that the Count would have crushed the Queen and King too if God had not come to the King's aid in this strait. But by God's grace, Count Tibald of Champagne (the same who later became King of Navarre) came to serve the King with three hundred knights, and by his aid, the Count of Brittany was brought to the King's mercy, so that, to make peace, he was obliged to relinquish to the King the county of Anjou (so it is said) and the county of Le Perche.

Now I must leave my subject for a while in order to rehearse certain matters that you shall now learn. We will say therefor, that the good Count, Henry the Generous (of Champagne) had two sons by the Countess Mary, sister to the King of France and to Richard of England, of whom the eldest was named Henry, and the younger Tibald. This elder one, Henry, took the cross and went on pilgrimage to the Holy Land, at which time King Philip and King Richard besieged Acre and took it. So soon as Acre was taken, King Philip returned to France, for which he was much blamed; but King Richard stayed in the Holy Land, and did many great deeds, so that the Saracens feared him mightily: for it is written in the book of the Holy Land that when the Saracen children cried, the women would scold them, saying, "Hush! King Richard is coming!" to quiet them. And when the horses of the Saracens or Bedouins shied at a bush, their riders would say: "Do you fancy that it is King Richard?"

This King Richard used his influence to give to Count Henry of Champagne, who had remained with him, the Queen of Jerusalem, who was direct heir to the kingdom. By the said Queen, Count Henry had two daughters, of whom the first was Queen of Cyprus, and the other was given to Lord Erard of Brienne, from whom has sprung a great lineage, as may be seen in France and Champagne. It is not of Lord Erard of Brienne's wife that I wish to speak now, but about the Queen of Cyprus.

After the King had crushed Count Peter of Brittany, all the barons of France were so stirred up against Count Tibald of Champagne, that they resolved to send for the Queen of Cyprus, she being daughter to the eldest son of the house of Champagne, in order to disinherit Count Tibal, he being son to the second son.

Some amongst them intervened to make peace between Count Peter and the said Count Tibald, and the upshot of the negotiations was that Count Tibald promised to take Count Peter's daughter to wife. A day was fixed for the Count of Champagne to espouse the damsel; and they were to bring her for the wedding to a certain abbey at Prémontrés which is close to Chateau Thierry, and is called, I believe, Val Secret. The barons of France, who were nearly all of kin to Count Peter, took much trouble in escorting the damsel to Val Secret for the wedding, and sent word to the Count of Champagne who was at Chateau Thierry. But whilst the Count of Champagne was on his way to get married, there came to him my lord Geoffrey de la Chapelle from the King with a letter of credentials, and said as follows: "Sir Count, the King has heard that you have covenanted with Count Peter of Brittany to take his daughter in marriage. Wherefore the King sends you word that, unless you wish to lose whatever possessions you have in the realm of France, you will not do this thing; for you know that the Count of Brittany has used the King worse than any man alive." And the Count of Champagne, by the advice of those that were with him, turned back again to Chateau Thierry.

2

How the barons of France ravaged the lands of the Count of Champagne, and how the king made peace; episode of Count Henry the Generous.

WHEN Count Peter and the barons of France, who were waiting for him at Val Secret, heard what had happened, they were all as it were beside themselves at the slight he had put upon them; and now they sent for the Queen of Cyprus; and so soon as ever she was come, they agreed with common accord to muster all the men-at-arms they could, and to march into Brie and Champagne from the French side; and the Duke of Burgundy, who had Count Robert of Dreux' daughter to wife, was to enter the county of Champagne on the Burgundian side, and take the city of Troyes if possible.

The Duke summoned as many men as he could muster, and the barons likewise. The barons came through, burning and destroying on one side, the Duke on another, and the King of France on another, seeking to come to battle with them. The Count of Champagne finding himself thus beset, began himself to fire his own towns before the approach of the barons, so that they might not find supplies in them. Amongst the other towns which the Count of Champagne burnt were Epernay, and Vertus, and Sézanne.

The burghers of Troyes, seeing themselves abandoned by their own lord, sent to Simon, Lord of Joinville (the father of the present lord) to come to their rescue. He, having summoned all his men-at-arms, set out from Joinville at nightfall, so soon as ever the tidings reached him, and came to Troyes before daybreak; and so the barons were disappointed in their hopes of taking Troyes, and passed by that city, and went and camped in the open, close to where the Duke of Burgundy lay.

The King of France, learning that they were there, marched straight to the place to give battle to them; and the barons sent to him begging that he would withdraw his person, and they would go and do battle with the Count of Champagne and the Duke of Lorraine and all the rest of his men, with three hundred knights less than the Count or the Duke should have. And the King sent them word that he would never fight against his own liegemen save in person. And they came again to him, and said that they would willingly incline the Queen of Cyprus to peace, if so he pleased. And the King sent them word that he would hear of no peace, neither suffer the Count of Champagne to hear of any, until they should have evacuated the county of Champagne. And they did withdraw in so far as to leave Ylles where they were, and go and camp below Juylli; and the King lodged at Ylles whence he had driven them. And when they knew that the King was gone thither, they went and camped at Chaorse, and durst not abide the King's coming, but went and camped at Langres, which belonged to the Count of Nevers, who was of their party.

Thus the King accorded the Count of Champagne with the Queen of Cyprus, and peace was made after this wise: that the said Count gave to the Queen land worth about two thousand pounds a year, besides forty thousand pounds that the King paid for the Count of Champagne. And the Count sold to the King, in exchange for the forty thousand pounds, the fiefs hereafter named: to wit, the fief of the county of Blois, the fief of the county of Chartres, the fief of the county of Sancerre, the fief of the vicounty of Chateaudun. There were people, indeed, who said that the King only held these aforesaid fiefs in pawn; but there is no truth in it, for I asked our holy King Louis about it whilst we were overseas.

The land which Count Tibald gave to the Queen of Cyprus is held by the present Count of Brienne and the Count of Joigny, because the Count of Brienne's grandmother was daughter to the Queen of Cyprus and wife to the great Count Walter of Brienne.

That you may know how the Lord of Champagne came by those fiefs that he sold to the King, I must tell you that the great Count Tibald, who sleeps at Lagny, had three sons: the first was named Henry; the second Tibald; the third Stephen. This same Henry was Count of Champagne and Brie, and was called, "Henry the Generous"; and rightly was he so called, for he was generous both towards God and the world: generous towards God, as appears by the church of Saint Stephen of Troyes and by the other churches which he founded in Champagne; generous towards the world, as appeared in the case of Artauld of Nogent and on many other occasions which I would relate to you, if I were not afraid of hindering the course of my story.

Artauld of Nogent was the burgher whom the King most trusted, and he was so rich, that he built the castle of Nogent l'Artauld with his own money. Now it chanced that Count Henry came down out of his hall at Troyes to go and hear mass at Saint Stephen on the day of Pentecost; and at the foot of the steps there knelt a poor knight, who thus accosted him: "Sir, I beseech you for the love of God, to give me out of your wealth the wherewithal to marry my two daughters whom you see here." Artauld, who was walking behind him, said to the poor knight: "Sir Knight, it is not courteous in you to beg from my lord; for he has given away so much, that he has nothing left to give." The generous Count turned round to Artauld, and said to him: "Sir Villein, you speak untruly when you say that I have nothing left to give, why, I have you yourself! Here, take him, Sir Knight! For I give him to you, and will warrant him to you." The knight was in no wise abashed, but took him by the cape, and told him that he would not let him go until he had come to terms with him; and before he could get away, Artauld had made fine with him for five hundred pounds.

Count Henry's second brother was named Tibald, and was Count of Blois; his third brother, named Stephen, was Count of Sancerre; and these two brothers held all their heritage with the two counties and their appurtenances in fee of Count Henry; and afterwards they held them of Count Henry's heirs who held Champagne, until the time when Count Tibald sold them to the King of France, as I told you above.

3

Of the feast that the King held at Saumur; and how the King of England and the Count of la Marche made war on King Louis.

LET us return to our story, and say as follows: that after these events, the King held a great court at Saumur in Anjou. I was there, and can bear you witness that it was the finest that ever I saw. For there ate at the King's table beside him the Count of Poitiers, whom he had newly knighted on a Saint John's Day; and next him sat Count John of Dreux, whom likewise he had newly knighted. Next to the Count of Dreux sat the Count of La Marche, and next him the good Count Peter of Brittany; and in front of the King's table, in a line with the Count of Dreux, sat my lord the King of Navarre, in a coat and mantle of samite, richly adorned with belt and clasp and circlet of gold; and I carved before him. Before the King, his brother the Count of Artois was trencher bearer, and the good Count, John of Soissons, carved. To guard the table, there was my Lord Humbert of Beaujeu (who afterwards became Constable of France), and my Lord Enguerrand of Coucy, and my lord Archibald of Bourbon. Forming a bodyguard behind these three barons were a good thirty of their knights, in coats of cloth of silk, and behind the knights a great crowd of sergeants clad in taffety stamped with the Count of Poitier's arms. The King had donned a coat of sky-blue satin, and a surcoat and mantle of scarlet satin lined with ermine, and on his head a cotton bonnet, which became him very ill, he being in those days a young man.

The King held this feast in the halls of Saumur, which were built, they say, by the great King Henry of England, to hold his great feasts. The halls are built after the fashion of the cloisters of the White Monks; but I trow there are no others so large by far. I will tell you why: for along the wall of the cloister where the King was dining, and he was surrounded by knights and sergeants who took up a great deal of room, there was a table at which were seated thirty other persons, bishops and archbishops; and again, beyond the bishops and at the same table, was seated Blanche the Queen Mother, at the opposite end of the cloister to where the King sat. The Count of Boulogne (who afterwards was King of Portugal) waited on the Queen, together with the good Count of St. Pol, and a German lad, eighteen years of age, who was said to be the son of Saint Elizabeth of Thuringia. It was said of him, that Queen Blanche used to kiss his forehead out of piety, because she heard that his mother had often kissed him there. At the end of the cloister, on the other side, were the kitchens, the butteries, the pantries, and the storerooms; and from this cloister they set bread and wine and meat before the King and Queen. And in all the other wings, and in the center plot, there feasted a vast number of knights, more than I can tell. Many people say that they never saw before at any feast so many surcoats and other garments of cloth-of-gold as were there; and that there must have been full three thousand knights in the place.

After this feast, the King brought the Count of Poitiers to Poitiers that he might take possession of his fiefs, but when the King was come to Poitiers, he would gladly have been back again in Paris; for he found that the Count of La Marche, who had eaten at his table on Saint John's day, had got together a number of men-at-arms at Lusignan by Poitiers. The King remained at Poitiers close on a fortnight, not daring to depart until he should be reconciled with the Count of La Marche. I know not how it came about, but I several times saw the Count of La Marche on his way from Lusignan to confer with the King at Poitiers; and he always brought with him his wife, the Queen of England, who was mother to the English king. And many people said that the peace which the King and the Count of Poitiers made with the Count of La Marche was an unsound one.

No long while after the King had got back from Poitiers, the King of England came into Gascony to make war on the King of France. Our holy King, with as many men as he could raise, rode forth to give him battle. Thither came the King of England and the Count of La Marche to do battle before a castle called Taillebourg, which lies on a dangerous river named the Charente, where there is no crossing save by a very narrow stone bridge. No sooner had the King reached Taillebourg, and the armies were face to face, than our men (who had the castle on their side) pushed on at great cost, and crossed over most hazardously by means of boats and the bridge, and rushed upon the English; and there began a general hand-to-hand engagement stiffly contested. The King perceiving this adventured himself into the thick of it along with the rest, for the English had four men for every one that the King had after he had crossed. Howsoever it so happened by God's will, that when the English saw the King cross over, they lost heart, and retired into the city of Saintes; and some of our men entered the city mixed up with them, and were taken prisoners.

Those of our people who were captured at Saintes related that they heard a great quarrel arise between the King of England and the Count of La Marche, the King of England saying that the Count of La Marche had sent for him to come over, and had assured him that he would find plenty of support in France. That very evening, the King of England left Saintes, and drew off into Gascony.

The Count of La Marche, seeing that there was no help for it, yielded himself prisoner to the King, together with his wife and children; and so, when peace came to be made, the King got a great slice of the Count's lands; but I do not know how much, for I was not present at this affair, not having yet donned a hauberk; but I heard say that, besides the land, the King carried off ten thousand pounds that he had in his coffers, and every year as much again.

Whilst we were at Poitiers, I saw a knight named Lord Geoffrey of Rancon, who, by reason, it was said, of a great outrage that the Count of La Marche had done him, had sworn by the holy relics, that he would never have his hair clipped in the fashion of knights, but would wear it long and parted as women do, until such time as he should see himself avenged on the Count, by his own hand, or by another. And when Lord Geoffrey saw the Count, his wife, and his children, kneeling before the King, and suing for pardon, he there and then bade them bring him a stool, and had his long locks shorn off in the presence of the King and the Count of La Marche and the company.

Out of this campaign against the King of England and against the barons, the King made many handsome presents, as I learnt from people who had come from it. And for no gifts nor expenses that he was put to in this campaign, nor in any others on either side of the water, did the King ever request nor take from his barons, nor from his knights, nor from his liegemen, nor from his good towns any aids that could be complained of. And no wonder, for he acted by the advice of his good mother who was with him, whose precepts he carried out, and those that were handed on to him by the wise men of his father's and grandfather's times.

4

How the king took the cross; the episode of the clerk and the three robbers; Joinville prepares to go on crusade.

AFTER the events above narrated, it happened, by God's will, that a great sickness overtook the King at Paris; whereby he was brought so low, as he used to relate, that one of the ladies who were nursing him declared him to be dead, and was about to draw the sheet up over his face; but another lady, who was on the opposite side of the bed, would not permit it, but said that his soul was still in his body. When he heard the two ladies disputing, our Lord worked in him, and presently sent him health, for he had been voiceless and could not speak. He desired that they would give him the cross, and they did so.

When the Queen, his mother, heard that his speech had returned to him, nothing could surpass her rejoicings; but when, as himself used to relate, she learnt that he had taken the cross, she made as great mourning as though he lay dead before her eyes. After he had taken the cross, Robert, Count of Artois took it, and Alphonso, Count of Poitiers, and Charles, Count of Anjou (who afterwards was King of Sicily)—all three the King's brothers; and Hugh, Duke of Burgundy crossed himself, and William, Count of Flanders, brother to Count Guy of Flanders, who was newly dead; and Hugh, the good Count of St. Pol, and his nephew, my Lord Walter, who bore himself right well overseas, and would have been a man of great worth, if he had but lived. And the Count of La Marche was one of them, and my lord Hugh le Brun, his son, and the Count of Sarrebruck, and his son, my lord Gilbert of Apremont, in whose company I, Lord of Joinville, crossed the sea in a ship which we hired, for we were cousins; and we crossed over twenty knights in all, of whom half were his, and half mine.

At Easter, in the year of Grace which was just striking 1248, I summoned my liegemen and my vassals to Joinville; and on the same Easter Eve, when all whom I had summoned were come, was born my son, John, Lord of Acerville, the child of my first wife, who was sister to the Count of Grandpré.

All that week we feasted and danced; for my brother, the Lord of Vaucouleurs, and the other rich men who were there entertained the company in turn, Monday, Tuesday and Wednesday.

On the Friday I said to them: "Sirs, I am going away overseas, and I know not whether I shall return. Now therefore, come forward; and if I have done any of you a wrong, I will right it, and will as my custom is redress in turn any grievances you may have against me or my servants." I put everything right with them as regards the public business of my estates, and in order that I might have no undue advantage, I left my seat on the council, and abode without dispute by their decisions.

Being unwilling to take any ill-gotten money with me, I went to Metz in Lorraine, and left a great quantity of my land there in pawn;

and know, that on the day I left our country to go to the Holy Land, I was not possessed of one thousand pounds of rent in land, for my Lady Mother was still alive. And so I set out, with nine other knights, myself the tenth, three of us being bannerets[3]. And so you see, that if God had not been ever at my side, I could assuredly not have held out through those long six years that I spent in the Holy Land.

Whilst I was getting ready to start, John, Lord of Apremont and Count of Sarrebruck by right of his wife, sent me word, that he had made arrangements for going overseas at the head of ten knights, and that if I liked, we would hire a ship between us; and I consented; and his people and mine hired a ship at Marseilles.

The King summoned his barons to Paris, and made them take an oath, that they would keep faith and loyalty towards his children if anything should happen to him on the way. He desired me to do so; but I would take no oath, because I was not his man.

Whilst I was on the road, I came across three men lying dead on a cart, whom a clerk had slain; and I was told that they were being taken to the King. Thereupon I sent one of my squires after them to learn what happened. The squire reported that the King, on leaving his chapel, went onto the steps to see the bodies, and asked the Provost of Paris how it had occurred. And the Provost told him that the dead men were three of his sergeants from the Chatelet, and that they used to go about robbing people on the high-roads; "and," said he to the King, "they fell in with this clerk, whom you see here, and stripped him of all his clothes. The clerk went off in his shirt to his house, and took his cross-bow, and made a child carry his falchion[4]. Directly he saw the robbers, he shouted to them, and told them they should die on the spot. The clerk wound his cross-bow, and let fly a bolt, and pierced one of them through the heart; and the two others took to their heels. The clerk took the falchion that

---

3 Knighted, feudal lords who have the right to lead their vassals to battle under their own banners

4 A one-handed, single-edged sword

the child was holding, and followed them by the light of the moon, which was bright and clear. One of them thought to escape through a hedge into a garden; but the clerk struck him with the falchion, and clean cut off his leg so that it hung only by the boot, as you can see," said the Provost. "The clerk set off again in pursuit of the third, who thought to take refuge in a strange house where the folks were not yet abed; but the clerk with his falchion struck him full on the head, so that he clove it to the teeth, as you may see, sir" quoth the Provost to the King, "And, sir, the clerk showed what he had done to the provost who lives hard-by the street, and then came and gave himself up in your gaol; and, sir, I bring him to you, and here he is, that you may deal with him according to your pleasure." "Sir Clerk," said the King, "your prowess has lost you your priesthood; and for your prowess I retain you in my pay, and you shall accompany me overseas. I deal thus with you, in order that my followers may see that I will not uphold them in any of their wickedness." When the people that were assembled there heard this, they cried on Our Lord, beseeching God might grant the King a safe life and a long one, and bring him home in health and happiness.

After this, I returned into our country, and we arranged, the Count of Sarrebruck and I, that we should send our baggage by carts to Auxonne, and thence by the River Saône as far as the Rhone. On the day that I left Joinville, I sent for the Abbot of Cheminon, who was reputed the best man in the White Order. I heard one testimony borne him at Clairvaux, on the feast of Our Lady, when the holy King was there; for a monk pointed him out to me, and asked, whether I knew him. "Why do you ask?" said I; and he replied: "Because I believe that he is the best man of all the White Order. Know too," said he, "that I heard from a worthy man who used to lie in the same dormitory as the Abbot of Cheminon, that once the Abbot had bared his chest, because of the heat, and this good man, lying in the same room where the Abbot was asleep, saw the Mother of God come to his bedside, and draw his gown across his chest lest the draught should hurt him."

So this Abbot of Cheminon gave me my scrip and staff, and

thereupon I departed from Joinville, and would not enter my castle any more, until I should come home again; and I set out on foot, barefooted, and in pilgrim's weeds, and visited Blechicourt and St. Urbans and other holy relics there; and all the while that I was on my way to Blechicourt and St. Urbans, I durst not cast my eyes back to Joinville, lest my heart should fail me for the fair castle and the two children that I was leaving behind me.

I and my companions dined at Fontaine l'Archeveque, hard by Donjeux. And there Abbot Adam of St. Urbans—God rest his soul!—gave me and my knights a great quantity of fine jewels. Thence we came to Auxonne, and went on with all our baggage (which we had placed in boats) down the Saône, from Auxonne to Lyons; and they led our big chargers alongside the boats. At Lyons we entered the Rhone on our way to Arles le Blanc; and in the Rhone we came upon a castle called the Rock of Gluy, which the King had caused to be pulled down, because the hue and cry was out against Roger, the lord of the castle, for robbing pilgrims and merchants.

End.